ETHNICITY AND NATION-BUILDING

ETHNICITY AND NATION-BUILDING:
Comparative, International, and Historical Perspectives

Edited by

WENDELL BELL
and

WALTER E. FREEMAN

SAGE PUBLICATIONS / Beverly Hills / London

For information address:

SAGE PUBLICATIONS, INC.
275 South Beverly Drive
Beverly Hills, California 90212

SAGE PUBLICATIONS LTD
St George's House / 44 Hatton Garden
London EC1 8ER

Printed in the United States of America

International Standard Book Number 0-8039-0173-9

Library of Congress Catalog Card No. 72-84045

FIRST PRINTING

PREFACE

This book is the result of the twelfth annual convention of the International Studies Association which was held March 17-20, 1970, in San Juan, Puerto Rico. Although we have subsequently asked a few additional people to contribute, most of the chapters were prepared for and presented at several sessions of the ISA convention, the participants having been invited and the panels organized by William J. Foltz and Leo Kuper, in addition to the editors.

Our theme was "Ethnicity in Nation-Building, Regional Integration, and International Conflict," and our discussions turned out to be among those happy intellectual occasions when a deep, common interest in a given subject matter washes away disciplinary distinctions. This was especially important because we are an interdisciplinary group composed of political scientists, sociologists, historians, community developers, anthropologists, and planners.

We were also gladdened by the sun, sand, and sea of the Caribbean and we all owe much for the pleasant surroundings, both physical and intellectual, to the Program Officers—Basil A. Ince, Fred W. Riggs, and Luis Vega. After the conference, the idea of bringing these papers together in a published volume was encouraged by Norman D. Palmer, Richard C. Snyder, and John E. Turner.

We wish to thank Lorraine Estra, of Yale University, and Kay McClellan Richard Gold, and Carol Gold, all of Pennsylvania State University, for editorial assistance. The first editor also wishes to thank the National Science Foundation for a grant (GS-2637) under which he was able to take the time to work on this volume.

—*Wendell Bell*
—*Walter E. Freeman*

CONTENTS

INTRODUCTION

*A*t the conference in Puerto Rico where most of these papers were presented, what struck us most was how much we had to say to each other that hit at the heart of our own individual work, despite the interdisciplinary—and theoretical—differences that existed among us and despite the diverse field experiences that we had had in a variety of countries and with quite different groups. This is not to say that there were no differences of opinion. There were and they are frankly retained in the following pages. Yet even though the situations discussed range widely over geographic space—Latin America, North America, Europe, Asia, Africa, and the Caribbean—and over time—old states as well as new—there exists a considerable consensus among the various authors about those aspects of the phenomena of ethnic and race relations that are both theoretically and socially significant.

First, it is clear from reading the following chapters that the proposition is reaffirmed: ethnicity is most importantly a question of group boundaries. When can an ethnic group be said to exist and on what basis does it exist?

Second, what other significant cleavages are correlated with the ethnic divisions? Every author, implicitly or explicitly, raises the foregoing questions, although, because of the different correlated cleavages and salient consciousness of them in different situations, different authors answer them somewhat differently. It is not always easy to decide what is a definition of ethnicity and what is a correlated cleavage, since in many situations *correlated* differentiating characteristics may dominate the way persons in the situation itself conceive of the groups involved and the way action and strife are organized. At minimum, perhaps, ethnicity may be defined as characteristic, distinctive *cultural* or *subcultural* traits that set one group off from others. Different beliefs, values, and patterns of behavior are involved as well as self and other identifications. Language differences may be so intertwined that they may in many circumstances be considered part of the definition, and this may be inherently so given the important connections between language and culture.

In gross terms, race is often correlated with cultural or subcultural distinctions, but to our minds this is not inherently so. There was a time, certainly, in the prehistory of humankind when gene pools and culture moved slowly and roughly together across geographical space or remained linked in relatively isolated pockets of density for long periods of time. But during historical times, this situation began to change. Today, and in the future, the technology of communication and transportation has—and will continue—to shrink the globe to the point where the prehistoric empirical correlation between gene pools and culture need no longer exist. This is, of course, not to say that it will disappear, because self-fulfilling endogamous practices alone would prevent that within the foreseeable future. But the socio-racial continuum described by Harmannus Hoetink among Iberian-dominated areas offers some indication that it could become smaller.

Much of the nature of ethnic relations can only be understood by investigating the nature of other cleavages and how they either cut across or correlate with ethnicity. In addition to race, our authors give prominent attention to religion, education, nationality, and social class (employment, occupation, ownership, wealth, prestige, and power). Regional and urban-rural differences are also mentioned. A recurrent theme is found in the questions of who controls the legitimate authority of government and how it is used in the competition and conflict of different ethnic and racial groups. And, of course, the question of what is legitimate raises the question of the nature of the ideologies that justify various structures and degrees of stratification. Colonialism, surely, is near an extreme end of a continuum where some ethnic and racial groups use governmental power and police and military force to dominate over other ethnic and racial groups. In this connection several of our contributors quite rightly point out the similarities between foreign domination of a geographically distinct colony and the discrimination and suppression of local ethnic and racial groups within a country by superordinate groups within the same country; i.e. "internal colonialism."

Third, ethnicity is an important factor in—and often a problem for—nation-forming and nation-building. The modern state is another way of defining group boundaries, one that is incredibly mixed up with ethnic divisions. Often, a state is composed of a variety of ethnic and racial groups; often, members of the same ethnic and racial groups are divided by the boundaries of states: Africans and East Indians in Guyana, various tribes in Ghana and Kenya, the Chinese in various countries of Southeast Asia, Catholics and Protestants in Northern Ireland, Basques in Spain and France, Afrikaners and Englishmen in South Africa, Blacks in the New World and in Africa, Ukrainians, Crimean Tatars, and Jews in the Soviet Union—the list goes on and on.

On the one hand, ethnicity has given a boost to the new nationalism of the 20th century. The correlation between the political domination characteristic of colonialism and ethnic cleavages meant in many cases that the struggle for political independence and nationhood could be in part cast as an ethnic or racial struggle as well, darker-skinned peoples of Africa, Asia, and the Caribbean struggling against the lighter-skinned peoples of Europe, the colonial masters. On the other hand, within the more than 60 new states that have been formed since World War II national unity was repeatedly threatened by internal racial and ethnic strife and compounding and cumulating conflicts based on religion, education, social class, and region that were more or less interlocked with the ethnic and racial divisions.

By "nation-building" we mean both the formation and establishment of the new state itself as a political entity and the processes of creating viable degrees of unity, adaptation, achievement, and a sense of national identity among the people. The first period may be characterized by years—even decades—of struggle, a period often of clandestine and illegal movements. Within the context of a politically dependent colony, one can say that a nationalist movement is a collection of politico-social beliefs, attitudes, emotions, and actions aimed at the creation of a nation-state, politically independent and autonomous, self-governing, and geographically distinct. Although much of the national character of the new state may be set during this early period, in a sense a state may never stop "nation-building," because ethnic, racial, class, and other cleavages may continually threaten the unity, legitimacy, and existence of the state, as they do, of course, in some of the old states, too.

Today, the nation-state is the dominant form of organization on every continent in that it, above all other organizations, demands the highest loyalty from the individual. It enforces that demand with a near monopoly on the (presumably) legitimate use of modern weapons systems. Yet, as Deutsch (1963) points out, humankind existed long before nations and probably will exist long after them. Given the tenacity with which ethnic memberships and identities persist it may be more than mere whimsy to seriously consider such alternatives as the hoped-for images of the future of some Basque nationalists reported by Pedro González Blasco: "the disintegration of the European historical states . . . and their substitution by a united Europe based on ethnic-linguistic-historical fatherlands or regions rather than states, reversing the process of national unification that took place through the last few centuries." Such an erosion of the authority of the state combined with generally smaller scale semi-autonomous units banded together in a supra-national federation or in several such federations may yet prove to be a viable alternative for the future political organization of the globe. The idea of supra-national political federations receives some support on other grounds as well, since, as Joel C. Edelstein says, the nation-state, though now at its height, is ironically anachronistic at a time when modern corporate imperialism has become international.

Fourth, we have stressed comparative, international, and historical perspectives in this volume because of the importance that we attach to each for an adequate understanding of ethnicity and nation-building. Some comparisons are explicitly made within the body of various chapters, such as those by René Lemarchand for Rwanda and Burundi, Roberta E. McKown for Ghana and Kenya, and Janet Merrill Alger for the northern, middle, and southern colonies of revolutionary America. Others are implicit and must be teased from a comparison of the different papers, although some of this is done in the theory papers in Part I, and in the commentaries and in the introductions to each of the other parts. Clearly, more must be done along comparative lines because it is only through such comparison that the causal effects of some variables and the spuriousness and confounding effects of others can be discovered.

Ethnicity and race have become internationalized, as Robert H. Mast, Locksley Edmondson, and Gordon K. Lewis say. They have become enmeshed in major global struggles against political and economic domination, both within and especially between capitalist- and socialist-dominated territories. They are affected within the new states, as described by Cynthia H. Enloe for the "soft states" of Southeast Asia and by Joseph B. Landis in the case of the United States Central Intelligence Agency in Guyana, by the foreign affairs—and foreign interventions—of other states, including the major world powers. And ethnicity and race are involved in supra-national networks of communication and influence, such as that composed of the Caribbean-Africa-Black America triangle, that carry ideas of destiny, of oppression, of struggle, and of an emergent identity that transcends the boundaries of any existing nation-state.

Furthermore, we agree that the time dimension is frequently—if not always—essential for an adequate understanding of the ethnic and racial factor. Facts concerning the origins and character-defining events in a group's history and, just as important, the collective memory of a group, the beliefs of shared experiences and common histories of struggle, value, and achievement that are perpetuated within a group, go far toward an explanation of the present situation of a group. For example, Paul F. Power traces sources of the recent conflict in northern Ireland back to the revolt and defeat of the Irish under Hugh O'Neill at the end of the 16th century and to William III's victory in 1690 at the Battle of the Boyne, the annual celebration of which has fueled divisiveness; Jeffrey E. Butler states that major historical celebrations, the memories of great deeds by folk heroes, and reminders of the wickedness of the historic enemy, Britain, among Afrikaners contribute to their exclusivist cultural nationalism; and Blasco relates modern Basque nationalism to certain aspects of the earlier state-building period in Spain.

This is not to say, however, that the immediate dynamics in any present situation have no independent effect nor that images of the future, aspirations and expectations, do not enter in. Quite the contrary. Every author acknowledges, at least implicitly, the importance of history, present conditions, and hopes and fears for the future in understanding both ethnicity and nation-building.

Fifth, the reader's attention should be directed to the importance of concepts dealing with the structure and ideology of equality and inequality in most of the following chapters. Although various terms may be used by different authors, clearly one of the major themes of this volume has to do with these ideas. There are several ways in which this is so. There are

(a) past and present inequalities in the distributions of various resources, goods, and services among groups

(b) perceptions and beliefs about what these inequalities were and are

(c) beliefs about what the causes of inequalities are

(d) expectations of the trends of change and expectations of resulting future inequalities

(e) evaluations of the legitimacy or justice of past, existing, or projected inequalities

(f) the creation and dissemination of images of possible alternative future arrangements in which more equality—or more inequality—is achieved and therefore more justice attained

(g) specific decisions, policies, and actions designed to create more equality—or sometimes to maintain the status quo—such as in employment, housing, or educational opportunity

(h) a variety of different types of more or less organized groups that actually make policy and take action to increase or decrease the degree of equality in any situation and that range from members of the established government taking legal or illegal action to members of revolutionary groups taking what will be surely described, unless they win their revolution, as illegal action

The struggle for equity, for justifiable equality or inequalities, in situations marked by systematic inequalities, we suggest, is an important part of what ethnicity and nation-building are all about. Of course, whether a given group views more equality as desirable or undesirable and whether they struggle to maintain existing inequalities or struggle to eliminate them remain complex and often highly contingent behaviors.

Several of the authors carry this argument, as it relates to the connections between ethnicity and the inequalities of social class, to the point of suggesting that socialism may be essential for depluralization and ethnic harmony. Yet, despite the "friendship of peoples" image presented in official Soviet sources, we know from data such as those presented by Frederick C. Barghoorn that the "establishment of a Soviet-type 'socialist,' or state-directed economy, does not eliminate nationality tensions and prejudices or the cultural oppression and even the economic exploitation of minority nationalities."

There are, of course, ways other than the Soviet model to bring about socialist change. Certainly, many of the theories and empirical cases offered in the following pages suggest that ethnic harmony would be promoted and ethnic conflict reduced if the many cleavages—especially perhaps the political and economic ones—could be broken loose from their linkages with ethnicity and race. The spread of equality—of opportunity, access, inputs, and outputs—would have this effect, but frequently ethnic and racial strife is precisely a disagreement concerning the desirability of increasing equality.

A way out of this dilemma was suggested to us by the following pages in that in some cases it appeared that situations of ethnic and racial conflict were misperceived by the participants as zero-sum games, some groups necessarily gaining only at the expense of others, when in fact all—or most—could gain through cooperation and negotiation and most would lose through conflict and violence. Our job as social scientists includes demonstrating this when it is in fact so.

There are other situations, to be sure, where there are irreconcilable differences and conflicts of interests. Solutions to these await the creative negotiations, emergent value consensus at least concerning the rules of the game, new structures of adjudication, and perhaps, though we hope not, still more human misery and death to spur the effort to negotiate.

Sixth, another set of recurring concepts in the following pages deals with the degree of self-determination or autonomy of a group. These concepts describe an important aspect of the relationship between a given group and some other group or groups. Again the authors use a variety of different terms that stress different points on the underlying continuum to which they refer and that are at different levels of abstraction. Indicative of these ideas are such terms as assimilation, integration, depluralization, incorporation, division, distance variables, ascriptive barriers, plural society, polarization, parallel systems, self-determination, autonomy, and independence. Indeed, there does seem to be an underlying continuum lurking behind these terms, one that ranges from full assimilation—i.e., the elimination of the boundaries separating a group from some other group or groups to the point of the disappearance of the group itself as a separate entity—to autonomy and independence—the self-determination of the group with its own integrity as a distinct and separate unit.

Both a variety of solutions to ethnic group conflict and a connection between ethnicity and nation-building can be understood better by keeping this continuum in mind. An individual cannot be discriminated against, exploited, or oppressed *as a member of a group* unless the group is demarcated and visible and also to some degree vulnerable, dependent, or defenseless. At the one extreme, under assimilation for example, the group as such would no longer exist. Its boundaries would have dissolved. At the other extreme, the group exists and is visible but it is autonomous and self-determining with defenses and a security system. Facing rejection from superordinate groups for assimilation or for just and equal treatment—the latter (equality) cannot really be divorced from the question of degree of autonomy in real situations—a subordinate group may turn to separateness and it may either create and develop its own sub-system or system in some form of accommodation with another group or groups or, in the most extreme case, it may strive to establish its own separate state and nation.

The following chapters are somewhat arbitrarily divided into four parts, roughly as they are grouped into different sessions at the Puerto Rican conference. None deals exclusively with any particular sub-topic, since the different concepts and themes described here recur in every part, and every paper takes up some aspect of both ethnicity and nation-building. Part I, however, concentrates somewhat more than the others on theory, Part II on status, Part III on conflict, and Part IV with old rather than new states.

Several years ago, many of us watching the creation of new states and the rise of the new nationalisms could not have believed that in the 1970s we would be focusing our attention on problems of ethnicity and race. We had concluded, as Enloe says, that "'primordial attachments' were fading away and the nation-state was the central actor in men's lives." Today, we find, as she says further, that "ethnicity appears to be attracting more emotional resources than ever." Hence, this book on *Ethnicity and Nation-Building*.

—*The Editors*

REFERENCE

DEUTSCH, K. W. (1963) "Nation-building and national development: some issues for political research," pp. 1-16 in K. W. Deutsch and W. J. Foltz (eds.) Nation-Building. New York: Prentice-Hall, Atherton Press.

Part I

THEORY

Chapter 1

ON THEORIES OF RACE RELATIONS

LEO KUPER

I

Many circumstances, relating both to the internal structure of societies and their international relations, combine to give a new significance to the field of race and ethnic relations, and to rescue it from the contempt into which it had fallen in academic circles.

The reasons for this contempt are not easy to understand. Students of race and ethnic relations were largely committed to an egalitarian ethic; they emphasized a common humanity, the universality of the human condition, and they were often oriented toward action against racial and ethnic oppression. Perhaps these commitments were distasteful in a milieu of social scientists, becoming increasingly dedicated to value neutrality and equating emasculation with scientific objectivity. There was also, no doubt, embarrassment over racial and ethnic discrimination. This would encourage its exorcism by subsuming it under other more general categories, as suggested by Harmannus Hoetink in the following chapter, and by indeed questioning the validity of race relations as a distinctive field of study, as if validity is derived from the phenomenon itself, and not from intellectual interests and academic organization. In the context of these rites of exorcism, race relations became somewhat epiphenomenal. It was viewed as an aspect of stratification, as indeed it is, or as purely an expression of class conflict, the racial difference permitting the more ruthless exploitation of labor, or as inherent in group formation, or as simply a particular form of the more general phenomenon of prejudice.

Yet, taken as a whole, there were important contributions to the study of race relations. The role of political domination and economic exploitation in the structure of racial oppression was obvious enough and indeed well recognized. The year 1948 was remarkable for the appearance of three outstanding studies. Edward Roux in *Time Longer Than Rope*, which bears the sub-title *A History of the Black Man's Struggle for Freedom in South Africa*, analyzed the structure and process of racial oppression from a perspective which was based on Marxism, and which derived emotional force from a strong identification with the racially oppressed. In *Caste, Class and Race*, Oliver Cromwell Cox, a black American, drew on the same tradition of Marxist analysis and deep commitment, combining extensive scholarship in comparative race relations and stratification with a critical review of rival theories of race relations. In a somewhat different tradition, J. S. Furnivall in *Colonial Policy and Practice: A Comparative Study of Burma and Netherlands India*, examined the political, economic, and social consequences of colonial exploitation, and outlined a theory of the plural society in which colonial domination imposes a forced union on the colonized peoples, and in which the rampant play, and the undisciplined primacy, of economic forces create a medley of peoples, lacking a common social life. And Furnivall's study was only one of many dealing with colonial exploitation.

Liberal perspectives contributed a variety of approaches. There was the search for regularities in the processes of race and culture contact. Many studies analyzed the forms and extent of discrimination, and the implications of discrimination for life expectancy, morbidity rates, life chances, and quality of living. Particularly in the United States, there was much interest in caste theories of race relations, which abstracted elements of the Indian caste system to emphasize similarities between the rigidities and inequalities of the caste system and those of structures of race relations. This gave rise to a lively controversy in taxonomy, but regardless of the validity of the theories, they served a significant ideological function. The concept of caste is so much the antithesis of the democratic ideal of equality of participation, that to characterize a racial structure, in the United States, for example, as caste was to condemn it utterly.

Theories of prejudice and discrimination became especially prominent, contributing studies of personality, of interaction, of the extent and forms of discrimination, and of the interrelations between prejudice and discrimination and between social situation and attitudes. Prejudice was often viewed as a cause of discrimination (see Hoetink), so that the problem became one of changing the minds and hearts of men. To this end, many strategies were devised resting on the conception of equal status contact, such as interracial holiday camps, and integrated housing estates. Against a background of preoccupation with prejudice, it is possible to understand the contemporary discovery of the institutional bases of racism, which one would have thought were surely obvious enough. Also, it is against this background that one can explain the persistence of strategies, apparently conceived in a sort of Walter Mitty fantasy, in which little flutters of elites are brought together in international airports; or in which supporters of South African apartheid are flown to the United States and exposed to a series of planned prejudice-shattering experiences, such as dining with a millionaire black banker. The effect of the American visit may merely be to add another item to a curriculum vitae, and to give a sort of international status to a henceforth more effective support of apartheid, while all the elite pugwashes deflect resources and energies away from more promising programs.

Both the radical and liberal perspectives share the fundamental premise that racial difference has no intrinsic significance for social relationships. They reject the conception that race has any greater primordial significance than, for example, predestination. Where racial difference becomes an important principle in the structuring of a society, it is because it has been selected, and socially elaborated, as a criterion of stratification, following conquest and colonization by people of a different race or consequent upon enslavement. Racial difference is not a sufficient condition for racial discrimination. There may be racial differences in a society, which remain quite irrelevant for the structure of the society; and conversely, groups of the same race, anthropologically speaking, may define their differences in racial terms.

At the present time, there appears to be a tendency among certain black and white scholars, to view racial difference as widely relevant for the qualities of groups and their interrelations. These theories I would describe as racist. I draw a distinction between racist theories of society, and theories of racist society.

Though Hoetink suggests that the somatic factor is an autonomous explanatory social element in the study of group relations in a multi-racial society, I do not think he is ascribing intrinsic significance to racial difference, and advancing a racist theory. His concern seems to be rather to develop a characterization of racist society; that is to say, a society in which mobility is to a high degree determined by membership in a given socio-racial category, and in which "special mechanisms of social selection generally tend to favor those whose somatic traits are most akin to those of the dominant socio-racial group, other things being equal." But I find great difficulty with the theory that the somatic norm image of the dominant group in these societies is a significant element in the system of stratification.

The somatic norm image may be highly inclusive, while the social system is rigidly exclusive. This seems to be the situation in South Africa, which has passed laws against the marriage of white and black, and against miscegenation between them, and which has built a system of rigidly exclusive racial categories. Yet the somatic norm image of the dominant whites seems highly inclusive, as indicated by a long history of miscegenation; the presence in the dominant group of very dark people, whose appearance is that of dark coloreds, but who are classified as white; the use of penal sanctions and police surveillance to prevent miscegenation; and the precipitation of white South Africans into the arms of African girls in the neighboring territory of Swaziland, creating a serious problem of prostitution for the Swazi Government.

II

In recent years, there has been a renewed interest in plural society theory. It seems to have explanatory value in a world where many societies experience sharp conflict between racial or ethnic groups, and where secessionist movements arise in countries which had been nationally integrated, so it would seem, for centuries. Unfortunately its explanatory value has been somewhat diminished by the fact that a good deal of confusion was introduced in the revival of the theory. Since I have contributed in part to this confusion, it seems appropriate that I should now attempt some clarification.

Furnivall applied the concept, in *Colonial Policy and Practice*, to colonial tropical societies, characterized by the separation and antagonism of their different peoples and the breakdown of cohesion in their separate communities. He thought that the driving force in these processes was the uncontrolled expression of economic interests in a context of racial difference and foreign domination, and he wished to determine what social arrangements might best ensure societal integration after independence. His theory was attached to a specific social situation.

M. G. Smith, in a creative paper on "Social and Cultural Pluralism" published in 1960, sought to revise the theory in such a manner as to give it a more universal significance as a general theory of society. In doing so, he introduced, in my view, two complications. The first lay in the comprehensiveness of his conception. Since he aimed at a general theory of society, which would at the same time be a critique of social functional theory, he saw no reason to limit the concept to situations where the basic cleavages fell along racial or ethnic lines. In his formulation, the plural society was constituted by incompatible cultural differences, and by pervasive social cleavages, between sections, who were held together by the political domination of a cultural minority, and by regulation rather than consensus. These sections might be defined by social class or race or ethnicity or religion. This was a matter of indifference, provided the sections were culturally differentiated and politically bound in a manner conforming to his conception of the plural society.

M. G. Smith's position was perfectly logical, but from a purely pragmatic point of view it would seem desirable to treat the class-structured society as a distinct category. Some of the more fruitful applications of plural society theory are precisely in the analysis of the relations between race or ethnicity, and class. Moreover, the extension of the concept to include certain types of class structure invites preoccupation with labels, whether, for example, a particular class-structured society should or should not be described as a plural society: this seems to me to close rather than to open inquiry. There is an overabundance of theories and concepts for the characterization and analysis of social classes, and I now feel that it is likely to be more creative, and less confusing, to apply the concept of the plural society primarily in situations of racial and ethnic pluralism.

The second complication lay in the emphasis on cultural difference. Whether or not it is correct to describe this theory as cultural determinism, it certainly gave a primary significance to cultural pluralism as imposing the necessity for domination by a plural section. The theory was immediately attacked by Caribbean scholars, and continues to be attacked, though M. G. Smith has moved to quite different formulations, and though, to the best of my knowledge, there are no protagonists for the theory of cultural pluralism.

M. G. Smith now distinguishes three levels of pluralism: at the lowest level, cultural pluralism, or institutional diversity; at an intermediate level, social pluralism, in which institutional diversity is associated with collective segregation; and at the highest level, structural pluralism, which adds the element of differential incorporation of the sections—that is to say, incorporation of sections into the society on a basis of inequality (1969: 440). The term plural society refers simply to a society characterized by both structural pluralism and minority rule. No primacy whatever is now given to cultural pluralism, no determinist role is assigned to it and cultural pluralism may be present without structural pluralism. Yet M. G. Smith's name still seems to be so ineradicably identified with a determinist theory of cultural pluralism, that the mere mention of his work on plural societies immediately evokes the performance of a ritual, initiated presumably in 1960.

Into this already complex debate, I injected further confusion in an introductory paper circulated to participants in a colloquium on plural societies ("Plural Societies: Perspectives and Problems," 1969: 7-26). I had found that when I spoke to American scholars and students about plural societies, the concept was given a very different meaning. As I gained more knowledge of the U.S., I realized that there was a widely accepted theory of "democratic pluralism," which serves as an ideology in the confrontation with communism. This theory attempts to specify the social conditions conducive to democracy, such as the separation of powers, checks and balances, competing political parties and competing interest groups organized to promote their interests, strong intermediate groups between the individual and the state, and cross-cutting affiliations. It came under strong attack by radicals, particularly when it was used as if descriptive of the U.S., on the grounds inter alia, that there were many sections which could not effectively exert pressure and were thus denied participation in the "democratic" process, and that issues of concern to them were excluded from consideration.

Since reference to plural society theory immediately suggested the theory of democratic pluralism, it was necessary to distinguish between them, and in "Plural Societies: Perspectives and Problems" I showed that they provided entirely different models of society, and indeed dealt with very different phenomena. Then most unfortunately, I asked how "plural societies," characterized by domination and conflict, might transform into societies of democratic pluralism and equilibrium. This not only introduced a somewhat irrelevant set of theoretical considerations, but naturally attracted the antagonism of radicals, who directed against plural society theory the conditioned reflexes they had already acquired to the theory of democratic pluralism. In fact, the problem I wished to raise was that of the transformation of racially or ethnically segmented systems of relationship into interracial or interethnic systems. Clearly this may be achieved in many ways, as envisaged, for example, in Marxism, race conflict being replaced by conflict between interracial classes, or as conceived in the extension of Durkheim's theory of the progressive division of labor, individuals detaching themselves from the racial or ethnic sections and entering into new interracial or interethnic relationships. There was no need to pose the problem specifically in terms of a transformation into democratic pluralism, and I am sure that it will assist thinking about plural societies to view the theory of democratic pluralism as rather irrelevant to the analysis of racially or ethnically plural societies.

Apart from these misconceptions to which writers on plural society theory have contributed, there is also misrepresentation and misuse of the theory. The misrepresentation consists in the charge based on excerpts out of context or on misquotation, that there is a basic assumption or postulate in the theory that the mere presence of ethnic differences creates a plural society and that ethnicity is, in and of itself, a sufficient cause of conflict. Nothing could be further from the truth. M. G. Smith in his analysis of "Pluralism in Precolonial African Societies" shows the quite variable consequences of contact between different ethnic groups, and concludes that:

"With the sole exception of band organization in its pure form, each societal type provides examples of all modes of interethnic accommodation, namely, segmental segregation, symbiosis, symmetrical or complementary consociation, amalgamation, assimilation, and differential incorporation.... Evidently, mere identities or differences of race have no uniform implications for the modes of consociation in such mixed societies. The same conclusion emerges when these materials are analyzed to isolate uniform patterns of consociation linked with particular conditions of ethnic composition" [1969: 136-137].

The plural society is only one possible consequence of the incorporation of different ethnic groups into the same society. Plural society theory does not assert that the mere presence of racial or ethnic difference is a sufficient condition for the structuring of a society on the basis of racial or ethnic identity. This is a point which has been made often enough, but perhaps bears repeating.

The significance which is attached to racial or ethnic difference in a society, particularly by the ruling section, is the result of the manner in which differences in race or ethnicity have been culturally interpreted and elaborated into a principle of social structure. It is not inherent in the racial or ethnic differences.

The misuse derives from a corollary which is drawn from plural society theory. The argument runs that the contact between people of different race or ethnicity inevitably results in conflict (which is of course *not* plural society theory), that the history of plural societies demonstrates that the attempt to integrate different races or ethnic groups into a single society is invariably attended by bloody strife, and that it is therefore in the best interests of all sections to adopt some such system of separation as South African apartheid. A new journal, Plural Societies, seems not unsympathetic to this point of view. Since I have always thought of South African apartheid as an abomination unto the Lord, and since I have always been dedicated to the ideal of a common society in which racial or ethnic difference would have no relevance for human rights, and in which there would be equality and freedom of association, I was much disturbed by this misuse of the theory. It seemed to me that the lack of a moral component in plural society theory, in contrast to Marxist or liberal theory, might have contributed to the misuse, until my nephew Adam Kuper reminded me how sadly the Sermon on the Mount had been misused. Clearly there is little relationship between a theory and the uses to which it is put.

If we can exorcise the theories of cultural determinism, and democratic pluralism, and narrow our concern primarily to racial or ethnic pluralism, and if we can set aside the misrepresentations of racial or ethnic determinism, then it should be possible to proceed with some clarity. Though I find utility in the concept of plural society as an ideal type, exemplified in practice by South African apartheid, which has made systematic racial discrimination a cardinal principle of social structure, I prefer, as does Pierre van den Berghe (1969: 68), to work with pluralism as a continuum. I distinguish the following dimensions: (i) particularism-universalism, which relates to the mode of political incorporation, whether persons are incorporated indirectly, through segmental identification, as members, for example, of an ethnic group, or directly on an individual basis; (ii) segregation-assimilation; (iii) cultural diversity-homogeneity, and (iv) inequality-equality in the differential access to, and distribution of, power, status and material resources. Discontinuity-continuity and superimposition-dissociation are suggested as two summarizing measures, the former relating to the structure of the society, and the distribution of its members in those structures, and the second based on the extent to which cleavages and issues of conflict are superimposed on each other or dissociated (Kuper, 1969: 473-479).

The value of plural society theory or of theories of ethnic and racial pluralism remains to be tested. The premise is that the social sciences were developed in a very different milieu from that which characterizes, for example, the colonial or white settler societies with their sharp racial or ethnic cleavage, or that at any rate, in the formulation of general social theories, little attention was paid to situations of racial or ethnic pluralism. It would seem therefore that some of these theories might not be appropriate for the analysis of pluralism, or might require modification. At the very least, pluralism would seem to introduce an intervening variable. Thus in the field of sociology of religion, it is difficult to apply Weber's concept of the varied elective affinities of different social strata for particular forms of religious expression. One cannot interpret the conversion of Africans to a Christian denomination as an expression of an elective affinity for that particular denomination, arising out of the social situation of the converts and their religious needs. There is a further variable, the elective affinities of the carriers of Christianity, and their religious needs and other interests. One must look not only to the elective affinity of the colonized, but also to the elective affinity of the colonizers and the interaction between them. If many educated Africans, in the colonial or white settler situation, were members of the Methodist Church, this does not necessarily imply an affinity of the educated strata for Methodism. It may be that the educated did not choose the Methodist Church, but that the Methodist Church, by providing the facilities for education, chose the educated.

In the use of liberal evolutionary models, pluralism introduces complications. If the evolutionary model is based on Durkheim's theory of the progressive division of labor, then the expectation would be that with increasing contact, interaction and differentiation, individuals of different racial groups would enter into relationships across the original segmentary divisions, and thereby progressively forge interracial solidarity. But in a plural society, the racial or ethnic solidarities may remain a potential basis for political action, and may be reactivated, even when the development of interracial or interethnic relationships is quite far advanced. The plural situation is very different from that of the industrializing European nations of Durkheim's analysis.

For Marxist theory, plural societies pose the problems of the failure in working-class solidarity between workers of different races, and the rise of movements of racial or national liberation, informed by racial or national consciousness. These phenomena raise questions in regard to the universality of the class struggle and the applicability of classical Marxist theories of revolutionary change to plural societies.

Thus the phenomena of pluralism provide a perspective for the critical examination of theories developed in a Western milieu.

III

Into this concern over the interpretation of internal structures of race relations, there has exploded the internationalization of race. The stimulus is so gross that preoccupation with the niceties of the analytical approach to the internal structure would seem to be somewhat meaningless, like seeking the explanation of some natural catastrophe in the life history and psychological tensions of its victims.

The internationalization of race, and the subjective awareness of it, are not, of course, new phenomena. The spread of colonialism over the world was a manifestation of this internationalization of race; and the colonizers' experience of races living in different territories throughout the world encouraged a more generalized conception of racial difference. General categories of racial thinking could hardly arise initially from the experience of members of a subordinate race, isolated within a particular territory. But propelled by the dynamic of material interests and ideological needs, they emerged quite readily out of domination over great empires. And critical analysis of colonialism, of racist theories, and of imperialist domination over subject peoples added to the international dimensions of the race question.

Yet, if the internationalization of race is not a new phenomenon, many circumstances now combine to give it greater significance, as Locksley Edmondson shows. He defines the phrase as referring to the factors and processes which influence the projection of domestic race issues into the international arena, and the intrusion of international influences on domestic race relations. Among these factors, he includes the still prevailing coincidence of power and race. He points out that this is associated with the rise of the Third World in the international system and a more universal organization of international relations. More effective channels are thus provided for articulating interests and demands, and for the regular expression of international concern. There result a greater visibility of racial problems, and a greater internationalization of race, with domestic parties promoting external interests, and external parties intervening in domestic disputes. Finally Edmonson argues that since race correlates with economic status both in the international system, and in the domestic situation in multi-racial societies, this encourages a convergence of national and international racial struggles for economic advancement.

At the same time, theoretical and ideological perspectives have developed in consonance with the increasing international salience of race. The conception of bourgeois and proletarian nations corresponds with the conception of the convergence of the national and international struggles. Transposing terms for the description of the internal class structure of a society to the relations between nations raises many analytic difficulties, and is no doubt somewhat misleading, but it offers a broad characterization for the moulding of political consciousness and action. Theories of neo-colonialism link the colonial situation with continuing hegemony by metropolitan powers after attainment of formal political independence. While the charge of neo-colonialism seemed initially rather exaggerated, much evidence now accumulates to document the political and economic dependence of the new states on the great powers, and to establish the somewhat illusory nature of the benefits received under many aid agreements. The concept of internal colonialism used by Leo Marquard (1943: 251; 1957) to describe the situation of Africans within South Africa, has gained currency in the very different context of the United States. It provides a concept for linking Black and other racial minorities in the United States with national liberation movements and with revolutionary movements against neo-colonialism.

The attempt by a subordinate racial group to seek outside support in its struggle for emancipation is usually viewed by the rulers as highly subversive, indeed treasonable; and I have always taken, as a rough measure of radicalism, the extent to which the movements externalized their struggles and related to outside forces. At the present time, however, these struggles are almost always internationalized, so that this in itself gives little indication of their political implications. Interpretation must rather be sought in the ideological and programmatic basis of the international involvement. Contemporary ideologies emphasize class conflict in its national and international dimensions, or race as a basis of worldwide solidarity, as in the Black Power movement, or a global equating of race and class. Against these perspectives, ideologies which seemed radical in the past may now be viewed as quite reactionary. This is the rather surprising charge against Pan-Africanism in some revolutionary circles. A generation ago, Pan-Africanism seemed a radical challenge to colonialism and to policies of fragmentation. Today, it is quite likely to be attacked, from a class perspective, because it is based on ties of race, and from a race perspective, because it is regionally oriented.

The increasing internationalization of race will certainly affect the significance of the internal structure of the society in domestic racial conflicts. However, my earlier comment that internationalization would seem to render preoccupation with the niceties of the analytical approach to the internal structure somewhat meaningless, is clearly exaggerated. During the last decade, in both the Rwanda and Algerian revolutions, the internal structures were important determinants of the struggle. In Rwanda, the signs of an impending violent conflict between Hutu and Tutsi were obvious to outside observers. The United Nations took steps to avoid a violent confrontation and to find a peaceful solution. The actions of the Belgian mandatory authority were under close scrutiny. There were discussions in the United Nations, and in conferences and in commissions, and there were site visits and investigations. Yet the revolution erupted much as expected, along the lines of traditional cleavage between Hutu and Tutsi. In Algeria, the large army of the metropolitan power was engaged in the struggle, while the revolutionary forces found outside bases and external support. But the dynamics of the struggle were conditioned by the internal relations between colonizer and colonized, and more particularly by the conflict between the colons and the indigenous peoples. Indeed, it seems likely that evolutionary solutions could have been found if it had not been for the rigid commitment of the colons to a highly privileged position shaped by the internal structure of the society.

Under present conditions of competing great power blocs, the salience of the internal structures may be greatly affected by strategic considerations. Where there is an active external involvement, then the conflict between the great powers may be expected to sharpen the internal conflict, either along lines of class antagonism or of plural (racial/ethnic) cleavages. It was for this reason that I suggested in an earlier paper that the peaceful resolution of internal conflict between racial and ethnic sections might very well be contingent on the reduction of international tensions and the movement toward a world community of nations. But Edmondson shows that racial and ethnic conflicts are themselves direct sources of international tension, so that the establishment of a world community is in some measure dependent on the resolution of internal racial and ethnic conflicts. Clearly there is interaction, and mutual reinforcement, between the national and international spheres in the heightening or reduction of racial and ethnic tensions.

REFERENCES

COX, O. C. (1948) Caste, Class and Race. New York: Doubleday.
FURNIVALL, J. S. (1948) Colonial Policy and Practice: A Comparative Study of Burma and Netherlands India. London: Cambridge University Press.
KUPER, L. (1969) "Plural societies: perspectives and problems" and "Ethnic and racial pluralism: some aspects of polarization and depluralization," in L. Kuper and M. G. Smith (eds.) Pluralism in Africa. Berkeley: University of California Press.

MARQUARD, L. (1957) South Africa's Colonial Policy. Johannesburg, South Africa: South African Institute of Race Relations.

——— [John Burger] (1943) The Black Man's Burden. London: Gollancz.

ROUX, E. (1948) Time Longer Than Rope: A History of the Black Man's Struggle for Freedom in South Africa. London: Gollancz.

SMITH, M. G. (1969) "Pluralism in precolonial African societies" and "Some developments in the analytic framework of pluralism," in L. Kuper and M. G. Smith (eds.) Pluralism in Africa. Berkeley: University of California Press.

VAN DEN BERGHE, P. L. (1969) "Pluralism and the polity: a theoretical exploration," in L. Kuper and M. G. Smith (eds.) Pluralism in Africa. Berkeley: University of California Press.

Chapter 2

NATIONAL IDENTITY AND SOMATIC NORM IMAGE

HARMANNUS HOETINK

I

*I*t cannot merely be a matter of semantic confusion between words like "race" and "ethnic group" which caused for so long the schools of the United States to deal with the sociological problems of racial (somatic) and cultural diversity, as if there were no essential distinction between them. Courses and books on "minorities" dealt with an astonishing variety of groups and phenomena.

The sociological rationalization of this approach was, that all these groups were subject to that mysterious—but, it was believed, ultimately eradicable—poison called "prejudice," which was viewed by quite a few as a final cause, rather than as a symptom of group conflicts, latent or active. They believed that diffusion of knowledge of the groups involved would detain prejudices or even make them disappear.

The analysis of the emergence and development of different types of group conflict (cultural, somatic, economic), their comparative study in different societies and periods, in short the analytical-comparative approach, had to retreat or be subordinated to ameliorative goals and ideologies (Rose, 1970). It is not improbable that this ameliorative tendency (widely popular in the social sciences already) was in this particular case strengthened even more because of a peculiar trait of U.S. society per se.

For its ethos as a typical immigrant society made it attractive to propagate the idea that all "immigrant" groups—including the Negroes—had, in principle, the same chances of social and economic improvement; having the same chances implied encountering the same obstacles, the same type of prejudice. Such a line of thought was especially attractive for those population groups—Irish, Jews, Italians—who in few generations had succeeded in considerably improving their relative position in the total structure (which, incidentally, increased their influence on social scientific thought). They could ascribe their improvement, in retrospect, to the cultural and economic qualities of the groups involved, implying that less successful minorities lacked these qualities, not necessarily through their own fault, but decidedly not through the fault of the former either, a line of analysis which, while perhaps not being entirely incorrect, was certainly comforting.

In the last two decades there are two tendencies in the U.S. social sciences which seem to inaugurate a less narrow approach to the problems of cultural and racial variety, and which certainly are a laudable effort to overcome the previously distressing parochialism. First I should like to mention the increasing number of comparative, cross-national studies of minorities of which Wagley and Harris's work (1958) is one of the early, good examples. In this type of research prejudice is no longer seen as a cause, but as a symptom of an "ongoing social conflict." Thus, the sociological, comparative approach began to gain on the psychological one: it became clearer now that prejudiced individuals view themselves as belonging to a specific group. They locate others, against whom they are prejudiced, in another group than their own. Such an identification implies the formation of an image of their own and the other's group in terms of their mutual relations.

This process of image-formation is a collective process (Blumer, 1961). But what was also preserved in this broader and more sociological approach was the generic definition of minority, which included, as in Wagley and Harris's work, the Negro in Martinique, the Jew in the United States, and the French-speaking person in Canada, among others.

Such a broad definition forced the theoretical analysis of the often admirably studied group relations to such a high level of abstraction, that the number of conceptual tools was kept limited to a deplorable minimum; "ethnocentrism" and "endogamy" were the type of key concepts with which under these circumstances Wagley and Harris and their followers had to operate. In a recent book in this vein (Mason, 1970) a very large number of "systems of inequality" are described, from the oldest times to the present, including master-slave, racial, cultural, and all kinds of colonial "patterns of dominance," but such an effort to extract from a maximum number of cases their sociological essence leaves us in fact with only one variable fit to be applied in comparisons within such a heterogeneous universe: the numerical relation between dominant and subordinate groups. One need not be a fanatic adherent of Stuart Mills' *A System of Logic* to entertain serious doubts about the assumption that our understanding of the problem is necessarily to be enhanced by the greater number of cases we study, especially if the problem has been defined in a rather loose way. Only God and the editors know whether the book in which this essay will appear belongs to this category. For if one's prime interest is in the study of multi-racial societies, then one precisely need not widen but rather narrow one's scope, not soften but harden one's analytical tools, not play down certain criteria of classification, but experimentally emphasize them. What are the differences between "cultural" and "racial" diversity? If the concept of "racial differences" has validity, is it then allowed to assume that some of these differences are greater (or are perceived as being greater) than others, and if we are not allowed to assume this, why not? Is "racial relations" synonymous with "socio-racial stratification" as some authors seem to believe? I intend to deal with some of these questions further on.

II

The second of the new tendencies to which I alluded, is the result of the increasing interest in the United States in the special position of its Black population group. Of those who endeavored to historically compare this special position with that of Negroes and mulattoes in other societies of the Western Hemisphere, Frank Tannenbaum with his *Slave and Citizen* (1947) was one of the first and most important. But his excellent pioneer work also introduced a spurious causality between "master-slave relations" and "race relations," which in the meantime has become virtually commonplace and therefore hard to eradicate.

He implied that where mild relations between masters and slaves prevailed (as he postulated for Latin America), there resulted mild race relations between white and Negro *outside* and *after* slavery and that severity or cruelty in slavery (as he assumed to have existed in British and Dutch America) led inexorably to a long-term crisis in the relations between the different socio-racial groups outside and after slavery. Tannenbaum linked both sets of relations in a causal way which later research has proven to be untenable. Yet, paradoxically, some of those who criticized Tannenbaum's emphasis on cultural factors as determinants of master-slave relations, and stressed—correctly, in my view—the link between economic conditions and slave treatment, nevertheless kept insisting on a close, even causal, link between slavery and the sociological problems of a multi-racial society: while Tannenbaum explained the nature of race relations out of the nature of master-slave relations, his formidable opponent, the Trinidadian historian Williams, stated that "racism" was the product of slavery as an economic system. Their well-known debate, published under the title *Race Relations in Caribbean Society* (Rubin, 1957), deals predominantly, in effect, with the conditions of different systems of slavery.

Of course, there did exist in several societies a historical sequence between slavery and the inception of a multi-racial society. But, equally obviously, there are also societies where an existing "race problem" was not immediately preceded by a system of slavery or serfdom and others where systems of unfree labor did not give rise to racial tensions (if only because the slaves or serfs were not physically distinguishable). The fact that—especially in the Western Hemisphere—such a historical sequence presented itself must not lead to its conversion into a sociological causality.

The characteristic differences in race relations between the different societies of Afro-America cannot be fully explained out of their slavery systems, but have to be understood in terms of the peculiar development of each *total* society, outside and after slavery. To give just one example: it is impossible to account for the curious absence in the United States of an intermediate (colored) stratum as a distinctly recognized social category on the basis of alleged peculiarities of the United States slavery system; it is possible, however, to develop hypotheses, which explain the emergence and maintenance of the North American black-white dichotomy in terms of peculiar traits of society at large (e.g., Harris, 1964). It is, incidentally, precisely this dichotomy, which makes it so tempting to postulate a causality between slavery and race relations in the United States; the master-slave dichotomy is seen as continued by the white-black dichotomy. But, as to the latter, the United States is a glaring exception in the entire Western Hemisphere! The presently booming historical research in "comparative slave systems" may increase our knowledge in many respects, but it is to be feared that our insight in the sociology of race relations will profit from it only indirectly.

The two tendencies, commented upon briefly, have produced then, on the one hand, a type of comparative study in which the distinction between cultural and racial relations is not or is hardly being explored, and, on the other hand, a type of research in which the explanatory factors of contemporary race relations are being traced back and converged toward a comparative study of the safely historical institution of slavery.

The disinclination to recognize the existence of racial differences and their sociological consequences as reality—in the philosophical sense—has to do with the general embarrassment that the word "race" provokes even among those who have made it clear from the start that they do not believe in hereditary mental or intellectual superiority or inferiority of any racial group.

Hence the eagerness with which phenomena (such as the Caribbean saying "A rich Negro is a mulatto, a poor mulatto is Negro"), which can be interpreted as a negation of an objectively functioning socio-racial classification, are emphasized by some researchers. Others try to undo the concept of "color" from its common-sense meaning, reducing it to a social metaphor, by speaking of "associational color," "structural color," and so forth.

This persistent inhibition of the somatic factor per se as an autonomous explanatory social element in the study of group relations in multi-racial societies, partly explains the success of two more general approaches, of which the tendencies we just discussed are only particular examples. I refer to the cultural-deterministic and the economic-deterministic approaches.

The Jamaican sociologist Michael G. Smith is probably the most articulate defender of cultural determinism in the study of race relations. His central idea is that what are viewed as "racial" tensions and conflicts are in fact the result of cultural (and hence institutional) diversity. A multi-racial society without institutionalized cultural differences would, consequently, have no "race problem" (Smith, 1965: 63). Smith distinguishes in a society such as Jamaica three "cultures" which he calls "white," "brown" and "black" and which are rather rigidly separated. But the concept of culture that Smith uses in his analysis has not so much to do with its anthropological connotation (language, religion, etc.) as with its sociological usage: culture is seen as a conglomerate of patterns of behavior and thought correlating with social position.

In this latter sense the Jamaican white group has indeed its own, namely, upper-class "culture," the mulatto group a middle-class, and the black group a lower-class "culture," grosso modo. But these cultural differences in the sociological sense are not greater than those in any predominantly agrarian society with a similar socio-economic structure. Nor are the cultural differences in the anthropological sense more distinct than those in any European society. This makes it difficult to understand why precisely these cultural differences have to be viewed as final cause of tensions expressed in racial terms. In a country such as the United States, where distinct cultural differences in the anthropological sense between blacks and whites are, comparatively speaking, not impressive at all, the militant blacks are precisely trying to *create* a culture of their own—which might be called an emancipatory culture—so as to emphasize *also* in linguistic expression, dress, hairdos, etc., the distinction which somatically already exists between them and the white group. This is clearly a case of cultural differences emerging out of an already existing socio-racial conflict.

It is not surprising that Smith's approach proves to be most successful if applied to societies where pronounced cultural differences in the anthropological sense are indeed clearly observable, as is the case in the Caribbean societies of Trinidad, Guyana, and Surinam, where there are vertical dividing lines between

(East—) Indian and Negro/colored segments, in certain multi-lingual European societies, as well as in several African societies where similar vertical "pillariza-tion" on a tribal-cultural basis exists. Smith's (1968) recent interesting research does indeed deal with these latter societies.

Just as Smith's culturalistic approach makes most sense where cultural-anthopological differences between component parts of a society are a paramount criterion of social distinction, the economic determinist approach is most defendable in the analysis of societies where economic achievement is indeed perceived as being more decisive in social categorization than either "race" or "culture."

Nineteenth century or "classical" sociology developed in industrializing European societies with a relative minimum of racial or cultural heterogeneity. The development of "class" out of "estate" systems of stratification consequent-ly attracted much of the new science's attention. Only certain linguistic and religious minorities in Central Europe posed enough of a political problem to be included in treatises on nationhood.

This Europe-centered sociology, fertile as it was, and with that fortunate historical orientation which is so deplorably lacking in most contemporary U.S. social science, had an impact great enough to have it granted universal applicability. This proclaimed universality of a mode of analysis, clearly tied to a particular time and place, has hampered rather than fostered our sociological understanding of racial—and, for that matter, cultural—conflicts.

By way of example, let me deal briefly with an engaging essay by Rodolfo Stavenhagen, the noted Mexican sociologist, in which he tries to analyze the "inter-ethnic relations" in Meso America (1970). With considerable justification he states that "the importance attributed by ethnologists to cultural elements of Indian populations has long concealed the nature of socio-economic structures into which these populations are integrated." In a similar vein he also rejects the significance of somatic differences between the different groups. A seemingly basic description by Alfonson Caso of an "Indian community" as one in which there exists "a predominance of non-European somatic elements, where language is preferentially Indian, possessing within its material and spiritual culture a strong proportion of Indian elements and finally, having a social feeling of being an isolated community within surrounding ones, distinguishing it from white and mestizo villages" is rejected by Stavenhagen, because, in his view, Caso introduces "racial considerations" and because in Caso's definition the elements that are needed for a study of the economic relations *between* Indian and mestizo are lacking.

But one cannot refrain from observing that in order to study these *relations* both groups have first to be defined culturally and/or somatically in much the same way as Caso is doing. While rejecting such definitions, Stavenhagen then proceeds to make statements such as "In Jilotepeque, laborers constitute 90% of the active population, of which only 9% are Ladinos," and "In Guatemala's coffee plantations, compulsory labor for Indians existed until recently, . . . yet no Ladino, even those possessing no land, was forced to perform this kind of work," and "in Jilotepeque, a Ladino laborer earns 50% more than an Indian laborer," and "the Ladino owners generally, possess more land than the Indian owners," all statements which make clear that within the economic categories of laborers, landless rural proletariat, and landowners, *other* observable distinctions exist between Ladinos and Indians which make it impossible to analyze their relations merely in terms of economic or "class" criteria. In fact, the *subordination* of economic factors to those of a cultural and/or somatic nature (in the subjective, but real, perception of both Indians and Ladinos) is implicitly recognized by Stavenhagen in a later part of his essay, where he makes such observations as "a Ladino will always be a Ladino, low as he may fall in the socio-economic scale" (1970: 265).

III

Several scholars who prefer to view racial relations from the perspective of economic exploitation speak in this context of "internal colonialism." They use this term with regard to the Amerindians in Central and South America and the Negroes in the United States. In my view, such a term is indeed appropriate; it is appropriate in Indo-America because we deal there with a subordinate autochthonous and culturally distinct population group; it is appropriate in North America as far as the black group's principal characteristics are described in terms of racial and even cultural differences as well as economic ones. For one of the unavoidable implications of the concept of "colonialism" is the recognition of the multi-racial and/or multi-cultural nature of the society to which the concept is being applied: the term is *not* used in cases of economic exploitation and subordination within culturally or racially homogeneous populations. Taken in this sense, the term "internal colonialism" is a recognition (albeit unintentional by most of its users) of the existence of racial and/or cultural diversity, and its sociological relevance.

Finally, there is also not a small touch of irony in the fact that some of the authors who tend to perceive racial conflicts mainly in economic terms, and hence supposedly belong to the materialist school of philosophic thought, in their eagerness to "explain away" the sociological impact of phenotypical group differences tend to resort to what they in other circumstances would regard as an instance of vulgar philosophical idealism: "color is in the eye of the beholder," they say (and class is not).

IV

Allow me now to briefly define my position vis-à-vis the contemporary currents that I—too sketchily—have indicated so far.

I am, with many of my colleagues, convinced that sociology as a discipline can only exist by the grace of the assumption that the social perspective, and hence, the "social consciousness" of the members of a social group are determined in great measure by the position which that group occupies in the total societal structure.

But this total societal structure is generally a conglomerate of diverse systems of social categorization and classification, which do not necessarily coincide. To mention just three of these: all societies have a socio-economic stratification (to which is linked a differentiation in "culture" in the sociological sense, correlated with socio-economic position); most societies have further a socio-cultural stratification (in the anthropological sense of socially relevant differences in language and religion etc.); some societies finally have a socio-racial stratification, with socially relevant differences between pheno-typical groups.

While a socio-economic stratification has horizontal lines of division (the socio-economic groups are vertically ordered), some socio-cultural and socio-racial stratifications have vertical lines of division. In this case the groups live next to each other, each with its own socio-economic stratification, and in some cases with its own territory within the joint political unit.

Now, to state that what matters in any of these three types of stratification is the difference in *power* between their component parts is to engage in a futile tautological exercise, because *every* type of stratification finds by definition its ultimate origin in, and is maintained by, differences in power.

What makes a given stratification sociologically interesting, however, are the criteria according to which this power is being allocated and distributed. Economic possession is one of the important attributes and instruments of power, but the *ways* in which such possessions are being distributed generally correspond to criteria of a non-economic character connected with differentiations along kinship, religious, socio-geographical, cultural, racial, friendship, clique and similar lines. It is the correlations with these criteria which convert the socio-economic stratification of a society from a mere statistical contraption into a sociological phenomenon.

The pure class society in which one's social rank is exclusively measured and allocated on the basis of achieved traits does not exist anywhere. But just as there are societies where, for purposes of comparison, the achievement-criterion may be considered predominant, so there are societies where membership in a certain cultural grouping or in a socio-racial category is of greater importance in the overall societal ranking than are wealth or education, the attainment of the latter being in such societies, for that matter, to a great extent *dependent* on one's membership in a given socio-cultural or socio-racial group.

Not only do these three types of stratification never occur in a pure and exclusive form, but the stratifications themselves are not necessarily rigid (though in some societies they are). In all societies, no matter which type of stratification predominates, cases of status inconsistencies occur.

The socio-economic, socio-cultural, or socio-racial position of a given individual may be evaluated differently by different members of his society: the ranking of an individual *is* to a certain extent "in the eye of the beholder"; yet, if the general concept of stratification is admitted as valid and useful for analytical purposes, a modicum of consensus on social stratification and its predominant criteria within a given society must implicitly be assumed.

In a society where a socio-racial stratification predominates, the frequency and distance of vertical social rise and fall are to a high degree determined by membership in a given socio-racial category: special mechanisms of social selection generally tend to favor those whose somatic traits are most akin to those of the dominant socio-racial group, other things being equal.

Insofar as the term racist is nowadays often used with reference to these mechanisms of selection, we may indeed speak here of racist societies, by definition, as it were.

Similarly, in a society where a socio-cultural stratification predominates, the membership in a given socio-cultural group determines the advantages or disadvantages in an individual's life cycle. We might, to further the parallel, speak here of a culturalist society.

Let me explain here why, in spite of obvious similarities between the two, we have for analytical purposes to distinguish between socio-racial and socio-cultural stratification. The necessity of such a distinction becomes clear as soon as we study in sufficient time-depth the development of societies which at their historical base line are both culturally *and* racially heterogeneous. In such societies, especially if they are of the horizontally layered type, there are often clearly observable differences in the rate of cultural exchange as compared to that of biological mixture-cum-social acceptance. Such a society, as is the case with many in the Western Hemisphere, can after some centuries attain a culture of remarkable homogeneity, while at the same time maintaining a rather rigid socio-racial stratification. This means, of course, that the factors determining cultural assimilation or rejection are different from those influencing racial assimilation or rejection. These latter have, for reasons previously mentioned, been neglected in the social sciences. They can only be studied in a comparative, historical context, which allows for taxonomic distinctions and diachronic analysis at the same time.

V

Continuity or discontinuity is one of the basic criteria for distinction between socio-racial stratifications.

A *continuous* socio-racial stratification is one in which none of the socio-racial groups in a society practices or is forced to practice a strict endogamy. Although in such a society color distinctions do have often great social significance, and the somatic traits of the originally dominant group are highly valued, this group has, in the course of time, formed socially recognized sexual unions with members of the contiguous intermediate socio-racial strata. This process of socio-racial mixture has thus produced a continuum, of which the extremes may be somatically very different, but in which numerous intermediate groupings make the socio-racial structure one of subtle gradations. In Afro-America, the societies colonized by the Spanish and Portuguese have achieved this type of stratification. As Seda-Bonilla observes:

> "A logical consequence of the Latin American conceptualization is that, though the social distance between the opposite groups, such as whites and blacks, is considerable, the social distance between contiguous categories is not that remarkable. If we measure the social distance between *grifos* and *mulatos,* between *negros* and *grifos,* between *blancos* and *blancos con raja,* we will find that it is considerably less than between the two poles in the continuum. . . . As the result of the 'tolerance' between contiguous categories, there is a marked tendency towards race-mixing between persons of contiguous categories so as to produce physical types with greater acceptability in society [for] . . . given the existence of racial prejudice, the hypogamic pressure is directed toward 'whitening'" [Seda-Bonilla, 1968: 577].

In the *discontinuous* type of socio-racial stratification we find that the dominant socio-racial group claims and clings to racial "purity." This is not to say that members of this group have not had sexual liaisons with members of the subordinate segments (to which the number of persons with mixed somatic traits attests). Nor does it means that no phenotypically "acceptable" offspring from the intermediate strata has ever been socially absorbed by the dominant socio-racial group. But this latter fact is apt to be denied by the dominant stratum which in its system of marriage selection and hence generally in its more intimate social contacts emphasizes the distance between itself and the stratum next to it in the socio-racial stratification. In the Western Hemisphere, the societies colonized by the British (including present-day United States), the French, the Dutch and the Danes, all belong to this discontinuous type, although there are obviously variations in the ways in which the non-intimate social relations between the different socio-racial groups are being carried out.

The discontinuous stratification of the United States is an exceptional one, because, while in all other discontinuous stratifications of the Western Hemisphere an intermediate group (coloreds, mulattoes) has always been given a position, distinct from both whites and blacks in the overall structure, in the United States this has not been the general case. There, a dichotomy—white-black—established itself, in which a person of mixed origins was and is defined as Negro or black.

VI

Let us at this point, schematically recapitulate the different socio-racial stratifications mentioned so far:

		Horizontal dividing lines	Vertical dividing lines
Continuous stratification		Societies colonized by Spanish and Portuguese	
Discontinuous stratification	With distinct intermediate strata:	Societies colonized by French, Dutch Danes, and British (except U.S.)	Trinidad Guyana Surinam
	Dichotomous:	U.S.	

Let us now briefly consider what effect the different types of socio-racial stratification may have on the awareness of national identity. Nineteenth-century European sociology tended to emphasize common origin in its definition of what constitutes a people. As such, the concept was virtually synonymous with what is called ethnic group in the United States today, defined by Shibutani and Kwan (1965) as those "who conceive themselves to be alike by virtue of common ancestry real or fictitious, and who are so regarded by others." Another school of thought, represented here by Karl Deutsch, prefers to disregard matters of (quasi-) biological origins and stresses the need for a "wide complementarity of social communication" which is considered characteristic of "membership in a people" (Deutsch, 1965: 97). Yet, both types of definitions have much in common. It is clear that communication is not fostered by socio-racial or socio-cultural barriers, and one need only read Deutsch's index references to intermarriage to discover that, in effect, he considers intermarriage between "distinctive units" a factor of importance in the growth of national identity. A prolonged process of intermarriage will in the end, of course, give form to, and justify, some belief in a common ancestry.

Maybe we can reconcile both approaches by saying that the strength or weakness of national identity depends on the degree to which the historical experiences of a nation are perceived and transmitted as *common* experiences.

VII

In countries like Surinam, Trinidad, and Guyana, where the somatic and cultural dividing lines between the main population segments run vertically, we observe in action a process of designing a national mythology, in which heroes and memorable feats are carefully distributed over the cultural heritages of the two main groups. In the light of the foregoing, the formation of such a national pantheon would seem to be a contradictio in terminis.

Theoretically, these types of societies have one advantage, however, as far as the fostering of national identity is concerned, over the horizontally layered ones: every type of horizontal solidarity that may emerge, such as that based on class position, will tend to mitigate the existing racial and cultural cleavages. In a horizontally layered multi-racial (or multi-cultural) society, on the other hand, such class solidarities rather tend to coincide with, hence strengthen, the already existing divisions of an ascriptive nature.

This explains the emphasis placed by those who would want to weaken the cultural and/or somatic group alignments in societies such as Trinidad, Guyana, and Surinam, on the similarities between Creoles and East Indians, as far as their historical roles as slaves, respectively contract laborers, is concerned, both groups being presented as equally suffering victims of colonial exploitation (Williams, 1964).

So far, there has been little indication that even those on the lower ranks of the economic scale have accepted these appeals to any effective degree (Nicholls, 1971). For the moment, then, these societies, with their short history of national autonomy or sovereignty, have a rather precarious sense of national identity. They would seem best fitted for a quasi-federative collaboration between the main component segments. The question is whether, due to differences in demographic growth and economic ethos, one of these groups—the East Indians—might not end up being dominant in the long run, the vertical lines of division thus becoming horizontal once again. The rate of growth of a common culture, and of intermarriage, will undoubtedly be crucial factors in these countries' future development and in their viability as a nation in the sociological sense.

VIII

In the horizontally layered societies of the rest of the Commonwealth, French and Dutch Caribbean, a growing awareness of négritude asks for its recognition on the level of national symbols, but finds some resistance from the intermediate colored sectors and the white élite.

Gordon K. Lewis has commented caustically on the controversies produced in Jamaica by the return, in 1964, of Marcus Garvey's ashes and "his elevation by the Jamaican government to the status of official hero" (Lewis, 1968: 176). In more general terms, Bell and Oxaal observed how "at the time of independence, some Jamaicans were reluctant to accept the growing emphasis upon African origins and slavery in the interpretation of Jamaica's past. . . . Such resistance . . . reflected either the rejection of identity with the Negro racial stock . . . or the principle . . . that the symbols of the African origins and slavery were somehow degrading" (Bell and Oxaal, 1964: 63). It is interesting to note that these authors expressed themselves strongly against "the story of the rise of the enslaved black man from Africa" becoming *the* history of Jamaica," because "some Jamaicans, perhaps all those who are not fairly dark-skinned Negroes, might be excluded from sharing in the new Jamaican history, perhaps from the new Jamaican society itself" (Bell and Oxaal, 1964: 64). Similar problems can easily be observed in other Caribbean societies with a discontinuous socio-racial stratification (Rapport van de Commissie, 1970).

Since in these societies the black population forms the overwhelming majority, its desire to substitute the traditional symbolism and history writing (which heavily emphasized the values of the originally dominant segment), by one, representative of their own socio-racial sector, is fully understandable. But since such a substitution would lead to the psychological exclusion of the creole white (quasi-) endogamous and the light-colored population groups, who lack the subjective potential for identification with the new symbols, compromises, at least as far as flags and national mottoes are concerned, have been worked out, which purport to symbolize and celebrate the racial "diversity." Such a symbolism in fact epitomizes the racial discontinuity, but this is being done in such a fashion (equally large circles, equally wide stripes for each socio-racial group) that an equivalence of the segments is suggested.

Such a symbolism, then, is not a reflection of real power or even numerical relations in these horizontally layered societies, but creates the fiction of a vertically segmented society, where all segments are equally powerful.

In the United States, where numerical proportions preclude a substitution of the traditional national symbols by one representative of the subordinate segment, a similarly divided pantheon of symbols would seem to be the only viable answer to the current wishes of the black group in this respect. The United States is, indeed, the only one of all societies under consideration where—as a result of its peculiar numerical proportions—black militants try to change society itself from horizontal to vertical segmentation and where this change, short of self-imposed political exclusion, can be considered as a final goal.

It seems clear that the particular vehemence of the blacks' struggle for social recognition in the United States is at least in part attributable to the absence in that society of an intermediate stratum in its socio-racial stratification. Light coloreds are also blacks there (though they may occupy a special position within the black segment).

Whether such a dichotomous, discontinuous stratification will in the end be favorable to the solution of the country's racial problems, as Talcott Parsons (1968), in an intriguing dialectic, tries to show, is too complex a matter to deal with here (Hoetink, 1971a, 1973).

Suffice it to say that, even on the basis of our brief observations here, it may be suggested that a discontinuous socio-racial stratification generally does not enhance the awareness of national identity; it is extremely hard for the groups involved to devise a history writing and a set of national symbols in which the commonalty of their past, as well as of their destiny, are convincingly demonstrated.

In spite of the often remarkable cultural homogeneity in several of these societies, there has always existed a tendency to consider one of the racial groups as alien. In the past the blacks were so conceived by the white segment, as the traditional symbolism and historiography clearly demonstrate. Today the tendency is in the reverse direction. Where, as in the United States, numerical proportions make such a reversal utopic, the black militants strive after some form of self-contained black community, in which their alienness in the society at large will be suffered from as little as possible. Some dream of exclusion, physical, cultural, and political, from white U.S. society.

It seems obvious that the self-image, and hence the image of the future, of the racial groups involved are strongly influenced by the type of socio-racial stratification of which they form a part.

Where, as in the United States, this stratification is dichotomous and discontinuous and the subordinate group is proportionally small, such images of its members will tend to be (self-) exclusion-oriented.

Where, as in the other horizontally layered discontinuous stratifications under discussion, the originally subordinated segment is large, there is now a tendency toward exclusion of the white group. Such a tendency has so far, however, been corroded by the curious buffer position of the intermediate (colored) strata.

While there is no need to dispute the fact of serious discrimination against the darkest strata in virtually all Afro-Latin societies, it does make a difference, both for the self-perception and the image of the future of the groups involved, that in these countries there does exist an inclusionist ideology of interracial mixing and that it *can* legitimately exist because there is indeed a socio-racial continuum. That in such an ideology emphasis is placed on the "whitening" of the population is virtually unavoidable in a multi-racial society where a racist ingredient in the mechanisms of social selection operates by definition. But it is also clear that the frequency of *connubium* between (often contiguous, yet different) socio-racial categories justifies the acceptance by all groups of an ideology of ultimate racial amalgamation (which therefore has an entirely different basis than the discredited melting-pot ideology in the United States, which never included the blacks anyhow). Hence the vision of the future can be inclusion-oriented for the darker strata, even if their present self-perception is being influenced by the, ideologically speaking, as yet functioning principles of racist selection.

While in the discontinuous stratifications we find that parts of the different socio-racial groups aspire to inclusion of the black population on the basis of an ideology of social equality, which ideology is constantly being undermined by social reality, we find in the continuous stratifications a national ideology of amalgamation, which ideology finds some justification in social reality.

It is not surprising to find that even in the traditional, colonial symbolisms of the Afro-Latin societies some dark-skinned heroes were included; the Wars of Independence added several more of these, without this being conceived by the creole whites as incompatible with their feelings of national identity.

The absence of clear-cut categories in the socio-racial stratification generally prevented racial animosities (though undoubtedly existing) from achieving the degree of articulation, and its concurrent impact on national symbolism and history writing, that we observed for the societies with a discontinuous socio-racial stratification.

IX

The comparative study of socio-racial stratifications in the Western Hemisphere has to focus, as the foregoing may show, on at least two highly intriguing and important questions. One is, why did not the discontinuous stratification of the United States develop a socially distinct, intermediate stratum, as was the case elsewhere?

The second is, why did a continuous socio-racial stratification only develop in the societies, colonized by Spain and Portugal? (In Haiti, the expulsion of the whites at the end of the 18th century left the country with a continuous socio-racial stratification—with sharp cultural differences between blacks and mulattoes. What interests us here, however, is the situation in societies where "creole whites" are present.)

The first question falls outside the scope of this essay. I shall address myself—albeit it briefly—to the second question, if only to justify the title of this contribution.

Quite a few efforts have been made to explain the emergence of a socio-racial continuum in the Iberian-American societies, and its absence elsewhere, using the type of explanatory factors that form part of the historian's or sociologist's normal stock in trade.

Thus there is the theory of the shortage of white females in the early Spanish and Portuguese colonies: the white man had to marry interracially and to socially absorb the offspring of such unions; the theory that economic conditions were consistently different between the two variants' components; the theory that mild slavery made the Negro in Latin America preserve his moral personality so that, once set free, he was on an equal footing with the rest of the population; the hypotheses that religion (Catholicism versus Protestantism), or legal traditions, or Moorish cultural influences, were responsible; the suggestion, finally, that an early creole culture gave a sense of collective identity to all socio-racial groups in the countries colonized by Iberians (and then fostered racial amalgamation) whereas such a creole culture did not develop elsewhere.

The trouble with most of such explanations is that the non-Iberian multi-racial societies of the Western Hemisphere (British, French, Dutch, Danish) show a very great variety between them in terms of economic history, cultural and demographic development, and so forth, making it virtually impossible to show convincingly that, say, factors of an economic or demographic nature, *present* in Afro-Latin America, were *absent* in *all* non-Iberian societies under discussion. The same goes for the supposed differences in religion, for the societies colonized by the French were Catholic, yet developed a discontinuous stratification. We therefore have to look for factors intrinsically part of the Iberian peoples and their cultural heritage and hence per definition absent elsewhere.

We have further to keep in mind that in essence the emergence of a socio-racial continuum—that is to say, the absence of rigid endogamous tendencies within the creole white group—is a problem of selection of marriage partners, confined to the creole white group and its nearest contiguous socio-racial groupings in the socio-racial stratification. Such a problem, then, is much more of a psycho-sociological than of a demographic or economic nature. This is not to say that marriage-markets generally do not have economic and geographic limits, but *within* those limits the selection of a partner, acceptable for marriage and the production of offspring, is an affair that generally transcends purely material considerations. In many of the discontinuous societies under discussion, white persons could also easily find economically attractive marriage partners from the intermediate strata, yet the frequency of such unions has, historically speaking, been distinctly greater in the Iberian-colonized societies.

Considerations such as these have led me to believe that there is a slight difference in the way a "light-colored" person is perceived in terms of physical attractiveness, between the Iberian and non-Iberian whites, and I think there is sufficient support in the existing literature for this idea.

Every society, of course, conceives some combination of physical features as attractive, and allows a certain margin around this ideal—which I call the somatic norm image—within which a person is still "acceptable" (Hoetink, 1971b). Since the very human concept of physical vanity simply cannot exist without there operating a socially approved somatic norm image, I think that fieldwork to prove the latter's reality by induction is superfluous where such a convincing deduction can be made. Yet, indirectly, its existence has been demonstrated empirically, also. In multi-racial societies, the ideal of physical beauty of the dominant group will in the course of time be taken over by the subordinated segments. This "one-way transference of the dominant somatic norm image" has been observed in all of these societies, recently again by Miller (1969) among a group of Jamaican adolescents.

It would seem that in the Iberian-American societies, where this process also operates, the white somatic norm image—which tends to correlate with the physical features of the group involved—is somewhat darker than its counterpart in the non-Iberian societies, so that persons, who would be called light-colored in, say, the Netherlands Antilles, would fall within the accepted margin of the white somatic norm image in one of the Spanish-speaking societies. The latter, as Rogler indicated for Puerto Rico (1943), may show a certain ambiguity about members of their societies who are perceived as being too blond or too white, and who would be entirely acceptable as creole whites in the non-Iberian societies.

If this type of analysis is correct, then the emergence of a socio-racial continuum, with its many favorable influences on the formation of an all-inclusive sense of national identity, would not predominantly be an economic, demographic, cultural, let alone moral phenomenon, but would rather be the result of the ways in which groups with particular physical characteristic and particular ideas about what is physically attractive (in the non-exotic sense) perceive each other. This would imply that a concept such as somatic distance would necessarily have to be introduced if we are to analyze and compare different societies with different socio-racial component parts.

X

All this is not to say that factors of an economic nature or of a cultural character do not influence the way contacts between different socio-racial groups in a given society are being carried out. Such factors undoubtedly have a great impact on race relations generally, on the way everyday social contacts are regulated, on the general atmosphere in which a particular multi-racial society lives. But, as Pitt-Rivers (1968: 277) observes: "Political or commercial alliances are not the same as alliances through marriage. Their products are of a different order. Profits are colorless, children are not. Hence, phenotype may not matter in commercial dealings, but it is never more important than in marriage." And, in a terminology reminiscent of ours, he writes: "Individual motivations are ordered to produce conformity with an ideal image of ethnic class."

It is this ordering of individual motivations conforming to the prevailing somatic norm image, which in my opinion, in certain societies has led to a socio-racial continuum, and not in others. And it would seem that such a continuum is an indispensable ingredient in the growth of an awareness of social cohesion, of sentiments of common descent and destiny, in the "complementarity of social communication," and in the subjective acceptance of the commonalty of collective experiences.

It is also such a socio-racial continuum, fostering and justifying an ideology of ultimate amalgamation which, once a population has achieved a certain degree of objective cultural homogeneity, helps to elevate this to a level of subjective solidarity, indispensable for a strong awareness of national identity.

REFERENCES

BELL, W. and OXAAL, I. (1964) Decisions of Nationhood: Political and Social Development in the British Caribbean. Denver: University of Denver.
BLUMER, H. (1961) "Race prejudice as a sense of group position," in J. Masouka and P. Valien (eds.), Race Relations: Problems and Theory. Chapel Hill: University of North Carolina Press.
DEUTSCH, K. (1965) Nationalism and Social Communication. Cambridge: MIT Press.
MARRIS, M. (1964), Patterns of Race in the Americas. New York: Walker.
HOETINK, H. (1973) Slavery and Race Relations in the Americas: An Inquiry into their Nature and Nexus. New York: Harper & Row.
––– (1971a) "Culture, race and national identity in the Caribbean," in J. Q. Campbell (ed.), Racial Tensions and National Identity. Nashville: Vanderbilt University Press.
––– (1971b) Caribbean Race Relations: A Study of Two Variants. New York: Oxford University Press.
LEWIS, G. K. (1968) The Growth of the Modern West Indies. London: MacGibbon and Kee.
MASON, P. (1970) Patterns of Dominance. London: Oxford University Press for the Institute of Race Relations.
MILLER, E. L. (1969) "Body image, physical beauty and colour among Jamaican adolescents." Social and Economic Studies 18: 1.
NICHOLLS, D. G. (1971) "East Indians and Black Power in Trinidad." Race 12: 443-459.
PARSONS, T. (1968) "The problem of polarization on the axis of color," in J. H. Franklin (ed.) Color and Race. Boston: Houghton Mifflin.
PITT-RIVERS, J. (1968) "Race, color and class in Central America and the Andes," in J. H. Franklin (ed.) Color and Race. Boston: Houghton Mifflin.
Rapport van de Commissie (1970) tot Onderzoek van de Achtergronden en Oorzaken van de Onlusten welke op 30 mei 1969 op Curacao hebben Plaatsgehad. Aruba: De Wit.
ROGLER, G. (1943) "The role of semantics in the study of race distance in Puerto Rico." Social Forces 22: 448-453.
ROSE, P. (1970) "The development of 'race studies': sociological views and expanding horizons," in G. Shepherd and T. Lemille (eds.) Race Among Nations. Lexington, Mass.: D. C. Heath.
RUBIN, V. [ed.] (1957) Caribbean Studies: A Symposium. Jamaica: Institute of Social and Economic Research.

SEDA-BONILLA, E. (1968) "Dos modelos de relaciones raciales: Estados Unidos y América Latina." Revista de Ciencias Sociales 4: 569-597.
SHIBUTANI, T. and K. M. KWAN (1965) Ethnic Stratification: A Comparative Approach. New York: Macmillan.
SMITH, M. G. (1968) "Institutional and political conditions of pluralism," in L. Kuper and M. G. Smith (eds.) Pluralism in Africa. Berkeley: University of California Press.
——— (1965) The Plural Society in the West Indies. Berkeley: University of California Press.
STAVENHAGEN, R. (1970) "Classes, colonialism and acculturation: a system of inter-ethnic relations in Meso-America," in I. L. Horowitz (ed.) Masses in Latin America. New York: Oxford University Press.
TANNENBAUM, F. (1947) Slave and Citizen. New York: A. A. Knopf.
WAGLEY, C. and M. HARRIS (1958) Minorities in the New World: Six Case Studies. New York: Columbia University Press.
WILLIAMS, E. (1964) History of the People of Trinidad and Tobago. London: André Deutsch.

Chapter 3

PLURALIST AND MARXIST PERSPECTIVES
ON ETHNICITY AND NATION-BUILDING

JOEL C. EDELSTEIN

I

*I*n his most recent formulation of plural society [1] theory, M. G. Smith proposes that "at the comparative or 'macro-sociological' level, we should distinguish societal types by basic differences of structure in their institutions of collective incorporation" (1969b: 437). Although the dominant political unit at this point in history is the nation-state, not all states are composed of a single group which shares common social, cultural, or even economic institutions. In some states, there exist two or more collectivities which share different institutional bases. In some of these (which Smith calls heterogeneous societies), the collectivities or categories differ only in respect to private institutions such as marriage and kinship. The result is only cultural differences. Everyone is equal in relation to public institutions such as in the legal and political spheres. In these societies, individuals "hold their citizenship directly and not through segmental or sectional identifications." In their relationships with public institutions which include all of the social collectivities in the state, each citizen acts and is perceived as an individual, rather than as a member of one of the collectivities within the state.

The two societal types described above (which Smith labels homogeneous and heterogeneous, respectively) differ only in that in the former, all institutions are shared while in the latter, differences exist at the private level. In both, individuals are incorporated into the society without respect to membership in any grouping or category.

Smith's classificatory scheme contains two other types. They differ from those described above in that institutional differences extend beyond the private realm to affect the relationships of members of these societies to public institutions. Individuals function in the public realm not as individuals, but as members of a collectivity which does not extend to the whole of the society. In some of these societies, the type called "social pluralism" by Smith, it is no more advantageous or disadvantageous to belong to one of the collectivities than another. In the remaining type, given the designation, "structural pluralism," an individual's group or collectivity membership is of considerable importance in his relations with public areas of life such as economic and political activity. In societies characterized by structural pluralism, the collectivities do not exist as equals. Instead, there exists a dominant-subordinate relationship which places

AUTHOR'S NOTE: I would like to thank Edna Bonacich, Leo Kuper, Michael Lofchie, Roberta Mapp, Helen Safa, Howard Sherman, and Benjamin Smith for their helpful suggestions during the development of this paper.

members of the subordinate collectivity at a disadvantage. Structural pluralism is most severe in societies in which the dominant group is a small minority.

Smith has made several significant changes in plural society theory since it was first developed by J. S. Furnivall (1945, 1948), a British colonial administrator. While Furnivall restricted its application to colonial, tropical, multi-racial societies in the historical period of European colonial expansion, Smith has raised the plural society theory to the status of a general theory, classifying all societies in its terms. Also, the emphasis in earlier formulations on cultural, racial, or ethnic differences as a cause of social division and the domination of one grouping by another is changed. In Smith's formulation, the denial of political and legal rights to a portion of society is the essence of structural pluralism. He states that this condition may exist in societies lacking racial and ethnic differences. Smith focuses on political domination as the key factor. While institutional differences usually exist prior to the establishment of the dominant-subordinate relationship as in the conquest of African and Asian peoples by the British, this need not be the case. The condition of discrimination and often segregation faced by subordinate populations will *cause* differences to arise. Moreover, the ruling group will promote institutional differences to maintain its control.[2]

For Smith, the essential condition of a structurally plural society is a status of members of subordinate segments of society as less than full citizens.[3] Structural pluralism is characterized chiefly by a differential distribution, either through law or extra-legal practice, of "civil and political rights and the economic, social, and other opportunities that these permit or enjoin" (Smith, 1969b: 430). Depluralization requires that citizenship be acquired by all segments of society. This does not imply that inequalities of power or economic and social opportunity need be abolished. Smith describes many societies of 18th-century Europe as examples of structural pluralism. He states that with some notable exceptions, they "were transformed into heterogeneous nation-states. We can summarize [the] processes of national development and integration as the progressive elimination of corporate categorizations in the social structure through the extension of citizenship from the oligarchy to all members of the corporate group" (1969a: 59). Thus, he sees whatever inequalities of access to political power which remain as a quantitative difference rather than the qualitative differentiation of structural pluralism.

Because of the marked division of 18th-century European nations into classes which were clearly socially and culturally different and because there is no doubt that the lower class was disenfranchised, Smith recognizes these societies as instances of structural pluralism. Over time, the franchise has been extended to the entire adult population. Portions of the working class have achieved some limited power within the capitalist framework through labor organizations and the majority of them vote for parties also supported by the upper class. The United States has experienced the same process. The only element of this society which, to Smith, suggests structural pluralism is the status of blacks.

Surely little of the 18th century can be recognized in contemporary industrialized, capitalist societies. There has been immense technological change, industrial development, and economic growth. The work day has been reduced and, especially in the United States, public education and mass consumption have developed considerably. But has depluralization occurred? Are these societies characterized by substantial equivalency of political citizenship and social and economic opportunity? Or is there, in Smith's terms, a "differential incorporation of social aggregates into a common political order"? In Marxist terms, are these societies divided into a ruling class based on ownership of the means of production and an essentially powerless working class?

We will briefly raise the key issues associated with the question as they relate to the United States. Since class consciousness is most lacking in American society, it would appear to provide the weakest case for a Marxist interpretation.

(I) Is American society divided into exclusive social categories? The American upper class has well-marked points of entrance (Mills, 1959: 47-70; Baltzell, 1962; Domhoff, 1967: 12-37), though individual movement into it does occur. This mobility, although numerically insignificant in relation to the working class, is probably responsible for the vitality of the upper class. Mobility is not theoretically problematic in Smith's terms, since its functioning is analogous to the assimilation policy of French, Belgian, and Portuguese colonies described by Smith as examples of structural pluralism (1969b: 431). No difficulty is presented by the character of the working class as a category including a number of social aggregates, some sharply delineated by race and ethnicity and others rather loosely defined by education, occupation, and consumption patterns. The collective character of inferior status is established by the exclusivity of the upper class.

(II) Is the upper social class a political class? This question depends upon whether or not the upper class has interests, shared by its members, which are distinct from the interests of the lower class. A Marxist view finds the maintenance of capitalism as such an interest, recognizing disagreements over how this goal is to be accomplished as secondary. In this view, alternate policies for the achievement of ruling-class goals constitutes the stuff of daily politics (together with simple competition for special interest legislation), which pluralists perceive as a representation of the full spectrum of reasonable political possibilities. If the pluralistic interpretation, that all interests are represented, is correct, then the significance of any power held by members of the upper social class is negated since these individuals would not be acting as a class in the political realm. Even if members of the upper classes occupy or control access to all major decision-making positions, the absence of a significant organized force favoring an alternative to capitalism leaves the situation open to several interpretations. While it may be that the upper class is able to immobilize, prevent, coopt or repress opposition to its rule, it is also possible that the upper class has no interests which are in conflict with the interests of the rest of society.[4] In the latter case, the upper social class would not be a political class.

(III) If the upper class is a political class, is it dominant? Power, the definition of the term and its application is a much disputed subject (Bachrach and Baratz, 1970: 3-51; Domhoff, 1967: 1-11, 141-156; 1971: 304-355; Dahl, 1963: 25-71). Until recently, the dispute concerning power in the United States focused on the merits of alternate methodologies. While this issue has not been resolved, one point of contact between the analyses of some pluralists and elite theorists has been established in the decision-making approach. This method of fixing the locus of power in those who occupy decision-making positions, used by some pluralists, has been adopted recently by Domhoff (1967). Examining the social class background of decision-makers in business, national politics, philanthropic foundations, and universities, Domhoff finds a proportion of upper-class members far beyond the proportion which would occur if selection for these positions were random from among the general population. With regard to decision-makers in dominant institutions who are not members of the upper class, Domhoff asserts that a demonstrated identification with upper-class interests is a prerequisite for access to these key positions. Pluralists tend to stress a separation between ownership of the means of production and control, while elite theorists point out that a share of ownership is conferred upon decision-makers, carrying with it upper class interests (Kolko, 1962: 65-69).

Of course, the reader must evaluate the evidence available with respect to the above-mentioned issues. A conclusion favoring the appropriateness of a ruling class model still does not necessarily imply that the United States is a structurally plural society. According to Smith, plural societies are distinguished from other highly stratified societies. However, his criteria are not entirely clear.

At one point, Smith states that "however variable the system may be in its specific conditions and properties, the collective character, and the scope of its substantive differentiations, must be sufficiently rigorous and pervasive to establish an effective order of corporate inequalities and subordination by the differential distribution of civil and political rights and the economic, social, and other opportunities that these permit or enjoin" (1969b: 430). If the United States is governed by a ruling class based on ownership of the means of production, then there is a qualitative difference in the political power of the respective classes.[5] The inequality of economic and social opportunities is undeniable. Smith also makes reference to legal recognition of social divisions, noting differential access to courts and administrative bodies and various forms of restrictive voting laws. However, he has specifically included "extra-legal practice" along with discriminatory law as a mechanism of structural pluralism, so that the de facto character of class rule and discrimination in the United States would not provide a basis for distinguishing this highly stratified society from structurally plural societies.[6]

At another point, Smith emphasizes that structural pluralism is based on "structural units and criteria . . . perceived as basic by the people concerned." It is clear that if a high degree of class consciousness is required to include the United States in the category of structurally plural societies, then the characterization would not be correct. However, while a knowledge of popular attitudes and opinions is essential to understanding social interaction and political dynamics, the state of consciousness of a population is hardly a sound basis for a fundamental categorization of societies at the macro-sociological level.[7]

Smith seeks to delineate "systematic conditions of differential incorporation," identifying "racial and structural divisions [which] cannot be regarded as merely incidental or contingent elements of social order, since they constitute its very foundations" (1969b: 431). However, while Smith's formulation of plural society theory offers the classificatory scheme described above, it provides little indication of the dynamics of change. He states that a society in which institutional practice in both the public and private spheres is shared (homogeneous society) may divide into sections which are socially and culturally different. When this occurs a transformation to the dominant-subordinate relationship among the sections (structural pluralism) may take place. Smith does not deal with these transformations systematically in the exposition of his framework. His analysis focuses on political domination and its consequences as the essential cause of the establishment and maintenance of structural pluralism. This emphasis is useful in correctly relegating cultural and institutional differences to a secondary, intermediate causal status. But, in not using a political-economic approach, Smith's formulation of the kind of change necessary for social integration and equality is too open-ended. Because it remains exclusively in the political realm, it fails to comprehend the specific political-economic context in which depluralization may take place.

II

A Marxist perspective is based on the observation that economy, understood as the way in which a society interacts with nature to sustain its existence, establishes a limited number of social and political alternatives for that society.[8] The division of labor required by a particular mode of production as shaped by physical conditions and the level of technology available creates different environments for members of a society. Cultural and social differentiation may result from these individual environmental differences. When social and political roles attach themselves to economic roles, social aggregates based on economic roles tend to develop. For example, miners and their families living in conditions of debt to the company store, threat of fatal accident, low access to education and travel, and possible eviction from a company-owned house, will develop a culture which differs from that of mine-owning families with respect to marriage, religion, political orientations, and so forth.

When environmental conditions and technological development permit the production of a surplus beyond the subsistence needs of the producers and access to the means of production is limited,[9] then corporate categories based on a differential relationship to the means of production are created. Even in an ethnically homogeneous society, the social, economic, and political conditions of owners of the means of production and those who must sell their labor become so different as to create distinct social aggregates within that society.

Although social and political position need not be attached to economic roles, this association is inescapable within capitalism. Private ownership of the means of production separates the owners and the workers into separate categories. The owners are the dominant section or class by virtue of the power derived from control of the means of production and control of other institutions based on their wealth. Differences in access to wealth, social institutions, and political position are cumulative. The wealthy are, for the most part, composed of owners. Their wealth provides access to a qualitatively different style of life from the conditions in which the rest of the population lives.

The dynamics of capitalist political economy requires that the owners appropriate a portion of the product of those who must sell their labor. The workers contribute to production with their labor and are paid less than the value of their contribution in wages. This appropriation is the basis of profit which is essential to the system. Therefore, the ruling class and the working class are possessed of inherently conflicting interests, though this not need be comprehended by the workers. The owners seek to maintain the system of private ownership by which the class division as well as the dominance of the owners is based, while it is in the interest of the workers to abolish it as the first step in the process of depluralization. Moreover, the classes do not merely coexist in a situation of dominance and subordination. Because the wealth of the ruling class is derived from the labor of the working class, they are related dialectically. In the final stage of development of this system, tendencies toward economic concentration and crises of overproduction posed by the disparity between the workers' contribution to production and their wages, polarize these classes and transform the working class into groups sufficiently organized and unified to overthrow the ruling class.

Smith has asserted that in the study of the segmented societies, we should define the unit of analysis as the common political system, that the examination of individual segments of society is misleading. In parallel fashion, a Marxist approach regards the economic system as the appropriate unit for study, rather than following formal political boundaries. Consequently, in the latter view, states which manifest significant economic interaction, particularly where monopoly-monopsony elements are present, are not usefully studied as individual political systems. A focus on these states separate from each other misunderstands fundamental aspects of their behavior. It is not immediately apparent that the United States is a structurally plural society because class polarization has not occurred within the nation. The nature of class cleavage is clarified when the unit of analysis is defined as the American empire.

The ruling class in the center of the empire, the metropolis, maintains client elites both within the mother country and in the neo-colonies. The working class throughout the empire is divided by three basic types of cleavage:

(1) Ethnic religious, racial, and culturally based cleavages among the working class are not caused by the process of appropriation of surplus, basic to capitalism. Agreeing with Smith, the differences on which this type of cleavage is based are neither necessary nor sufficient cause for the initiation or maintenance of this type of division. It comes about through a variety of circumstances. For example, competition among the work force generates antagonism. Competition may acquire a collective character based on existing ethnic, religious, racial or cultural lines, creating or exacerbating cleavage. While this may occur spontaneously, the ruling class will often assist the process when the division enhances its power. This type of cleavage may be congruent with either of the other types of division within the working class.[10]

(2) Colonial and neo-colonial cleavages are geographic divisions caused by the appropriation of surplus from dependent areas, both domestic[11] and international.[12] This type of division is basic to capitalism because it is rooted in an essential dynamic of capitalistic economics. The appropriation of surplus may result exclusively from the economic disadvantages of differential technological development, but is generally reinforced by economic and political manipulation. The process of decapitalization enhances the economic and technological disadvantages of the colonial or neo-colonial areas.

Cultural differentiation between metropolis and colony is considerable when the colonial area was at one time a separate and self-sufficient area. Increased contact between metropolis and colony tends to make the strata of the colonial area more culturally similar to corresponding strata in the metropolis. For example, in international colonialism or neo-colonial relationships, the client elites tend to become Americanized as functioning within North American-controlled institutions becomes more important with increased economic domination by the United States.[13] Moreover, as imperialistic economic forces penetrate rural portions of dependent areas, subsistence farmers, handicraft workers, and small capitalists are marginalized and induced to move to urban areas. As rural marginals become urban marginals, they tend to become more culturally similar to urban marginals in the imperialist nation.[14]

(3) In addition to racial, religious, ethnic, cultural, and colonial cleavages, the working class is divided on the basis of education, occupation, and income or consumption. Although all segments of the working class share the same fundamental relationship to the means of production, their environments differ due to differences in factors such as wages and salaries and the goods and services which can be acquired; availability and security of work; the nature of work and working conditions; status associated with employment; access to schooling, mass media and the arts; and the like.

Within the mother country, the structure of industrial capitalism has created a pattern of relatively closely graded strata within the working class. Due to the existence of foreign markets both in the empire and in other industrialized capitalist states, and the appropriation of surplus from the empire which increases the domestic market, the proportion of marginals and unemployed is relatively low. The structure supports a relatively large stratum of managers, technicians, professionals, and bureaucrats at a level of consumption which has given rise to doubt that class division is in fact significant.

While class polarization and division within strata of the working class within the metropolis has been discouraged by imperialism, the impact in the empire has been to intensify polarization and division. The appropriation of surplus from dependent areas limits the products available for distribution to middle and lower strata within the colony. The flow of goods into the colony, which are produced completely or up to the final stage in the metropolis, destroys the market for competing goods produced locally. The introduction of modern, capital intensive technology, while not possible on a scale generalized throughout the colonial economy, is significant in directing the surplus which remains in the colonial area into investments which displace employment provided by competing domestic producers operating at a lower technological level, without providing employment sufficient to replace jobs eliminated. Increased social mobilization and urbanization in this context leads to a swelling of urban marginals.[15] This pattern causes deep division between the very large group of marginals and other strata of the colonial working class. Consequently, economic stagnation and crisis perpetuated by the economics of imperialism bring about heightened polarization between large segments of the colonial working class and the client elite which represents the metropolitan ruling class.

The relationship among the three types of cleavage within the working class may be quite complex. An illustration, though necessarily oversimplified, is provided by the contemporary configuration facing the ruling class of the United States. In the century following the forced migration of Africans to the Americas, the status of blacks in North America was reduced from temporary indentured servitude, similar to the condition of voluntary European immigrants, to slavery. Differential incorporation was reinforced through segregation and denial of education (Handlin, 1957: 3-22). With the abolition of formal slavery, open competition between black and white workers was used to reduce the power of labor organizations. At this stage, a racially based cleavage was eufunctional for maintenance of the power of the ruling class.

In recent decades, a high rate of migration of blacks to urban areas has broken traditional ties and created conditions more favorable for political mobilization of blacks, while placing them in strategically important areas in which to disrupt society. Because of black militancy and disruptive activity, the maintenance of this racially based cleavage has become costly.

Ameliorating racial division would be expensive for the ruling class, politically as well as economically. White segments of the North American lower and middle strata of the working class have historically defended themselves against attempts to lower the price of their labor by eliminating black competition. Measures which would tend to integrate blacks and replace their subordinate position with a status equal to that of white segments of the working class would destroy this strategy and would increase opposition of the latter to the ruling class.[16] The struggle would be exacerbated by a deeply held racist ideology, generated in the course of white workers' efforts to maintain the price of their labor (Bonacich, 1971).

The upper and upper-middle strata of the working class are not threatened by most measures toward the amelioration of racial division in the working class.

Discrimination and segregation have kept blacks from acquiring resources to compete in the labor markets at levels occupied by these workers. The upper and upper-middle strata can use their salaries to maintain separation between themselves and all lower strata workers. Therefore their orientation toward integration of blacks tends to differ from that of white lower and middle strata. A ruling-class strategy of taxing the upper and upper-middle strata to pay for minimal social welfare and educational services for lower strata has also contributed to divisions among the working class.

The ruling class maintains its power by a variety of strategies, one of which is manipulating cleavages within the working class. Division in the domestic working class becomes dysfunctional when support is required to repress segments of the colonial working class in the empire. Costs of the Southeast Asia war, a revolution of a colonial working class against a client elite, has been paid for largely by the domestic working class through taxation and inflation. Ruling class attempts to unify the domestic working class under the banner of nationalism, widening the division between the domestic and colonial segments of the working class, has been only partially successful.

If the ruling class continues a policy of military imperialism, resistance to the costs involved could conceivably unite the domestic working class against the ruling class. More likely, however, is transfer of power to a portion of the ruling class which is aware of the dangers to the system and their position which would result. Unity among the working class would appear to require further development of the tendencies toward overproduction, crises, and polarization on an international scale.

III

In summary, the principle differences between Smith's conception and a Marxist perspective flow from the disagreements concerning the significance of economic and political arrangements for the maintenance of structural pluralism. For Smith, cultural and institutional differentiation depends upon political dominance of one section of society over others. In a Marxist perspective, political domination is a product of the political-economic system. Cultural and institutional differentiation is not only created by the ruling class, but is also a product of the systemic association of political and social conditions with economic position. Smith's view that social and cultural differentiation are fostered through the political power of the dominant section does not violate a Marxist understanding. However, in a Marxist view, differences in political power arise from differences in economic power in a relationship parallel to Smith's conception of the way in which political power and socio-cultural differentiation are associated.

A Marxist position finds class division to be the most significant feature of social structure in capitalist systems. It is inherent in all capitalist systems, its fundamental character remaining unchanged despite divisions among the working class into strata differentiated by education, occupation, and income or consumption. Therefore, capitalist society, from a Marxist perspective, conforms to the essential conditions of structural pluralism in the manner in which Smith applied this designation to 18th-century Europe. Since the fundamental cause of structural pluralism in capitalist society is the differential access to the means of production based on private ownership, socialism is essential to depluralization. With respect to divisions within the working class, ethnic, racial, and culturally based differentiation may be eliminated without displacement of the ruling class, if this division becomes dysfunctional for the maintenance of the system. The differential incorporation of colonial and neo-colonial areas cannot be overcome within the system because their relation to metropolitan areas is fundamental to the system, based on the dynamics of capitalist political economy. Therefore unless the system is displaced, colonial and neo-colonial areas can only change their situation by separation from the system.

While eliminating private ownership of the means of production is a necessary condition for depluralization, it is by no means sufficient. Given the nature of modern technology, a wide range of economic roles is unavoidable. Depluralization requires that access to goods and services be disassociated from economic roles so that individuals and groups do not become stratified socially or politically on the basis of type of employment. Nearly all societies have been functioning through the use of material, social and political advantage as a reward for work for so long that it is commonly thought to be an immutable fact of economic life flowing from a fixed human nature, rather than a product of historical conditions. To break the tie between the type of work an individual contributes and his or her position in society is consequently extremely difficult. This is particularly true in underdeveloped countries where socialism has been attempted. These nations require great increases in production and technical skills are possessed by only a few. Contributions to production will vary widely, and when the more productive and more technologically skilled are rewarded with economic and social privilege, a technocratic, bureaucratic elite is established. In the absence of material, economic incentives for high productivity, it is essential that the population maintain strong motivation to accept psychological rewards, a sense of satisfaction in contributing to society, for work. If this fails, the remaining incentive for work is the avoidance of negative consequences for underproducing, imposed by a political, bureaucratic elite.[17] For Marxists, when the ruling class has been deposed, the central task lies in defining a course which avoids the dangers of both the moral and the material incentive strategies.

NOTES

1. Some confusion has been introduced into the discussion of pluralism by the unfortunate similarity of terms used to designate the plural society theory originated by J. S. Furnivall (1945, 1948) and the older tradition of pluralistic society, represented in recent years in the followers of Parsonian functionalism. (For example, see Almond and Powell, 1966.) The concepts have been perceived as sharply opposed formulations: a society characterized by conflict stemming from sharp cultural differences among closed corporate sections as opposed to one of harmonious equilibrium based on dynamic adjustments among functionally differentiated groups. However, Furnivall's plural society in its original formulation was limited to tropical colonial societies. Pluralists of the second tradition have recognized the realization of their harmonious version of pluralism in modern industrialized societies. These concepts coexist easily when the use of the plural society theory is limited as in Furnivall's application.

In the literature of "nation-building" and development of the last two decades, the plural society appears as a less developed society characterized by sharp cleavages. Because one section is dominant over others and mobility between sections is limited, instability is present. Plural society theory has focused on institutional differentiation among the sections and a racial, ethnic, or cultural basis of cleavage, while the pluralistic approach has included ideological cleavage as well. Both traditions perceive a solution to the problem of instability in the uniform incorporation of the sections so that corporate social aggregates or classes with distinct and cohesive interests are superseded by closely graded strata.

Smith's reformulation differs significantly from Furnivall's conception and, in some respects, from his earlier work. Furnivall's restriction of plural society theory to colonial, tropical, multi-racial societies in the temporal period of European colonial expansion has been dropped. As a result, the relationship between the two traditions of pluralism has been clarified. By dropping cultural cleavage as an essential causal factor, Smith's formulation becomes congruent with the "equilibrium" school since the category of corporate sections which hinder national integration is broadened. Moreover, the apparent opposition of the two traditions as "conflict" and "equilibrium" theories is shown to be false since an analytical category exists in Smith's classificatory scheme for non-homogeneous societies characterized by an absence of dominance or conflict. It might still be charged that Smith ignores bases of integration in favor of emphasizing tendencies toward conflict in socially and structurally plural societies and is therefore a "conflict" theorist. However, this is not a difference between the plural society and pluralistic traditions. The disagreement between Smith and those who see integrative factors as dominant in societies characterized by differential incorporation, possibly because the latter assume that quiescence signifies harmony or equilibrium, is not a matter of theoretical approach so much as it represents conflicting appraisals of empirical data. In some instances, the position of these equilibrium theorists is in opposition to both Smith and the pluralistic tradition in their evaluation of the existence of harmony or stability.

Smith's scheme clearly parallels the pluralistic school. His view of the change from a condition of instability and conflict resulting from sectional incorporation toward a state of harmony and equilibrium is congruent to the nation-building approach of the pluralistic tradition.

Smith's approach and that of the pluralistic tradition are not identical. The most significant difference between them is apparent in comparing Smith's classificatory scheme and the framework of Almond and Powell. While Smith distinguishes among societies on the basis of the presence or absence of institutionally differentiated corporate sections and their mode of incorporation, Almond and Powell base their classification on the degree of structural differentiation and cultural secularization, considered as a single variable, and the degree of sub-system autonomy. Although Almond and Powell recognize that secularization does not always vary with specialization of structures, they appear to assume that it necessarily leads to universalistic incorporation. Their approach to change is therefore evolutionary, depending upon social mobilization (Deutsch, 1963: 582-603) to bring about change.

The second variable by which Almond and Powell classify political systems is sub-system autonomy. For them, an increase in the independence of specialized structures and systems is an indicator of political development. They are concerned for stability in the process of evolutionary change lest conflict bring into power an elite which would destroy sub-system autonomy. This school tends to value sub-system autonomy and, therefore, stability in the evolutionary process, as indicated by the recommendation that social mobilization should be slowed to avoid the stresses which it places on the system (Huntington, 1965).

While Smith agrees that corporate sections may be absent from modern, industrialized, capitalist society, in opposition to a Marxist approach, he differs from Almond and Powell in suggesting that differential incorporation may be an important aspect of such societies, that evolutionary increase in Parsonian variables may occur within differentially incorporated categories without affecting relations among the sections. Unlike the pluralistic approach, Smith observes the tendency of the dominant section in societies characterized by structural pluralism to exercise its power to maintain its position. Since equal access to legal and political institutions is for Smith the essential condition of depluralization, evolutionary solutions may in some instances be inadequate and political change accompanied by violence may be prerequisite.

We are now in a position to make a summary of this discussion of pluralism which will provide a point of departure for the presentation of a Marxist perspective.

(a) In the Furnivall tradition of pluralism represented by M. G. Smith's most recent formulation, societies are distinguished by structural differences in their institutions of collective incorporation. Almond and Powell's classificatory scheme which is representative of the pluralistic approach, focuses on the degree of sub-system autonomy as the crucial variable (see Dahl, 1963. Secularization and structural differentiation are given equal weight with sub-system autonomy by Almond and Powell, but the automatic character of growth in these indices, contrasted with the possible reversibility of sub-system autonomy relegates them to a secondary status for our purposes).

(b) Both traditions of pluralism have a preference for modern industrial society. Smith perceives the development in Western Europe in the 19th century as the breakdown of feudal corporate categories leading to a heterogeneous society characterized by a universalistic mode of incorporation after World War II (Smith, 1969a: 58-59). Smith finds nothing inherent in industrialized capitalist society which necessarily implies structural pluralism. Differential incorporation may or may not exist in this type of society. For Almond and Powell, socialism and particularly mobilizational socialism connote an absence of sub-system autonomy. Capitalism is necessary for their pluralistic society. In their scheme, the highest stage of development is reserved for liberal, capitalist, industrialized societies.

(c) The representations of both traditions of pluralism concur in the perception of evolutionary breakdown of Marxist corporate classes into integrated strata. They differ with respect to other types of corporate sections. Almond and Powell tend to rely on increased cultural secularization and structural differentiation to bring about integration through evolutionary means. In Smith's formulation, differential incorporation consists in political dominance of a corporate section. Alternative modes of incorporation require displacement of the political power of the dominant section of depluralization. Since the dominant sector attempts to maintain corporate sections, a transfer of political power not unusually accompanied by violent conflict is prerequisite.

The two traditions of pluralism are also discussed by Kuper (1969).

2. "... neither is differential incorporation confined to multiethnic or multiracial aggregates, nor is it always present in them; nor, even where present, is it always prescribed on biological grounds. Even ethnically homogeneous populations constitute plural societies under regimes of pervasive differential incorporation, while ethnically or racially diverse populations may either be unified under structures of uniform incorporation or consociated by incorporation as equal or complementary units. Further, although differential incorporation typically presumes antecedent institutional differences between its collective divisions, it also creates their institutional differentiation within the common public domain; and in consequence of this, even where the differentially incorporated sections initially lacked them, they invariably develop differing institutional practices and organizations in their several collective domains, and in other sectors also. Moreover, since its status and dominion are bound up with the maintenance and scope of this intersectional structure, the dominant section in such societies normally seeks not only to preserve its current control, but to enhance this by promoting further institutional and structural differentiation in other spheres, notably in cult, connubium, economy, education, military organization, and residential segregation" (Smith, 1969b: 436).

3. Social and cultural differentiation is also essential to structural pluralism. It is not mentioned here because, according to Smith, this differentiation will be induced by the consequences of lack of full citizenship rights, if it is not already present at the time that political domination is established.

4. Those who interpret quiescence in plural societies characterized by racial and ethnic cleavage as an indication of harmony, criticize Smith as a "conflict theorist," who fails to recognize integrative social factors. The problem of interpreting the lack of significant opposition to capitalism presents similar difficulties (see Marcuse, 1964: 1-120; and Edelstein, 1972).

5. In effect, the working class has a sizable role in choosing from among alternatives chosen by the ruling class (Domhoff, 1967: 84-103; Baran and Sweezy, 1966).

6. As enunciated by Anatole France, "The law in its majestic equality forbids the rich as well as the poor to sleep under bridges, to beg in the streets and to steal bread." Concerning the contemporary United States, see Lefcourt (1971), especially the chapter by Ken Cloke.

7. Class consciousness in the United States has waxed and waned with economic cycles throughout the 20th century, irrespective of any fundamental change in social divisions.

8. Marvin Harris (1968: 217-249) presents a particularly relevant discussion of determinism and alternatives in Marxist theory.

9. Caused, for example, by limited availability of arable land or by the substantial surplus labor necessary to produce the instruments of production in modern, industrial production.

10. Edna Bonacich (1971) presents an especially relevant and incisive explanation of racism as an ideology of an aristocracy of labor, developed in its conflict with business, to protect itself from udercutting by the use of cheaper labor. Also see the exchange between Harris (1969: 38-59) and Genovese (1969: 238-255).

11. One concept of internal colonialism has been presented by Gonzalez Casonova (1969: 118-139). A. G. Frank has responded to this concept directly (1969: 318-332) and developed a wider theory (1967, 1969).

12. Examples of the large body of literature dealing with imperialism and colonial relationships are Magdoff (1969), Jalée (1968, 1969) and Fann and Hodges (1971) and bibliography cited therein.

13. This effect extends beyond the client elite. For example, bilingual secretaries receive higher pay than native schoolteachers in many dependent capitalist countries. The

implications are clear. Of course, this tendency is not limited to "Americanization." For example, as Japanese tourism becomes more important in the economy of the state of Alaska, the natives (i.e., the American citizens residing in Alaska) find it advantageous to learn to speak Japanese.
14. Many followers of the Weberian-Parsonian school have mistakenly interpreted this process as one of integration, erroneously equated "modernization" with "development." In reality, it is an aspect of polarization.
15. For example, see Dillon Soares (1968: 186-201) and Quijano Obregón (1968: 289-328; 1971).
16. The Nixon administration's flirtation with an equal-employment policy in the construction industry in 1970 illustrates the problem. The reaction of white workers indicates that they saw the move as an effort to reduce their bargaining power by increasing the supply of labor in the industry. This perception would appear to be accurate, since the government at that time also reduced the demand for labor in construction by reducing expenditures in this area as part of a program of induced recession to control inflation. The move was met by street demonstrations on the part of white construction workers.
17. Of course, the problem of moral or psychological and material or economic incentives is not a question of absolutes. One approach, focusing on the size of the economic unit as an important variable, is Dumont's (1970) discussion of Cuba, based on his observations as an advisor to the Cuban Government in the early 1960s. An excellent treatment of the problem in general is the exchange between Sweezy and Bettelheim (1972).

REFERENCES

ALMOND, G. A. and G. B. POWELL, Jr. (1966) Comparative Politics: A Developmental Approach. Boston, Little, Brown.
BACHRACH, P. and M. S. BARATZ (1970) Power and Poverty. New York: Oxford University Press.
BALTZELL, E. D. (1962) An American Business Aristocracy. New York: Collier Books.
BARAN, P. A. and P. M. SWEEZY (1966) Monopoly Capital. New York: Monthly Review Press.
BONACICH, E. (1971) "A theory of ethnic segmentation: the split labor market." Department of Sociology, University of California, Riverside (mimeo).
CHILCOTE, R. H. and J. C. EDELSTEIN [eds.] (1974) Latin America: The Struggle with Dependency and Beyond. Cambridge, Mass.: Schenkman.
DAHL, R. A. (1963) Modern Political Analysis. Englewood Cliffs, N.J.: Prentice-Hall.
——— (1961) Who Governs? Englewood Cliffs, N.J.: Prentice-Hall.
DEUTSCH, K. W. (1963) "Social mobilization and political development," pp. 582-603 in H. Eckstein and D. E. Apter (eds.) Comparative Politics. New York: Free Press.
DILLON SOARES, G. A. (1968) "The new industrialization and the Brazilian political system," in Latin America: Reform or Revolution? Greenwich: Fawcett.
DOMHOFF, G. W. (1971) The Higher Circles. New York: Vintage Books.
——— (1967) Who Rules America? Englewood Cliffs, N.J.: Prentice-Hall.
DUMONT, R. (1970) Cuba: Socialism and Development. New York: Grove Press.
EDELSTEIN, J. C. (1972) "Mobilizational, immobilizational and spontaneous forms of fascism," in Politics and Society 2(Spring): 363-375.
FANN, K. T. and D. C. HODGES [eds.] (1971) Readings in U.S. Imperialism. Porter Sargeant.
FRANK, A. G. (1969) Latin America: Underdevelopment or Revolution. New York and London: Monthly Review Press.
——— (1967) Capitalism and Underdevelopment in Latin America. New York: Monthly Review Press.
FURNIVALL, J. S. (1948) Colonial Policy and Practice. London: Cambridge University Press.
——— (1945) "Some problems of tropical economy," pp. 161-184 in R. Hinden (ed.) Fabian Colonial Essays. London: George Allen & Unwin.
GENOVESE, E. (1969) "Materialism and idealism in the history of Negro slavery in the Americas," in L. Foner and E. Genovese (eds.) Slavery in the New World, Englewood Cliffs, N.J.: Prentice-Hall.
GONZALEZ CASANOVA, P. (1969) "Internal colonialism and national development," pp.

118-139 in I. L. Horowitz, J. de Castro and J. Gerassi (eds.) Latin American Radicalism. New York: Vintage Books.
HANDLIN, O. (1957) Race and Nationality in American Life. New York: Doubleday.
HARRIS, M. (1969) "The myth of the friendly master," and "The origin of the descent rule," pp. 38-59 in L. Foner and E. Genovese (eds.) Slavery in the New World. Englewood Cliffs, N.J.: Prentice-Hall.
HARRIS, M. (1968) The Rise of Anthropological Theory. New York: Thomas Y. Crowell.
HUNTINGTON, S. P. (1965) "Political development and political decay," pp. 386-411 in World Politics 17, 3.
JALEE, P. (1969) The Third World in World Economy. New York: Monthly Review Press.
––– (1968) The Pillage of the Third World. New York: Monthly Review Press.
KOLKO, G. (1962) Wealth and Power in America. New York: Praeger.
KUPER, L. (1969) "Plural societies: perspectives and problems," pp. 7-26 in L. Kuper and M. G. Smith (eds.) Pluralism in Africa. Berkeley and Los Angeles: University of California Press.
LEFCOURT, R. (1971) Law Against the People. New York: Random House.
MAGDOFF, H. (1969) The Age of Imperialism. New York: Monthly Review Press.
MARCUSE, H. (1964) One-Dimensional Man. Boston: Beacon Press.
MILLS, C. W. (1959) The Power Elite. New York: Oxford University Press.
QUIJANO OBREGON, A. (1971) Nationalism and Capitalism in Peru: A Study in Neo-Imperialism. New York: Monthly Review Press.
––– (1968) "Tendencies in Peruvian development and class structure," pp. 289-328 in J. Petras and M. Zeitlin (eds.) Latin America: Reform or Revolution? Greenwich: Fawcett.
SMITH, M. G. (1969a) "Institutional and political conditions of pluralism," pp. 27-65 in L. Kuper and M. G. Smith (eds.) Pluralism in Africa. Berkeley and Los Angeles: University of California Press.
––– (1969b) "Some developments in the analytic framework of pluralism," pp. 415-58 in L. Kuper and M. G. Smith (eds.) Pluralism in Africa. Berkeley and Los Angeles: University of California Press.
SWEEZY, P. M. and C. BETTELHEIM (1972) On the Transition to Socialism. New York: Monthly Review Press.

Chapter 4

SOME THEORETICAL CONSIDERATIONS
IN INTERNATIONAL RACE RELATIONS

ROBERT H. MAST

THE LIMITS AND CHALLENGE
OF SOCIAL SCIENCE

*T*his topic causes me some trepidation in presenting myself as having some insight into theories of international race relations because of my derivation from white, Anglo-Saxon, Protestant, middle-class, male America. I know that this restrictive background is an extremely limiting factor in the proper approach to both local and international race relations analyses because I have had enough personal and literary contact with my progressive racial, class, nationality, and sex opposites to be concerned about intellectual imperialism.

It is simply a fact that different assumptions, approaches, political identities, and philosophies produce different theories, data categories, information, and conclusions. To a large extent, this intellectual process is ethnic- and class-bound, notwithstanding the norms of science and objectivity. All one has to do is read the mainstream of British and American race academics and compare them with the writings of Third World radical intellectuals to know that where one stands in the international order largely determines one's science.

Perhaps we should reflect some 30 to 40 years—before the current obsession with mathematical models, developmentalism, urbanization, industrialization, and so on—to the time when the present form of the social sciences was being forged. Perhaps we should re-read Karl Mannheim as he attempted to sort out the major components of the so-called cultural sciences: "Weltanschauung," historicism, intellectual syntheses, the sociology of knowledge, the rejection of "vulgar" positivism and empiricism—in order to reorient our perspectives. I think that by so doing we might re-evaluate much of what has become academic gospel, and such re-evaluation would be strongly enhanced by a careful look at the patterns of racial and ethnic experience since World War II. I submit that something went wrong in the way we analyze the world, and I further submit that much is the fault of academia in taking much too seriously the ministrations of such philosophers of science as Ernst Nagel, Norman Campbell, and Karl Popper who, difficult as it is to accept, enhanced a cult of elitist science, buttressed the status quo, and made social analysis into a most conservative enterprise.

White, Western academics skillfully assemble a vast amount of "intellectually respectable" information according to one or another conceptual scheme. But there are several major problems in their work. The first is that most of their work is bland and uninspiring. Another and more important problem is that they seldom seem to capture the major issues in race and ethnic relations. Furthermore, they are inadequately self-conscious and, although they are trained to assess and understand the social roles and functions of the professions, they seem disinclined, if not unable, to make such deliberations upon themselves. Finally, as judged by the crisis of relevancy in social science today, and by the tendency on the part of victims of racial dominance and exploitation to sternly reject social scientism, the white, Western academic may be criticized as being basically irrelevant in terms of helping to solve the problems faced by racial and ethnic minorities.

Academic fads tend to determine the intellectual enterprise, while political, economic, and prestige support structures tend to determine the nature of the fads. Where are we to turn then for answers that permit us to set priorities which will help in achieving analytic relevancy? The answer to this is crucial. I see relevancy as the main responsibility of social science, and this mandates the search for an egalitarian utopia. Relevancy in this context must have certain philosophical and moral bases which stress service to those who are the victims of discrimination, exploitation, and subjugation, with opposition to those who are the perpetrators of such injustice. We must have a philosophy or set of ideologies for intellectual guidance and compassionate understanding and we must have direct experience in the real world.

The notion of the real world requires considerable reflective judgment so as to avoid projecting a monolithic and elitist perception. One must determine what reality and whose reality is under consideration, and be able to differentiate these realities from that to which the social scientist lays claim. The point is that the subjective reality of a given group is also that group's objective reality. Too often, the social scientist's "objective" reality is a blinder for his own subjectivity and is also a kind of elitist deception of those possessing fewer professional credentials. I am arguing for a cleansing away of self-deception, experiencing the realities of others, and taking on an egalitarian social philosophy. Out of this process, theory emerges—not predetermined by some logico-deductive scheme, but developed out of experience and philosophy.

Is there any question that the prevailing philosophies in the different international power blocs determine the theories that are used by social scientists in each bloc? Mainstream social scientists in the Western, capitalist nations have applied their craft to the service of the political order in which they function and are supported. And this is likewise true for academics in the Eastern European socialist nations, for those in the Third World whose governments orient to the capitalist West, or to socialist Eastern Europe or to China, and for those in the so-called "non-aligned" Third World nations. Academics in all these areas claim to seek truth, to apply unbiased methods, to pursue the canons of science. Upon inspection, it is found that development of knowledge is dependent upon the prevailing social and political conditions. American sociology today shows somewhat of a trend away from a functional analysis and towards a conflict analysis, thus reflecting the "true" conditions prevailing in the United States, while Soviet sociology increasingly accepts functionalism as a correct theoretical predisposition to analyzing the conditions prevailing in the Soviet Union. One could conclude that academics in both systems are selecting the available faddish theories that appear to them to reflect the reality they perceive, but one could cynically suggest also that both sets of academics select those theories which are both politically acceptable and tend to mirror certain obvious phenomena. I suggest that there are more fundamental, and perhaps more simple, conceptual dimensions that can capture a larger chunk of human experience and conceivably take us much further in performing a relevant social role.

One approach we should avoid is that of partial or middle-range theory. Such theory is of quite limited use because it does not speak to fundamental and central problems; it is not committed to relevancy; it is unable to take diversity into account; and it does not manifestly make critical inquiry. Until quite recently, the results of partial theory have been seen, for example, in efforts to explain urban American black insurrection in terms of motivational psychology theory; student militancy and hippie movements in terms of Freudian theory; the Cold War in terms of communication theory; white-black relations in terms of attitude theory; decision-making and priority-setting on such issues as poverty and underdevelopment in terms of bureaucratic or mass society theory. These are not particularly useless approaches and can feed into more general applications. But too often these partial approaches are used as the major explanatory vehicles for a wide range of experience, and they always fall short. Worse still, they represent theory development of the capitalist West and much of it is not relevant to the oppressed in *that* sector of the world, let alone the rest of the world.

When I suggest that general theory is required, I mean that there must be some priority of concepts that are considered, above all others, to be most important; that this priority is more applicable to the masses of people in the world than any other priority set; that this priority can take into account a greater range of human experience in diverse situations and account more successfully for observed structures, social processes and cultural ideology than any other conceptual arrangement. Thus, a total approach is needed that takes a sweeping historical and comparative look at the mechanisms and ideas that seem to be responsible for the development and continuance of human oppression. Relevance is enhanced by this approach, but relevance is not fully achieved until a full consideration of non-oppressive arrangements is made. We may do this by speculating on and encouraging the development of utopian social arrangements. We also have at our disposal, if we were only permitted to make use of them, a number of experimental societies with which to make comparisons. Chief among these is China. Where else is such a massive social experiment being undertaken? But because of international politics, there is little possiblity of finding out the extent to which oppression is being eliminated there, whether there is a process of redefinition of oppression being undertaken or whether other forms of oppression are developing. Short of reports of brief visits by journalists or businessmen, we are unsure how theory and practice merge to make the people full social participants or how the Maoist and Trotskyist concepts of the "permanent revolution" are articulated in behavior which is ostensibly intended to remove old oppressive forms and abort new ones.

As social scientists, we ourselves are repressed by the realities of our own political milieux, and thus we find it difficult to make free inquiry and promote the development of egalitarian social arrangements. We find that we are bound to conservative norms of an academic discipline and to the outer society that nourishes that discipline. We may not freely inquire into, nor criticize the system in which we function, for that invites censure and ostracism. No wonder the oppressed of the world increasingly reject our fumbling efforts. They know our inquiries are limited by political exigencies and, from their point of view, are of little direct value to their self-interest.

OPPRESSION: THE SUBJECT MATTER OF
INTERNATIONAL RACE RELATIONS

It seems essential today for social analysts to free themselves of traditional professional constraints and conventions and to unashamedly look at the world around them with a view toward increasing their personal relevancy. Their optimism and efficacy will be raised by a fresh look at life, by a free association of ideas and hunches and, most important, by drawing on the intellectual products and experience of those who are the victims of oppression.

I have learned from such victims that the fundamental subject matter of international race relations is oppression. In his book, *The Colonizer and the Colonized,* Albert Memmi said that oppression is "the greatest calamity of humanity." But oppression is a vague concept, one that is not readily amenable to operationalization, definition, and measurement; so our computers become a bit redundant. What we must do is study oppression through the minds and feelings of the oppressed; so we must try to get into those minds and take their role. To a great many of us, their roles are foreign, and we use our own values and political loyalties as guidelines to understanding or feeling and seldom catch the essence of oppression as lived and felt by others. But it may not be as difficult as all that since everyone has suffered one form or another of oppression: young people invariably suffer from the hypocrisy and double standards of adult authority; women from sexism and male chauvinism; workers from bureaucratic impersonality and alienation, and so forth. It is possible to transpose one form of oppression into other forms by a cognitive operation based on personal experience, and this is immeasurably enhanced by careful observation and careful listening to those whose oppression is manifestly different, and thus more difficult to empathise with.

I suspect that revitalized anthropolgy, the return to participant observation and the development of ethnomethodology in the United States, as well as the renewed interest in existentialism and phenomenology in Europe, reflect a felt need to capture the meanings of oppression which were suppressed, perhaps for 25 years, in academia's bid to copy the natural sciences and locate the universal laws that govern human association. If the study of oppression is the major challenge in race relations, we are forced into asking a number of most difficult questions: what is oppression; what are its manifestations; who are the oppressed; who are the oppressors; what are the origins of oppression; how is it maintained; what are its functions; and, by no means least, what are the alternatives, and how can they be achieved? Inquiry into these difficult areas requires a sustained commitment to the development of general theoretical postures within which *diverse* group experience may be subsumed.

If we do study the causes of oppression with a general theoretical perspective, we must analyze the political and cultural constraints to the achievement of egalitarianism. Thus, we analyze the structure of power in the local and international context as well as the cultural ideology that supports and buttresses such structures; but we must do so from the point of view of how political and cultural factors operate *against* the interests of oppressed people. To a limited extent, we may define oppression objectively; at least, in terms of opportunity structures, available choices, and income equality. But the full definition of oppression rests with the oppressed people themselves. There is too much evidence available that objective definitions of oppression reflect the norms and values of social science practitioners, rather than the people they study. The evidence comes from the very incisive analyses which non-academics are making of their own conditions and the challenges they are rendering to the conclusions of textbook social science. Indeed, such people challenge the political and cultural systems in which they live—which is something few social scientists do. Rather, they have been content to describe and partially explain how a system came to be, instead of challenging the system as being intolerant or immoral. Many of the movements today throughout the world are challenging, rather than explaining the systems in which they exist; and these include Third World liberation movements, black liberation, youth counter-culture, women's liberation, and the rest.

The full face of racial oppression cannot be seen without first taking into account the political and cultural material that is present in any race relations context. This mandates an analysis of class relations, internal to a nation, and colonial relations in the international context. A class analysis necessarily starts from Marxian assumptions about the relations surrounding the means of production. Expanding many of the insights from this into the international sphere, a colonial model seems most appropriate. Woven into the class and colonial nature of human relations is cultural ethnicity: group identity which results in racism, tribalism, or communalism. Thus class, race and culture are essential starting points for analysis.

We must look at the distribution of power and ownership and the ideological roots which legitimate such distribution. Once this has been done, we must look at the racial and ethnic patterns within this distribution. But we must also know what racial and ethnic identity or consciousness *is* in order to understand the patterns. Finally, we must assess the cultural origins and maintenance of racism and colonialism. This immensely broad framework allows somewhat of a theoretically integrated approach to the relations between groups and nations and blocs of nations at any level of analysis we choose, whether it is urban, rural, national, regional, or international. With this, we are able to approach an empirical level—for example, the city—with certain assumptions about the nature of human relations. This empirical level can be seen as a special case requiring knowledge of the unique character of, for example, urbanness, the capability of measuring or at least taking into account certain variables in that level and an analysis of the relations of specific group experience in that level (political economic relations, cultural ideology, ethnic identity) to the general set of propositions that come out of the colonial, class, and cultural contexts. If we do not begin in such a way, we flounder in a sterile sea of verbiage and indecisiveness. An integrated theoretical approach to race relations is the challenge before all of us.

THE NATURE
OF ETHNICITY

The definition of ethnicity depends on the socio-political condition prevailing at a given time and place. In some situations a condition of ethnic pluralism may exist in which self-determination and relatively equal power pertains for co-existing groups. But generally, it is more the case that pluralism, with tolerance and without conflict, is a myth enunciated by the ideology of liberal democracy. This seems especially true in capitalist countries (although communist countries are not exempt), as well as in those Third World nations which are in a state of economic and political schizophrenia, split among the forces of feudalism, oligarchical elitism, or colonial control. In these nations, "divide and rule" has been the historic policy of the colonial powers, and such divisions have often been on the basis of the religious, racial, tribal, language, or custom differences of the people. One does not know for certain how nations with egalitarian social policies—such as Cuba—are handling the question of ethnicity which, in the colonial, capitalist period, was divisive and white supremacist. Reports indicate that insidious racism, as we know it, is essentially non-existent or reduced in Cuba, though there may be evidence that non-structural, attitudinal racism operates as a residual in the older generations.

Social science, assuredly, has made elaborate classifications of ethnicity into which almost everyone can be placed, either by objective techniques or by subjective identity. The objective aspect of ethnicity is a function of anthropological skill in observing and recording qualitatively different cultural characteristics, and these alter with changing political and economic conditions. Thus, a large body of literature has grown up around cultural dynamics and theories of assimilation.

The subjective aspects of ethnicity may be approached in several ways. One basis of subjective ethnicity is natural and historically continuous group pride and identity. This is most visibly manifested in situations where there is population homogeneity; that is, where there is relative non-pluralism. One illustration would probably be Sweden, and there are others in the Third World countries of Africa and Asia. Of course, this kind of subjective ethnicity may be too obvious to be important. But it leads into what I think is one major issue in race and ethnic oppression, and that is that ethnic identity is an important and necessary defense mechanism against the forces of oppression, or against prejudice and discrimination, to use common jargon. (Compare Landis on African defensive racialism in Guyana). Subjective ethnic identity is then really synonymous with the idea of ethnic or racial consciousness, which is considered an absolutely central component in the development of political will. In principle, it does not differ from the idea of class consciousness or, for that matter, of sexual consciousness if we are considering women's liberation.

In this general sense, subjective identity can be seen as a strategy in the process of political development, though the strategy is based on the reality of oppression of a group, a set of groups, a nation, or a bloc of nations by some external forces. To use a political explanation for what might be called a social-psychological process in no way denies the anthropological categories which classify people according to their cultural characteristics. This may demonstrate however, how interlocked the social science disciplines are and how a general theory is most desirable. Indeed, some of the cultural classifications may be more apparent than real. If they are used by cultural groups themselves to politically organize on the basis of oppression, the classifications become somewhat of a self-fulfilling prophecy. Likewise, the classifications become self-fulfilling when used by oppressive and divisive elites, whether at the international, national, or locals levels, to manipulate such ideas as "manifest destiny," "racial superiority," or "the chosen people."

The illustrations are voluminous. The obvious illustration of Nazi Germany becomes overshadowed by the historical and contemporary examples everywhere. It has been noted by some that the Hindu-Muslim conflicts in India were exaggerated by local elites and British colonial policy. Likewise, the same divisive forces of oppression have created artificial tensions more recently between India and Pakistan. The Ibo-Hausa conflict in Nigeria was exacerbated by neo-colonial capital interpenetration. Wherever Britain imported one of its colonial nationalities into another of its colonies, it manipulated the local political and economic conditions so that, ultimately, intergroup tension and hostility were created. Clear illustrations of this are seen in Kenya (introduction of Asians) and Malaysia (introduction of Chinese). In another British ex-colony, Ceylon, one rift is based on language (Singalese versus Tamil). The conflict in Northern Ireland is by no means based exclusively on Protestant-Catholic difference, though that is of some importance; it rests also on the artificial division of Ireland and the divisive imperial political and economic practices of Westminster. Indeed, within Britain, one sees constant elite manipulation of ethnic groups and ethnic ideology (Irish, Pakistanis, West Indies, Indians), as one does in Western European countries (Spaniards, Algerians, Turks, Indonesians). In these instances, cheap labor is imported from former colonies and then, when an economic slump comes and white workers fear displacement, elites make political hay of growing tensions and further mystify those who are socially and economically marginal. The historical and current pattern of ethnic manipulation by elites in the United States is too well known to spend time on here. There are numerous examples elsewhere.

The main idea is that subjective ethnic identity, as a defense mechanism, may result more from the divisiveness and manipulation by the forces of oppression than from antipathies produced by the *fact* of difference, though the fact of difference is something that has been played up by social science and cashed in on by elites who benefit both politically and economically by creating or perpetuating myths. If this is true, then one main focus in the study of race relations must be on the forces of oppression themselves, with special attention to the manipulation of ethnic groups and nations by those with superior power. Race relations study becomes, to a large extent, the study of political control and the means by which such control is wrested away from oppressive forces.

RACE, CLASS AND CULTURE

We need to adopt a perspective in which oppressed racial or ethnic groups are not viewed in the same way as the lower-class sectors of dominant groups. Robert Blauner at Berkeley, California, and others—especially those who are victims of racist oppression—warn us not to reduce race relations to class relations. Racist social relations have different cultural origins and consequences than class relations. Though in the West the white working class is oppressed by the capitalist system, as are people of color in the Third World, it does seem apparent that racial and ethnic oppression has a life and quality of its own which must be understood in its manifestations at all levels of social relations. We should not underestimate the importance of subjugation and humiliation that results from the lack of dignity and equality. This is borne out by the fact that the economically poorest Third World colonizer or white American can and does feel superior to the Third World colonized or black American. In his article, "Black Culture: Myth or Reality" in the volume, *Afro-American Anthropology,* Blauner said that racism insults and violates dignity and degrades personalities in a much more pervasive way than class exploitation. He notes further that racist and class oppression, though intimately related, have diverse consequences for group formation, for the salience of identities based on these groups, and for individual and group modes of adaptation and resistance. Class exploitation per se does not stimulate ethnic and national cultures and liberation movements, but colonialism and domestic racism do.

Following these insights of Blauner, some of the same intellectual tools that are used in the study of internal, domestic racism can be applied to the study of colonialism at the international level. We must deal with the two major interrelated factors of politics and economics. As William Tabb mentioned in his book, *The Political Economy of the Black Ghetto,* there are two key relationships which must be proved before the colonial analogy can be accepted: economic control and exploitation, and political dependence and subjugation. Both necessitate separation and inferior status. Tabb went on to say:

> "In defining colonialism, militants argue that the spatial separation of colony and colonial power is secondary to the existence of control of the ghetto from the outside through political and economic domination by white society."

Thus, if we merge the two Tabb criteria, economic exploitation and political subjugation, with Blauner's cultural racism, we have a beginning theoretical synthesis with which to approach the idea of oppression. This does not seem like a very new or startling synthesis. Oppressed minorities throughout history have been conscious of political, economic, and ideological control over their lives, and they intuitively have known much about the structures and processes of such control. Social scientists, however, have paid too little attention to these fundamental ideas, and it is about time we set the matter right.

ANALYSIS BY THE OPPRESSED

I am rapidly reaching the conclusion that the only people who can properly analyze oppression are those who themselves are the victims of it. Everyone is oppressed in some way, but if there is a priority of suffering from oppression, then those at the bottom are the most eligible to initiate analysis and tell the social science technicians what the research priorities should be. This turns social science into a service for the people, rather than for elites.

What do we find from the writings of the oppressed minorities? We find a closer approximation to the total theoretical approach for which I have argued, and this results from their having lived and felt oppression. As Jean-Paul Sartre said, "Oppression means, first of all, the oppressor's hatred for the oppressed." Oppressed minorities understand this, whether they are blacks in the Harlem ghetto; West Indians in London's Notting Hills district; Spanish Basques; Algerians in Paris; the French-speaking in Quebec; darker-skinned Brazilians; Australian Aborigines; Peruvian Indians; working-class Trinidadians; Bangladesh refugees; Palestinian Arabs; black Rhodesians; or those being mercilessly violated by a foreign power, like the Vietnamese. Those who can best describe and analyze oppression turn out to be such people as Franz Fanon or Albert Memmi who emphasize its cultural-psychological aspects; or Kwame Nkrumah who, in

Neo-Colonialism: The Last Stage of Imperialism, vividly described the debilitating effect of foreign control; or London's C. R. Hensman who, in *From Gandhi to Guevara* and *Rich Against Poor,* traces the process of anti-development of poor nations resulting from external political-economic control. These intellectuals are increasingly assisted by those who themselves are not direct victims of oppression, but are sensitive to it and wish to destroy it: Regis DeBray, Rene Dumont *(False Start in Africa),* Andre Gundar Frank, David Horowitz, G. William Domhoff, Paul Sweezy, Ernest Mandel, and many others.

This rich mixture of intellectuals is creating a sensitive projection of the major dimensions of race relations analyses in the international context. They share a left-wing political perspective, and this fact may reduce their legitimacy in the eyes of more politically conservative scholars who are tied in to the capitalist West or in the Third World nations that orient to the capitalist West. But this does not reduce the meaningfulness of their scholarship and analysis. It is no accident that Stokely Carmichael, in his consciousness-expanding quest, ends up with Nkrumah in Guinea, after having visited Cuba, Vietnam, Algeria, and Tanzania; nor is it an accident that his and Hamilton's book, *Black Power,* resulted in the application of the colonial model to the American ghetto. These represent stages in history and points in black consciousness. The international tour of Robert Williams is also no accident; nor is the Algerian refuge of Eldridge Cleaver; nor the mass dropping-out of Western youth from the social system they have inherited; nor the women's liberation movement; nor the creation of such works as *Trial* by Tom Hayden (1971: 167) in which he said:

> "But the fact that so many different people are moving at once for their own liberation suggests an inspiring possibility. We are living in a time of universal desire for a new social order, a time when total revolution is on the agenda: not a limited and particular 'revolution' for national identity here, for the working class there, for women here . . . but for all of humanity to build a new, freer way of life by sharing the world's vast resources equally and fraternally. The world's people are so interdependent that a strike for freedom anywhere creates vibrations everywhere. The American empire itself is so worldwide in scope that humanity has, for the first time, not only a common spirit but a common enemy. Through their particular struggles, more and more revolutionaries see the possibilities of the 'new man' envisioned by Che Guevara. Formed in an international upheaval, such a human being would be universal in character for the first time in history. To become such a whole person in the present means fighting, not only around immediate self-interest, but against all levels of oppression at once."

Thus Hayden, unblack, unyoung any more, and unpoor by Third World standards, articulates the main dimensions of general, relevant theory at a universal level which come out of a philosophy stressing egalitarianism, freedom, and humanity. Hayden can produce this because history has arrived at a point when such writing must happen. The consciousness of oppressed people now orients toward the political and economic dimensions of oppression buttressed by cultural racism and a mentality of imperialism.

THEORY OPERATIONALIZATION

How do we articulate and operationalize the kind of theory for which I have been arguing? We should be past the point of playing games with computer or rigorous deductive models. They tend to underrate the intangible, but vitally important, dimensions of people's will, feelings, and culture. How, for example, does one measure racism? But it is one of the most important aspects of race oppression, at any level of analysis. Perhaps we can measure the *product* of racism, however, if we think in terms of the degree to which minority groups and minority nations have control over their lives and have equal access to economic resources. We can measure, or at least describe, the economic and political results of imperialism in the Third World.

In so doing, we find that the motivations of the imperial powers were always out of self-interest. Because of the colonial mentality, they exploited the colonies for self-gain, even though the forms of exploitation have been somewhat different-looking: British paternalism, French metropolitan elitism, American monopoly capital. They operated, and continue to operate, on illusive assumptions about Western cultural, social, technological, and political superiority, along with the operational premise that cultural, technological, and other transplants from the West are in the best interests of the Third World. The most recent expression of colonialism is aid programs to the Third World. These are seen by many to inhibit real internal development, but still operate under the guise of economic growth, measured in such terms as GNP increase. On inspection, it is seen that those who benefit most from increases in such indices are the old and newly developing elites, not the masses of people. What results is an increase in internal segmentation, rather than increased nationalism; but this merely continues the trend of "balkanization" which took form in the division of Africa after World War I and was continued after World War II by the British, French, Dutch, Belgians, and Italians when the Third World nations achieved political independence.

Third World aid has political strings attached. The United States provides the largest gross amount of aid, but in interesting ways. To political "neutrals," such as India, aid is provided in the form of interest-bearing loans; but it is now recognized that India's debt costs are almost equal to the amount of new aid it receives. To political friends, such as South Korea and nationalist China, aid is mostly given in the form of direct grants. And the aid figures become greatly inflated when we find that a great portion of it is direct or indirect military aid. China, on the other hand, provides interest-free aid as well as technicians. The products are tangible; for example, four factories in Cambodia and the beginning of the Tanzam railway. No developed nation, with the possible exceptions of Sweden and Japan, comes close to reaching the Pearson recommendations that 1 percent of GNP should be provided to the Third World with no strings attached. Hensman (1971) says that, although official British aid to Third World nations in 1968 was £221 million, when reduced by the amounts of loan repayments, interest payments, profit margins on goods which have to be bought in Britain, and the additional business which accrues to British interests, little actual aid occurs. We must add to this the insane set of economic priorities evident in today's international order. Total international military expenditure is estimated to be in excess of $120 billion (U.S.), and it may be double that figure if we consider space and indirect military expenses. The various aid programs from the wealthy nations obviously are designed to buttress or expand their particular sphere of interest, and to a large extent, it is a direct result of the different ideological and political differences among the major power blocs. The Third World nations are the ones that suffer.

Corporate investments from the developed nations add a major burden on the backs of Third World nations. Such investments are made mostly in high profit yield commodities and in the extractive industries upon which the West is increasingly dependent. Though seemingly in the interests of Third World nations, such selective investing tends not to develop local economics in any great measure but, instead, it encourages the development of affluent indigenous elites and a small middle class, while the masses' lot gets little better. Third World nations have bad balances of payments because their prices of export goods fall while Western prices rise as a result of inflation, higher costs, and an effective freeze on First World/Third World profit ratios. Markets for Third World products are declining. Too little attention appears to be given to the special needs of the various economic sectors in Third World nations: factory industries, extractive industries, plantations, peasant farming. All the relevant and applicable literature suggests that many of the causes of these problems are to be found in the patterns of interpenetration by international monopoly capital, the rather selfish and shortsighted cooperation by Third World elites and bureaucrats, and the aid programs from developed countries that place a political imprint and legitimation for the manipulative use of private capital.

REVOLUTIONARY CONSCIOUSNESS

There are new developments occurring that have great political significance. These frequently develop around economic criteria, such as protection of coffee prices in Africa and the recent confederation of Middle East oil-producing states to collectively bargain on prices with the oil corporations of Europe and America. More important, a growing consciousness on the part of Third World people is developing. This takes the form of being increasingly conscious of the conditions of exploitation, how it occurs, and what the sources are. With such awareness, there is a growing consciousness of kind; of the racist aspects of economic and political exploitation; in short, of the conditions of neo-colonialism. This consciousness is only partially economic, though that certainly is a manifestation, in the political economy, of Western racism against Third World nations. There is furthermore a growing consciousness that the agencies of international development and divisions and decision-making bodies of the United Nations have strong ethnocentric overtones. Thus, national liberation movements develop to challenge this arrangement both locally and in broader political divisions. Not only do such movements exist to throw off oppressive imperialism in such places as Mozambique, Angola, and Portuguese Guinea, but they exist in places where an internal colony—such as in South Africa, Rhodesia, and the United States—struggles to gain freedom from tyranny. This is rapidly growing and is an integral part of race relations throughout the world. Third World peoples are challenging the international order. They are challenging the right of Western culture and the capitalist economic system to dictate what the conditions of life should be in their lands. They are challenging the profit motive; the excessive individualism, rather than communalism, that emanates from Western practice; the mania for industrialization and urbanization and the plastic culture and life styles that seem to be produced by these particularly Western processes. C. R. Hensman (1971: 70) summed it up:

"To assume that the peoples of Latin America, Asia and Africa are now entering the eighteenth and nineteenth centuries, rather than preparing to enter the twenty-first, is to imply that these peoples will *never* escape being backward, inferior and underdeveloped. (It is also to ignore the fact that these peoples did experience the 'development' of the past few centuries.) Since, according to this racial theory, the way to *modernity* in society, thought, politics and industry is necessarily pioneered by western democracy, western science, western industrial know-how, and western leadership qualities generally, whatever the underdeveloped peoples do to develop their own societies and thus to modernize them will lead to something other than modernization . . . as development theory, it is nonsense."

A. Sivanandań in London noted the dynamics of culture, identity, and politics in the June 1970 issue of *Liberator:*

"Black culture today is too self-conscious and too vibrant to submit itself to white hegemony, yet not strong enough economically to withstand white capital. By sequestering itself from meaningful political action over a wider area, it runs the risk of falling prey to the system. To move against the system, even as one discovers one's identity, is to prevent such a contingency. Furthermore, to seek one's identity in seclusion is to become inbreeding, self-righteous, and, to that extent, inhumane. It keeps one from finding in Fanon's indomitable phrase, 'the universality inherent in the human condition' " [p. 12].

Sivanandan argues for the universality in the human condition. I agree, and add that the study of race relations in the international context must try to operationalize, or at least take into account, such abstractions as "the human condition" and "oppression," and develop a utopian vision of the egalitarian alternatives for the future. This is a major theoretical challenge. But the effort should take us closer to much-needed relevancy. I have not offered rigid definitions, nor have I suggested explicit hypotheses. We need flexible, general models that consider the political and economic factors in race relations contexts; the cultural causes and consequences of racism and colonialism; the consciousness of their position in a social order that comes to oppressed racial and ethnic groups as they further understand their situation; and their struggle for freedom through revitalized political organization. Ecological space and sense of community become important dimensions in this process, because where people live is where they are oppressed, where they share their culture and where they organize politically. The major theoretical challenge in international race relations is to develop means by which we can study the forces of oppression as well as the forces of counter-oppression.

REFERENCES

BARAN, P. A. and P. M. SWEEZY (1966) Monopoly Capital. New York: Monthly Review Press.

BLAUNER, R. (1970) "Black culture: myth or reality," in N. E. Whitten, Jr. and J. F. Szwed (eds.) Afro-American Anthropology. New York: Free Press.

CAMPBELL, N. (1952) What is Science. New York: Dover Publications.

CARMICHAEL, S. and C. V. HAMILTON (1967) Black Power: The Politics of Liberation in America. New York: Vintage Books.

DeBRAY, R. (1969) Essays on Latin America. New York: Monthly Review Press.

DOMHOFF, G. W. (1967) Who Rules America. Englewood Cliffs, N.J.: Prentice-Hall.

DUMONT, R. (1966) False Start in Africa. London: Andre Deutsch.

FANON, F. (1963) The Wretched of the Earth. New York: Grove Press.

FRANK, A. G. (1969) Capitalism and Underdevelopment in Latin America. New York: Monthly Review Press.

HAYDEN, T. (1971) Trial. London: Johathan Cape.

HENSMAN, C. R. (1971) Rich Against Poor. London: Penguin Press.
——— (1969) From Gandhi to Guevara. London: Penguin Press.
HOROWITZ, D. (1969) Imperialism and Revolution. London: Penguin Press.
MANDEL, E. (1971) "What is U.S. imperialism," in The Red Mole (January 16-31, 1971): 6-7 (London).
MANNHEIM, K. (1952) Essays on the Sociology of Knowledge. London: Routledge & Kegan Paul.
MEMMI, A. (1965) The Colonizer and the Colonized. New York: Orion Press.
NAGEL, E. (1961) The Structure of Science. New York: Harcourt, Brace & World.
NKRUMAH, K. (1965) Neo-Colonialism, The Last Stage of Imperialism. London: Nelson & Sons.
POPPER, K. R. (1961) The Logic of Scientific Discovery. New York: Science Editions.
SIVANANDAN, A. (1970) article in Liberator 10, 6 (June): 11.
TABB, W. (1970) The Political Economy of the Black Ghetto. New York: W. W. Norton.

Chapter 5

CARIBBEAN NATION-BUILDING AND THE INTERNATIONALIZATION OF RACE: ISSUES AND PERSPECTIVES

LOCKSLEY EDMONDSON

*T*his essay addresses itself to two interrelated matters. Initially, it will touch on some very broad considerations on the role of race factors in contemporary international relations with some attention being focused on the impact of black nationalist and internationalist assertions on the internationalization of race. The main portion of this study will then attempt to relate some issues bearing on racial challenges in Caribbean nation-building to the wider environments of external black nationalisms, Caribbean international relations, and race in the international relations setting. In pursuit of the latter task, the intention is less to try to arrive at definitive conclusions than to discuss some practical issues and pose some theoretical perspectives which appear amenable to further enquiry.

RACE ANALYSIS AND BEHAVIOR: INTERNATIONAL DIMENSIONS

While there have been numerous national and comparative studies of race relations, relatively few academic efforts have been made to expand analytic horizons to the international relations stage. Nor have international relations scholars been too concerned with exploring the relevance of racial factors in the complexities of international relations behavior. The overwhelming majority of the all too limited number of studies sensitive to international relations dimensions of race has been narrowly confined to selected issue or area concerns, as is evident in a recent bibliographical collection of major contemporary studies on race and ethnic issues in various regions of the world (Shepherd et al., 1970).

But there have been some recent encouraging academic signals of a developing internationally oriented focus among race relations analysts as well as a race-sensitive focus among students of international relations. The former is illustrated in the setting up, in 1969, of a unit on international race studies in the Institute of Race Relations (London); the latter is reflected in the establishment in that same year of a Center on International Race Relations at the University of Denver. And in addition to such institutional developments, some individual researchers have already taken the plunge in trying to comprehend in conceptual or practical terms the role of race factors in international relations (e.g., Edmondson, 1969a; Gardiner, 1968; Isaacs, 1969; Le Melle and Shepherd, 1971; Preiswerk, 1970; Rosenau, 1970; Shepherd, 1970). The distinctive aspect of the studies cited here is that they attempt to assess the role of race not as an isolated but as an integral part of international relations behavior patterns. But there is no unanimity among these writers as to the analytic tools or approaches required, or on the importance of race relative to earlier historical phases of the international system or relative to other behavioral variables or issues in the contemporary international system.

The premise of this essay is that there are clear indications of a growing political potency of race issues at the international level. This phenomenon is here conceived of as an *internationalization of race,* a phrase which refers to the factors and processes influencing a projection of domestic race issues into the international arena and conversely encouraging an intrusion of international influences on domestic race relations. In order to assess the dynamics of this phenomenon it is necessary, first, to reflect on the tendencies and forces in the contemporary international system which have influenced the scope and style of the internationalization of race and, second, to discuss the primary dimensions of the outstanding international challenges of race.

In dealing with the subject of international system tendencies and forces, certain hypotheses developed in and out of previous studies by the present writer (Edmondson, 1969a, 1971, 1973) will be advanced:

(1) There have undoubtedly been positive changes for the better in the twentieth-century global race relations climate, most significantly in the relative decline of the once solid entrenchment of international white power and the rising (and partially rewarded) counter-challenges in the searches for non-white empowerment.

(2) But the still prevailing coincidence of power and race—with few exceptions—and the changing circumstances under which the interests and demands of the less powerful can be more readily articulated and consistently projected, have influenced the trend towards an internationalization of racial concerns.

(3) Of fundamental importance to the previous considerations is the rise of the Third World in the international system which in and of itself constitutes a change in the racial composition of the basic international relations actors and which in turn affects the style and scope of articulated interests and demands which in the fairly recent past could find only limited expression through the formal channels of the international political system.

(4) The globalization of international relations, affected substantially by the democratization of the primary actor base, has influenced the trend towards an increasing sense of interdependence in the international system—a trend reinforced by communications and other technological advances—which has contributed to: (a) more visibility of racial problems; (b) more regular expressions of international concern; and, (c) a greater likelihood of a spillover of racial cleavages across national frontiers, or, of a projection of racial issues and interests from the domestic to the international sphere.

(5) Situations influencing a transnational projection of racial interests and activities have encouraged racial groups per se to seek legitimacy as regular international relations actors.

(6) The rise and consolidation of the international organization movement (global-type, regional, or functional) not only reflects a growing sense of interdependence but also, in furnishing ready-made mechanisms for concerted pressure, affects positively the frequency with which interests are internationalized. (In this connection it is essential to note the increasing importance of race issues in the concerns of the United Nations, the Organization of African Unity, and the Commonwealth.)

(7) The continuing search for an international political community, spurred on by a rising structure of interdependence, has contributed to a heightening sense of urgency of the need for racial adjustments in encouraging an awareness of the contributory potentialities of race to international conflict and in encouraging a search for remedies through internationally organized action.

(8) But the search for an international political community has simultaneously been accompanied by an expanded entrenchment of the bases of territorial nationalism and by a heightening of nationalistic aspirations. One consequence of the latter trend is that it has served to reinforce the political importance of race and ethnicity as significant motivating forces in the dynamics of self-determination. This has been especially evident in the anti-colonial struggle at large, and it is still relevant not only in many post-colonial situations but also in other longer established polities. International systemic inducements (see hypothesis 4) appear increasingly to reduce the prospects of most such struggles being confined to a domestic habitat, by encouraging: (a) demonstration (emulative), or counter-demonstration (reactive) external responses; or (b) the promotion of external interests by domestic parties, or the intervention of external parties.

(9) The correlation between race and economic status in the international system, being the domestic situation in multi-racial societies writ large, encourages a convergence of national and international racial struggles for economic advancement and reflects the realities of the outstanding remaining hurdles confronted in the search for non-white emancipation. Some observers (Drucker, 1968; Fanon, 1968: 95-106; Nyerere, 1969; Russett, 1965; Segal, 1967; Smith, 1965, 1968: 1-5) have indeed drawn attention to the prospects of international race cleavages or conflicts being conditioned or exacerbated by the persistence of international economic stratification patterns along racial lines.

The most important dimension of international racial challenges in their historical and contemporary phases has concerned the issue of black-white relations. In order to understand the significance of this dimension it is necessary to consider the conditions under which race and color factors were first injected into the dynamics of the modern international system. The root of the problem historically lay in white power expansionism, and the most crucial historical determinant originated in the institutionalization of transatlantic slavery. Once slavery was linked to the ongoing predominating transitions in the international economic system, sustained by the primary actors in the emerging modern international political system, and rationalized in terms of inherent race superiority, the stage was set for the internationalization of the linkages of race, economics, and politics. It is appropriate here to quote Talcott Parsons (1968: 366):

> "the primary historic origin of the modern color problem lies in the relation of Europeans to African slavery, as that became established along the whole Atlantic coast of the Americas from the Southern North American Colonies to Southern Brazil, *very much including the Caribbean area" [my emphasis]*.

With this background in mind, the triumph of European colonialism is best considered as an institutional reinforcement and extension of white power, insofar as it affected African peoples. As a function of its pervasive application throughout the non-white world, colonialism historically considered has been the most important influence in the globalization and internationalization of race issues. But considering both the traumatic impact of slavery on Africa and within the African diaspora, and the problems and legacies deriving from the colonial intrusion in Africa and colonial constructions in the Caribbean, the intensity and urgency of racial adjustment has traditionally assumed the most acute dimensions in the relations between black and white.

Thus, viewing the problem of race in its most significant evolutionary *global* dimension, it is clear that it was primarily as a function of European political and economic expansionism that race domination became pervasive in scope, politicized in practice, systematized in effect, and internationalized through necessity. W.E.B. DuBois (1920: 42) succinctly underscored the conditions of the injection of race factors in the modern international system in the following terms:

"Such degrading of men by men is as old as mankind and the invention of no race or people. Ever have men striven to conceive of their victims as different, in soul and blood, strength and cunning, race and lineage. It has been left, however, to *Europe* and to *modern days,* to discover the eternal *world wide* mark of meanness—color" [my emphases]!

A more recent commentary (Isaacs, 1968: 75) captures well the nature of the historical legacies, contemporary realities, and future international challenges of race relations:

"Skin color has served as the badge of master and subject, of the enslaved and the free, the dominators and the dominated. Of all the factors involved in the great rearrangement of human relationships taking place, skin color is the most glandular. Hence none is more sensitive, more psychologically explosive, or more intimately relevant to each individual's involvement in the process of political change."

To comprehend the dynamics of the internationalization of race, it is essential to understand the fundamental impact of the politicization and internationalization of black emancipation struggles (Edmondson, 1968); and to assess the implications of black nationalist strivings around the world it is necessary to pay attention to the wider influences and transitions in the functioning on the international system which encourage an internationalization of race.

THE INTERNATIONAL CONTEXT OF CARIBBEAN NATION-BUILDING

A study of the Caribbean region naturally lends itself to a consideration of the two perspectives posed in the foregoing paragraph.[1] A crucial test in Caribbean nation-building lies in the challenging of establishing viable multi-racial societies; the future of multi-racial viability will predominantly be conditioned by the capacities of the regional political and economic systems to satisfy the aspirations of the black masses; and regional traumas are inherently complicated by the international situation.

Whether as a result of its historical origins or contemporary positioning, the Caribbean cannot escape being inextricably tied up in the cross-currents of international political, economic and race relations. With reference to the region's history, in no other part of the world were the original international links of racial, political, and economic oppression as systematically defined and institutionalized. Genocide (through which the indigenous elements almost totally disappeared), slavery (which in its Caribbean application was more pervasive as a societal shaping force than elsewhere), colonialism (which literally constructed the region as we know it), and the plantation system (being a political, social, and economic system all wrapped up in one, and a dominant system through which human and economic exploitation was regularized), explain the very origins of the modern Caribbean. The region was at once the laboratory of modern political and economic imperialism and the incubator of modern internationalized racism. The symbolic and strategic positioning of the Caribbean viewed temporally or spatially in the dominant global struggles against racial, political, and economic oppression has accordingly been incisively assessed by Sivanandan (1971: 230), a Ceylonese resident in Britain. The Afro-Caribbean, he maintains, being

"a product both of colonialism and slavery . . . is the common denominator in the struggles of Afro-America and the Third World alike. He is the link that connects the enslaved peoples and the colonized, the blacks of America and the peoples of Afro-Asia."

But apart from the Caribbean's historical importance (and as a consequence the region's lasting symbolism) as the focal point of the unholy trinity of human, political, and economic exploitation, the region too has a special significance as an arena in which dominant international cultural, racial, political, and economic forces have interacted with a high degree of frequency. Politically subordinated either to Europe or North America through a common colonial experience but fragmented as a consequence of differing colonial contacts; politically linked (in certain cases) through Commonwealth ties to nations on all continents; geographically bridging North and South America, and (in some instances) consolidating hemispheric organizational linkages through the Organization of American States; subservient to, and substantially controlled by, external economic forces and particularly susceptible to the forces of international economics; racially shaped predominantly by Africa and Asia and culturally molded in a large degree by Europe; objectively located in the Third World but in most instances subjectively identifying (at least at the official level) with the Western world—the Caribbean, while occasionally appearing to indicate some promises in the search for an internationalist ideal, more often than not has been a mirror of the seamy side of international relations history.

More to the issue at hand, the foregoing considerations underscore my previous contention that as a function of historical legacies and contemporary positioning, the Caribbean is naturally sensitive to the influences—some contradictory, others reinforcing—of external forces and international currents. It follows that the study of race factors in nation-building in the Caribbean cannot be divorced from a consideration of the wider international context of race.

In exploring the interrelations of the regional (Caribbean) and international dimensions of race, there are three important regional factors with wider implications or symbolism which should be noted. These factors have bearing on the politics, economics, and psychology of the contemporary dynamics of racial struggle.

The first is that despite differing national clusters of racial mixture or degrees of racial balance, the Caribbean racial experience is predominantly influenced by an African presence. As George Lamming (1966: 49), the Barbadian writer, once put it in relation to the West Indies—an assessment that might be extended to the Caribbean region at large:

"in spite of this diversity of peoples, stratified in this period of transition by the policies of race and colonialism, the African presence . . . has worked its way like oxygen into every ethnic and cultural pore of West Indian consciousness.

"It is this presence—to be found everywhere and in numerical superiority on the islands—that makes for the essential continuity of West Indian reality."

Secondly, the contemporary economic predicaments of the Caribbean can be initially assessed in terms of the historical economic functions and evolution of the area. No other region of the world has ever been as dependent on slave labor for economic viability; nor have there been more significant examples of societies being invented as economic servicing units for metropolitan powers. Here matured the historical linkages of racial and economic domination as an international relations phenomenon.

It has indeed been argued that the West Indies' wealth was crucial to the emergence of Britain as the first industrial society (Walvin, 1970; Williams, 1964). But whatever the Caribbean impact on European economies might have been, the continuing reality of Caribbean economies has been their entrenched subordination to external interests. The present unabated power of foreign (white) economic exploitation highlights the relationships of international race and class factors. The racial ordering of the economic sphere is further reinforced by the historical formalization in the region of economic power along racial and color stratification lines which, while modified in some degree over time, still persists as an important operative variable. Such is the kind of situation which dramatically illustrates my earlier hypothesis concerning the inducements to a convergence of national and international racial and economic liberation struggles.

Thirdly, on the psychological level, Gordon Lewis (1968: 55) has pointed out that in the Caribbean "not only the dominant institutions but also the controlling attitudes of the society have been shaped, to a great extent, by the white European influence" (more often than not by the "less attractive attributes of Europe," he adds). The challenge to the Caribbean is to transform these inherited attitudes, but this challenge, too, underlies one of the outstanding predicaments of global black existence. The individual and collective searches for identities within the black world are enmeshed in the psychology and politics of contemporary global race relations.

The realities of the Caribbean multi-racial structure are much too complex to pin down solely to the dimension of black-white relations. But any assessment of the broad regional characteristics and regularities in the evolution of race relations systems must focus primarily on that subject, especially if these concerns are related to international racial considerations. And even if we tried to focus attention exclusively on the regional (as opposed to the international) *racial* dimension, the issue sooner or later comes back to the unfulfillment of black aspirations as the common element in a region where black predicaments have basically originated from a subjection to white domination. "West Indian society," in the words of a Jamaican (Nettleford, 1971), has been characterized by "the persistence of the struggle between Europe and Africa on foreign soil and the primacy of this struggle over all other considerations." This is the unfinished struggle underlying much of the Caribbean experience and which complicates the searches for national identities and the strivings for substantive measures of national emancipation.

These reflections on some international aspects of the Caribbean dilemma would be incomplete were consideration not attached to the question of population mobility. A most influential conditioning force in the Caribbean experience has been the original wholesale construction of immigrant societies in the region and the area's subsequent role as a population exporting base.

As a consequence of the former, the traumas of nation-building have been complicated by the historical imposition of minority (colonialist) cultures, the survival of some original cultural heritages, or the conscious attempts in some quarters to try to retain (or recapture) a psychological linkage with the past. The Caribbean thus remains highly susceptible to the variety of external cultural and racial (and, as well, racist) influences which helped to mold the region's history. Trinidad and Tobago's Prime Minister, Eric Williams (1962: 281), was aware of some of these attendant external complications in the search for nationhood when he warned:

> "There can be no Mother India for those whose ancestors came from India. . . . There can be no Mother Africa for those of African origin, and the Trinidad and Tobago society is living a lie and heading for trouble if it seeks to create the impression or allow others to act under the delusion that Trinidad and Tobago is an African society. There can be no Mother England and no dual loyalties. . . . There can be no Mother China, even if one could agree as to which China is the Mother; and there can be no Mother Syria and no Mother Lebanon. The nation, like an individual, can have only one Mother. The only Mother we recognise is Mother Trinidad and Tobago. . . . And no possible interference can be tolerated by any country outside in our family relations and domestic quarrels, *no matter what it has contributed and when to the population that is today the people of Trinidad and Tobago*" [my emphasis].

The latter consideration—the Caribbean as an emigrant-producing region—reinforces my thesis that a combination of operative forces makes for a natural internationalization of Caribbean concerns and interests, not least in the area of race. It is no accident that the questions of immigration policies and domestic race practices of the immigrant-receiving countries are entrenched in the regular foreign policy concerns of most Caribbean regimes. But of far more importance to the present and future is that in the contemporary setting of a rising structure of race protest and struggle within the main (British and North American) centers of the Caribbean diaspora, the relationship of Caribbean migrants to these race struggles abroad is likely to prove of major consequence to the climate of race relations back home. Indeed, the present-day predicaments of the Caribbean migrant have a wider meaning relating to the linkages of international political, economic, and racial issues. Sivanandan's (1971: 230) perceptive assessment of the dilemmas of the West Indian migrant in Britain is very relevant to the latter consideration:

> "In view of the massive and ongoing exploitation of his own country, his choice is between psychological servitude here and economic servitude back home—which is no choice at all. He is therefore faced with the dual problem of overcoming injustice and discrimination in this country and overthrowing the neo-colonial set up in his own."

In this light, instructive are the recent angry denunciations of "American oppression" of Puerto Rico made by a Puerto Rican nationalist spokesman (Gonzales, 1971) who, in so doing, pointed out that her relatives, having fled the island to escape "the oppressive conditions perpetuated here by U.S. capitalism," had "failed to find the American Dream in New York."

As a hint to what the future might hold in store in terms of the impact of the Caribbean diaspora on the Caribbean homeland, mention should be made here of the disproportionate contribution of Afro-Caribbeans in exile to the cause of black internationalism. Moreover, such a consideration may shed some light on some factors influencing a natural internationalization of important Caribbean concerns.

BLACK INTERNATIONALISTS AND INTERNATIONALISM: NOTES ON THE CARIBBEAN CONTRIBUTION

"The persistence" of the "West Indian factor . . . in all-African movements is remarkable," as George Shepperson (1962: 356) asserts, but this phenomenon while also recognized by other writers (e.g., Cruse, 1967: 115-147; Edmondson, 1969b: 57-63; James, 1963: 391-418; Mazrui, 1966) still remains to be fully explored and assessed.

The Caribbean has produced a notable crop of individuals who can best be collectively treated under the label of black internationalists, a description which would include those motivated primarily by racial interests as well as those who were relatively less so.[2] It would also embrace those of either evolutionary or revolutionary persuasions. But whatever their individual motivations or persuasions, a common link has been that in no case could they afford to be unconcerned about the politics of race at the international level.

It is not necessary here to enter a detailed catalogue of the Caribbean contribution to black internationalism. Names which immediately spring to mind are Edward Wilmot Blyden (Virgin Islands) and Marcus Garvey (Jamaica) —the most illustrious "pan-Negro" spokesmen of their day; H. Sylvester Williams, George Padmore, C.L.R. James (all of Trinidad), and T. R. Makonnen (Guyana) who, with others in the English-speaking and French-speaking Caribbean (Edmondson, 1969b: 58, 72-73; Langley, 1969), were important catalysts of the evolution and institutionalization or political pan-Africanism; Aimé Césaire (Martinique), Leon Damas (French Guiana), Jean Price-Mars (Haiti), Claude McKay (Jamaica)—recognized pioneers of cultural pan-Africanism; Frantz Fanon (Martinique), and Stokely Carmichael (Trinidad)—leading theorists of contemporary Third World and/or Black Power revolution.

Linking the historical record of the Caribbean black internationalist contribution to the dynamics of the contemporary black revolution in the African diaspora, there is some justification in the following report (Johnson, 1970):

"While conceding the great impact of the black revolution in the United States, activists here [in the Caribbean] quickly add that West Indians, such as . . . Marcus Garvey and . . . Stokely Carmichael, have played crucial roles in the development of black pride in the United States. Thus, they say, black-power convictions are not entirely a United States export, but also something of a West Indies reimport."

What are the reasons for the significance of the Caribbean contribution? I suggest two interrelated sets of considerations, the first set also helpful in explaining the notable Afro-American impact on black internationalism, and the second highlighting the more unique aspects of the Caribbean situation.

Among the first set of considerations we might include:

(1) the impact of enslavement and a long history of subordination to white power in heightening sensitivities to race oppression;

(2) a long exposure to, and intimate knowledge of, the gap between the stated ideals and actual performances of Western civilization in its treatment of black men the world over;

(3) the operational base, in that being located within or tied directly to European and North American focal points of world power and being automatically involved in the concerns of these centers of global influence, this facilitates the promotion of a black internationalist vision;

(4) a natural sensitivity to continental African affairs because of Africa's all-pervading influence on the past and present situation of black people around the world.

But there are at least three additional factors directly relevant to the Caribbean experience. The first concerns issues earlier raised, namely, the global positioning and mobility of Caribbean peoples which has facilitated a diversification and enrichment of experiences. In most of the previous examples we have cited, the internationalists have had some face-to-face contact with the United States racial experience and, equally important, they, unlike most Afro-Americans, have been directly linked to Europe which for so long set the tone for the international dynamics of politics and race. Further, a greater likelihood of direct face-to-face and diversified contacts with both Afro-Americans and continental Africans (in Europe and elsewhere) has aided in an internationalization of concerns. Second, the cultural diversity within the Caribbean region has encouraged a cultural diversification of external linkages, thus widening the scope of contacts with, and interests in, pan-African affairs. Third, there is the matter of the strategic positioning of the Caribbean region in black liberation struggles. While concerned (like Afro-Americans) with a quest for black dignity as a function of similarities in historical predicaments, the more conscious Caribbean nationalist would (like continental Africans) be highly sensitive to colonialism which in its classic formal manifestation was an experience shared by both. Viewing the matter in this light, the Caribbean "has been positioned strategically and symbolically between continental African and Afro-American struggles against white domination" (Edmondson, 1969b: 59). The major international manifestations of racial cum political cum ecnomic oppression are part and parcel of the Caribbean experience.

CONTEMPORARY AND FUTURE IMPLICATIONS

But if, as has been seen above, the Caribbean has been in a special position to make significant contributions to black internationalist strivings and black revolutionary struggles abroad, why then is the Caribbean region, with the notable exception of Cuba (and perhaps—though this is as yet uncertain —Guyana), so plagued with conservative political regimes? And why, as the history of the West Indies Federation suggests, is the region so beset by parochial political forms? Is it that the crop of black internationalists such as those discussed above were so out of tune with the Caribbean mood that most of them deliberately sought external platforms for the promotion of their appeals? Is it the case, as C.L.R. James (1970) observed, that West Indians are only good at fighting other people's revolutions, a conclusion also drawn by Harold Cruse (1967: 135) in one of his few undistorted assessments of the Caribbean scene?

One thing seems clear. If Caribbean-born internationalists and revolutionaries are at all representative of latent Caribbean urges then the Caribbean potential at home has yet to be realized. Two contemporary factors appear to be crucial to the present and future political direction of Caribbean emancipation struggles.

The first is that, thanks to the decline of formal political colonialism in much of the region, the existence of territorial sovereignty and the formal indigenous control of political machineries may help to furnish more potentially viable operational bases than in the past, and may help to create stronger psychological inducements for those dedicated to meaningful change to mount an unrelenting pursuit of regional liberation strategies. (As a variation on the theme, mention should be made of an apparent demonstration effect of West Indian independence on the Puerto Rican nationalist movement.) Thus many of those who in the past might have been tempted to seek expression of their political talents on external platforms are now more likely to redirect their energies inward at this crucial stage of Caribbean evolution.

Second, those Caribbean-born political activists who still prefer to seek a wider international political stage, are now more likely than before to identify a natural congruence between their external concerns and regional Caribbean immediate needs, in an international situation more conducive to a politicization and internationalization of struggles against racial domination.

It is in such evolving contexts that the contemporary thrust of Caribbean Black Power movements are best understood. For the first time in Caribbean political history of the post-slavery period have arisen the phenomena of grassroots-inspired or grassroots-focused political movements seeking a substantive reshaping of regional political and socio-economic orders, which in the process are helping to mold a wider recognition of the similarities in the Caribbean predicament and are seeking to forge a sense of a wider Caribbean identity. Black Power challenges to the legitimacy of the prevailing political and economic orders naturally feed on the urgency of a need to reorder existing racial stratification systems. These challenges are combined with a recognition of a need to contain external forces of economic exploitation and, to some extent, political direction. Thus a situation where black establishment leaders are themselves under attack because of their failure to relate to the needs of the economically deprived (predominantly black) masses, and on account of their general insensitivity to the problems of foreign (white) economic domination, is tailor-made for a merging of class struggle (against the leaders from within) and race assertion (against the dominant internal and external economic forces and combinations).

Undoubtedly, the situation is complicated by racial suspicions within the non-white groupings, notably in Trinidad and Tobago and Guyana. But it is of interest to note that within the West Indian political leadership ranks Cheddi Jagan, of East Indian descent, was one of the first to endorse Black Power (Edmondson, 1968: 29);[3] and a major thrust in the 1970 Trinidad uprisings was the conscious effort by Black Power leaders to legitimize the movement as a means of overcoming Indian-African racial divisions entrenched in the established political order (Best, 1970).

In the societal structure of the Caribbean any viable Black Power movement while being necessarily sensitive to black needs cannot afford to be racially exclusive in means or ends.[4] As argued by a black Guyanese (Rodney, 1969: 28):

"Today, some Indians (like some Africans) have joined the white power structure in terms of economic activity and culture; but the underlying reality is that poverty resides among Africans and Indians in the West Indies and that power is denied them. Black Power in the West Indies, therefore, refers primarily to people who are recognisably African or Indian."

Whether Black Power strivings result in a diminution or exacerbation of such intra-regional racial cleavages remains to be seen. The real test ahead in such cases is whether Black Power, in mounting the necessary challenges in the search for emancipation of the masses, can serve as a catalyst for a merger of race and class protest directing attention away from existing racial competition for limited political and economic spoils to an overriding unifying multi-racial search for meaningful national power and for full emancipation of all races traditionally oppressed.

But such considerations cannot be divorced from the external dimensions of race, economics, and politics. In the first place, contemporary patterns of Black Power nationalism in the Caribbean invite reflection on the wider patterns of black nationalism in external environments and on the contemporary mood of black internationalist or global strivings in terms of certain futuristic implications which I have elaborated elsewhere (Edmondson, 1973), namely:

(a) the general processes of political resocialization—"a process of induction into new political values and styles qualitatively different from those generally accepted in the past"—among youth in the black world-at-large;

(b) the prospects and consequences of a heightening interaction of interests within, and forging of closer nationalist links between various parts of, the black world, which not only might aid in extending the scope and intensity of race cleavages but also bring into the picture the question of

(c) trans-socialization political impacts—defined as situations where socialization patterns spill over from one arena of political action to influence positively behavior in other external political arenas—which would, for example, involve considerations of the probable impact of the political behavior of Caribbean exiles abroad on those at home and vice-versa.[5]

Pitching our concerns beyond the specific focus of external and international black nationalist strivings, special consideration should be devoted to the prospects of a direct spillover of racial tensions from external environments,[6] an issue which could prove very important in the Caribbean future in view of

(a) relatively recent massive Caribbean migration flows to various parts of the white world which has

(b) contributed to tensions of race adjustment in the latter at a time when

(c) the prospects are more conducive to a politicization and internationalization of racial issues and at a time when

(d) the search for racial power and full national emancipation in the Caribbean becomes more urgent in the aftermath (or latter stages) of decolonization which

(e) is, however, exacerbated by the continuing subordination of the region to the power of the dominant manifestations of international white power originating from the very sources perpetuating discrimination against those who have fled these conditions in search of better economic opportunities abroad.

I have been arguing that two of the most influential historical factors in the shaping of the Caribbean region have been its racialization and its internationalization. The legacies of the past pervade the present. The political future of the region will largely be determined by the challenges of multi-racial existence and economic advancement of the masses. But both factors are tied up in the international order of white power dominance.

Moving to the wider international context of race relations, I argued initially that a combination of tendencies and forces has influenced an internationalization of racial issues and that consequently race has become enmeshed in major global struggles against political and economic domination. I further observed that some have already drawn attention to the conflict potential of race at the international level. If these interpretations are correct, the future of race relations in the Caribbean may well be ultimately determined more by external, than by the strictly internal, influences.

Leo Kuper (1969: 486) has argued that "The peaceful resolution of internal conflict between racial and ethnic sections may very well be contingent on the reduction of international tensions and the movement toward a world community of nations." But once we admit of the possibility of race and ethnicity as direct sources of international tension, it would follow that the resolution of internal racial and ethnic conflicts would prove that much more problematical.

NOTES

1. There are a variety of usages of the term "Caribbean" (see, e.g., Preiswerk, 1969: 1-2, on various definitions). In the present essay the "Caribbean" is used to refer to all the islands in the region, the Guianas, and British Honduras (Belize); the "West Indies," when specifically identified, refers to the English-speaking component. Much of what is hereafter said about the Caribbean is in fact based on the West Indian situation, but the Caribbean situation as discussed here can in most cases be generalized from the West Indies experience.

2. Some of these will be identified below by country of birth and early upbringing. Some later changed their nationality.

3. Since then, Jagan's main political opponent, Guyanese Prime Minister Forbes Burnham, has openly identified himself with elements in Black Power movements in his country and elsewhere. He is the only regional leader in power (besides Fidel Castro) who appears sympathetic to Black Power styles and goals. But Burnham's strategy is as yet unclear. Is he coopting Black Power strategically to disarm potentially revolutionary forces? Or is he engaging in race politics which is not uncommon in the recent Guyanese political tradition? Or does he genuinely perceive Black Power as a path to full national integration and emancipation? Jagan, on the other hand, has seemed less vocal on Black Power ideas in recent times. These developments appear to suggest that the present structure of race politics in Guyana is such that efforts to forge a mass trans-racial movement under a Black Power banner will face greater challenges than in most other parts of the Caribbean. But it should be recalled that in Guyana of the early 1950s there emerged briefly a de facto one-party system with strong ideological content and class appeal which transcended racial lines.

4. It is clear that to reduce Black Power in the Caribbean to a purely racial slogan is to misunderstand and distort the Caribbean situation and to misrepresent Caribbean needs. Stokely Carmichael's description of Fidel Castro as "one of the blackest men in the Americas" has been approvingly cited by one West Indian Black Power proponent who, by contrast, has labeled the predominantly black Jamaican government as a "White Power" establishment (Rodney, 1969: 23, 31).

5. In this latter context it is relevant to wonder if the apparent closer forging of linkages in Britain between West Indians of African and Indian descent may result in a spillover encouragement of closer cooperation and unity between these racial segments back at home; or whether intra-regional racial cleavages may exacerbate (or intra-regional searches for national advancement through racial unity may advance) the prospects of closer cooperation among the various racial elements in the Caribbean diaspora.

6. A recent case in point was the way in which race tensions in Canada were an important catalyst for the Black Power uprising in Trinidad (Best, 1970: 9).

REFERENCES

BEST, L. (1970) "The February revolution: causes and meaning." Tapia (Trinidad) 12 (December 20): 9-13.

CRUSE, H. (1967) The Crisis of the Negro Intellectual. New York: William Morrow.

DRUCKER, P. (1968) "A warning to the rich white world." Harper's (December): 67-74.

DuBOIS, W.E.B. (1920) Darkwater: Voices From Within the Veil. New York: Harcourt, Brace & Howe.

EDMONDSON, L. (1973) "Africa and the African diaspora: interactions, linkages, and racial challenges in the future world order," in A. A. Mazrui and H. H. Patel (eds.) Africa in World Affairs: The Next Thirty Years. New York: Third Press.

––– (1971) "Race and human rights in international organization and international law–and Afro-American interests: analysis and documentation." Afro-American Studies 2 (December): 205-224.

––– (1969a) The challenges of race: from entrenched White Power to rising Black Power." International J. 24 (Autumn): 693-716.

––– (1969b) "George Padmore's place in the study of Pan-Africanism." University of East Africa Social Sciences Council Conference 1968/69: Political Science Papers (Kampala: Makerere Institute of Social Research): 56-74.

––– (1968) "The internationalization of Black Power: historical and contemporary perspectives." Mawazo 1 (December): 16-30.

FANON, F. (1968) The Wretched of the Earth (C. Farrington, trans.) New York: Grove Press.

GARDINER, R.K.A. (1968) "Race and color in international relations," pp. 18-33 in J. H. Franklin (ed.) Color and Race. Boston: Beacon Press.

GONZALEZ, G. (1971) Comments at a Press Conference held by the Young Lords Party; reported in "Young Lords Denounce U.S., Ferre," San Juan Star (March 19).

ISAACS, H. R. (1969) "Color in world affairs." Foreign Affairs 47 (January): 235-250.

––– (1968) "Group identity and political change: the role of color and physical characteristics," pp. 75-97 in J. H. Franklin (ed.) Color and Race. Boston: Beacon Press.

JAMES, C.L.R. (1970) A Commentary on "George Padmore" on a Panel at the 55th Annual Meeting of the Association for the Study of Negro Life and History. Philadelphia, October 22-25.

––– (1963) The Black Jacobins: Toussaint L'Ouverture and the San Domingo Revolution (2nd ed. rev.). New York: Vintage Books.

JOHNSON, T. A. (1970) "Black Power flourishing in the Caribbean." New York Times (April 24).

KUPER, L. (1969) "Ethnic and racial pluralism: some aspects of polarization and depluralization," pp. 459-487 in L. Kuper and M. G. Smith (eds.) Pluralism in Africa. Berkeley: University of California Press.

LAMMING, G. (1966) "Caribbean literature: the black rock of Africa." African Forum 1 (Spring): 32-52.

LANGLEY, J. A. (1969) "Pan-Africanism in Paris, 1924-36." J. of Modern African Studies 7 (April): 69-94.

LeMELLE, T. J. and G. W. SHEPHERD, Jr. (1971) "Race in the future of international relations." J. of International Affairs 15, 2: 302-313.

LEWIS, G. K. (1968) The Growth of the Modern West Indies. New York: Monthly Review Press.

MAZRUI, A. A. (1966) "The Caribbean impact on African nationalism." East Africa J. 3 (June): 17-20.

NETTLEFORD, R. (1971) "Caribbean perspectives," a lecture delivered at the Institute of International Relations, St. Augustine, Trinidad; reported in the Jamaican Weekly Gleaner (June 30).

NYERERE, J. K. (1969) "Stability and change in Africa" address at the University of Toronto (October). Reprinted in C. Legum and J. Drysdale (eds.), Africa Contemporary Record: Annual Survey and Documents, Vol. II, 1969-70: C30-C39.

PARSONS, T. (1968) "The problem of polarization on the axis of color," pp. 349-369 in J. H. Franklin (ed.) Color and Race. Boston: Beacon Press.

PREISWERK, A. R. (1970) "Race and colour in international relations." Year Book of World Affairs, 1970 Vol. 24: 54-87.

––– [ed.] (1969) Regionalism and the Commonwealth Caribbean. Trinidad: Institute of International Relations, University of the West Indies.

RODNEY, W. (1969) The Groundings With My Brothers. London: Bogle-L'Overture Publications.

ROSENAU, J. N. (1970) "Race in international politics: a dialogue in five parts," pp. 61-122 in G. W. Shepherd, Jr., and T. J. LeMelle (eds.) Race Among Nations: A Conceptual Approach. Lexington, Mass.,: D. C. Heath; also in Rosenau (1970) The Scientific Study of Foreign Policy, Free Press.

RUSSETT, B. M. (1965) Trends in World Politics. New York: Macmillan.

SEGAL, R. (1967) The Race War. New York: Viking Press.
SHEPHERD, G. W., Jr. (1970) "The study of race in American foreign policy and international relations," pp. 1-22 in G. W. Shepherd, Jr. and T. J. LeMelle (eds.) Race Among Nations: A Conceptual Approach. Lexington: D. C. Heath.
——— C. KAHN, and D. SEEGMILLER. (1970) "The racial factor in American foreign policy: a selected bibliography of the 1960's," pp. 163-215 in G. W. Shepherd, Jr., and T. J. LeMelle (eds.) Race Among Nations: A Conceptual Approach. Lexington: D. C. Heath.
SIVANANDAN, A. (1971) "Black Power: the politics of existence." Politics and Society 1 (February): 225-233.
SMITH, A. (1968) Second Report of the Commonwealth Secretary-General: September, 1966-October, 1968. London: Commonwealth Secretariat.
——— (1965) Manchester Guardian Weekly, July 1; p. 242 in A. A. Mazrui, On Heroes and Uhuru-Worship: Essays on Independent Africa, London: Longmans, 1967.
WALVIN, J. (1970) "W. I. Wealth helped push British industries to top," report of a speech by Dr. James Warvin, University of York, England, delivered in Jamaica; Jamaican Weekly Gleaner, December 16.
WILLIAMS, E. (1964) Capitalism and Slavery. London: Andre Deutsch.
——— (1962) History of the People of Trinidad and Tobago. Port-of-Spain: PNM Publishing.

Chapter 6

A COMMENTARY

CYNTHIA H. ENLOE

I

Black Power, the Third World, neo-colonialism—each concept is gaining prominence as scholars follow on the heels of political activists in an effort to explain the continuing, widening gap between rich and poor, powerful and powerless. An older internationalism, with roots back to Woodrow Wilson, presumed that diplomatic forums, democracy, and legal self-determination would ensure world peace and progress. Today most colonial administrators have been retired to gentlemen's clubs back "home," democracy in one form or another is cited to legitimize independent polities, and Geneva hosts international conferences ad infinitum. Yet injustice persists in international relations. Observers seeking to understand the failure of decolonization to herald an era of world harmony talk more now about subtle forms of oppression that defy sovereignty. In the United States it is said that southern desegration had to be fought for with courage, whereas racial justice in the North has to be secured through analysis. Similarly, colonialism, like de facto segregation, is a relatively simple sort of oppression; there's little mistaking its existence. On the other hand, neo-colonialism, like California's or New Jersey's racism, is considerably more subtle; it has to be carefully scrutinized before productive battles can be waged against it. A principal feature of post-colonial relations is a racial inequality built into economic structures which themselves seem to have little relevance to race: corporations, national and multi-national; trade groups; international banks; foundations; state agencies. Persons on the short end of international relations are beginning to surrender their faith in the promise of decolonization. At the same time they are fashioning new concepts of oppression—e.g., neo-colonialism—together with new ideologies and notions of identity. In a sense, then, the concepts of neo-colonialism and Black Power are opposite sides of the same coin, each reflecting a sophisticated analysis of contemporary political and economic power distributions.

Despite their basic agreement on these points, Mast and Edmondson hold different estimations of racial identity as a factor in transforming patterns of power. Essentially, Mast implies that racial solidarity among newly militant black peoples is reactive. Black Power and negritude are negative responses to white oppression. If human relationships, including those between nation-states, were genuinely egalitarian, as Mast thinks is natural, then there would be no need for symbols such as the Black Power salute or ideologies such as espoused by Senghor and Fanon. Mobilization of black identity movements in the United States, the Caribbean, and Africa testifies to society's imperfection. For social scientists interested in ethnic politics, therefore, it is crucial to admit that oppression is more than merely a rhetorical term; it is an empirical fact worthy of analysis. Oppression should be carefully dissected. Social scientists are indebted to the ethnic-racial activists in the Third World. They are compelling us to take oppression seriously when, typically, we feel most comfortable studying conditions for stability, the pathology of violence, or the deviances of a "culture of poverty." Afro-American solidiers in Vietnam who proudly announce that they have been "blackanized" and feel little obligation to follow white lieutenants' orders, are not, however, exposing personal maladjustments. They should be seen as recorders of racially founded inequalities at the core of the U.S. military establishment and American society. A young blackanized G.I. is proof of the oppressive character of the American polity; were it just and egalitarian, such defiant racial militancy would be unnecessary or irrelevant. Mast and other critics of contemporary social science are making the same point as the soldier: political relationships are not just a matter of disembodied socio-economic conditions, but are concerned with power. Ethnic militants in the United States and elsewhere are underscoring the irony of political science's development. As the discipline has grown more and more sophisticated, it has progressively lost sight of the central element in politics—power. The dark side of power is oppression. Thus the understanding of ethnic or racial militancy as healthy witness to injustice, instead of a form of pathology, will help redirect social science back to a concern for power and forms of oppression.

Locksley Edmondson sees the same phenomenon, the mobilization of black people and the internationalization of ethnic politics. He makes specific what Mast notes in general—i.e., that pride in blackness has been most forceful in the Caribbean, because there men are acutely vulnerable to forces beyond their national control. However, Edmondson parts ways with Mast on the question of the reactive quality of black identity. His portrayal of black ideologies assigns more weight to their positive attributes and functions. Pride in blackness and in an African heritage is more than a strategy to counter neo-colonialism in places like Trinidad; it is a valuable foundation for psychological and social well being. Disappointment over the slim rewards of decolonization and frustration over persistent foreign influence may have stimulated a sense of black separateness. Still, it is doubtful whether an early decline of that penetration would bring a corresponding dilution of black identity. All this is to suggest that, while rising black solidarity and oppression tinged with racism both are important parts of the reality social scientists must investigate, they may not be as intimately related to each other as Mast implies. Racial or ethnic identity may perform functions beyond self-defense. Particularly in societies marked by impersonal bureaucratization and automation, ethnic references seem to be gaining new relevance. Ethnic communalism could be more appropriate to the *modern* social milieu than anti-traditional nation-builders typically believe.

Edmondson's analysis makes it clear that other social boundaries besides the nation-state can exert a powerful influence on individuals as they seek a sense of belonging and self-definition. Most of the literature on political development— the same literature which neglects power—assumes that development occurs within the confines of the nation-state. Thus decolonization and independence are considered great steps forward on the path to development in that they legitimize the nation-state as the area for modernization. Though few writers lay it out so plainly, the common presumption is that men progress from fragmented ethnic groups subject to external rule to mobilized independent nation-states and, only later, to some sort of supra-national community. Consequently, development, nation-building, and integration are analyzed as if they were virtually synonymous. If this is so, what are we to make of the black nationalist ideologies spreading outward from the Caribbean in a period when nations remain fragile and immature? Black identity derives from an interweaving of racial and historical consciousness that reaches out to a broader group than any Caribbean island can contain. Furthermore, it excludes some people—e.g., Indians—who are citizens of the new nations. At the same time, paradoxically, black identity is promoting national mobilization while it builds international reference groups. Mutinous Trinidadian soldiers calling for Black Power claimed to be urging more national pride, not less. In the United States, by contrast, Black Power is more ambiguous regarding the nation. To the extent that a firmer sense of self-confidence and communal pride encourages greater political efficacy, black identity movements must be said to foster political development, despite the fact that development is not easily marked off by national boundaries.

Once again, the occurences of ethnic mobilization are shaking social scientists out of facile assumptions and biases. While Mast argues for treating power and oppression more seriously, Edmondson's study should lead us to carefully separate "political development," "integration," and "nation-building." The three phenomena often do reinforce one another, but not inevitably. Black Power advocates and Pan-African spokesmen remind us of the complexity of relationships that can exist among development, integration, and nation-building in pluralist societies vulnerable to international forces.

Mast's and Edmondson's papers are weakest when they fail to clarify distinctions between racism in general and white-black racial conflict in particular. Both also slight differences between racial mobilization and non-racial ethnic mobilization. These lapses are obstacles to dissecting oppression or determining the role of the nation-state in the more general process of development. Crucial to both endeavors is the question: to what extent and in what various ways does *race* shape distributions of power and formation of vehicles for development?

Only recently, Leopold Senghor, the poet-President of Senegal and leading exponent of Negritude, visited Quebec, Canada. There he found ardent Quebec separatists claiming common cause with blacks, labeling themselves "White Niggers." And yet are there not critical differences between oppression and conflict in a Canadian context, where the chief protagonists share the same race, though different languages, than in Africa or the Caribbean, where physical appearance and its symbolism play such a significant role? True, there is also the element of foreign intrusion in Quebec in the form of massive American capital investment, but, again, culture not race, sets the corporate director and local laborer apart. To nail down the racial factors in both oppression and in communal mobilization we need to carry on many more comparative studies.

Furthermore, we need more information concerning the differences between white-black relations on the one hand and white-Asian or black-Asian relations on the other hand. This is especially relevant for Caribbean studies, given the large East Indian populations in Trinidad and Guyana. But it also is important for the study of such African countries as Kenya and South Africa, where inequities and political tensions revolve around white-black, but also black-Asian group relations. Increasingly, studies of British politics must come to grips with these differences. If, for instance, Black Power is an ideology springing from white colonial and neo-colonial domination, how has it affected black-Asian relations? It may be found upon examination that, while the *racial* component of black communalism is strong in white-black relations, the more purely *cultural* factors will play a larger role in black mobilization in Asian-black relations. Of course, the specific character of black-Asian relations is apt to vary according to local political and economic conditions, so that Kenya, Britain, and Guyana, for instance, will have to be compared in order to determine essential similarities. One might also ask why an Asian equivalent of Black Power (or American Indian "Red Power") has not developed among Asian communities in the Caribbean, Africa, and elsewhere.

II

Social science probably has never been as immune to headline chasing as its proponents believe. But this may be a factor for gratitude, not lamentation. Were we left to our own predilections, we might be content to concentrate on those phenomena which are easiest to isolate and study dispassionately. Since the mid-1960s, however, events and activist interpreters of events have intruded on various disciplines forcing them to redirect their attentions and re-examine settled theories. No trend has contributed more to academic second thoughts than ethnic mobilization. Just at the time when we—especially those of us interested in political development—had concluded that "primordial attachments" were fading away and the nation-state was the central actor in men's lives, ethnicity appears to be attracting more emotional resources than ever. Furthermore, ethnic movements within nations and spilling over national boundaries are not confined just to traditional societies or transitional societies. They are preoccupying governments in the allegedly "developed" countries as well. What is the real value of classifying Britain, the Soviet Union, and the United States as "developed," and Sudan, Burma, and China as "underveloped" if in fact all six at the same time are struggling with problems of ethnic mobilization and counter-mobilization?

Mast points to the element of oppression in social arrangements and sees ethnic-racial identity as a dramatic—and rational—reaction to that state of affairs. Edmondson focuses on the international vulnerability of certain peoples and notes its part in stimulating black awareness. Each author is alerting us to the deficiencies in social science research that can be at least partially overcome if we listen carefully to ethnic spokesmen. We should listen to them not as we would patients in a mental hospital but as we would sharp-eyed messengers from the battlefield.

Chapter 7

A COMMENTARY

GORDON K. LEWIS

The papers by Mast, Edmondson, Hoetink, and Edelstein constitute yet another installment in the ongoing debate on the sociology of race relations that has been unleashed by the historic rise of black nationalism and Third World revolution since 1945. They all reflect a fine dissatisfaction with the conventional wisdom of orthodox sociology which is undoubtedly persuasive. Thus, Hoetink is surely right in exposing the theoretical inadequacy of the integrationist assumptions of the American melting-pot thesis, based as it has been on at once the narrow experience of American immigration patterns and on a facile optimism even about the realities of that experience; although an English observer is tempted to note that those assumptions continue to shape British official theories about race relations. Similarly, although the other three contributors (Edelstein, Mast, Edmondson) are essentially Marxist in their analysis, all of them show an acute perception of the inadequacy of a doctrinaire Marxist approach, if only because Marx, set as he naturally was within a Eurocentrist sociology, albeit revolutionary, failed fully to appreciate the independent power of idea systems, whether race, religion, or nationalism, to shape social behavior. It is indeed not the least ironic aspect of this that the orthodox Marxist dialectic shares with conventional Parsonian system sociology the assumption that the race issue can be contained within the formal categories of class-group conflict inside the modern industrial nation-state, a view ending logically in the thesis of Marxist sociologists like Cox that class conflict must be seen as the primordial factor in ethnic group relations. The strength of Marx, of course, is that he set the problem within the particular boundaries of historical time and place (which Hoetink properly applauds), and that, further, he saw clearly the economic roots of prejudice (which Hoetink, to my mind, improperly underestimates). His weakness is that (1) he failed fully to appreciate the deep, institutionalized relationship between capitalism and slavery, although his great chapters on capital accumulation show that he knew about it, and (2) he failed to emphasize the independent contribution that the black under-class of the Americas made, ever since Haiti, to the theory and practice of revolution. It has been left to Eric Williams to rectify the first omission, and to C.L.R. James to rectify the second. What we euphemistically today call "nation-building" in the Third World can only be understood in the light of their achievement.

What all this means is that a really satisfactory social science must seek a persuasive reconciliation between the twin concepts of race and class, between, that is to say, two distinct ways of looking at society, through ethnic-racial identifications or through social class identifications. Certain leading principles emerge from these papers. The first is a recognition that prejudice and discrimination, whether racial-based or class-based, are equally evil. To debate whether one is less desirable, or structurally more appropriate, is an arid exercise, not unlike the old discussion as to the comparative benignity of slave codes. That latter discussion, expressed in Tannenbaum's work, has been effectively demolished in Marvin Harris' forthright essay, "The Myth of the Friendly Master." Correspondingly, Edelstein has no difficulty in showing the inadequacy of the school of American liberal political sociology which posits corporate integration on the basis of class stratification and class values. For, as he argues, the nation-state is anachronistic when modern corporate imperialism is international; the real locus of power in American capitalism is not, as M. G. Smith urges, political dominance but business ownership of which political phenomena are only a secondary expression; effective depluralization, then, necessitates a socialist change. It follows from this that the mere appropriation by the subordinate black group of the class philosophy of the dominant white group merely means the replacement of a white Protestant ethic with a black Protestant ethic. There are serious implications in this argument about the Black Power theme which Edelstein does not spell out. But it is clear that, from this viewpoint, the answer to Life magazine is not Ebony magazine; any more than in, say, the Caribbean area the answer to ethnic pluralism is the class stratification argued for by some of Smith's West Indian critics. That way lies the new forms of Creole-class dictatorship emerging in the colonial post-independence societies. Absolute power corrupts absolutely, black or white, as the record of *duvalierisme* surely demonstrates.

The second consideration is that, since in the real world in which we live both race and class are facts of life a radical sociology must take both into account. Too much of the debate has assumed that they are mutually exclusive whereas in fact they constitute parallel constituent elements at times in conflict with each other, at times mutually reinforcing. As Edmondson notes of the Caribbean situation, it is tailor-made for a merging of the two, of the class struggle against the internal class oppression and of race assertion against the dominant economic forces of international capitalism. It is a fine sentiment. Yet the main thrust of the Edmondson essay itself shows how agonizingly difficult it will be to marry the two protest forms. For it is possible to argue that its insistence that the Caribbean racial experience has been predominantly influenced by the African presence fatally overlooks the multi-culural reality. It is no accident that his leading quotation comes from the Barbadian novelist George Lamming. For Barbados, overwhelmingly black, ethnologically speaking, by 1700, tells us little, if anything, about the poly-ethnic conglomerate societies of Trinidad, Guyana, and Surinam, not to mention Puerto Rico, the majority of whose people regard themselves, within the Caribbean color classificatory system, as white. He also quotes Dr. Williams' trenchant declaration of an all-Trinidadian nationalism. But he fails to add that all recent studies on Indian Trinidad—Klass, Bahadoorsingh, Malik, Nicholls—emphasize the continuing intractability of subordinate ethnic-religious loyalities stubbornly resisting incorporation into the mainstream national culture which is regarded by them as a vehicle of Negro-Creole dominance; and to this day Dr. Williams remains a sectional chieftain rather than a national statesman. To deny this is to indulge in romantic fantasy.

The Caribbean situation, in fact, is irritatingly complex. Two points need to be made: (1) If emphasis is placed on racial, ethnic or religious identity resources, it becomes more difficult to emphasize national identification along objective class lines. But the harsh truth is that this is indeed the emphasis of the Edmondson paper. And it has serious consequences. For to the degree that the Black Power advocate stresses his racial self as a counterweight to the white imperialist cultural pollution Edmondson so eloquently analyzes, or that the Puerto Rican *independentista* stresses his Hispanic identity as a counterbalance to American colonialism, or that the French Antillean accepts a continuing relationship with Parisian culture and the myth of the Gallic civilizing mission, to that extent each one of them enlarges the distance between himself and the rest of the Caribbean. (2) It is even difficult to accept the thesis of an African presence, as if it were a monolithic entity. For there are cultural and insular differences between Afro-Caribbeans themselves. Within Trinidad and Tobago itself there is the crucial distinction between Tobago Creole and Trinidad Creole attitudes, due to their different historical evolution, with a black rural village economy developing in Tobago and with similar development frustrated in Trinidad because of the counter-pressures of Indian indenture and the internal urban imperialism of Port of Spain; not to mention the disturbing fact that, in the American Virgin Islands the most virulent disruptive force is perhaps the cultural contempt that native Virgin Island blacks feel for the black "down islanders" who constitute perhaps the latest manifestation of the old evil system of Caribbean indenture. It is this type of pheonomenon which justifies Hoetink's insistence on the validity of the cultural-deterministic component, in which membership of a separate cultural grouping or a socio-racial category is of larger importance than the rival criteria of wealth, education, or occupational achievement. All this is not to say that I am in agreement with the "plural society" thesis, for the thesis has its own internal weaknesses, especially its assumption of social statics, that is, its assumption that there exists more or less timelessly a constant identification of the individual with his plural section under all circumstances. It is to say, rather, that, being in essential agreement with Edmondson for a root-and-branch assault upon the neo-colonialist system, I do not think it helps the cause to oversimplify the rich, complex data of the Caribbean reality.

By the same token I find myself sympathetic to the main thrust of the Mast paper. He is surely correct in his insistence that the study of race relations is a study of the exploitation of the Third World peoples by Euro-American imperialism. He is right to argue that racial oppression is qualitatively different from class exploitation, for it imposes a terrible wound upon the colonial psyche that in both degree and kind sets it apart from the phenomenon of white working-class experience under the capitalist system. I would only like to qualify that latter point with the reminder that argument about "oppression" can itself divide the "oppressed," for I have heard myself angry discussions between West Indian blacks and Indians as to who suffered most, the black slave or the Indian indenture laborer, not to mention equally angry discussions in New York between blacks and Jews on the relative iniquity of the slave trade and the Nazi holocaust. Surely the only proper point to make—and I am sure Mast would agree—is that the Nazi gas chamber, as compared with the European slave trader, simply illustrates the awful advance in the technology of white genocide. This sort of futile argument can do nothing but serve the interests of the oppressor agencies, including the colonial black bourgeoisie which both Mast and Edmondson castigate. Nothing, indeed, is so depressing in Caribbean societies as the ease with which the metropolitan Uncle Sam produces, by response, the colonial Uncle Tom.

Having said all that, however, I think there is room for dissent. There is a sense of shame for the white record in the paper which is commendable. But it becomes too easily an abject apology for being white, an embarrassingly deferential attitude to the sufferers which seems to me, frankly, to invite psychiatric rather than philosophical treatment. The rest of the argument suffers as a result, for it spoils with excess. So, it is one thing to note the "divide and rule" imperialist strategy, quite another to overlook the native, indigenous sources of racism and communalism. It is one thing to note the colonial use of cheap labor, quite another to argue that the imperial employing classes deliberately foster and manipulate intergroup fears and tensions. Mast hates the general system so much, indeed, that he consistently attributes (a thoroughly unMarxian procedure) motives to the imperialists instead of recognizing that their behavior is the simple and logical consequence of the system they represent. Similarly, it is the unstated assumption of his spirited attack upon all the sociologists with whom he disagrees that they are "tied in" to the capitalist West and, by inference, selling their talent. It does not apparently occur to him that they might write as they do out of intellectual conviction. And even when he does mention those white intellectuals who have contributed to what he terms the literature of "subjective ethnicity" it has curious omissions. For surely—to speak only of Puerto Rican oppression—Sidney Mintz and Oscar Lewis have helped the victims to speak for themselves. But the picture must be presented in such a way as to suggest that only left-wing intellectuals have done this kind of work. Yet the academic exposure of capitalism and imperialism can claim other names—Veblen, Hobson, E. D. Morel, Leonard Woolf. For the Caribbean, there are the books of Lord Olivier, for Southeast Asia the remarkable books of Maurice Collis. The list of names cited by Mast is curiously contemporary; the cynic might be tempted to observe that this may be so because Americans are born without a sense of the past. Black Power, after all, commences with the slave revolts of the plantation period; white humanitarian effort on behalf of the slave person goes back to Las Casas. But it is the historian, not the sociologist, who tells about that best.

Hoetink's contribution to all of this is a reiteration of the concept of the somatic norm image as constituting the key to a satisfactory understanding of the differentiations that mark the three leading culture areas of the Americas: the North American society, Brazilian society, and Caribbean society. Much of the argument is persuasive enough: its insistence on the non-economic factors in intergroup relationships, its exposure of the flaws in the Eisenstadt-type graded system of immigrant adjustment in plural societies, its careful separation of the cultural and racial components in the toal mix of such societies, its emphasis upon the absence of an intermediate colored stratum as a buffer group in the evolution of North American society. It is illuminating to be told that the religious factor has minimal importance, since the color-class structure imposed by the French Catholic culture differed significantly from that imposed by the Hispanic Catholic culture (although one wonders if the piquant fact that all of the centers of the great American bacchanalian carnival-féte—Rio, Port of Spain, New Orleans, Havana—are all historically Catholic cities, mixing both French and Iberian influences, does not mean that there has been something about the

European Catholic ethic, whether French or Spanish, diffentiating it from the Protestant ethic, that helps to explain the variants of the general social-sexual relationship).

Yet, as Hoetink's critics elsewhere have noted, there are difficulties about the concept of the preferred physical beauty image. There are too many plausible alternative theories. It is arguable that the peculiarly unsophisticated brutality of North American race relations is due to the fact that the United States, almost from the beginning, was pure capitalism, seeing the black person in exclusively economic terms, while the other colonizing powers in the Americas were diluted capitalisms, bringing with them an inherited baggage of pre-capitalist values; so, in American society, "money talks," in the New World societies colonized by the European powers "money whitens." It is equally arguable that the racial association variant in the Hispanic islands can be traced to the more widespread Creolization process, as Mintz has propounded in an interesting essay. For the Spanish, unlike the English, say, or the Dutch, undertook a widespread settlement pattern, accepting the overseas settlements as their permanent home, and thus effectively Creolizing themselves. The outcome of that process was a more successful amalgamation, racially and culturally, with the native groups, which in turn generated that gentle, subterranean nationalism that today, for instance, permeates every corner of the Puerto Rican psyche, and releases most Puerto Ricans from the psychic anxieties of identity.

Hoetink's special recipe for viable nation-building, then, is that of ultimate racial amalgamation leading to a "whitening" of all groups based on the somatic norm image. It is possible that the recipe cavalierly overlooks difficult problems of acceptance and application. There is , first, the problem of the time element involved. For it is palpably obvious that the ultimate erosion of race problems by means of this sort of biological admixture, including intermarriage, would consume an incalculably lengthy period of time to complete itself; so lengthy, indeed, that it takes on the shape of a Wellsian, cosmic future that can mean little, if anything at all, to contemporary Caribbean man. There is, secondly, the problem of consent. For if the new Caribbean nationalism is to be fully democratic it cannot afford the dictatorial leadership which, in the manner of Rousseau's Grand Legislator, will impose its grand social plan upon the willing citizen body. There is much resistance in Caribbean segmental attitudes to the amalgamatory process Hoetink advocates. The Trinidadian East Indian group, to take one example only, occupies a lesser somatic distance from the white French Creole group than do the black Creoles, which should lead—if the norm image thesis is correct—to intermingling of both. Yet this has not occurred, and the failure is surely traceable to the religious and cultural factors that divide them from each other. Similarly, to take another example, the recent emergence of black nationalist ideology among the region's black people (going back in fact to the earlier négritude theme) adds a further barrier to amalgamation. From the Black Power viewpoint, indeed, the Hoetink concept invites them to a "whitening" process they fiercely resist; and it is difficult not to feel that the "somatic norm image" is nothing much more than a sociological disguise for the old "white bias." Class, cultural, and religious factors in brief, invalidate the attempt to make the racial factor into an independent aesthetic determinant. Not the least ironic aspect of this is that Hoetink criticizes both the culturally deterministic and the economically deterministic theses of his fellow Caribbean scholars, but in the end proposes to replace them with a psycho-biological determinism less rooted than either of those alternatives in the firm ground of empirical evidence. Not withstanding, then, the scholarship that accompanies the argument it looks too much, in the end result, like—to employ Herbert Spencer's phrase—a beautiful theory murdered by a gang of brutal facts.

What, then, emerges from all this? A reading of these four papers suggests some general thoughts on the common problem of ethnicity and nation-building with which they deal.

(1) The growing importance of the international factor is unquestionable. Its basis is probably the massive character of the cyclical intercontinental movements of human populations in the modern period. In a sense, today we are all immigrants. Modern nationhood is no longer identifiable with insularity, as the return to ethnicity on the part of the older, European immigrant groups in North American society demonstrates. Edmondson's emphasis on the factors that have made the Caribbean, for example, sensitive to external forces and linkages is thus peculiarly apt, as well as his analysis of the contribution that Caribbean thinkers and activists have made to the international struggle. The employment of the homeland-diaspora dichotomy is especially enlightening. It generates a debate not unlike the historic debate within Zionism of an earlier period. It perceives that the relationships between the homeland and the forces of the diaspora is not to be seen as one of irreconcilable loyalties but of a creative, enriching tension from which both benefit. The one feeds the other. That can be seen, to take another example, from the new black experience in English society; for under the pressures of the English subtle, genteel racialism the black immigrant sees himself less and less as a West Indian in English society and more and more as a black man in a hostile white world. That process is fed by both the new ideology of the African return and the new militancy of the North American black revolt; and so the old triangular slave trade is replaced with a new triangular idea trade. Having said this, however, I merely wish to express doubt about the danger of exaggerating the international component. We are not yet, by any means, the global village. To talk about a global race war is to overlook everything we know about the persistent tenacity of local pride and prejudice. Even a generic term such as Third World oversimplifies the rich complexity of the reality behind it. And that this is so apparent enough from Mast's attempt to bring a variety of human conditions, from the Harlem ghetto to Vietnam, into the common frame of what he terms, conceptually, "oppression;" the term is so abstract that it tells us nothing, anthropologically, about the essential particularity of each individual situation. The theorists of the united international struggle must ponder the implications of the fact—reporting now from San Juan—that many of the young warriors of the growing *independentista* force in Puerto Rico have no desire to be saved by any outside elements, however revolutionary they may be; they want, quite simply, to make their own revolution.

(2) The papers reflect the urgent necessity for theoretical formulation. Merely descriptive sociology is not enough; we need the intellectual capacity to identify the general laws that lie behind all experience, to make the experience meaningful. There are two dangers present in this exercise. The first is the temptation of the intellectual mind to construct grand theory, which produces what Sir Ernest Barker, speaking within a different discipline, aptly termed the

fallacy of the "pure instance." Edelstein notes how Smith has thus attempted to expand his plural society thesis into a general theory to encompass all societies. Yet these papers themselves are tempted at times to do the same thing, and the Marxist authors among them ought perhaps to remember that it was a temptation that Marx himself, when looking at non-European systems, resisted. The second danger is that the radical in race relations sociology, situated within the now classic black-white confrontation, may be tempted, like the disciple Peter on the morning of Calvary, to deny both himself and his discipline as a result of his disillusionment with the orthodox sociology. This leads him, as in the Mast paper, to argue for a "peoples' social science" in which the common people will create their own analysis of their condition. The answer to that is surely, as Edelstein points out (speaking of the Smith thesis), that the state of consciousness of a population is hardly a sound basis for a fundamental categorization of societies at the macro-sociological level. To say that the victim must report his own experience, even that he should have opportunities to do so that are denied him by the class-color system, is one thing. To say that only he can fully understand the system is to indulge, Sartre fashion, in a vulgar Rousseauistic romanticism, so that the idealized proletarian hero-figure of the leftwing world of the 1930s is curiously followed by the idealized Che-cult figure of the black militant of the 1970s. This is not radical theory. It is revolutionary rhetoric.

(3) The complex problem of the relationship between cultural segmentalism, racial identity, and nation-building clearly requires some fresh formulation. In what is almost a passing aside Hoetink suggests that societies like Trinidad, Guyana, Surinam might best be suited for some sort of quasi-federative collaboration between the main component segments. This assumes—counter to the national integration thesis—the separate evolution of group religious-cultural institutions. What form of relationship they would have to the central state order suggests that the older pluralist theory in the political science field of an earlier period might provide the answer. That theory sought to establish the rights of personality of groups in the modern state—churches, trade unions, cooperative societies—as against the erastian claims of state sovereignty; we could fruitfully apply it to the contemporary situation. The breakdown of the modern nation-state—proceeding equally in the older European states, as with the Welsh and Scottish movements in Britain, and in the newer Third World states, as the theory and practice of secessionism challenge their new governing elites—makes the application peculiarly imperative. The Victorian liberal slogan of "a free church in a free state" is as appropriate for the Trinidadian Hindu or the Surinamese Catholic today as it was for the Free Church of Scotland in 1843.

(4) That involves, further, a theoretical reformulation of the relationship between socialism and nationalism within the framework of the non-white world all of these papers seek to analyze. That reformulation must start from a categorical rejection of the conventional political sociology of the American Almond-Deutsch-Lipset variety the theoretical inadequacy of which Edelstein sufficiently demonstrates. For the anti-socialist bias of that school only makes sense to the degree it assumes that socialism means the centralized état administratif of the Soviet and Fabian models. But—as Aneurin Bevan asserted in a well-known remark—there is no immaculate conception of socialism. Third

World socialist discussion—whether one thinks of the Tanzanian discussion in the African setting or, say, the Trinidad *Tapia* group discussion of localization in the Caribbean setting—already addresses itself to its pecular conditions: the agricultural base, the need for mass participation, the search for defensive mechanisms against elitism, and the centripetal pull of new state bureaucracies. It is worth noting, again, that there is much to learn from the European debate here, for a book like Horace Davis' *Nationalism and Socialism (1967)* sufficiently demonstrates how that debate has sought throughout to accommodate the nationalist fervor of sub-groups to the socialist ethic: Bakunin's Panslavism, Marx on the Irish question, the exchange between Kautsky and Rosa Luxemburg on Polish national independence. A satisfactory theory, this is to say, urgently requires a fructifying marriage between the twin socialist and nationalist concepts. For the socialist idea, by itself, can easily lead to a merely abstract internationalism that leaves out of account the pride and prejudice of local nationalism. In its turn, the nationalist idea, by itself, can equally lead to a mindless "my country right or wrong" attitude, no less dangerous to civil liberties in Jamaica than it is in Germany. The plural society needs plural loyalties.

(5) It is frequently urged by Third World protagonists that this analogy with the historic European experience is not pertinent since Europe equates with white history. We need, they say, neither Marx nor Jesus, only black consciousness. There is an important half-truth secreted in this attitude. For although, historically, slavery predates the rise of European civilization, it is nonetheless true that its more brutalizing and dehumanizing forms have been coterminous with that rise. A book like Kiernan's *Lords of Human Kind (1969)* is testimony enough to the general feelings of contempt, arrogance, and racialist amusement which imperialism engendered in the English people toward their subject races. Yet it is historically erroneous to see Europe either as a white or a completely racialist society. Its origins go back to the brown Mediterranean trading cities of the Graeco-Roman-Hellenistic period; Egypt and Abbysinia added their influence; and the contribution of North African science and philosophy to Medieval thought is well known. And—speaking for modern Europe—it is a black ideologue like C.L.R. James and not an evil-minded white ideologue like myself who has paid tribute (in his Montreal lectures of 1966) to the emancipating influence of the European intellectual tradition, from Hegel and Michelet to Marx and Lenin. Anyone, furthermore, who has carefully read Fanon will recognize the deep influence upon him of the pre-Marxian French humanist socialist tradition; not to mention the influence of the English Lockeian tradition on the young Castro. No one trained in the Marxist dialectic is likely to elevate skin color to the status of a final cause, and it is worth noting that the Marxist-oriented papers in this symposium avoid that mistake. If this line of argument is correct, it follows that Europe and, say, the Caribbean are not to be seen as mutually hostile polarities but as mutually complementary worlds, with the potential of learning from each other. Another way of putting this is that it is the West Indian poet like Derek Walcott, with his perception of how the West Indian psyche has been shaped by both the African and the English tradition, rather than his fellow poet Edward Brathwaite, who embraces the apocalyptic vision of Africa, who expresses more correctly the cultural reality. The African component, undeniably, is vital. But I hazard the guess that

the idea of Africa will play the role, in Caribbean nation-building, of a general, revolutionary energizing idea, in much the same way as the idea of America fed the social criticism and the utopia-making of the *philosophes* of the European enlightenment.

(6) What, finally, should the role of the professional academic be in all this? It is, I suggest, threefold. In the first place, the task of adding to the general storehouse of knowledge in the field of his Afro-American-Asian studies. There are large lacunae still in Caribbean studies. The smaller, Lilliputian island-societies have been neglected, and a book like Julia Crane's on Saba, *Educated to Emigrate (1971)* shows what can be done. There has been a tendency for anthropologists to study the more exotic groups, with a consequent neglect of work on the Creole white groups, and how they stand with relationship to nation-building, and a book like Frances Karner's *The Sephardics of Curaçao (1971)* again shows what can be done. Secondly, there is the task of building up a viable theory of reality based on this empirical investigatory work. This requires, perhaps, a complete renovation of first principles, for it is doubtful if any really new dialectic can come out of the mechanistic structuralism of the conventional positivist sociology of the day. Too much of that sociology is little more than rationalization of the status quo, facilitated by its general characteristics—the Latinate ponderosity, the confusion of profundity with obscurity, the preoccupation with finding complex answers to simple problems—which flow out of the complex labyrinth in the American university leading to the Ph.D. A booklet like Ivar Oxaal's recent *Race and Revolutionary Consciousness (1971)*, dealing with the urban *jacquerie* of Trinidad in 1970, with its style of happy irreverence, shows that sociology can easily dispense with all of that baggage and still succeed—despite its author's anxiety to prove that he is as good a West Indian as the rest of them. Third, and finally, we need a service sociology, dedicated to the end of the popular emancipatory struggle. Perhaps we ought to remember that the young Clarkson's commitment to the great cause of the abolition of the slave trade started with the composition and publication of his winning prize essay as a senior bachelor at Cambridge in 1785, so that what started as—in his words—a trial for academical reputation became transmuted into the production of a work which might be useful to injured Africa. We could set ourselves no better example.

REFERENCES

CRANE, J. (1971) Educated to Emigrate: The Social Organization of Saba. Detroit: Gale Research.

DAVIS, H. (1967) Nationalism and Socialism. New York: Monthly Review Press.

HARRIS, M. (1964) "The myth of the friendly master," in Patterns of Race in the Americas. New York: Walker. Reprinted in Black Society in the New World. New York: R. Frucht (ed.) Random House, 1971.

KARNER, F. (1971) The Sephardics of Curaçao: A Study of Sociocultural Patterns in Flux. New York: Humanities Press.

KIERNAN, V. G. (1969) Lords of Human Kind: Black Man, Yellow Man and White Man in an Age of Empire. Boston: Little, Brown.

Part II

STATUS

Chapter 8

ETHNICITY, STATUS, AND CONFLICT

WILLIAM J. FOLTZ

*T*he chapters by Frederick Barghoorn, Jeffrey Butler, and René Lemarchand deal with ethnic-based political conflict in widely different geographic and social contexts. In all of them, however, ethnic distinctions have to some extent reflected distinctions of status, and to some degree all of the conflicts have been motivated by individual or group status considerations. In this chapter I should like to relate some of the basic points made in these three chapters to a general consideration of the ways status and ethnicity may interact and affect group conflict.

As the patient reader of a volume such as this one must be aware, clear definition of "ethnicity" at a high enough level of generality to be analytically useful in the wide variety of situations for which it is commonly applied is no simple matter. Nor is one much advanced by passing the definitional buck via a statement such as "ethnicity is that quality which distinguishes ethnic groups one from the other," though such a partial definitional effort does have the virtue of directing our attention to particular human collectivities and away from more transcendent commonalities. In both common usage and in more formal social science codification, an ethnic group is assumed to be distinctive by virtue of its sharing of certain properties not shared, ideally at all but more realistically to the same degree, by members of other groups. These properties may be summarily grouped under four headings:

(1) Biological. Members of a group will draw from a particular genetic pool which they will perpetuate over time. Thereby they will share certain physical characteristics.

(2) Cultural. Members of the group will share certain common ways of doing things and of choosing what things to do. They will "think differently" from other people and evaluate both people and things differently.

(3) Linguistic. Members of a group will communicate more easily among themselves than with members of other groups, in the extreme case to the point of complete mutual unintelligibility. The "different thoughts" will be expressed "differently."

(4) Structural. Members of the group will organize their joint relations differently from the way other people do. They may evolve different social roles, and even where common roles exist pattern their relationships differently from the way others do.

Such a checklist of itself is quite useful for distinguishing ethnic divisions from other divisions, such as class, power, or religion, which, depending on circumstances, may either cut across or be congruent with ethnic divisions, but like any checklist it is most easily applied in a dichotomous manner—either one possesses or does not possess a particular property. Such an application would clearly not be helpful in any real-life situation (Barth, 1969: 10-31). A checklist may more profitably be used if, rather than looking for the presence or absence of a trait, one assumes that it will be found unequally distributed across a broader population and looks for relatively high-density clusters of a trait surrounded by areas of relative discontinuity. The scatter dot map replaces the fixed line boundary. Such a probabilistic approach to group identification has been admirably used in the study of nationalism (Deutsch, 1953), and in addition to its greater intellectual rigor has the great advantage of facilitating quantification of many of the key variables. The "scatter dot" approach calls attention to the fundamental relational aspect of ethnicity: an ethnic group can define itself as such only by virtue of contact and comparison with other people whom its members define as being different.

The most carefully done and methodologically sophisticated study of the relative distribution of ethnic traits will still not by itself tell us in any immutable way what ethnic identity a person has. Not only are such identities subject to change over time, more importantly they change in terms of the specific relational situation. An individual may be a member of a nuclear family, an extended family, minimal and maximal lineages, a linguistic community, a territorial nation, a "race," and for some the list does not stop there. Each of the identities may be marked by clusterings of traits an individual considers as ethnic and separated from the next more inclusive identity by relative discontinuities. Which of these identities affects a person's action will depend on the situation in which the person finds himself. A striking and classic example of the situational quality of ethnic identity is to be found in the studies of the Nuer and related peoples of eastern Africa whose essential political structure can be said to consist of a set of rules for supporting and opposing one another in feuds (Evans-Pritchard, 1940). The definition of who are one's "brothers" in a particular feud depends on who is one's opponent. The greater the social distance between the opponents, the larger and more inclusive the identity principle upon which the feuding alliances will be based. Studies of migrant workers in Africa have revealed a phenomenon of "supertribalization" (Rouch, 1956; 163-164) whereby workers from a variety of small ethnic groups redefine their identities when away from home in terms of the identity common to the largest group represented. This in no way prejudices their resumption of their original identity once they have returned to their original homes. Nor, of course, is such a process confined to Africa or other exotic areas. Recent re-examinations of the American melting pot have testified not only to the persistence of ethnic identification unto the third and fourth generation, but also to the selective combination and recombination of various partial identities depending on the situational context (Glazer and Moynihan, 1963: 16-20; Lenski, 1961: 362-366). The popular acceptance of "ethnic American" or "hyphenated-American" into United States political terminology reflects a need to find a convenient term to summarize a politically relevant and superordinate ethnic identity which is mobilized in some situations, but which in no way inhibits resumption of subordinate ethnic identities in other contexts. Indeed, the superordinate identity requires that subordinate ethnic identities lurk in the background.

Without reference to a particular situation, then, it is impossible to say what level of identity will influence action, or indeed which particular identity trait will appear most relevant. In some situations a single trait, language especially,

WILLIAM J. FOLTZ [105]

may detach itself from other traits to define a cleavage and provide a principle for association. Without knowing the structure of a particular relational situation (for example, the precise degree of supposed kinship between two antagonists) one cannot predict the trait or level of identity that will operate. However, the relational phenomenon itself suggests that once a confrontation has been initiated there will be strong pressures to define a situation in mirror-image terms; i.e., if one party defines itself according to a particular trait and calls in allies at a particular level of identity, the other side will reciprocate by emphasizing his own distinctiveness in terms of that trait and/or by calling in allies at the same level. In straight confrontation situations something of an escalation process may develop as each side tries to call in wider and wider ranges of supporters, and most societies where feuding is endemic construct elaborate procedures and saanctions to prevent such escalation taking place (Gluckman, 1956: 1-26).

In real-life confrontations ethnicity must be seen as more than an abstract principle of organization; by its very nature it lends certain qualities to a confrontation situation which it structures and thereby, in collaboration with other significant contributing factors, influences the duration of a confrontation, the methods used to maintain or end it, the way people explain a confrontation to themselves, and the sorts of people who will rise to positions of leadership. The first and most important of these qualities is emotion. Ethnicity evokes sentiments touching the most private and emotionally powerful relationships with which an individual is involved. Any ethnic confrontation touches the family and both reinforces and threatens the emotionally powerful bonds that hold it together. As all social distance research has shown, family relationships ("Would you like your daughter to marry one?") are the most sensitive of all possible relationships and the most fiercely protected against incursions from outsiders (compare, e.g., Banton, 1967: 315-333). Ethnic confrontations are those most likely to evoke slogans of the "Protect Our Women" variety and to provoke rumors of rape and lurid allegations of astonishing sexual proclivities on the part of the opposite side. Nazi propaganda directed not only against Jews, but against opposing military forces, particularly Soviet Asian, French African, and American Negro soldiers, is an extreme case in point which followed quite easily from defining the German side in ethnic (Aryan race) terms. As the example also shows, fictive kinship can be as effective an organizing principle as biological kinship under proper propaganda circumstances.

Emotional intensity is further reinforced in that ethnic organizational principles imply that everyone in a group is involved. Figuratively, there is no distinction between frontline troops and civilians; indeed when conflict is not highly organized, women and children may carry out much of the direct confrontation with the other side. At the very least this means that an individual involved in a confrontational contact receives frequent reinforcement for any hostile attitudes from his most significant others. While there may be many arenas in a person's daily existence in which confrontation with the other side does not take place, most of those peaceful arenas are influenced by the family and thus emotionally reinforce the symbols on which the confrontation is based.

Such reinforcement involves large numbers, and a high proportion, of the people significant to an individual and includes also those people least likely to be flexible in their emotional attitudes toward outsiders. Or more precisely, the conflict will be evoked and made emotionally relevant in the context of familial relations and thereby cannot summarily be revoked without threatening, at least symbolically, the ties between the family members. This helps account for the familiar situation in which a wife, as an element of her marital relations, may hate her husband's enemies with a more perfect and lasting hatred than her husband himself. Whatever the psychological or social mechanisms involved, such reinforcement not only provides frequent reminders of the salience of the ethnic cleavage, it makes it more difficult for a leading protagonist in a confrontation to call it off, since by doing so he calls into question the domestic social and emotional support relations the confrontation has reinforced. Both through its emotional intensity and through the reinforcement mechanisms it calls forth, the mobilization of ethnic identity in a confrontation tends to persist over time, perhaps long after the initial cause for the confrontation has been resolved or ceased to be relevant. In some of the most severe situations the initial cause of a confrontation may become irrelevant, as the emotionally intense principles of ethnic alignment and opposition suggest other and less easily resolvable reasons for continuing or exacerbating a confrontation.

Because ethnic confrontations potentially involve such a wide spectrum of social attributes and activities, they are particularly likely to call forth stereotypes of the other side, and to endow those stereotypes with great emotional intensity. Stereotyping is one way in which the mind summarizes large amounts of information, indicates which items are salient, eliminates or overrides seemingly contradictory items, and attaches value judgments to the whole package. It is closely related to such respectable intellectual tools as ideal type or national character analysis, and is probably an inescapable part of human existence. For most people involved in confrontations characterized by a significant amount of social distance between the parties, it serves much the same information processing and interpretation function as a formal ideology. Indeed, stereotyping and ideology may be seen as functional substitutes one for the other. When ideology is vulgarized, it frequently declines into stereotyping, or, equally important, is interpreted in stereotypic terms by the intellectually unsophisticated. Since this sort of person will, as argued above, play a particularly strong role in an ethnically structured confrontation, stereotyping and action based upon stereotypes become all the more common.

When stereotyping is used to characterize the other side in an ethnic confrontation, it commonly selects out those individuals and traits perceived as most nearly opposite to traits considered descriptive of one's own group and then generalizes these traits to all (or most) members of the opposing group. The more significant the trait is considered for one's own group, the more significant and intense the feeling of opposition is likely to be. Stereotyping is, however, a two-way process. By producing a stereotyped image of how the other side differs from one's own, one not only simplifies the description of the other side, one invariably defines one's own side in a simplified manner. This in turn heightens the salience of certain ethnic traits considered distinctive, if for no other reasons than that they serve to distinguish one's own group from one's opponent and to bind group members together. Such stereotyping introduces a further rigidity into both inter- and intra-group relations.

One further characteristic of stereotyping should be mentioned here: it greatly facilitates scapegoating, the "unrealistic" projecting of responsibility for negative events onto a safe target (Coser, 1956: 48-55). Under some circumstances scapegoating can be used as an economical device for reducing inter- or intra-group tensions, though not to remove any objective cause for those tensions (Gluckman, 1956: 81-108).

The interaction of situation and these distinctive qualities and mechanisms of ethnic confrontation will affect the definition of leadership roles and the weight attached to various individuals' attributes as political resources in the competition for those within each side. The interplay between individual attributes, role definition, and the structure of confrontation is constant and complicated, and the interaction between these variables defies simple assignment of priority or causal direction. At any point in time the definition of a confrontation situation suggests the way a side should organize itself, and therefore the sorts of leaders it should have. Often it suggests the combative techniques it should use as well. At the same time potential leaders will compete to define the situation in terms which would heighten the value of their own particular attributes, skills, and social position. It is through the mobilization of leadership roles and the competition of individuals for leadership positions that ethnic confrontation passes from the purely social or psychological realm into the political. Once that step has been taken, the interplay between the purely ethnic and the political will be constant and reciprocal. In his study of caste in Indian politics Rajni Kothari (1970: 5) concludes, "Where caste itself becomes a political category it is futile to argue as to whether caste uses politics or politics uses caste." The same may be said more broadly of ethnic conflict. Such a conclusion should not be taken as an admission of analytic failure but rather as a reminder to stay out of chicken-and-egg controversy and an invitation to direct attention to such classic political elements of conflict analysis as the structure of competition within each side, the effects of such competition and the resulting alignments on the other side, possibilities for harmonization of interests between leaders and non-leaders of the different sides, and the interaction of all these in escalating, stabilizing, or de-escalating conflict.

An essential part of any such analysis is the delineation of the degree of reinforcement between ethnicity and other sources of cleavage in society. It is now a well-established line of argument that the more ethnicity and such other lines of cleavage reinforce one another, the more rigid will the lines of confrontation be and the more intense and all-encompassing will conflict be, should it break out into the open (compare, e.g., Dahrendorf, 1959: 239 and passim). The innate plausibility of this proposition should not blind one to the necessity in any concrete instance to demonstrate measures of rigidity and intensity which are independent of the terms in which the confrontation structure itself is defined. It must also be noted that the proposition says nothing whatsoever about the probability that open conflict will break out. Though one may suspect that rigidity contains within itself the presumption of at least short-term stability, more strictly construed the idea of rigidity suggests only that change of any sort, when it comes, will have far-reaching effects likely to shatter the whole structure rather than to modify it in minor details.

Lipset has developed similar lines of thought in a variety of contexts. Of particular interest is his Tocquevillian reminder that democracy as well as stability depend over the long run on the existence of secondary cleavages which cut across, rather than reinforce, social cleavages like religion and ethnicity, and of the importance for the development of stable and legitimate government that it be allowed to confront and resolve major cleavage-producing issues sequentially, rather than being obliged to fight all the major battles not only at the same time, but over and over in a situation such that when one particular issue is raised, all the others become immediately relevant in the minds of the people involved (Lipset, 1963: 71-82). Issues expressed in ethnic terms can have particularly disruptive effects in that they both summarize and emotionally evoke great numbers of issues at once through stereotyping, and recall all sorts of past conflicts through the lag effect.

One must qualify assumptions of rigidity based on cleavage reinforcement by reference to the number of groups involved in any social situation. The more groups involved, the greater the flexibility of the system and the greater the opportunity for individual, sub-group, and group maneuvering. That the Indian caste system has shown itself able to preserve its essential elements while permitting numerous groups to modify some aspect of their status in part results from the sheer number of groups involved on the status ladder. Thus any single confrontation, despite the fact that it involves groups separated from one another by all manner of cleavages, does not threaten the total social order. Such a threat would be more likely to come about if a high proportion of existing groups were to be involved on one side or another of a cleavage line, whatever that line might represent. However, such a system provides few incentives for an activist group to polarize society, since a successful caste-climbing strategy depends on picking one small fight at a time, while scrupulously keeping other groups from being involved (Bailey, 1970: 95-100).

In general terms there seems no reason to disagree with the assumption that open conflict between only two parties rigidly divided along multiple lines of cleavage, including the ethnic, is the most likely to be violent, to evoke total emotional commitment, and to produce radical structural change, with the greatest possibility of complete status reversal or total elimination of the losing side. Such situations are extremely rare, and are generally maintained by such a balance of power in the hands of the superior group that large-scale group-based violence has little chance of breaking out, isolated slave rebellions to the contrary. More commonly, the development of strong ethnic consciousness and the activation of stereotyping produce perceptions which override "objective" realities of cross-cutting cleavages that ought to mitigate conflict, and under such circumstances a complex situation may subjectively be reduced to a straight two-party confrontation. As Lemarchand observes was the case in Rwanda, the longer such conflict goes on, the closer to objective reality does this stereotype become, as the conflict itself forces people to one side or the other of the cleavage line. The Zanzibar revolution of 1964 appears to have followed a similar course when two distinct groups, the mainland Africans and the Shirazi, submerged their differences under a composite African ethnic identity and slaughtered the Arabs who as a group had dominated politics and some of whom had controlled a substantial part of the economy (Lofchie, 1965; Kuper, 1971). In his discussion of the Zanzibar situation, Kuper (1971: 100) shows clearly that there were many poor Arabs and some well-off Africans, and concludes that since "Arabs were slaughtered, regardless of class," the "encompassing principle" of the conflict was racial (or ethnic) rather than economic. While certainly agreeing with Kuper that Zanzibar hardly presented a class conflict in the classic European sense, I differ marginally with him in that I think it more helpful not to make a clear distinction between two types of conflict in such a case. Rather, as in the Rwanda case, once status differences were transformed into political issues for conflict purposes, they came to be explained stereotypically in ethnic terms of African versus Arab. This ethnic description was a close enough approximation and provided an easy enough basis for association and opposition that the conflict reified this particular ethnic cleavage into the handiest possible rule of thumb for whom to hit when violence broke out. Implied in this formulation, but not, I think, in Kuper's, is the sad prediction that in any violent conflict situation where class and ethnicity substantially overlap, ethnicity will provide the basic rule of thumb for whom to hit. To infer original cause from an analysis of who did what to whom would understate the role status grievance played in initiating conflict.

One problem with a simple version of the reinforcing cleavage argument is that it uses the same terms to explain the results of instability as it must to explain the persistence of stability during the period before the instability breaks out. To escape this dilemma some have introduced the additional element of "structural violence," implying that the original order was based on some principle of well-clothed repressive force exercised almost unconsciously by the more privileged group, to explain the prior existence of relative stability. However useful the structural violence argument may be in other contexts (Galtung, 1971; Moore, 1966: 3-39, 505-508) it can be lopped off with Occam's razor in many cases of ethnic relations. First, it is important to distinguish two different sorts of cleavages which may cumulate or cut across ethnic cleavages. The first are based on qualitative attributes, of which two, religion and mode of livelihood, are of pre-eminent importance. The second are purely relational or status attributes, which possess no absolute quality of their own. Though the number of such status attributes may be very large, they may adequately be summarized in three classic categories, wealth, prestige, and power.[1] Clearly any of these five attributes may be distributed randomly between ethnic groups under some circumstances, or may correlate very strongly with some level of ethnic identity. When the qualitative attributes coincide with ethnicity (however defined), they are likely to be viewed by the people involved as part and parcel of their ethnic identity. Even so universal a phenomenon as the Roman Catholic religion is likely to take on a variety of ethnic flavors in a multi-ethnic community large enough to support several parishes. Under many circumstances—modern/urban as well as traditional/rural—mode of livelihood also may be taken into ethnic identity, and like religion, may serve to reinforce the distinction between an ethnic group and outsiders. Through stereotyping and self-stereotyping, a group may behave as if all members of the other side share a distinctive or modal occupational or religious attribute and at the same time enforce extension of occupational or religious symbols to all members of one's own group.

Where ethnicity, religion, and mode of livelihood cumulate, they may function as distance variables to soften the effects of status discrepancies between groups. Under appropriate circumstances, sufficient social distance will allow different groups possessing widely different characteristic status positions to live side by side without coming into conflict. Why should this be so? Two mechanisms appear to operate. First, clear-cut and reinforced ethnic cleavage diminishes the salience of status comparisons with other groups. If the other group is clearly of a totally different sort from one's own, its peculiar value position does not threaten one. One must extend one's own identity far enough to include the other group, at least symbolically, for the comparison to make sense, and thereby motivate action. This is, I think, the important core of Lerner's (1958) empathy hypothesis. The second mechanism reducing group conflict is that sufficient social distance permits the elaboration of a separate status system within the group which either is not dependent at all on the principles through which status is allocated in other groups or in the dominant society of which the group makes up a part (the case of prestige and power, for instance) or assigns different subjective appreciations to different absolute value levels (the case of wealth, though this also may be calculated in a different manner from that of the larger society). It is essential for any analysis of ethnic relations, as Lemarchand and Butler remind us, to pay as much attention to the status distribution within groups as to the distribution between groups, and further to understand such distinctions in the same terms they are understood by the group members.

The definition and the distribution of status are no more fixed over time or conceivable without reference to context than are those of ethnicity. Individuals will seek to manipulate group ethnic identities as a way of securing status advantages, either within or across ethnic boundaries, and this manipulation may either reduce or promote conflict across ethnic lines or between ethnic groups. Abner Cohen's (1969) fine study of Hausa migrants in Ibadan, Nigeria, shows us a case in which ethnicity is reinforced to produce status advantages for some individuals and at the same time to reduce conflict between a minority ethnic group and its ethnically distinct hosts. Cohen (1969: 14) argues that "Hausa identity and Hausa ethnic exclusiveness in Ibadan are the expressions not so much of a particularly strong 'tribalistic' sentiment as of vested economic interests." Protected by the slogan "Our customs are different," Hausas were able to organize and control certain highly profitable economic activities (some forms of trade, crime, and begging) of both high and low prestige, and to isolate their group from outside interference by maintaining rigid physical and moral boundaries between themselves and the dominant community within which they lived. This boundary was maintained by ruling out of the ethnic community those Hausa who lived among or married with Yoruba, and by responding to an increased rate of Yoruba conversion to Islam, the Hausa religion, by the mass adoption of a special sect *(wird)* which in Ibadan (though not elsewhere) was purely Hausa. Although as a group the Hausa occupied an inferior position, at least when viewed from the perspective of the larger community among whom they lived, the community as a whole enjoyed a fairly high absolute level of wealth and within itself elaborated distinctions of wealth, prestige, and power which were of considerably more moment to the group members than were those of the dominant community.

The stability of the relationship between the Hausa and the dominant Yoruba society depended on the maintenance of a clear and single structure of power within the Hausa community and the limitation of formal political contacts between the Hausas and their hosts to negotiations undertaken by a single recognized leader of the community. The introduction of party politics and competition for power first among the Yorubas by individuals who sought Hausa allies for purposes of fighting Yoruba battles, and then among the Hausa, as individuals responded to these new opportunities for purposes of increasing their wealth, prestige, and power within the Hausa community, breached the ethnic identity wall and initiated a period of confrontation within the Hausa ethnic community and, inevitably, between the community and the Yorubas. Put in general form, the breakdown of some qualitative cleavages initiated open conflict between groups in which power within each group was the major prize sought. In this and in many analogous situations, the introduction of a structural violence explanation for the long period in which open conflict did not take place adds nothing but a moral judgment to our appreciation of the situation.

A further limitation of the simple reinforcing cleavage argument is that it says nothing about what initiates open group conflict. Since Aristotle discussed the disruptive consequences of giving people education while denying them access to political and social rewards, scholars have sought to explain the origin of conflict in terms of status discrepancy or disequilibrium. Such explanations share either the assumption that when people attain a higher status in one aspect of their lives, they are highly motivated to bring other aspects of their lives up at least to that level, or the assumption that when people identify slightly with strangers occupying higher status situations, they will be motivated to attain such situations for themselves or for those close to them. By itself, however, status discrepancy is just a condition, not a principle for action, and furthermore it is a condition that most people are in most of the time. Slightly more precision is achieved by introducing the idea of "relative deprivation," defined most simply as "actors' perception of discrepancy between their [status] expectations and their [status] capabilities" (Gurr, 1970: 24). Relative deprivation is most usefully understood in a dynamic or diachronic sense. Gurr (1970: 46-56) summarizes the principal dynamic deprivational models under three headings: decremental deprivation, where one's expectations remain constant while one's capabilities decline; aspirational deprivation, where one's capabilities remain constant while one's expectations rise; and progressive deprivation, in which during an initial period both expectations and capabilities rise, but capabilities subsequently level off or decline (the "J-curve model") while expectations continue to rise. The first may be epitomized by the old elites whose status suffers as new groups rise; the second by that instant cliché, the "revolution of rising expectations," and the third by the leveling off of the rate of improvement in the situation of the American black during the 1960s.[2]

Whether the analyst uses it in a dynamic or static sense, relative deprivation relates a social situation to a psychological state and suggests that the cause of conflictive action must ultimately be analyzed in psychological terms. This is both true and not very helpful. The most closely related branch of elegant psychological theory, that dealing with cognitive dissonance, by itself tells us little about the varieties of human group action that may be used to relieve dissonant tension (Runciman, 1970: 177-181). Nor are we much helped by reference to basic drives, instinctual or other. The difficulty is, basically, that not all status discrepancies lead to feelings of relative deprivation, and not all relative deprivation leads to conflict. Whatever the psychological mechanisms involved, they will remain obscure enough that in looking at any particular situation the sociologist and political scientist will find no escape from the necessity to attempt explanation in terms of the structural and behavioral variables that are the stock in trade of his discipline. At most, the analysis of status cleavages and discrepancies tells us something approximate about potential for conflict of some sort. Any further analysis must deal with the particularities of structure, societal resource base, repressive capabilities, learning capacity, ideology, and the like, as well as the positions and abilities of leaders and potential leaders and their relations with different societal and political structures.

In building up explanations from the status situation of individuals who become or might become leaders of combative ethnic groups, generalizations based on status or relative deprivation are only partially helpful. A schematic explanation would begin something as follows: An individual in some form of status disequilibrium somehow feels relatively deprived. For some reason he connects his deprivation with some level of ethnic identity and somehow mobilizes some other people bearing some relation to a similar identity to take some sort of conflictive action. All of the "somes" must be elaborated in something other than the initial status terms. Such complexity of explanation is nothing new to social science, and status or relative deprivational arguments are not to be faulted because they increase rather than decrease the complexity of the analytical task. At the same time one should be aware that many satisfactory explanations of important aspects of status-connected ethnic conflict can be carried on without reference to disequilibrium or relative deprivation, and that even where those terms form part of the analysis, the interplay of situation, instrumental strategies, and such properties of ethnic mobilization as emotion and lag may have determinate independent effects on the outcome of any confrontation. The South African and Soviet cases illustrate some of this interplay.

The Afrikaner people of South Africa, an amalgam of primarily Dutch, French, and German immigrant stock, developed a highly integrated ethnic identity during the nineteenth century and during the first two-thirds of the twentieth used that ethnic identity as a basic organizing principle of political conflict. Following the defeat of the Boer armies and the creation of the Union in 1910, the Afrikaners were a subordinated and politically divided people.[3] As a group, they ranked below the English population on every measure of development or status, except that they had equal access to political rights, and had a latent numerical advantage which could be turned to general political advantage if (a) politics could be restricted to whites, (b) immigration did not shift the balance, and (c) they could hold themselves together as an ethnic political force.

It was, however, not at all clear to the majority of Afrikaners in 1910 (and to a few even today) that they wished to activate that latent advantage. The defeated Boer generals Botha and Smuts sought a policy of "accommodation" with the English which implied the integration of the Afrikaners into a white imperial identity, substantially on English terms, and at first a majority of the Afrikaner electorate supported them. J.B.M. Hertzog vigorously opposed this policy and argued for the creation of a separate and "pure" Afrikaner ethnic and political identity of which language and religion would be the cornerstone. Hertzog's strategy was to build up and mobilize Afrikaner identity to the point at which it would be strong enough to withstand the appeals of the higher status

English way of life, and then to come together with the English population on the basis of political and ethnic equality. By 1929, Hertzog's National Party succeeded in winning a clear parliamentary majority in its own right, and, citing the need for a "broader white unity" against the "Black peril," in 1934 Hertzog led the party into fusion with Smuts' primarily English party. Hertzog failed to carry the Afrikaners with him and six years later was driven out of political life, because the forces building his cherished Afrikaner identity could not be put to such flexible use. The schoolteachers, journalists, and particularly the religious leaders "set their faces against any flexibility of policy" (De Villiers, 1971: 390) and through organizations like the secret *Broederbond,* gave their support to the ethnic separatist policies of D. F. Malan, himself a former minister of the Dutch Reformed Church and newspaper editor. It was not until the mid-1960s that the triumphant Afrikaner political leaders moved tentatively toward a reconciliation with the English population, and then clearly on terms of Afrikaner cultural and political dominance and under the threat of newly salient ethnic opposition from the black population.

Hertzog's defeat seems a clear case of the lag effect of ethnic mobilization, and its mode of operation reminds us to look at the role of special groups—here the religious and linguistic specialists—who have emotional as well as status interests in emphasizing a particular level of ethnic identity and in maintaining a cleavage, no matter what the cost. Indeed, it is within these groups that the present *verkrampte* opposition toward accommodation with the English is centered. English ethnicity, as Butler shows, was never called on to the same degree as an instrument of political combat, and those English teachers and preachers who have played political roles have often acted in the name of ethnically transcendent principles. In addition, the social distance between the white populations, including the crucial absence of a common scale of status, has meant that the English community as a whole did not feel threatened by Afrikaner ethnicity, or even by its political success. Now in continuous political power since 1947, the Nationalists have tightly bonded their ethnic principles to a repressive political structure which not only has left the English population with very few political options, but has enforced a maximum amount of ethnic disunity among the South African black population. Now that the political structure has become an instrument of ethnic power, opposition of the *verkrampte* sort may no longer be as effective as it was against Hertzog. The futher rapprochement of the white communities on Afrikaner terms and even the eventual creation of a common status scale through Afrikaner promotion in the economic sphere seems unlikely to weaken the political experession of Afrikaner ethnic ideals, nor overcome the dominant cleavage between blacks and whites.

The Soviet case demonstrates the persistence of a high degree of ethnic awareness under circumstances in which a common scale of individual status is rigidly enforced, and in which all status indices correlate highly. Despite official claims to the contrary, ethnic group status appears to be ranked according to a single scale, with the "elder brother" Great Russians at the top, and the exiled groups, rehabilitated or not, at the bottom. The only way for most individuals to escape this de facto group status ranking is by linguistic and cultural russification, and beyond that by active service of the political structures that reinforce both the individual and the group status rankings. As would be predictable from relative deprivation analysis, the greatest resentment against the system seems to come from the Jews who as a group have apparently been in the best position to russify themselves and whose efforts to reap the promised benefits have been decisively rebuffed. In their case, individual repression has virtually created a new consciousness of ethnic identity and "revitalized Zionist sentiments . . . to a degree that has not been evident for a half a century" (Friedberg, 1970: 26).

Perhaps the most striking aspect of the Soviet situation is, as academician Sakharov points out, the linking of general political opposition in the national republics to ethnic issues: "In the national republics the movement for democratization, surging up from below, inevitably takes on a nationalistic character" (quoted in Barghoorn, Ch. 9: 130). The comparative liberalism of the Khrushchev era allowed both the democratization and national movements to come to the surface, and the comparative repressiveness of his successors presumably has both exacerbated the feelings of grievance and facilitated the union of the two movements. Within the national republics it would seem today as if ethnicity offers the most obvious principle of political association between the dissatisfied of varying individual status positions. For the moment, the ideology of democratization permits a certain coordination of the various national movements, under primarily intellectual leadership. In the unpredictable circumstance that the national movements did attain enough power to express themselves openly, there is no guarantee that they would retain either their present type of leadership, their operative unity, or a democratizing ideology. Such a reversion to repressive ethnic chauvinism seems at the heart of both Sakharov's and Amalrik's concerns. The alternatives seem even more unthinkable repression by the authorities, or elaboration of a more open society, admitting ethnic pluralism and some degree of independent elaboration of status positions.

As Barghoorn points out, there are many reasons why the authorities may be reluctant to move toward implementing Leninist prescriptions of a more pluralist—or at the very least non-discriminatory—Soviet order. In addition to the factors he mentions, our analysis would lead us to pay particular attention to the persistence and influence of Great Russian ethnic consciousness and its close bonding with state structures yielding significant status advantages which are shared, at least symbolically, by the Soviet Union's largest single ethnic bloc. One would further expect that in the absence of institutional buffers, increased ethnic consciousness among the "lesser" nationalities is likely to exacerbate that of "elder brother."

In conclusion, the papers and additional cases considered here illustrate some essential points about ethnic and status conflict. Ethnic awareness and ethnic conflict are closely related to status issues in multiple ways. In particular, status discrepancies interpreted in ethnic terms are likely to initiate ethnic conflict, and the presence of status cleavages which reinforce ethnic cleavages is likely to exacerbate such conflict once it has started. However, when ethnicity is suitably reinforced by other "distance variables," it may be possible for different ethnic groups to live side by side peacefully over considerable periods of time, if each group is allowed to create and enforce its own independent status system. In political situations, ethnicity is a malleable principle of association which can be mobilized for conflictful purposes and connected with many different ideological principles by many different sorts of leaders. In research on ethnic conflict it must be a main task of the analyst to specify the precise conditions permitting the mobilization of a precise level of ethnic identity. Finally, ethnicity is a very potent political resource and a very difficult one to control. The passions ethnic appeals arouse and their embodiment in particular institutions providing individuals with new advantages, make it likely that a leader who tries to reduce or redirect ethnic appeals will be challenged by a new set of leaders in the name of the principles he once enunciated. Though status considerations may prompt the original mobilization on ethnic lines, they are likely to be overriden by other concerns in the heat of conflict.

NOTES

1. See the discussion in Gurr (1970: 26) where following Runciman (1966) he relates Maslow's need hierarchy and Lasswell and Kaplan's value categories to three such attributes. My own labels differ from Gurr's and Runciman's out of a desire to avoid terminological complications, particularly those implicit in the use of "economic class" instead of "wealth," and "status" instead of "prestige," when "status" is also used as a general description of all such relational attributes. For a convincing discussion of the adequacy and logical independence of these three attributes, see Runciman (1970: 102-140).
2. On the limitations of the "revolution of rising expectations" approach, see Oberschall (1969). On the J-curve model and the American black, see Davies (1969).
3. The following discussion is based heavily on De Villiers (1971) in addition to the points made by Butler.

REFERENCES

BAILEY, F. G. (1970) Stratagems and Spoils: A Social Anthropology of Politics. Oxford: Basil Blackwell.
BANTON, M. (1967) Race Relations. London: Tavistock Publications.
BARTH, F. (1969) "Introduction," pp. 9-38 in Barth (ed.) Ethnic Groups and Boundaries. Boston: Little, Brown.
COHEN, A., (1969) Custom and Politics in Urban Africa: A Study of Hausa Migrants in Yoruba Towns. Berkeley: Univ. of California Press.
COSER, L. (1956) The Functions of Social Conflict. New York: Free Press.
DAHRENDORF, R. (1959) Class and Class Conflict in Industrial Society. Stanford: Stanford Univ. Press.
DAVIES, J. C. (1969) "The J-curve of rising and declining satisfactions as a cause of some great revolutions and a contained rebellion," in H. D. Graham and T. R. Gurr (eds.) Violence in America: Historical and Comparative Perspectives. Washington, D.C.: National Commission on the Causes and Prevention of Violence.
DEUTSCH, K. W. (1953) Nationalism and Social Communication: An Enquiry into the Foundation of Nationalism. New York: John Wiley.
De VILLIERS, R. (1971) "Afrikaner nationalism," pp. 365-423 in M. Wilson and L. Thompson (eds.) The Oxford History of South Africa, Vol. II. Oxford: Clarendon Press.
EVANS-PRITCHARD, E. E. (1940) The Nuer: A Description of the Modes of Livelihood and Political Institutions of a Nilotic People. Oxford: Clarendon Press.
FRIEDBERG, M. (1970) "The plight of Soviet Jews." Problems of Communism 19, 6: 17-26.
GALTUNG, J. (1971) "A structural theory of imperialism." J. of Peace Research 2, 1971: 81-118.
GLAZER, N. and MOYNIHAN, D. P. (1963) Beyond the Melting Pot: The Negroes, Puerto Ricans, Jews, Italians, and Irish of New York City. Cambridge: MIT and Harvard Univ. Presses.

GLUCKMAN, M. (1956) Custom and Conflict in Africa. Oxford: Basil Blackwell.

GURR, T. R. (1970) Why Men Rebel. Princeton: Princeton Univ. Press.

KOTHARI, R. (1970) Caste in Indian Politics. Bombay: Orient Longmans.

KUPER, L. (1971) "Theories of revolution and race relations." Comparative Studies in Society and History 13, 1: 87-107.

LENSKI, G. (1961) The Religious Factor: A Sociological Study of Religion's Impact on Politics, Economics, and Family Life. Garden City, N.Y.: Anchor Books.

LERNER, D. (1958) The Passing of Traditional Society. New York: Free Press.

LIPSET, S. M. (1963) Political Man: The Social Bases of Politics. Garden City, N.Y.: Anchor Books.

LOFCHIE, M. F. (1965) Zanzibar: Background to Revolution. Princeton: Princeton Univ. Press.

MOORE, B., Jr. (1966) Social Origins of Dictatorship and Democracy. Boston: Beacon Press.

OBERSCHALL, A. (1969) "Communications, information, and aspirations in rural Uganda." J. of Asian and African Studies 4, 1: 30-50.

ROUCH, J. (1956) "Migrations au Ghana." J. de la Société des Africanistes 26: 1-2, 163-164.

RUNCIMAN, W. G. (1970) Sociology in Its Place and Other Essays. Cambridge: Cambridge Univ. Press.

――― (1966) Relative Deprivation and Social Justice. Berkeley: Univ. of California Press.

Chapter 9

SOVIET DISSENTERS ON
SOVIET NATIONALITY POLICY

FREDERICK C. BARGHOORN

*T*his study is an interpretive report on critical opinion and protest directed, since about 1965, by some Soviet citizens against the policies of the Soviet political authorities toward national minorities in the USSR, particularly Ukrainians, Crimean Tatars, and Jews. In most of the cases examined, it is clear that the Soviet authorities regarded the opinions in question so incompatible with official doctrine as to require that they at least be denied publication, or that their authors be subjected to sanctions varying from verbal chastisement to long terms in corrective labor camps. Attention is focused on the ethnic groups named above because some members of these groups have been bold enough to insist upon articulating their dissent from official policy, even at the risk of severe punishment. Considerable data have become available on the attitudes of these dissenters toward Soviet nationality policies.

Concentration of attention on the above ethnic groups does not imply the belief that the aspirations of other nationalities in the USSR are politically insignificant, or even that demands made by some minorities, especially the Turkic Moslem peoples of Central Asia and the Caucasus, whose rate of population growth far exceeds that of the dominant Russians (often called Great Russians to distinguish them from the other Slavic peoples, such as the Ukrainians), may not over the long run present the most difficult challenges to the cohesiveness of the Soviet polity. However, the political elites and intellectuals of these peoples, except for the Crimean Tatars, seem content for the time being to abide by the rules of the game of Soviet politics; thus, in contrast to some Ukrainian, Crimean Tatar, and Jewish intellectuals, counterpart members of most of the Turkic–and other–non-Russian minorities have refrained from aggressive articulation of views on nationality problems that differ conspicuously from official doctrine.

The fact that non-Russian minorities constitute close to half the total Soviet population renders dissent from official policy among members of these ethnic groups politically significant. The volume and intensity of such dissent grew during the early years after the ouster of Nikita Khrushchev from the Soviet leadership, as Khrushchev's successors moved to snuff out the expression of unorthodox opinion in this and other areas of political life which Khrushchev had grudgingly tolerated. The significance of protest against official nationality

AUTHOR'S NOTE: The author wishes to acknowledge assistance from the following: Yale University for a Senior Faculty Fellowship enabling him to devote the academic year 1970-1971 to full-time research; the Research Institute for International Communist Affairs of Columbia University for a Senior Fellowship providing financial and research assistance; the American Philosophical Society and the American Council of Learned Societies-Social Science Research Council for grants of assistance.

policy was heightened when prominent participants in the Moscow-centered "democratic movement," as has come to be called the expression of protest against violations by the authorities of the constitutional and legal norms in the name of which they profess to act, have increasingly lent support to the efforts of some members of particular national groups to defend cultural and political values shared by many members of the former. Support, on the part of such prominent leaders of the "democratic movement," as academician Andrei Sakharov, for the aspirations expressed by dissenting members of non-Russian minorities, has brought these aspirations to the attention of segments of world opinion to which they might otherwise have been unknown. It has also perhaps fostered solidarity between minority group dissenters and members of the "mainstream," largely Russian and Russian Jewish dissent movement.

As is true in general of opinions expressed by Soviet citizens that challenge the official Soviet policy line, much of the critical opinion discussed herein was first disseminated in the USSR in *samizdat* (literally, self-published) form, because it could not be legally published in that country. Some of the information on which this study is based is widely known in Soviet intellectual circles, as a result of unauthorized distribution in mimeographed or photocopied organs, such as Chronicle of Current Events (Khronika tekushchikh sobytii), which, since the fall of 1970, has been published in English translation by Amnesty International of London, England. The first English-language issue of the Chronicle to be published was No. 16, dated October 31, 1970. Interested Soviet citizens derive much of their information about the contents of samizdat publications by listening to Western radio broadcasts, from which, often for the first time, they learn of the publication abroad, in Russian or Western languages, of works by their fellow countrymen. The Chronicle is the most comprehensive single source of information on Soviet dissent. It has been compiled and distributed since April 1968 by anonymous Soviet citizens.

The sharply negative evaluation of the treatment of non-Russians by the Soviet state and the Communist Party of the Soviet Union (CPSU) and of the state of ethnic relations generally in the USSR, contained in the dissenters' testimony, of course stands in stark contrast to the image of the "friendship of peoples" presented in official Soviet sources. The official image is well known and need therefore be only briefly outlined. It bulks large in the stream of political communication continuously and systematically disseminated by Soviet mass media and also by millions of oral agitators, propagandists, scholars, teachers, and others engaged in implementing the Kremlin's political socialization program. The tone of Soviet statements regarding ethnic and national relations in the USSR is dogmatically optimistic and intolerant. Its doctrinal premise is that "socialism" eliminates the class oppression that breeds national tensions and the oppression of national minorities by governments. Hence, there is no place for these remnants of an unhappy "capitalist" past in the Soviet Union and other socialist societies. As a Soviet study, published under the auspices of the Academy of Sciences of the Uzbek Soviet Socialist Republic puts it, "Building a new society, free of exploitation and oppression, the Soviet Union not only eliminated the grievous heritage of capitalism in the sphere of nationality relations, and resolved the nationality problem, but it demonstrates by its example . . . paths to further perfection and development of relations of friendship, cooperation, mutual aid and rapprochement among the peoples."

The same work typically asserts (Khonozarov, 1963: 9) that Soviet experience has "inestimable significance" for other countries that have chosen "the path of non-capitalist development." Wielding the conductor's baton in this harmonic symphony of friendship is the "elder brother" Russian people. An especially important role is assigned to the Russian language (Kammari, 1963: 7-8), "one of the indispensable elements of that new historical community of the toilers of various nations—the Soviet people—which has grown up as the result of the social transformations of . . . the Soviet system." This concept of the core role of the dominant Russian, or Great Russian, nationality in the Soviet family of peoples—which bears significant resemblances to some of the concepts of the tsarist regime—was developed by Stalin in the 1930s. Although since Stalin the complex of doctrines and policies of which it is a central element has been dubbed "Leninist," it in fact differs sharply not only from Lenin's but also from Stalin's earlier doctrine, which severely condemned—but not after 1930—all manifestations of "Great power chauvinism."[1]

To complete this sketch of the official nationality doctrine we should point out that its predominantly positive and self-satisfied orientation is occasionally, and vaguely, qualified by admissions that it is precisely in the sphere of national sentiments, and behavior associated therewith, that "survivals of the past" are especially strong, tenacious, and pernicious, in spite of proclaimed progress in elimination of their officially postulated social class roots. Unauthorized criticism of, not to mention organized or "conspiratorial" resistence to, official nationality policy, is at least condemned as "bourgeois nationalism" and is uusually severely punished, in many instances by sentences to long terms in labor camps. It is difficult if not impossible to determine whether official charges, at trials of alleged nationalists in 1961 and 1967, in Lviv—that the latter had organized to work for the secession of the Ukraine from the USSR—were true, or were merely security police propaganda. Soviet secrecy regarding these cases and the character of the meager evidence available about them, supports the latter interpretation. Ironically, as the accused pointed out, in the 1961 trial, in Lviv, of seven Ukrainians accused of secessionist activity, advocacy of secession should scarcely be regarded as criminal, since the constitution of the USSR and of its constitutent republic, grants the right of secession to the latter (Maistrenko, 1968; Anonymous, 1971: 64-66).

Soviet nationality policy, as administered by Stalin, Khrushchev, or Brezhnev is condemned by some Soviet intellectuals, both non-Russian and Russian, as a flagrant violation of Leninist principles of "proletarian internationalism." The history of Soviet nationality policy and the harassment and persecution of Soviet citizens who criticize it, suggests several propositions, which, in our opinion, tend to be verified by the evidence presented herein. First, establishment of a Soviet-type "socialist" or state-directed economy does not eliminate nationality tensions and prejudices or the cultural oppression or even the economic exploitation of minority nationalities. Indeed, Soviet-type systems, unless modified, as in Yugoslavia by institutional checks against dominance of larger over smaller national groups, may perhaps repress national-cultural diversity as severely as even the most reactionary non-socialist societies. Second, widespread resentment, indignation, and concern have been aroused by Stalin and post-Stalin Soviet nationality policies, among both non-Russian intellectuals and their Russian sympathizers and co-participants in the contemporary Soviet dissent movement. Finally, there is evidence to support the prognosis in Brzezinski's Foreword to the Chornovil Papers (1968) that "It is not inconceivable that in the next several decades the nationality problem will become politically more important in the Soviet Union than the racial issue has in the United States."[2]

Criticism by Soviet citizens of official nationality policy of course is related to a wide variety of situations and is shaped by the specific experiences and personalities of its authors. Although much of the testimony available is extraordinarily interesting and moving, some of it is also heterogeneous and fragmentary. Dissenters' testimony, produced in defiance of censorship, adminis-trative, legal and police controls, and often in response to what its authors regard as exceptionally outrageous governmental actions, tends to be unsystematic in structure, although often surprisingly objective and detached in style. It must be constantly borne in mind, in evaluating this testimony, that criticism of the official policy in the sphere of relations among nationalities perhaps involves more risk to those who engage in it than any other kind of political dissent in the USSR.

Dissenting opinion on Soviet nationality policy displays a substantial degree of consensus. As is the case with unofficial criticism of other CPSU policies, that directed at official nationality policy is couched partly in terms of broad moral and legal principles, such as human rights and civil liberties. Critics also assail the authorities for policies specifically related to ethnic questions, such as assimilationist and russifying pressures which they perceive as weakening, suppressing, or destroying ethnic diversity and national self-expression. Also, some dissenters point out that not only does the CPSU demand that non-Russians internalize the norms and act in accordance with the behavior patterns of a dominant political culture which is indulgent toward the Russian language and the culture patterns conveyed by it and discriminates against non-Russian languages and traditions, but that the very authorities who demand that Jews, for example, in effect become Russians nevertheless refuse to accept russified Jews as full-fledged Russian and Soviet men.

Another widely voiced criticism of the incumbent Soviet leaders is that in respect to entire peoples, such as the Volga Germans and Chechens, or more particularly the Crimean Tatars, victimized by Stalin's near-genocidal policies, they have been guilty of moral outrage in their failure to take more than token measures to redress the grievances of these peoples.

UKRAINIAN RESISTANCE

In September, October, and November of 1965 the security police of Kiev and Lviv, in the Ukrainian Soviet Republic, arrested about thirty Ukrainian intellectuals on charges of conducting anti-Soviet agitation and propaganda. It appears from study of the campaign of repression thus inaugurated against dissident Ukrainian intellectuals that the authorities sought to crush resistance to russification measures first imposed by Khrushchev in the late 1950s and continued by his successors. Article 9 of the 1959 "Law on the relations between school and life," which abolished the previous obligatory study of a non-Russian language in schools in the non-Russian republics in which the basic language of instruction was Russian, and substituted, for the previously obligatory study of a non-Russian language, a provision making such study elective, at the request of parents, seems to have aroused alarm and resentment among those non-Russians who cared deeply about the continued effective use of national languages. As a leading American student of Soviet nationality policy notes (Aspaturian, 1968: 173), the law referred to was calculated to accelerate the Russianization and russification of the Soviet non-Russian nationalities. Without going into the intricacies of this complex subject, it should be pointed out that one of the main reasons why both Western scholars and concerned Soviet citizens regarded the 1959 reform as a russification measure was that while it left the study of non-Russian languages at the discretion of parents, it also left unchanged the previous legal provision requiring that, in schools in which the basic language of instruction was not Russian, study of Russian was nevertheless obligatory. Actually, although the legal provisions were important, they were probably less so than the political and administrative pressures for russification that they symbolized. In the Ukraine, these russification policies were sharply criticized in two major works. The first of these, the already-mentioned Chornovil Papers, compiled by the young television journalist Vyacheslav Chornovil—arrested because he became sympathetic with the dissenters whose trials he was assigned to cover—consists of a lengthy protest petition addressed by Chornovil to the public prosecutor of the Ukrainian Soviet Socialist Republic and the other top political leaders of the Ukraine, and of writings by and information about arrested Ukrainian dissenters such as Svyatoslav Karavansky, Mykhailo Masyutko, and others, assembled by Chornovil. The second of these major works, entitled *Internationalism or Russification?*, is an eloquent, comprehensive, and coherent polemic and analysis, subtitled "A Study in the Soviet Nationalities Problem," by the Ukrainian literary critic and scholar Ivan Dzyuba (1968).[3] Dzyuba, a man of greater reputation and status than Chornovil, and also more tactful in his approach to the political authorities, was not arrested or even expelled from the Ukrainian Writers Union, a fact indicative of support therein for his views, but he was subjected to severe criticism and, among other actions taken against him, he was for more than two years prevented from publishing any of his writings.

In 1965 another Ukrainian writer, Svyatoslav Karavansky, wrote two of the most vigorous denunciations of official Soviet nationality policy to be composed in the post-Stalin era. One of these was an essay pointing out that the above-mentioned Article 9 had, among other things, led to the closing of many Ukrainian-language schools in the Ukraine. In the course of this essay Karavansky also touched upon another major grievance of some Ukrainian and other non-Russian intellectuals, namely, the bias in favor of admission to higher educational institutions of Great Russians and russified non-Russians, and against non-Russians, resulting from the requirement that to be admitted to a higher educational institution in the USSR it is necessary to pass entrance examinations in the Russian language, and in Russian literature. Probably, however, in the eyes of the authorities the other major protest document on the subject of russification drafted by Karavansky, to wit, a petition to the prosecutor of the Ukrainian Republic, demanding that Dadenkov, the Republic's Minister of Higher and Secondary Education, be indicted for "violation of national and racial equality" and other provisions of the Ukrainian criminal code, seemed even more objectionable than his vigorous essay.

Karavansky was arrested in November 1965 and was sentenced, without investigation or trial, to eight years and seven months in severe hard labor camps. Although he had been freed from a labor camp in 1960, where he had been serving a twenty-five-year sentence imposed for alleged anti-Soviet nationalist activity, he was now sentenced, or resentenced, to complete the remainder of his twenty-five-year term. These details are mentioned because they may shed some light on the sensitivity of the Soviet authorities to protest against official nationality policy, even if, as seems to be the case with Karavansky and almost all other non-Russian critics of the Kremlin's nationality policy, there is no evidence that these critics either advocated or organized for secession of their peoples from the USSR (Chornovil Papers, 1968: 166-221).

In April 1970, Karavansky, although serving the sentence reimposed in 1965, was subjected to yet another trial and this time received an additional sentence of five years in a camp at hard labor and three years' deportation, presumably to be served at the expiration of the twenty-five-year term that he was already serving (Ukrainian Quarterly, 1971: 109).

The criticism of Soviet nationality policy in the Chornovil Papers was by no means confined to discrimination against Ukrainians in use of their language and in regard to access to higher education. It also dealt in considerable detail with failure to allocate adequate resources in funds and manpower to Ukrainian cultural institutions, forced migration of Ukrainians to Siberia, economic exploitation and underdevelopment of parts of the Ukraine, settlement of Russians in Ukrainian cities, and scorn and derision directed by Russians against Ukrainians who wished to maintain their cultural identity.

However, such subjects were dealt with most fully by Dzyuba. For example, Dzyuba (1968: 102-113) in his discussion of the impact upon the Ukraine of centralized USSR economic policy, asserts that "economic overcentralization" damages and "fetters the existing possibilities of development of a number of republics, the Ukraine in particular." He argues that one cannot "speak of the sovereignty of the Ukraine, when for thirty years, till 1958, the Ukrainian SSR did not compute its national income or national product—that is to say, those indices without which no idea can be formed about the economy of a country," adding that "in any case, it is not easy to compute economic indices in a Republic which in fact has no economy of its own." Dzyuba adds that it is impossible to calculate in detail the effects of administrative and economic centralization on the Ukraine because of official secrecy. Thus, the production in the Ukraine of industrial enterprises directed from Moscow is an "uncharted area." In his discussion of economic exploitation, Dzyuba deals with many other topics, including the assignment of Russians to manage such major economic installations in the Ukraine as the Kiev hydroelectric station. He links the Soviet centralized economic administration, and Moscow's policy of the "exchange of cadres," with linguistic russification, pointing out that "When the managers and highly skilled workers do not understand Ukrainian . . . the Ukrainian worker cannot help losing the desire to use his language anywhere outside his own dwelling or hostel room." Dzyuba's book, with its wealth of telling data and eloquent argumentation provides impressive evidence of the persistence of Ukrainian national consciousness, despite Moscow's centralizing and assimilationist pressures. On the other hand, many statements contained in the writings of Chornovil, Karavansky, Dzyuba, and other Ukrainians can be regarded as manifestations of despair resulting from awareness of the power and impact of the Kremlin policies opposed by them. For example, in his comment on the existence of a group of more than ten million persons who, according to the 1959 census, had changed their language from their previous native language to Russian, Dzyuba (1968: 189) notes that the fact that "these 10.2 million are described as a great success of our nationalities policy . . . implies: that the friendship of nations is synonymous with Russification." Later, referring to "the painful national differences between the Ukrainian village and the Russian city," he (Dzyuba, 1968: 194) expresses the opinion that such evils as "demoralization, indifference and drunkenness" could in part be explained by "a sense of doom hanging over the nation, the lack of national prospects and of national growth beyond the village boundaries, the denationalizing pressure from above."

Although we are drawing our data primarily from the writings of Soviet citizens, it should be noted that data confirming the opinions of Chornovil, Karavansky, and Dzyuba are provided in a book, based upon personal experience in the Ukraine, by a former Canadian communist of Ukrainian extraction (Kolasky, 1970), whose experiences as a student at the Higher Party School of the Ukrainian Communist Party, in Kiev, in 1963-1965, led to his break with the Communist Party of Canada. It would appear that Kolasky's experience not only provided Western readers with much information regarding Soviet nationality problems but also exerted influence in the Ukraine itself. This is indicated by the fact that Karavansky in a petition he addressed in September 1965 to Wladyslaw Gomulka, then First Secretary of the Polish United Workers Party, wrote, of Kolasky (Chornovil Papers, 1968: 182-183), that "If after a stay of one year in Kiev, under the effect of reality he began to doubt the justice of the Russification of Ukrainian life . . . this fact should have compelled the leadership of the CPSU to ponder whether it is carrying out the right nationality policy in the Ukraine, whether this is the Leninist policy, and whether it serves to strengthen the international communist movement." It is also reported (Chornovil Papers, 1968: 66-67) that when Karavansky was arrested in November 1965, "The only charge was that his petition to the prosecutor somehow found its way into the hands of a Canadian communist." Clearly, Chornovil here refers to Karavansky's petition, mentioned earlier, and to Kolasky.

An effort to conduct what might be termed spiritual and aesthetic resistance to russification is associated with the names of Valentyn Moroz and Oles Honchar. Moroz was one of the Ukrainian intellectuals punished for alleged anti-Soviet propaganda and agitation in 1965-1966 (Choronovil Papers, 1968: 150-152). Released from camp in September 1969, Moroz was again arrested in June 1970. After a secret trial he was sentenced in November 1970 to nine years at hard labor. Word reached the West (The Times, 1971: 7; Anonymous, Ukrainian Quarterly, 1971: 13; Anonymous, Chronicle, 1971: 41-43) that in connection with Moroz's 1970 arrest seven house searches were made and thirty persons were interrogated. Although warned they would be dismissed from work if they sought to attend Moroz's trial, some persons nevertheless came, but were refused admittance to the hearing. Among witnesses asked to testify at the trial were Chornovil and Dzyuba, who refused to do so on the ground that a secret trial was illegal.

It is clear that Moroz's second arrest resulted from his continued expression of opposition to russification (Boiter, 1970: 4; Anonymous, Ukrainian Quarterly, 1971: 13-37), especially as expressed in his essay, "A Chronicle of Resistance." In this work, Moroz praises the Hutsuls, a little-known sub-group of the Ukrainian people, for their defense of their national cultural heritage against assimilationist pressures. The Hutsuls are a mountain people of Ukrainian origin and Uniate, or Eastern Rite, Roman Catholic, religious tradition, inhabiting an area now incorporated in the Stanislav oblast of the Ukrainian Soviet Republic. Prior to 1945, when they were incorporated within the USSR, they were scattered in Poland, Hungary, and Czechoslovakia. Their national shrine is a museum, named after their legendary hero Dovbush, and located in the village of Kosmach. Before 1959, this museum had functioned as a church. In 1963 its most important art and religious objects were ostensibly borrowed from it and, later, in violation of an agreement to return them, transferred to the museum of Ukrainian art in Kiev. From 1964 on, the director of the Dovbush museum in Kosmach, supported by a number of well-known Ukrainian intellectuals, including Honchar, and leading historians and artists, sought to have these treasures, among which the most important is the altar screen of the former church, returned to their ancestral setting. Moroz sees this issue (Boiter, 1970: 4) as epitomizing healthy "self-preservation" of a nationality group against false modernization, mass culture, and other pressures leading to "deculturization, alienation, dehumanization, the loss of the core." He cited the Ukrainians, except for two groups, the Hutsuls, and the Mordovian people, as examples of Soviet nationality groups whose culture had been badly undermined. On the other hand, he expressed admiration for the Georgians, the Armenians, the Germans living in exile in Kazakhstan, and the Chechens, as peoples who had stubbornly and successfully resisted assimilation. He pointed out that the struggle for preservation of cultural identity was based upon the feeling that to surrender a traditional way of life amounted to the loss of an essential part of an individual's personality. Moroz also heavily stressed the vital role of religion as a factor in national cultural identity. While defending tradition, and arguing that revolutionary interference with tradition is destructive, Moroz at the same time was far from advocating either national exclusiveness and intolerance or rejection of progress and innovation. On the contrary, he advocated respect for cultural diversity and pluralism, combined with acceptance and incorporation of new elements within a frame of reference created over the centuries.

In his novel Sobor *(The Cathedral)* Honchar symbolically championed the spiritual values embodied in Ukrainian folk culture against a kind of bureaucratic industrialization that, as he perceived it, was fatal both to the national values inherited from the past and to true individuality. Like Moroz, Honchar was clearly not propagating a narrow exclusive nationalistic perspective but was attempting to show that the suppression or perversion of particular national values amounted to the destruction of values common to all people, both as individuals and as members of distinctive cultural groups. Honchar's novel was sharply attacked in the official press of the Soviet Ukraine but it was praised by various Ukrainian communists in Poland, Czechoslovakia, and Canada.

In May 1971 Honchar lost his position as president of the Union of Ukrainian Writers, probably because of Moscow's irritation over his opposition to russification, and for related reasons, such as his defense of Dzyuba's views (Radio Free Europe Research Report, 1968; Radio Liberty, 1971).

Although the fragmentary nature of data on resistance to official nationality policy renders generalization hazardous, it seems clear that the opinions reported thus far are representative of a determined and—from the point of view of the authorities in Moscow and Kiev—troublesome and dangerous current of Ukrainian intellectual opinion. It is impossible to know how Ukrainian public opinion as a whole would respond to the largely suppressed views of these "nationalists," if repression were to be replaced by freedom of expression, but there is evidence that their views are shared by a substantial number of persons. For one thing, in 1965 scores of people were reportedly subjected to searches and hundreds were questioned by the security police (Chornovil Papers, 1968: 53). Also, besides Chornovil and others who were arrested, many Ukrainians, including distinguished writers, composers, scientists, aircraft designers, and others addressed petitions to the Ukrainian political leadership in protest against the secrecy of the trials of most of the accused, and against the exceptionally severe sentences meted out to them. Also perhaps indicative of public support for the opinions of Ukrainian dissenters is the fact that at least in the cases of Dzyuba and Honchar, there was a certain amount of open discussion of their views in the official press. However, the limited toleration displayed toward these men was probably also a reflection of the fact that many foreigners, especially Canadian Ukrainians, publicly indicated their sympathy and support for them.

TATAR PROTEST

After the Slavic peoples of the USSR—Great Russians, Ukrainians, and Belorrussians (also called White Russians)—the most numerous Soviet peoples are those of Turkic origin, such as the Uzbeks, Kazakh, Turkmen, Azerbaidzhanians, and others. Among these Turkic peoples, whose culture was largely shaped by Islam, a group that is of special interest to students of the dissent movement in the USSR are the Crimean Tartars—the Crimean Tatars should not be confused with the Tatars of the Volga region, whose capital is Kazan. With the exception of the Jews, the Crimean Tatars have produced more vocal and persistent protesters and demonstrators against official nationality policy than any other Soviet national group. Also, the Crimean Tatar cause was championed by leading members of the Moscow dissent community, in particular by the late writer Aleksei Kosterin, and by retired Major General Petr Grigorenko. The latter's insistence, in 1969, on going to Tashkent, capital of the Uzbek Republic, where a number of Crimean Tatars were on trial, led to his incarceration in a mental institution. Grigorenko went to Tashkent in response to a request reportedly signed by 2,000 Crimean Tatars. Academician Sakharov (1968: 53, 68; Kirimal, 1970: 70-97) also characterized as "disgraceful" Moscow's treatment of the Tatars.

A quarter-century of repressive Soviet policies toward the Crimean Tatars culminated in 1944 when the entire Crimean Tatar population was deported, mainly to Central Asia, charged with having collaborated with the Germans while they were occupying Crimea. In 1967, however, the Crimean Tatars were "rehabilitated" but they were not granted permission to return to their homeland, although according to Kirimal (1970), 148 families were permitted to return. Crimean Tatars, dissatisfied with a merely conditional rehabilitation, organized numerous demonstrations and other protest actions. For example, in March 1968, a number of Crimean Tatars at a celebration in Moscow in honor of Kosterin's seventy-second birthday, demanded the right to return to the Crimea and re-establish the autonomous Crimean Soviet Socialist Republic. It was on this occasion that Grigorenko began his activity as an outspoken supporter of the demands of the Crimean Tatars. A month later, there was a mass procession of Crimean Tatars on the occasion of Lenin's birthday, in the town of Chirchik in Uzbekistan, which was dispersed by police detachments and followed by many arrests. After a number of other demonstrations and arrests, numerous Crimean Tatars were put on trial in Tashkent. The defendants included outstanding writers and other representatives of the Tatar intelligentsia. Probably the best-known defendant was the renowned physicist Roland Kadiyev. On August 5, 1969 hundreds of Crimean Tatars staged a protest against the verdict in the above trial at the prosecutor's office and the building of the Communist Party of Uzbekistan in Tashkent. Because of the vigor of their protests, and the support they received from non-Tatar intellectuals, the Tatars' plight was reported in major world newspapers, such as Le Monde and the New York Times and received considerable coverage in Turkey, a country with traditional religious and cultural links with the Tatars. Although since 1969 open, large-scale Tatar protest appears to have been effectively suppressed by the Soviet authorities, this writer has received reports, from sources he considers reliable, that some Tatars, counseled by Jewish friends in the dissent movement, have, in 1971, followed the example, set by Soviet Jews, of applying for permission to emigrate from the USSR, in their case to Turkey, as, one might surmise, a "functional equivalent" of Israel.

JEWISH ASPIRATIONS

In the whole tangled web of ideological, political, and cultural relationships involved in the Soviet "nationality problem" none are more complex, contradictory, and paradoxical than those that have shaped the destiny of Soviet Jewry. Because of such factors as the articulateness of Soviet Jews, and their links with Jews abroad, far more data on their situation are available than is the case with other Soviet ethnic groups. Roughly until the period of Stalin's bid for dictatorial power, in the mid-1930s, Soviet Jews who were ideologically committed to Marxism-Leninism and thus by implication to militant atheism, benefited perhaps more than any other ethnic or national group in the USSR, in terms of social mobility and other outcomes of the Leninist transformation of society. Partly because they prospered under Soviet rule, and for other reasons, including, in particular, the fact that unlike almost all the other minority nationalities, they lacked a territorial base, and were largely concentrated in major cities, such as Moscow, Leningrad, Kiev, and Odessa, the Jews were the nationality group most easily assimilated into the dominant Soviet Russian cultural pattern. However, their security and welfare were threatened from the mid-1930s on by powerful internal and external factors. Stalin, increasingly dependent upon a Russian-oriented concept of "Soviet patriotism" as an instrument of foreign and domestic propaganda and socialization, and involved in bitter political conflict with Trotsky and other Jewish communists, found it expedient, and perhaps congenial, to make increasing use of covert anti-semitism as an instrument of policy. After the establishment of the state of Israel, support for which the USSR regarded, for a short time, as a useful instrument against British power in the Middle East, Soviet anti-semitism became increasingly overt—though never expressly admitted—and intense. Soviet Jews, having experienced the horrors of the Nazi policy of extermination in German-occupied Soviet territories, now underwent the rigors of campaigns against their "passportlessness." They were derided as "rootless cosmopolitans," and were made victims of intimidation, harassment, arrests, and, in some instances murder, as in the case of prominent Jewish cultural figures, such as the poet Itzik Feffer and the Shakespearean actor Solomon Mikhoels. The Stalinist phase of Soviet anti-semitism culminated in January 1953 when it appeared that Stalin was planning to utilize charges that Jewish doctors had plotted against high military and civilian officials as the pretext for launching a vast new purge.

Soviet Jews, like all other Soviet citizens, benefited from the lessened reliance upon coercion as an instrument of social control that has characterized Soviet rule since Stalin's death. On the other hand, they suffered relatively more than other minorities, including other formerly "privileged" nationalities, such as the Georgians and the Armenians, within the framework of post-Stalin intensification of pressures for russification, as well as intensified anti-religious propaganda.

Finally, the adversities confronting Soviet Jews have been compounded by shock waves emanating from the Middle East, especially since the six-day war of 1967. In this new and highly unfavorable phase of their history, Soviet Jews, partly in desperation but also in a new spirit of positive affirmation of national identity, have increasingly posed demands, in particular the demand for permission to emigrate to Israel, which the Soviet political leadership regards as almost intolerable (Kochan, 1970: 321-336; Bociurkiw, 1970: 13-20; Bordeaux, 1970: 24-27). Within a few years a people deprived since World War II of almost all organizational resources for national, cultural, and religious self-expression and apparently regarded by the CPSU as "a non-territorial nationality scheduled for early assimilation" (Aspaturian, 1968: 179-180), has found itself in contention and confrontation with the Soviet state. It is of course impossible to know how many Soviet Jews would opt for emigration if they could freely choose. Many in the West find it difficult to understand why the Soviet authorities have been unwilling to permit more than a trickle of emigration, in contrast to the policy of communist Rumania, which has permitted emigration on a very substantial scale. The Soviet authorities, it must be admitted, find themselves in a painful dilemma in respect to Jews who wish to emigrate. Permission for large-scale emigration would conflict with Soviet Mid-Eastern policy and would hardly be compatible with official claims about Soviet progress, "friendship of peoples," etc. It might set a dangerous example to other non-Russians. Also, as Katz (1970) emphasizes, the Soviet Union, under conditions of intense scientific and technological rivalry with other advanced industrial nations, might be seriously weakened by the emigration of Jews, who are represented in the arts and sciences, in medicine, in education, and in other occupations in percentages far out of proportion to their weight in the total Soviet population. At the same time, however, Jews are discriminated against in such fields as political leadership, the military, the security agencies, diplomacy, and other "sensitive" areas. They are, in effect, treated as second-class citizens, to be used but not trusted.

The plight of Jews in the USSR may be illustrated by the fate of Boris Kochubiyevsky. In December 1968, Kochubiyevsky, a young Soviet Jewish engineer who had, incidentally, married a Ukrainian girl, was arrested and charged with disseminating "anti-Soviet slander." The apparent reasons for his arrest were his stubborn refusal to support the official Soviet position, condemning "Israeli aggression" in the 1967 war, and his application for himself and his wife to emigrate to Israel. In May 1969, Kochubiyevsky was sentenced to three years in a labor camp. In the meantime, his wife had been expelled from the Pedagogical Institute where she was studying and had been pressured to divorce him, which she refused to do. In May 1968, Kochubiyevsky had written an essay, entitled "Why I Am a Zionist." A few weeks before he was arrested he addressed a letter to Leonid Brezhnev and to the First Secretary of the Ukrainian Communist Party, Petr Shelest, requesting permission to leave for Israel and presenting arguments in support of this request. In the first of these documents, Kochubiyevsky asked the rhetorical question

"Why is it that the most active sector of Jewish youth, raised and educated in the USSR, still retains a feeling of Jewish national unity and national identity? How is it possible that Jewish boys and girls who know nothing about Jewish culture and language, who are mostly atheists, continue to feel so acutely and be so proud of their national affiliation?

"The answer is simple: Thanks for that, in large measure, can be given to anti-semitism—the new brand which was implanted from above and, as a means of camouflage, is called anti-Zionism; and the old anti-semitism which is still alive among the more backward sectors of Soviet society. It is precisely this anti-Zionism and anti-semitism which prevents us from relaxing and welds us closer together."

Continuing, Kochubiyevsky referred to discrimination against the Jews, "in the absence of Jewish schools, in religious persecution, when looking for jobs or applying to institutes of higher learning." Turning then to criticism of other aspects of Soviet policy, particularly "assistance provided by the government of the USSR to the Arab Fascist fanatics," Kochubiyevsky concluded his essay by asserting that "the Jews no longer are the mute, disunited and cowed creaters of the past whom one could abuse with impunity, but individuals . . . who are strong." He stated further that "More and more Jews are coming to understand that endless silence and patience—leads straight down the road to Auschwitz."
Kochubiyevsky began the above-mentioned letter as follows:

"I am a Jew. I want to live in the Jewish state. This is my right, just as it is the right of a Ukrainian to live in the Ukraine, the right of a Russian to live in Russia, the right of a Georgian to live in Georgia."

He followed up these statements with arguments similar to those contained in his essay. For example (Decter, 1970; Brumberg, 1970), he asked how he could be accused of "slandering Soviet reality," when there were no Jewish theatres or Jewish newspapers in the USSR and when in the multi-national Soviet state only the Jewish people could not educate its children in Jewish schools. [4]

THE SIGNIFICANCE OF NATIONALITY DISSENT

Is protest against the CPSU's nationality policies merely a reflection of narrow, parochial national sentiments? Is it true, as CPSU propaganda seems to say, that non-Russian national identity and national pride are prejudices inherited from the "bourgeois" past? Do the non-Russians have in common only animosity toward the Great Russians? To what extent does the Soviet regime rely upon the exploitation of nationalist attitudes, especially Great Russian chauvinism and anti-semitism, as a psychological resource, and can it continue to do so? Upon the answers to such questions depends, in large part, one's estimate of possible future developments in relations among the national components of the present Soviet multi-national state and perhaps of the future viability of that state.

Not surprisingly, the writings of Soviet dissenters (Chornovil Papers, 1968: 222-226; Dzyuba, 1968: 27, 62-63, 101-102; Sakharov, 1968: 50, 53-54, 66) provide somewhat contradictory responses to such questions. On the one hand, the testimony not only of embattled Soviet Jews but also of the Ukrainian Dzyuba and the Russian Sakharov deplores the widespread persistence among Great Russians and Ukrainians of anti-semitism and other nationalistic prejudices. It is probably true that "Old animosities between nationalities remain psychologically dominant in the masses of the people" in the USSR (Boiter, 1970: 10). On the other hand, there is much evidence that, among both non-Russian and Russian participants in the "democratic movement," particularistic traditionalism in the perception of nationality relationships has been transcended. There seems to be a growing appreciation of the compatibility of universal democratic values and cultural pluralism. Moreover, there also seems to be a growing tendency to acceptance of the idea that freedom and autonomy for one people require freedom and autonomy for all. Solidarity of sentiments and coordination of actions seem to be replacing isolation among representatives of the Russian and non-Russian democratically oriented intellectuals. Thus we find Ukrainian General Grigorenko championing the rights of the Crimean Tatars. The appeal to the United Nations sent by fifty-two members of the "Initiative Group for the Defense of Civil Rights in the USSR" included the trial and sentence of Kochubiyevski among the violations of such rights which it protested. The Chronicle of Current Events frequently reports instances of cooperation among members of diverse national and religious groups. A few hours before his arrest in 1969 for protesting the trials of dissident intellectuals, the Pole Ivan Yakhimovich, former chairman of a collective farm in Latvia, wrote a letter in which, inter alia, he addressed himself to Poles, and to "Latvians, whose land has become my homeland, whose language I know as I know Polish and Russian. Do not forget that in the labor camps of Mordovia and Siberia are thousands of your fellow countrymen! Demand their return to Latvia. Watch carefully the fate of everyone deprived of freedom for political reasons." Yakhimovich thus called attention to the solidarity of interests of the various peoples of the USSR and at the same time linked national values to general democratic values (New York Times, 1969).

In addition to Sakharov's *Progress, Coexistence and Intellectual Freedom,* to which references have been made, other major "programmatic" dissent documents of recent years have included criticisms of established Soviet nationality policy and, in some cases, demands for alternative policies. Thus the "Reply of the Estonian Technical Intelligentsia to the Brochure of Academician Sakharov," published in the West in the Frankfurter Allgemeine Zeitung first contained a demand for the "just regulation of the nationality problem and the granting of the right of peoples to sovereign, independent State existence." The

"Program of the Democratic Movement of the Soviet Union," released by "Democrats of Russia, the Ukraine, and the Baltic Area," in 1969, dealt at considerable length with "national discrimination," in connection with which it referred to mistreatment of the Crimean Tatars, the Chechens, the Ingush, the Kalmyks, the Volga Germans, a "suspicious attitude" toward the peoples of the Baltic area, and also "Ukrainophobia" and anti-semitism. Among other things, this document *(Programma demokraticheskogo dvizheniya sovetskogo soyuza,* 1970) asserted that the Soviet Union was the "greatest colonial power" and it recommended that self-determination of the nations of the Soviet Union be assured by a referendum conducted under the auspices of the United Nations. The letter addressed in March 1970 by academician Sakharov, the physicist V. Turchin, and the historian R. Medvedev, recommended abolition of the requirement that an individual's nationality be entered in internal passports and questionnaires, and demanded the gradual elimination of the entire internal passport regime. It also demanded the restoration of the rights of all nations forcibly resettled by Stalin, as well as of their national autonomy, and facilitation of their return to their homeland.

What trends or future projections do Soviet dissenters who have studied nationality problems perceive? The young Soviet historian and essayist, Andrei Amalrik, sentenced in September 1970 to three years in a labor camp for alleged slander against the Soviet state, has given us a startling prognosis regarding the future development of nationality relations in the USSR. His essay, "Will the Soviet Union Survive until 1984?" predicts that, at the beginning of the Soviet-Chinese war that he forecasts, there will be a flare-up of Russian nationalism but that as the war progresses "Russian nationalism will decline while non-Russian nationalism will rise." He foresees that, as difficulties connected with the war with China mount, "The nationalist tendencies of the non-Russian peoples of the Soviet Union will intensify sharply, first in the Baltic area, the Caucasus and the Ukraine, then in Central Asia and along the Volga." The most positive of the outcomes of this situation would be the creation of a federation, "similar to the British Commonwealth or the European economic community," but it is also possible that the USSR "will begin to disintegrate into anarchy, violence and intense national hatred."

Sakharov, both in his 1968 analysis and in his later program (Sakharov et al; 1970: 21-22) warned that unless the regime overcame its rigidity and conservatism and carried out fundamental reforms, there would be "a sharpening of national problems, for in the national republics the movement for democratization, surging up from below, inevitably takes on a nationalistic character. This perspective becomes especially threatening, if account is taken of the danger of Chinese totalitarian nationalism (which in historical perspective we regard as temporary, but very serious in the next few years)." Thus the prognostication of Sakharov and his colleagues resembles that of Amalrik.

Myhaylo Masyutko, one of the most severely punished victims of the purge of Ukrainian intellectuals in 1965, wrote (Chornovil Papers, 1968: 145-147) that "The experience of the times of Stalin's personality cult has shown that the use of suppression to cover up social deficiencies leads to antagonism between the government and the people, because behind every groundlessly condemned individual stand not only scores of his relatives and friends, but also the weight of opinion of the entire public." He added that if the authorities continued to imprison people whose sole offense consisted of thinking regarded by them as objectionable, the desire to defend the Soviet rule would "turn into its antithesis," and there would be "an anti-Soviet agitation such as no enemy of Soviet rule could devise."

How seriously should the futurological speculations in this sphere of Amalrik, Sakharov, and other leading Soviet dissenters be taken? There are good grounds for thinking that these prognostications must be taken quite seriously, even though it is probable that the Soviet authorities may by the use of massive coercion be able to successfully continue for a long time to contain the disintegrating pressures of national discontent. Even if they can do so, they may only succeed in postponing the adoption of policies which if undertaken in time and with good will might enhance both the domestic morale and the international image of the USSR. In the sphere of nationality relations, as in other areas to which the "democratic movement" addresses itself the costs of a lack of responsiveness on the part of the regime may be high. Such a surmise seems warranted, on the basis of evidence both of growth of the dissent movement as a whole, indicated by reports of widening dissemination of samizdat literature and in particular by the increasing tension between the Soviet regime and the Jewish community of the USSR.

It must, of course, be recognized that in the sphere of nationality policy the Soviet leadership confronts difficult choices. For example, Moscow may well perceive a clash between concessions to the non-Russians in language policy and its goals of maximizing efficiency in public administration and economic development. It may also see a conflict between state security and increased political autonomy for national sub-groups. It may fear that the free and open discussion of national questions demanded by men like Dzyuba would only encourage disintegrative tendencies. Like other rulers of multi-national polities, past and present, the men in the Kremlin face the dilemma between suppression of national aspirations, leading to increased alienation and possible conspiracy and rebellion and reforms which might only encourage their beneficiaries to pose further demands, perhaps incompatible with continued Moscow control over lands and peoples regarded by the central political authorities as necessary for the survival of the Soviet state. The Soviet rulers' ability to skillfully reconcile conflicting demands appears to be limited by extreme rigidity, shaped by the despotic and overbearing Russian political culture. This tradition seems to exert a particularly baneful influence on Soviet official attitudes toward the Jewish problem, which could, one would think, be considerably alleviated if Moscow were willing to permit greatly expanded emigration and at the same time to allocate greater resources for Jewish cultural facilities. But, of course, in connection with the question of Jewish emigration whatever impulses of rationality actuate Kremlin policy makers would appear to clash with the "messianism" and excessive ambition attributed by Sakharov, Turchin, and Medvedev to Soviet foreign policy, for reasonableness on this issue is scarcely compatible with an expansionist policy in the Middle East.

NOTES

1. Lowell Tillett, in *The Great Friendship*, has delineated the development of Soviet nationality doctrine in the field of historiography; on the exceptional ferocity with which

Stalin's purges were conducted in the non-Russian Soviet republics, see Zbigniew K. Brzezinski (n.d.), and Robert Conquest (1968). For attempts at systematic analysis of the nationality factor in overall Soviet political development, see Frederick C. Barghoorn (1956), and Vernon V. Aspaturian (n.d.).

2. The Chornovil Papers were published under the auspices of the Ukrainian National Federation of Canada, with foreword by Zbigniew K. Brzezinski and introduction by Frederick C. Barghoorn.

3. Dzyuba's book, published in London, has an introduction by Peter Archer, M.P., and was edited by M. Davies. Neither it nor Chornovil's book could be legally published in the USSR, although some copies of Dzyuba's book were circulated, for discussion and information purposes, at upper levels of the Ukrainian organization of the CPSU.

4. Much of the evidence available on the political attitudes of Soviet Jews indicates that many Soviet Jews, especially young ones, have ceased to be "Jews of Silence" and have begun to stand up vigorously for their rights as Jews and as free men. Much of the available evidence also supports the view that the new Jewish group consciousness is, as Kochubiyevski maintained, a reaction against discriminatory official Soviet policy. This writer has heard from sources he considers reliable of such incidents as vigorous resistance offered by Jews in Moscow in the fall of 1970 to KGB efforts to break up a throng of thousands of Jewish celebtants gathered at the central synagogue and of telephone calls placed by Moscow Jews to the Israeli Mission to the United Nations in New York.

REFERENCES

AMALRIK, A. (1971) Will the Soviet Union Survive until 1984? New York: Harper & Row.
ANONYMOUS, (1971) "The trial of Valentyn Moroz." Chronicle of Current Events (April): 41-43.
――― (1971) "Trials of recent years." Chronicle of Current Events (April): 64-66.
――― "A chronicle of resistance." Ukrainian Q. (1971): 13-37.
ASPATURIAN, V. (1968) "The non-Russian nationalities," pp. 143-200 in A. Kassof (ed.) Prospects for Soviet Society. New York: Praeger.
――― (n.d.) "The non-Russian republics."
BARGHOORN, F. C. (1968) Introduction. Chornovil Papers. Toronto: McGraw-Hill.
――― (1956) Soviet Russian Nationalism. Cambridge: Oxford Univ. Press.
BOCIURKIW, B. (1970) "Soviet religious policy and the status of Judaism in the USSR." Bull. on Soviet and East European Jewish Affairs 6 (December): 13-20.
BOITER, A. (1970) "The Hutsuls: tribulations of a national culture in the USSR." New York: Radio Liberty Dispatch (October 22); 4, 10.
BOURDEAUX, M. (1970) "Religious Minorities in the Soviet Union." Minority Rights Group (December)' London: 24-27.
BRUMBERG, A. (1970) "Russia creating Zionists." Washington Post (June 28).
BRZEZINSKI, Z. K. (1968) Foreword. Chornovil Papers, Toronto: McGraw-Hill.
――― (n.d.) The Permanent Purge.
Chornovil Papers (1968) Toronto: McGraw-Hill.
Chronicle of Current Events. London, England: Amnesty International.
CONQUEST, R. (1968) The Great Terror. New York: Macmillan.
DECTER, M. [ed.] (1970) "A Hero for Our Time"; "Redemption! Redemption! Redemption!" New York: Academic Committee for Soviet Jewry.
DZYUBA, I. (1968) Internationalism or Russification? London: Weidenfeld & Nicolson.
KAMMARI, M. D. (1963) Foreword, in K. Kh. Khonozarov, Sblizhenie natsii i natsional'nye yazyki v sssr (Coming Together of Nations and National Languages in USSR). Tashkent.
KATZ, Z. (1970) "After the six-day war," pp. 321-336 in L. Kochan (ed.) The Jews in Soviet Russia since 1917. London: Oxford Univ. Press.
KHONOZAROV, K. Kh. (1963) Sblizhenie natsii i natsional'nye yazyki v sssr (Coming Together of Nations and National Languages in USSR). Tashkent.
KIRIMAL, E. (1970) "The Crimean Tatars." Studies on the Soviet Union 10 (January), Munich: 70-97.
KOCHAN, L. [ed.] (1970) The Jews in Soviet Russia Since 1917. London: Oxford Univ. Press.

KOLASKY, J. (1970) Two Years in Soviet Ukraine. Toronto: Peter Martin Associates.
MAISTRENKO, I. [ed.] (1968) Ukrainski yuristi pid sudom KGB (Ukrainian Jurists Tried by the KGB). Introduction. Munich.
New York Times, 1969 (April 13).
Programma Demokraticheskogo Dvizheniya Sovetskogo Soyuza (1970). Amsterdam: Alexander Herzen Foundation.
Radio Free Europe Research Report (July 16, 1968). "The discussion on 'Sobor' spreads further afield." Radio Free Europe, New York.
Radio Liberty [Radio Svoboda] (1971) "Oles Gonchar smeschen s posta predsedatelya pravleniya soyuza pisatelei ukrainy" ("Oles Honchar Removed as President of Union of Writers of Ukraine") No. 177/71. Radio Liberty Committee, New York.
SAKHAROV, A., P. TURCHIN, and R. MEDVEDEV (1970) Po voprosu, imeyushchemu bolshoe znachenie. Torino, Italy.
SAKHAROV, A. (1968) Progress, Coexistence and Intellectual Freedom. Introduction, Afterword and Notes by H. Salisbury. New York: W. W. Norton.
TILLETT, L. (1969) The Great Friendship. Chapel Hill, N.C.: Univ. of North Carolina Press.
The Times (1971). London, England (February 17).
Ukrainian Quarterly (Spring 1971) 27: 109; 28: 13. New York.

Chapter 10

STATUS DIFFERENCES AND ETHNIC CONFLICT: RWANDA AND BURUNDI

RENE LEMARCHAND

*T*he aim of this paper is to arrive at testable generalizations about untestable pheonomena on the basis of limited empirical evidence drawn from two notoriously deviant cases. This is not meant as an apology for what some might regard as an unwarranted predilection for political pathologies, but to specify at the outset the limits of this discussion.

Although the countries selected for analysis present enough similarities from the standpoint of their stratification systems to make the task of controlled comparison between them both feasible and meaningful, the very nature of these similarities significantly reduces their comparability with other African states. Rwanda and Burundi exemplify those relatively rare situations in tropical Africa where the "differential incorporation" of ethnic segments within a single political unit becomes the hallmark of the stratification system as well as the key criterion for the exercise of authority (Kuper and Smith, 1969: 473). Both shared the formal attributes of caste societies (i.e., of societies made up of predominantly endogamous, hierarchically organized groups with a relatively high degree of occupational specialization), and ultimate control over the allocation of political resources was in each case the privilege of a culturally or ethnically differentiated minority. Each state thus exhibited in its most extreme forms the characteristics of the "plural society" analyzed by M. G. Smith (1965).

Rwanda and Burundi are not only conspicuously "deviant" cases but among the most disconcerting candidates for analyzing the etiology of ethnic strife in contemporary Africa. For if both have experienced ethnic violence, the timing, scale, and outcome of violence were in each case very different. Ethnic violence in Rwanda occurred not only at a much earlier point in time than in Burundi, but on a far more devastating scale. The reversal of traditional statuses effected through the impact of modernity unleashed a revolutionary upheaval for which there is as yet no parallel in Burundi. Whereas in Rwanda this upheaval resulted in the enthronement of lower-caste elements, in Burundi the result of ethnic confrontations has been precisely the opposite.

Given the very different implications of what appears on surface to be a fundamentally similar type of stratification system, the question arises as to whether there is any point in focusing upon status differences as an independent variable for explaining the contrasting responses of their ethnic segments to political modernization. Nor are the inferences to be drawn from available indices of social and economic modernization all that illuminating. One may note in this connection the extreme deviations they offer, jointly or individually, from most predictive models of ethnic or civil strife. Matched against the findings of recent statistical analysis of civil strife, Rwanda and Burundi far exceed the usual range of standard deviations (see, e.g.; Gurr and Ruttenberg, 1967: 100-106).[1] Finally, many of the theoretical explanations of ethnic violence which seem applicable to one state appear invalidated by the data obtainable from the other. Thus if "conflict pluralism" provides a reasonably sound explanation for ethnic violence in Rwanda, its explanatory power is obviously much weaker when applied to Burundi; if the notion of "class conflict" is at all applicable to Rwanda one wonders why apparently similar conditions did not produce similar results in Burundi; alternatively, if the lower incidence of violence experience by Burundi can be attributed to the stabilizing properties of the functional reciprocities of the caste system, one is impelled to wonder why these compensating mechanisms did not come into play in Rwanda.

One obvious way out of this thicket is to start from the assumption that even though both societies exhibited the same *generic* type of stratification system, they each exhibited different forms and levels of differentiation. Here the problem is not only one of descriptive analysis but one of interpretation and evaluation: on the basis of what criteria can one best evaluate status discrepancies within each society? How much weight should one give to any of these criteria to explain the different degrees of vulnerability of their social systems to ethnic strife?

Before providing tentative answers to these questions, let me begin with a brief sketch of the premises from which I start.

SOME PRELIMINARY ASSUMPTIONS

A basic assumption underlying this discussion is that ethnic conflict is as much a reflection of objective status differences—whether defined in terms of class, caste or ethnicity—as a consequence of the perceived status transformations it tends to generate among the protagonists. Hence no satisfactory attempt at understanding the roots of ethnic conflict in either society can be made unless one is prepared to treat status differences both as a dependent and an independent variable. Rather than asking ourselves what type of status difference is most likely to generate ethnic conflict, a more relevant question is: what type of conflict is most likely to engender polarization of status differences along ethnic lines?

Implicit in this assumption is the existence of dialectical process between intergroup differentiation and intergroup conflict, each interacting with the other in such a way as to produce shifting pattern of identifications, in turn leading to a displacement of conflict from one segment of society to another.

Another point implicit in what we just said is that status solidarities can be activated at many different levels depending on how the protagonists happen to define the boundaries of conflict. (for a somewhat similar argument, see Anderson et al., 1965). Our main assumption here is that in Rwanda as in Burundi the boundaries of ethnic conflict were defined primarily through subjective reinterpretations of status differences which at first bore little relation to the "objective" realties of either society. This is not meant to suggest that perceptions of ethnic identities were unrelated to conditions of ethnic pluralism. All we intend to suggest is that in each case the framework of subjective meanings attached to intergroup conflict has tended to arbitrarily reify a particular indicator of status (ethnicity) at the expense of all other criteria of differentiation.

Nor is this element of subjectivity limited to the perceptions which individual actors may have of themselves. It also has a direct bearing upon the observer's own "motivational understanding" of any given conflict situation (for further elaboration of the concept, see Schutz, 1967: 25). How one deals with the analysis of ethnic conflict depends on how one chooses to define the context in which ethnic conflict takes place; or, to put it somewhat differently, the explanation one may offer of any given conflict depends on how one defines the actors in the drama as well as their relationships with each other. Just as conflict often originates in the consciousness of the protagonists, explanations of conflict are likely to reflect the analyst's own conception of the social structure (Kuper, 1970). Whether originating in the minds of political factors or in the biases or prejudices of outside observers, subjective definitions of status differences may be just as instrumental in stimulating ethnic conflict as the objective conditions with which such differences tend to be associated.

INDICATORS OF STATUS DISCREPANCIES: CASTE, CLASS, AND ETHNICITY

The standard image conveyed by much of the literature of Rwanda and Burundi is that of a hierarchical order in which cleavages of caste, class, and ethnicity were generally consistent and cumulative. According to this view in each state a dominant Tutsi minority held sway over the subordinate Hutu majority, with the numerically and politically marginal Twa relegated to the very bottom of the heap. Insofar as each of these categories was assigned a specific economic role, and to the extent that different social rankings and privileges inhered in these roles, one might conceivably argue that in each society ethnic differences tended to coincide with caste and class differences.

Although criteria of caste, class, and ethnicity may help us achieve an "objective" understanding of status differences, these categories seem far too general or ethnocentric to do justice to the empirical realities of stratificatory phenomena in Rwanda and Burundi.

Because cleavages of caste and class were somehow more "visible" and analytically manageable than the narrower differentiations arising from intra-caste (or intra-class) cleavages, the latter have received relatively little attention from social scientists. Yet if one accepts Weber's definition of status, as "the way in which social honor is distributed in a community" (Gerth and Mills, 1958: 181), one must also include as possible indicators of status such differences as were traditionally associated with the positions of chief and sub-chief, chief and subject, patron and client; with membership in particular clans or kinship groups; or with cultural or residential ties. Quite aside from the distortions involved in the use of such simplified labels as "Hutu-Tutsi," "pastoralists-agriculturalists," and "upper-caste" and "lower-caste" elements, the very multiplicity of status differences in existence in each society correspondingly increases the potential margin of error involved in our assessment of any particular conflict situation. What may seem on surface to be an opposition of interests between different castes or classes, may in fact express a very different type of opposition.

In addition to the multiplicity of criteria by which one might evaluate status differences, another problem concerns their mutability. As Berreman (1967: 359) recently argued, "a social hierarchy is continually redefined, affirmed, challenged and validated by interaction, even as interaction is continually constrained by the hierarchy." This is true not only of the narrower differentiations we just noted but of the more inclusive ones as well. What may be regarded at a particular point in time as a reasonably valid indicator of status discrepancies may no longer be so at a subsequent stage. Because the boundaries of caste, class, and ethnicity are so indeterminate, both spatially and temporally, they can only provide us with provisional identification tags for defining social reality.

Moreover, the stratificatory phenomena to which they refer may be apprehended from widely different angles depending on how one wishes to define class, caste, and ethnicity. Just as ethnicity has in recent times been used to designate different levels of identity, caste may be used to refer to very different degrees of separateness among groups. Even more ambiguous are the connotations and criteria attached to the concept of "class." Should the term be used to refer to a traditional form of inferior-superior relationships rooted in economic role specialization, as between pastoralists and agriculturalists? Should it be reserved to designate an incipient opposition of interests between the relatively wealthy and educated elites on the one hand and the peasant masses on the other? Or should the main criterion be the degree of collective self-consciousness displayed by a particular socioeconomic category in relation to another? In the absence of definitive answers to these questions the problem of separating status differences along sharp and well-defined boundaries becomes all the more vexing.

The crux of the problem is summed up in Apter's (1970: 222) lament that "our analytical categories are too general when they are theoretical, and too descriptive where they are not." Not only too general, but in this case too static and ethnocentric. A possible escape from this dilemma is to recognize that the loss of descriptive accuracy involved in the use of some of these categories is partially made up by the heuristic value they offer from the standpoint of comparative analysis.

The argument may be summarized by reformulating and extending the concepts of class, caste and ethnicity along the following lines:

(1) Insofar as they connote different orderings of relationships among ethnic groups, the concepts of caste and ethnicity point to a major variation in the structure of intergroup differentiations between Rwanda and Burundi. Of special relevance here is the distinction drawn by Weber (Gerth and Mills, 1958: 189) between "caste structure" and "ethnic coexistence," a distinction analogous to that recently drawn by Horowitz (1971: 232 ff.) between "horizontal" and "vertical" ethnic differentiation. Although both states shared the characteristics of a "caste structure," involving, according to Weber, "the transformation of ethnically segregated groups into a vertical social system of super- and subordination" (Gerth and Mills, 1958: 181, 189), on the eve of the European penetration this transformation had been achieved on a significantly broader scale in Burundi than in Rwanda. In Rwanda the incompleteness of this transformation resulted in a structural bifurcation along "vertical" and "horizontal" lines, so that elements of "caste" and "ethnicity" tended to coexist within the same political unit. In Burundi by contrast the inclusiveness of the caste system left virtually no room for ethnic coexistences. The potential for ethnic conflict originating from conditions of "mutual repulsion and

disdain"—as opposed to the conditions of functional integration characteristic of the caste structure—was therefore comparatively higher in Rwanda than in Burundi.

(2) Another axis of differentiation concerns the span and shape of their respective caste structures. By "span" is meant the degree of social distance discernible among the constitutent ethnic segments of each society; "shape" refers to the levels of differentiation between the upper and lower echelons of the social pyramid. On the basis of these criteria the social structure of Burundi was not only more flexible but infinitely more variegated that that of Rwanda. The caste structure of Burundi incorporated a variety of social rankings for which there was no counterpart in Rwanda—as between (1) princely and non-princely families, (2) "low-caste" Tutsi-Hima and "upper-caste" Tutsi-Banyaruguru, (3) prestigious and less prestigious lineage affiliations within the latter category as well as within the Hutu stratum. Unlike the Rwanda pattern, where social and ethnic differentiations tended to cluster, the "pecking order" of Burundi society suggests a far greater complexity of social rankings. The absence of a clear-cut relationship between ethnic and social differentiation tended to diminish the social distance between ethnic segments to an extent unparalleled in Rwanda.

(3) Although the concept of class in the Marxist sense has little explanatory power in the context of this discussion, once reformulated along the lines suggested by Dahrendorf (1959: 139) its descriptive connotations may help us understand yet another difference between Rwanda and Burundi. If one starts from the assumption that "classes are neither primarily nor at all economic groupings," but involve "participation in the exercise of authority," only in Rwanda can it be argued that the Tutsi stratum shared the characteristics of a class; even so, only a small fraction of this stratum would then qualify as a class. There was no counterpart in Burundi for the degree of control exercised over political institutions by the Tutsi in Rwanda. Political institutions in Burundi were the monopoly of princely families, collectively referred to as *ganwa*. What Huntington (1968: 20) refers to as the "autonomy" of a society's political institutions thus points to a major difference between Rwanda and Burundi: in questioning Tutsi supremacy, the Hutu of Rwanda questioned not only the social and economic supremacy of a particular caste but its political supremacy; in Burundi, by contrast, opposition to ganwa rule tended to invite a strengthening of political solidarities between Hutu and Tutsi.

(4) A fourth criterion of differentiation concerns the degree of institutionalization of stratificatory norms. Lacking the pervasiveness of the "premise of inequality" which characterized Rwanda society, Burundi was distinctly more tolerant of deviations from institutionalized norms. The official "image" of the stratification system was far less clearly articulated than in Rwanda, and the "culturally elaborated image of the 'admirable man' " far more difficult to pin down (Fallers, 1963: 162).

On the basis of the foregoing, a convincing case could be made for the view that the Rwanda system of stratification was on the whole more vulnerable to the destabilizing consequences of modernity than that of Burundi: the higher degree of discontinuity and hierarchization among strata, the higher congruence of social and ethnic cleavages, the greater pervasiveness of the "premise of inequality," can all be cited as evidence in support of this contention. Whether defined in terms of literacy, urbanization, diffusion of communication media, or social mobilization, modernization engenders new aspirations, and where these aspirations are consistently thwarted by the constraints of the stratification system (as was so evidently the case in Rwanda), the potential for revolutionary strife becomes all the more threatening.

A major difficulty with this line of argumentation is that the one society (Burundi) which experienced the lowest incidence of violence is also the one where the impact of modernization was the most widely felt; another is that even if modernization were taken as a constant variable, that one society exhibited a higher potential for ethnic conflict than the other leaves unanswered the question of how this potential was actually converted into ethnic violence. This question can best be answered by reversing the postulates of conventional wisdom. Rather than asking ourselves why a revolution did not occur in Burundi, a more pertinent question is: why did Rwanda experience a revolution in the first place?

OBJECTIVE VERSUS SUBJECTIVE
CORRELATES OF ETHNIC STRIFE

Just as "ethnic conflict" has often been used as an all-inclusive label to designate very different forms of opposition, explanations of conflict have tended to reduce a variety of social forces to a single common denominator.

In the case of Rwanda this reductionist bias has generally taken the form of caste- or class-centered explanations, the former emphasizing the disruptive effect of modernization and nationalism on the caste structure, and the latter the potential for conflict inherent in the exploitive relationship between a dominant and a subordinate class. "Wherever caste organization occurs," according to Berreman (1967: 365), "it is acutely jeopardized by modernization and nationalism." The assumption is that "caste systems are held together by power, concentrated in certain groups." Under the impetus of modernization and nationalism, however, "there is unprecedented pressure for and the means to cultural homogeneity; the direction is toward conformity, consensus and the 'replication' of uniformity in place of the traditional pluralism or cultural diversity." In short, modernization and nationalism imply consensus and homogeneity, whereas caste systems are "systems of cultural pluralism maintained by enforced differential association."

According to this view ethnic violence in Rwanda expressed the attempt of the Hutu majority to substitute a consensual and ethnically homogenous order for a system based on enforced differential association, or, to quote from Helen Codere (1962: 63) "an attempt on the part of the majority to achieve a social and political order based on consent."

Class-centered explanations, on the other hand, emphasize the economic contradiction inherent in the traditional ordering of relationships between Hutu and Tutsi. Reduced to its simplest expression, the argument runs as follows: Hutu-Tutsi relationships involved the systematic exploitation of the peasant masses by their Tutsi overlords through corvée labor, taxes, and prestations; given the nature of this relationship the Hutu and Tutsi strata can be regarded, in Maquet's (1964: 557) words, as authentic social classes; with the emergence of an educated Hutu elite a conscious effort was made to instill a consciousness of their inferior economic status and numerical strength among the peasant masses, culminating in a genuine class struggle between haves and have nots.

Each of these interpretations is derived from a tautological model of Rwanda society. Since the nature of the conflicting groups as well as the character of the opposition between them is specified in advance by the postulates of the model, the root cause of ethnic conflict is in each case foreordained.

By way of a corrective to the nomalist or determinist biases inherent in this approach, the following points are worth bearing in mind:

(1) The reduction of ethnic antagonisms to caste antagonism is doubly objectionable. Besides making unduly short shrift of the dimension of horizontal differentiation (or "ethnic coexistence") noted earlier, the vertical solidarities associated with dyadic ties of the patron-client variety are totally left out of the picture. Against the view that caste systems are based on "the concentration of power in certain groups" (Berreman, 1967: 365), one might usefully stress the merits of the "conservative thesis," with its emphasis on the cohesive, consensual aspects of inter-caste relationships. It is not a matter of pure coincidence that those areas which proved the least susceptible to the ferment of ethnic strife were also those where the caste structure had been longest in existence.

(2) Assumptions of class antagonisms, on the other hand, grossly exaggerate the extent to which the Hutu as a group had become conscious of their class interests, i.e., of their differential access to social and economic rewards. To argue that a segment of the Hutu community, through its exposure to modern socioeconomic forces, had become aware of its interest as a class is by no means the same as to argue that the Hutu as a group were "class conscious." Not only did the Hutu fail to evince a "class consciousness" in the Marxist sense, but also the processes of restratification which had taken place within the Hutu stratum as a result of its exposure to modernization make it equally difficult to identify the Hutu as a group with an "objective" social class. In short, and to borrow Marx's dichotomy, the Hutu failed to qualify either as an *"an sich"* or *"fur sich"* class.

(3) Even if it could be shown that caste or class antagonism did occur at one point between segments of the Hutu and Tutsi communities, the mere presence of such antagonisms would not suffice to detect the roots of ethnic conflict. Cleavages of caste or class are by no means the only empirical referents from which ethnic antagonisms might be inferred. At best these cleavages point to different stages and levels of activation; at worst they may conceal the implications of cultural, regional, or political cleavages and thus mask the initial directional tendencies of ethnic conflict.

In short, there is no self-evident correlation between any particular characteristic of the stratification system and the crystallization of ethnic antagonisms. Just as the boundaries of conflict have tended to shift from one geographical or political arena to the next depending on the nature of the political resources made available at any given time, status self-perceptions have been activated at different levels at different points in time. Ethnic self-perceptions were not activated overnight, but as a result of "perceived similarities among the subgroups taken together vis-à-vis the other groups they confronted in society" (Horowitz, 1971: 239). Ethnic conflict in this sense may be seen as the ultimate phase of a process of interaction which gradually moved from the stage of sectional or parochial oppositions to that of a nationwide, ethnically centered confrontation.

A convenient starting point for analyzing the dynamics of ethnic conflict is offered by the distinction drawn earlier between "caste structure" and "ethnic coexistence." Much of the evidence available supports Horowitz's (1971: 232) contention that in situations of "ethnic coexistence" ethnic conflict rarely aims at a drastic transformation of the established social order but "at the exclusion of other parallel groups from power." Whatever incompatibility of interests may exist among the protagonists does not necessarily imply incompatibility of institutionalized norms. In situations of vertical differentiations, by contrast, the internal dynamics of ethnic strife tend to reflect a conscious attempt at reversing the hierarchical basis for intergroup relationships. The aim is not merely to substitute one category of incumbents for another but to operate a fundamental restructuring of society. In this case ethnic conflict inevitably takes on the characteristics of social revolution.

This generalization gives us an important clue to an understanding of the sources of discontent involved in the intial stages of the Hutu-Tutsi conflict. Nonetheless, several qualifications are in order. One is that the situation of ethnic coexistence prevailing in the north did not simply involve the juxtaposition of two sharply differentiated ethnic groups conventionally labeled "Hutu" and "Tutsi." Ethnic coexistence was also a characteristic feature of group differentiation among non-Tutsi elements. Only through a process of ethnic redefinition were non-Tutsi elements able to perceive themselves as members of the Hutu stratum. Until this happened status self-perceptions were generally oriented toward clan or regional affiliations. Nor was this process of ethnic redefinition achieved overnight. Contrary to what is generally assumed, the introduction of electoral processes in the north was accompanied by an extraordinary fragmentation of "ethnic" self-perceptions among non-Tutsi elements.

Another qualification concerns the limitations placed on the development of revolutionary activity in areas where the "caste structure" prevailed over "ethnic coexistence." We have already noted the added cohesiveness imparted to the caste system by the existence of patron-client ties. Another source of cohesion stemmed from the very limited incidence of non-institutionalized mobility among Hutu elements, a fact which also tended to limit the range of "status incongruencies" among lower caste elements. "Mobility," writes Germani (1964: 371) "has its most disruptive effects on the social order when it is non-institutionalized mobility and when there is an imbalance between aspirations and actual chances of mobility. . . . Non-institutionalized mobility by definition introduces status incongruencies. It involves opening some dimensions while the dominant norms and values (or at least the norms and values of the dominant groups) remain geared to the requirements of the previous structure. . . . This situation is a powerful source of social tension because the groups involved tend to reequilibrate their status." To put it in somewhat different terms, the wider the gap between subjective and objective status, and the greater the obstacles in the way of a peaceful adjustment of status, the greater the chances of a violent social upheaval (Lemarchand, 1966). What Germani refers to as "status incongruencies," and what others might describe as a disjunction between "objective" and "subjective" statuses, is certainly a key factor in the background of the Rwanda revolution. What must also be stressed is that on the eve of the revolution only a tiny fraction of the Hutu community had achieved enough social mobility to experience this kind of disequilibrium. In these conditions mobility can scarcely be regarded as the only motive force behind the development of nationwide ethnic antagonisms.

Which brings us to the critical issue: how do we pass from a situation of limited ethnic interaction, characterized by different types of oppositions to one of generalized and violent ethnic strife? Following up Coser's (1968: 53 ff.) insights into the "social functions of violence", the Jacquerie of November 1959 suggests at least one possible answer. Not only did it shift the locus of interaction between Hutu and Tutsi from a parochial to a national level, but also the quotient of violence involved in the peasant uprising fostered a new sense of solidarity among non-Tutsi elements. As ethnic violence gathered momentum status self-perceptions came to reflect a dichotomous conception of ethnic similarities and dissimilarities, thereby enhancing the chances of further ethnic violence. Ethnic conflict was the cause as well as the symptom of a restructuring of status perceptions along ethnic lines.

The explanation is not so much erroneous as it is incomplete. One crucial omission concerns the role of the trust authorities during and after the peasant uprisings of November 1959. By no stretch of the imagination can these uprisings be regarded as a class conflict; yet that they happened to be interpreted in precisely these terms by the Belgian authorities is directly relevant to this discussion. By defining as an incipient "class struggle" what was actually a peasant revolt and by anticipating a possible concurrence of interest between the goals of international communism and those of the Hutu leadership, the Belgian authorities felt that they had no choice but to "canalize this claimant movement while publicly recognizing its existence" (Lemarchard, 1970). In practice this meant a systematic attempt on the part of the tutelle to guide the entry of the insurgents into the political arena, while at the same time depriving the incumbents of the uses of force, the key political resource through which they might have stayed in power.

Moreover, the inability of the incumbents to effectively meet force with counter-force rapidly accelerated the dissolution of patron-client relationships, thereby elimanating a major source of interethnic cohesion. Meanwhile, as they were allowed to gain access to an increasingly wide range of political resources, including authority, status and wealth, the insurgents were placed in an ideal position to act as surrogate patrons to the peasantry and to appropriate for themselves the role of benevolent protectors heretofore assumed by their "oppressors." Once redefined along ethnic lines the patron-client nexus could serve both as an instrument of political mobilization and as an additional source of ethnic solidarity between the insurgent leadership and the peasant masses. This relationship, however, could not have materialized as long as the insurgents were barred from legitimate access to political resources, including force. Only through a deliberate choice of the tutelle could these resources be made available to the insurgents.

Thus in seeking to elucidate the variations noted earlier in the patterns of ethnic strife evidenced by Rwanda and Burundi, it is not enough to point to the differences inherent in their systems of stratification. While these have certainly affected the structure of conflict in each state in radically divergent ways, a more critical issue relates to the subjective meanings attached to the structure of conflict by the trust authorities.

As far as the relationship between social stratification and ethnic strife is concerned, much of the evidence available from Rwanda and Burundi confirms the results of recent investigations into "the politics of communalism" or "ethnic politics" (Horowitz, 1971; Melson and Wolpe, 1970). The lower incidence of ethnic violence experienced by Burundi, together with its comparatively late manifestations, can be explained on the basis of any or all of the foregoing factors:

(1) The greater multiplicity of status distinctions encountered in Burundi, ranging from unilineal descent groups among princely families to differential rankings of prestige within each caste (i.e., Tutsi and Hutu), has contributed to extend the sequential dimension of ethnic conflict over a longer time-span; unlike what happened in Rwanda, where the passage from clan or region to ethnicity involved relatively few

intermediary stages, in Burundi a far greater variety of structural thresholds had to be crossed before ethnic cleavages could become activated on a nationwide scale.

(2) The conspicuously greater autonomy of Burundi's political institutions acted as a further brake on the activation of ethnic cleavages. As noted earlier, whereas in Rwanda political institutions were the monopoly of the Tutsi caste, in Burundi this monopoly was exercised by princely families, or ganwa, whose ethnic identities were regarded as separate from those of either Hutu or Tutsi. The comparative evidence on this score abundantly confirms the hypothesis that "the subordination of political institutions to the interest of particular communal groups tends to reinforce and politicize communal conflict" (Melson and Wolpe, 1970: 1120).

(3) A third explanation refers to the relative weakness of ideological and normative sanctions which underlie Burundi's system of stratification. If "cultural pluralism is in some measure an ideology of domination or of conflict in a struggle for power between different groups" (Kuper and Smith, 1969: 16) one can see why the situation of cultural pluralism exemplified by Burundi should have implied a lower potential for ethnic conflict than that of Rwanda. Although Rwanda's official ideology could conceivably lend itself to different interpretations, its inegalitarian bent was nontheless far more pronounced than in Burundi.

None of the differences noted above enables us to make valid predictions about the actual occurrence of ethnic strife. Even in the case of pre-revolutionary Rwanda, where most of the conditions of generalized ethnic strife seemed satisfied, these conditions were not sufficient to predict violent conflict. "Cultural sections," as Despres (1967: 29) observed, "do not clash by chance or because their structures express incompatible values: they clash because certain individuals and groups have decided that something can be achieved by way of making them clash." From this perspective the onus of responsibility for the Rwanda revolution clearly lies with the trust authorities. In making this assertion our intention is not to deny the sense of revolutionary purpose which once animated the Hutu elites; nor is our intention to rehabilitate Barruel's conspiracy theory of history. Our sole objective is to point to the significance of the subjective meanings attached to patterns of social stratification for an understanding of political change, or indeed the absence of political change. Attention has already been drawn to the motivations which governed the intervention of the Belgian authorities during the initial stages of the Hutu-Tutsi confrontation. By attaching the meaning of a class struggle to a jacquerie phenomenon, the Belgian authorities in Rwanda found it politically expedient to throw their weight on the side of the insurgents; what initially might have been dismissed as a false interpretation eventually thus acquired the qualities of a self-fulfilling prophecy. There is yet another point to be stressed, namely, that the support given to the Tutsi stratum until World War II stemmed from a similarly distorted view of stratificatory phenomena. Paradoxically, the same motivations that led the trust authorities to support the Hutu in 1959 led them to support the Tutsi until World War II. The fear that a shift of policy in favor of the Hutu masses might engender a situation of anarchy leading to a "fiercely anti-European brand of Communism" became one of the chief motives for perpetuating Tutsi hegemony in the social and political sectors (De Lacger, 1969: 524). By 1959, however, the fear that the Hutu leadership might succumb to communist ideology and propaganda provided the main justification for Belgian intervention.

CONCLUSION

"Stratification," writes M. G. Smith (1964: 142), "is a process as well as a state of affairs". From the evidence presented in this discussion stratification might also be viewed as a state of mind.

The subjective underpinnings of status discrepancies can be apprehended at several levels: at the level of vertical rankings in a stratification scale; at the level of horizontal solidarities, on a continuum of cultural similarities or dissimilarities, ranging from family or kinship ties to regional or ethnic identification; and at the level of the social consciousness of the outside observer. Our main contention is that greater predictive benefits can be gained from these phenomenological perspectives than from the analysis of objective status differences.

The first of these distinctions draws attention to the potential for conflict involved in perceived discrepancies between objective and subjective status. As Hyman (1942) reminds us, subjective status may not necessarily coincide with accorded status; attempts to bring them in line with each other inevitably generates tension. When the "slices" of the stratification hierarchy coincide with ethnic discontinuities and where little or no opportunities exist for a peaceful adjustment of status, the potential for ethnic conflict is likely to increase in proportion to the perceived distance between the status objectively accorded to individuals and their subjective definition of where they deserve to be. At least some of the impetus behind the emergence of ethnic conflict in Rwanda can be explained in these terms.

The horizontal dimension of status self-perceptions is clearly illustrated by the shift of solidarities which in Rwanda accompanied the enlistment of northern Hutu elements into the revolutionary movement. As the scope of ethnic interaction widened and the quotient of ethnic violence increased, regional and clan solidarities were rapidly superseded by ethnic solidarities. The point was eventually reached where ethnicity emerged as the only meaningful referent in the stratification pyramid. A very similar situation developed in Burundi as a result of the projection of the Rwanda model into the context of domestic politics: the Tutsi-Hutu cleavage rapidly permeated every sector of society, in the end substituting a sharply dichotomous conception of status differences for the multiplicity of ethnic and social rankings in existence in the traditional society.

The "external" dimension of the phenomenology of ethnic strife is again illustrated by the case of Rwanda. However remote from the empirical realties of the situation, the cognitive schema of the trust authorites had a determining effect on the intensification and outcome of ethnic conflict.

That our view of social phenomena cannot be divorced from our own biases and preconceptions, any more than the explanations we give of such phenomena, has been emphasized time and again by social scientists—and in particular by Max Weber. "For a science which is concerned with the subjective meaning of action explanation requires a grasp of the complex meaning in which an actual course of understandable action thus interpreted belongs" (quoted in Schutz, 1967: 25). Similarly, for social scientists concerned with the impact of status differences on ethnic conflict, explanation requires a grasp of the subjective meanings attached to stratificatory phenomena. In Kuper's (1970: 97) words, "the objective structure and the conception of the structure cannot be sharply separated. In an important sense, the conception is the structure." This is true not only of the actors' own conception of their social structure, but, in some instances, of the interpretation of the social structure conveyed by outside observers.

NOTE

1. The scale and intensity of violence experienced by Rwanda far exceeds Gurr's predictions, while Burundi falls below most other predicted levels of violence.

REFERENCES

ANDERSON, C. W., F. von der MEHDEN, and C. YOUNG (1965) Issues of Political Development. Englewood Cliffs, N.J.: Prentice-Hall.
APTER, D. (1970) "Political studies and the search for a framework" pp. 213-224 in C. Allen and R. W. Johnson, African Perspectives. Cambridge, Eng.: Cambridge University Press.
BERREMAN, G. (1967) "Caste as a social process." Southwestern J. of Anthropology 23 (Winter): 351-371.
CODERE, H. (1962) "Power in Rwanda." Anthropologica 4 (Special Issue): 45-85.
COSER, L. (1968) Continuities in the Study of Social Conflict. New York: Free Press.
DAHRENDORF, R. (1959) Class and Class Conflict in Industrial Society. Stanford, Calif.: Stanford University Press.
De LACGER, L. (1959) Ruanda. Kabgaye, Rwanda.
DESPRES, L. (1967) Cultural Pluralism and Nationalist Politics in British Guyana. Chicago: Rand McNally.
FALLERS, L. (1963) "Equality, modernity and democracy in the new states," pp. 158-219 in G. Geertz (ed.) Old Societies and New States. New York: Free Press.
GERMANI, G. (1964) "Social and political consequences of mobility," pp. 364-394 in N.J. Smelser and S. M. Lipset, Social Structure and Mobility in Economic Development. Chicago: Aldine.
GERTH, H. H. and C. W. MILLS (1958) From Max Weber: Essays in Sociology. New York: Oxford University Press.
GURR, T. and C. RUTTENBERG (1967) The Conditions of Civil Violence: First Tests of a Causal Model. Princeton, N.J.: Princeton University Press.
HOROWITZ, D. (1971) "Three dimensions of ethnic politics." World Politics 23 (January): 232-244.
HUNTINGTON, S. (1968) Political Order in Changing Societies. New Haven, Conn.: Yale University Press.
HYMAN, H. H. (1942) "The psychology of status." Archives of Psychology 269 (June): 5-91.
KUPER, L. (1970) "Race structure in the social consciousness." Civilisations 20, 1: 88-103.
KUPER, L. and M. G. SMITH (1969) Pluralism in Africa. Berkeley: University of California Press.
LEMARCHAND, R. (1970) Rwanda and Burundi. London: Pall Mall Press.
――― (1966) "Political instability in Africa: the case of Rwanda and Burundi." Civilisations 16, 3: 2-29.
MAQUET, J. (1964) "La participation de la classe paysanne au movement d'independence du Rwanda. Cahiers d'Etudes Africaines 4, 4: 552-568.
MELSON, R. and H. WOLPE (1970) "Modernization and the politics of communalism: a theoretical perspective." American Political Science Review 64 (December): 1112-1130.
SCHUTZ, A. (1967) The Phenomenology of the Social World. Evanston, Ill.: Northwestern University Press.
SMITH, M. G. (1965) The Plural Society in the British West Indies. Berkeley: University of California Press.
――― (1964) "Preindustrial stratification systems," pp. 141-176 in N. J. Smelser and S. M. Lipset, Social Structure and Mobility in Economic Development. Chicago: Aldine.

Chapter 11

SOCIAL STATUS, ETHNIC DIVISION, AND POLITICAL CONFLICT IN NEW NATIONS: AFRIKANERS AND ENGLISHMEN IN SOUTH AFRICA

JEFFREY E. BUTLER

A distinction can be drawn between the two broad types of stratification system in multi-ethnic societies, and the distinction between them is essentially a political one: "In vertical—that is hierarchical—systems stratification is synonymous with ethnicity. . . . There are superordinate and subordinate ethnic or racial groups. . . . In horizontal systems . . . parallel ethnic structures exist . . . [and] the groups are not, in a general social sense, definitely ranked in relation to each other" (Horowitz, 1971: 232).[1] The distinction is, therefore, on the extent to which ethnicity becomes the basis of hierarchy, in social and economic, as well as in political spheres. Where ethnicity has such a pervasive influence the state may become an active agent in the definition and maintenance of ethnic cleavages (Kuper in Plotnicov and Tuden, 1970: 77-78). As Horowitz suggests, however, both types of system can exist simultaneously in a single society, with deep divisions and conflict on both sides of a dominant cleavage. Furthermore, though politicians may use a language of permanence, group identities are not stable and extensive amalgamation of sub-groups can take place.

In spite of a complexity comparable to that of the United States, South Africa has at least one engaging simplicity: it contains a cleavage which determines the allocation of power, status, and reward, a cleavage with a long history, and one which defines both the actors and the issues of political conflict. It is in the allocation of power that the cleavage is most precise; indeed, the restriction of power in national politics to whites is the cardinal tenet of apartheid, and is hardly questioned by the major opposition party (Thompson, 1966: 8, 92-94). The population is divided on the basis of race into those with power and those without it: the 3.6 million whites (19.0 percent) are politically dominant over 1.9 million (9.9 percent) Coloreds, .6 million (3.0 percent) Asiatics, and 12,750 million (68.1 percent) Bantu[2] (Buro of Statistics, 1968. All estimates for 1967). At 18, whites are entitled to vote and stand for office in national and local elections. They, and only they, are eligible for positions in a legislative, judicial, and executive system which has responsibility for the whole area of South Africa and Southwest Africa, and rules the whole population, enfranchised and unfranchised alike. Although there are specialized, ethnically defined institutions which govern separate non-white groups in certain aspects of policy, the subordinate character of those institutions is explicit, and national politics remains exclusively a white preserve.[3]

Along this dominant cleavage, therefore, political and ethnic stratification correspond. Furthermore, powerlessness and ethnic identity are not simply a residue of history but are legally defined and enforced. The dominant cleavage is a classic example of an ascriptive barrier where the power to define or redefine identity is not left to individual choice. The state defined first, and most important, the distinction between whites and non-whites, i.e., the distinction between superordinate and subordinate groups; second, the distinctions between Asiatics, Coloreds and Bantu; and third, the distinction between various Bantu groups. Ethnic identity, particularly important in the case of marginal groups like Coloreds and "detribalized" Africans, is determined by a comprehensive system of registration: where there is doubt, the state decides.

The dominant whites, however, in spite of a minority situation which creates many pressures toward unity, have not consistently behaved like a beleaguered garrison facing a fate worse than death, and therefore willing to sink all those other differences which are the normal lot of men in society. White society has been divided, on both class and ethnic lines, and these divisions do not coincide. The origin, nature, and changing content of political conflict between whites form the subject of this paper.

I

Before proceeding to discuss South African white political conflict, one definitional, and four historical points must be made. First, the very language of identification is confusing and controversial, terms which meet linguistic criteria fail on ethnic or racial ones. "South African" tells one nothing except citizenship; "white South African," race and citizenship but of little value when looking at white politics. "English-speaking South African" and its "Afrikaans-speaking" equivalent are precise but awkward, and politically valueless because linguistic barriers cross racial ones: English speakers and Afrikaans speakers include many who are not white. "Afrikaans- (or "English-) speaking white South African" is the minimum that can be used to be precise, but it tells one nothing about origin. Even "Afrikaner" has many meanings: it may refer to origin, not necessarily to present cultural and political affiliation; it can also have a highly charged political meaning—not merely an Afrikaans speaker but a true son of the *volk*. There is no term equivalent to Afrikaner for English-speaking white South Africans: "Briton," "Englishman," "Britisher" are all anachronistic or inaccurate to some degree. For the purposes of this paper, therefore, "Afrikaner" refers to language habitually spoken, but not to political affiliation. "Englishmen" refers to those of British origin who habitually speak English; when we wish to include Jews, or German immigrants who speak English, we shall use the more general "English speakers." It should be noted however, that the overwhelming proportion of English speakers *are* originally from the British Isles, though it would be foolhardy in certain circles, especially Irish circles, to call them "British."

Historically, South Africa has four important features. First, it is from an earlier generation of new states, having already celebrated the sixtieth anniversary of the promulgation of its constitution, the South Africa Act (1909). It was the last of the white frontier societies of the nineteenth century to achieve its modern constitutional form. South African society has, therefore, a much longer political history to draw on than the new states founded since 1945 though, like many of them, it may well be questioned whether it can be described as a new nation. A white-dominated society was not, however, created by the South Africa Act: the four self-governing colonies which united in 1910 were already the Union of South Africa in miniature, with some important variations between Cape Colony on the one hand, and Natal, Transvaal, and the Orange Free State on the other. Since 1910, the celebrated "Cape liberal tradition" has been whittled away, but the assault on that tradition began long before the present government came to power in 1948, indeed, even before 1910 (Walker, 1957: 431-432). The obliteration of a modest and faltering attempt at political and legal, but not social, assimilation has not altered the nature of the traditional dominant cleavage: it has merely made the cleavage precise, rooting it more and more in law and regulation, not convention.

Second, since World War II, South Africa has come to be widely regarded as an anachronism, not because it has undergone a basic change but because it has not: the world outside it has changed, and particularly that part of the world to the north of it. The new nations regard South Africa as a survival of colonialism; South Africa is, in many respects, "a colonial power with all the problems that face those European states that hold dominion over Non-European peoples" (Marquard, 1962: 269).

South Africa has not escaped the effects of these changes: there have been major challenges, internal and external, to the very survival of the state in its present form, leading to serious limitations on such hallowed liberal institutions as habeas corpus, freedom of the press, and freedom of organization, which were part of the British and Dutch legal traditions, and were not limited to Cape Colony. But however repressive the system has been in relation to its non-white majority, and to those whites who challenge the very existence of the dominant cleavage, the constitution has "worked" in several senses (Gluckman in Kuper and Smith, 1969: 375). As a legislature, the South African parliament has functioned successfully in adapting South African law to the conditions of rapid industrialization and ensuring the continued maintenance of white power. Administration—judicial, civil, and military—has effectively enforced the decisions of the parliamentary executive. An interesting indication of the stability of these institutions, almost entirely British in origin, is that when South Africa became a republic in 1961, thus achieving a basic Afrikaner nationalist ambition, the amendments to the constitution were entirely technical and verbal (Thompson, 1966: 57-58). This acceptance of British institutions is remarkable because Afrikaners have a constitutional tradition of their own. As a functioning system, British parliamentary and administrative practice has met the needs of the white minority: the long attack on those institutions by Afrikaner nationalists before 1948 was purely political, based on resentments from past conflict, and the continued presence of British symbolism in day to day acts of government (Stadler, 1969: 209-11).

Third, these two aspects of continuity have an important implication for social change and political conflict among whites. As important as the effective separate functioning of the arms of government, and the stability of the system as a whole, was the relation of the "powers" in the constitution to each other. The military accepted civilian control, judges showed vigorous independence at a time of high national feeling, in spite of their political and social origin, and, most important of all perhaps, politicians accepted the verdict of the ballot box and of the courts.[4] A political system came into being which gave South

Africa's enfranchised population "a politics . . . of moderation," at least up to 1948 (Le May, 1965: 215). Discussion was as uninhibited as anywhere, political conflict between whites was often violent, but order never seriously broke down, except during the rebellion of 1914, and the general strike of 1922. Even there, and in other celebrated incidents involving non-whites, order was quickly restored. It was, in fact, for white men, government by consent and a regime subject to the rule of law.

Since 1948 South Africa has been ruled by a party which is both radical and conservative. Determined to apply a comprehensive policy governing the relations of white with non-white, the Afrikaner National Party government embarked on an ambitious program of legislation summed up in the word *apartheid.* Though ill-defined in 1948, there was little doubt among politically conscious non-whites that apartheid would involve increased resistance to redistribution of power in their favor. The resistance by non-whites and white sympathizers to the implementation of policy, especially in the early sixties, provoked a determined government reaction: there followed considerable elaboration of a security system to control and frustrate the activities of those who seriously questioned the distribution of power in South African society. These changes have radically altered the context in which political activity, by whites as well as non-whites, takes place: we have now a "politics of security" (Stultz, 1969: 19-20). But for those whites who accept the dominant cleavage, the regime remains essentially unchanged and legitimate. Within the white community, therefore, though it is a community in only a limited sense, social change has taken place since 1910 in an atmosphere of freedom and institutional stability.[5]

Fourth, though there has been a considerable expansion of state activity in political economic and social spheres, there has been no attempt to police all boundaries in the society. As we shall see, ethnic factors have been of major significance in white politics, but the state has not intervened directly, e.g., by proscribing intergroup marriage, to maintain the boundaries between white groups, as they have those between white and non-white.

II

South Africa has been undergoing rapid industrialization since 1910, and especially since 1932 when abandonment of the gold standard revived the mining industry (Houghton, 1964: 15-17). The white population enjoys freedom of movement and opportunity and consequently is divided by income and occupation in addition to linguistic divisions inherited from the past and sustained by religion and informal residential segregation. Both white groups have been in South Africa for long periods—Afrikaners since the mid-seventeenth, Englishmen since the early nineteenth, centuries. There has been considerable intermixture, each having absorbed individuals from the other, from non-white groups, and from European societies. Last names are unreliable as indicators of ethnic identity. Afrikaner society absorbed Huguenots in the seventeenth century, and the Scotch Presbyterian pastors recruited by the British government in the nineteenth century in the vain hope of creating an anglicized but still Calvinist reformed church; many Afrikaners were completely anglicized. But two separate cultures have survived in spite of mobility between them.

The language habitually spoken, the language chosen by a speaker if there are not constraints from outside, is the major determinant of life style and political and cultural loyalties. Language is not an invariant determinant because the relations between language group, political party, and issue have varied. Because of its bicultural heritage, and a history of conflict and compromise, South African political and administrative practice and symbolism are shot through with dualisms: two legal traditions, two languages, two capital cities, formerly two flags and two anthems. But for all the insistence on training in both official languages in schools, the use of both in public offices, and the intermingling referred to above, a fundamental social dualism persists. Individuals use the other language only when the job demands it, they attend an entertainment in the other language, or they read a newspaper for a specific purpose unrelated to political or cultural affairs. Such crossing of the language barrier is probably more frequent for Afrikaners than it is for Englishmen, because of cultural arrogance among many of the latter, the continuing importance of English in economic life, and the vigor and enterprise of the South African English press, especially in covering sport and business (Thompson, 1966: 124-125). Most films shown come from an English-speaking world beyond South Africa and the market does not justify "dubbing" in Afrikaans.[6] To adapt Furnivall's definition of a plural society, members of different language groups "meet only in the market place," where language is often dictated by the situation or commodity supplied, not by the user's individual choice.

One indication of the unilingual character of most voluntary situations can be found in census data. The number of whites who record themselves as using both languages habitually in the home is ramarkably small.

1960 Census: Home Languages of Whites (in thousands)

	Urban	Rural	Total	% Urban
Afrikaans	1,369	420	1,789	74
English	1,068	74	1,142	93
Afrikaans and English	45	4	49	92
Other	92	7	99	93
Total	2,574	505	3,079	84

Less than fifty thousand, out of a total white population of just over three million, regarded themselves a bilingual at home (Buro of Statistics, 1968: A29). It would be interesting to know who regard themselves as bilingual, even though unilingual at home, and whether their number is rising. Though in recent years Afrikaners have made notable advances in industry and commerce and the use of Afrikaans has generally increased, it is not clear yet that the proportion of habitually bilingual people is increasing or that a merging of the languages is taking place.

Afrikaans speakers come under a large number of influences which reinforce their cultural identity. Schools for white children are officially segregated on the basis of medium of instruction; in some areas the decision as to home language was taken away from parents, an indication of the desire on the part of Afrikaner nationalists to prevent Afrikaans-speaking parents from having their children educated in English (Thompson, 1966: 99-100). The creation of a segregated education system for whites is one of the important developments of the twentieth century, for now an Afrikaans child can go from kindergarten to graduate school in an Afrikaans environment. Furthermore, if an individual goes to church, he probably goes to one of the Dutch Reformed churches. The correlation between language and religion is extremely close, in spite of attempts by Presbyterians to accommodate Afrikaners, and the odd Dutch Reformed church that gives services in English (Cape Times, September 8, 1969). Out of 3 million whites, 1,615,000 gave their religious affiliation as Dutch Reformed, a figure close to the total of Afrikaans speakers, 1,689,000, though undoubtedly many of the declarations of church membership reflect merely formal or past membership (Buro of Statistics, 1968: 36).

Apart from religion, leisure time activity is also segregated: sports clubs reflect the language of their community, and while there is competition between clubs, especially in rugby, the national winter sport for men, individual clubs often have relatively homogeneous membership. During World War II militant Afrikaners partially turned their back on the white sporting world—all of whose games were of British origin—and developed some games of their own. Perhaps the most notable was *jukskei,* a variant of horse shoe, played with the separator from an ox-yoke, an artifact with many resonances in Afrikaner pioneer folk lore (Patterson, 1957: 114-115). They did not, however, abandon the sports which have become traditional for whites, rugby and tennis in particular, and recently Afrikaans schools have begun to take an interest in cricket, a game played largely in English-speaking areas and in English schools before World War II.

These mechanisms for the maintenance of Afrikaner identity have shown themselves to be remarkably effective, in spite of major economic and social changes in the twentieth century. Indeed, Afrikaners have gone through changes of occupation, income, and residence far more fundamental than those of their English-speaking contemporaries, most of whom came to South Africa with urban occupations and have retained them. Afrikaners came into existence as a rural people on South African frontiers between the seventeenth and nineteenth centuries, developing ultimately a homogeneity of language and *weltaan-schauing,* and a remarkable capacity for rapid mobilization when threatened, in spite of their considerable disperson. During the first stage of industrialization, they seemed to be in danger of extinction as a distinct people, unable to compete with Englishmen from Britain or the colonies in the development of mining and industry, or with non-whites in the field of unskilled or semi-skilled labor. They also faced the cultural threat of one of the world's "universal" languages (Thompson in Kuper and Smith, 1969: 355, 362-364). In the twentieth century, however, they moved from countryside to town until today, according to South African census criteria, they have become 77 percent urbanized. In industry, construction, transport, and government they have profited from deliberate discrimination against non-whites (Ford in Adam, 1971a: 260-61). In the twenties and thirties Afrikaners took the place of the upwardly mobile British worker. More recently, they have moved substantially into commerce and the upper levels of every kind of business activity, producing a group of entrepreneurs active in the world of high finance inside and beyond the borders of South Africa (Welsh, 1969: 270). This diversification has removed any conflict there might have been at one time between cultural identity and personal ambition. A young Afrikaner today has wide opportunities for education and subsequent employment, in institutions of distinctively Afrikaans character, if he so chooses.

One of the weapons used by Afrikaners to resist the forces of anglicization was a superbly articulated "machine" made up of religious, charitable, and cultural organizations dedicated to advancing Afrikaners and the Afrikaans language in every way possible, along with businesses which aimed to break the hold of the Englishman and the Jew on commerce and industry (Patterson, 1957: 260-270; Stadler, 1969; Danziger in Adam, 1971a: 287-288). Cooperation among Afrikaners was hardly left to informal and public processes. Quite apart from the effect of interlocking memberships of governing bodies, there existed from 1918 a secret society, the *Broederbond*, which set itself the task of coordination. The range of activity of Afrikaner organizations became so great that it became virtually impossible for an Afrikaner to avoid taking part in political activity (De Villiers in Wilson and Thompson, 1971: 381-382). Major historical celebrations, like the centenary of the Great Trek in 1938, were successfully appropriated to the purposes of an exclusivist cultural nationalism, appealing to historic loyalties by reviving memories of great deeds by folk heroes, and of the wickednesses of the historic enemy, Britain. In addition to recalling the Trek itself, local Voortrekker celebrations were often accompanied by the dedication of "women and children" monuments, i.e., monuments to those who died in British concentration camps during the South African War.

South African Englishmen do not have a comparable awareness of the past and do not "mine" it as effectively as do Afrikaners. Yet they live in a world equally effective in maintaining their identity. Englishmen hardly form a community in the sense that Afrikaners do (Stadler, 1969: 213 note 3). Their roots in the society are historically and psychologically shallower than those of Afrikaners, although this has not made them subject to acculturation. The development of mining, and later of industry, gave the English-speaking group formidable reinforcements in terms of numbers, but maintained the spatial segregation among these groups until the impoverished Afrikaner came to town. Unlike the Afrikaner, however, the Englishman brought to South Africa his world culture, universal language, and self-confidence that was to be unrealistically encouraged by British intervention on his behalf in the South African War (Thompson, 1960: 480-482). Moving steadily to living in large cities, he left small town commerce, teaching, civil service, and working-class occupations generally; he goes to an English church, if at all, reads English papers, lives in a largely English suburb, and sends his children to English-medium schools, public or private. His patriotic, service and sporting clubs—Sons of England, Free Masons, South African Legion, Memorable Order of Tin Hats—tend to be based on historic connection and loyalty, conduct their proceedings in English, and have little on which to base an appeal to Afrikaners.

With two such communities intermingled in cities and at work, it might be asked whether intermarriage and urbanization have not played a part in breaking down cultural divisions between the white "races," leading perhaps to a new culture, or the victory of one of them. As we saw above, the boundary between the white communities has not been policed by the state, and no legal sanctions attach to cross-cultural marriages as they do between white and non-white. The only area of white social interaction in which the government has intervened directly to deny the citizen freedom of choice, has been in the definition of home language for choice of medium of instruction. But that policy has not been systematically applied, and it may only have regional significance; i.e., in the Transvaal (Personal communication: H. Van der Merwe). Intermarriage has, indeed, been frequent but it has not produced a recognizable new social animal and a new group—"Anglo-Afrikaner" or "Boer-Brit"—developing a new language, culture, and self-consciousness.

The conditions for cultural assimilation of one group by another, or the creation of a new culture out of both, have hardly existed in South Africa. In the United States in the nineteenth century, many, perhaps most, immigrants were willing, even eager, to be absorbed, well aware of their interest in full membership of a new society, and few American school systems made concession to the language of immigrants. In colonial Africa, those Africans who became assimilated to the metropolitan cultures were equally aware of the advantages of doing so. But in South Africa neither white group was willing to lose its identity, particularly as expressed by language, Englishmen from a sense of self-confidence and superiority, Afrikaners from a fear of assimilation by a more powerful culture. This fear is hardly surprising when one remembers the attempts by British policymakers, notably Lord Miner after the South African War, to find a means of acculturating Afrikaners out of existence (Le May, 1965: 155-56).

In such a situation neither the school nor intermarriage could become a major agent of assimilation. In the case of the school, it became for Afrikaners an agent of cultural survival; in the case of marriage, an alliance across the language barrier became for many nationalist Afrikaners an act of ethnic treason, especially if the married couple were to live in an English-speaking context. Movement across the barrier tends to be complete for one of the parties to the marriage. There does not seem to be reliable and conclusive evidence as to how the direction of movement is correlated with home language of mother, relative income and status, urban or rural origin, religion, political view, and so on. Because, as we shall see, political structures are not exactly correlated with language, we need evidence of the frequency and effect of marriages when political loyalties of the parties are different. Until recently an English supporter of the Afrikaner National Party was rare, whereas Afrikaans-speaking supporters of the opposing parties were not; culturally mixed marriages, therefore, were not necessarily politically mixed. The bulk of such marriages might well have had no political significance at all, merely confirming the political positions of both parties, and perhaps increasing the tendency for the anglicization of already "moderate" Afrikaners.

The closeness of groups to each other in the modern city is frequently only geographical. The South African city has not yet proved to be a cultural "melting pot" for whites as many liberals hoped, and many Afrikaners feared. The same spontaneous segregation of urban neighborhoods has taken place as in the American city. The Dutch Reformed churches have made a major attempt to follow their people from the countryside to the town, unlike the Anglican church in the English industrial revolution; the Afrikaans city high schools have played the equivalent secular role of maintaining a persistently Afrikaans-speaking environment. Similarly, South African private schools virtually all use English as the medium of instruction. The large South African cities, with the exception of Bloemfontein and Pretoria, still retain a predominantly English character in spite of rapid increases in the Afrikaans-speaking populations of all cities. Afrikaners in the city are frequently in the position of an immigrant minority, often concentrated in certain areas with their own social institutions, and marked by low income and status within the white community. Despite the blurring of the earlier pattern of English-speaking town/Afrikaans-speaking countryside (except for the English-speaking areas of eastern Cape and Natal), and a thorough mixing of whites in work, play, and areas of residence in the cities, the mechanisms for the maintenance of both identities have been successful in preventing wholesale acculturation in either direction.

Even though Afrikaners have achieved power and a considerable redistribution of income and wealth in their favor, the threat of anglicization remains (Adam in Adam, 1971a: 97-99). A recent study (1968) of elites in South Africa found that of 925 subjects interviewed 471 were born in Afrikaans homes; 79 of these were no longer predominantly Afrikaans-speaking; while 51 percent were born Afrikaans-speaking, only 43 percent remained Afrikaans-speaking. Finally, though only 35 percent were born in English homes, 46 percent were English-speaking (Van der Merwe and J. J. Buitendag, n.d.: 9). It is conceivable, however, that this anglicization is an elite phenomenon which could co-exist with a movement in the opposite direction lower down economic and social scales.

There is evidence that major changes are taking place among urbanized Afrikaners. The move to the cities by Afrikaners took place in the twenties and thirties; i.e., those who went to the cities as children are in mid-career, thirty to fifty years old; their children are only now moving into adulthood. The occupational diversification of Afrikaners is probably more recent still, much of it taking place since World War II (Ford in Adam, 1971a: 260-261). A recent study of young Afrikaans-speaking business executives in Cape Town showed a growing convergence with their English-speaking contemporaries, particularly in material and social aspirations. Furthermore, one result of this study touches the question of identity itself: a large number recorded a dislike of the word "Afrikaner" and a preference for "South African," a geographically based national label rather than an ethnic and cultural one, which may imply a degree of conciliation with English-speaking contemporaries (personal communication: Van der Merwe). In spite of action by the Dutch Reformed churches, Afrikaners in the cities are becoming secularized and are beginning to question the strict enforcement of Sunday observance (Welsh, 1969: 269-270). Secularization does not necessarily involve a loss of cultural identity, however; nor does a return to a set of national sports in which all whites participate and which happen to have a foreign origin. Intimate intermixture for specific purposes can exist in leisure time activity, just as it can in economic life, without loss of traditional loyalties and identity.

What is happening among South African English speakers requires examination. At the anecdotal level there is evidence of a willingness on the part of young people to speak Afrikaans and quite self-consciously to acknowledge without resentment the facts of Afrikaner power. The number of English-speaking students at Afrikaans universities may be rising. There are frequent references to English-speaking supporters of the National Party. At the same time as accommodating themselves to a political regime in which they have little formal say, South African English speakers have suffered the loss by emigration of thousands of their most highly trained members in the professions. The scale of this new diaspora is not known, much less its effect on the capacity of the group which remained behind to maintain its cultural identity. Recently teachers of English have called for the development of a vigorous English-speaking South Africanism which may be the beginning of a linguistic sub-nationalism which parallels that of Afrikaners sixty years ago (Cape Times, July 5, 1969). It has, however, poorer prospects of success if the cleavage between whites is maintained, and English speakers continue to decline as a proportion of the white population.

Ethnic identities, therefore, appear stable and have survived substantial changes of income, occupation, and residence, especially in the case of Afrikaners. The mechanisms of cultural maintenance, organized and articulated among Afrikaners, spontaneous and uncoordinated among Englishmen, had a major political implication: if ethnic identity were stable and remained the basis of politics and public policy, relative population growth-rates and immigration became crucial. British policymakers before Union had looked to industrial development to increase the proportion of Englishmen in the white population in the hope that an anglicized South Africa would at least remove one major conflict and lay the basis for a stable relationship between Britain and South Africa. But none of the immigration programs, official or unofficial, from 1820 to the present day succeeded in creating a wave of settlement which would have produced an English majority among whites, let alone a white majority in the population as a whole (Ford in Adam, 1971a: 249-253). South Africa could not attract immigrants on the basis of its agricultural resources, and its industry had limited absorptive capacity because of the industrial color bar and the availability of non-white labor for unskilled work.

Afrikaner nationalist strategists saw from an early date that immigration could become a threat as serious as deliberate anglicization in the schools. Immigrants were a threat even if they were not English: though the evidence is scanty it is probable that most twentieth-century immigrants, including those from Holland and Germany, have ended in English-speaking groups. After the publication of the results of the census of 1936, it was clear that if it were a matter of domestic growth rates, the future lay with Afrikaners. For every 100 English speakers over 21, there were 115 Afrikaans speakers over 21; for every 100 English speakers under 7 there were 212 Afrikaans speakers under 7 (Roberts and Trollip, 1947: 159). The obvious strategy for Afrikaner nationalists, therefore, was to limit immigration, to resist anglicization, and to appeal to ethnic loyalties, thereby correlating cultural and political identities. It is hardly surprising that one of their first acts after achieving power in 1948 was to cancel the immigrant ships which were bringing in settlers (mostly British) at a high rate, and at the same time to make it more difficult for British immigrants to become citizens (Carter, 1958: 51-59). The reversal of immigration policy in 1961 may be evidence of a decisive change in attitude—a shift from an Afrikaner to a white nationalism. But it may merely be a recognition that Afrikaner power has little to fear from immigration which could give essential allies in the defense of white power, without eroding the social base of Afrikaner organizations. However, *verkrampte* politicians continue to complain of the immigration of "unassimitable" groups (Adam, 1971b: 129-130; Adam in Adam, 1971a: 99)[7]

III

Given that white language groups have considerable stability in spite of rapid social and economic change, what are the relations between them? Where has there been conflict and what is it origin? Intergroup conflict has its origins in the social and political consequences of South Africa's industrial revolution and the subsequent intervention of the imperial power. It was not until the coming of diamonds and gold mining that Afrikaners came into serious conflict with British settlers, as distinct from the British government. Before the industrialization of South Africa, British settlers were largely farmers like their Afrikaner contemporaries, facing similar problems on the frontier, and equally suspicious of the "negrophilist" sympathies of the Colonial Office. When the English townsman or farmer from Natal or the eastern Cape joined Colonial and British regiments to fight the Boers between 1899-1902, he was reflecting a national loyalty to the Queen Empress, meeting a challenge from a group which was consorting with the Queen's potential enemies, and denying equal rights to his countrymen in the Transvaal.

The roots of the conflict for the British farmer settler did not lie in day-to-day abrasive contact, or competition for scarce resources or jobs, or fundamental differences over native policy. Rather the conflict stemmed from already developed national loyalties and its focus was in the city, in Johannesburg, where the discovery of gold brought a heterogeneous group of settlers—mostly British in origin and all in urban occupations—into the heart of a pastoral community (Danziger in Adam, 1971a: 293-294). These foreigners, or *Uitlanders*, not only offended the religious and social beliefs of Afrikaners, but also threatened the independent existence of the state. They brought with them the arrogant self-confidence of Englishmen whose own society was showing all the symptoms of an imperially enthusiastic people. It was, as has often been said, a conflict of centuries, as well as of people, a conflict which common assumptions of the superiority of white men did little to mitigate. On the one hand was a belief in a British manifest destiny, on the other a dour refusal to bow before it.

However, even as in the case of the farmers, there was little actual contact between the two groups until the war broke out. Until shortly before the South African War it was a conflict between elites, a modern one demanding a say in affairs of state from a traditional elite in power. In standing up against Cecil Rhodes and his friends, Paul Kruger, President of the Transvaal, ultimately involved both imperial and South African colonial interests, touching off a colonial and civil war which devasted part of the South African countryside, conquered the Afrikaner republics and their Afrikaner rebel allies from the British colonies, and laid the basis for the constitutional settlement of 1910. In the long term, it also produced that sense of grievance which gave leaders an opportunity to recreate an Afrikaner nationalism embracing Afrikaners through-out South Africa and not merely in the former Republics of the Transvaal and Orange Free State (Patterson, 1957: 35, 37).

The South African white groups, therefore, live in a parallel structure allowing for a type of ethnic coexistence which, as Weber wrote, conditions "a mutual repulsion and disdain but [allows] each ethnic community to consider its own honor as the highest one" (Kuper in Plotnicov and Tuden, 1970: 84;

Horowitz, 1971: 233). Furthermore, such parallel structures frequently have
their origin in both migration and "incomplete conquest" (Horowitz, 1971:
235). It was not so much the migration, but the attempt at conquest which
exacerbated the conflict between South African whites. An imperial power
intervened with massive force on behalf of colonists who had crossed beyond the
frontiers of the empire in the hope of creating a new, consolidated,
white-dominated state in which the domestic balance of power would be
permanently altered in favor of English-speaking groups. The attempt failed but
many Afrikaners understandably came to regard the South African English-
speaking group as a kind of Trojan Horse. But that major basis of conflict has
now been removed by an agreement on the hostile contemporary role of the
former imperial power, historic enemy of one group, and once mother country
of the other.

Today, South African whites are still socially, but not geographically, isolated
from each other. This isolation is correlated with an absence of a common scale
of status. Indeed, the lack of a common scale may be a consequence of isolation.
An examination of the social columns of the major newspapers shows clearly,
not only how isolated the groups are from each other, but that status is accorded
to different roles: English newspapers do not follow closely the social activities
of Afrikaner cabinet ministers and their wives, but the parties and weddings of
the rich, their appearances at race tracks, and the arrivals and departures of such
people from overseas, particularly from Britain; Afrikaans newspapers follow the
activities of their leading politicians, businessmen, and ministers of religion.

Afrikaners are, however, far from withholding status from the rich, and they
now face a clash between traditionalism and modernity for which there is no
equivalent among English speakers; the "new men" of Afrikaner business are
coming into conflict with traditional leaders and policies. The rapid growth of
Afrikaner-controlled businesses, and the widespread appointment of Afrikaners
to boards of directors where there were only English speakers before, are
certainly breaking down the isolation of the groups from each other. These
trends may be leading to the development of a common scale of status in the
cities giving the same types, if not yet the same individuals, equal status. One
South African author claims that Afrikaners have developed a system of social
snobbery remarkably similar to that among English speakers: Afrikaners, he says
regretfully, have been apt pupils (Galpin, quoted in Van der Merwe and
Buitendag, n.d.: 10).

More important than criteria within groups is the relative ranking of
communities in relation to each other. Although there is "mutual repulsion and
disdain" between the groups, there are also some agreements on questions of
status, quite apart from questions of race. One of the most effective appeals of
Afrikaner leaders in the twentieth century has been to the fear that Afrikaner
culture would be obliterated in the twentieth century in the face of the
competition of a "world language" (Thompson in Kuper and Smith, 1969:
364-365.) Afrikaners do not question the existence of the cultural riches open to
anyone with command of English. Their activity in the twentieth century has
been precisely to defend the "poor thing but mine own," to give it a worthy
literature, and to make it a vehicle for commercial and intellectual life.

We have already seen that, although there may well have been a serious
conflict of interest for Afrikaners between group membership and personal

ambition, such a conflict has probably disappeared. The question is important not only in relation to identity but in relation to group conflict. Mobility up the social scale may increase the resources of Afrikaners to survive culturally; but simultaneously by increasing the number of social contacts, it may increase the sense of threat, not on the part of those who make the contacts but on the part of those who do not. As segregationists believe that contact between cultures is the basis of conflict, Afrikaners, if they continue to control government, could well move to policing the boundary between the white cultures in ways they have not done before. There is, however, little evidence of an intention to do so, though the verkrampte faction in and out of the National Party is based partly on dislike of increasing cooperation with English speakers, and on the long-standing fear of acculturation (Welsh, 1969: 273-274).

Englishmen, however, did not face, or thought they did not face, any threat to linguistic and cultural survival. Indeed in 1910 they faced the future with confidence, and some of their Afrikaner allies, such as Generals Smuts and Botha, assumed that ultimately English would become the dominant national language (Hancock, 1962: 239-243). Many English speakers regard Afrikaans with disdain as the patois of a nation of farmers, and probably support "dual medium" education on the assumption that, given an equal showing, English would eventually become the major language (Stadler, 1969: 205). For the young Englishman in 1910 there was little conflict between group membership and personal ambition,even though certain professions were beginning to be closed to him. This was notably true for the government services, where the rule of equal competence in both languages was used steadily in Afrikaner favor by both major parties (Stadler, 1969: 204-205). Sufficient work was available in business and industry, then mostly under English control, for Afrikaners and Englishmen to avoid major conflict over jobs, one of the frequent occurrences in parallel structures (Horowitz, 1971: 237).

Though the two groups have their own criteria of status, and institutions which make it possible both to preserve identity and to avoid much conflict, there is no mechanism for a definitive ranking relative to each other which both groups would accept. Differences in wealth and income remain significant: though Afrikaners have increased their control in industry and commerce— especially the latter—the ratio of Afrikaner to other white incomes has remained constant: 100 : 128 in the mid-thirties, 100 : 126 in 1960 (Welsh, 1969: 270). Differences in levels of education remain; the percentage of English-speaking matriculants is still twice as high as that of Afrikaans-speaking matriculants (12.9 percent versus 6.4 percent); furthermore, only 45 percent of total white income is earned by Afrikaners (Adam in Adam 1971a: 97). It may well be that urbanization has made Afrikaners more aware of the wealth of many English speakers, but there does not seem to be a tendency towards increasing the class element, as opposed to the ethnic element, in their attitudes towards each other. Far more serious from an Afrikaner nationalist point of view are the social consequences of the diversification of occupation and therefore of income within the Afrikaner community. Several Afrikaans writers have drawn attention to the "danger of proletarianisation"; but a recent study has shown that the tension between traditional and modern groups is closely correlated with class, not with urbanization: "Many of the changes that Afrikaner families are undergoing, including the drift away from the Church, are occurring in rural areas as well. In a comparison of rural and urban Afrikaner families . . . the major differences in family position, structure, values, morals, etc., were between social classes, and not between rural and urban families" (Van der Merwe and Buitendag, n.d.: 13). Such a development may well mitigate Anglo-Afrikaner conflict while exacerbating class divisions in the white community as a whole.

Contacts between the two groups have always been limited except for "the market place." It is hardly surprising, therefore, that it was in commerce that there was considerable hostility between the Jewish, Asian, or English shopkeepers on the one hand, and the poorer Afrikaner customers on the other. Afrikaners in the cities resented the unwillingness of shop assistants in the cities to speak their language, but this is probably declining as an issue because of the rapid growth of Afrikaner-owned retail stores: between 1939 and 1966 Afrikaner control of trade went from 8 percent to 30 percent (Van der Merwe and Buitendag, n.d.: 10). Furthermore, there has been greater attention to bilingualism in stores controlled by English speakers. "Afrikaans Week" in Cape Town in 1969, an organized attempt to make shopping in the city more congenial to Afrikaners, was conducted without the production of evidence either of resistance by English speakers or resentment by Afrikaners (Cape Times, August 8, 1969; September 8, 1969).

South African white society exhibits, therefore, many of the characteristics of a parallel system in which one group is unquestionably dominant politically, but it is not so economically, or socially in the form of wide acceptance of its values. One major basis for conflict—the close emotional tie between South African English speakers and the United Kingdom—has been removed, and the social differentiation engendered by industrial development may be removing another. In the late nineteenth century the clash between traditionalism and modernity corresponded closely but not exactly to the ethnic division between Englishmen and Afrikaners. Even before the South African War, Afrikaners in Cape Colony and the Transvaal were divided as to whether they should welcome the new world of industrialism or try to preserve Afrikaner society unchanged. After the war that conflict continued as Afrikaners were drawn into the cities and both groups became enmeshed in an industrial economy. For a time after 1948 it appeared that a form of traditionalism had triumphed, but since the mid-sixties the conflict has broken out anew, this time within the Afrikaner community itself (Adam, 1971b: 175-178).

IV

What has been the relation between these stable, conflicting ethnic groups and political parties?

White politics since 1910 have been ethnic in two senses: first, ethnic factors have determined the principal social base of all parties, though one of the major parties has always been explicitly non-ethnic in its appeal. Both language groups have been appealed to by exclusivist parties, but only one of them, the National Party, was successful in overcoming historic regional differences, and loyalties based on the South African War, so as to achieve power without having to go into coalition with a non-Afrikaner party. Exclusivist parties based on English groups have had little success, even among Englishmen. Second, the ethnic appeal by parties has inevitably affected the content of political debate, and much conflict has centered on historical tradition, political symbolism, and language.

Neither ethnic group has ever been united behind a single party. To take Afrikaners first: in 1910 they were united behind their founding fathers, Generals Botha, Smuts, and Hertzog, who had played major roles in bringing Union into existence. Though the unity of the leaders was fragile, sufficient agreement existed to fight South Africa's first general election as a party of "conciliation"—the South African Party. But even during the election there were disputes over precisely what conciliation meant. Soon the leaders were quarrelling publicly, Hertzog questioning whether Botha and Smuts could be trusted with the preservation and development of Afrikaner life, and whether, in fact, political conciliation would lead to cultural assimilation of Afrikaners (Thompson, 1960: 465-469). After the founding of the National Party by Hertzog in 1914, Afrikaner exclusivism had its political expression. Steadily increasing its hold over the Afrikaner electorate, this party was to last until Smuts and Hertzog formed in 1934 the second coalition dedicated to conciliation, i.e., a revival of the consensus of 1910 (Stadler, 1969: 208).

The pattern of 1910-1914 was then repeated. Once more an Afrikaner leader, Dr. Malan, went out in the wilderness to build a "pure" Afrikaner movement. Again, after a period of extreme and bitter factionalism, his Reunited National Party asserted its control of Afrikaner organizations, narrowly achieved victory in 1948, and steadily increased its proportion of the Afrikaner vote thereafter (De Villiers in Wilson and Thompson, 1971: 370). Once again, pressures towards conciliation were effective even though the context had changed. In the early sixties, Dr. Verwoerd began to make friendly noises at English speakers, just as Hertzog had done in the thirties (Stultz, 1969: 14). Verwoerd's successor, John Vorster, has followed the same course. In reaction to this implied abandonment of Afrikaner exclusivism, the National Party has recently split, with the verkrampte faction demanding a re-dedication to the pursuit of Afrikaner ideals. The process of fission among Afrikaners is being repeated, but it has yet to run its course. The National Party remains an Afrikaner party appealing predominantly to Afrikaners, but the tension persists between those willing to combine or ally with others, formally or informally, and those wanting to "go it alone".

There have, nonetheless, been two major changes in party alignments since 1910. For some time generals of the South African War played a major role in politics, and Afrikaner voting was heavily based on personal loyalties (Kruger, 1958). Divisions among Afrikaners had a strongly regional character: Hertzog, who had led an Orange Free State commando in the South African War, built up an impregnable base in that province: from the 1915 election to that of 1933 the National Party won all seats but one in every election. In the Transvaal, though the position was less clear, Smuts retained strong support in the Afrikaner countryside as late as 1948 (Carter, 1958: 449). However, by the late thirties these loyalties were being undermined and were decisively lost by both Smuts and Hertzog. Though historic wrongs were still used for political mobilization, personal loyalties based on former military roles were no longer sufficient, especially if the leader concerned had used the language of conciliation. Indeed, the two generals were defeated by men who could claim no glorious war record.

Second, Afrikaner nationalist organizations have acquired an urban as well as a rural base, something which had always been a characteristic of their opponents. In the twenties Afrikaner nationalism had secured some urban support but only through a coalition of the National Party with the Labour Party, which had English leadership and a mixed following. By the beginning of World War II the strength or urban working-class Afrikaner nationalism was beginning to become clear: the trade union movement became deeply divided, partly as a result of an attempt by Afrikaner nationalists to gain control of the powerful Mineworkers Union (Sachs, 1952: 166-170). Furthermore, the National Party made its first gains in urban constituencies in the general election of 1943, gains they have since expanded and consolidated.

English-speaking South Africans have shown a comparable factionalism from time to time, and a similar drift to a single national organization, which is not, however, ethnic in orientation. In 1910 Englishmen were divided between those who supported conciliation of Afrikaners, those who supported strong imperial ties and a more explicitly British future for South Africa, and those who supported the Labour Party. In the voting in South Africa's first general election, the ethnic basis of voting between the major contenders was clear, English voters supporting the Unionists, Afrikaners supporting the Afrikaner-led party of conciliation, the South African Party (Thompson, 1960: 477-478). In 1921 Smuts, who had long been opposed by the Labour Party and who was steadily losing support of Afrikaners, was forced to amalgamate with the Unionists; in 1924 the Labour Party made a coalition with Nationalists. When Smuts and Hertzog formed their coalition in 1934, a small group of Englishmen, from the English-speaking areas of Eastern Cape, Border, and Natal, kept alive exclusive pro-British sentiment in the Dominion Party. Many English working men, largely in the Transvaal, continued to support the Labour Party, but its base was being undermined as the proportion of nationalist Afrikaners in industry increased, and the party became deeply divided on the issue of "native policy." World War II, by returning many English-speaking working men to historic allegiances, gave the Labor and Dominion parties a brief lease of life. Yet it was a spurious extension, hardly related to the central issues the parties were respectively supposed to represent. Since 1948 they have both been eliminated as political forces (Carter, 1958: 33, 36, 340-346, 448-449).

As a minority group, and as a group which is declining as a proportion of whites, English speakers have had a steadily decreasing number of options. If they were to control or have dominant influence in any affairs of state, they had to form a coalition with another group. Their influence depended on continued division among Afrikaners. The consolidation of English-speaking voters behind a single moderate party, and the recent tendency of some to vote for the National Party, may be directly related to the abandoment of the hope either that immigration would produce an English majority, or that Afrikaners would become deeply divided once more, with one faction willing to ally itself with a largely English supported party. It may also be that the apparent move of English voters back to the United Party in 1970, and its net gain of 4 seats, are a direct consequence of hope of renewed Afrikaner factionalism. However, if there is consolidation of English-speaking voters, it is not paralleled among the elites: a recent study has shown a far greater disperson of political loyalties among English speaking elites than among their Afrikaner equivalents (Van der Merwe and Buitendag, n.d.: 20).

V

Even though most of the alignments of social groups with political parties have had a strongly ethnic character, and politics frequently became violent at the local level, the degree of conflict has not been so great as to require a great deal of coercion of whites to ensure the functioning of government. The fact that one of the major parties, the South African Party, and its successor, the United Party, always appealed to both white groups probably contributed to maintaining a system of electoral politics. Even exclusivist Afrikaner parties have been unable to maintain their exclusivism, and both before and after 1948 they appealed for the support of English speakers (Stadler, 1969: 205). The use of coercion against whites in the 1960s did involve the imprisonment of many English speakers. This happened not because they were English but because they were liberal, and were attacking the very existence of the dominant cleavage (Stultz, 1969: 5-6). Acceptance of that cleavage is part of the consensus on which South African white politics has been based ever since Union sixty years ago.

In 1910 the political consensus had three major elements. First, all but a very small proportion of whites, shared a belief in the importance of the "color line" and its correspondence with a distinction between civilization and barbarism. Second, there was agreement on the necessity to police that boundary, though there were disagreements over the method of doing so. Power in the constitution was retained clearly and explicitly in white hands, however much some hoped for the extension of the Cape liberal tradition. Third, there was a commitment to democratic procedures within the white community. Both Englishmen and Afrikaners had participated in colonial and republican governments before the South African War which had been effective in varying degrees in giving expression to the wishes of constituents. Breaches with democratic tradition and the rule of law have been justified by the nature of the threat perceived to white government. In spite of the development among Afrikaners of fascist type movements in the late thirties, a fully developed totalitarian regime with close analogies to Nazi Germany has not appeared (Van den Berghe, 1967: 83-85). As noted above, the government has been frequently checked by the judiciary.

What then was the content of political debate from 1910 to 1948 within that consensus? The national coalition on which the Union was created lasted for only a short time. The resentment of the South African War, the reconstruction which followed it, and the economic weakness of the Afrikaner community, became the basis of three sets of issues fought out in both local and national arenas. The first concerned the question of external relations, particularly relations with Britain, and especially the question of neutrality in a war in which Britain was involved. Indeed, the issue was whether relations with Britain could properly be called "external." Consequently, both world wars became major political issues in South Africa, the first leading to rebellion, the second to a period of acute instability which limited the country's capacity to send troops overseas. South Africa has had, as a result, an incongruous combination of compulsory military service in peacetime but volunteer service in wartime. At the national level, moreover, there was serious conflict over republicanism and membership of the Commonwealth, often in the form of debates over symbols: anthems, flags, and changing the name of the major military base from "Roberts

Heights" to "Voortrekkerhoogte." (Lord Roberts was British commander-in-chief during the South African War, and one of the conquerors of the Afrikaner Republics.) Locally, such issues frequently led to small-scale violence—fights in pubs, or during the playing of the anthem at the end of movies, much of it due to a deliberate political "coat-trailing" comparable to that which goes on in northern Ireland. During World War II there were major riots in large cities, particularly in Johannesburg, and some serious sabotage.

A second major set of issues can be called cultural which is hardly surprising in a society where language is the major differentiator within the white group. Education had already become a key problem before 1910. Fearful of cultural swamping by the English, exclusivist Afrikaners campaigned for equal treatment of languages by law in the constitution. Having secured that in the South Africa Act, they then demanded the replacement of Dutch by Afrikaans. At the same time they pressed for "mother tongue" instruction, usually in separate schools. Schools were controlled by education boards which were elected locally. Consequently, education became a major issue, and in evenly balanced communities especially, choices of school principals, language of instruction, and the whole cultural tone of school activities became sources of conflict. As the generation of Scotch and English schoolteachers recruited after the South African War retired, some of them in protest to compulsory bilingualism, their places were taken by Afrikaners. Between 1926 and 1946 the proportion of Afrikaners among male schoolteachers rose from 27 to 73 percent (Ford in Adam, 1971a: 261). Local school board elections, which had long been fought on a non-party basis, more and more reflected the division at the national level. In 1943, Provincial council elections were fought throughout the country on the issue of "dual medium education," i.e., the teaching of some subjects in the official language other than the pupil's home language.

A third group of issues are social and economic—"bread and butter" questions. Throughout the twentieth century, poor whites, largely Afrikaans-speaking, have been leaving the countryside for the cities. In the twenties and thirties they faced on the one hand competition by Coloreds, Asians, and Africans for scarce jobs, and on the other, a commercial system dominated by Englishmen and English-speaking Jews. The National-Labour coalition of 1924-1933 adopted "civilized labor" policies; these gave whites sheltered employment in national and local government, state-controlled corporations, and the military services, and they were put to wide use as the depression increased the flow of impoverished Afrikaners to the cities. Consequently, the rural poor were successfully absorbed into urban occupations and the poor white was rapidly becoming a memory (Van den Berghe, 1967: 60).

The tension between class and ethnic antagonism can be seen most clearly in labor history and the development of the industrial color bar. From the earliest days in South African mining, white miners, at first largely British, have demanded the legal or conventional control of recruitment and apprenticeship on a racial basis. The difficulties faced in all labor movements of persuading all workers to behave as a class with common interests, were compounded by the racial antipathies within the labor force, and even a communist-led movement in 1922 resorted to the slogan "Workers of the world unite for a white South Africa" (Walker, 1957: 591). As the white working class became more and more Afrikaans-speaking, the attempts of employers to reduce labor costs by employing more blacks, reconciled class, race, and ethnic interests of workers, at least for a time. Both the Afrikaner and the English miner could see the Chamber of Mines as a common class and race enemy. For a brief period then, there was an explicit political alliance on a class basis—agrarian Afrikaner nationalists allied with Afrikaner and British working men against a capitalist, upper-income group, English and Afrikaner moderate, combination. But that alliance was achieved only by a temporary abandonment by socialists of their socialism and of Afrikaner republicans of their republic in the interests of maintaining the dominant cleavage within the society.

The alliance proved to be fragile, however, once its program had been largely realized. No party in South African white politics could allow itself to appear as the enemy of the white worker, who had been enfranchised since 1931, when an income qualification was removed. The attempt to change the structure of the work force without the concurrence of organized white labor was not repeated. Furthermore, the Labour Party suffered, as did the United Party, from trying to base itself on both white groups at a time when ethnic appeals to Afrikaners were more effective than those based on class. The great realignment of parties in 1933 which was supposed to herald the end of Afrikaner exclusivism and Anglo-Afrikaner conflict destroyed the basis of the old National/Labour Pact. Another realignment in 1939 on the outbreak of war divided Afrikanerdom anew and put the Labour Party into combination with its old capitalist enemies, not on a class, but on an historic issue. Many Afrikaner working men, whose economic interests were not threatened by the war—rather the reverse—refused to follow their English-speaking contemporaries into the armed forces. Their opposition to the war was soon reinforced by the fear that the war was leading to renewed assault on the industrial color bar.

By 1948, the balance was changing between the essentially political and historical issues of relations with Britain and cultural issues dividing whites on the one hand, and the social, economic, and political issues of relations with the South African majority on the other. Afrikaner nationalists were deeply divided during the war, but not over the issue of the war itself. Indeed opposition to involvement in the war was one of the few things on which they agreed. Reiterating a winning formula used in 1929, the election of 1948 was fought by exploiting various "threats", Red and Black, internal and external, to white, and to Afrikaner, South Africa. Issues of foreign policy, such as participation in the war, were played down (Carter, 1958: 35). Having achieved power, Nationalists embarked on an ambitious program, largely domestic and almost entirely concerned with white/non-white relations. In 1957, however, the government decided that "God Save the Queen" and the Union Jack were no longer to be used on state occasions; it is a measure of change in South Africa that the decisions caused hardly a ripple whereas "thirty years previously either would have sent the country into paroxysms of excitement and anger" (De Villiers in Wilson and Thompson, 1971: 394).

With the postwar changes in the Commonwealth, Afrikaner attitudes toward it became ambivalent, not uncompromisingly hostile as one would have expected from a supposedly republican party. In 1951 Dr. Malan deplored Britain's tendency to lay down the white man's burden in Africa and elsewhere; after his attendance at the coronation of Elizabeth II in 1953, he claimed that South Africa could not be freer than it was (Walker, 1957: 825, 843). But during the

fifties, and especially after the independence of Ghana in 1957, the Commonwealth became an instrument of intervention in South Africa's internal affairs,
and South Africa left the Commonwealth in 1961, after a narrow vote on a
plebiscite (Stultz and Butler, 1963: 87). Events since then have clearly put that
issue beyond doubt: the vote for the Commonwealth today would be extremely
small, especially since UDI in Rhodesia. Indeed the editor of the *Cape Times*
noted in 1969 that young white South Africans showed far less interest in the
Commonwealth issue than did those who served in one or both world wars (Cape
Times, September 1, 1969).

   In the period before 1948, then, and perhaps even to 1960, white politicians,
and their constituents generally, appear to have felt sufficiently confident of
their ability to maintain the system of white power so as to concentrate most of
their political energies on historic and cultural conflicts among whites. This is
not to say that no attention was given white/non-white conflict but to argue that
the major conflicts were not concerned with "native policy." Indeed, the major
legislation of 1936, which removed qualified Africans in the Cape from the
voters roll, was carried by an overwhelming majority, much the same
combination of forces that brought into existence the Union of 1910, and
passed the Native Lands Act of 1913. Though there was a steady move toward
segregationist policies, or rather toward making segregation both more precise
and legally rather than conventionally enforced, political debate centered on
traditional, historical, and cultural issues, with "bread and butter" issues
between whites playing a minor role.

   Since 1948, the development of serious internal and external challenges to
the political system—and particularly to its restriction of full political participation to whites—has been accompanied by a fundamental change in the content
of debate. The introduction of the term apartheid into political discourse,
combined with an elaboration of the machinery of security since 1960, has
meant an increasing preoccupation with the dominant cleavage. The age-old
question of "solving" the "native problem" has moved to the center of the stage
where it is likely to remain.

   In all its essentials, therefore, the 1910 consensus survives. The "color line"
has been defined and redefined and neither major party means to abandon it as
the boundary of political power. Within that consensus, and within a new body
of law covering many aspects of political behavior, we still have vigorous debate
but it is a regime which limits severely those who want to abolish the boundary
by reaching across it. But such limitations do not preserve the boundary from
attack. The issues which dominate South African politics are now far more
concerned with race than they were before 1948. The programs of Afrikaner
nationalists in relation to national identity—republic, flag, anthem, and so
on—and in relation to language and culture have been achieved. External
relations have taken a new form: those with African states, who regard South
Africa as a major threat; those with the Western powers whose investment in
South Africa has increased rapidly but who find South Africa's internal policies
offensive and embarrassing; and relations with the non-governmental world of
sport, covering both visiting sportsmen and the participation of South Africans
overseas. South African white politics are now ethnic politics only in the sense
that one of the major parties is still predominantly from one ethnic group; and
they are class politics only in the sense that the governing party is heavily

dependent on the votes of white working men who feel they have most to lose by changes in the dominant cleavage.

VI

We have then in South Africa a society in which both "vertical" and "horizontal" systems of stratification co-exist. On the white side of the dominant cleavage there is ethnic co-existence, in which there has been considerable restraint in the use of power by one white group against the other. That restraint, however, persisted only so long as the dominant cleavage was accepted as legitimate, inside and outside the country. With the development of a large body of opinion hostile to the regime, South African whites who accept the dominant cleavage have drawn together. They have accepted serious limitations on freedom of the press and organization and an elaborate security system, which is used against white and non-white alike. While the preservation of the cleavage has always been part of the consensus on which parliamentary politics was based, it has never before been so seriously threatened. Though most of those who attack the dominant cleavage today are English-speaking, the issue is a general one of political morality on which both language groups are now divided.

The change in the content of white politics has important implications for Afrikanerdom. Between 1914—the date of the founding of the National Party—and today, a party based on an ethnic appeal, which included an exploitation of historical, cultural and economic issues, achieved most of its major objectives in its conflict with the South African British and those Afrikaners who were prepared to ally themselves with them. The party, though successful, is now faced with all the consequences of its own success and of major social changes in the nature of the ethnic group it represents.

Leaving aside the small minority of South African whites who want a major redistribution of power, it seems that resentment by Afrikaners of status differences between Afrikaners and English speakers has declined with the rapid occupational diversification of the past twenty-five years. Similarly, although South African English speakers still take the superiority of English culture for granted, they now take Afrikaners and their culture more seriously. Within Afrikaner society there has been a rapid change in the nature of its elites. In 1910 political leaders were recruited from the church, farming, and the law. In the thirties they were joined by young intellectuals from universities. The National Party is still led by these groups. The new men of business have yet, however, to make their mark in politics, and may well precipitate a conflict between traditional and modern leaders as they reflect major interests unrepresented in Afrikaner ranks until recently. Are ethnic issues likely to remain of importance to them, or are they likely to develop common interests with English-speaking equivalents?

If intra-white ethnic conflict is being superseded by black/white conflict and a search for white unity, what form will political conflict take? One of the characteristics of a parallel system is that relationships between communities are often like international relations; contact is made by negotiation between elites (Horowitz, 1971: 234-235). If one elite, the Afrikaner, is radically changed in character, and old issues lose their interest and relevance, it may be that the parallel system will break down, or at the very least, there will be a radical realignment of social groups and parties, and consequently of the issues of politics.

As Stultz (1969: 18) has pointed out, the danger of a success can easily be exaggerated: though it is easier to make a revolution than to sustain it, Afrikaner political objectives were profoundly conservative and securely based in the fears of a people hoping for a return to a golden age. "When ethnic conflict occurs horizontal groups usually aim, not at social transformation, but at the exclusion of other parallel groups from power, and often at reversion to an idealized, ethnically homogeneous *status quo ante*" (Horowitz, 1971: 235). However a major change in issues *has* already taken place and apartheid and economic development between them are changing the nature of non-white elites. In the theory and practice of apartheid, non-white elites or selected portions of them play an important role, though it can hardly be said that in practice the dominant whites really negotiate with them. But that is precisely the issue that is beginning to divide national Afrikanerdom, because ideal apartheid has as its model a classic parallel system of ethnic co-existence where there is contact between elites in politics and administration, and between the people, if at all, only in the marketplace.

Whether to negotiate with non-whites or to command has long been an issue, as it has been before in rapidly industrializing societies in which political rights were limited. In South Africa, however, there is a condition that militates against the development of a class structure among whites which would produce leaders capable of developing cross-cutting political ties with non-white groups. The whites at the bottom of the scale of income and status feel they have most to lose by a change in the dominant cleavage. "Since most white settlers are distributed towards the base of the white occupational structure, there is in the class situation of these settlers, who constitute a majority of voters and are most exposed to competition by subordinate groups, the social basis for politics of racial extremism" (Kuper in Plotnicov and Tuden, 1970: 90). White working men are enfranchised and mobilized and largely, but not entirely, Afrikaans-speaking.

There exists, therefore, a continuing basis for a political appeal combining ethnic and class elements, hardly new in South African politics, and one at which Afrikaner politicians have been adept (Stadler, 1969). Those sections of the white elite, and especially Afrikaners, who want to change the distribution of power, status, and reward may well continue to find themselves isolated, and the dominant cleavage may remain, in spite of the development of a new form of ethnic co-existence among whites.

NOTES

1. Vertical systems are divided by horizontal cleavages; horizontal systems by vertical cleavages.
2. "Bantu" is the term used by the South African government; it is synonymous with the modern use of "African"; both terms are used in this paper.
3. I use "racial" to define the dominant cleavage; "ethnic" to define sub-groups on each side of that cleavage.
4. Van den Berghe (1967: 181), writes: "Should the Nationalists have any prospect of losing an election, they would not allow the election to take place, or they would fake the results." This is, of course, merely an opinion.

5. I do not enter here into the thorny question of whether a genuine parliamentary regime on the British model survives.
6. The costs of "dubbing" are reportedly a major issue in the debate over the introduction of television (Washington Post, July 13, 1970).
7. Afrikaner nationalists are divided into two factions: *verkrampte,* inward looking, restricted; *verligte,* enlightened.

REFERENCES

ADAM, H. [ed.] (1971a) South Africa: Sociological Perspectives. London: Oxford University Press.
––– (1971b) Modernizing Racial Domination. Berkeley: University of California Press.
Buro of Statistics (1968) South African Statistics. Pretoria: Government Printer.
Cape Times (1969) July 5.
––– (1969) August 8.
––– (1969) September 1.
––– (1969) September 8.
CARTER, G. (1958) The Politics of Inequality: South Africa since 1948. New York: Praeger.
HANCOCK, W. K. (1962) Smuts: The Sanguine Years 1871-1919. Cambridge: The University Press.
HOROWITZ, D. L. (1971) "Three dimensions of ethnic politics." World Politics 23, 2 (January): 232-244.
HOUGHTON, D. H. (1964) The South African Economy. Cape Town: Oxford University Press.
KRUGER, D. W. (1958) The Age of the Generals. Johannesburg: Dagbreek Book Store.
KUPER, L. and M. G. SMITH [eds.] (1969) Pluralism in Africa. Berkeley: University of California Press.
LeMAY, G.H.L. (1965) British Supremacy in South Africa 1899-1907. Oxford: Clarendon.
MARQUARD, L. (1962) The Peoples and Policies of South Africa. London: Oxford University Press.
PATTERSON, S. (1957) The Last Trek. London: Routledge & Kegan Paul.
PLOTNICOV, L. and A. TUDEN [eds.] (1970) Essays in Comparative Social Stratification. Pittsburgh: University of Pittsburgh Press.
ROBERTS, M. and A.E.G. TROLLIP (1947) The South African Opposition 1939-1945. London: Longmans Green.
SACHS, E. S. (1952) The Choice Before South Africa. London: Turnstile Press.
STADLER, A. W. (1969) "The Afrikaner in opposition, 1910-1948." J. of Commonwealth Political Studies, 7, 3 (November): 204-215.
STULTZ, N. and J. BUTLER (1963) "The South African general election of 1961." Political Science Q. 78, 1 (March): 86-110.
THOMPSON, L. M. (1966) Politics in the Republic of South Africa. Boston: Little, Brown.
––– (1960) The Unification of South Africa 1902-1910. Oxford: Clarendon Press.
VAN DEN BERGHE, P. (1967) South Africa: A Study in Conflict. Berkeley: University of California Press.
VAN DER MERWE, H. W. and J. J. BUITENDAG (n.d.) "Some sources of differentiation among white South Africans." Cape Town: Abe Bailey Institute. (mimeo)
WALKER, E. A. (1957) A History of Southern Africa. London: Longmans Green.
WELSH, D. (1969) "Urbanisation and the solidarity of Afrikaner nationalism." J. of Modern African Studies, 7, 2, (March): 265-276.
WILSON, M. and L. THOMPSON [eds.] (1971) The Oxford History of South Africa. Volume II. New York: Oxford University Press.

Chapter 12

A COMMENTARY

ANTHONY P. MAINGOT

*I*n this commentary and critique it is assumed that the purpose of comparative analysis is to arrive at a set of generalizations which have an applicability beyond the case studies on which they are based. It should be clear that the vast factual and specialized knowledge and the richness of the conceptual and theoretical postulations contained in these four papers make any pretense at synthesis difficult if not completely absurd. Thus, I will limit myself to two broad comments, or, better, critiques, of all the papers, making reference to specific papers only when directly called for by the treatment of the two points.

The first critique deals with the failure in all these papers to deal with the formal institutions, political, legal, economic, of the societies treated. In what way have ethnic group relationships been purposeful creations of the state or at least consequences of specific political or legal measures? As behaviorally oriented social scientists, we often tend to disregard or at least minimize the social effects of formal institutions, especially constitutions, methods of selecting the political leadership, and legal institutions. It is clear that formal institutions such as constitutions and electoral systems are created by specific decisions which can affect the nature of the social system which a country develops in a permanent way (compare Lipset, 1961; Duverger, 1962).

The second critique is intimately related to the first. Since two of the three case studies—USSR and South Africa—are totalitarian societies, examples par excellence of manipulated social structures, one has to enquire to what extent can generalizations be derived from the study of status and conflict in totalitarian societies? To limit the analysis of South African politics to the political participation among whites is illusory; for the majority of South Africans the state is clearly totalitarian, legislating on even the most minute aspect of their existence. Since the concept of the "plural society" is utilized in two of the case studies it might be illuminating to discuss the two points raised above in terms of Furnivall's original use of the concept plural society.

A fundamental part of Furnivall's thesis is his view that the plural society was not created by fiat, by a series of policies, but rather these policies were dictated by economic circumstances. "The plural society," he noted, "was not planned; it happened" (Furnivall, 1945: 169).

> "present conditions have not arisen out of statements of policy in the past. There was no deliberate choice between indirect rule, direct rule and the dual mandate. They were dictated by economic circumstances; they happened" [Furnivall, 1945: 169].

And it happened because no one group monopolized power, no one group could structure the institutions of society in its favor or in its image. What one had, therefore, was two or more groups living side by side, without intermingling.

Each group retained its own standards and ideas concerning what was right and proper (Furnivall, 1939: 445-50, passim). Since none of the groups has political, social, or economic predominance, the society is kept together only by pressure from the outside. "The plural society is in fact held together only by pressure exerted from outside by the colonial power; it has no common social will' (Furnivall, 1945: 168).

It is wrong to assume that such a society was conflict-free; to Furnivall, the most obvious characteristic of the plural society was that the tension existing everywhere between classes with conflicting economic interests was intensified in a plural society by a corresponding cleavage along racial lines. But again, this conflict was not a result of explicit state policies or legislation; it was a "natural" result of competition.

To turn to the South African case, one has to note that not only did the South African state become an agent in the "definition" and "maintenance" of ethnic cleavages, but rather that the "state" in fact created and institutionalized a specific type of cleavage or stratification system. One finds in South Africa not merely a form of government but also a theory of government which provides official behavior a solid philosophical underpinning. A particular vision of the ordering of groups was embodied in the institutions and laws of the state which in turn assured the creation of just such an order of events. The interaction between theory or ideology and formal institutions goes deep in Afrikaner history. As early as 1858 the Frontier attitude was embodied in the Constitution of the Transvaal: "The people will admit no *gelykstelling* (putting on an equal basis) between the White and the Coloured inhabitants either in Church or State" (Mason, 1970: 201). Butler's statement that South African society "contains a cleavage which determines the allocation of power, status, and reward . . ." should rather read: "The white sector monopolizes power which allows them to determine the allocation of status and rewards and thus the nature of the cleavage in the society."

It is a question of power, of purposeful use of that power to insure continued retention of that power. Note Butler's analysis:

> "powerlessness and ethnic identity are not simply a residue of history but are legally defined and enforced. The dominant cleavage is a classic example of an ascriptive barrier where the power to define or redefine identity is not left to individual choice. *The state defines first,* and most important, the distinctions between white and non-whites . . . between Asiatics, Coloreds, and Bantu; . . . between various Bantu groups" (p. xxx, emphasis added).

Contrary to the classical "plural society," thus, the relationships between the various sectors of South African society have largely been determined by the institutional structure of the society.

To understand the attitudes of present-day white organized labor toward the African laborer it is important to understand the step by step construction of legal barriers to African competition: the Mines and Works Act, 1911; the Apprenticeship Act, 1922; the Industrial Conciliation Act of 1924; the Wage Act, 1925; and finally, the frankly uncivilized Civilized Labour Policy which gave whites priority for employment and higher wages over non-whites. Similarly, the population movements which began as a natural consequence of economic development soon were covered by the general doctrine of the state, and enforced by another law, the Group Areas Act of 1950.

It is crucial, then, to focus on the nature of the state organization, its political and legal institutions.

To see the ordering of society, its major cleavages, as an attribute rather than a process is misleading. Social processes can be directed this way or that by the types of decisions made by those in power. Phillip Mason (1970) has suggested that the conflict between whites in South Africa began as a conflict between town (Cape Town especially) and Frontier. His analysis (p. 200) is worth quoting at some length:

> "From the view point of the Cape, the Frontier and its sharp distinctions were far away. There was no need to divide the world into 'us, the people' and dangerous enemies, the Bushmen with their poisoned arrows, the Xhosa and the Zulu with their assegais. There was a gradation of rank, status, and wealth among whites; some free blacks had property. The influence of Europe was perceptible and was an influence for moderation and conciliation. There was much to suggest a development similar to that of Brazil, where racial origin, though important, is only one element in social identification."

Crucial in the eventual emergence to political power of the Frontier and consequently its theory of government was the voting system which, as Mason (1970: 213) notes, "in their optimism the British Government had allowed to be titled so as to over represent the rural, that is, the Afrikaner vote." Had power remained in the urban centers the processes of ethnic group identification and status distribution conceivably would have been different.

As distinct from the plural society which just "happens" it is clear that the cleavages in South Africa were created.

The focus on formal institutions leads to the second major question and substantive critique of these papers: to what extent can any generalization be derived from case studies of authoritarian, if not totalitarian, societies? Or the reverse, are theories of race and ethnic group relations which are derived from politically plural societies, applicable to totalitarian or authoritarian systems?

Alex Inkeles (1964) has noted that the first things the totalitarian does once in command of state power is to destroy, or at least shape to a new mold, all independent associations, groups or other potential centers of power. Ethnic groups are invariably among these (also see Friedrich, 1964). The purpose is the forced creation of a perfect new society, a purposeful reordering of the status and role assignments in the society. The official ideology or doctrine covers all aspects of man's life in society and is supposed to be adhered to uniformly—the state-dictated laws and police machinery see to that.

Thus, we have here the opposite of the plural society which has no collective or central will of its own; there is nothing forcing the different ethnic groups to abandon their own traditions and approaches to life; the society is kept together only by the material benefits to be derived from a common marketplace and by outside pressures.

In this regard it is important to note that a crucial feature of the authoritarian system is its relative immunity to outside influence. Again, the case of South Africa is that of an ethnic group, the Afrikaner, which broke any and all ties, except of course marketplace ones, with the metropolis. The rising wave of Labor Party and socialist opposition to colonial rule of the early twentieth century had little or no effect on the bulk of South African whites, much less of course on the Afrikaner. That immunity has increased and is today shared by the

Portuguese enclaves in Africa. Even the English southern Rhodesians have not been able to withdraw totally from the currents of broad world opinion, though important sectors of the dominant white group seem willing to sever international ties in exchange for a free hand at home.

It is no surprise, on the other hand, that intensified articulation of ethnic group identities in the USSR has followed Krushchev's de-Stalinization program; that is, the liberalization of the Soviet's "official doctrine" as described by Barghoorn. A mobilized world opinion has definitely played a role in the agitation of Soviet Jews.

To conclude, then, the minimizing of the role of formal institutions in shaping the character of ethnic groups has led to two positions which need querying: (1) the implicit acceptance of major cleavages in the society as attributes of the social structure, rather than as consequences of a clear process of political and ideological action. The secondary consequence of this is an underestimation of the capacity of the state (i.e., of power wielders) to either create or remove barriers to the homogenization of ethnic groups; and (2) the indifference as to the nature of the society from which social science models are derived and to which they are applied. Clearly, a closer look at formal institutions is called for even if it does mean putting some traditional reins on the galloping horse of behavioralism. (For an insightful study on how the comparative analysis of formal institutions provides valuable leads for the study of race relations, see Goveia, 1960.)

REFERENCES

DUVERGER, M. (1962) Political Parties. New York: John Wiley.
FRIEDRICH, C. J. (1964) "The unique character of totalitarian society," pp. 47-60 in C. J. Friedrich (ed.) Totalitarianism. New York: Grosset & Dunlap.
FURNIVALL, J. S. (1945) "Some problems of tropical economy," p. 169 in R. Hinden (ed.) Fabian Colonial Essays. London: George Allen & Unwin.
––– (1939) Netherlands India. Cambridge: Cambridge University Press.
GOVEIA, E. V. (1960) "The West Indian slave laws of the eighteenth century." Ciancias Sociales (Puerto Rico), 4, 1 (March): 75-105.
INKELES, A. (1964) "The totalitarian mystique: some impressions of the dynamics of totalitarian society," p. 99 in C. J. Friedrich (ed.) Totalitarianism. New York: Grosset & Dunlap.
LIPSET, S. M. (1961) Party Systems and the Representation of Social Groups. Berkeley: University of California Press.
MASON, P. (1970) Patterns of Dominance. London: Oxford University Press.

Part III

CONFLICT

Chapter 13

FUNCTIONS OF ETHNIC CONFLICT
AND THEIR CONTRIBUTIONS TO NATIONAL GROWTH

WALTER E. FREEMAN

In the evolution of nations and the emergence of ethnicity, patterns of sub-cultural survival occur in such a way as to appear to mitigate the growth of nationhood and the existence of a national identity Analyses of national growth and ethnic conflict patterns often focus upon societies which are achieving national status after years of colonization and Western domination. Societies seeking nationalism not only are attempting to achieve a higher degree of internal ethnic identity, but are struggling to divorce themselves as much as possible from cultural attributes acquired through years of assimilation to political and economic institutions which, if not totally inappropriate to their now existing problems afford embarrassment and confusion to pressures placed upon them as they attempt to achieve a new sense of sovereignty and national purpose.

Added to the conflict brought about by past identification with external cultural systems has been the inheritance of years of internal divergence created in part by ruling nations which gained advantage through maintaining and encouraging strong and separate ethnic identities in competition with one another. Such identities were often the outcome of previous struggles between other invading forces which had merely preceded the contemporary masters.

Further examination of the struggle between ethnic groupings in national growth calls for a comparison between "developing" nations and "developed" nations in the nation building process. In a functional sense, the process of nation-building is continuous and only terminates with the demise or radical change in the national existence. Ethnic competition and conflict appear to play a functional part in the maintenance and existence of any societal system when observed in the framework of national growth. Although the subject of this paper cannot be considered as breaking new ground in the discussion of cultural and social pluralism, it is hoped that the points discussed might lead to further exploration in the analysis and taxonomy of ethnic conflict and the contribution of that analysis to an understanding of nation-building and nationalism.

An analysis of many stages of nation-building and a wider range of ethnic identity is clearly needed to understand nationhood and ethnic conflict. The collection of papers within this book contributes to that purpose. In Part III attention has been paid to newly developing nations of the post-colonial period. Further interest in ethnic conflict should extend to all cases found in the readings of this book. In the study of developing nations, greatest attention is paid to incipient conditions which relate to the past, but may well result in ethnic divisions in more established and strongly identified nations of the future.

Ethnicity and nationhood are in constant change and the product of continuing pressures of new social relationships, both internal and external to the nation. It is often the case that conflict manifests a high degree of hostility. Such hostility may be the result of ethnic competition for power, status, and wealth within the national system. Though conflict may result in hostility it is also a means of reducing more serious impediments to social interaction, such as insularity, subjugation, alienation, and attrition (Caplow, 1964: 326-330).

Ethnic conflict contributes to national growth through the major functions of intensifying interaction and social communication, increasing social solidarity and development, and of calling for individual and group commitment to a national identity (Himes, 1966: 1-10).

Conflict over desired goals draws ethnic groups together if for no other reason than to contest the rights of the competing parties. Divergent groups which might by choice seek avoidance of one another are prevented such an alternative through the necessity of interacting in a state of competition. In short they must agree to disagree and this state of acceptance calls for an acknowledgment of participation. Studies of racial conflict have emphasized the solidarity that grows from this interaction (Suttles, 1969: 99-148; Waskow, 1966; Wolf, 1970). Struggles for power result in coalitions of diverse groups, draw together groups with weak identity, and bring concerted efforts for cohesive action. Competing parties seek some source of arbitration and acceptance of a greater source of authority which assists in the growth of national identity. Further discussion will point out the interdependence that brings about such a condition, but first some consideration of the character of conflict itself is necessary.

Coser emphasizes that "Conflict is not always dysfunctional for the relationship within which it occurs; often conflict is necessary to maintain such a relationship. Without ways to vent hostility toward each other and to express dissent, group members might feel completely crushed and might react by withdrawal" (Coser, 1954: 48).

Maintenance of national identity and the persistence of the national system calls for release mechanisms for conflict and hostility which are dysfunctional.

Release mechanisms are developed within a society in such a way as to avoid social dissolution and may be manifested in substitution of groups and objects for the displacement of hostility from other more critical objects of conflict (Coser, 1954: 48-49). This results in avoiding the direct source of conflict and disagreement. Scapegoating and the emphasis of ethnic differences have played an important role in the development of many nations and have served to direct more serious questions of disagreement toward less significant areas of conflict. In such cases, maintenance of ethnic differences when not aimed directly at a contest of power or desired national goals sustains a competitive position for all groups and denies the possibility of a national unity based upon superiority or dominance of any one sub-culture (Glazer and Moynihan, 1963). Ethnicity, then, may reinforce the certainty of competitive group interests and the maintenance of equal opportunities within the system for the achievement of desired positions in the societal hierarchy. Nations which have emerged with a number of significant ethnic divisions in their early stages of development may maintain this system of competitive differentiation as long as the essential conflicts among them do not revolve around critical goals of national growth or develop in such a way as to call for total or complete dominance on the part of any one elite group or ethnic party. When this becomes the case, ethnic differences become related to contests of "realistic conflict" (Coser, 1954: 48-49). "Conflicts which arise from frustration of specific demands within the relationship and from estimates of gains of the participants, and which are directed at the presumed frustrating object, can be called realistic conflicts, insofar as they are means toward a specific result." When specific goals conflict in such a way as to point toward subjugation of any particular ethnic group, then ethnic conflict may no longer be viewed as a means of releasing hostility but instead, until such conflicts are resolved, may continue as a force which inhibits national growth and development.

All realistic conflict, however, need not result in threats to national growth and unity. It may well lead to increased communication, unity, and national identity.

COMMUNAL ETHNICITY

Most often ethnic conflict becomes realistic conflict as ethnicity becomes defined communally. Communal ethnicity requires some degree of locality identity upon the part of people. It further requires a condition where major social functions are met in a community sense and shared in common by ethnic members to some degree; production and consumption, socialization, social control, and cohesiveness must be maintained in common to sustain communal ethnicity.

Communal relationships are focused upon the sharing of social interaction within a common locality. It is within the community setting that one finds the microcosm of societal living and in fact when dealing with tribal and kinship units, community and society often become interchangeable concepts. Societal institutions become articulated in communal activities and when geography, climate, and history have provided people with a relative degree of insularity from contacts with other human societies, these communal relationships provide for a homogeneity of patterned beliefs and sentiments. The normative system of people living in communal isolation provides the basis for the commonality of local endogamy, linguistics, and religion. Such commonalities give foundation to ethnic structure prototypes. For this reason ethnicity considered beyond communal origin weakens in its capacity to attract and hold adherence to the generic value system. When contact and interaction with other groups take place, ethnic communities seek to maintain territorial boundary arrangements (Barth, 1969: 9-38).

TERRITORIAL CONFLICT

Whether belief systems regarding property ownership are collective or individual, institutional arrangements regarding land and property still define clearly the insider from the outsider. Territorial conflict appears to be a fundamental consequence of ethnic integrity. Most theories regarding the growth of civilization and cultures lay emphasis upon the collective response for protection and fortification. Theories of city growth have emphasized the concept of the "natural area" for the maintenance, identity, and semi-autonomy of homogeneous groups (Park, 1952; Stein, 1960: 22-27). Human ecologists have documented their theories with studies of the struggle between groups of people for scarce space and the accommodation that is necessary for man to make as a consequence of these struggles. Thus, competition, concentration, centralization, segregation, invasion, and succession become the major processes which shape the city and help form the subcommunities or cultural islands (Martindale and Neuwirth, 1958; Stein, 1960). All struggles for land space, whether in the city or village, are dependent upon the concentration of people. The amount of land available to the number of people a community supports determines conditions which affect spatial competition. The studies in this section which reflect ethnic conflict show a wide range of population density features, ranging from the most extreme population densities in Pakistan to relatively sparsely populated areas in Ghana and Kenya and in all but the coastal area in Guyana. Also density relationships vary among local ethnic groups within nations. The variance in density features frequently determines the intensity of any ethnic conflict and the extent to which the competing parties will struggle for dominance over one another.

Internal conflict within nations over territorial demands may serve as a way of determining accountability of sub-cultural groups since clearly delineated community boundaries provide national leadership with the means of identifying local leadership in the implementation of national goals. Conflict with external national forces can also draw otherwise conflicting ethnic groups together for purposes of defending common territory in which future disputes may still take place.

HOMOGENEITY OF COMMUNITY SOCIAL STRUCTURE

When density features are such that they provide less and less opportunities for dominance to be expressed in terms of the struggle for space, the growth in the complexity of the "division of labor" results in ranking of groups and the people within the groups. "The roomier the environment, the more likely it is that order will be achieved through territorial spacing; the denser the population the more likely will it be that societies must turn to rank order as an organizing principle" (Ardrey, 1971: 240). Although a greater degree of homogeneity may be expected with less dense a population, errors have been made through assumptions regarding homogeneity of populations in communities which are relatively less urban, smaller in size, and agricultural or of a peasant structure (Steward, 1950). These errors are partly a result of the preoccupation of early social theorists to stress the great historical processes which led to changes transforming feudal societies to modern contractual ones (Tonnies, 1957). Taxonomies which polarized folk-urban, sacred-secular, Gemeinschaft-Gesellschaft, etc. have resulted in oversimplified generalizations of community structure applied in part to communities found in developing cultures (Loomis & Beegle, 1959). Traditional peasant communities vary according to the development of nationhood in the countries where they are found, the character of kinships structure, and the rigidity of flexibility of their class or caste hierarchy (Lewis, 1958). Many of these communities on a continuum of measurement between structural homogeneity and heterogeneity might appear more complex and varied in their social structure than small communities in more developed nations.

When communities are composed of a social structure which is primarily homogeneous, strong ethnic identity exists; especially if such identity is determined by some degree of competition and challenge from neighboring and competing communities. Communities with more heterogeneous structures maintain sub-cultures within them and where strong sub-communal identity is to be found are able to sustain strong ethnicity among the smaller groups. This is often the case in caste societies which have developed "para-communities" (Rudolph and Rudolph, 1967) through more flexible arrangements within their social ranking. Where class interests within a community become defined more as special group or quasi-group interests (Dahrendorf, 1959: 179), some decline in communal ethnicity may appear evident. This does not mean that less conflict exists between interests groups than exists between sub-community groups but there would appear to be more areas of agreement open to those groups in conflict which hold in common a greater degree of locality interdependence through the sharing of economic, social, and political needs at the community level. It is at the point of locality interdependence that the horizontal patterns of group efforts to function with one another are evident. A community's horizontal pattern of relationships is "the structural functional relation of its various social units and sub-systems to each other. The term 'horizontal' is used to indicate that, roughly speaking, the community units, *insofar as they have relevance to the community system,* tend to be on approximately the same hierarchical level . . . as opposed to a state, regional, national, or international level of authority . . . " (Warren, 1963: 161-163). At the horizontal level of conflicting interests, issues and controversies become determined in the light of local authority, and the decision-making.

VERTICAL AND HORIZONTAL DIMENSIONS OF CONFLICT

Whether homogeneous or heterogeneous in structure, the community in a systemic sense maintains the horizontal dimension of cohesiveness through local unity. Such a condition poses structural problems for nation-building (MacIver, 1928). There is a vertical dimension to communal ethnicity which calls attention to this basic conflict between locality identification and nationalism. This vertical dimension refers to all locality relationships and their functional dependence upon extra community systems (Warren, 1963: 161-163). It is necessary to build in any nation a system of interrelated locality units which provide sub-systems having some degree of economic, social and political self-sufficiency. When community structure is weakened, ethnicity has become a chief obstacle for growth in many developing countries. Changes in the traditional economy have resulted in imbalance. Marketing changes in Africa shifting from subsistence levels to national agricultural production have weakened locality identity and tribal self sufficiency in order to accommodate large-scale national economic plans (Bohannan and Dalton, 1965).

National leaders may not seek to weaken or eliminate ethnic identity but they must in the process of national planning rearrange communal ethnic functions in order to compete in an industrial society. National elites develop concern and suspicion regarding ethnic groups (Rudolph and Rudolph, 1967). The very existence of such a pressure brings to most ethnic minorities a fear of destruction, and a wariness of all other sub-cultural groups which are competing for new economic and political goals. The functions changed may not be economic alone. Efforts to move Village Aid programs to more efficient forms of local control and autonomy were included in plans for Basic Democracies of Pakistan (Inayatullah, 1967). Although encouraging the maintenance of locality control, new and increased accountability in the use of development funds and increased contact with outside officials did much to threaten the insular characteristics of village units. The concept of Basic Democracies, while allowing for greater participation of local leaders in the national policy-making, often coopted their power and reduced effectiveness at the local level.

Efforts on the part of Britain and the United States to shape national policy in Guyana threatened the communal balance of two major rural and urban groups. Africans and Asians had in the past found through interdependence between rural-urban needs a means of balance in the struggle for power in this growing nation. It is not unlikely that as Guyana grew and new economic forces emerged in its relationship with the world market the same or similar conditions would have resulted, brought about by a dependence upon other economies. Vertical dimensions of international economic and political functions create problems for nations as well as smaller communities.

Large social changes, that have brought to newly developing nations the modernity of the twentieth century, are in themselves indicators of future problems leading to ethnic conflict and point to the basic areas of disagreement which grow out of a struggle for power as new alignments to communal control take place (Rudolph and Rudolph, 1967).

Modernity witnessed in the Western world has resulted in inherent qualities of conflict as the major social changes of urbanization, indistrialization, and bureaucratization shifted locality self-sufficiency to greater interdependence at provincial, regional, and national levels. Local communal structures, as they have become reformed, do not disappear; people have held to local identity as they have grown to recognize expanded identity (Merton, 1957). Roles to be performed at the community level have become complicated as they may well serve functions locally, provincially and regionally at the same time. Such overlapping territorial functions have created conflict of identity for the people seeking to meet needs satisfied at the local level, but unobtainable if not affected at the regional or national level.

Since the major forces of social change (industrialization, urbanization, and bureaucratization) are inseparable conditions of contemporary national growth, attention must be paid to the structural balance of community functions within nations and to the shifts in interdependence which affect local identity. The horizontal patterns of community life are radically changed as nations become part of the international world. Nations seek greater integration of functions, wish to reduce internal dysfunctional competition, and attempt to acquire healthy intercourse among other nations. All such attempts have a way of reducing the horizontal function of the local communities. When too-rapid pressure for national growth exists, the horizontal function weakens, and national leaders witness growing dissatisfaction among local areas. New coalitions form and incipient forces of rebellion emerge. National programs in community development are often a recognition that this problem exists or are attempts to avoid its occurrence (Brokenshaw and Hodge, 1969: 161). Efforts to bring about strong local participation toward national goals are frequently enhanced by ethnicity.

CONFLICT TERMINATION

Ethnic conflict has been seen to be structurally determined by horizontal and vertical patterns of community life where ethnic groups are either to be found in semi-autonomous and self-sufficient communities, in para-communities subsumed in larger community structures or in quasi-interest groups which compete for goals represented by contests in the national arena of decision-making. Processes of conflict may be examined as they determine the direction taken by ethnic groups in their struggle for national status and power.

Caplow offers three heuristic typologies or patterns of conflict which are situationally oriented to group competition (Caplow, 1964: 335-365). *Episodic* conflict continues over an extended period of time, the conditions regarding conflict are known in advance, and there are more or less clearly defined means for achieving agreed upon goals. Episodic conflict calls for objective measurement of organization strength, procedures appropriate for conflict, and overlapping polarization of interests, and written rules accepted by all parties. Episodic conflict tends to maintain the equality or the agreed upon inequality of the combatants. *Continuous* conflict is less structured and gains are to be reached within the situation of conflict itself. Continuous conflict most often takes place between well-structured organizations or groups and between nations during times of peace. Continuous conflict can result in more intense struggles for power and lead to the third form of conflict which is terminal.

Terminal conflict involves competing parties in a struggle for a redistribution of power. In its extreme it calls for the destruction of the opposing party or parties. Few instances of terminal conflict take place where competing groups accept the conditions of total annihilation as they engage in a contest. Zero-sum games are rarely played even in the most intense rivalries between competing ethnic groups. In the termination of conflict losers may not concede to total loss nor winners be assured of complete victory (Coser, 1968: 37-51).

In conflict, episodic situations are most often reached as nations are established. Para-community structures blend with quasi-interest groupings in order that all parties seeking some gain in the national polity can be assured of protection and judicious arbitration from government elites. Tribal, kinship, and caste groups may form coalitions of power to maintain gains for their particular ethnic interests. As ethnic groupings become more vertically committed to the national ethos, as such groups find that the major communal functions of production and consumption, socialization, social control, and cohesiveness are met by the vertical dimensions of nationhood rather than through self-sufficient localities, and as ethnic groups become less tied to territorial struggles and more concerned for specific economic and political gains, conflicts which are ethnic in character may be intense and realistic in their consequence but may provide through the functional interdependence of all competing parties, a national identity which is strong enough to cope with vertical dimensions of the international world. When external forces threaten national existence, the network of interdependent relationships brought about through episodic periods of conflict relationship may serve as a means of meeting such threats.

Strong communal ethnicity most represented in autonomous and self-sufficient localities is often found in developing nations. Conflict which is internal to the nation is most often displayed in continuous conflict between these ethnic groups. There is always the implicit threat that such a condition may lead at any time to terminal conflict and the disruption that such conflict often obtains. The recent terminal event between West and East Pakistan resulting in Bangla Desh, clearly emphasizes the potential threat that continuous conflict holds for national development. Other nations have had to cope with such problems in different ways as demands for nationhood have created pressures upon ethnic minorities. Treatment of the Massai in Kenya by coalitions of other tribal groups has led through continuous conflict to lesser identity and to weaker communal strength on the part of these nomads. Their loss of territoriality and communal identity need not be as dramatic as the case of the Ibo in Nigeria but in a sense of continued national pressure events may lead to as drastic a climax and even greater a loss for the Massai than was the case of the ill-fated Biafra.

Of all terminal extremes in the studies provided in this section, Arab-Israeli tension illustrates the tenuous condition of conflict which may swing between efforts to terminate the struggle by complete annihilation or efforts to arrive at an uneasy condition which maintains continuous conflict allowing combatant parties to find some grounds for limited gains. Law regulating the Arab interests in denying Israeli legitimacy to its territorial claims and at the same time preventing Israeli interests from demanding international acceptance of its territorial conquests is aimed primarily at maintaining continuity of conflict rather than efforts to allow any party the freedom of coercion leading to termination.

Although terminal conflict has been illustrated in Pakistan, there are still significant areas of ethnic cleavage which are communal and largely territorial in scope. The Sind and the Northwest Frontier still offer serious problems of continuous conflict for the more powerful Punjabi elite. Unless more successful efforts are made to provide for the vertical articulation of communal needs through some form of government as has been tried with Basic Democracies, future terminal efforts on the part of these ethnic groups are more than likely.

The "soft states" of Southeast Asia illustrate extremes of widely separated ethnic groups bound by insularity and autonomy as well as more densely populated minorities existing in close proximity, where episodic conflict is often necessary. "Ethnic pluralism" among indigenous people as described by Enloe illustrates the necessity for some recognized system where controlled arrangements exist and some guarantee of arbitration is evident. Ghana and Kenya grow with tribal coalitions providing dominance in efforts to nationalize and "Africanize." Local tribal units are discouraged from their subsistence level of living and encouraged to produce cash crops for the national market. Both countries display a remarkable concern on the part of local minorities for some commitment to vertical competition for education and preferred positions in the occupational hierarchy. As elite groups hold desired positions, efforts must be made to enlarge occupational opportunities which elevate previously subordinate positions. With the encouragement of agricultural education in Kenya (Sheffield, 1967) and the development of this agricultural sector, larger number of ethnic groups deprived of limited education and limited job opportunities may be able to find greater opportunities in the economic and social stratification of the nation. Finally in the case of Guyana, ethnic identity, which has polarized more from external economic and political influence, may accommodate to more satisfactory levels of competition when the nation seeks adjustment to an industrializing economy. Past rural-urban interdependence has provided for controlled ethnic conflict through segregated labor functions. As Africans and Asians adjust to a more diversified economy brought about by the trends in the world market rather than just by ideological pressures from more powerful nations, conflicts that emerge in the future may be determined more through economic stratification than in any other institutional area. Newly formed interest groups may have to determine the nature of the continuous and episodic conflict which has existed in the nation in the past.

Nationhood for the most part seems to deny the probability of terminal conflict for ethnic groups except in the case of the most extreme minority examples where strong territorial identity challenges the existence of a functional national unity. Ethnic conflict although extremely difficult to manage for developing nations neems to be critical to their growth and strength. Few ethnic groups, even majorities, wish to eliminate contests for power at the expense of national growth and stability. Whether groups are subordinate or superordinate there always will be efforts to maintain a system by which conflict can be determined in advance, efforts to gain power for all groups exist, and conditions of the struggle whenever possible can be predicted.

REFERENCES

ARDREY, R. (1971) The Social Contract. New York: Dell Publishing.
BARTH, F. (1969) Ethnic Groups and Boundaries, Boston: Little, Brown, and Company.
BOHANNAN, P. and G. DALTON [eds.] (1965) Markets in Africa. Garden City, N.Y.: Doubleday.
BROKENSHAW, D. and P. HODGE (1969) Community Development: An Interpretation. Chicago: Chaldler Publishing.
CAPLOW, T. (1964) Principles of Organization. New York: Harcourt, Brace & World.
COSER, L. (1967) Continuities in the Study of Social Conflict. New York: Free Press.
––– (1954) The Functions of Social Conflict. New York: Free Press.
DAHRENDORF, R. (1959) Class and Class Conflict in Industrial Society. Standord, Calif.: Stanford University Press.
GLAZER, N. and D. P. MOYNIHAN (1963) Beyond the Melting Pot. Cambridge, Mass.: MIT Press.
HIMES, J. S. (1966) "The functions of racial conflict." Social Forces 45 (September).
INAYATULLAH, [ed.] (1962) Bureaucracy and Development in Pakistan. Peshawar, Pakistan: Pakistan Academy for Rural Development.
LEWIS, O. (1958) Village Life in Northern India. Urbana, Ill.: University of Illinois Press.
LOOMIS, C. and J. A. BEEGLE (1950) Rural Social Systems. New York: Prentice-Hall.
MacIVER, R. M. (1928) Community: A Sociological Study. New York: Macmillan.
MARTINDALE, D. and G. NEUWIRTH [trans. & eds.] (1958) "Prefatory remarks," in Max Weber, The City. New York: Free Press.
MERTON, R. (1949) "Patterns of influence: a study of interpersonal influence and of communication behavior in a local community," in Lazarsfeld and Stanton, Communications Research 1948-1949. New York: Harper & Bros.
PARK, R. E. (1952) Human Communities. New York: Free Press.
RUDOLPH, L. and S. RUDOLPH (1967) The Modernity of Tradition. Chicago: University of Chicago Press.
SHEFFIELD, J. R. [ed.] (1967) Education, Employment and Rural Development. Proceedings of a conference held at Kericho, Kenya 1966. Nairobi: East African Publishing House.
STEIN, M. (1960) The Eclipse of Community. Princeton, N.J.: Princeton University Press.
STEWARD, J. (1950) Area Research: Theory and Practice. Bull. 63. New York: Social Science Research Council.

SUTTLES, G. (1968) The Social Order of the Slum. Chicago and London: The University of Chicago Press.
TONNIES, F. (1957) Community and Society. [trans. & ed.] C. Loomis. East Lansing, Mich.: Michigan State University Press.
WARREN, R. L. (1963) The Community in America. Chicago: Rand McNally.
WASKOW, A. (1970) Running Riot. New York: Herder & Herder.
WOLF, M. (1970) Lunch at the Five and Ten, The Greensboro Sit-Ins. A Contemporary History. New York: Stein & Day.

Chapter 14

THE PALESTINIANS AND THE ARAB STATES

DAVID P. FORSYTHE and J. L. TAULBEE

*O*ver the last few years there has been a revival of interest in the relevance of law as a mechanism for conflict resolution. These same years have seen a demonstration of the undeveloped state of international law, particularly with regard to intra-state conflicts. That there is such wide disagreement as to questions of fact, legal consequence, and world order implications of internal war is a telling commentary on the current problems in applying legal standards to such conflicts. A major part of the disagreement can be explained in terms of the specific problems relating to fact determination and authoritative inter-pretation engendered by the nature of the environment in which the international legal order must function. Part can also be attributed to the ambiguous and emotionally charged atmosphere which is characteristic of all international actions where force or the threat of force is involved.

The Arab-Israeli conflict clearly raises the further question of whether or not the traditional approaches and concepts of international law are adequate to characterize the range and variety of contemporary internal disorders and the types of involvement by third states. It is the nature of many international legal norms that they are not specific enough in content to allow "illegal" behavior to be identified with confidence. This is especially true of norms purporting to limit the use of coercion. Under the general heading of "minor coercion," many different forms of coercive influence have remained largely undifferentiated in law. The major problem here is not the perennial one of making appropriate judgments about state behavior but the more complex problem of constructing categories that will accurately reflect the changed and changing milieu in which the law must function.

This is a challenging and perhaps insuperable task. The most fundamental obstacle to clarification remains the decentralized nature of the international legal order, which, when coupled with the normal presence of complementary patterns of norms, permits national decision-makers to reach authoritative determinations as to fact and legal consequence by their own "adversary" representations.[1] Even where there is a consensus in support of desired behavior, there is no uniformity of legal technique, or established framework with substantial agreement on usage to encourage a convergence of views. Often a single label is used to refer to several different phenomena, and a similarity in labels does not necessarily imply a similarity in factual points or legal reference.[2]

Yet there remains a need for third-party inquiry into the relevance of international law to conflicts such as the Arab-Israeli confrontation, and in particular into the status of Palestinian claims to use violence to change the present status quo. With due regard for the limitations of third-party observations, [3] it bears emphasizing that law—especially as understood by third parties—is both a technical language for the rational discussion of emotion-filled issues [4] and a framework of analysis leading to an understanding of what is a reasonable solution in the context of the conflict. [5] It is with these functions of law in mind that we make a tentative overview of the Arab-Israeli conflict.

One further series of comments is in order by way of introduction. No doubt some would insist on distinguishing political from legal considerations, and would argue that politics rather than law will determine the future of the Arab-Israeli conflict. It is the position of the present authors that this is not a viable distinction, that there are no inherently political disputes. [6] There is no antipathy between law and conflict over public policy; that is, normally one should not speak of a breakdown of law when conflict occurs. Law and conflict are intimately connected: conflict often produces legal norms by making explicit the issues in context, and by providing conditions for the development of "normative sets" that may help prevent future conflicts (Gould and Barkun, 1970: 190). Moreover, while law does function as a restraint system in pursuit of order, it also functions to promote and protect other public policy goals subsumed under the general heading of "equity." Thus law exists to promote cooperation in support of public policy as well as to restrain conflict. [7] Law constitutes the formal aspect of a particular conflict relationship and expresses the more lasting interests of the parties involved. This is only to point out that in most conflict situations the parties have shared as well as disputed interests (Ikle, 1963: 118 ff; Schelling, 1966: 35; Rapoport and Chammah, 1965). Law may then be characterized as a mediating structure—a mechanism which provides a common framework, a common point of reference for the control of cognitive divergence (Glenn et al., 1970: 37). [8]

LEGAL STATUS OF THE PALESTINIANS

The central issue in the Arab-Israeli conflict is the status of the Palestinians. The question has at least two dimensions: territorial control and personal identity. The former may be amenable to rational settlement, the latter may not. Most fundamentally the Arab-Israeli conflict reflects a mutual denial of national and personal identity (Glenn et al., 1970: 40; Peretz, 1970: 322; Harkabi, 1970: 209 ff). An increasingly major factor in the situation since 1967 has been the use of violence by various Palestinian organizations. Through various activities the fedayeen [9] have attempted to coerce not only Israel but certain Arab states as well. Thus it is clear that regional stability depends upon an equitable settlement of Palestinian claims. Is is toward an evaluation of such demands that international law becomes centrally relevant.

There is nothing to be gained from rewriting the history of the struggle for Palestine. Both Zionist and Arabs have numerous grievances and all have been subject to considerable extra-regional manipulation (Hurewitz, 1950; Khouri, 1969; Laquer, 1968). The initial problem in evaluating these grievances is characterization of the situation. For the purposes of this inquiry, there is reason to characterize the core Israeli-Palestinian struggle as a civil war for control of smaller Palestine. [10]

Arab claims regarding the non-legislative nature of the partition resolution (A/Res/147) purporting to divide Palestine between Zionists and Arabs have merit (Falk, 1970: 174; Asamoah, 1966: 11 ff; Lande, 1966; Onuf, 1970). There is considerable evidence to support the Arab contention that the terms of the original Mandate, the Balfour Declaration and Article 80 of the Charter plus continued and effective local control for over a thousand years guaranteed Palestinian rights in the territory (Elarby, 1968; Wright, 1970b: 277; Bousky, 1965: 265 ff). If the Assembly resolution is not legally binding, and if the United Kingdom were unable, as claimed, to protect the rights of the indigenous population in the territory, then the conflict is most accurately regarded as a civil war within the territory of Palestine, the Palestinians representing the potential incumbent regime of the state of Palestine.

Under the law of the Charter, intervention into such situations is forbidden. By contrast the customary law provides no authoritative prohibition against intervention (Brownlie, 1963: 322; Farer, 1968: 508, 515). In lieu of effective United Nations action, the participation of the Arab states in the 1948 fighting was defensible under customary law. However, despite the continued insistence of the relevance of these considerations by the Arab states, they are largely irrelevant to judgments about contemporary claims. Israel, as a successfully challenging regime in a protracted civil war, has acquired legitimacy through Arab acceptance of the partition resolution post-1948; Israel's admission to the U.N.; the general acceptance of Israel in bilateral recognition by most states; and the effective exercise of state functions over the territorial limits. Israel must be regarded as a legitimate state by any system of law that emphasizes order. The Palestinians then can be regarded as the challenging faction in a continuing struggle.

An important contemporary consideration is the legal relationship of the Arab states to the state of Israel as a backdrop to the core struggle. The Arab states have interpreted the four Armistice Agreements of 1949 as a temporary military cease fire pending settlement of the state of belligerency in a formal peace treaty. Accordingly, that state of belligerency is said to still exist. The status of an armistice seems to be a question not fully resolved in contemporary international law. The traditional interpretation favors the Arab view, while more recent developments tend to undermine it. Security Council practice has indicated that no claim of belligerency should be permitted under an armistice which envisages progress to peace and which expressly prohibits a return to hostilities. United Nations practice has apparently established the position that if U.N. machinery is in operation, an armistice under U.N. auspices establishes a legal situation in which the provisions of the Charter have been applied, thus ruling out any claim to a status of belligerency (Higgins, 1970, 1967: 214 ff).[11] Further, a claim to belligerency as enforcement of the right of the Palestinians to repatriation, rejected by Israel, cannot be accepted, given the controversy over the obligations established under that Assembly-established right in 1948 and Arab official statements challenging the legitimacy of Israel.[12]

These above considerations pertain to interstate relations, and may not directly apply to the Palestinians. Two basic questions remain of central importance: the validity of Palestinian claims vis-à-vis Israel, and permissible actions with respect to enforcement of these claims; and the legal relationship of the Arab state to the Palestinians. We now turn to this further area of complexity.

PALESTINIAN CLAIMS

There can be no challenge to the historical fact that Arabs constituted an overwhelming majority of persons and property owners in pre-1947 Palestine (Safran, 1969: 23-26; Peretz, 1954). While there is some challenge and controversy over responsibility for the exodus of Palestinian Arabs from their homes during 1947-1948, objective third-party inquiry cannot overlook the examples of concerted Zionist efforts to harass Arabs or the lack of empirical evidence to support arguments that Arab leaders encouraged flight (Stevens, 1952; Davis, 1968: 53-60; Safran, 1969: 35).

From these facts stem two types of Palestinian claim—a collective claim to national self-determination, recently endorsed by the General Assembly, and an individual claim to a choice between repatriation or resettlement with compensation, acknowledged yearly by the Assembly since 1948. These two types of claim can, in one form, be said to constitute one general claim. If repatriation of some 1.5 million Palestinians were to occur at once, the probability is that Israel as a Zionist state would cease to exist shortly thereafter either through violence or through peaceful means such as a higher birth rate.[13] Thus the two claims, when the possibility of larger-scale repatriation is left unqualified, can be viewed as complementary.

The claim to national self-determination presents rather obvious difficulties when asserted as a legal principle, despite repeated endorsements of the concept in the Assembly during the last decade. Historically the status of the concept in law has been murky (Tung, 1968). Moreover, it is obvious that the states that assert the principle as law restrict its application decidedly.[14] Of course black peoples are said to have the right to self-determination vis-à-vis white regimes. But what about Kurdish people in Iraq; Armenians in Lebanon; Georgians in the USSR; Navajos in the U.S.? There is, in short, no general application of the principle. Despite this rather major restriction on the development of national self-determination as a part of customary law, it seems relevant to note the fact that non-Western and socialist states assert quite strongly a claim that struggles for national liberation are "just" under the "higher" law of anti-imperialism.

The claim to choice between repatriation/resettlement is at once more complex and more simple. Freedom of choice in matters of repatriation has little standing in international law, except that there is agreement in opposition to focused repatriation, whether to the USSR in the 1940s or to North Korea in the 1950s. Moreover, the Palestinians have never claimed to be "stateless persons," in the precise meaning of that term. It is clear, however, that repatriation or resettlement is a community-desired choice for the Palestinians, as presented by yearly endorsements of the paragraph eleven of A/Res/194 (III) in each Assembly, plus numerous efforts to actually implement the principle over the past two decades via U.N. and U.S. efforts. The state of Israel is virtually a minority of one in opposition to recognition of the validity of the principle.

Part of the difficulty lies in the studied ambiguity surrounding Arab pronouncements concerning a "just solution to the refugee question." If the state of Israel be regarded as legitimate, as argued here and as supported by general state practice, then unqualified repatriation as a weapon against Israeli security cannot be permitted. There is little reason to believe, moreover, that unqualified repatriation could lead to a democratic, secular, binational state of Palestine; rather, there is every reason to anticipate violent opposition to, and violent struggle in that transformation.[15]

On the other hand, lack of equity and resettlement can lead to violence as well. Lack of equity for Palestinians forced from their homes by the state of Israel is obviously a condition conducive to extremist politics as recent events have demonstrated. Moreover, resettlement into Lebanon would upset the Christian-Moslem balance crucial to Lebanese stability; and resettlement into Jordan would likewise exacerbate the Palestinian-Jordanian split that has brought civil war once to that nation in the past years.

These considerations and the logic of the situation suggest that a feasible legal framework for satisfaction of Palestinian claims would center on the ideas of the Johnson Mission of the early 1960s (Johnson, 1964; Forsythe, 1971a). This Mission suggested a listing of preferences for the Palestinians, qualified by the right of the receiving state (Israel, Arab, or otherwise) to veto admissions for security reasons. Thus freedom of choice was to be qualified by legitimate state security interests. Nothing in this approach would preclude the process of resettlement from leading to the creation of an Arab state of Palestine in the West Bank area. Both Israel and Jordan might indeed endorse such a trend as a solution to certain problems. For both regimes, a state of Palestine in the West Bank area might reduce the charge of ignoring the self-determination rights of the Palestinians, thus reducing pressures for more violent actions.

While this line of reasoning does not endorse either the position of Israel, which rejects repatriation and choice per se, or that of the Palestinians, who demand unqualified choice and the demise of the Zionist state, the argument does possess the merits of its demerits. It is close to the policy position of both the United States and USSR, who endorse A/Res/194, Paragraph Eleven and the legitimacy of Israel.[16] Thus there would be some hope for a convergence of law and power. Moreover, recent statements by influential states such as the UAR and Jordan seem compatible with equity for the Palestinians and security for Israel.[17] Thus there would be some hope of support for this form of settlement from important elements in the Arab world.

ARAB STATES AND PALESTINIAN VIOLENCE

Given the above determination of the status and claims of the Palestinians, what then is the responsibility of the Arab states toward the Palestinians? The question, like the question of status and claims, is not easy to subsume under legal judgment. The focus of the controversy is the extent of Arab state responsibility for Palestinian violence against Israel.

The factual relationship between fedayeen groups and states, while complex, lends itself to some systemization. There is one fundamental differentiation among Arab states: (1) those which organize and control guerrilla groups as governmental policy, and (2) those which offer support to the guerrillas in various forms but who have neither initiated the groups nor control them. While virtually all Arab states offer either money, arms, logistical support, territorial bases, or verbal endorsement to the fedayeen, only a few Arab states have sought direct governmental control over particular groups. The UAR was the sponsor and patron of the original Palestine Liberation Organization (PLO) in the mid-1960s; Syria created Al Siquah as an adjunct of the Ba'ath party in the late 1960s; and Iraq has sought to control the guerrilla movement by forcibly opposing groups that do not adhere to governmental policy (Cooley, 1970: 5; Hudson, 1969; Sharabi, 1970; Harkabi, 1968). The major guerrilla organization post-1967, PLO-Al Fatah, is largely independent of direct governmental control, as are several active smaller groups, sometimes in and sometimes out of the larger framework, such as the Popular Front for the Liberation of Palestine (PFLP). Relative independence has been achieved through the popularity of "the cause" in the Arab world, independent financial wealth coming in from Palestinians particularly in Kuwait and Saudi Arabia, and small arms from China (through Kuwait), as well as from Russia (through the UAR and Syria).

A secondary factual differentiation is not without importance. Some Arab states support Palestinian guerrillas from a relatively voluntary commitment to the Palestinian movement as anti-Zionist and/or anti-imperialist. While no Arab state wishes to place itself on public record as opposing the Palestinian movement given the regional ideology of Arab unity, at least two Arab states, Lebanon and Jordan, show an unmistakable historical record of reservations toward support of the Palestinians. The Hussein government finally undertook direct military action against the guerrillas in September 1970. The several Lebanese governments, lacking both the military capability and a mandate from the electorate to move decidedly against the fedayeen, have, nevertheless, built a record of some non-involvement in anti-Zionist affairs of the Arab world. Internally, Lebanese governments have challenged Palestinian activities from time to time; and, while the governments are as fragmented as the larger Lebanese society, the general outcome of governmental policy has been distinctly different from Iraqi, Syrian, and UAR policy on the question of Palestinian support.

Hence the factual situation is characterized by general but uneven Arab state support of Palestinian violence against Israel. Neither PLO-Al Fatah activities nor those of other groups are currently controlled by these states. It is to be noted that the factual situation demonstrates a dichotomy between Palestinian interests and a given state's interests (most notably in the Jordanian civil war).

State claims as to responsibility in this factual context vary considerably. A particular problem in dealing with the Arab-Israeli conflict is distinguishing public pronouncements intended for certain domestic or foreign communities from legal claims intended to coincide with actual public policy.[18] There being no sure legal standard for this task, one has to take careful note of state practice over time.

In prima facie form, Charter norms prohibiting the use of force have proven to be irrelevant to the realistic assessment of claims. Particularly with regard to guerrilla operations, Charter provisions are inadequate to deal with the problems created by guerrilla violence (Taulbee, 1971). In such situations it appears useful to resort to a second-order level of legal inquiry.[19] Such a mode of inquiry becomes relevant where charter norms are vague or by-passed for practical considerations.[20] Such a second-order level in this case would comprise the customary law of war and neutrality. Often, however, the norms embodied in second-order levels are not self-sufficient in their historical form, and so they must be modified in the interest of relevancy and concomitant probability of obedience by a contextual analysis of the factual situation (Falk, 1969: 430-431).

The traditional Arab public posture has been to claim first aggression by Zionists in seizing control of Palestine in 1947-1948. In the words of Foreign Minister Bourguiba of Tunisia, " . . . it is the very existence of Israel which constitutes permanent aggression" (GAOR, 1967: 32). This Arab argument then follows with the claim that war and lesser violence is permitted as a sanction against the continuing aggression. This is the essential position of states such as Syria, as well as the position of spokesmen such as Baroody of Saudi Arabia, whatever the official policy of his government.[21] It is also the position of the Palestinian fedayeen when their revolutionary ideology is translated into legal terms.

As argued above, while this position may have had legitimacy in the late 1940s it cannot be accepted in the 1970s. Though law may be largely irrelevent in a revolutionary political setting, there must be agreement on avoiding threats to existence for mutually advantageous laws to become operative (Hoffman, 1961; Deutsch, 1968). A claim to an unlimited right to threaten a state's existence when not supported by state practice or community expectations, tends to undermine all restraining norms. Palestinians cannot realistically expect implementation of the emerging law on refugee choice or the general law on proportionality in reprisal when such unlimited claims are made. In addition, state practice increasingly rejects the assertion that Israel is a colonial state and the legitimate target of violence under the higher law of anti-colonialism. Not only do the Western and Latin American states reject that assertion, but also Jordan, the UAR and the Soviet Union have recognized the basic legitimacy of Israel,[22] Claims to exercise violence against the very existence of Israel cannot now be accepted by any legal order seeking minimum public order, whether the perspective of the claimant be traditional interpretation of specific law, philosophical interpretation of specific law, philosophical interpretation of "natural rights," state practice, or community expectations.[23]

The traditional Arab claim, and with it the right to give total support to the fedayeen, has been significantly altered by some states since 1967. Jordan, the UAR, the USSR and others now focus on the territory occupied since 1967 by Israel, claiming a right to support Palestinian violence or direct governmental violence against Israel's presence in these areas (U.N. Monthly Chronicle, 1968, 1969). While the Palestinians themselves recognize no such difference in Israeli-controlled territory, these other states lay claim to the permissibility of violence for two reasons: (1) this territory is said to be clearly colonialist in nature, thus the higher law of violent struggle against colonialism is controlling; and (2) there is a right to resist otherwise legal occupation during time of war, when an end to the state of war is offered, yet the occupier will not withdraw.

The competing Israeli claim is that with the collapse of the 1949 Armistice Agreements in both 1956 and 1967, states have become bound by the specific prohibition against coercion contained in the Security Council's cease fire resolution dating from the summer of 1967 (Bowett, 1970). Behind this legal stance is the Israeli concern that reference to post-1967 occupied land is but a prelude to characterizing all of Israel as illegally occupied, which is of course the position of the Palestinians and some supporting states such as Syria.

The starting point for evaluation is that if states such as Jordan and the UAR make this argument, they must perform their obligation to curtail guerrilla activity from their territory directed against the existence of Israel per se. Both law and logic are clear on this point (Brownlie, 1963: 322-323). It is to be noted that such an obligation is not absolute, but only one of "due diligence." There is no doubt that the Egyptian government has the capability to exercise this obligation. Events during the fall of 1970 indicate that Jordan also has the capability to police its own territory, although the costs have been rather high in terms of overall stability. At present the territory seems well under government control. Lebanon is not altogether free of the same obligation.[24] Syria, the fourth staging area for Palestinian raids, has increased its control over the fedayeen since the military ousted the more leftist politicians in early fall of 1970, and while it has yet to accept S/242 or renounce a policy of total support, it too falls logically under these same constraints.

It would seem there is no obligation to prohibit the operations of groups who direct their attacks to military targets in the areas occupied since 1967. This may be read as a legitimate challenge to Israeli occupation (Jennings, 1963: 52 ff). The responsibility for the origin of the 1967 war makes no difference in this regard as a point of law, especially if it is held, as is extremely reasonable in the light of the facts, that both Israel and the UAR were aggressive.[25] Violence in resistance to occupation, however, must clearly demonstrate a difference from attacks against Israel per se. The most obvious differentiation is the limitation of targets to the occupied territories and to military targets. It would reduce unnecessary destruction if this norm were matched by the avoidance of population centers, whether refugee of national, by the fedayeen, in anticipation of Israeli reprisal. Rather than being naive and legalistic restraints, these points have been largely agreed upon in the past between the fedayeen and governments in a compromise between guerrilla interest in raids and government interest in avoiding reprisal. In the period 1968-1970, such agreements were negotiated by both Lebanon and Jordan. In the Lebanese case, there is still something of a free-fire zone in southern Lebanon where the guerrillas operate with the understanding that they stay out of the cities. If the legal order cannot establish an effective law *for* behavior, then it can lend its support to the best available law *of* behavior (Deutsch, 1968: 64).

It may seem somewhat artificial to urge that violence be contained within territory occupied since 1967 in order to demonstrate that the activity is directed toward impermissible occupation rather than Israel's security per se. But it is not. While it is true that bomb damage in Tel Aviv is as destructive as in Ramalah, the former does not achieve the stated objective of resisting occupation. It has the reverse effect of increasing Israeli determination to stay in the occupied territories for security reasons. Military effectiveness has long been an underlying support for the laws regulating coercion (McDougal and Feliciano, 1961: 520 ff); thus it is in the military as well as the legal interest of those legitimately resisting illegal occupation to contain violence within the occupied territories.

However, some question as to rights acquired by conquest in the occupied territories arises because of certain Israeli actions in East Jerusalem and the West Bank which clearly are in violation of its obligations and rights as *occupant* power. Since there is no clear rule of law regarding the acquisition of territory by *conquest,* the discussion might more usefully focus upon the economic and political factors that must be considered in any eventual legal judgment.[26]

The occupied territories can be divided into two categories: those to which the Palestinians have some claim, and those which formed part of the de facto or de jure territory of the adjacent Arab states. East Jerusalem, Gaza, and the West Bank area fall into both categories. Thus, there is a potential divergence in interest between the Arab state and the Palestinians concerning the eventual disposition of certain occupied territories. It might be fruitful as well to distinguish between those territories in which Israeli interest is primarily strategic, and those in which its interest is potentially economic or ideological.

In Jerusalem the original partition plan provided for the establishment of Jerusalem as separate from the proposed Jewish and Arab states, but integrated into a projected economic union. The Arabs resisted the plan, the Israelis accepted it as the price of partition. Several plans for internationalization of the city were drawn up but never implemented (Wilson, 1969; Pfaff, 1969). Despite a number of General Assembly resolutions for internationalization, both Israel and Jordan formally incorporated the areas controlled at the Armistice in 1948. Thus neither side had any strict legal title to the portion it controlled before the June 1967 war. To the extent that military decisions are subject to change by subsequent military actions, the Israeli action in incorporating the whole city is not barred by the Armistice. Israel has done no more than Jordan did in 1949. Israel of course is obligated to protect the rights of the Arab population and others who hold the city sacred, but the prima facie case for return of East Jerusalem to Jordan is a weak one (Schwebel, 1970; Jennings, 1963).

This does not argue that the case for internationalization is irrelevant. Internationalization under a plan more or less similar to the original proposal would clearly accomplish Israel's stated goals of unifying the city and ending an artificial division. It is probable that this solution will not be acceptable to either side. It should be noted, however, that the Armistice line does not have to be regarded as the presumptive starting point for negotiations on the status of Jerusalem.

In Sinai the problem is different. The territory involved is Egyptian, and no other state or faction has a claim to it. The same is true of the Golan Heights of Syria. From the standpoint of a status injuriae with respect to an Israeli security interest, the occupation of these territories is legal until a treaty of peace is signed (Greenspan, 1960: 213; Von Glahn, 1957: 27; Stone, 1959: 108-109). However, the legality of occupation is affected by the overall context of occupation. There are several considerations in this regard. It would seem that a satisfactory guarantee of Israeli security such as the permanent demilitarization of Golan and the Sharm el Sheikh is not only the prerequisite of any settlement but also would remove any justification for continued occupation. Given the contemporary tendency for armistices to serve the function of peace treaties, and given the recent proposals of the UAR to the Jarring Mission, continued Israeli occupation seems increasingly unreasonable.

Gaza and the West Bank may be grouped together since they were both to be part of the originally projected Arab-Palestinian state. When the projected state did not emerge, the Egyptians took Gaza, while the Jordanians annexed the West Bank. Again, if the Armistice lines are purely military and not political, these territories are not part of the respective states. As with Jerusalem, though Israel does not have a greater right to these territories, it does not have a lesser right either.

The principal distinction to be made here, and one which strongly endorses the Jordanian claim, but not the Egyptian, is the importance of the West Bank to the Jordanian economy. There is some question as to Jordan's ability to survive as a viable state without the West Bank. This is not the case with Gaza, which is in no way vital to the Egyptian economy, and is separated from the central part of Egypt by the Sinai desert. This point has relevance for the whole problem: when the claims on both sides are equally unclear, and when both sides demonstrate little concern for law, the solutions of necessity have to be on the basis of other than narrow legal considerations.

CONCLUSIONS

We have been focusing on the type of law that seeks to regulate coercion, rather than on other types of law such as that which establishes a framework of jurisdiction or which lays a foundation for community building (Hoffmann, 1961; Coplin, 1966). We have found that within this law of regulation there may be several orders, or levels of legal inquiry. The first, that of the Charter, has proved generally uninstructive in efforts to evaluate claims on the basis of order and equity in the complex factual situation of the Arab-Israeli conflict in the 1970s. The second order of restraining norms, that of the customary law of war, measures short of war, and neutrality, has also proved itself somewhat deficient in clearly illiminating controlling legal principles. This is the case with regard to Palestinian claims to refugee choice and with regard to Israeli claims to reprisals against targets in Jordan, inter alia. Thus we have ultimately resorted to a third level of legal inquiry, that of the relevance of these customary norms when modified by a contextual analysis of the contemporary features of the Arab-Israeli conflict—such as the validity of claims to the "higher law" of national liberation and anti-imperialism, and claims to reprisal based on an assertion of state responsibility for guerrilla activity. It is our view that the normal scope for creativity in legal reasoning, found in all legal systems, must be expanded under the international legal order (Cardozo, 1921). Revolutionary changes in state perspectives, modes of coercive interaction, and community value judgments make this imperative.[27]

The function of this law, while maximally to restrain behavior in keeping with community expectations, is multifaceted. The persistent weakness of centrally organized and managed sanctions obviously undermines the effectiveness of law as a restraint system. But law as a tool of communication and framework for analysis, perhaps the major roles for law in coercive processes, is not so weakened. States can at times bypass third party legal inquiry when the power configuration permits. But it is increasingly clear that they do so at some sacrifice and cost to their real, long-term interests (Henkin, 1970: 270-271). Reasonable interpretors of international law have been trying to communicate to Arab actors for some time the interests derived from acceptance of the legitimacy of Israel. These same interpretors are now trying to communicate to Israel the futility of a quest for regional stability when law and equity are ignored—whether in regard to territory or legitimate claims of the Palestinians. If actors fail to pursue their real national interests, it is in part because they fail to observe what law is trying to convey. The question of sanctions remains "separable from the question of whether the core law itself is present" (Barkun, 1968: 155).

The Arab-Israeli conflict has generated certain normative sets which we hold relevant for a broader range of situations: the impermissibility of imperialism but the need to restrict that term to situations clearly so defined by state practice and community judgments; the impermissibility of title by conquest but the need to direct resistance to illegal occupation rather than legitimate state security per se; the impermissibility of state surrender of authority in relation to guerrillas but the need to recognize situations in which a government does not have the capability to control guerrilla activity. As with other types and orders of international law, the implementation of these sets and their derivative specifics depend upon a system of mutual reciprocity that in turn reflects the shared interests of the actors in a conflict situation.

NOTES

1. On the difference between adversary arguments and transcendental legal judgments see Falk (1969b: 334-335). For different view see McDougal (1960: 337).

2. For example, does the term "intervention" denote delictual conduct, or is it a neutral term; does it denote a fact or a supposed legal judgment; or perhaps a prior question, what are the legally permissible forms of involvement by states in the internal affairs of other states? Some observers think of intervention in terms of standards to which behavior ought to conform; others see it as a certain set of consequences stemming from behavior; still others see it as certain forms of behavior; and, many equate it with certain intentions underlying behavior. Thus, we have discussions of military, diplomatic, ideological, and economic intervention. The concept has been defined in such a general way that even inaction whenever certain consequences follow can be regarded as intervention. Logically this can produce such absurd conclusions as the inference that the inaction of the United States with respect to Indochina in 1954 *and* our heavy involvement there a decade later both constitute intervention (Rosenau, 1969: 153; Wright, 1968).

3. For example see the debate between Rostow (1970) and Wright (1970b).

4. On the subject of law as a language and tool of moderation see Falk and Hanrieder (1968: 1-11).

5. McDougal (1960) argues that there are opposing normative sets applicable to every situation. However, in context not all normative sets are equally convincing. So far as disputes are concerned, it is a commonplace observation that international law is used as a means of bolstering political claims. In this law is merely one more weapon in the armory of national rhetoric. Appeal to legal considerations is one way of mobilizing international support. Hence, the Israelis, for example, have attempted to rationalize normally illegal actions, such as their activities in East Jerusalem, in legal terms. However, this is a very cynical and narrow view of the function of law. In that policymakers do feel compelled to give some attention to legal justification, law must be perceived to be more than a simple exercise in rhetoric, more than a systematic ex post facto rationalization (see further Henkin, 1969).

6. For an elaboration of this argument see Franck (1968: 171).

7. On control paradigms see Converse (1968: 472-474).

8. It should be noted that "communication" does not imply either understanding or acceptance of claims. The use of a common framework is no guarantee against misperception; and, the nature of the communication may predetermine the response. The communication may convey a threat to basic values. Then too, there must be some correspondence between reality and language. If reality and language are totally divergent, that is, if the legal principles invoked are inappropriate to the facts as known, then law is destroyed as a language which parties hold in common. For example, note the Soviet position on Czechoslovakia (SCOR, 1968).

9. Fedayeen is used as a synonym for "guerrilla." Of the approximately three million individuals who identify themselves as Palestinians, perhaps 50,000 are active in various armed organizations and would, therefore, be classified as fedayeen in the most precise sense. This set of terms is preferred to more subjective alternatives available such as terrorists, freedom fighters, resistance fighters, etc.

10. The following points should be made about this language: (a) smaller Palestine refers of course to western Palestine, or that part of greater Palestine remaining after the United Kingdom granted independence to Transjordan in 1946; (b) in referring to Palestinians as Arabs, the authors are aware that a number of Jews are also indigenous to Palestine; but,

these have now become Israelis. The word Palestinian is now a useful way to refer to Arabs who so identify, even though there remains some necessary overlap between Palestinians and Arab Israelis.

11. In the 1949 Agreements all parties affirmed the principle of no aggressive action by either's armed forces to be undertaken, planned or threatened against the people or armed forces of the other. It was agreed that no military or para-military force of either party would commit any hostile act against the forces of the other or otherwise violate the international frontier or the sea or air space of the other party. The Agreement also delineated the Armistice Demarcation Line, but stated that it was not to be considered in any sense as a political or territorial boundary. Non-military claims were specifically left open for later agreement: "It is emphasized that is it not the purpose of the Agreement to establish, to recognize, to strengthen, or to weaken or nullify in any way, any territorial, custodial or other rights, claims or interests which may be asserted by either party in the area of Palestine or any part of locality thereof covered by this Agreement, whether such asserted rights, claims, or interests derive from the Security Council resolutions . . . or from any other sources. The provisions of this Agreement are dictated exclusively by military considerations and are valid only for the period of the armistice" (SCOR, 1949).

12. For a detailed account of the bargaining in 1949 over repatriation and related issues, see Forsythe (1971).

13. Controversy over the original number of refugees does not affect this point, whether that number be 700,000 or 750,000 or some other number (see Forsythe, 1971b).

14. The inclusion of the right to self-determination in two covenants accepted by the General Assembly in the late 1960s is counterbalanced by lack of definitions, sanctions, and ratifications. For a discussion of problems in applying the higher law of self-determination see Emerson (1968: 153-174).

15. Peretz (1970: 31) and Reisman (1970: 44, 80) both make an argument for a democratic, secular, binational state of Palestine. The problems with this approach are two: there is nothing in it for the Zionist elite, and thus they will oppose it with force if necessary; and, should they not oppose it, the subsequent state will be dominated by Jews more accustomed to democratic procedures and more socially aggressive, which will lead to antagonisms and eventually violence within that projected state. There are any number of subsidiary questions involved as well such as the right to armament by the projected state, its relationship to Gaza, etc.

16. The United States has reportedly explored the possibility of an Arab Palestine in the West Bank with Palestinian leaders. The Soviet Union has reportedly informed those same leaders that the Palestinian movement should unify behind realistic goals (Cooley, 1971: 2).

17. Both the UAR and Jordan have accepted S/242, which implies an indirect recognition of Israel's legitimacy, and have publicly stated their willingness to recognize that legitimacy through treaty.

18. While this problem exists in evaluations of most governmental claims, it is accentuated in the Arab-Israeli conflict. Observers have long noted especially the Arab tendency to extreme and provocative public statements frequently at variance with actual policy; although Israel, too, has misrepresented claims, as when it argued in the Security Council that the UAR carried out an armed attack in 1967 before Israel's air strike on the UAR air force. On the Arab tendency see Lie (1954: 97). On this problem in general see Deutsch (1968: 57).

19. One can distinguish several different "orders" of legal considerations. Recognition of differing levels or orders of law merely reflects the complexity of the international system. Geographical and ideological diversity, the various processes of rule formation and application, the heterogeneity of situations to be regulated all suggest the utility of such a distinction (see McDougal and Lasswell, 1959). Claims based upon the Charter would be claims of the first order. These general principles are, however, at such a level of abstraction that normative guidance from them in concrete situations is impossible. Such guidance must come from the network of consensual rules, or rather second order considerations, which arises out of the everyday interaction of states. Often these, too, are vague, and so there is the possibility of even a third order of considerations.

However persuasive this argument is in analytic terms there is a problem with it in practical terms. Its relatively unconventional nature means that it is either unknown or irrelevant to policymakers. It is arguable that the functions of law operate whether policymakers are aware of them or not; but, the fact remains that officials will still regard clear statements of general principles as substantive rules of law whenever it suits them. Even if the above argument is good and explains a good deal, its credibility with practitioners is limited. As a result the present confusion over the law of civil war and other uses of coercion short of general war is perpetuated (for an elaboration of this argument with respect to reprisals, see Onuf, 1970a).

20. Both the Arab states and Israel justify their actions by a claim of action in self-defense. Since under the Charter this is the only allowable exercise of force, it is to be

expected that all parties to a conflict will invoke such a claim. Given the paralysis of the U.N. peacekeeping machinery, and further, the controversy over the scope of the right under Article 51 and Article 2.4, the Charter provides little guidance for the evaluation of claims (for a sample of the debate see Stone, 1958: 92-103; Brierly, 1963: 416-420; Bowett, 1958; Brownlie, 1963: 268; Higgins, 1967: 167-235).

In the absence of authoritative guidance from the Charter, a case can be made that the customary law is still effective. However, this is of little help, since the scope of the customary right is equally vague and uncertain. In the absence of authoritative third-party review, the customary right is often affirmed to cover not only threats to a state's territorial integrity, but its vital interests of "existence" in a broader sense as well. Similarly, there are no clear guidelines to evaluate the proportionality of force used in self-defense. There is considerable disagreement as to whether proportionality applies to objectives pursued or to the size and character of the aggression; that is, whether a state may act to remove the cause of aggression, or simply to repel the aggression. The response and consequent justification of the United States in the Cuban missile crisis in 1962 demonstrates the difficulty of the problem.

21. The debate in the Security Council, as summarized in the U.N. *Monthly Chronicle* (1969: 14-36), after the Israeli raid in the spring of 1969 is illustrative in this respect. The focus on this raid caused most governments to clarify their positions on the legal points at issue since 1967 for the first time.

22. Soviet policies and legal claims on this series of issues have been something less than fully consistent. This is pronounced with regard to the actions and claims of the fedayeen. In general, the Soviets endorse the "sacred right of all peoples that are determinedly fighting for the liquidation of racist and colonial regimes and are fighting against imperialist aggression" (S/P.V. 1437: 22 in Bowett, 1970). Yet the Soviets have also argued, "Ill-considered and rash actions which do no substantial harm to Israel's military potential cannot solve the problem of eliminating the consequences of the Israeli aggression, and . . . may even help the Israeli extremists . . . " (Dimitriev, 1970: 23). These positions, coupled with Soviet arguments in the Security Council, seem to support resistance to occupation but not violence against Israel per se.

23. For a relevant argument that pursuit of minimum order is more likely to lead to justice than the pursuit of absolute justice at the expense of order see De Visscher (1967).

24. Lebanon is one Arab state that has historically maintained a de facto posture of neutrality. Its forces were not involved in either the 1956 or the 1967 actions. To the extent that the government has control over the situation, neutrality has been maintained since 1967. There seems to be a general recognition in the Arab world of the imperatives of the Lebanese situation; and, consequently, with the exception of Syria, there is no demand from other Arab states that Lebanon should overtly support the guerrillas. This understanding is a prudential calculation based upon Lebanese domestic politics. The Moslem-Christian split is such that any overt action either in support of, or in opposition to, the Palestinian guerrillas will jeopardize the stability of the government. While it is true that the guerrillas use Lebanese territory as a base for their operations, the Lebanese government can do little to control them. Given the position of Lebanon in the history of the conflict, the Israeli raid against the Beirut airport seems unreasonable in context (see Falk, 1969a; Taulbee, 1971).

25. It is perhaps generally assumed in the West that only the UAR was aggressive in ordering the withdrawal of UNEF, mobilizing troops and deploying them in Sinai, ordering a blockade on the Gulf of Aquaba, and making bellicose statements. But Israel had exercised certain threats against Syria and most importantly was the first to initiate armed attack while the UAR was beginning to negotiate with the U.S. on how to avoid war. Thus Israel initiated violence when the threat of imminent attack probably was declining (Yost, 1968; Copeland, 1969: 276-277; Laquer, 1969).

26. This point has engendered considerable debate. In the traditional pre-United Nations view, acquisition of territory by conquest and subsequent annexation was recognized, though at times with great reluctance, as the logical consequence of the legal status of war. McMahon (1940) provides a good survey of the literature. Under the Charter, nations are not to reap the benefits of a resort to force, and so it would seem that territory gained by conquest cannot be legitimately kept. The Security Council, General Assembly, major states, and numerous other states have recently endorsed that concept.

27. We speak here of the addition of non-Western and non-capitalist states, the proclivity to guerrilla activity, and the growing importance of collective review of state assertions (see further Falk, 1970).

REFERENCES

ASAMOAH, O. A. (1966) The Legal Significance of the Declarations of the General Assembly of the United Nations. New York: Columbia University Press.

BARKUN, M. (1968) Law Without Sanctions: Order in Primitive Societies and the World Community.New Haven: Yale University Press.
BOWETT, D. W. (1970) "Reprisals." Washington, D.C.: American Society of International Law. (mimeo)
——— (1958) Self Defense in International Law. Manchester: Manchester University Press.
BOUSKY, T. (1960) "The claims of the Arabs and Jews to Palestine." Papers of the Michigan Academy of Arts and Sciences 45 (Winter).
BRIERLY, J. L. (1963) The Law of Nations. New York: Oxford University Press.
BROWNLIE, I. (1963) International Law and the Use of Force by States. London: Oxford University Press.
CARDOZO, B. (1921) The Nature of the Judicial Process. New Haven: Yale University Press.
CONVERSE, E. M. (1968) "The war of all against all." J. of Conflict Resolution 12 (December): 471-532.
COOLEY, J. K. (1970a) "Principal Palestinian groups." Christian Science Monitor (July 5, 1970).
——— (1970b) "Middle East increasingly polarized." Christian Science Monitor (October 3, 1970).
COPELAND, M. D. (1969) The Game of Nations. New York: Simon & Schuster.
COPLIN, W. D. (1966) The Functions of International Law. New York: Rand McNally.
——— (1965) "International law and assumptions about the state system." World Politics 17 (July): 615-635.
DAVIS, J. (1968) The Evasive Peace. London: J. Murray, Ltd.
DEUTSCH, K. W. (1968) "The probability of international law," in K. W. Deutsch and S. Hoffmann (eds.) The Relevance of International Law. Cambridge: Schenkman.
DE VISSCHER, C. (1967) Theory and Reality in International Law. Princeton: Princeton University Press.
DIMITRIEV, Y. (1970) "The Arab world and Israel's aggression," International Affairs, Moscow (September): 20-23, 28.
ELARBY, N. (1968) "Some legal implications of the 1947 partition resolution and the 1949 armistice agreements." Law and Contemporary Problems 33 (Winter): 97-109.
EMERSON, R. (1968) "The new higher law of anti-colonialism," in K. W. Deutsch and S. Hoffman (1968) The Relevance of International Law. Cambridge: Schenkman.
FALK, R. A. (1970) The Status of the International Legal Order. Princeton: Princeton University Press.
——— (1969a) "The Beirut raid and the international law of retaliation," Amer. J. of International Law 63 (July): 415-443.
——— (1969b) Legal Order in a Violent World. Princeton: Princeton University Press.
——— and W. HANRIEDER [eds.] (1968) International Law and Organization: An Introductory Reader. Philadelphia: Lippincott.
FARER, T. (1968) "Intervention in civil wars: a modest proposal," in R. A. Falk (ed.) (1968) The Vietnam War and International Law. Vol. I. Princeton: Princeton University Press.
FORSYTHE, D. P. (1971a) United Nations Peacemaking. Baltimore: Johns Hopkins Press.
——— (1971b) "UNRWA, the Palestine refugees, and world politics, 1949-1969." International Organization 25 (Winter): 26-45.
FRANCK, T. (1968) The Structure of Impartiality. New York: Macmillan.
General Assembly Official Records [GAOR] (1967) Emergency Session. A. P. V. 1543.
GLENN, E. R. JOHNSON, P. KIMMEL, and B. WEDGE (1970) "A cognitive interaction model to analyze culture conflict in international relations." J. of Conflict Resolution 14 (March): 35-48.
GOULD, W. and M. BARKUN (1970) International Law and the Social Sciences. Princeton: Princeton University Press.
GREENSPAN, M. (1960) The Modern Law of Land Warfare. Berkeley: University of California Press.
HARKABI, Y. (1970) "The position of the Palestinians in the Israeli-Arab conflict and their national covenant." N.Y. J. of International Law and Politics 3 (Summer).
——— (1968) "Fedayeen action and Arab strategy." Adelphi Papers 53, London: Institute for Strategic Studies.
HENKIN, L. (1970) How Nations Behave. New York: Praeger.

HIGGINS, R. (1970) "The place of international law in the settlement of disputes by the security council." Amer. J. of International Law 64 (January): 1-18.
——— (1967) The Development of International Law through the Political Organs of the United Nations. London: Oxford University Press.
HOFFMANN, S. (1961) "International systems and international law," in K. Knorr and S. Verba (eds.) The International System. Princeton: Princeton University Press.
HUDSON, M. (1969) "The Palestinian Arab resistance movement." Middle East J. 23 (Summer): 291-307.
HUREWITZ, J. (1950) The Struggle for Palestine. New York: Norton.
IKLE, F. (1963) How Nations Negotiate. New York: Praeger.
JENNINGS, R. Y. (1963) The Acquisition of Territory in International Law. Manchester: University of Manchester Press.
JOHNSON, F. E. (1964) "Arab v. Israeli: a persistent challenge." Middle East J. 18 (Winter): 2-13.
KHOURI, F. (1969) The Arab-Israeli Dilemma. Syracuse: Syracuse University Press.
LALL, A. (1968) The U.N. and the Middle East Crisis. New York: Columbia University Press.
LANDE, G. R. (1966) "The effect of resolutions of the United Nations General Assembly." World Politics 19 (October): 83-105.
LAQUER, W. (1969) The Road to War. London: Weidenfeld & Nicholson.
——— (1968) The Arab-Israeli Reader. New York: Bantam.
LIE, R. (1954) In the Cause of Peace. New York: Macmillan.
McDOUGAL, M. (1960) "Some basic theoretical concepts about international law: a policy oriented framework of inquiry." J. of Conflict Resolution 4 (September): 337-354.
——— and F. P. FELICIANO (1961) Law and Minimum World Public Order. New Haven: Yale University Press.
McDOUGAL, M. and H. LASSWELL (1959) "The identification and appraisal of diverse systems of public order." Amer. J. of International Law 53 (January): 1-29.
McMAHON, M. (1940) Conquest and Modern International Law. Washington, D.C.: Catholic University of America Press.
ONUF, N. G. (1970a) "The current status of reprisals." Washington, D.C.: American Society of International Law. (mimeo)
——— (1970b) "Professor Falk on the quasi-legislative competence of the General Assembly." Amer. J. of International Law 64 (April): 349-355.
PERETZ, D. (1970) "Arab Palestine: phoenix or phantom?" Foreign Affairs 48 (January): 322-333.
——— (1954) "Problems of Arab refugee compensation." Middle East J. 8 (Autumn): 403-416.
PFAFF, R. H. (1969) Jerusalem: Keystone of an Arab Israeli Settlement. Washington, D.C.: American Enterprise Institute.
RAPOPORT, A. and A. CHAMMAH (1965) Prisoner's Dilemma: A Study in Conflict and Cooperation. Ann Arbor: University of Michigan Press.
REISMAN, M. (1970) The Art of the Possible. Princeton: Princeton University Press.
ROSENAU, J. N. (1969) "Intervention as a scientific concept." J. of Conflict Resolution 13 (March): 149-171.
ROSTOW, E. P. (1970) "Legal aspects of the search for peace in the Middle East." Amer. J. of International Law 64 (September): 64-70.
SAFRAN, N. (1969) From War to War. New York: Pegasus.
SCHACHTER, O. (1964) "The quasi-judicial role of the Security Council and the General Assembly." Amer. J. of International Law 58 (October): 960-965,
SCHELLING, T. (1966) Arms and Influence. New Haven: Yale University Press.
SCHWEBEL, S. S. (1970) "What weight to conquest?" Amer. J. of International Law 64 (April): 344-347.
Security Council Official Records [SCOR] (1968) 22nd year, 1441st meeting.
——— (1949) 4 Spec. Supp. 3 UN Doc. S/1264/Rev. 1.
SHARABI, H. (1970) "Palestine guerrillas." Washington, D.C.: Georgetown Center for Strategic and International Studies.
STEVENS, G. (1952) "Arab refugees: 1948-1952." Middle East J. 6 (Summer): 281-298.
STONE, J. (1959) Legal Control of International Conflict. London: Stevens.
——— (1958) Aggression and World Order. Berkeley: University of California Press.

TAULBEE, J. L. (1971) "Reprisals and state responsibility for the acts of guerrillas and other irregular forces." Washington, D.C.: American Society of International Law. (mimeo)
TUNG, W. (1968) International Law in an Organizing World. New York: Appleton-Century-Crofts.
United Nations Monthly Chronicle (1969) April 6: 14-36.
——— (1968) April 5: 1-27.
VON GLAHN, G. (1970) Law Among Nations. New York: Macmillan.
——— (1957) The Occupation of Enemy Territory. Minneapolis: University of Minnesota Press.
WILSON, E. M. (1969) Jerusalem: Key to Peace. Washington, D.C.: Middle East Institute.
WRIGHT, Q. (1970a) "The Middle East problem," Amer. J. of International Law 64 (April): 270-281.
——— (1970b) "The Middle Eastern crisis," Amer. J. of International Law 64 (September): 71-77.
——— (1969) "Non-military intervention," in K. W. Deutsch and S. Hoffman (eds.) The Relevance of International Law. Cambridge: Schenckman.
YOST, C. (1968) "How it began." Foreign Affairs 46 (July): 304-320.

Chapter 15

PROVINCIAL CONFLICT AND NATION-BUILDING IN PAKISTAN

ALBERT E. LEVAK

BRIEF HISTORY OF AN EMERGING NATION

A detailed historical statement on the evolution of Pakistan as a nation is not the intent of this article.[1] However, it is important to review certain personalities and formal acts which illustrate the country's preoccupation with protecting minority rights not only as they pertain to the overriding emphasis on the minority status of the Muslim religion in the Indian sub-continent, but, with particular reference to the repeated identity of ethnic enclaves and their autonomy.

One can begin with the Government of India Act of 1919 which introduced ministerial government in the provinces and created an increased demand for minority safeguards. The Government of India Act of 1935 proposed a federal constitution providing for government by responsible ministers in the provinces (linking the provinces under a central government bureau with the princely states) to be responsible to the Secretary of State for India in London. But the Muslim League, a political party formed in 1905, felt that the Hindu majority had shown little concern for the rights of minorities and so became active again under the leadership of Mohammed Ali Jinnah. The Muslim League disagreed with the federal part of the constitution because of the large voice it gave to the authoritarian Indian princes. Since none of the princes was willing to accede to the federation, the federal portion of the Act was never put into force.

Jinnah, a lawyer-politician, led the move to preserve the culture of the sub-continent's Muslim community against the threat of destruction by the Hindus through the ballot box. An ally in this effort was Sir Muhammed Iqbal, a Muslim philosopher and politician who had been elected President of the Muslim League in 1930. In his inaugural address his concern for a separate state was evident. He declared:

> "I would like to see the Punjab, Northwest Frontier Province, Sind and Baluchistan amalgamated into a single state. Self government within the British Empire, the formation of a consolidated Northwestern Indian Muslim state appears to me to be the final destiny of Muslims, at least of Northwest India" [quoted in Weekes, 1970: 81].

The Cripps Mission of 1942 was another step in the dissolution of the sub-continent. Sir Stafford Cripps offered to grant India Dominion status if it would cooperate with the allies during World War II. Among his proposals was the recommendation that the concept of Pakistan was feasible if certain regions wished to secede from the Indian Union. While his proposals were rejected by the Indian leaders, Cripps found it necessary to reaffirm the British government's position of its duty to protect minorities.

On March 23, 1940 the Muslim League session at Lahore formally adopted the goal of independence for the Muslim areas of India.

"Resolved ... that no constitutional plan would be workable in this country or acceptable to the Muslims unless it is designed on the following basic principles, *viz.*, that geographically contiguous units are demarcated into regions which should be so constituted with such territorial readjustments as may be necessary that the areas in which the Muslims are numerically in a majority, as in the north-western and eastern zones of India, should be grouped to constitute 'Independent States' in which the constituent units shall be autonomous and sovereign" [Rajput, 1948: 79-80].

One other important formal act was the Cabinet Mission Plan issued on May 16, 1946. It attempted to preserve the unity of India with a three-tiered constitution. Cognizant of the Hindu-Muslim problem, the Plan linked the provinces in two Muslim-majority groups (in the northwest Baluchistan, the Northwest Frontier, Punjab and Sind; the the northeast Assam and Bengal) and one Hindu majority (all the remaining provinces) under a central government with minimal powers. Jinnah recommended to the League the acceptance of this Plan but he also stated that the ultimate objective of the Muslims continued to be the attainment of a separate nation—Pakistan.

On February 20, 1947 Prime Minister Atlee made it clear that the British would withdraw from the sub-continent no later than June 4, 1948. He sent Lord Mountbatten as Viceroy of India in February 1947 to make the necessary arrangements. Within three months after his arrival Mountbatten announced and put into operation plans for independence, partition, and secession.

Jinnah and his followers pieced together Pakistan out of those areas of the sub-continent which were predominantly Muslim. In the West there were the provinces of Sind and the Northwest Frontier, the western part of the Punjab, the Baluchistan Agency, and the small princely states of Amb, Bahawalpur, Chitral, Dir, Kahan, Las Bela, Makran, and Swat. Certain Pathan tribes along the Afghanistan border also swore allegiance to the new government. In the East there was the eastern half of Bengal Province, a portion of Assam and the tribal territories of the Chittagong Hill Tracts.

Summarizing the situation rather succinctly Wheeler (1970: 36) has written:

"Seven short years after the adoption of the Lahore Resolution a separate state had been achieved. The emergence of Muslim political separatism—the demand for separate representation, then minority safeguards, then provincial autonomy and federalism, and finally a separate state—had occurred well within an adult lifetime, and an entire population was confronted with the psychological adjustments of the transition from minority to nationality. The Pakistan movement had appealed to diverse aspirations among the urban middle classes of the Provinces that were to remain India, the rural aristocracy of the Indus valley, and the peasant masses of eastern Bengal. There were, too, those Muslims—both traditionalist and secularist—who did not support the Pakistan idea at all, and also non-Muslims whose destinies had perforce been shaped by the surge of Muslim nationalism. This variegated people was to give institutional form to a new state, with a heritage from British India of parliamentary democracy and of autocracy, and at the same time a heritage of repudiation of both of these. From such diverse aspirations and traditions would be built a state and a society in which Islam would have definite meanings."

PAKISTAN

On August 14, 1947 Pakistan emerged on the world scene as a new nation.[2] It was an anomaly for two reasons. First, it was a nation founded on Muslim religious ideology and religion as a basis of nationalism is unique in the modern world. Second, it was physically divided into two distinct land units separated by over 1,000 miles of India. These two land areas were identified as East Pakistan and West Pakistan with the central government located in Karachi in West Pakistan.

East Pakistan, abutting India on its northeast border, has a considerable portion of its land area made up of the deltas of the Ganges and Brahmaputra rivers. It consists of only 15 percent of the total land area of Pakistan and yet has 55 percent of the total population. It is predominantly agricultural with rice, tea, and jute as the primary crops.

Ethnically the East Pakistanis are a relatively homogeneous group with the exception of small communities like those found in the Chittagong Hill Tracts. Approximately 95 percent of the population speaks Bengali and they are more like their neighbors in West Bengal than their fellow nationals in West Pakistan. The diet of East Pakistan consists of rice and fish as staples and meat as a luxury. They are liberal and secular in their interpretation of Islam. Physically the Bengalis are petite in structure and dark in complexion as are the other inhabitants of Southeast Asia. Tempermentally they are light-hearted, intense, volatile, expressive in the arts, democratic, and sophisticated in politics.

West Pakistan, on the other hand, is not homogeneous even in language. Urdu is considered to be the official language of West Pakistan but it is only spoken by approximately 15 percent of the population. West Pakistan includes four distinct linguistic and cultural ethnic areas: Sind, the Northwest Frontier, Baluchistan, and the Punjab.

The Sindis are probably the oldest ethnic group. The area in which they are located is divided into large landholdings and many of the inhabitants work as tenants. Sindi is the principle language. The mass of the Sindis are socially and physically isolated from the mainstream of Pakistani life. As a result they know little of the efforts being made by the national leaders to assist them.

The Pathans of the Northwest Frontier include those who reside in the cities and villages of that region as well as the tribal groups who live in the mountainous areas. Pashtu is the principle language of the area. The tribal groups do not always conform to the laws of the land but, as were the British, the government is sensitive to their folkways and allows for considerable latitude in the enforcement of laws. Complicating the identity of the Pathans with Pakistan is the fact that a number of the related tribal groups also reside in Afghanistan. There has been constant pressure to allow these tribal Pathans to establish a separate nation, to be known as Paktoonistan which would be based on their ethnic uniqueness.

The Baluchis are also a tribal people, some of whom also live in Iran and Afghanistan. They too speak a separate language. They are one of the least advanced groups in terms of economic development and are somewhat belligerent in their concern for their independence.

The dominant ethnic group in West Pakistan is the Punjabi, making up approximately 60 percent of the population of that wing. The Punjab has long been a major source of food, and the British, while in a ruling position, established in the Punjab the largest irrigation system in the world. While the Punjab has many villages engaged in the production of food it also has the highest degree of urbanization in all of Pakistan. The principle language in that area is Punjabi.

The dominance of the Punjab is felt in more than sheer numbers or as a source of food supply. The Punjab has played a significant role in the development of Pakistan in many ways. The Muslim elites and intellectuals from this area provided the leadership of the Muslim League during the struggle for independence. It was in Lahore, the heart of the Punjab, where the Muslim League formally adopted the goal of independence. Lahore is known for its educational institutions—the University of Punjab, the Civil Service of Pakistan Academy and the Administrative Staff College are all located there. It is also known as an established center of journalism and literature, a cultural center, a commercial center, and as a headquarters for government. Punjabis interpret Islam in an orthodox manner. They are a stolid people, more adjusted to autocratic and military rule, who prefer to govern and to soldier. The leaders of this region perceive themselves to be the elite of the country and attempt to impose their value system on the remainder of Pakistan.

Ethnicity and Nationalism

Pakistan, in its relatively brief history as a nation, has been struggling to establish and maintain national unity. Rupert Emerson (1960: 27) discusses the role of nationalism in creating pressures on the lives of people who have been traditionally bound by the norms of their ethnic identity. In all countries, regardless of their stage of advancement, there are pockets of people who have not been brought into the broader national society. Emerson speaks of the demands of the linguistic communities in India. He speaks to Pakistan's split from India where " . . . even the assertion that there is a single nation embracing the peoples concerned may be successfully denied."

The long struggle in Pakistan for independence, along with the development of the spirit of nationalism, may have given the nation an illusory sense of national unity. The Center for International Studies (1960: 1203) studying social, economic, and political change in developing countries concluded:

"Once independence is achieved . . . the old ethnic, linguistic, religious, or tribal loyalties reassert themselves with renewed strength. This has been particularly true wherever the new national leadership has been recruited largely from a single region or ethnic group, or where it is a conspicuously westernized elite trying to impose alien values on their society."

In defining ethnic groups Litt (1970: 4) has stated rather tersely

" . . . for there to be 'brothers' there must also be 'others.' Boundaries, whether they be geographical or psychological, have a way of being both cohesive and divisive."

The importance of ethnic identity to the Pakistani is demonstrated by his adjustment in a foreign society. In studies of immigrants in England (Oakley, 1968; Rose et al., 1969) it was discovered that Pakistani migrants were not randomly distributed in the cities. Rather, kinsmen from the same village or group formed close-knit enclaves in the towns where they settled. In Bradford, where there are bachelor dormitories, there is no sharing between the Pakistanis from different regions—Pathan tribesmen live on their own and there is a division

ALBERT E. LEVAK [207]

between Punjabis and non-Punjabis. In other areas regional loyalties are also evident. Punjabis, Kashmiris, Pathans and Bengalis seek to set themselves above each other by fostering their own localized loyalties in patronizing businesses established by kinsmen.

Local Urdu papers treat exogamy as a deviant pattern of behavior and a threat to the culture of the community. Other factors, such as linguistic differences and the diversity of cultural origins between one regional group of Pakistanis and another, militate against the development of cross-regional organizations. Patterson (1969: 317) points out that Pakistani organizations in Britain tend to be based upon an East-West regional identity and a village-kin language identity. Finally, to identify oneself as a Pakistani rather than as a Kashmiri or Bengali is rare. It becomes important only when conflicts with other nationalities arise, particularly with Indians over the Kashmir dispute.

Because of limited mobility, limited forms of communication and a high incidence of endogamy, the members of the linguistic-cultural ethnic groups in Pakistan share a common historical background. These groups each have a language with its ramifications in the socialization process, particular patterns of thought and feeling, and certain identifiable physical characteristics. In the continuing drive for nationalism and modernization these subcultural differences cannot be ignored, suppressed or their importance reduced.

Governing a New Nation

The decision for partition came so rapidly and independence so quickly the new nation was without a Constitution. The Government of India Act of 1935, as modified and amended by the accepted authority in the new Pakistan government, provided the basis for rule in the first four years of independence. But problems were numerous. During the first year of independence the fledgling government had to cope with boundary disputes over Kashmir that had begun prior to Pakistan's independence. Another factor adding to the unsettled pattern during the first few years of the new nation was the untimely death of Jinnah in September 1948, only eleven months after the founding of Pakistan.

In an attempt to provide political unity the Establishment of West Pakistan Act was passed on October 14, 1955. This Act amalgamated the provinces into one unit, a system resulting from a bureaucratic coup brought about by Machiavellian methods. Instead of promoting political unity it gave rise to a host of regional grievances. Politicians from the West wing gave stiff opposition because they were unwilling to accept the extinction of their separate ethnic identities.

A number of significant events at the national level contributed to major shifts in policy. These included the continuance of the conflict over Kashmir; two Constitutions in 1956 and 1962; Field Marshall Ayub Khan taking over the reign of government in a military coup and later becoming President; the 1965 war with India; General Yahya Khan's takeover from Ayub Khan which led to his present position as President and chief martial law administrator.

After a long seige of martial law, President Yahya Khan on March 28, 1970 issued Legal Framework Order, 1970, more aptly described as the Constitutional Framework Order. He recognized democracy as the guiding force in the establishment of Pakistan and advocated adhering to the democratic principles. To this end he dissolved the "one unit" scheme, called for an election on the basis of one-man-one-vote, and sought greater provincial autonomy.

The dissolution of the "one unit" system was supported almost unanimously by both East and West Pakistan. In particular it satisfied a long standing demand of West Pakistan's different linguistic, cultural, and ethnic groups. Under this order West Pakistan would consist of the three former provinces of Punjab, which would now include Bahawalpur; the Northwest Frontier including Dir, Swat, Chitral, and Malakand; and Sind including Karachi; and a fourth one, the new province of Baluchistan. The tribal areas and the national capitol, Islamabad, would be administered by the central government. The new structure was designed to rectify regional imbalances and prepare the ground for the evolution of a new pattern of political life based on administrative equality and reciprocal economic benefit.

Conflict Areas

The "one unit" system in Pakistan attempted to merge the various linguistic and cultural ethnic groups by governmental fiat and continued rule through martial law. Language differences, competition for the resources of the society and differential power served as obstacles to the development of nationalism. With restructuring the problem became one of welding variant groups into a single nation through the democratic process. However, Pakistan has a form of ethnic stratification which may serve as a continuing obstacle to the development of nationalism. Historically, the Punjab ranks as the dominant ethnic group in Pakistan. Bengal, Sind, Baluchistan, and the Northwest Frontier are subordinate to the Punjab at this time, but their relative position to each other is unknown in the absence of research on ethnic stratification in Pakistan.

While nationalism attained through the democratic process may be a desirable goal, it is a complex process and a number of questions need to be raised. How will government maintain a relatively equitable distribution of the economic resources of the nation in the form of foreign aid, foreign export income, and the growth of the gross national product? How is authority to be kept in balance between central government and the Provinces, and among the Provinces? How are the variant linguistic and cultural ethnic groups to be incorporated into a nation as they see their cultural heritage and value systems conflict with each other?

Economic distribution. Once power has been transferred from an outside imperialist power to an indigenous national government, the need for a high degree of ideology will remain in order to help foster the long-time objective of economic development. Pakistan has been implementing economic growth through a series of Five-Year Development Plans. One would assume the purpose of economic planning would be to minimize regional differences and to facilitate redistribution of income to the lower income sectors of the society. But such was not the case in Pakistan. Griffin (1965: 603-613) observed that planning was intentionally designed to skew distribution of the increased income in favor of the already wealthy. His observation was confirmed by an advisor to the Pakistan Economic Planning Commission who has written (Papanek, 1967: 241-43) of development in Pakistan. He did acknowledge the inequalities between East and West and spoke of the resulting tensions between the two Provinces as being serious. He also wrote that the inequalities in personal income and wealth were directly related to the pattern of Pakistan's development. He states, "The problem of inequality exists, but its importance must be put in perspective . . . the inequalities in income contributes to the growth of the economy, which makes possible a real improvement for the lower-income groups. The concentration of income in industry facilitates the high savings which finance development. Allowing the more enterprising and wealthy peasants to sink tube wells is a major factor in expanding agricultural output. . . . Great inequalities were necessary in order to create industry and industrialists. . . ." Another author (MacEwan, 1971), writing on Pakistan's development, asserts in his preface, ". . . the narrow scope of the book and the use of a formal planning model as the principle tool of analysis is essentially independent of social organization . . . in my opinion, one cannot speak of planning as independent of social organization."

On July 1, 1970 the nation initiated its fourth Five-Year Plan which will be in effect through June 30, 1975. Under the "one unit" system central government had greater control in the allocation of the resources to the various regions of the country. Under the present structure, a new ideology of planning must be developed to take into consideration the decision-making process and political viability of each of the new Provinces.

An aid to Pakistan consortium, held in Paris under the auspices of the World Bank, noted on July 24, 1970 Pakistan's considerable progress in overall economic growth despite several difficulties. Consortium members expressed concern over some of the strains apparent in the social aspects of development and regional imbalances. They noted the emphasis in the Fourth Plan on the need to "give greater weight" to the objectives of social justice and accelerating economic growth in the less developed regions of the country (Asian Almanac, 1970: 4065). But the problems are not easy to solve.

Language. The nation-state, as we are familiar with it in the West, has been the result of cultural assimilation and absorption. Both religion and language have been key elements in creating a sense of nationhood. Even though there are exceptions, a common language has often served as an integrating force. A classic exception is the case of Yugoslavia where the two largest ethnic groups, the Serbs and the Croats, have not resolved their linguistic differences and this continuing conflict has ramifications in the area of economic development as well as in having a stable form of nationalism.

Tinker (1962: 123) reports the Asian pattern as a different story from the West. Two States, Japan and Thailand, have linguistic homogeneity and a number of others have a recognized major language, as in China, Vietnam, and Burma. Most of the other countries have created a national language by compromise, coercion, or synthesis. However, in a number of countries the complexity of the problem appears to defy any simple resolution.

Pakistan has thirty-two distinct languages and a large number of dialects (for a brief but incisive discussion of the language problems in Pakistan, see Das Gupta, 1970: 26-28). English has continued to be the de facto language of national unity since independence and is used for all official purposes by provincial and central governments. However, in 1948, Jinnah made his national policy quite clear before a convocation at Dacca University when he said, "There can be only one lingua franca . . . and that language should be Urdu" (Mahmood: 1970: 10). East Pakistan protested and as a compromise Bengali was established as the official language of the East wing and Urdu as the official language of the West wing.

Authority. Desiring to return authority to the people, President Yahya Khan in his March 28, 1970 speech to the national provincial legislature announced his decisions on elections and on the drafting of a Constitution. Elections to the National Assembly of 313 members would be held on October 5, 1970. Thirteen of these seats were reserved for women. On the basis of population distribution, 169 of the 313 seats were allocated to the East wing. The Assembly would have the responsibility of drafting a Constitution within 120 days of their first sitting.

His Legal Framework Order, 1970 ruled that the new Constitution must promote and preserve the Islamic ideology, ensure Pakistan's independence, territorial integrity and national solidarity, and preserve the territorial unity of Pakistan in the federal union. His Order ruled that the Constitution must also embody free and periodic elections on the basis of population and direct adult franchise. It must be a "true federal one," with provinces having the maximum autonomy and the federal government having adequate powers to discharge its responsibilities in the country's external and internal affairs. And, it must include a statutory provision for removal of all disparities, in particular economic disparity, among the various provinces within a fixed period.

Many of the provisions of the Legal Framework Order, 1970 are substantially taken from the Constitutions of 1956 and 1962. The most sensitive and crucial issue occurs in Clause 4 of Article 20 of the Order (Munir, 1971: 4).

"All powers including legislative, administrative and financial, shall be so distributed between the Federal Government and the Provinces that the Provinces shall have maximum autonomy, that is to say, maximum legislative, administrative and financial powers to discharge its responsibilities in relation to external and internal affairs and to preserve the independence and territorial integrity of the country."

President Yahya Khan said he would accept and authenticate the new Constitution only if it upheld the directive principles envisaged in the Order issued by him. If it did not, he threatened to dissolve the National Assembly and call for new elections. While he was reluctant to install the Army in politics, as in the Turkish Constitution which provides for forceful representation for the Army in the national government, he indicated that they would be standing by until a stable government was finally established.

EAST PAKISTAN

Pakistan government officials concede that the East wing, with 75 million people compared to 55 million in the West wing, has been consistently short-changed politically, economically and socially for the twenty-three years of Pakistan's independence. This disparity is demonstrated by comparisons of per capita income. During the period 1951-1952 the per capita income of the East was 85 percent that of the West. In 1967-1968 the inequity was increased to the point that per capita income in the East was only 62 percent of that of the West (Nulty and Nulty, 1971: 19). In recent years, per capita income has risen 42 percent in the West while during the same period it rose only 17 percent in the East. This disparity in income, in conjunction with the fact that prices are higher in the East than in the West, accentuates their perception of relative deprivation. In addition, there is considerable instability of their income due to their dependence on agriculture in an area with devastating climatic conditions.

The production and exportation of rice and jute by East Pakistan earns the

ALBERT E. LEVAK [211]

vast majority of foreign exchange for Pakistan. However, most of this money is spent in West Pakistan, which also receives approximately four times as much foreign aid. In addition, about twice as much of the nation's development funds have been allocated to the West wing. In total, over the past 23 years four-fifths of the national budget from all sources has been spent in the West wing.

East Pakistanis feel that they are merely an outlet for West Pakistan's products. They are the largest single export market for the West. Business leaders in the country report that the industrial firms in the West export 40 percent of their output to the East wing. In addition, many of the industrial and commercial firms in East Pakistan are simply branches of large firms whose headquarters are in West Pakistan. According to official records, twenty-two families of West Pakistan control 60 percent of the nation's industrial output, 80 percent of the total bank assets, and 75 percent of its insurance assets. These families have dominated West Pakistan's social and political arena and have exercised considerable control over East Pakistan through these economic resources.

East Pakistanis have also been deprived along other lines. Authority has been in the hands of the military since the advent of martial law in 1958. As a consequence many view the Army as the cohesive force binding Pakistan into a nation. Martial law has been discriminatory against East Pakistan because approximately 90 percent of the Army is made up of Punjabis and Pathans who have little respect for the East Pakistani. Another binding force in administering rational authority is the civil service bureaucracy. The training academies for the various levels of civil servants are located in West Pakistan. Approximately 85 percent of the civil servants are recruited from the West wing and many of them are posted at all levels in East Pakistan. It is not necessary for these civil servants to know the Bengali language. It is obvious that the West wing has dominated the government bureaucracy, industrial community and the military.

Ill feelings between East and West were further exacerbated by government's reaction to the cyclone and tidal wave that swept over the coastal areas of East Pakistan on November 12, 1970. Hundreds of thousands were killed while unknown numbers were homeless, ill, and hungry. The central government, dominated by the Punjabis, was slow to react. Their delay and bureaucratic red-tape cost an inestimable number of lives.

The East Pakistanis have felt these acts of discrimination in all facets of life but for twenty-three years they did not revolt. They were tied to Government by the ideology of Islam even though their interpretation was more secular than the inhabitants of the West.

Possibly some of the East Pakistanis saw hope in the actions of President Yahya Khan after eleven years of martial law under Ayub Khan who had refused to delegate authority. Yahya Khan encouraged discussion in government. He has served as President and Chief Martial Law administrator since March 1969 when Ayub Khan resigned. He has curbed business monopolies, brought corruption charges against hundreds of former government officials, raised minimum wages and increased allocations for education and development.

Also of significance to the East Pakistanis were the various radio proclamations and press releases in which Yahya Khan pointed out that the people of East Pakistan had not had their full share in the decision-making process on vital national issues. He agreed they were justified in being dissatisfied with the state of affairs. He vowed to end economic discrimination and the fourth Five-Year Plan gives evidence of his intentions. In addition to the national capitol in Islamabad he planned to build another national capitol in Dacca where the National Assembly could sit for six months of the year. He also ordered the release of all political prisoners and declared political parties legal once again.

Another significant contribution of his martial law regime was the announcement in July 1969 of a new educational and language policy. The Constitution of 1962 provided that the use of English for official purposes would continue until 1972 at which time a Commission was to be appointed "to examine and report" on the question of its replacement. However, to demonstrate his sincerity, President Khan announced the replacement of English by Bengali and Urdu in each of the two provincial governments by 1974 and in the central government by 1975. All civil servants are expected to acquire a working knowledge of both languages by 1973 (Pakistan Times, July 4, 1969: 1).

DEMOCRACY AND REBELLION

The President's expressed desire to return to democracy and his willingness to allocate seats in the National Assembly on a one-man one-vote basis, encouraged the East Pakistanis. However, in the election campaigns of each wing violence erupted on the political scene. In light of the continued general unrest, the President postponed the elections until December. The cyclone and tidal wave that occurred in mid-November caused the President to consider postponement once again. However, Sheikh Mujibur Rahman, the leader of the Awami League, a leading political party in East Pakistan, protested and threatened violence if the elections were not held when scheduled.

On December 7, 1970 the first free universal adult franchise election since 1954 was held in Pakistan. It was peaceful and well conducted. The Awami League, which was to the right of center in the political spectrum won 167 of the 169 seats allocated to East Pakistan in the National Assembly. This was an overwhelming victory because the Pakistan People's Party, which was to the left of center, led by Zulfikar Ali Bhutto was able to win only 82 seats of the 144 seats allocated to the West. All but two of these were in Sind and Punjab. (The remaining two were in the Northwest Frontier in an area peripheral to the Punjab.) This mandate was reinforced by the results of the election on December 17, 1970 to the East Pakistan Assembly. Campaigning on the issue of full provincial autonomy, the Awami League won 288 seats in the 300 member Assembly.[3]

The victory of the Awami League centered on the Six Points advocated by Mujib. These points called for a federal parliamentary government which would leave very limited powers with the center and a national government responsible only for defense and foreign affairs (the latter to be restricted by certain provincial rights). Mujib also called for two separate, freely convertible currencies, one for East and one for West, or, if a common national currency, a system that would give East and West the right to prevent the transfer of resources and flight of capital from one wing to another. He demanded that the provinces collect taxes, sharing out an agreed proportion for the support of the national government. Mujib also called for provincial control of foreign exchange earning and provincial authority to maintain their own militia for provincial security. In short, these demands, while negotiable, were designed to grant greater economic and political autonomy to the provinces, and particularly to East Pakistan.

These six points were not merely contrived for this general election. As early as 1966 Mujib gained international prominence when his Awami League launched a mass movement in East Pakistan in support of his autonomy program. The London Times in March 1969 (Van Der Hat, 1969: 1) reported that representatives of Mujib handed the President a six-page plan for reform of the Constitution. Included were proposals for federal legislation on a population basis and for state assemblies in East and West. Mujib also demanded division of the West wing into four provinces, hoping that this would help to ensure autonomy for the East and allow them to dominate the federal government.

Negotiations

The immediate post-election period was one of optimism for East Pakistan because they had achieved a decisive victory through the democratic process. The almost unanimous victory in the East was a mandate from the people for the six points. However, to suddenly impose the demands of the six points in an immediate categorical manner would have created chaotic conditions in the country. Recognizing this the leaders of the Awami League were agreeable to negotiations. In mid-January Yahya Khan and Sheikh Rahman met and on January 27 Ali Bhutto and his group met with representatives of the Awami League. Neither Yahya Khan nor Bhutto made any constructive proposals to replace or modify the six points in these meetings. The assumption was, on the part of all participants, that everything was going well and the meetings would continue after the representatives from West Pakistan returned to their home constituencies for further discussion, or the elected representatives would meet in the National Assembly. The President had set February 15 as the first meeting of the Assembly but Bhutto wanted more time and a new date of March 3 was set.

Bhutto boycotted the meeting and attempted to coerce the other parties holding seats in the National Assembly in an effort to keep them from attending. Nevertheless, all members of the Assembly from West Pakistan, except members of Qay-vum Muslim League and the Pakistan People's Party, had booked flights to Dacca. Within the Qay-vum Muslim League only half the members arranged to attend the Assembly and there were signs of revolt in the Pakistan People's Party. Faced with this breakdown, Yahya Khan yielded to Bhutto on March 1 by postponing the Assembly *sine die*. The reaction to this decision in East Pakistan was predictable. The people took to the streets and the entire civilian administration, including the police and civil service, refused to fulfill their duties. The East Pakistanis pledged their support to the Sheikh. From March 1 through March 25 non-cooperation was total. Sheikh Rahman, however, continued to seek a political settlement even though there was massive public sentiment for independence. He continued to discuss what might be done to resolve the issue with President Yahya Khan and his officials. Throughout the talks during the month of March there was no reason to believe that Yahya Khan was assuming a position which was non-negotiable. As late as March 24, 1971 the Awami League was of the opinion that a final drafting session could be held between the advisors of Mujib and Yahya Khan to complete an interim constitution [for a comprehensive discussion of personalities, events, and effects related to the upheaval in Pakistan, see Durdin (1971), Singh (1971), Time (1971) New York Times (1971), Newsweek (1971), Kann (1971)].

Bangladesh

On the night of March 25 East Pakistan's hopes for representative government were shattered. Simultaneously throughout the towns of East Pakistan the Army moved in a surprise attack to destroy the Awami League and the cultural and political leaders of East Bengal.

During the negotiations the industrial sector of the society based in Lahore and Karachi petitioned the military government to come to a settlement, even if it meant the granting of broad powers of autonomy to East Pakistan. They supported their arguments with data on the economic costs of non-settlement to the economy of the West and consequently to the nation. Nevertheless, Bengali nationalism was viewed by the military leaders as the creation of a small group of extremists who could be isolated and destroyed. The military felt that eliminating the extremists would put an end to Bengali nationalism. President Khan's strong sense of Pakistani nationalism succumbed to the strong urging of the military leaders to allow the military to intervene. Unfortunately, neither the President nor the military took into consideration the depth of the ideological commitment to the concept of Bengali nationalism on the part of the East Pakistan population.

The Army's tactics only served to solidify public support behind the resistance movement. This support goes beyond the boundaries of East Pakistan to West Bengal, where similar language and cultural characteristics have precipitated a strong sympathy with the resistance movement in East Bengal (Sterba, 1971: 10C). This gives some evidence of the strength of ethnicity, over religion alone, as a binding force (East Bengal is predominantly Moslem, West Bengal is predominantly Hindu).

One last example of the Army's lack of understanding of the human factor is their attempt to eradicate Bengali culture by re-naming streets. According to one report (Newsweek, 1971) Shankari Bazar Road is now called Tikka Khan Road after the martial law commander in charge of the troops in East Pakistan. General Khan is an authoritarian who lives by military rules and is recognized as a responsible figure in planning resolution of East Pakistan's demand for autonomy by military action rather than by political compromise. Naming a street after the General can only serve as a continuing symbol for unifying the Bengalis into a more determined force.

There has always been a small core of Bengali nationalists whose rebellious attitudes have been subdued through the efforts of those who preferred to work through the existing system. The recent election results gave them some promise of success within the system but their unjust treatment by Yahya Khan spread the rebellious attitude throughout the Province and resulted in insurgence. On April 17, 1971, three weeks after the initial attack, East Pakistan was named Bangladesh (Bengal Nation). In a statement following the proclamation, Tajuddin Ahmed, Prime Minister of the new sovereign state said:

"Bangladesh is at war. It has been given no choice but to secure its right of self-determination through a national liberation struggle against the colonial oppression of West Pakistan."

WEST PAKISTAN

Whether East Pakistan is successful in seeking independence or is "conquered" by central government, there is a lesson to be learned from the Bengali rebellion. West Pakistan may still face a similar problem with its own distinctive linguistic and cultural ethnic groups. The division of West Pakistan into four Provinces has been followed by a sharp rise in parochial and provincial bitterness over linguistic differences, competition for resources and distribution of power.[4] One reporter (Lelyveld, 1971: 3) suggests that West Pakistan might have to face claims by the Pathans, Baluchis, and Sindis who have often indicated their resentfulness of Punjabi domination.

Some evidence of this resentfulness and the strength of ethnic identity of these minorities can be found in the recent elections and negotiations. Both the Northwest Frontier and Baluchistan were strong supporters of provincial autonomy. As a result of the election only two seats went from the Northwest Frontier electorate to Bhutto's Party that supports the concept of a strong central government. During the negotiations the representatives of the Northwest Frontier and Baluchistan had supported Mujib in his struggles for provincial autonomy. However, Mujib, during the negotiations, in hopes of getting the Army out of East Pakistan, conceded to the demand for separate sessions of the National Assembly. This concession was designed to appease Bhutto who feared a joint session might allow Mujib to join forces with the Pathan and the Baluch. Joint action could neutralize Bhutto's power and could even impose the six points on West Pakistan. As a result of Mujib's concession, the Pathan and Baluch leaders left the negotiations because they felt they had been sacrificed to a Bhutto-Mujib entente. They flew home to look after their own defenses (Sobham, 1971: 3).

Additional evidence of resentfulness and ethnic strength is found in linguistic and religious concerns. There is a strong undercurrent of opposition by the people of the smaller Provinces against Urdu as the official West Pakistan language. Opposition is based on two counts. First, a Pathan, Sindi, or Baluchi does not normally speak Urdu. He has to learn it as he has to learn English. Second, Urdu is not readily capable of assimilating the rapidly expanding vocabulary of a technological science; although this may be corrected by developing or borrowing new words. Further complicating the issue is the argument by those who have a fundamentalist approach to Islam that Arabic ought to be adopted in order to inculcate a sense of oneness and translate into reality the dream Iqbal saw in Pakistan.

Since the dissolution of the "one unit" system the language issue has received considerable attention. In spite of opposition to Urdu as the West Pakistan language, there was a riot of university students in Karachi favoring Urdu. The riot was sparked by actions of the Board of Intermediate and Secondary Education in Hyderabad making Sindi the medium of instruction for the entire Sindi Province. Little thought was given to the non-Sindi speakers who comprise almost one-half the population of Karachi, a former federal area, occupied by many refugees and migrants from other provinces attracted by available work (The Khyber Mail, January 23, 1971: 1). Among these migrants were approximately 800,000 Pathans who has been encouraged to come to Karachi to support Ayub Khan. He hoped to establish a strong Pathan community to counter strong opposition to his autocratic rule. The Pathan leaders urged government to rehabilitate these Pushtu speaking tribesmen in November 1969 (Asian Recorder, January 15-21: 9366).

A group of poets, writers, and philosophers demonstrated in Lahore to press their demands for the Punjabi language. In addition to their language demands, they wanted all roads and squares re-named for Punjabi poets, writers, and thinkers and they also wanted the ban on Punjabi dress in government offices and first class hotels to be lifted (The Pakistan Times, September 4, 1970: 6).

Some leading Punjabi politicians have lent support to the demand for creation of a separate province of Bahawalpur State to include the districts of Multan, Dera Ghazi Khan, and Dera Ismail Khan. This suggestion was made on grounds that people in these areas speak a language different from Punjab. Other leaders have opposed the suggestion on grounds that the language was merely a Punjabi dialect (Asian Recorder: February 5-11, 1970: 9380).

Economic factors are also evident in influencing potential internal strain in West Pakistan. The fourth Five-Year Plan which was designed to protect the special needs of the less developed areas of West Pakistan has run into some obstacles. The Punjab which averages 66 percent of the total revenues of West Pakistan decries this intent. An editorial appearing in The Pakistan Times editorialized "Punjab ... seems in for a spell of penalization. The planners' emphasis on a 'wider geographical dispersal of investment and ... a better inter-provincial distribution' is quite justified, but his concept seems likely to be over-simplified. . . . The villages of Punjab are as undeveloped as anywhere else; and the bulk of the population is as poor in this province as in another" (The Pakistan Times, September 25, 1970: 6).

The Northwest Frontier Province also protested the fact that since the dissolution they are actually going deeper into poverty and they are concerned over the prospect that production and employment will continue to go down. An editorial in The Khyber Mail (February 6, 1971: 4) argued, ". . . the province is still being deprived of its due share in the import trade of West Pakistan. Despite the break-up of the 'one unit' and the promises of making amends for earlier lapses, the pattern remains very much the same. The industry is being treated on par with industrially developed 'islands of affluence' in West Pakistan."

CONCLUSION

It is difficult to arrive at conclusions while the rebellion continues in Pakistan. However, on the basis of the causes of the rebellion and the expressed discontent among the Provinces of West Pakistan, some factors are evident.

The Islamic religion was the basis for the founding of Pakistan. In the past twenty-three years it has been considered the binding force for uniting Pakistan as a nation. While religion may have been appropriate as a force during the early years of the nation, it is an error to assume that continuing appeal solely to religious sentiments will suffice to maintain a unified nation. Other social institutions cannot be ignored because a relative balance among them is necessary to a state of equilibrium. Evidence of the importance of other factors in the common identity of East and West Bengal is on the basis of ethnicity, even though their religions—Muslim and Hindu— are radically different.

Some form of ethnic stratification exists in all societies comprised of heterogeneous ethnic groups. In the developing countries, well-intended economic planning commissions have contributed to magnifying ethnic stratification. Economic development is important for these countries but its impact has not always been considered in the ethnic context of the society. Until recently, these planning commissions have given little recognition to the power of the human factor of ethnicity and some degree of economic determinism has been the basis of their planning.

The case of Pakistan is an example. For the past twenty-three years East Pakistan has been used as a colony for the products of West Pakistan. Even though East Pakistan made significant economic contributions to the country's development, they received very little in return. Their discontent has long been articulated—but they were ignored. Economic benefits Pakistan may have derived from their first three Five-Year Plans have been seriously eroded by the social factor of ethnicity.

Nation-building is not synonymous with economic development. Even the most economically advanced nations in the world have internal conflicts among racial and ethnic groups. The United States began with an implicit national policy of Anglo-conformity. Newcomers were expected to put aside their cultural heritage and assimilate the Anglo value system. In spite of this view, and a later idea of the melting pot (which assumed a biological merger of the various ethnic groups), intergroup problems are still quite visible in American society.

In Pakistan, rebellion was not brought about simply by the negative reaction of Government to a modified form of Provincial autonomy but grew out of twenty-three years of social, political, and economic discrimination coupled with governments' refusal to practice the democracy it espoused.

In Pakistan the Punjabi are the dominant ethnic group. Since the rebellion began communications media have constantly referred to the Punjab as synonymous with Pakistan. Newspaper, radio and television reporters refer to the Pakistani Army as the "Punjabi" Army, of Government in Pakistan as the "Punjabi regime." These factors augment the suspicions held by the other linguistic and cultural ethnic groups in West Pakistan, and portend serious questions about the possibility of achieving a stable nation-state even after the current rebellion is resolved.

In light of Yahya Khan's desire to return to democracy, assuming he implements that desire after the rebellion, he might achieve stability by establishing a policy of cultural pluralism. Such a policy would allow ethnic groups to maintain their communality and culture while operating within the context of Pakistani citizenship. Cultural pluralism could also permit political and economic integration of Pakistani society. The ethnic groups will continue for generations. To attempt to impose a Punjabi conformity upon them would be an error not unlike the attempt to impose Anglo-conformity upon the immigrants to American society.

A nation-state must develop loyalty to its value system and this system cannot be that of only one of the ethnic groups in the society. If cohesiveness is to be attained, there must be effort by central government to establish equal opportunity for all citizens to make contributions to a pluralistic society and a new emerging culture resulting from such contributions.

EPILOGUE: FEBRUARY 22, 1972

The civil war in East Pakistan raged for nine months with the military forces of Pakistan overpowering the resistance forces of the Bengali independence army. On December 3, 1971 India became involved in the war against Pakistan. Within two weeks the Indian army had encircled Dacca, the capitol city of East Pakistan, and surrender negotiations with the Pakistan forces were completed on December 16. Final surrender documents were signed on December 17 when Pakistan accepted a cease fire on the western front. The result of the prolonged conflict was the dismemberment of a Moslem nation. In its stead emerged a new nation—Bangladesh, and a new Pakistan which would require a reformation.

Bangladesh

Bangladesh as a new nation faces enormous political, economic, and social problems. The destructive tactics of the Pakistan army in systematically annihilating the leadership of East Bengal compounds the problem. Among these leaders were politicians, professional men, intellectuals, students, and skilled administrators.

The new leadership of Bangladesh, limited by inexperience, must build a nation from a society in chaos. In addition to the destruction of human life, bridges, communication lines, airports, factories, and roads were also destroyed or badly damaged. Machinery was made useless and crops have gone unattended. Many villages were partially or completely razed. Approximately nine million refugees fled to India during the course of the conflict and must now be repatriated.

Sheikh Mujibur Rahman, after his return from nine months' imprisonment in West Pakistan, declared that Bangladesh would be a secular, democratic socialist state. He established a provisional constitution setting up a parliamentary form of government to be governed by a Prime Minister and cabinet. Sheikh Mujib, the unquestioned leader of the East Bengalis, became Prime Minister. He assumed personal responsibility for the ministries of Defense, Home Affairs, Cabinet Affairs, and Information.

Bangladesh has already been recognized as a sovereign state by thirty-three nations. As an independent state, Bangladesh will have economic independence. It will no longer be subject to economic exploitation by West Pakistan. This will be a challenging period of economic development for the new nation. A number of factors indicate reasons for optimism. There is freedom now to exchange goods with other nations, especially India. However, the fledgling economy must avoid being overwhelmed by the export demands of India. Because the threat of war is remote only a small share of the gross national product will be required for defense expenditures, thereby allowing a greater proportion to be used for development. Finally, the national spirit fostered by the new independence, prompts willingness of the population to forego immediate pleasures with the ultimate goal of building a productive economic and political system.

The new nation has a serious social problem based on ethnicity. At the time of the partition of the sub-continent, a large number of Moslems from the Indian State of Bihar migrated to East Pakistan. This groups still speaks Urdu and has made no conscious efforts to become assimilated into the Bengali culture. Today there are approximately 1.5 million of these non-Bengali Moslems, known as

Biharis, residing in Bangladesh. Large numbers of them are in the towns of Mirpur and Mohammadpur near Dacca. The rest are scattered in towns throughout the country. The problems of integrating the Biharis into the new nation lie with their partisan involvement in the recent conflict. Large numbers of them identified with the Pakistan cause. During the period of occupation the Pakistan army used the Biharis as members of "Peace Committees." They served as informers on the civil administration as well as on the general population. They were also responsible for confiscating and redistributing lands and shops from Hindus and pro-independence Bengalis. To lend protection to their efforts they recruited armed vigilantes known as razikars.

Sheikh Mujib gives law and order top priority in getting the new nation underway. Yet since the signing of the surrender terms, the Biharis have become the oppressed and are subjected to Bengali brutality. The savagery is being applied indiscriminately to the Biharis regardless of whether or not any individual Bihari collaborated with the Pakistan army. The Indian army has attempted to protect them and Sheikh Mujib has asked the Mukti Bahini (pro-Bengali independence guerrillas) to turn in their weapons so that they might not be used against the Biharis. To a certain degree Mujib has been successful but the role of the Biharis during the war will remain in the minds of the Bengalis for generations to come. The Biharis may stay in Bangladesh but they will surely be subjected to constant discrimination. The problem could be solved by their migration to a safe territory, but little help is available. Bhutto, the President of Pakistan, has protested the genocide of these Biharis but his first concern is with getting his own troops and civil servants out of India. Thus, the problem of the Biharis remains unresolved.

Pakistan

On December 20, 1971, following the surrender, Zulfikar Ali Bhutto became President of Pakistan. He appointed himself Foreign Minister, Minister of Defense, Minister of the Interior, Minister of Interprovincial Coordination, and Chief Martial Law Administrator.

Bhutto walks a thin line. His leadership role in rebuilding a nation which has suffered defeat by a historic "enemy" will not be a simple one. He must be equally careful in dealing with the traditional leadership of the society and in fulfilling his campaign promises to the general population. Because of the military defeat, and the strong support of the general populace, he was able to purge the military and place some of its leadership under house arrest. However, the military is still a strong force in Pakistan and provides a basis for a possible coup d'état.

Bhutto removed a number of high level civil bureaucrats when he took office. The remaining civil bureaucracy needs to be handled diplomatically because it is through this avenue that the presidential plans must be implemented. Bhutto has also taken strong action against the "twenty-two wealthiest families" by withdrawing their passports and threatening them with prosecution unless they return the foreign exchange held abroad. He has also placed under house arrest the heads of two of these families.

Bhutto is a pragmatist. The military leaders he removed had no power. It is doubtful that the civil servants who have been removed and the heads of the two families placed under house arrest would have been able to exercise enough power to create a problem for his leadership.

In a Radio Pakistan broadcast, speaking in English because he is somewhat inadequate in Urdu, Bhutto announced the nationalization of most of the country's major heavy industries (iron, steel, auto manufacturing, and heavy construction) but said this action would not affect foreign investment. However, he did not nationalize cotton textile manufacturing, which is the largest single industry in the country. Nor did he mention agriculture, which accounts for more than one-half of the national income of Pakistan and employs two-thirds of the work force. He did make it clear that he had no intention of extending governmental controls over small industries.

In the past two months Bhutto has done a skillful job of moving the Pakistani populace to accept these new conditions. The problems he has resolved have been immediate ones. He must still face the long-range problems of potential interprovincial conflict and the language issue. It seems likely he has learned from recent past experience the lesson of planning for economic development. Hopefully he recognizes the need to put these plans into the context of the changing social organization of the country.

NOTES

1. Materials for the section on the brief history of an emerging nation are based on the following sources: Stephens, 1963; Tinker, 1962; Weekes, 1964; Wheeler, 1970; Wilber, 1964; Wilcox, 1963.

2. Undocumented materials presented throughout the remainder of the text have appeared in many different acceptable sources. It would be a cumbersome task and would reduce readability of the text if all were to be cited individually. There has been a frequency and consistency of the items in the following sources: Asian Almanac, Asian Recorder, The Japan Times, The Khyber Mail, The London Times, The Manchester Guardian, The New York Times, Newsweek, The Pakistan Times, and Time Magazine.

3. Elections to the constituencies in the cyclone hit areas of East Pakistan were held on January 17, 1971.

4. The thesis of provincial conflict in West Pakistan resulting from the dissolution order was the basis of a paper given by the author on March 20, 1971 at the International Studies Association annual meetings in San Juan, Puerto Rico. The status of East Pakistan was acknowledged and the threat of armed conflict, which erupted six days later, was covered in the discussion period.

REFERENCES

AHMED, T. (1971) Bangladesh: A Statement by Tajuddin Ahmed, The Prime Minister. (mimeo)

Asian Almanac (1970) "Development plans." (July 18): 4065-4067.

Asian Recorder (1970) "Pathans demand rehabilitation" (January 15-21).

––– "Demand for separate provinces in West Pakistan" (February 5-11).

Center for International Studies, Massachusetts Institute of Technology. (1960) "Patterns and problems of political development." United States Foreign Policy: Compilation of Studies, Vol. II. Committee on Foreign Relations, United States Senate. Washington, D.C.: Government Printing Office. Chapter VI: 1203-1210.

DAS GUPTA, F. (1970) Language Conflict and National Development. Berkeley: University of California Press.

DIL, A. A. [ed.] (1965) Perspectives on Pakistan. Abbottabad, Pakistan: Bookservice.

DURDIN, P. (1971) "The political tidal wave that struck East Pakistan." The New York Times Magazine (May 2): 22, 25, 88, 90, 92-94.

EMERSON, R. (1960) "Nationalism and political development." J. of Politics 22 (February): 3-28.

GRIFFIN, K. B. (1965) "Financing development plans in Pakistan." Pakistan Development Review (Winter): 603-613.

KANN, P. R. (1971) "A nation divided." Wall Street Journal (July 23): 1, 14 and (July 27): 1, 18.

THE KHYBER MAIL (1971) "Troops called out in Hyderabad." (January 23).

――― "Northwest province seeks economic development." (February 6).

LELYVELD, J. (1971) "Pakistan born of a shaky abstraction." New York Times (April 7): 3.

LITT, E. (1970) Ethnic Politics in America. Glenview, Ill.: Scott, Foresman.

MacEWAN, A. (1971) Development Alternatives in Pakistan. Cambridge, Mass.: Harvard University Press.

MAHMOOD, S. (1970) "The problem of national integration." The Pakistan Times (May 17): 10.

MUNIR, M. (1970) "The constitutional framework." The Pakistan Times (April 14): 4.

NEWSWEEK (1971) "Bengal: the murder of a people." (August 2): 26-30.

NEW YORK TIMES (1971) "Excerpts from World Bank report on East Pakistan." (July 13): 8C.

NULTY, T. and L. NULTY (1971) "The busy bee route to development." Trans-action 8 (February): 18-23.

OAKLEY, R. [ed.] (1968) New Backgrounds: The Immigrant Child at Home and at School. London: Oxford University Press.

THE PAKISTAN TIMES (1970) "Artists, poets demonstrate for Punjabi language." (September 4): 8.

――― (1970) "Plea for Punjab." (September 25): 6.

――― (1969) "Pakistan to speed end of English language." (July 4): 6.

PAPANEK, G. F. (1967) Pakistan's Development: Social Goals and Private Incentives. Cambridge, Mass.: Harvard University Press.

PATTERSON, S. (1969) Immigration and Race Relations in Britain 1960-1967. London: Oxford University Press.

RAJPUT, A. B. (1948) Muslim League, Yesterday and Today. Lahore.

ROSE, E.J.B. et al. (1969) Colour and Citizenship: A Report on British Race Relations. London: Oxford University Press.

SINGH, K. (1971) "Why they fled Pakistan—and won't go back." New York Times Magazine (August 1): 12-15.

SOBHAM, R. (1971) "Prelude to an order for genocide." The Manchester Guardian (June 5): 3.

STEPHENS, I. (1963) Pakistan. New York: Praeger.

STERBA, J. P. (1971) "Indian volunteers sought to go to aid East Pakistan." New York Times (March 30): 10C.

TIME (1971) "Pakistan the ravaging of golden Bengal." (August 2): 24-28.

TINKER, H. (1962) India and Pakistan: A Political Analysis. New York: Praeger.

VAN DER HAT, D. (1969) "East Bengal demand for control of Pakistan." The London Times (March 25): 1.

WEEKES, R. V. (1970) Pakistan: Birth and Growth of a Muslim Nation. Princeton: D. Van Nostrand.

WHEELER, R. S. (1970) The Politics of Pakistan: A Constitutional Quest. Ithaca: Cornell University Press.

WILBER, D. N. (1964) Pakistan: Its People, Its Society, Its Culture. New Haven, Conn.: Human Area Relations Files.

WILCOX, W. (1963) Pakistan: The Consolidation of a Nation. New York: Columbia University Press.

Chapter 16

FOREIGN POLICY AND ETHNICITY IN "SOFT STATES": PROSPECTS FOR SOUTHEAST ASIA

CYNTHIA H. ENLOE

*A*ll too often foreign policy studies appear written as if such policies were made in the unreal context of war rooms and elite strategy sessions. Perhaps this explains the unfortunate gaps in communication between social scientists working in the foreign policy field and their colleagues concerned with socio-political development. But it is precisely in underdeveloped nations that foreign and domestic affairs are most intimately related. Nowhere are they complete divorced, but it is easier for French or Swedish policymakers to make foreign policy decisions without an overwhelming preoccupation with their internal ramifications than it is for their Indonesian or Guyanese counterparts. For the very nature of underdevelopment includes insufficient integrity, acute vulnerability to outside forces. Foreign affairs constantly intrude upon domestic realms when (1) a nation's sovereign legitimacy is uncertain, or (2) a nation has minimal control over internal-external transactions. Swedish sociologist Gunnar Myrdal pinned the label "soft state" on those nation-states with inadequate authority to make and implement decisions affecting common welfare. A government which is not assured of other nations' respect for its legitimacy and which has little control over external factors touching its vital interests reigns over a "soft state." Underdevelopment, politically speaking, is in large measure characterized by inadequate authority and it is the international environment that greatly influences the degree of authority a government enjoys.

Ethnically diverse countries are not automatically "soft." Effectiveness of an authority structure to come to decisions and carry them out does not require communal homogeneity. Likewise, even remarkably homogeneous countries (though few on earth are totally devoid of ethnic diversity) at some historical stage have been limited developmentally because they were being buffeted about by external forces—e.g., China in the nineteenth and early twentieth centuries, Germany and Japan following World War II, England in the turbulent seventeenth century. Still, in those culturally divided countries ethnic hostilities can compound an already weak government's troubles in handling external pressures.

Nowhere has this been clearer than in Southeast Asia. Much of the literature dealing with ethnic complexities in Southeast Asian regional affairs has focused on the mainland, particularly the territories of former Indochina (see Connor, 1969, and the excellent collection of studies in Kunstadter, 1967). There the presence of hill tribes situated on strategic border points and barely conscious of lowlander-dominated national regimes have made ethnic pluralism's relevance to foreign policy vital. Yet much of the discussion revolves around geographic borders; what starts as an analysis of ethnicity's impact on foreign relations rapidly declines to an exercise in cartography. The following remarks, therefore, are devoted instead to *insular* Southeast Asia. The absence of guerrilla bands (though clever smugglers abound) and the lesser significance of disputed frontiers (Borneo's role in the archipelago is a major exception) may help to keep our sights on the theoretical relationships between underdevelopment, ethnic pluralism, and foreign policy.

Insular Southeast Asia embraces three island nations—the Philippines, Indonesia, and Singapore—as well a one island-cum-peninsular nation—Malaysia. The latter was created in 1963 out of a merger between the nine states of the Malayan peninsula and Britain's two unwanted Borneo colonies across the water, Sabah and Sarawak. Each of the four nations contains several distinct ethnic communities, attracted to the country or reinforced in their separateness by European colonial administrations in the past. The ethnic dimension of southeast Asian political underdevelopment has its roots in imperialist convenience. "Ethnicity," however, takes on several different meanings in the archipelago, just as European overlords pursued several different policies toward communities. Social scientists readily acknowldege that Malaysia's and Singapore's Chinese, Indians, and Malays form separate ethnic communities, as do Indonesi's Chinese and Indonesians and the Philippines' Chinese and Filipinos. But, additionally, these unstable nations have to reconcile another sort of ethnic divisiveness, not as blatant but surely as politically sensitive as that between indigenous and immigrant groups. This is ethnic pluralism among the indigenous peoples themselves. Both types of ethnic fragmentation have shaped the relationship between political development and foreign policy.

For example, calculations leading to the formation of the Malaysian Federation included an assumption by the Alliance Party leadership in Malaya that the critical line of cleavage in the Borneo territories was between Chinese and "indigenous" communities. Indigenous origins were thought to provide a solid foundation for collaboration among Borneo Malays, Ibans, Kadazans, and Dyaks. Together they would offset Chinese interests and put Sabah and Sarawak firmly on the side of the Malays over on the peninsula. This ethnic analysis proved incorrect, and the miscalculation opened the new federation up to serious external pressures in its first years. Instead of natural friendship and shared outlooks, there was resentment felt by non-Malay indigenous groups on Borneo toward the historically dominant Malays. After federation the antagonisms were refueled by the central government's moves to bolster Malay politicians, the Malay language and Islam (see Anonymous, 1971). The resultant instability within Sabah and Sarawak and between each and the central government not only delayed important programs but stimulated outside interference from the Philippines, claiming Sabah as its own, and from Indonesia, charging that the whole federal scheme was a neo-colonialist plot designed in London. Both feuds retarded Southeast Asia's tentative progress toward regional cooperation.

The Philippines has experienced two kinds of conflict among indigenous groups, each with foreign policy ramifications. The Muslim minority in the southern provinces was never fully subdued ("integrated" often is just a euphemism for subjugation) by the Spaniards or Americans. Now they are figuring more importantly in independent Filipino politics. Muslims attracted attention during the Philippines—Malaysia dispute over Sabah because it was the traditional jurisdiction of the Muslim Sultan of Sulu on which Manila based its claim and Manila encouraged Muslim identification with Sabah. More recently, however, the central regime has been at odds with Muslims. There have been violent clashes between Muslims and Christians who have been prompted to migrate to the less developed southern islands with Manila's sponsorship. The second interethnic division among indigenous Filipinos is along linguistic lines. Studies have found that the country's language groups, which also inhabit distinctive regional areas, tend to vote communally in national legislative elections (Ando, 1969). Moreover, in the abortive Huk rebellion of the 1950s it was the Pampangano-speaking peasants of central Luzon who formed the backbone of the insurgency. Had it not been for linguistic-ethnic barriers the Huks might have been able to cast their net wider (Mitchell, 1969). Filipino officials and their American Advisors at the time, however, defined the rebellion ideologically, not ethnically. Treating the Huks simply as communists served to harden the Philippines' position in the anti-communist, anti-Peking camp internationally and to increase its reliance on the United States for the maintenance of national security.

Given its close ties with its former colonial master, as well as its Christian majority, the Philippine sense of nationalism and identification with Asia has always been ambiguous. A new generation of political leaders and the retreat of Americans from direct responsibility for security in the area together have set off a search for Filipino and Asian identity. As with so many fragmented nations, it is a common "national" language that is the principal mechanism for generating pride and consolidation. This has been true in Malaysia, Indonesia, and the Philippines. Singapore, though 75 percent Chinese, elevates four languages to the status of national language in order to insure internal peace and to allay anti-Chinese suspicions among its neighbors. The language chosen to serve as the national language for the Philippines is Tagalog, originally spoken by people on the main island of Luzon. Tagalog is now officially referred to as "Filipino" in order to reduce its ethnic connotations. Still, some non-Tagalog communities have expressed unhappiness with the national language policy.

In terms of development and foreign policy, the language issue is significant insofar as deliberate governmental pursuit of a distinctly Filipino (as versus Spanish, American, or general Christian) identity is part of the broader efforts to adjust the changing Great Power relationships and regional potentials. Critical to development is the maximization of options, the creation of policy choices relevant to the present demands but amenable to change. Philippine reliance on U.S. aid and protection may have served developmental needs a decade ago; it is questionable whether it does today. But extricating itself from the American embrace calls for revised patterns of internal integration, patterns which alter Tagalog-nonTagalog relations and prompt Manila to urge settlement in the south despite Muslim antagonisms.

Ethnic differences among Indonesia's indigenous groups have received more attention from social scientists. Perhaps this is because their impact on power rivalries has been so obvious. The most prominent cleavage is between the Javanese and the non-Javanese peoples of the "outer islands," though the latter are composed of a myriad of cultural groups. Suspicion of Javanese attempts to control the central government and thus the entire nation-building process has been mirrored in the country's political party alignments (no party is strictly ethnic, however) and in splits within the Indonesian army. The Java-outer island tensions took on direct foreign implications in the unsuccessful rebellion of 1957. At that time the Socialist Party and the modernity-oriented Muslim party, Masjumi, collaborated with Sumatran dissidents in an attempt to upset the Java based regime of President Sukarno. Sukarno denounced the United States, charging it was covertly aiding the rebels as a means of limiting his government's anti-neocolonialist activities. Sukarno and the central government on Java withstood the assault, but in the process the U.S. became the regime's bete noir and Indonesian strategists turned toward the communist world for allies. Ethnically-motivated regionalism became almost inseparable with anti-Sukarnoism and sympathy with the neocolonialist West.[1]

In each instance just cited interethnic conflict among indigenous groups compelled resource-poor governments to devote men, money, and popular emotional energy to non-growth areas. In terms of international integrity, each communal dispute had at least one of the following results:

(1) it induced greater dependency on a foreign power, often at the price of stunted national pride and consciousness;

(2) it allowed other countries to meddle in the nation's development, frequently covertly and illegitimately, thus prolonging and escalating domestic violence; and

(3) it forestalled such intra-regional cooperation in the archipelago as might have fostered economic rationalization and a sharing of development costs.

A new decade finds the nations of Southeast Asia still searching for enduring solutions to hostilities between their respective indigenous communities. Yet one signal of their progress toward political development—i.e., the capacity to utilize public resources to satisfy public needs—is their broadened outward orientations.

From the time of the isolationist strategies of Japan's Tokagawa shoganate and the newly independent administration of America's George Washington up to the present xenophobic policy of Burma's military regime, developing countries have tried to avoid those foreign "entanglements" which dissipate their resources and undermine their political authority. Or, as in the case of the Philippines and its dependence on the United States, developing nations have put all of their foreign policy eggs in a single basket. This formula is actually a modified form of isolationism in that it severely narrows the diversity of external contacts. Multi-ethnic countries suffering under the strains of development are prone to one sort of isolationism or another partly as a means of keeping the lid on communal tensions. Another variant on this formula is to have a multitude of contacts, but to restrict most of them to a ceremonial level, rather than risk commitments and genuine partnerships. A powerful patron can be called upon to lend assistance in times of domestic turmoil and to act as a buffer against other outside interference. Malaysia's seemingly tepid anti-colonialism and its reliance on Britain for military aid during the Communist (and largely local Chinese) Emergency of 1948-1960 is a striking example of this policy pattern.

Singapore is so small and its economy so urban and dependent on international trade that it would be almost impossible for it to be isolationist. Its refusal to choose any one ethnic culture as *the* Singaporean culture reflects this international fact-of-life. As we will see, however, there are elements in the Singapore polity which deem this developmental decision unsatisfactory, for it undervalues the Chinese identities of the vast majority of the island-nation's citizenry. Of all the archipelago countries, Singapore is the last to attain independence and really it is only now beginning to fashion a foreign policy which acknowledges Britain's departure. Indonesia, too, seems to be an exception to the general rule, for it has been in the vanguard of international, "Third World" organizers ever since it defeated Dutch returning colonialists in 1949. But the regional civil war of 1957 cut it off from the United States, while disputes with Malaysia over Borneo severed that likely tie. The violent coup and "counter-coup" which sent communists to the hills and Chinese to internment camps in 1965 also ruined its warm relations with China. Each conflict and subsequent retraction of overseas contacts involved questions of interethnic relations.

As these countries gain political confidence—a requisite as well as a product of political development—there is a greater willingness and need to expand serious external contacts. For any state in Southeast Asia such expansion means above all a coming to terms with mainland China. In the archipelago such a crucial reorientation can be accomplished only if foreign ministers take their own local Chinese into account.

A major factor separating ethnic politics between indigenous communities and ethnic politics between indigenous and "overseas" communities (Indian as well as Chinese) is the importance assigned to citizenship. To some social analysts citizenship sounds like a rather old-fashioned element, rarely discussed in sophisticated analyses of development. But in any nation comprised in part of immigrants, controversies over the qualifications and obligations of formal citizenship can be as divisive as conflicts over ideology. Although Tagalog and non-Tagalog speakers in the Philippines may argue over the linguistic character of Filipino national identity, neither denies the other's claim to citizenship. This restricts the debate and limits its potential disintegrative force, because the question must be settled among them; no one can pretend that the other community will "go back to where it came from." Indonesians contend over Java's predominance, but when the local Chinese appear to be involved in a coup d'état the first solution adopted by outraged officials is deportation.

Integration frequently is made synonymous with "nation-building." In that process resolving differences over citizenship has been central. The problem is aggravated in Southeast Asia because Peking insists on continuing to think of overseas Chinese as mainland citizens. Added to this is the split between Peking and the nationalists on Taiwan over who has the right to grant Chinese citizenship in the first place. Local politicians from Manila to Kuala Lumpur have accused their own Chinese residents—renowned for their pragmatism—of opportunistically going along with domestic governments while hiding Mainland and Taiwan Chinese passports under their pillows "just in case." A good deal of an overseas Chinese leader's time is spent trying to assuage these fears and prompting his own communal followers to go the extra mile in demonstrating allegiance to their country of residence. If a leader pushes the latter point too energetically, however, he risks losing his ethnic supporters.

Just what stand should overseas Chinese spokesmen take when the issue of foreign relations with Peking comes up? Singapore, Malaysia, the Philippines, and Indonesia face certain common problems in deciding how to adjust their foreign policies to meet the changing role of Peking:

(1) scarcity of resources—funds and experienced personnel—required for extensive diplomatic contacts (an embassy abroad is a big item in a budget already stretched);

(2) continuing suspicion by indigenous groups that immigrant allegiance to the nation is only skin-deep and would shift quickly if their "mother country" were given a position of prestige;

(3) minimal control over the international environment in which security must be assured and economic growth pursued—the Nixon administration's sudden about-face on Peking made this clear once again;

(4) lack of common borders with China and thus at least some sense of "breathing space" as contrasted with countries such as North Vietnam and Burma.

Yet policies toward China have taken quite dissimilar paths. Among the variables affecting policy orientations is, first, the extent to which a government relies on an anticommunist power for maintenance of internal security, including the supply of military equipment and police training. The four countries differ in such a reliance and they differ too on a second variable: the intensity of any fear of Chinese domination domestically; the local Chinese might lend valuable assistance to rebels in the Philippines, but they could actually take over the machinery of government in Malaysia and Singapore.

Third, the degree of political self-confidence of non-Chinese policy-makers and their followers varies from nation to nation and influences their outward perspectives. Although all four states have been granted formal independence and hold seats in the United Nations, their acceptance as truly legitimate states is not identical. Singapore, especially, suffers from a lack of acceptance from immediate neighbors and consequently is wary of any foreign maneuver further undermining its regional security. A fourth variable is the degree of coherence between Peking's ideological outlook and that of the bulk of local Chinese residents. If resident Chinese seem solidly bourgeois it is likely to reduce anxiety over Peking penetration; whereas if their is a strong radical streak among local Chinese, then giving Peking an entré could seriously jeopardize internal order. The Malaysian Chinese, for example, are almost indistinguishable in many Malay minds with the Communist insurgents of the 1950s, whose remnants still carry out ambushes on the Thai border. In the Philippines, by contrast, although the Chinese are often considered pariahs, they are not merged in the public mind with the Huks. Finally, enthusiasm for a reapproachment with Communist China will be affected by the likelihood of balancing that relationship with other new contacts. Offsetting relationships could be either with nations having cultural affinity with local non-Chinese groups or with countries having no special connection with any of the resident communities. Australia or Japan could play the latter role and the Muslim states of the Middle East could play the former for Indonesia, for instance.

It is rather surprising to old Southeast Asia hands to see these variables currently at work. They have acted so as to put Malaysia out in front among Peking's new suitors: Malaysia, the country whose very viability has been profoundly shaken by Chinese-Malay hostilities and whose ruling Alliance Party is one of the most conservative and pro-Western in the area. Observers' surprise stems from their inattention to developmental changes. For, paradoxical as it may seem, it is the escalation of Malay ethnic militancy that has caused the Alliance leaders' turn-about on China. The communal riots of May, 1969, compelled the the older English-speaking, cosmopolitan Malay elite to take greater interest in the interests of their politicized Malay-speaking constituents. Malay leaders loosened their ties with the Chinese elite and pledged to Malayanize developmental programs. What Arend Lijphart (1969) has called "consociational democracy," in which social fragmentation is papered over by elite cooperation, had come apart at the seams.[2] Although Chinese are still in parliament and the ministries, the Kuala Lumpur regime is more Malay than it has ever been since independence.

With this domestic redistribution of power has come a revised outlook on Malaysia's external intersts. It has been reinforced by three other events. First, the British have pulled most of their military out of Malaysia and closed the famous navy yard in Singapore, forcing Malaysians to reduce dependency on the U.K. and the West in general. Second, ascendency of anti-Sukarno military officers in Indonesia ended the war in Borneo, with all of its ethnic overtones, and lessened the role of China in Djakarta. Less direct in its impact is, of course, the United States military pull-back from Asia.

As one might expect, Malaysia's changes could be seen first in its relations with countries culturally associated with the now assertive Malays. Talks between the Philippines, Indonesia, and Malaysia, which had ended sourly in 1963, began again. There was the assumption that these three "Malay" populated nations were natural partners and could form the nucleus of any wider Southeast Asian cooperative scheme. In another direction, Kuala Lumpur stepped up communications with Islamic states such as Saudi Arabia and Egypt. Ties with Islamic Pakistan are more delicate, however, given Malaysia's 10 percent Indian population. But the role of religion, more important to Malay sense of ethnic identity than to Chinese, is bound to gain in significance and serve as a bridge to broader international involvement. It is noted, incidentally, that as Malaysia was sending diplomats and students to Cairo, Singapore was accepting aid and advice from Israel.

Previously, Malaysian leaders grounded their country's stability—and their own personal security—in careful compromises among three ethnic elites (though Malays were still "first among equals" in the Alliance) and a firm attachment to Britain. Termination of both formulas has generated a greater number of options for foreign policymakers. The bloodshed of 1969 is not forgotten, but there appears to be less obsession with caution and ambiguity in governmental actions. At home this has meant clearer ethnic priorities favoring Malays, while abroad it has meant greater independence from the West. In other words, Malay militancy has limited local Chinese influence internally and raised Chinese influence externally. So long as the government was led by a tri-communal leadership, any move toward China would have angered and frightened the Malay masses whose participation had to be kept at a low pitch if the Alliance system was to operate. Malay mobilization was something that neither the Malay or Chinese elite could afford. But the Malay government of the seventies has less to fear from Malay rank and file. In May, 1971, Malaysia sent a trade delegation to China, headed by a Malay royal prince. Reconciliation with China, at the same time, could mollify Malaysian Chinese, who are unhappy about promotion of Malay language in schools and other ethnic programs. The Prime Minister, therefore, in a year when the China issue will be critical, chose as the country's deputy U.N. representative Miss P. G. Lim, a well known Chinese lawyer in Kuala Lumpur.[3] For the first time in its history, Malaysia finds that the ethnic interests of both Malays and Chinese coincide on the question of China.

These same variables make Singapore notably hesitant in cultivating Peking. This again comes as a surprise, for Singapore is heavily Chinese and its Chinese-led People's Action Party (PAP) regime is more explicitly socialist than any other in Southeast Asia, except North Vietnam and perhaps Burma. But it is precisely because Singapore is 75 percent Chinese, wholeheartedly internationalist, and programmatically socialist that Prime Minister Lee Kuan Yew had bided his time while Malaysians flew to Peking. The key variable here is international acceptability and legitimacy. Singapore leaders know that their country is "a Chinese island in a Malay sea." The phrase means insecurity. It is less for home consumption than for external impression that Singapore has four official languages, that its party program eschews ethnic goals, that a Malay is in the post of ceremonial chief of state and that an Indian serves as foreign minister. In fact, Singapore is the only nation in Southeast Asia presently to have a member of an ethnic minority heading its foreign policy machinery. Not all Singaporean Chinese concur with the PAP coolness toward China and preoccupation with neighboring Malay regimes. Thus the ethnic aspect of Singapore's foreign policy process takes the form of conflict within the Chinese community itself. So long as Lee Kuan Yew gives top billing to economic growth for the sake of rapid social development, he must follow a path that protects national autonomy and integrity. Consequently, the PAP's show of independence and flexibility in the aftermath of Britain's withdrawal and the "Nixon Doctrine" has been in its relations with the Soviet Union, a country having no ethnic connotations for Singapore.

It would be foolish and misleading to assume that even in as self-consciously a pluralistic nation as Malaysia ethnicity is the sole or even preeminent factor shaping foreign affairs. Yet domestic interethnic relations usually cannot be quarantined. They spill over into external matters. This is particularly true in underdeveloped polities, since there issues tend to blur and authority structures are too immature to prevent outside interference. What is needed to complement general analysis like the preceding is close empirical investigation of the foreign policy decision-making process in such countries as those of the Southeast Asian archipelago. For example, does it really make any difference that Singapore's foreign minister is Indian? On what evidence did Indonesian generals determine that local Chinese collaborated with Peking and coup organizers? Students of development and ethnicity need the assistance of foreign policy students to answer these questions.

But the assistance should be mutual. Perhaps foreign policy studies would be more pertinent to the rest of the social sciences if their authors worked in closer collaboration with students of political change. More account could be given to the impact of domestic social cleavages on foreign policy decisions. Projections for future Southeast Asian relations therefore must include interethnic data as well as national defense expenditures.

NOTES

1. Nawawi (1969) has studied Indonesian regional conflicts and concluded that economic and social stagnation is a more basic cause of regionalist sentiment than ethnic cultural allegiances alone. Ethnicity rarely, in fact, is solely cultural; the cultural divisions are burdened with social and economic dissatisfactions.

2. Lijphart (1969) focuses on such European plural democracies as the Netherlands and Belgium, but the concept is applicable worldwide.

3. Malaysia and China signed their first direct trade agreement in August, 1971, making diplomatic ties a possibility in the near future. For a summary of Malaysia's foreign policy since the riots, see Polsky (1971).

REFERENCES

ANDO, H. (1969) "A study of voting patterns in the Philippine presidential and senatorial elections, 1945-1965." Midwest J. of Political Science 13, 4 (November): 581-586.

Anonymous (1971) "Porkboys' complaint." Far Eastern Economic Rev. 71, 1 (January): 12-14.

CONNOR, W. (1969) "Ethnology and the peace of South Asia." World Politics 22, 1 (October): 51-86.

KUNSTADTER, P. [ed.] (1967) Southeast Asian Tribes, Minorities and Nations, Vols. I and II. Princeton N.J.: Princeton University Press.

LIJPHART, A. (1969) "Consociational democracy." World Politics, 21, 2 (January): 207-225.

MITCHELL, E. J. (1969) "Some econometrics of the Huk rebellion." Amer. Pol. Sci. Rev. 62, 4 (December): 1167-1169.

NAWAWI, M. A. (1969) "Stagnation as a basis of regionalism: a lesson from Indonesia.'. Asian Survey 9, 12 (December): 934-945.

POLSKY, A. (1971) "Razak and the new order." Far Eastern Economic Rev. 73, 31 (July): 29-31.

Chapter 17

THE IMPACT OF EDUCATION ON ETHNIC
GROUPS IN GHANA AND KENYA

ROBERTA E. McKOWN

*T*here are ethnic tensions within the new nations; the possibility that education might preserve or intensify them is a real one. Many of these tensions may be traced to the uneven impact of the colonial experience (new commercial and communications facilities, urbanization, and cultural forces) on pre-existing ethnic groups. Because education is such an important determinant of an individual's ability to move into the limited modern sector of the economy in these countries, it has been one of the most sensitive policy areas of post-independence politics.

High expectations were held, by both sympathetic foreign observers and the political leaders of developing nations, for the results of the rapidly expanding educational systems. Schools and colleges were seen specifically as sources of the needed new technical and economical cadres and generally of a nationally oriented, civic citizenry. We do not intend to deal here with the degree of success education has had in creating both a common sense of national identification and a willingness to accept other ethnic groups as fellow citizens. Not only is there discouraging behavioral evidence, but there is a prior aspect of the educational impact that requires examination: its purely structural impact on lines of horizontal ethnic division.

Before education can perform its integrative role of socialization of diverse groups into a common political culture, it must reach them. Ethnic groups in African states tend to be geographically localized and existing educational institutions tend to be part of a pattern involving urbanization and economic development. Thus, the local resources to maintain and expand education are concentrated in areas that are already ahead in providing schools. Educationally backward areas, on the other hand, tend to be less developed in economic and social modernization as well. Either pattern will tend to be maintained unless national policy and resources are directed toward equalizing development and educational opportunity. Yet, it is often more economically rational to concentrate development resources in areas where some development has already taken place. This is so because:

"Short-run inequality maximizes capacity ....On the other hand, a premature and excessive effort to impose or to realize equality may so disperse meager resources that system capacity is gravely weakened, if not destroyed [Coleman, 1965: 31-32].

AUTHOR'S NOTE: The student sample for which data is reported here was obtained in 1966. Financial support for the research was provided by the National Science Foundation and by the Institute for International Studies and Overseas Administration of the University of Oregon. The author accepts responsibility for the interpretation of the data.

Until the national budget is able to provide nearly universal access to education, certain families and localities will continue to have a better opportunity to gain elite status than others. Thus, ethnic or tribal divisions (the cultural or other lines that divide the population into distinguishable and self-conscious groups) may be not only maintained, but also, because of the same economic-efficiency considerations, intensified. A short-run solution might be found in policies designed to equalize access without expanding the number of schools or places within them. However, one thereby runs the risk of antagonizing the previously favored groups (who are likely to be the individuals called upon to make or implement such a policy).

We will also note some evidence of the relationship of education to emerging class lines, but our major emphasis is on ethnic groups as component national units. The following brief description of the two nations is intended only as the broadest sort of scenario for those without a prior knowledge of either or both countries.

THE CONTEXT OF COMPARISON

Ghana and Kenya provide an apt comparison for a number of reasons. They share certain characteristics that make comparison meaningful. The patterns of ethnic diversity are similar. Ethnic fragmentation is not as extreme as in countries such as Tanzania nor as divisive as in Nigeria or Rwanda. No one group is sufficiently dominant to be able to rule alone as do the Libero-Americans of Liberia. Both countries have had their share of ethnic-based political conflict: the Ashanti-centered United Party coalition as the major anti-Convention People's Party grouping in the early years of independence or the Luo-Kamba coalition that surfaced in 1965 as the Kenya People's Union in opposition to the ruling Kenya African National Union. Both have also successfully weathered secessionist threats—that of the Somalis in northern Kenya or the Ewe in eastern Ghana. Unity is the political goal and "tribalism in politics" is uniformly decried although each party to a conflict generally accuses the opponent of practicing it.

Each country has its relatively neglected Muslim northern regions as well as a few groups who profited disproportionately from the advantages of colonialism, emerging after 1946 as the politically most organized and efficacious. Both were British colonies and protectorates with the pragmatic admixtures of direct and indirect rule as local circumstances dictated. They are reasonably similar in geographic and population size. Nonetheless, there are differences that should be noted. The first is simply the length of the external impact. There was little European influence on the East African Coast until the late nineteenth century whereas the Gold Coast had been a trading center—for slaves, gold, and then agricultural products—since the fifteenth century.[1] The first school was established in one of the Gold Coast slaving 'castles' in 1644 (Foster, 1965: 44) and the first missionaries were on the scene a century later, while European education did not arrive in Kenya until after 1900. Gold Coasters were traveling to Britain for higher education at least a hundred years before the first Kenya African enrolled at Makerere in 1928. Both countries effectively became colonies the same year: 1910, when Ashanti and the northern territories were incorporated into the Colony and Protectorate of the Gold Coast, and the railroad from the Coast to Lake Victoria opened up the interior of Kenya to trade and settlement.

Ghana was also fortunate in having two truly enlightened governors, Maclean in the 1830s and 1840s, and Guggisberg in the 1920s, whilst those in Kenya seemed to have to pass a test of acceptability to the local white settlers before appointment (for the most blatant example see Bennett, 1963: 50). Ghana had the "good fortune" to be located on the Guinea Coast with its malarial mosquitoes and other hazards to health and attracted very little permanent European settlement. The Kenya Highlands were at the opposite end of the scale—temperate, fertile, and inviting.[2] The European farmers who took advantage of the opportunity to settle quickly established the typical pattern of superior-inferior relationships common still in the southern part of the continent.

The presence of European farmers in the Kenya "White Highlands" had some modernizing economic consequences for the adjacent tribal groups, but the major impact seemed to be a stifling of African social and political development and a freezing of ethnic groups into their geographic compartments. Legal rules and informal practices tended to keep the African on his tribal reserve, reduced urbanization, and generally restricted his horizons to the parochial. This was in marked contrast to the Ghanaian experience. British imperialism in Ghana had been more hesitant and hence literate, politically aware Gold Coasters had early formed protective associations (the Aborigines' Rights Protection Society being the most famous) to resist the worst effects of colonialism and to press their demands for benefits. There was nothing comparable in Kenya in the late nineteenth century, where Stanley was describing the natives as a disagreeable hazard on the way to Uganda, to be avoided if at all possible. The impact of imperialism was thus sudden, disagreeable, and highly disruptive in Kenya compared to Ghana, where the Foreign Office (and later the Colonial Office) took its responsibilities to the natives more seriously.[3]

Hopes of the European settlers for self-government in Kenya were not finally and officially dashed until the Hilton-Grigg Commission report of 1929. Neither the government nor the settlers took this to portend any change in the existing racially stratified hierarchy of relationships for several generations. Until 1944 the Africans were felt to be adequately represented on the Legislative Council by missionaries or other Europeans. In the Gold Coast, the growth of ethnic associations, improvement societies, and pressure groups had provided a firm base for the political parties that appeared after 1946. There had also been some experience for both chiefs and urban intellectuals on various quasi-legislative councils and a limited franchise was in effect. The British had viewed the Gold Coast with some pride as an example of what enlightened colonial adminis-tration could do. A limited but very good secondary school system was producing graduates comparable to those of the British system, the colony was prosperous, the people loyal (the West African regiments served honorably in World War II), and political development appeared to be progressing in accord with an orderly, if long-range, plan.

The appearance of mass-based politics in the Gold Coast and the rural guerrilla warfare of the Mau Mau uprising in Kenya in the immediate postwar period caught the British somewhat unaware. The particular form of political activity in each colony was in many ways typical of the level of social and political change that had been allowed by the respective regime. The lagging of Kenyan modernization behind the Ghanaian pace combined with the apparently

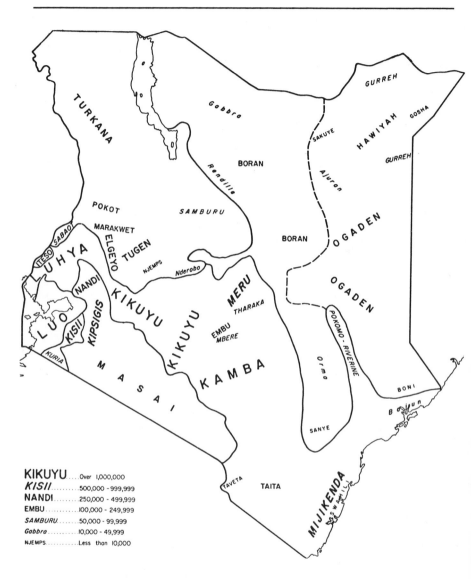

KIKUYU .... Over 1,000,000
KISII ....500,000 - 999,999
NANDI ....250,000 - 499,999
EMBU ....100,000 - 249,999
SAMBURU........50,000 - 99,999
Gabbra ....10,000 - 49,999
NJEMPS............Less than 10,000

Source: W.T.W. Morgan and N.M. Shaffer: (1966) Population
of Kenya, Density and Distribution. Nairobi:
Oxford University Press. p. 33.

Figure 1: PREDOMINANT TRIBE IN THE AREA, KENYA

entrenched minority power to produce extra-legal violence rather than political action. In both instances, after some uncertainty, the British accepted the inevitable and turned the colonies over to majority self-government. Ghana became the first black African colony to gain independence in 1957, and Kenya followed in 1963 as the first white-settler colony to attain independence with majority rule.

The differences in the two countries chosen for analysis are thus reflective of the two types of British African colony: the "administered" colony versus the "settler" colony.

ETHNIC DIVERSITY

With independence and majority rule, the politically relevant ethnic lines are those within the African population alone. Cultural, linguistic, and even physical differences within the Kenya African population are more marked than in Ghana. There are three major racial groups in Kenya—Bantu, Nilotic and Nilo-Hamatic—each in turn composed of several distinct tribes.[4]

The Bantu are the largest group, with about 39 percent of the total African population and within this broad category the Kikuyu and the closely related Embu-Meru-Kamba tribes are the largest (Republic of Kenya, 1966: 36). They are sometimes referred to as the "Central Bantu" because of their location near Nairobi. The most famous Kikuyu, of course, is Jomo Kenyatta. The second most important tribe would be the Luhya (a name coined by missionaries to cover a large number of small tribes) near Lake Victoria, followed by the Gusii and a number of small tribes on the coast.

The Luo are the only Nilotic group in Kenya—their ethnic relatives are in Uganda and the Sudan. Like the Bantu, they are farmers, constricted in a heavily populated area near the Lake. They are chronically restive under the Central Bantu political dominance and the fate of the two leading Luo politicans —Mboya assassinated and Odinga jailed—does not auger well for future ethnic political harmony.

The third group, the Nilo-Hamitic, occupies the greatest area, largely the barren areas of the North and Southwest, as nomadic pastoralists. The Masai are the romanticized representative of the group, although not the largest tribe. With the exception of the Kipsigis, they have been relatively passive politically. The Somalis actively sought to withdraw from the state, in the long series of *shifta* incidents only recently resolved through diplomacy.

If the traditional political structures of most Kenya tribes has been characterized as lacking in chieftancy or other centralized authority structures, the opposite generalization would hold for the Gold Coast. The great symbolic authority of the chiefs often masked considerable decentralization of authority and elements of popular control but were nonetheless impressive in their symbols, titles and ceremonies. Tribal lines are complex, the official census lists over 400 (Gil et al., 1964) with seventeen major linguistic divisions, all belonging racially to the so-called "true Negro" stock (as do the Bantu).

The major group, the Akan, are relatively recent arrivals, coming in three waves from the North. The first wave, the Guan, are historically and presently of little importance. The second, the Fanti, settled along the coast and have the longest tradition of European contact. They often solicited the aid of the British

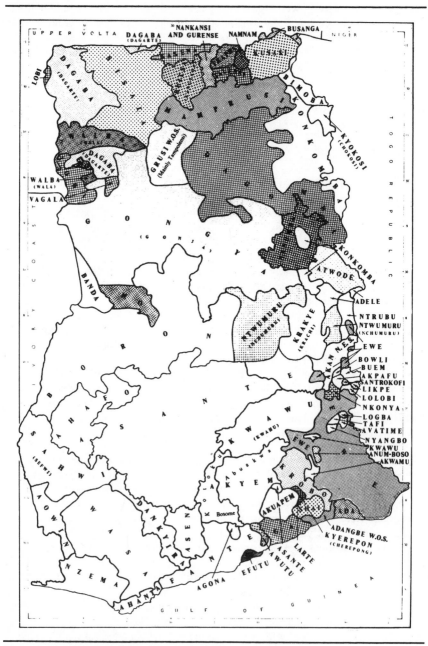

Figure 2: PREDOMINANT TRIBE IN THE AREA

against the restless energy of the Ashanti, the third wave of Akan. The Ashanti (or Asante) occupy the center of Ghana and required a series of wars lasting a century before they capitulated to British rule. They acquired the head of one British governor in the process, for symbolic and decorative purposes, and as the nucleous of the opposition to Nkrumah often boasted they would have his head as well. Reasonably satisfied with the colonial modus vivendi, they were not in the vanguard of nationalists. The present Prime Minister, Dr. Kofi Busia, is of the royal family of Wenchi, one of the wing chiefdoms of Ashanti.

The remaining important southern tribes are the Ewe and Ga-Adangbe, immigrants from the East. Since many Ewe are located in Togo, there was considerable sentiment for unification with the French Togo Ewes. The Ga surround Accra and are highly urbanized but nonetheless prone to form ethnic protective associations.

The Mole-Dagbani of the northern half of the country are the second largest group, predominantly Muslim or Animist, economically and educationally isolated and backward. They, too, were footdraggers as independence approached and still evidence a defensive posture toward the more modernized South.

THE STRUCTURAL IMPACT

The political question is often phrased in Lasswellian terms: who gets what? Our "what" is educational access or advantage and the "who" is "which of the diverse tribal/ethnic groups?"

We promised to comment on the "class" or vertical integrative impact. Without getting into the debate on the relevance of class analysis for Africa, we may simply note that (a) there is a very limited private modern economic sector, (b) most "status" well paid (relatively, of course) employment is in the civil service and other governmental institutions and enterprises, and (c) that access to these positions is generally based on educational attainment.

Longitudinal data (Koplin, 1968: 144-59) for Ghana may be summarized on this point. The information available indicated increased access to education for children of illiterate and farming parents over time, although higher status groups remain disproportionately represented in terms of their position in the total population. Longitudinal data are not available for Kenya but on the basis of the 1966 data, access to education is open to children from lower economic strata, more so in fact than in Ghana. Yet, at the same time, the advantage of being from an "elite" family background in Kenya, if one would obtain higher education, is greater than in Ghana. This is due to the lack of any appreciable middle class (such as the small traders or richer farmers found in Ghana) in Kenya between subsistence peasants and the elites.

Perhaps the most striking evidence of the advantage of family background is in the comparison of the educational attainment of the fathers in a 1966 student sample with those of the general adult male population. We may compute a selectivity index: a ratio of the proportions of student's fathers and the general male population with the given characteristic.[5] An index of 1.00 would indicate no difference between the two groups. Thus, university and secondary students in both countries are only half as likely to have an illiterate male parent as the distribution of non-literate males would produce randomly but five to

TABLE 1

GHANA AND KENYA STUDENTS' FATHERS COMPARED TO ADULT
MALE POPULATION, EDUCATIONAL SELECTIVITY INDICES[a]

Level of Educational Attainment	Ghanaian Students, 1966			Kenya Students, 1966		
	4th Form	6th Form	Univ. of Ghana	4th Form	6th Form	Univ. Col. Nairobi
None	.47	.55	.39	.51	.54	.52
Elementary and middle school	1.69	1.84	2.07	1.69	1.52	1.77
Secondary, teacher training, technical	8.84	5.52	8.84	7.07	9.14	5.28
University	33.33	28.66	31.00	11.25	16.26	10.00

a. The comparison is with adult males, aged 25 and over. The ratio is: (percentage of students' fathers)/(percentage of adult males).

eight times more likely to have a father with some secondary level education. It is at the level of university education that the "selectivity" becomes most marked and the ratios are much higher for Ghanaian than Kenyan students,[6] indicating that higher levels of education in Ghana are "preserves of the existing elites" to a greater extent than in Kenya. One must, to some extent, concur with the findings of another study which concluded that:

"One might even suggest that the presence in secondary schools of children of the underprivileged groups is due largely to the fact that there are more secondary school places than there are children of the elite to fill them" [Hurde, 1967: 238].

As long as the number of places in universities and secondary schools continues to increase, education is not likely to be the institution that creates a barrier between the traditional majority and the modern elite.[7] This is particularly true if achievement criteria are the basis for access to modern elite occupations, for the possession of a university degree denotes achievement par excellence.

It should also be noted that an educationally defined (self-perpetuating) elite need not lead to vertical (class) divisions within African societies as long as there is a continuing network of traditional social obligations based on kinship and the extended family system.[8]

Ethnic divisions may be very broadly defined as those cultural, linguistic, racial, religious, or other factors that differentiate within national populations, creating distinguishable and self-conscious groups. Within tropical Africa, these ethnic divisions are typically described in terms of tribes, and we have indicated the ethnic environment in each country.

Much of the disparity in access to education can be attributed to the fact that the geographic concentration of tribal groups often coincides with localized patterns of educational development, regardless of the reasons why the latter may have occurred. We indicated some of the reasons for the continuation of such patterns. The degree of "tribal compartmentalization" in the two countries will be assessed before evaluating the extent to which particular tribes appear to monopolize educational opportunity.

The dual problems of uneven development and tribalism are linked inexorably if tribes continue to be located in their traditional and separate rural areas. The pervasive force of traditional land tenure custom and law combines with habit, intertia, and the presence of family and friends to preserve such traditional residence patterns. Tribal compartmentalization is greater in Kenya than in Ghana because permanent urban migration has only become common since independence. The Kenya census concluded that:

"The concept of a tribe's home district is not unmeaningful, and may be broadly interpreted as those districts in which the majority of the tribe is normally resident and in which they own land" [Republic of Kenya, 1966: 36].

The residential patterns for selected tribes in Kenya and Ghana are presented in Table 2. The general public impression—that members of the Kikuyu tribes provide a disproportionate share of the "modernized" element within the Kenya African population—is supported if we use mobility as one criterion.[9]

The extent of tribal compartmentalization is not as easily determined in Ghana because the census data are in terms of a much smaller spatial unit—a "locality"—and the comparison is between "locality of birth" and the next

TABLE 2
RESIDENTIAL PATTERNS OF SELECTED TRIBES, GHANA AND KENYA, 1962

Kenya[a]		Ghana[b]		
			% Enumerated Who were Born in:	
Tribe	% Resident "Home" District	Tribe	Same Locality	Same Region[c]
Bantu		All Akan	60.4	85.3
Kikuyu	69.4	Asante, Ahafo	62.2	87.0
Kamba	87.6	Akyem	71.0	88.4
Meru	98.1	Akuapem, Akwamu	35.8	69.3
Other Central Bantu	94.8	Ga-Adangbe	50.0	72.8
Luhya	82.8			
Kisii	95.0	Ewe	53.9	68.7
Coast Bantu	86.6			
Nilotic		Northern Tribes		
Luo	89.3	Mole-Dagbani	69.0	88.8
Nilo-Hamitic				
Kipsigis	83.5			
Turkana	92.3			
Masai	90.7			
Other Nilo-Hamitic	88.2			
Hamitic				
Ogaden	99.6			
Other Hamitic	98.2			
All Kenya Tribes	85.4			

SOURCES: Kenya Population Census, 1962, Vol. III, African Population, p. 36. 1960 Population Census of Ghana, Special Report "E", Tribes in Ghana, Appendix "C," Statistical Supplement, pp. C-12, C-15.
a. Kenya statistics are based on the complete sample.
b. Ghana statistics are from a partial sample in which several groups are not included, particularly the Twi-Fante (Fante).
c. The census concept of "locality" defined a very small area, such as a settlement or village. Those born in "different locality, same region" are included in the percentage for "same region." A figure roughly comparable to the Kenya "home district" percentage might be derived from the mean of the two Ghanaian percentages.

largest unit, a region. However, one may assume that an average of the two percentages, "born in same locality as enumerated" and "born in different locality, same region as enumerated" would give a figure somewhat comparable to the Kenya figures for "resident in home district." These, then, would range from the low of 52.5 percent for the Akuapem/Akwamu, through 72.4 for all Akan to highs of 78.4 percent for the Mole-Dagbani and 79.2 for the Akyem group of Akan. These figures are considerably lower, on the whole, than for any Kenya tribe excepting the Kikuyu. Yet, the persistence of quite high percentages of individuals who were enumerated in the "locality of birth" indicates that it is still relevant to consider much of non-urban Ghana in terms of geographic tribal areas.

The apparent higher degree of mobility among Ghanaian than Kenyan groups appears to be due to two factors. Neither has anything specifically to do with education and while they have been mentioned earlier, they may be emphasized again in this context. The first is simply that Ghanaian contact with British and other external influences dates back much farther than that of Kenya. This would tend toward a greater break down of traditional social patterns, including those having to do with residence. The second may well have been the absence of *Kapande* (pass) laws during the colonial period. Ghanaians were allowed much freer movement than Kenya Africans. In Kenya, the pass laws interacted with the low wage rates for urban and agricultural unskilled labor to render it nearly impossible for Africans to leave their tribal areas on a permanent basis and move with their family into urban areas. There were legal restrictions on property ownership that further curtailed African urban migration (Goldthorpe, 1958: 248-277).

High living costs and housing shortages in Kenya's urban centers have continued to limit migration of family units to urban centers, to some extent, despite the removal of the legal and social obstacles of the colonial period. The larger Ghanaian cities present a picture of considerable tribal heterogeneity but this is not true of the countryside. In terms of the major tribal groups in Ghana, rural residential homogeneity remains high.

"With respect to major tribes, almost two-thirds of the 69 local authorities containing almost two thirds (62.6%) of the total country population show a homogeneity index higher than 50% and about one-fourth of local authorities (16) comprising one-fifth of the total population—an index higher than 75% [Gil et al., 1964: xxv].

As the first pair of figures indicated, the maps of either country may be drawn in terms of tribal boundaries. It is instructive to compare those with a second pair which indicates levels of literacy in the two countries. [10] They effectively demonstrate that within each nation there are wide variations in literacy levels on purely geographic lines. A composite of the pair of maps, tribal and literacy, for each country would yield an intuitive picture of the correlation between tribe, location, and access to education.

It is not necessary to construct such a map for Ghana, because the census data have been broken down in terms of tribe and education. We are thus able to carry forward the analysis done by Foster (1962: 133) using the less reliable 1948 census data, in which he computed a selectivity index based on his sampled students in relation to the ethnic proportions in the general population. An ordering of tribal groups, from most to least advantaged in access in his fifty-nine-school sample would be: Akuapem, Guan, (various) Nigerian, Asante,

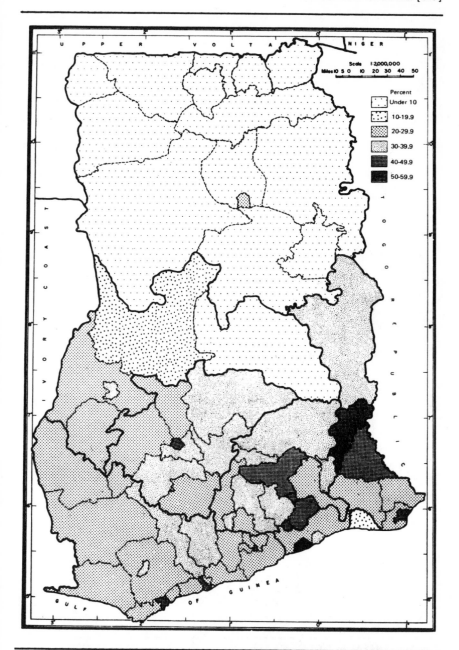

**Figure 3: SCHOOL ATTENDANCE—PAST AND PRESENT, OF PERSONS AGED 6
AND OVER**

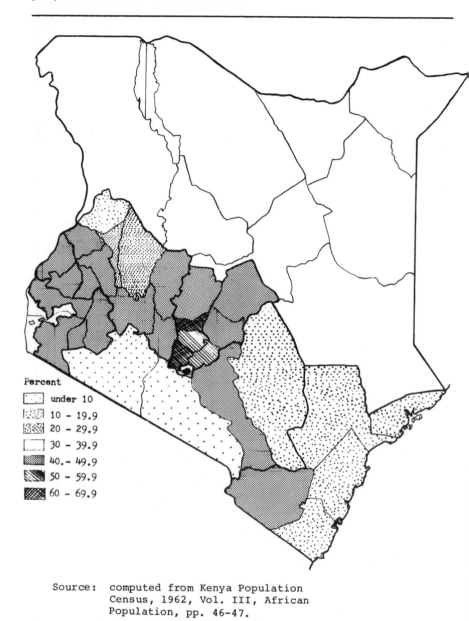

Percent
under 10
10 - 19.9
20 - 29.9
30 - 39.9
40.- 49.9
50 - 59.9
60 - 69.9

Source: computed from Kenya Population
         Census, 1962, Vol. III, African
         Population, pp. 46-47.

Figure 4: PERCENTAGE OF LITERATE POPULATION 15 YEARS OR OLDER,
KENYA, 1962

Fanti, Ewe, Ga-Adangbe, Akim, other Akan and Brong (tied), northern tribes. Contrary to his prior expectation, however, he did not find evidence that particular ethnic groups were doing better than others in terms of getting admitted to the so-called "elite" as opposed to "other" secondary schools.

A major advantage stemming from use of census data is the discrimination introduced in the Ga-Adangbe category when they are separated. As the graphic presentation in Figure 5 shows, the Ga move to the top of the rank-ordering when they are considered separately from the closely related Adangbe. A more accurate ranking of the tribes in Figure 5, plus those in Foster's listing for which the census data are available would be as shown in Table 3. It should be noted that the tribes at the bottom of the list are those who conform to the pattern for "all tribes" in that present percentage in school is greater than the "past school attendance" percentages. This reflects not only attempts to redress past imbalances—whether through government, mission, or private response to demands for education as these groups came to realize the correlation between education and social mobility—but may also simply reflect "saturation" in terms of schools in areas occupied by tribes at the top of the list. That is, percentages of the six to fourteen-year males presently in school among the Ga, Akim, and

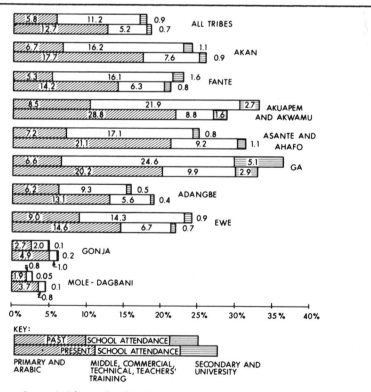

Sources: Computed from 1960 Population Census of Ghana, Special Report "E," Tribes in Ghana, Tables 18 and 21.

Figure 5: PAST AND PRESENT SCHOOL ATTENDANCE, MALES AGED 6 AND OVER, GHANA, SELECTED TRIBES

TABLE 3

GHANAIAN TRIBES, RANK-ORDERING BY EDUCATION (in percentages)

Tribe	Males Over 6 Years Who Have Never Attended School
Ga	30.7
Akyem	34.0
Akuapem-Akwamu	38.1
Asante and Ahafo	43.5
"All Akan"	49.8
Ewe	52.8
Fante	55.8
Guan	60.5
All Tribes	63.6
Adangbe	64.9
Gonja	89.1
Mole-Dagbani	92.7

Asante (77.0 percent, 76.7 percent, and 71.3 percent respectively) may be close to the contemporary possible upper limit. The Adangbe or the Ewe (44.7 percent and 51.4 percent on this dimension), on the other hand, are still moving toward universal primary education, and the Mole-Dagbani (16.5 percent) have barely begun.

It is clear that past educational advantage is being preserved in that specific tribes—the Ga and Akuapem, for example—who have enjoyed past absolute advantages in access to education are continuing to maintain this advantage in the present. Education seems to be a factor in preserving horizontal cleavages. A possible measure of this effect will be considered in a final section—that of correlations between tribe and certain status occupations. First, however, a similar comparison of tribal group and educational attainment in Kenya is necessary.

The Kenya comparison must be in more impressionistic terms. An approximation of tribal literacy rates can be derived from the use of figures for specific administrative districts because of the fact noted above (see Table 2), that all tribes except the Kikuyu show very high percentages resident in specific "home" districts. There are no census data on either past or present levels of education by tribe. The data in Figure 6 are derived by the literal application of the earlier suggestion that the ethnic distribution map could be superimposed on the map of geographic literacy distributions.

A district has been used to represent data for a tribe if it is the "home" district of only that tribe (i.e., administrative districts that are shared with another tribe as "home" districts have been eliminated). Even though the Kikuyu are not as heavily resident in "home districts," they do dominate the population in such districts—their places have not been taken by migrants from other tribes.

The educational lead of the two major Bantu tribes—the Kikuyu and Luhya—and of the Luo is as marked as was that of some tribes in Ghana. The Masai (Nilo-Hamitics) are as non-literate as the Mole-Dagbani were in Ghana. If the Kenya census had reported statistics for the Northern Province, one might have had a continuum from the 61.1 percent of the Kikuyu in Kiambu District to nearly zero percent for the Boran or Turkana tribes.

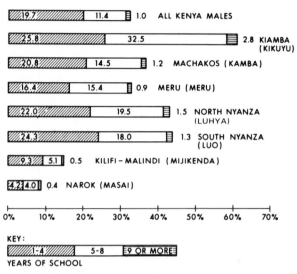

19.7	11.4	1.0 ALL KENYA MALES
25.8	32.5	2.8 KIAMBA (KIKUYU)
20.8	14.5	1.2 MACHAKOS (KAMBA)
16.4	15.4	0.9 MERU (MERU)
22.0	19.5	1.5 NORTH NYANZA (LUHYA)
24.3	18.0	1.3 SOUTH NYANZA (LUO)
9.3 5.1		0.5 KILIFI – MALINDI (MIJIKENDA)
4.2 4.0		0.4 NAROK (MASAI)

0%   10%   20%   30%   40%   50%   60%   70%

KEY:

1-4 | 5-8 | 9 OR MORE
YEARS OF SCHOOL

Source: Kenya Population Census, 1962, Vol. III, African Population, Table VII; 3 pp. 46-7, and Table V.2, page 36.

Figure 6: SCHOOL ATTENDANCE, MALES 15 AND OVER, BY HOME DISTRICTS OF SELECTED TRIBES, KENYA

Although we cannot discriminate between past and present educational attainment with these data, it is not unreasonable to assume that Kenya distributions on this dimension would show patterns similar to those in Ghana. In both countries there are rather large statistical differences in education by tribe. The graphs indicate that the advantage tends to be general—the more primary- and middle-school-level attainment, the higher the percentage for secondary and higher education. The discrimination possible in the Ghanaian data between past and present school attendance indicated that present distributions are related to past advantage.

The brief consideration of the elite-mass gap led to the conclusion that the offspring of high-education (and high-status occupation) fathers were over-represented in both secondary and university samples. It is pertinent to examine the relationship between tribe and certain high status occupations to determine whether or not the educational advantage enjoyed by some tribes has resulted in their overrepresentation in high-status occupations. A recalculation of Ghanaian occupational statistics is possible, giving percentages by tribe in specific occupations.

The percentages would, if all tribes were included, add to one hundred across the table rather than down. This means, to use the Fanti as an example, that this tribe represents 11.3 percent of the total Ghanaian population but only 10 percent of males fifteen years or older who are employed in some occupation. They are overrepresented in professional occupations (where 14.6 percent of all employed in this category are Fanti) both in terms of their proportion of the working population and in the total population. Similar comparisons may be made for the other occupational categories and other tribes. The low degree of

TABLE 4

RELATIONSHIP BETWEEN TRIBE AND HIGH-STATUS OCCUPATIONS, GHANA, 1960, MALES,
15 AND OLDER (in percentages)

					Percentage of Occupational Categories Who are Members of					
	Fante	Akuapem	Asante	Ga	Adangbe	Ewe	Guan	Gonja[b]	Mole-Dagbani	n
Percentage of total population	(11.3)	(2.2)	(13.3)	(3.5)	(3.5)	(13.0)	(3.7)		(15.9)	
Occupational Category:										
All occupations	10.0	2.0	10.7	2.8	3.1	12.5	3.3	.1	19.5	1,565,590
Professional, technical and related	14.6	4.6	16.9	5.7	2.7	14.8	4.7	.4	5.0	46,190
Administrative, executive and managerial	15.6	4.8	19.1	12.3	1.5	10.9	3.4	.2	4.1	10,120
Government[c]	18.6	5.0	14.0	15.3	2.4	8.3	5.2	.2	4.2	4,240
Business[c]	10.4	4.4	23.6	9.1	.3	16.2	2.4	.1	4.7	2,970
Clerical workers	18.7	5.3	17.1	13.5	2.1	13.1	3.2	.2	1.7	40,170
Working proprietors, wholesale trade	7.4	2.5	12.6	1.3	.8	4.6	2.6	.8	9.5	6,100

SOURCE: Gil et al. (1964). Computed from Tables 26 and S26.
a. Percentages do not add to 100 because several tribes are not considered here.
b. Percentage for Gonja also included under Guan.
c. Administrative, executive and managerial is the larger category, figures for those within it who are in government or business are given separately. The census report does not specify where those not included in government or business are located.

access by the Mole-Dagbani is perhaps the most striking impression to be derived from the table.

A second impression is that the category "working proprietors, wholesale trade" is not a prestigious one, for the selectivity indices for the Ewe (3.54) and the Mole-Dagbani (5.97) were the highest. It is therefore excluded from Figure 7 which compares several tribes on the basis of an occupational selectivity index. The place of the tribe in the rank-ordering on the literacy dimension is also indicated. A correlation between rank on the various occupational selectivity indices and literacy would be nearly perfect, providing evidence of a strong relationship between education and the horizontal cleavages of tribe.

The data presented in Table 5 represent a survey of Kenya elites carried out in 1963 in which income (over $2,800 per annum), position, and power position of posts occupied were criteria for inclusion.[11] The present distribution of "elected or appointed representatives" is probably quite different than the one reported by Wilson, for the 1964 constitution eliminated many of the positions

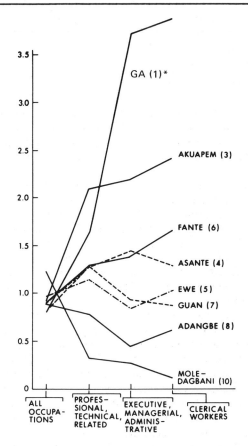

*Figure in parentheses indicates rank in literacy-ordering (see Table 3).

Figure 7: OCCUPATIONAL SELECTIVITY PROFILE, GHANA

TABLE 5
RELATIONSHIP BETWEEN TRIBE AND ELITE STATUS, KENYA, 1962
(in percentages)

Tribe	Total Kenya Elite[a]	Civil Servants[a]	Elected or Appointed Representatives[a]	All Others[b]	All Adult Males[c]
Kikuyu	23.0	29.0	17.0	27.0	19.7
Kamba, Embu, Meru	9.0	10.0	13.0	8.0	18.6
Luhya and other Western Bantu	22.0	21.0	18.0	25.0	20.0
Luo	19.0	23.0	12.0	26.0	13.8
Coast Bantu	–	6.0	14.0	7.0	6.7
Nilo-Hamitic		7.0	17.0	2.0	16.5
Hamitic	25.0	–	2.0	–	4.6
Other Kenya		–	2.0	–	–
Tanganyika	2.0	2.0	–	3.0	–
	(n=457)	(n=123)	(n=190)	(n=183)	

SOURCES:
a. Wilson (1966: 445, 448).
b. Ibid. This includes commerces, industry, trade union politicans, education, professional, cooperative/trade, religious/welfare, agriculture and miscellaneous.
c. Kenya Population Census, 1962, Vol. III, p. 36.

reported in 1963 as the power of the central government now eclipses that of the former regions. It is not likely, on the other hand, that the Luhya-Luo-Kikuyu predominance in the civil service will have diminished, for access to that occupational category (certainly at that income level) remains dependent upon education.

A selectivity index profile was also constructed for the Kenya elite by tribe, but the relationship with educational rank-ordering is not as clear as in Ghana. This may point to an inadequacy in the data as much as to the null hypothesis. Certainly there is a rough correlation apparent in the profile suggesting that tribe, education and elite status are not unrelated in Kenya.

Another measure of the effect of education on ethnic cleavages may be derived by a cross-tabulation of the student samples by tribe and socio-economic status. The students were assigned a socio-economic rank on the basis of father's occupation, education, and income

Table 6 confirms the earlier conclusion that the "middle and upper sectors" are nearly absent in Kenya. the majority of Kenya African students could only be assigned to the low group on an objective evaluation of family background. The Kenya students conform much more closely to what must be the class distribution in the general society while the Ghanaian students are skewed in favor of the two higher socio-economic groups. This conclusion is highly impressionistic, of course, but one may begin with the fact that two-thirds of Kenya adult males must be considered either as unemployed or subsistance farmers and that less than 1 percent are in occupations that rate higher than unskilled, and it is difficult to arrive at an idea of the Kenya class structure that is not heavily weighted at the bottom.

In terms of tribe and socio-economic status, the Kenya student distribution points to a confirmation of Kikuyu predominance, a belief that is popularly held

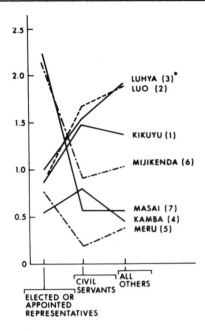

*Indicates rank-ordering of tribe by literacy (see Figure 6).

Figure 8: ELITE SELECTIVITY PROFILE, KENYA

in Kenya but that did not come out in the limited occupational data for the total population. The Kikuyu are the Kenya tribe most overrepresented in "high" SES in terms of their percentage in the total sample. This is true, but to a lesser extent, of the composite groups of Nilo-Hamatic and "other Bantu" (predominately coastal tribes). At the other extreme, one may see some socio-economic justification for the political discontent of the Luo and the Kamba that was expressed in the formation of the KPU in 1966.

The Ghanaian distributions simply reinforce the conclusions derived from the earlier consideration (see Table 4 and Figure 7) of aggregate data. The Ga-Adangbe, Ewe, other Akan and Fante are overrepresented in the "high" SES category while the northern and "other" tribes are overrepresented in the "low" category.

CONCLUSION

The impact of education on ethnic sources of societal tension appears to be mixed. As long as the number of school and university places continues to expand the less advantaged groups in the society will gain in absolute terms even though "elite" groups may maintain or even increase their relative advantage. In terms of the elite-mass gap, whether considered as a traditional-modern dichotomy or as an educated-illiterate one, this advantage of the "elite" need create no integration problems as long as the educational systems expand. If, however, the size of university enrollment should be fixed (whether for financial

TABLE 6
TRIBE AND SOCIO-ECONOMIC STATUS, GHANA AND KENYA
STUDENTS, 1966 (in percentages)

Tribe	n	Socio-Economic Status		
		High	Medium	Low
Ghana				
Ga-Adangbe	170	28.8	37.7	33.5
Fanti and Akim	78	30.8	48.7	20.5
Asante	91	20.9	38.5	40.6
Other Akan	104	29.8	41.4	28.8
Ewe	84	32.1	25.0	42.9
Northern	96	5.2	13.5	81.3
Other	47	14.9	19.1	66.0
Total Sample	670=100%	24.2	33.3	42.5
Kenya				
Kikuyu	185	12.4	20.6	67.0
Kamba, Embu, Meru	105	4.7	14.3	81.0
Luhya	111	9.0	15.3	75.7
Other Bantu	44	13.6	9.1	77.3
Luo	73	8.2	15.1	76.7
Nilo-Hamitic	15	13.3	26.7	60.0
Total Sample	533=100%	9.8	16.7	73.5

reasons or policy decisions based on projected manpower needs), the advantage of elite family backgrounds would be intensified in the competition for limited places and this aspect of the general national integration problem could quite easily become much more salient.

It is the other dimension of the national integration problem—that of ethnic divisions—that emerges as potentially more important. In both countries it appears that tribes do not share proportionately in the total distributions between educated and uneducated, between high-status occupations and low-status occupations. Specific ethnic groups are visibly, and measurably, located higher up on the socio-economic pyramid than others. An economic and status differential is thus added to the cultural, linguistic, and historic bases that divide tribes. The availability of earlier studies on Ghanaian students, and of educational data for the population as a whole by tribe, indicated that these advantages were to some extent continuing and that the educational system was a contributing, if not a major, factor in the creation of economic and status differentials between tribes.

We have established that the two dimensions of integrative cleavages overlap and that tribal differences have also become socio-economic differences. The relevant question now is whether or not attitudinal variations among the student samples are a function of tribal differences, socio-economic differences (or some combination of these two), or whether the level of education or some other variable is more important. The strong structural impact of education which alone would have to be considered as potentially mal-integrative, will be lessened if the process of education reduces perceptual and attitudinal differences among students. To the extent that student's attitudes are "detribalized" by increasing levels of education, the cause of national integration will be served. Other data, collected as part of the larger study, only a portion of which is reported here, show that increasing amounts of education do not, in fact, make an appreciable impact on the ethnocentric attitudes held by ethnic groups toward one another (Mapp, 1972). Thus, the problem is an escalating one, as past disparities feed present disadvantages and few of the resulting ethnic tensions are "washed out" by educational resocialization.

NOTES

1. We can do no more than indicate some of the historical salients here. The interested reader should begin with Oliver and Fage (1962), Apter (1963), Ingham (1965), Bennett (1963), Rosberg and Nottingham (1966), Kingsley (1899), Fage (1964).
2. The Kikuyu were not the only tribe to have large areas of land alienated for white settlement; the Nandi, Kipsigis and Masai were equally misfortunate but did not parlay their loss into political capital as did the Kikuyu.
3. There was no overall British policy for her African colonies—what might be semi-official policy in one was likely to be illegal in another (Oliver and Fage, 1962: 196 ff). It was the Africans who were chiefly affected by these anomalies and their lack of intercolony organization prevented the discrepancies from being publicized or corrected.
4. This discussion is indebted to Goldthorpe (1958: 20-50). A fourth racial group is included by many others, the Hamatic, but since it includes only the Somali and Galla, both small tribes, we will follow Goldthorpe and include them with the closely related Nilo-Hamatic. We will also avoid the overly self-conscious circumlutions for the world "tribe" despite its present lack of academic favor.
5. This eliminates the bias that use of absolute or percentage figures would introduce, since levels of educational attainment are generally higher in Ghana than in Kenya.
6. In part this may be the result of the difference in census reporting of educational data. While the Ghanaian census discriminates between secondary and university, the Kenya census reports in terms of years of schooling and their category "13 years or more" would include those of the sixth form attainment as well as those who had gone to universities. If one were to assume that roughly half the .16 percent of the adult males over 25 reporting this level of education had actually been secondary rather than university students, then the selectivity indices for Kenya students at this level would be 22.5, 32.5, and 20.
7. For a much less sanguine view of the situation, see Kiwanuka (1967).
8. Goldthorpe (1965: 32-48), brings out the wide range of educational and occupational levels within the immediate family circle of former Makerere students. He notes that "we have stressed how closely linked they are by kinship to the world of illiterate peasants and unskilled manual workers, and how virtually all of them have at least some relatives who can neither read nor write (46)." He later points out the problems that this can create, as uncles or cousins expect to share in the material benefits that education has brought to the individual (75-76). The wide range of interaction between "elite" and "mass" within the same family or kin group is an integrative function of ethnicity that should be added to those put forward by Wallerstein (1965).
9. Supporting survey data for this generalized impression, from a large adult sample, is reported by F. G. Burke (1965). District boundaries in Kenya have been radically redrawn since the 1962 census, to bring them into closer conformity with ethnic lines.
10. The Northern District proved a difficult area in which to conduct a census and the special volume promised on that area does not seem to have been published. It should be noted that the data illustrated by each map are not exactly comparable, but the Kenya census statistics would not permit the drawing of an exactly similar map. The maps do, however, prove our basic point.
11. For the full explanation of criteria of selection for elite status see Wilson (1966: 423-433).

REFERENCES

APTER, D. (1963) Ghana in Transition. New York: Atheneum.
BENNETT, G. (1963), Kenya, A Political History: The Colonial Period. London: Oxford University Press.

BURKE, F. G. (1965) Unity and Diversity in East Africa—A Synthesisless Dialectic. Syracuse: Syracuse University, Maxwell School of Citizenship and Public Affairs, The Program of East African Affairs.
COLEMAN, J. S. (1965) "Introduction," in J. S. Coleman (ed.) Education and Political Development. Princeton, N.J.: Princeton University Press.
FAGE, J. D. (1964), An Introduction to the History of West Africa. Cambridge: Cambridge University Press.
FOSTER, P. J. (1965) Education and Social Change in Ghana. Chicago: University of Chicago Press.
——— (1962) "Ethnicity and the schools in Ghana." Comparative Education Rev. 6.
GIL, B. et al. (1964) 1960 Population Census of Ghana, Special Report "E", Tribes in Ghana. Accra: Census Office.
GOLDTHORPE, J. E. (1965) An African Elite: Makerere College Students 1922-1960. Nairobi: Oxford University Press for the East African Institute of Social Research.
——— (1958) Outlines of East African Society. Kampala: Makerere University College Department of Sociology.
HURDE, G. E. (1967) "Education," in W. Birmingham, I. Neustadt, E. N. Omaboe (eds.) Some Aspects of Social Structure in Ghana. Evanston, Ill.: Northwestern University Press.
INGHAM, K. (1965) A History of East Africa. New York: Praeger.
KINGSLEY, M. (1899) West African Studies. London: Macmillan.
KIWANUKA, M.S.M. (1967) "The Crisis of education in Uganda: rich man's harvest?" East Africa J. 4 (May).
KOPLIN, R. E. (1968) Education and National Integration in Ghana and Kenya. Eugene: University of Oregon, Department of Political Science doctoral dissertation.
MAPP, R. E. (1972) "Cross national dimensions of ethnocentrism." Canadian Journal of African Studies, 6.
MORGAN, W.T.W. and N. M. SHAFFER (1966) Population of Kenya, Density and Distribution. Nairobi: Oxford University Press.
OLIVER, R. and J. D. FAGE (1962) A Short History of Africa. Baltimore: Penguin.
REPUBLIC OF KENYA (1966) Kenya Population Census, 1962. Vol. III, African Population. Nairobi: Ministry of Economic Planning and Development, Statistics Division.
ROSBERG, C. G. Jr., and J. NOTTINGHAM (1966) The Myth of "Mau Mau": Nationalism in Kenya. New York: Preager for the Hoover Institution on War, Revolution and Peace.
WILSON, G. M. (1966) "The African elite" in S. Diamond and F. G. Burke (eds.) The Transformation of East Africa. New York: Basic Books.
WALLERSTEIN, I. (1965) "Ethnicity and national integration in West Africa," in P. L. van den Berghe (ed.) Africa: Social Problems of Change and Conflict. San Francisco: Chandler.

Chapter 18

RACIAL POLARIZATION AND POLITICAL CONFLICT IN GUYANA

JOSEPH B. LANDIS

*I*n many multi-racial societies the nation-building process has been seriously threatened or brought to an end by the polarization of politics along racial lines. In Guyana, then known as British Guiana, racial polarization of politics in the late 1950s was followed by several rounds of racial-political violence in the early 1960s costing about 175 lives and delaying independence for four years.

There are at least three possible theoretical explanations of the racial polarization of politics and the violence that sometimes follows in multi-racial societies. First, the theory of cultural pluralism would attribute the polarization and the violence to cultural differences between the racial groups or to socio-economic differences resulting from the cultural differences.[1] Second, Marxian theory would attribute the polarization and violence to class conflict between the different racial groups. A variant of Marxian theory would explain the polarization and conflict as the result of a divide-and-rule policy by the ruling class of the society or by foreign imperialists. If such a variant is not to contradict the basic principles of Marxian theory, however, it must predict some movement toward increasing class consciousness and unity within the working class. Third, intergroup relations theory would attribute the racial polarization of politics and the violence to racial or other intergroup attitudes and to psychological processes such as selective perception which results from identification with an in-group.

In this chapter, I will compare the validity of these three theoretical positions as explanations of the polarization of politics along racial lines and the subsequent racial-political violence in Guyana. The intergroup relations theory may appear to have an advantage in this comparison since it assumes that conflict can occur among and between many different types of group—e.g., racial or ethnic groups, classes, political parties, nations, or even groups of nations—depending on the attitudes and perceptions of these groups toward each other and the salience of group memberships. But, in order to reject the theory of cultural pluralism and Marxian theory in favor of the intergroup relations approach, it will be necessary to show that the polarization and the violence in Guyana were caused by intergroup attitudes and perceptions associated with cleavages other than cultural or class cleavages.

DEMOGRAPHIC AND HISTORICAL BACKGROUND

The territory that is now Guyana had been a series of three Dutch colonies in the 1600s and 1700s and the British colony of British Guiana from 1804 until political independence in 1966. The two major racial groups in Guyana are the descendants of African slaves brought to Guyana between 1650 and 1808 and the descendants of indentured laborers brought from India between 1840 and 1918 to replace the slaves as cheap labor on the sugar plantations. Smaller numbers of Portuguese and Chinese laborers were also imported.

In 1960 Guyana's population of slightly over a half-million was 48 percent Indian, 33 percent African, 12 percent mixed (primarily African-European), and 4 percent Amerindian (American Indians), with the remaining three percent made up primarily of Chinese and Portuguese. The Indian population had been growing faster than the other groups since the 1930s and was to become a majority of the Guyanese population in the mid-1960s.

Four-fifths of the Indians in Guyana live in rural areas, making up two-thirds of the rural population. Half the Africans and most of the Portuguese, Chinese, and individuals of mixed descent live in the three larger towns or cities, with these groups forming at least three-quarters of the population in each of the urban areas.

In the first election held under universal adult suffrage in Guyana in 1953, the majority of Indian and African voters supported the People's Progressive Party (PPP). The PPP was led by Cheddi Jagan, a Marxist-oriented Indian dentist, and by Forbes Burnham, an African barrister who was a more moderate socialist. The PPP won the 1953 elections, but the British government deposed the PPP government 133 days later charging that there was a plot to turn the colony into a communist state subordinate to Moscow (British Government, 1953).

In 1955 the PPP split into a radical faction led by Jagan and a moderate faction led by Burnham. The split was not initially a racial split, but by the time of the 1957 elections over 90 percent of the Indian voters supported the Jaganite faction and over 90 percent of the Africans supported the Burnhamite faction or a smaller predominantly African party and an independent candidate who later joined with the Burnhamite faction. The Jaganite faction won the 1957 elections and retained the title PPP. The Burnhamite faction and its allies reorganized as the People's National Congress (PNC). In both the 1961 and the 1964 elections the PPP won over 90 percent of the Indian vote and the PNC won over 90 percent of the African vote.

THE RACIAL-POLITICAL VIOLENCE

In the 1961 elections the PPP won 57 percent of the seats in the Legislative Assembly with 42.6 percent of the popular vote. The PNC won 31 percent of the seats with 41 percent of the popular vote. The United Force (UF), a new party led by Peter d'Aguiar, a Portuguese businessman, won 11 percent of the seats with 16 percent of the vote. The PPP's disproportionate success in winning seats was due to the fact that Indians form the majority in practically all the rural constituencies in Guyana. Thus, the leaders of the PNC and the UF came to the conclusion that they would not be able to defeat the PPP in future elections unless the electoral system were changed from a single-member constituency system to a proportional representation system. The opposition parties were in a strong position to force a change in the electoral system because they had the support of three-fourths of the urban population and a solid alliance with the urban labor unions, and because the United States government was opposed to Guyana achieving independence under a Marxist-oriented PPP government.

In February 1962, a UF campaign against independence under Jagan, a civil service dispute resulting in a politically timed government worker's strike, and a demagogic campaign culminating in a general strike against the PPP's tough bootstraps budget coincided to cause a riot in which much of the center of Georgetown, the capital city, was burned. The violence was not directly racial in form but had racial overtones since it was directed against an Indian-supported government and many of the businesses burned belonged to Indians.

In the fall of 1962 the British Guiana Independence Conference was held in London, but the PPP and the opposition leaders were unable to agree on the terms of independence. The opposition wanted the electoral system changed to a proportional representation system and wanted new elections before independence. The PPP rejected these two demands and countered with a demand that the voting age be lowered from 21 to 18.

In the spring of 1963 the PPP introduced a Labour Relations Bill designed to allow elections in industries in which there were jurisdictional disputes between rival unions. If elections were held in the sugar industry, where the vast majority of workers are Indians, a pro-PPP union could have won recognition over the recognized sugar workers union which was strongly anti-PPP. This would have increased the PPP's influence in the labor movement considerably since half the organized workers in Guyana in 1963 were sugar workers. The urban labor unions, however, resisted by going out on an 80-day general strike against the Labour Relations Bill and ultimately against the PPP government. U.S. labor organizations and the U.S. Central Intelligence Agency supported the strike with over a million dollars' (U.S.) worth of aid (Meisler, 1964). Although it was successful in defeating the Labour Relations Bill, the strike was not successful in forcing the PPP government to resign. The strike had begun peacefully, but the last two months of the strike saw a considerable amount of violence costing ten lives and including the first widespread racial violence between Africans and Indians in Guyanese history.

The Independence Conference resumed in the fall of 1963. Again, the PPP and opposition leaders were unable to settle the three issues that had divided them in 1962. The British Colonial Secretary, Duncan Sandys, offered to decide the three issues and, when the Guyanese leaders accepted, decided all three issues against the PPP, thereby giving the forthcoming elections to the opposition parties.

The PPP reacted by organizing a campaign against Sandys' decisions and having the pro-PPP sugar workers union call a recognition strike in the sugar industry in the spring of 1964. If the strike were successful, the PPP would at least have a solid base from which to carry on the fight against imperialism. If the strike were resisted, the PPP could use the strike to stir up violence and disruption to pressure the British government and the local opposition to compromise on Sandys' decisions. The sugar companies and the recognized union refused to yield on the recognition issue, and the British government and local opposition refused to compromise on Sandys' decisions. The strike persisted for five bloody months. The violence remained nonracial during the first two months of the strike but became racial and escalated sharply during the last three months. By the end of the summer, 165 persons had been killed and thousands had been injured or forced to flee their homes. The PPP finally ended the strike when it realized that it was on the losing end of the fight.

From the end of the summer of 1964 through the time of this writing, (July,

1973) there has been no significant African-Indian violence in Guyana. In the elections held in the fall of 1964 the PPP won 46 percent of the popular vote, the PNC won 41 percent of the vote, and the UF won 12 percent. Under the proportional representation election system, the PNC and the UF together won a majority of seats in the National Assembly and formed a coalition government. This coalition government was still in office in 1967 when the research on which this chapter is based was conducted.

RESEARCH METHODS

The analysis of the racial polarization of politics in this chapter is based on a survey of the racial attitudes, political opinions, and voting behavior of 456 Indians and 372 Africans from different parts of Guyana. The survey was conducted during the summer of 1967 by interviewers from the University of Guyana who worked under the supervision of the author. The interviewers were assigned in such a way that they were usually of the same race as the respondent. The sample was selected from the voting lists for 28 polling divisions in different parts of Guyana. Urban Indians were deliberately overrepresented, constituting 31 percent of the Indian sample but only 14 percent of the Indian population. African females were accidentally overrepresented, constituting 58 percent of the African sample, but only 52 percent of the African population. Except for these departures, the Indian and African samples were reasonably representative of the Indian and African populations in Guyana.

An index of non-racial voting was constructed to facilitate analysis of the racial polarization of politics. Respondents were classified as nonracial voters if (1) they had voted for a party other than the one associated with their race in one or more of the elections between 1957 and 1964 or preferred such a party at the time of the survey, or if (2) they had not voted in one of the elections between 1957 and 1964 because they could not decide who to vote for or if they had no party preference at the time of the survey. A quarter of the Indian respondents and a fifth of the Africans were classified as non-racial voters.

The discussion of the racial-political violence in this chapter is based primarily on interviews with over 50 Guyanese political influentials and on a review of Guyanese newspapers for the 1960-1964 period.

EVALUATION OF THE
CULTURAL PLURALIST EXPLANATION

Anthropologists have not been able to agree on whether Guyana is a culturally plural society. M. G. Smith (1967) and Leo Despres (1967) have argued that Guyana is a plural society, while Raymond Smith (1962: 198) and Chandra Jayawardena (1963) have concluded that Africans and Indians in Guyana "share a common cultural equipment." Both Africans and Indians in Guyana speak English as their major language and thus are able to communicate with each other freely. There are, however, substantial differences between Africans and Indians in family and kinship patterns and religion. For the purposes of my analysis it is not necessary to determine whether Guyana is a culturally plural society but only whether the cultural differences that do exist were a basic cause of the racial polarization of politics and the subsequent racial-political violence.

Religious differences are among the most important cultural differences between Africans and Indians in Guyana. Practically all the Africans are Christians with nine-tenths being Protestant and one-tenth Catholic. Over two-thirds of the Indians are Hindus, about a fifth are Moslems, and about 12 percent are Christians, 9 percent Protestant, and 3 percent Catholic.

Table 1 shows the relationship between religion and non-racial voting for Indians and Africans. Most of the small number of Indian Catholics in the sample were non-racial voters, lending some support to the theory of cultural pluralism. Most Africans in Guyana are Protestants, however, so that if religious differences were a major cause of the racial polarization of politics, one would expect Indian Protestants to be much less racial in their voting than Indian Hindus and Moslems. Since Indian Protestants were no less racial in their voting than Indian Hindus or Moslems, religious differences explain only a small proportion of the pattern of racial voting.

Education has been a major avenue of acculturation for Indians in Guyana. Thus, if cultural differences were a major cause of the racial polarization of politics, one would expect Indians with several years of education to be less racial in their voting than Indians with little or no formal education. Indians with seven or more years of education, however, were no more likely to be non-racial voters (23 percent, n = 65) than Indians with less than seven years (26 percent, n = 355).

Cultural differences do not appear to have been a cause of the racial-political violence in the early 1960s. Religious and other cultural differences were not issues in the conflicts; moreover, when respondents in the survey were asked whether they would rather see the different racial groups in Guyana mix and merge completely or maintain their separate identities and traditions, three-fourths of the Indians and 95 percent of the Africans favored mixing and merging.

Data from the survey also indicate that there are more diffuse relationships between Africans and Indians than cultural pluralists had assumed. Despres (1967: 175-196), for example, has asserted that relationships within racial groups in Guyana are "relatively diffuse and predicated upon a general value consensus, whereas the relationships between them are highly specialized and segmented." To the contrary, half the African respondents reported that they had Indian close friends and 43 percent of the Indians reported that they had

TABLE 1
PERCENTAGE OF NONRACIAL VOTERS BY RACE AND RELIGION

| | Percentage of Nonracial Voters | | | |
| | Indians | | Africans | |
Religion	%	n	%	n
Catholic	87	(15)[a]	25	(32)
Protestant	20	(50)	18	(317)
Moslem	28	(81)	—	
Hindu	22	(271)	—	
(sig. test)[b]	(p <.001)		(n.s.)	

a. The number of cases on which the percentages are computed is given in parentheses.
b. The significance tests reported in this and subsequent tables are based on chi square tests.

African close friends. Three-fourths of the Africans and 70 percent of the Indians reported that they had had friends from the other race while they were growing up and going to school. Thus, many Africans and Indians do share enough of a value consensus to form diffuse relationships.

EVALUATION OF MARXIAN EXPLANATIONS

Marxian theory would attribute the racial polarization of politics and the subsequent racial-political violence to class conflict. The theory of cultural pluralism also might claim some validity if the polarization and violence were associated with socio-economic differences which might reflect cultural differences between Africans and Indians.

Africans and Indians in Guyana are relatively equal in overall socio-economic status. There are, however, some important differences in occupational patterns. About four-tenths of the employed Indian males in Guyana but only about a tenth of the Africans are engaged in agriculture, while two-thirds of the Africans, but only a third of the Indians, are engaged in non-agricultural blue collar occupations. Although about a quarter of the employed males from each group are engaged in white-collar oocupations, about a tenth of the Indians but only about three percent of the Africans are businessmen, while a tenth of the Africans but only about five percent of the Indians are civil servants or teachers.

Table 2 shows the relationships between occupation and income and non-racial voting. There were no significant differences in the level of non-racial voting between white-collar and skilled or unskilled blue-collar workers for either Indians or Africans, thus showing no support for Marxian theory among non-agricultural workers. The lower level of non-racial voting among Indian

TABLE 2

PERCENTAGE OF NONRACIAL VOTERS BY RACE AND OCCUPATION
AND BY RACE AND HOUSEHOLD INCOME PER MONTH

| | Percentage of Nonracial Voters | | | |
| | Indians | | Africans | |
Independent Variable	%	n	%	n
Occupation[a]				
white collar	32	(92)	18	(55)
skilled workers	32	(63)	24	(118)
unskilled workers	34	(67)	16	(70)
agricultural other than sugar	19	(63) }	32	(19)
sugar workers	6	(68) }		
(sig. test)	(p $<$ .001)		(n.s.)	
Household Income per Month[b]				
$150 or more	33	(90)	14	(93)
$50-149	20	(243)	21	(157)
$0-49	29	(77)	19	(93)
(sig. test)	(p $<$ .05)		(n.s.)	

a. Refers to the occupations of the male respondents and of the husbands of the female respondents.
b. Household income per month in Guyanese dollars. One Guyanese dollar was equivalent to about .60 U.S. dollars at the time of the survey.

agricultural workers, especially Indian sugar workers, and the higher level of non-racial voting among African agricultural workers suggests that class conflict or cultural differences between agricultural and non-agricultural workers may have contributed to the polarization of politics. These occupational differences, however, explain only a small proportion of the polarization since two-thirds of the Indian non-agricultural workers and two-thirds of the African agricultural voters were racial voters.

The relationship between income and non-racial voting bears a slight resemblance to Marxian theory. If the second income category is identified as the proletariat, as distinguished from the bourgeoisie and the lumpenproletariat, Marxian theory would predict that the PPP would draw most support from the proletariat and least from the bourgeoisie, as it does. The relationship is relatively weak, however, and does not help to explain the racial polarization of politics since Africans and Indians have relatively similar income distributions.

The rural-urban differences between Africans and Indians may reflect cultural or class differences or both to some extent. Urban Indians were somewhat more likely to be non-racial voters (39 percent, n = 128) than rural Indians (19 percent, n = 294). The rural-urban differences, however, explain only a small proportion of the pattern of racial voting since most urban Indians were racial voters and rural Africans were no more likely to be non-racial voters (18 percent, n = 162) than urban Africans (23 percent, n = 196).

Marxian theory might appear to be quite relevant for explaining the racial-political violence in that all of the violence occurred during strikes, either by the urban labor unions in 1962 and 1963 or by the sugar workers in 1964. But these strikes do not fit the Marxian model. In 1962 and 1963 the urban labor unions were striking not against their capitalist employers but against a Marxist-oriented government. In 1962 the urban workers (except for the government workers) were allied with their employers against the government; and in 1963 the urban unions were allied with the major imperialist power in the Western hemisphere. In short, the urban proletariat, designated as the leading revolutionary class in Marxian theory, was engaging in a counterrevolution. The sugar workers strike in 1964 might appear to fit a Maoist version of Marxian theory, but neither the majority of the African sugar workers nor any other African workers joined the strike.

The Marxian view that would attribute the racial polarization of politics and the racial-political violence to a divide-and-rule policy by the ruling class or by foreign imperialists is harder to test than the more straightforward Marxian explanation. The Guyanese working class was united behind the PPP until the British government deposed the PPP government in 1953 and let it be known that Guyana would have to mark time in its advance towards independence until the PPP leaders changed their approach or were replaced by more moderate leaders (Robertson, 1954). The divide-and-rule explanation, however, cannot be applied to Guyana without contradicting some of the basic principles of Marxian theory. Marxian theory predicts that class conflict will increase the class consiousness and unity of the working class. In Guyana, this consciousness and unity, rather than increasing when the PPP government was deposed, practically evaporated. Marxian theory also posits that class consciousness is potentially stronger than other types of social consciousness. Thus if Marxist leaders are on hand to instill class consciousness in the working class, class consciousness should replace other types of social consciousness. In Guyana Marxist leaders have preached class consciousness and working-class unity continually for two decades, but if anything, class consciousness has lost ground to racial consciousness.

EVALUATION OF THE
INTERGROUP RELATIONS EXPLANATION

In order to evaluate the intergroup relations explanation of the racial polarization and violence it is necessary to give a brief description of the attitudes and perceptions that Guyanese Africans and Indians have toward each other.

Most Indians in Guyana have superordinate attitudes toward Africans, while most Africans have defensive attitudes toward Indians. Four-fifths of the Indian respondents, for example, said they would object to their son or daughter marrying an African, while less than a fifth of the Africans said that they would object to their son or daughter marrying an Indian. Only half the Indians who objected to intermarriage with Africans also objected to intermarriage with Chinese or Portuguese, two higher-status groups.

An important element in Indian superordinate racialism and in African defensive racialism is the belief that Indians are more thrifty or ambitious than Africans. When asked whether they thought Africans and Indians had different outlooks on life, 59 percent of the Indian respondents and 58 percent of the Africans gave some version of this belief. When asked whether they or their spouses in fact had any savings, Indians were no more likely to report that they had any savings or to report larger savings than Africans. A belief such as this, however, does not have to be accurate to convince many Indians that they deserve to be better off than Africans or to convince Africans that they may not be able to compete with Indians economically.

African defensive racialism is also based upon recognition that Indians are becoming the majority of the voting-age population of Guyana and on African awareness of Indian attitudes toward Africans. When respondents in the survey were asked what they thought most Indians think of Africans, 86 percent of the Africans (and 87 percent of the Indians) said they thought most Indians had negative attitudes toward Africans. In response to a separate question, 86 percent of the Africans said they thought most Indians would object to their son or daughter marrying an African.

Table 3 shows the relationship between attitude toward intermarriage and non-racial voting and between Indian and African perceptions of each other's racial attitudes and non-racial voting. More than half the Indians who accepted intermarriage with Africans, but less than a fifth of those who did not, were non-racial voters, suggesting that superordinate racialism is an important cause of Indian racial voting. Indian superordinate racialism combined with African defensive racialism also may be an important cause of African racial voting. In 1957 Indians lined up behind the Jaganitee PPP more rapidly and more solidly than Africans did behind the Burnmite PPP, indicating that African racial voting may, to some extent, be a reaction to Indian racial voting. Also, as shown in the second part of Table 3, Africans who perceived Indians as having negative attitudes toward Africans were more racial in their voting than other Africans.

Racial attitudes and perceptions are not the only intergroup perceptions that

TABLE 3
PERCENTAGE OF NONRACIAL VOTERS BY RACE AND ACCEPTANCE OF INTERMARRIAGE AND BY RACE AND PERCEPTION OF EACH OTHER'S RACIAL ATTITUDES

| | Percentage of Nonracial Voters | | | |
| | Indians | | Africans | |
Independent Variable	%	n	%	n
Acceptance of intermarriage with other major race				
accept	55	(74)	22	(283)
object	18	(334)	12	(68)
(sig. test)	(p < .001)		(n.s.)	
Perception of other race's attitude towards own race				
favorable or neutral	29	(52)	32	(41)
negative	21	(289)	17	(252)
(sig. test)	(n.s.)		(p < .05)	

have contributed to the racial polarization of politics. Indians in Guyana appear to have identified with the PPP, or with its Indian leader, and to have developed strongly selective perceptions favoring the PPP. Africans, on the other hand, have identified with the PNC, or with its African leader, and have developed equally strong selective perceptions favoring the PNC. One question in the survey asked, "Do you think the economy of Guyana is doing better now, or was it doing better when the PPP was in office?" "Now" referred to the time of the survey when a PNC-UF government was in office. Four-fifths of the Indians thought the economy had been doing better when the PPP was in office, while 84 percent of the Africans thought the economy was doing better at the time of the survey. In a second set of questions respondents were asked whether they thought the PNC-UF government was favoring Africans over Indians and whether they thought the PPP government had favored Indians over Africans. Three-fourths of the Indians thought that the PNC-UF government was favoring Africans over Indians but that the PPP government had not favored Indians over Africans. Eighty-four percent of the Africans thought the opposite: that the PPP government had favored Indians over Africans but that the PNC-UF government was not favoring Africans over Indians. In a third set of questions respondents were asked what they thought of the three party leaders. Three-fourths of the Indians but only two percent of the Africans gave more favorable opinions of Jagan than of the other two leaders; while 58 percent of the Africans but only one percent of the Indians gave more favorable opinions of Burnham.

Table 4 shows the relationships between each of these perceptions and the respondents' voting intentions at the time of the survey. The majority of the Indians who thought the economy was doing better at the time of the survey did not intend to vote for the PPP in the next elections, and the majority of the Africans who thought the economy had been doing better when the PPP was in office did not plan to vote for the PNC. The relationship between perception of discrimination and nonracial voting intentions was equally strong, though very few respondents believed that only the party associated with their own race had been or was discriminating. Finally, the majority of the respondents who favored

TABLE 4
PERCENTAGE OF RESPONDENTS WITH NONRACIAL VOTING
INTENTIONS BY RACE AND SELECTED POLITICAL PERCEPTIONS

| | Percentage with Nonracial Voting Intentions | | | |
| | Indians | | Africans | |
Political Perception	%	n	%	n
Economy was doing better when:				
PPP was in office	12	(331)	57	(21)
about the same	45	(51)	28	(25)
at time of survey	62	(21)	5	(241)
(sig. test)	(p < .001)		(p < .001)	
Government seen as discriminating:				
PPP only	(4)[a]	(4)	5	(291)
neither or both	38	(94)	20	(49)
PNC-U.F. only	12	(306)	(2)	(3)
(sig. test)	(p < .001)		(p < .001)	
Favored leader of party associated with:				
other race	79	(19)	(6)	(9)
no preference	28	(78)	10	(130)
own race	12	(303)	4	(200)
(sig. test)	(p < .001)		(p < .01)	

a. When the number of cases in a category is less than 10, the number of respondents with nonracial voting intentions is given in parentheses rather than the percentage. For the significance tests these categories were combined with the contiguous category.

the leader of a party other than the one associated with their race did not plan to vote for the party associated with their race.

The selective perceptions of politics developed by Africans and Indians and the strong relationships between these perceptions and voting behavior suggest that selective perception was a powerful factor in the polarization of politics along racial lines. The process of selective perception may have begun as soon as Jagan and Burnham split or may have begun only when the Jaganite and Burnhamite PPPs began to be seen as Indian and African parties during the 1957 election campaign. Whenever the process began, it became a driving force in further polarizing the parties.

I am not prepared to argue that the racial attitudes and political perceptions of Africans and Indians in Guyana are a sufficient explanation for the racial-political violence in the early 1960s. Africans and Indians in Trinidad and Surinam have racial attitudes (and cultural and socio-economic backgrounds) quite similar to their counterparts in Guyana (Bahadoorsingh, 1968; Speckman, 1965). Although politics has become polarized along racial lines in Trinidad and Surinam, there has been no widespread African-Indian violence in either country. Thus some additional factor is necessary to explain the African-Indian violence in Guyana.

The difference which appears to explain the racial-political violence in Guyana is the fact that two additional intergroup cleavages were superimposed on the racial and political cleavages.[2] These were the international cold war and the cleavage between Marxists and non-Marxists within the Guyanese political elite. Because of the identification of the government and opposition parties with opposite sides in the cold war, each side could expect, and did receive, substantial amounts of aid from its foreign allies. The fact that the opposition parties were on the same side in the cold war as the United States, the most powerful nation in the hemisphere, and Great Britain, Guyana's colonial master, meant that the opposition could use strategies that opposition parties normally would not dare. Within Guyana the cold war ideology and implications of the struggle between the PPP and the opposition made each side more militant and less willing to compromise than it might otherwise have been. Each side saw itself as part of a worldwide struggle against the dangerous monster of "capitalist imperialism" or "totalitarian communism."

CONCLUSIONS AND IMPLICATIONS

From the data presented in this chapter it can be concluded that cultural differences and class conflict explain only a small proportion of the racial polarization of politics in Guyana. Indian superordinate racialism, African defensive racialism, and the selective perceptions of politics developed by Africans and Indians explain a much larger proportion of the pattern of racial voting. Thus the intergroup relations explanation of the polarization of politics received much more support than the cultural pluralist or the Marxian explanations. Intergroup relations theory also provided the most adequate explanation of the racial-political violence, attributing the violence to the superimposition of the international cold war and the cleavage between Marxists and non-Marxists in the Guyanese political elite on the domestic racial and political cleavages.

The results of this study suggest three ways of reducing the racial polarization of politics in Guyana, and perhaps in similar multi-racial societies:

(1) The provision of equal opportunities in all sectors of the economy, including government employment;

(2) reduction of Indian superordinate and African defensive racialism; and

(3) reduction of the selective perception of politics.

The provision of equal opportunities in all sectors of the economy is necessary, but may not be sufficient, to reduce African defensive racialism and African and Indian perceptions of discrimination and to increase the socio-economic similarities between Africans and Indians.

The strong relationship between political perceptions and voting behavior suggests that individuals who break out of the patterns of selective perception are more likely to vote for the party favored by their perceptions or to abstain from voting than to vote for the party associated with their race. An important question, of course, is whether enough Guyanese voters are capable of breaking out of the patterns of selective perception, and whether there is enough consensus among these voters to create a swing vote large enough to change the government of Guyana from time to time as circumstances warrant. In other words, can democracy work in Guyana?

To help answer this question, Table 5 presents the data on voting behavior by race separately for the three elections between 1957 and 1964 and on voting intentions at the time of the survey in 1967. Between 1957 and 1967 there was a small but steady decrease in support for the PPP among both Africans and Indians. Between 1964 and 1967 there also was a slight decrease in support for the UF and a slight increase in support for the PNC among both groups.

TABLE 5

VOTING BEHAVIOR BY RACE IN THE 1957, 1961, AND 1964 ELECTIONS AND VOTING INTENTIONS AT THE TIME OF THE SURVEY BY RACE (in percentages)

Date	Race	PPP[a]	PNC[a]	UF	Other	Total	Total n
1957	Indian	98	2	—[b]	0	100	(247)
	African	3	91	—	5	99	(214)
1961	Indian	95	1	4	0	100	(333)
	African	2	95	3	0	100	(301)
1964	Indian	93	1	5	1	100	(399)
	African	1	95	3	0	99	(352)
1967	Indian	91	5	3	1	100	(364)
(voting	African	1	97	2	0	100	(329)
intentions)							

a. The PPP percentages for 1957 refer to the percentages of voters supporting the Jaganite PPP and the PNC percentages refer to the proportion of voters supporting the Burnhanite PPP.
b. The U.F. had not been formed in 1957.

Although these changes all were small, the fact that they were in the same direction for Africans and Indians resulted in the creation of a small swing vote favoring the PNC. The fact that twice as many Indians (12 percent) as Africans (six percent) had no party preference at the time of the survey also could be expected to benefit the PNC in the next election. If the elections held in December of 1968 were not rigged, as the opposition parties have claimed, the PNC did benefit from an effective swing vote. In the 1968 elections the PNC won 50.8 percent of the domestic vote,[3] turning a 5 percent PPP plurality in 1964 into a slight PNC majority in 1968.

The conclusion that the racial-political violence in Guyana was caused by the superimposition of the international cold war and domestic ideological cleavage on the racial and political cleavages suggests that the best way to prevent violence in the future is to disengage these cleavages from each other. The United States, the Soviet Union, and China can contribute to such a disengagement by refraining from interfering in the politics of smaller nations and by attempting to transcend the cold war. Guyanese political leaders can work toward such a disengagement by developing ideologies that are more differentiated from the major Western (or East-West) ideologies and by attempting to reach enough consensus on their economic and political objectives that they will not be tempted to welcome foreign intervention.

NOTES

1. In his study, Despres (1967) argues that whether or not politics will become polarized and whether violence will occur in a culturally plural society depend on the organizational strategies adopted by political leaders. To the extent that Despres uses the theory of cultural pluralism to explain the polarization and the violence, however, the polarization and the violence are attributed to cultural differences and socio-economic differences resulting from the cultural differences.

2. Several social scientists have suggested that violent conflict is more likely when several cleavages coincide or are superimposed on one another (Dahl, 1967; Lipset, 1960). The superimposed-cleavages explanation follows from the basic assumptions of intergroup relations theory. If intergroup cleavages are seen as the basic sources of social conflict, but if no one type of intergroup cleavage is seen as the predominant source of conflict in all or most societies, then it is logical to conclude that conflict would be most likely when several cleavages coincide.

3. For the first time in Guyanese history, Guyanese living abroad were allowed to vote in the 1968 elections. The PNC won 94 percent of the "overseas vote," raising its percentage of the total vote to 55.8 percent.

REFERENCES

BAHADOORSINGH, K. (1968) Trinidad Electoral Politics. London: Institute of Race Relation.

British Government (1953) White Paper. Cmd. 8980.

DAHL, R. (1967) Modern Political Analysis. Englewood Cliffs, N.J.: Prentice-Hall.

DESPRES, L. (1967) Cultural Pluralism and Nationalist Politics in British Guiana. Chicago: Rand McNally.

JAYAWARDENA, C. (1963) Conflict and Solidarity on a Guianese Plantation. London: Athlone Press.

LIPSET, S. M. (1960) Political Man. New York: Doubleday.

MEISLER, S. (1964) "Dubious role of A.F.L.-C.I.O. meddling in Latin America." The Nation 198 (February 10): 131-138.

ROBERTSON, J. (1954) [Chairman] Report of the British Guiana Constitutional Commission. London: H.M.S.O. Report, Cmd. 9274.

SMITH, M. G. (1967) Forward to L. Despres (1967)

SMITH, R. (1962) British Guiana. London: Oxford University Press.

SPECKMAN, J. D. (1965) Marriage and Kinship among the Indians in Surinam. Assen: Van Gorcum.

Chapter 19

EFFECTS OF ETHNIC CONFLICT ON NATIONAL DEVELOPMENT: A COMMENTARY

MARGARET E. GALEY

*I*n this age of international organization, a striking contrast to the increasing numbers of such organizations is the retribalization or revitalization of ethnic consciousness (Alger, 1970: 694-697). Revival of ethnic consciousness, much like the revival of religious fundamentalism, seems anachronistic in scientific, technological, or high-energy and highly politicized societies. Thus from one perspective, revitalized ethnic consciousness symbolizes a remnant from the past and people that are out of the mainstream, for one reason or another. From another perspective, it symbolizes the strength and security of tradition amid the frustrations of modernization. And from still another perspective, it says that political regimes have been unresponsive to the needs of constituents either by forcing too rapid a pace of development, by turning a deaf ear, or by simply not knowing how to retard or accelerate innovation.

Revitalization of ethnic consciousness challenges scholars of various persuasions to rethink the complex and multiple processes of nation-building and to take into account the particular role that ethnic conflict plays in these processes. By way of commenting on the very interesting preceding papers in this regard, I propose in the following paragraphs to do some rethinking about the role of ethnic conflict in nation-building. Central to this effort is the clarification of the concepts of national development and ethnic conflict.

National development has been a subject of considerable interest to social scientists and there is no dearth of literature on its various and interrelated dimensions. More particularly, there seems to be a growing consensus that national development involves several processes. These processes are not unilinear or additive; one cannot add each and sum total the lot and expect to have a neat figure for this or that country's national development. A process operative on one level affects other processes with multiplier effect rather than a sum total effect. Having said this, let us look briefly at the various processes involved in national development.

Studies of human development appear in less abundance than those on political, social, and economic development though McClelland's *Achieving Society* (1961), Hagen's *Theory of Social Change* (1962), Pye's *Personality, Politics and Nation-Building* (1962) and Frantz Fanon's contributions are to be noted. The impact of public policy on the individual's growth and development is suggested as an area for profitable inquiry.

Economic and social development refers to the increase in productivity of

AUTHOR'S NOTE: The author wishes to thank the Maurice Falk Medical Fund for the opportunity to conduct research on American race and ethnic problems, 1970-1971, and colleagues at UNITAR in New York for comments on the paper.

human and material resources. Measures of it include increased GNP resulting in increased per capita income, new urban centers, improved transportation and communication (TVs and radios), increased levels of skill, and the formation of new groups (political parties, for example). Increase in the level of skill of the population—a function of education—is critical to a society's ability to convert and use material resources. Similarly, the increased organization of people for productive work is also essential. Economic and social mobilization thus generate new interest groups, associations, and labor unions. These are not equivalent to ethnic groups although a particular ethnic group may indeed dominate the rank and file of a new group, be it labor union, political party or status group.

Political development is closely related to economic and social development. Political development, however, refers to an increase in the channels or institutions of communication between the newly formed interest groups and the central policy makers. More specifically, decision makers have channels, e.g., bureaucracy, legislature, political parties, newspapers, perhaps schools and churches through which they receive and respond to demands from constituents. Groups other than elites may also have channels, e.g., associations and limited legislative and bureaucratic representation. The increase in channels of communication means that groups will increase, for example, their legislative representation or the priority of their demands on the elites.

Political development supposes the increase of such channels as well as the increase in the level of skill of these groups and their organization of information. As they are mobilized and become absorbed into the politically relevant strata, they adopt strategies to shape and share in policy making. A relation here between social and economic development and political development is obvious. If we think of political power as the monopoly of information or access to it then one access route to power is through education. One question for ethnic groups within a politically developing society as Roberta Mapp writes is who (ethnic groups) gets what (education); and if we continue Lasswell's formulation, we might ask how (what strategies), when (what point in the developmental context and in the group's history), and why (were elite attitudes favorable, did the cultural tradition of the group permit it, and so forth). Further, social and economic mobilization do not mobilize all groups for more intensive communication. Deutsch (1966: 127-130) makes a useful distinction in this regard between total population, mobilized population, underlying population, differentiated and assimilated populations. These are helpful in an analysis of a particular nation-state's development, and I submit more useful than thinking in the less precise terms of majority/minority relations which tend to obscure the variety of interminority relations.

Cultural processes are intimately related to nation-building. Styles of living, value orientations, and patterns of behaving are learned and passed on to new generations through family, tribe, ethnic group, school, and so on. These may encourage resistance and/or openness to change. In this context, it is appropriate to discuss ethnic groups.

Ethnic groups have been variously defined. Schermerhorn (1970: 12) writes that an ethnic group is a "collectivity within a larger society having real or putative common ancestry, memories of a shared past, and a cultural focus on one or more symbolic elements defined as the epitome of their peoplehood." Milton Gordon (1964: 23) defines an ethnic group as a group which shares "a common culture in which a principal element [is] a set of religious beliefs and values shared more or less uniformly by all members of the group and a common racial background ensuring an absence of wide difference in type." The problem with these definitions is that they do not convey the significance of ethnic person and ethnic group behavior nor do they illuminate ethnic identity. Nevertheless both are important to understanding ethnic conflict.

Von Mering's (1971: 34) insights are especially helpful. He conceives of ethnicity as the complex summation of race, religion, language, class, and national origin; the individual experience and social reality of ethnic identity. Thus, there is the "individual way" of perceiving and living with ethnicity, of behaving according to a special sense of "coming face-to-face and to terms with one's own." There is also the "group way" of ethnicity, a pattern of living and working, or presenting oneself and of performing among fellow man with historical symbols, special legends and conventional "social pieties" or actualities. For the person or the group, having and using ethnicity may be a matter of behaving one of several ways:

(1) presenting and demonstrating to selectively targeted "other people," or to "outsiders" in general, the visible signs and symbols, both traditional and fictive, of "race," creed, and national origin.

(2) calling, naming, and blaming another person or group; picking on and labeling a thing or event as one sees it, yet claiming to "tell it as it is,"

(3) claiming for one's group an indefinable, unique aura of special sensitivity in order to classify "other kinds of people" into immutably lesser social beings and forms of existence;

(4) elaborating one's consciousness of kind for the purpose of controlling, influencing, or posturing with a likeminded following inside a circumscribed social area,

(5) practicing ritual acts of alienation on particular outgroups by making them into "unpersons" and nonpeople, by perpetrating "rhetorical harm" on them, and by predicting if not actually committing a "final solution" on designated "strangers," "aliens," or all "enemies of the people" [Von Mering, 1971: 34].

Though no human group has the capacity to identify totally with all of these modes of self-presentation and action, these ways of men offer ever-present options for developing lasting negative-mirror images of self and other, and as such account for a major source of ethnic conflict. Moreover, such ways of behaving may be viewed as process, the continuous interrelation of personal group and the interaction of groups with other groups. Thus one can speak of the process of *becoming* an ethnic person or member of an ethnic group, or of developing ethnic identity, and the process of group interaction (Von Mering, 1971). In regard to the former, Von Mering writes that ethnic identity involves:

(1) a growing up of discovery and struggle with the "familial inheritance" or world and characterological assets and liabilities,

(2) growing into and learning to accept or reject a special sense of personal origin, family history and locality,

(3) a growing older or searching and finding a "rightful or false direction of self-expression and life work,

(4) living into and with a personal conviction of having a "just" and "deserved" place or an "unequal" and "undeserved" status among peers and contemporaries,

(5) working toward and with a lasting personal stake, or working to fit into a "power niche" or moving about "going no place" in the existing social order,

(6) *preparing for* individual and social change in the course of taking active leave from selected fulfilled obligations, loyalties and commitments for the benefit of peers and younger people; or resisting change by "holding in" whatever activities there are, grasping to the point of becoming alienated from one's talents and making strangers of one's fellow men,

(7) *becoming* a respected elder in later life, and perhaps a "laudable ancestor" thereafter by the timely turning over of secular reigns to the next generation for the future social order; or declining into has-been-personhood and enduring as a declasse person of fixed motives, only to end up in memoriam as a forgettable and perhaps blameworthy forebear [Von Mering, 1971: 35-36].

Developing ethnic identity must be viewed as a continuous interrelation of person and group. Ethnic community is an important dimension of this process. Studies have shown that migrants from rural or overseas areas moving into urban areas tend to settle with those of similar ethnic background and life style. This phenomenon characterizes settlement pattern of migrants in squatter settlements in urbanizing areas much as it characterized settlements of immigrants from Eastern Europe to the urban areas of the Unites States in the nineteenth and twentieth centuries. Ethnic communities provide "newcomers" with the security of the familiar—amid the "foreign" and unfamiliar. As such these communities offered a moratorium from the immediate pressures of adapting and adjusting to the "host" community (Park and Miller, 1921: 146; Leiberson, 1962: 677; Brody, 1969: 11; Fitzpatrick, 1966). Within communities groups have established institutions, e.g., associations, churches, and schools. These naturally helped shape and perpetuate ethnic identities. Interaction and behavior of the ethnic group with other groups in society may lead to modifications of groups' cultural patterns, resistance to change and/or developing for itself a place among other groups in society.

In the opening paragraphs, I noted that the persistence of ethnic identities and communities in an age of increasing international organizations and high-energy societies, appears anachronistic. It connotes being separate from society, out of the mainstream, looking inward or backward to a golden age, or resisting change. However, if we view this anachronism in historical perspective, it confirms the fact that development processes are not additive and do not proceed at the same rate. The multiplier effect does not mobilize all groups equally. Some groups may remain outside the mainstream. Thus in examining groups it is useful to think of the continuities and discontinuities with the group's past that present ethnic identities represent, e.g., which cultural practices—endogamy, religious beliefs, languages—have persisted or have changed over a period of time. Such historical perspective enables comparative assessment of the effects of external events—international, national, intranational—on the processes of developing ethnic identity and of behavior of groups with other groups in society.

In this regard, we need finally, though briefly, to distinguish between nationality and ethnicity. Deutsch (1966: 96) writes that nationality is the alignment of large numbers of individuals from middle and lower classes who are linked to regional centers and leading groups by channels of social communication and economic intercourse, both directly and indirectly (Deutsch, 1966: 101). Nationality may be said to refer to the identity of a large group of people with the territory, heritage, and traditions of the nation-state. Thus one speaks of Americans, British, Mexicans, Poles, Brazilians, and Russians. Ethnicity, however, refers to the identity of groups who share a particular cultural heritage and tradition, but whose identity referent may not be the nation-state. For example, various ethnic (cultural) groups comprise the American people; there are those of English, Irish, German, Polish, Italian, Japanese, and Czech origin. Yet the label-hyphenate-American may obscure the more specific and telling cultural heritage and tradition. For example, Italian-American does not specify whether Sicilian, Florentine, Roman, Neapolitan, first, second, third, or fourth generation Italian-American.

The extent to which a nationality exists could be measured by the extent to which the diverse cultural groups within society share complementary habits of social communication and economic intercourse and are linked through these to decision makers. For the United States, the dominant ethnic group—WASP— for many years dominated government, commercial, and other decision positions; tradition of this group provided the model to which newcomers aspired and adapted. Modeling themselves after the WASP, other groups developed habits of compliance and communication that enabled them to live in American society. The current intensity of ethnic revitalization in the country suggests that some groups have not incorporated these habits of compliance.

Three points are to be made now in concluding these brief thoughts about the processes of national development. First, development and process imply growing toward or achieving some goal. Goals may include improving the quality of life, offering greater educational opportunity, or achieving a higher GNP. Suffice it to say that this is a significant concern that could form another paper, but one generally agreed-upon goal is survival. We may think of these processes in terms of their promoting the survival of the society.

Second, though the investigation of particular processes has usually fallen to particular traditional disciplines, the orientations of these have been and are being fertilized with concepts and techniques of related fields. Political scientists, for example, in seeking to explain the dimensions of the political processes have found the techniques of anthropologists, sociologists, and economists useful in their research. Moreover, there is little doubt of the growing influence of psychology in these endeavors. As its vocabulary is absorbed, however, caution must be exercised in assuming conceptual equivalencies across disciplines or in employing reductionist arguments. For example, integrity for the individual is quite a different thing from the integrity of the nation-state; individual growth may or may not be a touchstone of political development; similarly, different levels of human organization may or may not be autonomous. While the autonomy of different levels of organization may be desirable, and operational definition of autonomy for the individual and for the nation will mean different things. Such concepts as integrity and autonomy have heuristic value for developing hypotheses about national development, but it is important to recognize the context and processes in which they are used.

Third, these processes are interrelated and the complex pattern of their interaction will vary from nation to nation. Despite this and as an aid in thinking about ethnic conflict in national development, the dynamics of these processes may be pictured in the following simplified model.

Ethnic groups make demands for increased income, political representation and/or distribution of resources on other groups, specifically elites of dominant ethnic groups through channels. They also provide what Easton calls supports for the regime. Elites (government, military, business, and sociocultural) respond

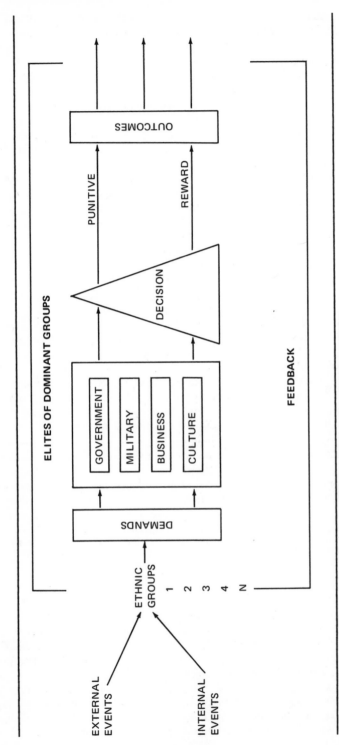

Figure 1: SIMPLIFIED MODEL OF ETHNIC GROUPS IN NATIONAL DEVELOPMENT

through their channels to demands by making decisions. Information about a decision is communicated or returned through channels to decision makers and ethnic groups, and is technically known as feedback. Such information engenders a response (outcome) from ethnic groups as well as decision makers. It is suggested that ethnic groups may interpret a decision as rewarding or punitive and respond by increasing or decreasing their level of suport for the regime or by reformulating previous demands. Decision makers respond to information about a decision by "correcting their behavior," that is, by establishing new measures, or readjusting previously formulated policies (Easton, 1965; Wade, 1972).

An illustration will clarify the notion of feedback and outcome. Albert Levak writes that the Establishment of West Pakistan Act passed in October 1955 (policy decision) had these outcomes. It amalgamated the provinces into one unit and thereby encouraged a number of regional grievances. The politicians from the West perceived the act as tantamount to the extinction of their separate ethnic identities inasmuch as the one-unit system aimed to merge groups by government fiat. Despite ethnic grievances, martial law continued. In 1970 President Khan decided to call democratic elections. The outcomes of his decision were: (1) postponement of elections, (2) continuation of martial law by President Khan as the army attacked East Pakistan, (3) spreading of the resistance to the Khan regime beyond East Pakistan to West Bengal, and (4) hostilities between East and West Pakistan. Feedback in this context refers to the information about Khan's decision which has been communicated to groups and the consequences or outcomes of the perception of that information by ethnic groups. The groups responded in this case by withdrawing support and formulating new demands on the political system.

In regard to the basic model and the preceding papers, the role of ethnic conflict in national development can be profitably discussed. In particular it becomes possible to talk of sources and effects of conflict, though they often appear indistinguishable.

The following sources of conflict have been identified by the authors of the preceding papers. (1) Ethnic diversity of populations, Guyana, Indonesia, Malaysia, Philippines, Pakistan, Ghana, and Kenya. This fact in itself suggests that in multiethnic societies the probabilities for conflict exist. (2) Selective perception of Africans and Indians in Guyana were reinforced by national and international ideological positions. Thus respective parties to the conflict saw themselves as part of a world struggle against either the monster of capitalist imperialism or totalitarian communism. (3) The soft authority structures of governments in Southeast Asia—Malaysia, Philippines, and Indonesia—enhance the vulnerability of groups to events in the external environment. (4) The legal status of Palestine which involves the territorial control and integrity of Palestine. (5) The punitive decisions of the Pakistani government which have threatened the ethnic identities of population groups. (6) The structure of education in Ghana and Kenya which has preserved the opportunity for education for those having past advantage.

In addition, the rate and location of social and economic mobilization of population, lack of political communication, and the strength of cultural traditions have contributed to intensifying and spreading of ethnic conflict within and beyond national boundaries. But basic to all of these sources of conflict, are the misperceptions of self and other, or "we" and "they." Whether misperception, selective perception or negative mirror image, these form the bedrock of conflict among ethnic groups be they majority or minority groups.

The effects of ethnic conflict on national development may be examined in the context of: (1) demands made by groups on other groups, most particularly elites of dominant ethnic groups, and (2) the effects or outcomes of elite decisions on the groups.

The demands which ethnic groups have made on elites include the following: groups have demanded the use of their own language, (e.g., Bengalis in East Pakistan; Sindi, Baluchis, and Pathans in West Pakistan; and presumably some non-Tagalog communities in the Philippines); preservation or restoration of cultural autonomy; a stake in political decision-making, control of the government (e.g., Javanese efforts to oust Sukarno, Papangano-speaking peasants to overthrow the Philippine government, Portuguese and African efforts to unseat the Indian majority in Guyana); and a greater stake of the economic pie (e.g. East and West Pakistan).

A common channel through which groups articulate their demands is the political party or coalitions of parties. Other channels such as cultural or ethnic fraternal associations have not been discussed. However, it should be noted that these institutions have often been important channels for groups' demands and/or a resource base for a political party in some states (Smock, 1971).

Ethnic groups have employed various strategies and tactics to achieve their demands ranging from nonviolent strikes and threats of violence to outright rebellion, guerrilla maneuvers, and invocation as in the case of the Arab States of legitimacy of violence. Though not described in any of the papers, a certain amount of naming, blaming, labeling, protesting, and demonstrating of groups against other groups occurs. What, however, is the response to these demands and tactics?

Here we may speak of the decisions of elites and the effects or outcomes of these decisions on groups. More particularly, decisions may be either punitive or rewarding. An example of a punitive decision is President Khan's imposition of martial law and the sending of the army to occupy East Pakistan (Levak). In contrast, Singapore's decision to elevate four languages to the status of national language is rewarding (Enloe). There appears to be a mixed category of punitive decision, e.g., Khan's decision to hold democratic elections, his postponement of elections, and the reestablishment of martial law.

What effects or outcomes do these decisions have? In respect to the singular rewarding decision, Cynthia Enloe writes that the intent was to ensure internal peace and allay anti-Communist suspicion among Singapore's neighbors. No note is made of whether in fact these outcomes were accomplished, but one can suppose that this has diffused rather than fostered interethnic conflict.

Most decisions referred to in these papers are punitive and a number of these have been based on misperception of the situation by elites. The effects of these decisions have encouraged violence, intensified ethnic conflict, slowed the process of national development, and encouraged foreign intervention. In Malaysia, for example, the ruling Alliance Party bolstered Malay politics, language, and religion, and in so doing—according to Cynthia Enloe—fostered instability in Sarawak and Sabah, delayed important development programs, encouraged interference from the Philippines and Indonesia, and retarded regional cooperation. Another example: the misperception of the Board of Education of Hyderabad with respect to the ethnic composition of Karachi led to their decision to make Sindi the medium of instruction in the schools. This precipitated a riot by university students. Finally, the claims and counterclaims of parties to the Arab-Israeli dispute have perpetuated hostilities and postponed the settlement of the status of Palestine.

A third kind of decision—mixed punitive and rewarding—is illustrated by Roberta McKown's study of the impact of education on ethnic groups in Ghana and Kenya. She writes that government elites for the sake of efficiency provide educational facilities for those regions where economic and social development is already under way. Educational structure thus preserves the past advantages of those developing groups at the expense of other groups who have limited or no access to education simply because their area is not developing economically. Regional disparities in terms of economy and education reinforce existing cultural disparities. One wonders with Roberta McKown whether education of advantaged groups will foster attitudes favorable to providing equal educational opportunity to disadvantaged groups. If the evidence from other countries including the United States is valid, education may not affect necessary attitude change that is anticipated.

Ethnic conflict plays an important role in the processes of national development. In the cases examined, conflict has arrested, retarded, or threatened to retard national development. Despite these negative effects, does ethnic conflict contribute to development?

From the viewpoint of Taulbee and Forsythe, conflict is contributive as it produces legal norms by making explicit the issues and by providing the development of normative sets to help prevent future conflict. Normative sets could be also referred to as the rules of the game or "shared habits of compliance." While international legal analysis of the Arab-Israeli situation, or similar conflict situations is highly instructive, a practical problem is the difficulty of persuading elites that are party to such conflict to agree on terms, to settle their differences, and to develop normative sets to prevent future conflict. Because of the multiethnic character of national societies and the nascent world community, the process of developing normative sets is neither easy nor rapid. Nevertheless within national societies, discussion among ethnic groups has led to the development of national norms of conduct. In this respect, ethnic conflict has contributed to defining rules of the game and thereby promoted national development. Yet such norms require continuous redefinition to reflect changing priorities. This appears to be one reason why the development of international law proceeds at a tortoise-like pace.

At issue in the role of ethnic conflict in national development is the capacity of the elites to accommodate conflict (perceptions and management of the situation in the context of scarcity), and the degree to which the rules of the game are already established. For various reasons, elite capacities vary. In contrast to the elite behavior described in these papers is that of the Founding Fathers of the "first New Nation" (Lipset, 1967). They chose to avoid entangling alliances; moreover, international communications and migration then by comparison with the recent past were very much smaller. Because the United States had "breathing space," because of the numerical strength of its dominant WASP culture, and because the elites more or less agreed on the rules of the game, authority structures could accommodate conflict. Ethnic conflict that occurred did foster certain normative sets, e.g., demands brought legislation on rules for labor organizations, strikes, bargaining, and so forth, but did not overwhelm authority. Despite the current revitalization of ethnic consciousness in the United States which raises serious demands for a larger share of relatively scarce resources, access to channels, to more goods and services, and benefits, there remains withal a relative capacity of the elites to accommodate differences.

Having said this, ethnic conflict within the developing nations which today figures as a source of weakness may in future generations become a source of strength for the nascent world community. If the "soft" authority structures of nation-states cannot control the impact of external communications and events on immigrant or indigenous groups, it may be that those groups that survive in the process of adjusting to these circumstances will achieve a new cosmopolitanism appropriate to living and working within world social processes. This possibility is partly predicated on elite behavior within these societies. It is also predicated on the assumption that the developed states, in the course of their further rapid scientific and technological growth, will not make the peoples and groups of the developing countries targets for elaborating their superior consciousness of kind, or make them into nonhuman objects unworthy of the company of their equals or betters.

In conclusion, the subject of ethnicity is receiving increasing legitimation in professional meetings, research projects, scholarly communication, and community activities. The avenues for basic research are vast as scholars of many disciplines have long neglected or avoided the subject almost as if it were the skeleton in the closet. The research orientations of all of the preceding papers are very useful. However, much could be gained through comparative analysis of developing with developed countries. Such comparisons may serve to highlight issues, e.g., influence of ethnic conflict on comparative foreign policies, and to contribute to the enlightenment of local and international leaders.

REFERENCES

ALGER, C. (1970) "Problems in global organization." International Social Science J. 22: 691-705.

BOZEMAN, A. (1971) The Future of Law in Multi-Cultural Societies. Princeton: Princeton Univ. Press.

BRODY, E. (1969) "Migration–adaptation: the nature of the problem." American Behavioral Scientist 13, 1 (September): 5-13.

DEUTSCH, K. (1966) Nationalism and Social Communication. Cambridge: MIT Press.

EASTON, D. (1965) Systems Analysis of Political Life. New York: Wiley.

FITZPATRICK, J. P. (1966) "The importance of community in the process of immigrant assimilation." International Migration Rev. 1, 1 (Fall): 5-16.

GORDON, M. (1964) Assimilation in American Life. New York: Oxford.

HAGEN, E. (1962) Theory of Social Change. Homewood, Ill.: Dorsey Press.

LEIBERSON, S. (1962) "Suburbs and ethnic residential patterns." American Journal of Sociology 67.

LIPSET, S. (1967) First New Nation. New York: Doubleday.

McCLELLAND, D. (1961) The Achieving Society. Princeton: Van Nostrand.

PARK, R. and H. MILLER (1921) Old World Traits Transplanted. New York: Harper.

PYE, L. (1962) Personality, Politics and Nation-Building. New Haven: Yale Univ. Press.

SCHERMERHORN, R. A. (1970) Comparative Ethnic Relations. New York: Random House.

SMOCK, A. (1971) Ibo Politics: The Role of Ethnic Unions on Eastern Nigeria. Cambridge: Harvard Univ. Press.

VON MERING, O. (1971) "Rethinking ethnic identity: the group and the person," in Evolving Patterns of Ethnicity in American Life. Washington: National Center for Urban Ethnic Affairs.

WADE, L. (1972) Elements of Public Policy. Columbus, Ohio: Charles C Merrill.

Part IV

NEW AND OLD STATES

Chapter 20

ETHNICITY, DECISIONS OF NATIONHOOD, AND IMAGES OF THE FUTURE

WENDELL BELL

"... cultural sections do not clash by chance or because their structures express incompatible values: They clash because certain individuals and groups have decided that something can be achieved by way of making them clash."

—Leo A. Despres
Cultural Pluralism and Nationalist Politics
in British Guiana, p. 29

*I*n referring to the above quote, I join two other contributors to this volume, Landis and Lemarchand. I do so despite the fact that I can not really agree that chance does not sometimes play a role in ethnic conflict nor that values do not enter in. Furthermore, the theory I wish to stress, a decision-making approach, contains a somewhat different perspective than that adopted by Despres in most of his analysis. But Despres is a perceptive field worker who spent considerable time in Guyana and he saw the importance of "decisions" in the situation despite the theoretical filter he was using.

Decisions, moreover, are involved not only when groups clash, but also when they exist in peace and harmony. They are involved as well in the formation and the dissolution of groups, in their growth and decline, and in the other ways in which they change.

My task in this chapter is to explain a decision-making approach to ethnicity and nation-building. The particular approach discussed involves some assumptions about a framework of historical trends, a set of abstract concepts, and a theory that appears to apply equally well to both old and new states. The trends can be summarized as "increases in the scale of society" and they are offered as factual descriptions of certain long-term changes through time in the course of the development of human communities and societies.

The concepts and theory importantly involve the notions of decision, choice, and images of the future as keys to understanding history, culture, and social structure on the one hand and individual behavior on the other (Bell and Mau, 1971; Eulau, 1958). The realities of social existence are viewed as including the definitions of the situation and meanings attributed to social relationships by different individuals and groups. Consciousness and differential perception, individuals' images of alternative or possible futures, the choices and decisions individuals make, and of course the resulting actions they take enter into the creation, maintenance, and change of the boundaries of groups, including those of racial and ethnic groups and of the nation-state.

INCREASES IN THE SCALE OF SOCIETY

Both ethnicity and nation-statehood are forms of identity and organization that can be conveniently viewed as stages in the development of the human group from small face-to-face locality bands of prehistoric times to large regional units that today link or command large territories or populations, such as the large nation-states, the Catholic church, Standard Oil, and the European Common Market. They exist as occasionally coalescing, more frequently criss-crossing, cleavages and, combined with other cleavages such as race, social class, rural-urban differences, and religion, they create a complex of social worlds of overlapping, alternative, and sometimes competing modes of organization more or less correlated with specific chunks of land. If we add the millions of other groups to which individuals belong such as families and neighborhoods, hobby clubs and sports associations, business firms and professional societies, merchants' organizations and trade unions, to mention but a few, one begins to get a picture of the world of social organizations in which modern humans live, compartmentalized yet manifoldly interpenetrating and overlying. Perhaps modernization may be quite adequately measured by the number of organized groups of whatever type that exist in a given social and geographical space relative to the total number of persons there. If the trend continues, one can easily imagine some future time where there will be more organizations than people, modernization thereby reaching an apex. For the present, of course, this trend obviously affects some individuals more than others. Some people, such as those in the interior of Brazil or New Guinea, may live today little differently than they did hundreds—even thousands—of years ago. Other people, such as those in the most affluent classes of the most affluent societies, already live in a world different from that which the "average" member of an advanced society experiences today. New organizations are created, often without replacing the old, and the old ways of life frequently continue into the present, coexisting with the new ways in a human system of relationships that in some respects becomes increasingly heterogeneous.

The trend toward increasing numbers of organizations is one part of a trend toward the increase in degree of organization of human society. Another is the trend toward increasing size of some organizations. Generally, human society has been expanding in people, in total power, in internal inclusiveness, in space, and in time (Bell, 1964). This is, of course, not to say that there have never been contractions in scale in the course of human evolution. There have, but the long-term non-repetitive movements of the time series have been toward the increase in the scale of society: the scope of social interaction and interdependency has increased for most of the people on earth (Wilson and Wilson, 1945).

More and more people are being linked together and drawn into networks of relations that have been expanding territorially with increasingly dense and extensive patterns of communication and transportation. Also, human society has been expanding through time by the spread of literacy, increasing education, the writing and reading of history, and by the increasing knowledge of the distant past resulting from archaeological research. More contemporary humans are "in touch" with more of the past than ever before (Bell, 1964). Thus, consciousness both of past times and other peoples and places contemporaneously has expanded.

Along with the expanding consciousness of widening relations and dependence on past and contemporaneous groups has come an increased awareness of the future. Most people may still be focused on the present and the near future, tomorrow or next week. But one can see that the trend is toward a longer view of the future, a greater concern with the future consequences of present actions, and an increase in expectations that some future time will be better—or can be *made* better—than the present in important respects. Both the revolution of rising expectations and the conception of the earth as a single system from the ecological point of view reflect the spatial and temporal increase in the scale of society.

Increased mobility is another aspect of increasing scale. There are, of course, the great interregional migrations, including the slave trade, that redistributed the earth's population. There are also the flows, in the United States for example, from farm to city, south to north, east to west, and city to suburb, as the case may be. There is also the sheer increase of movement, both change of residence and travel per se, between and within countries and cities, including the daily or twice-daily currents between home and work.

The increase in the scale of society is not offered as a cosmic principle or an impersonal social force. Rather, one assumes that there are definite advantages in increased scale that are weighed against the disadvantages by some persons who then decide for or against taking those actions that they hope will result in achieving the advantages they perceive. There seems to be a dialectic at work whereby political and economic domination—to some extent causes, effects, *and* concomitants of economic expansion—frequently have been the means by which scale was increased, capitalism, imperialism, and colonialism being prime examples in modern times; and then the people oppressed under the system demand changes, not usually a return to smaller scale, but often a just share in the benefits that have derived from the larger-scale organization, socialism, democracy, and nationalism being typical reactions, sometimes increasing social scale still more, though, it must be added, not guaranteeing the elimination of oppression.

SCALE, ETHNICITY, AND RACE

Ethnicity and race are involved in the trend toward increasing social scale in a number of ways. One is, as William Foltz points out, that ethnicity and race are fundamentally relational: "an ethnic group can define itself as such only by virtue of contact and comparison with other people whom its members define as being different." Thus, ethnicity and race are in this sense created as social phenomena by increases in scale, both through increased geographical movement of people and the redefinition of society to include more and more people in the same society (Shevky and Bell, 1955: 7). Although the contacts between diverse groups may create ethnic and race "relations," they also create the preconditions, short of mere chance parallel developments in the case of ethnicity, for the reduction of ethnic and racial heterogeneity for the population of the earth considered as a whole. This is so because social interaction among diverse groups makes possible, although it does not make certain, cultural diffusion, exchange, and innovation and because social interaction permits sexual interaction leading to mixed biological types and often mixed social and cultural types as well. This can occur, of course, even when there is conflict.

Another way in which ethnicity and race are involved in the trend toward increasing scale is that each is itself a way of organizing people. Depending on what ethnic group or what race one considers, of course, the scale created by ethnic or racial identity and organization could vary. Some would be very large, such as those defined by the Chinese or Western civilizations. Even if the latter were subdivided into French-speaking and English-speaking units, for example, the resulting collectivities would be relatively large in scale, while many other ethnic groups such as the Bretons in France or the Kurds in the Middle East would constitute units relatively small in scale.

With respect to race, one finds in the examples of *négritude* or Black Power an effort to combine people who are otherwise quite diverse in language, culture, tribal and national affiliation into a unity of a shared past and a common destiny. The mobilization of all blacks, for example, into a cohesive organization would result in a large scale unit, but it has an obvious limit: Brown, yellow, red, and white people, to use rather inadequate terms, would be excluded at the point of largest scale permitted by the racial criterion of organization and "by definition" could have only "external relations" with blacks.

Conceivably, the criterion of ethnicity would permit the crossing of cultural boundaries through assimilation into a single culture, perhaps by all of earth's people assimilating toward an emergent global culture. Although this may in fact turn out to be the case, one cannot safely predict, given the known persistence of some culture traits, that it could come about within three or even four generations. In an ethnically homogeneous world, there would be no "ethnic conflict," but one could not be sure that there would not be conflict of other kinds. Furthermore, even if perfect harmony and communal efficiency on a global basis were thus achieved, it would be because of the introduction of a new order of restriction and the suppression of human variations, some of which are delightful and give pleasure and others of which may have survival value for creature sapiens. Stereotypy remains stereotypy even when uniformly applied to all, if that is all there is to total cultural life.

The increase in the scale of society has meant an increase in total human power, an increase in social mobilization. It has meant more coordination, control, and direction and the rise of managerial and supervisory personnel which has taken a variety of different forms of legitimacy and authority and has included such diverse entities as United Fruit, General Motors, the government bureaucracy of the Soviet Union, and new governing bodies of the new states, although in the latter case their power is small compared to that of both governments and some corporations in the developed societies.

Such power and control, of course, has developed systematically into some hands and not others, hands in large part that are differentiated by race and ethnicity. Thus, if the fruits of development have been unequally distributed and if exploitation and oppression have occurred, as they obviously have, then an equally obvious by-product has been ethnic and racial inequality, exploitation, and oppression. There are, of course, individual exceptions in that some members of oppressed groups may escape economic insecurity and social degradation one way or another. But the general social context is nonetheless defined in the language and by the presumed virtues of the ethnic and racial groups who hold power and it is defined to their benefit. Distinctive characteristics of the ethnic and racial groups who do not hold power become, also by definition, "inferiorities." And the mark of oppression in the form of lost dignity, self-deprecation, and low self-esteem can often be seen long before members of subordinate groups reach young adulthood.

It is also no surprise to learn that it is frequently members of oppressed groups who decide that they should favor equality, freedom, participation, autonomy, respect for others, human dignity, and the like, as principles that should be applied to all humans, since in so doing their own position in a future social system based on such principles would be improved. Such persons, of course, do not always support such notions, sometimes because they are not aware or conscious of the injustices of their situation. They need to perceive the realities of their condition and to evaluate them in a certain way to achieve that, something that often requires the work of intellectuals. Sometimes, even though they have reached a certain level of consciousness, it is because they fear reprisals if they make demands or because they are benefiting individually by working for or cooperating with the oppressors. This is not to say that some members of dominant ethnic and racial groups do not support the same beliefs about the nature of existing social realities and do not share the same values. Some of them usually do because such ideas have a life of their own that affects commitment and action. Also, some additional support may be found in the demands of interchangeability, impersonality, and rationality involved in the large-scale organizational need for adequate performance, though such a need, perhaps, has been exaggerated. It cannot be denied that an ever present motive force for the attachment to such ideas is, as Robert H. Mast says, the fact of oppression itself as felt and experienced by the oppressed, their recognition and rejection of it, and their struggle to overcome it.

SCALE AND NATIONHOOD

The breakup of the European empires after World War II may superficially appear to be a reduction in scale, since the geographical size of the empire on which the sun never set seems obviously larger than the geographical size of the many new states that have been made out of the former imperial territories. Yet *social* scale was in fact increased by the rise of the new nationalist movements and the transition to nationhood. The reason is that the empires reflected large geographical scale, not so much large social scale, the far-flung units being held together by thin strata of ruling elites at the top of a pyramidal structure most of which—from the middle to the base—was composed of "outsiders," the masses of "natives" in their own lands. The nationalist movements involved the mobilization of these masses, and the transition from dependent colony to independent state involved the redefinition of society to include them into the newly established polities on the basis of equality of citizenship. It is true that the resulting new "nationality" became a new barrier, sometimes where little national identification existed before, between the peoples of the different new states and the peoples of other states, both old and new. The founding of the new states, however, and the drive toward nationhood widened the scope of interaction for most members of the former colonies, who had formerly been isolated in small communities and who had had local orientations, by bringing them into systems of national networks of communication, participation, and identification. New loyalties were created at the national level, internal inclusiveness was increased, and a new and more thorough-going internal unity began to be forged. The population pyramid was no longer like an iceberg with two-thirds or more hidden from view and lost from consciousness.

The "integrative revolution," as Clifford Geertz (1963) has called it, was under way. Primordial sentiments, ethnic and racial—as well as religious, tribal, and others—were under attack by new nationalist leaders who hoped to create a new civil order and an overarching national loyalty. Compared to the colonial inequalities that submerged huge proportions of native populations, the new states were at once larger in scale with the beginning of mass participation and the creation of national citizenries.

But primordial groups have frequently conflicted with the emergent nationality of new states—or even the existing nationality of old states as we see in several of the chapters that follow in this volume—for the domination of individuals' highest loyalty and provide alternative ways of organizing and identifying. Sometimes they are smaller in scale than the state itself and promote separatist tendencies, sometimes they are larger and promote a sense of political dismemberment and a desire for unification on a larger scale based on primordial ties such as the cases of pan-Arabism, greater Somalism, or pan-Africanism.

Yet the relationships between nationalism and ethnicity are complex. There is the rare instance where the boundaries of the state are nearly coterminous with the boundaries defined by ethnicity or race, although the absolutely perfect fit may exist nowhere even among the old states. More characteristically, ethnicity and race, even while competing with the emergent nation, have sometimes become redefined on a larger scale than before as a result of nation-building activities. After reviewing the cases of several new states, Geertz (1963: 153-154), for example, concluded that one common developmental tendency stood out:

"... the aggregation of independently defined, specifically outlined traditional primordial groups into larger, more diffuse units whose implicit frame of reference is not the local scene but the 'nation'—in the sense of the whole society encompassed by the new civil state. The leading principle in terms of which this lumping is mainly carried out varies—region in Indonesia, race in Malaya, language in India, religion in Lebanon, custom in Morocco, and quasi-kinship in Nigeria. . . . It is a progressive extension of the sense of primordial similarity and difference generated from the direct and protracted encounter of culturally diverse groups in local contexts to more broadly defined groups of a similar sort interacting within the framework of the entire national society.

"The emergence of a nation-wide system of 'ethnic blocs' engaged in 'total relations with one another' sets the stage for a direct clash between personal identity and political integrity in the new states. By generalizing and extending tribal, racial, linguistic, or other principles of primordial solidarity, such a system permits the maintenance of a profoundly rooted 'consciousness of kind,' and relates that consciousness to the developing civil order. It allows one to continue to claim public acknowledgment of one's existence and import in terms of the familiar symbols of group uniqueness, while at the same time becoming more and more drawn into a political society cast in a wholly different mold than the 'natural' community those symbols define. But, on the other hand, it also simplifies and concentrates group antagonisms, raises the specter of separatism by superimposing a comprehensive political significance upon those antagonisms, and, particularly, when the crystallizing ethnic blocs outrun state boundaries, stirs international controversies.

Statehood, then, although it may not do away with primordial attachments, may transform them and raise them to a higher level of scale by shifting the focus of attention to the relationships between large sub-populations on the national stage. To take an example with which I am familiar, the conception of Jamaican society, popularized by M. G. Smith (e.g., 1965), as being plurally divided into white, brown, and black sections could arise only if Jamaica were in some important sense a single social unit. For a small island-society such as Jamaica such unity may have occurred earlier, but certainly the riots and disturbances of 1937-1938 and the transition to political independence which began in 1944 and culminated in 1962 gave impetus to the idea of Jamaica as a single society, while also, *pari passu,* increasing the validity of the tripartite ethnic-racial divisions identified by Smith, themselves larger in scale than the various regional and community types that had further sub-divided Jamaica.

SOME DECISIONS OF NATIONHOOD

When men decide to form a new nation-state, they embark upon a task that involves them in changing, or attempting to change, the boundaries, membership, degree of autonomy, coalitions, organizational structure, internal relationships, history, and personal character of some existing pattern of relationships. At each step of the way they are confronted with possible alternatives that must be perceived and choices that must be made (Bell and Oxaal, 1964; Bell, 1967). Generally, they advance reasons they think are important in explaining the decisions that they make.

We have called these decisions, "the decisions of nationhood," since it is incumbent upon those who wish to create and build a nation-state to face them: some geographical boundaries must be established, some type of government must be formed, some policies must be set to deal with competing claims from ethnic and racial groups, the government must play some role in the affairs of the economy—even if the decision is to play a minimal one, some kind of relations with other nation-states must be established or the decision taken to establish none, etc. We view our list of the decisions of nationhood as deriving in part from problems of internal and external affairs that all organizations must face, although the particular form they take in this case is shaped by the fact that the organization under consideration is the nation-state; in part from the definition and conception of the nation-state itself that is more or less generally shared by the relevant actors involved; and in part from the nature of the physical and social environments in which the action takes place. In the latter case, for example, the problem of boundaries involves the fact that geographical territories are surfaces of a sphere, at least in their most salient aspect (control of outer space is causing additional intriguing problems), and often cannot be solved without taking into account competing claims for the same territory raised by other centers of power (Bell and Oxaal, 1964).

Equality and Nationhood

The decision that has priority over all others in time and in importance is: Should we become a politically independent state? It has priority since the other decisions of nationhood may never arise if this one does not and since the purposes and objectives behind the desire to create a politically independent state have implications for particular preferences with respect to the alternative outcomes to most of the other decisions of nationhood.

In answering "yes" to this question, the founders of nation-states, both old and new, have, with perhaps some deviant or debatable cases, affirmed their democratic and egalitarian ideologies. For example, in his excellent comparative summary of nationalist movements Konstantin Symmons-Symonolewicz (1970, 1968) regards modern nationalism as different from earlier forms of group loyalty and solidarity with which it is frequently lumped " . . . in that it is expressly based on the idea of nationhood, represents a new secular world-view, and *is a product of revolutionary democratic ideology"* (italics added). He says further that the "first stimulus toward nationalism" for the " . . . various 'non-historical' peoples of Europe—that is, those which became politically submerged early in their development and survived as depressed classes, or 'half-societies' with certain ethnic traits, rather than as culturally distinct whole societies . . . was the *principle of equality* among individuals and among nations brought to all the countries of Europe, and to some outside of it (Turkey, Egypt), by the shock-wave of the French Revolution" (italics added).

R. R. Palmer (1959, 1964) in his two-volume work, *The Age of the Democratic Revolution,* summarizes "what happened in the world of Western Civilization in the forty years from 1760 to 1800"

"as a single movement, revolutionary in character, for which the word 'democratic' is appropriate and enlightening; a movement which, however different in different countries, was everywhere aimed against closed elites, self-selecting power groups, hereditary castes, and forms of special advantage or discrimination that no longer served any useful purpose. These were summed up in such terms as feudalism, aristocracy, and privilege, against which the idea of common citizenship in a more centralized state, or of common membership in a free political nation, was offered as a more satisfactory basis for the human community" [Palmer, 1964: 572].

Although Palmer uses the term "democratic" to refer to the general revolution he analyzes, thereby acknowledging its political aspects, he also uses it to signify "a new feeling for a kind of equality" (1959: 45). He says, in fact, that the democratic movement had as an overriding central theme "the assertion of 'equality' as a prime social desideratum" (1964: 572).

Since the end of World War II, more than 60 new states have been created. In important respects, the nationalist movements that have brought them into existence can be validly viewed as a continuation of the democratic and egalitarian revolution that began in the latter part of the eighteenth century. I will not attempt to document this statement here except to summarize a small part of the field research done by myself and my associates on the new states of the former British Caribbean and the overseas departments of the still French Antilles.

From our work in the West Indies, we can conclude that in a colonial situation of political dependency, the question, "should we become a politically independent nation-state" is affirmatively answered:

(1) if there exists a significant amount of inequality (civil, political, economic, social, or cultural), especially inequality between "the natives" or local inhabitants and representatives or agents of the foreign power that is institutionalized, legitimated, and enforced by the imperial rule;

(2) and if such inequality is so perceived by a significant number of local people, that is if they become conscious of it,

(3) and if there exists an "enlightened elite" among the local people, that is an elite that is committed to the ideology of equality and that usually is also committed to the values of democracy, fraternity, the use of reason in the conduct of human affairs and the belief in the possibility of progress and the "perfectibility" of humankind;

(4) and if political independence is perceived as feasible by a significant number of local leaders, in the sense both of successfully attaining political separation from the imperial power and of successfully becoming a viable political and economic unit after independence;

(5) and, I add with less certainty than the above, if there exists at least a core of local cultural integrity identifiably free from the cultural dominance of the imperial power.

As early as 1958 in Jamaica, four years before independence was to be achieved, I asked a sample of Jamaican leaders: "Does Jamaica have more to gain or lose as a result of political independence from the United Kingdom?" Of the 234 top- and middle-level elites who answered, 66 percent thought that Jamaica had more to gain. When divided according to their responses to an index of egalitarianism, there was a small correlation between favorable attitudes toward equality and thinking that Jamaica had more to gain than to lose from political independence, 74 percent of the egalitarians favoring independence compared to 57 percent of the inegalitarians (Bell, 1962). Two aspects of equality were related to favorable attitudes toward independence, one was the equality of citizenship as compared to the citizens of other nation-states and the other was the equality between different races, ethnic groups, and social classes within Jamaica itself.

On the eve of independence in late 1961 and early 1962, Charles C. Moskos, Jr. (1967) extended my earlier study to include not only Jamaica, but also Trinidad, Guyana, Barbados, each of which is now independent, and the still dependent territories of Grenada and Dominica. Restricting his sample to top leaders and using a more valid set of measures to determine attitudes toward political independence than I did, he constructed a typology of nationalist types: *True nationalists* were those persons who favored immediate independence and actually engaged in pro-independence public activity, such as participating in nationalist political parties, pamphleteering, public speaking, etc. *Acquiescing nationalists* included *reluctant* leaders who favored political independence as a long-range goal, but did not want it now or in the near future, typically saying that the ". . . West Indies are not ready for independence now" (Moskos, 1967: 35); the *dutiful* who ". . .supported the nationalist movement because they thought it was an expression of the will of the people" (Moskos, 1967: 36), even though they were not personally in favor of it; and the *opportunistic* who engaged in pro-independence public activities although they were privately favorable to maintaining the colonial order. And, finally, the *colonialists* were those persons ". . . who opposed political independence for the

West Indies in the present or future and favored an indefinite continuation of colonial rule" (Moskos, 1967: 37). The distribution of nationalist types among the 112 West Indian leaders interviewed by Moskos is as follows:

True Nationalists		39%
Acquiescing Nationalists		25
Reluctant Nationalists	11	
Dutiful Nationalists	5	
Opportunistic Nationalists	9	
Colonialists		36
Total		100%
Number of cases		(112)

SOURCE: Moskos, 1967: 38.

I will not pause here to discuss these findings, except to point out that even on the brink of independence over a third of the leaders (mostly those who were more likely to be very well-off economically, planters and merchants, white or near-white, older, Anglo-European in life styles, and secondary-school-educated rather than more highly or lowly educated) opposed the transition to statehood. But what concerns us here is any evidence that tests the hypothesis linking nationalism with the democratic revolution. Moskos also collected data on attitudes toward the rights of man: liberty, equality, and fraternity. Liberty was measured by asking the West Indian leaders ". . . if they thought the democratic form of government was the best suited for their territory, the referent being a British parliamentary type system based on adult suffrage and the existence of civil rights (Moskos, 1967: 49); equality was measured by attitudes toward equality of opportunity; and fraternity was measured by attitudes toward social inclusiveness, that is, the relative emphasis leaders placed on reducing social barriers between groups (e.g., racial, religious, or class) within their own society as compared to increasing their contact with persons outside the West Indies. The nationalist types by attitudes toward the "rights of man" are given in Table 1.

In the case of each of the rights-of-man variables the differences in attitudes toward political independence are large, democrats being more likely than non-democrats to be true nationalists, egalitarians more than inegalitarians, and inclusivists more than exclusivists. Note that the largest differences occur between egalitarians and inegalitarians with 100 percent of the former and none of the latter being true nationalists. At least for the case of the West Indies, the interpretations of historical materials linking nationalism and the democratic revolution are clearly borne out, and they are borne out by a quite different type of data: systematic interviewing of the leaders during the time that history-making events were taking place. We have other types of data also, such as participant-observations, sample surveys of the lower classes, interviews with sugar workers, questionnaires filled out by students, etc., that generally support the same conclusion, and the reader is referred to them for more detailed and complete information and interpretation (Bell, 1964, 1967, 1973; Bell and Oxaal, 1964; Mau, 1968; Moskos, 1967; Murch, 1971; Oxaal, 1968, 1971).

TABLE 1
NATIONALIST TYPES BY ATTITUDES TOWARD THE RIGHTS OF MAN[a]
(in percentages)

| The Rights of Man | West Indian Leaders Who Were | | | |
	Colonialists	Acquiescing Nationalists	True Nationalists	Total
Liberty (political democracy)				
Democratic	5	36	59	100 (56)
Non-Democratic	66	14	20	100 (56)
Equality				
Egalitarian	0	0	100	100 (44)
Inegalitarian	59	41	0	100 (68)
Fraternity (priority of concern with social inclusiveness)				
Greatest need is for reducing social barriers at home (inclusivists)	6	13	81	100 (48)
Greatest need is for increasing contact abroad (exclusivists)	58	34	8	100 (64)

SOURCE: Moskos (1967: 46).
a. The number of cases on which the percentages are based is given in parentheses.

In examining the goals and values that led some people to want and work for independence and others to oppose it, we have also touched upon two other decisions of nationhood. "What kind of social structure should the new nation have?" is in part answered by knowing that the new nationalist leaders struggled for power, both by getting control of legitimate government authority through independence and then by expanding the role of government in the affairs of the society, in order to make their images of a future egalitarian and inclusivist society, where there would be equality of opportunity and no ascriptive barriers based on race, ethnicity, and class, into a social reality. And "What should the form of government be?" is in part answered by knowing that democrats were more likely to be true nationalists than were non-democrats, although it should be added that there was an important minority (20 percent) of non-democrats who were also true nationalists. Furthermore, one must remember that (1) half or more of the West Indian leaders were self-proclaimed authoritarians, inegalitarians, and exclusivists, (2) existing structural inequalities carried over from colonialism are great, and (3) foreign economic dominance and exploitation have continued into the period of political independence.

Social and Cultural History

Two other decisions of nationhood that have obvious and important connections to ethnic and racial distinctions are "Should the state and nation be coterminous?" and "What should the new state's cultural traditions be?" Here, the distinction between the state as a political entity and the nation as a cultural entity must be made and the notion of cultural management taken into account. Should the political boundaries of the state also define a single, homogeneous cultural unit and what features should distinctively characterize the national culture? Of course, cultures have been transformed in the past without intentional policy, but increasingly, with modern means of communication, the manipulation of culture becomes possible (compare Moskos and Bell, 1965). With respect to the new states, McKim Marriott (1963: 29) says:

"The possibility of educating their citizens to a newly chosen way of life, of mobilizing them in support of deliberately cultivated values, of representing them to the world according to a consciously created image—all these are open to the elites of the new states, either in actuality or in prospect. Whoever in the new states commands mass communications cannot avoid taking decisions and choosing among alternatives that shape cultural development."

Sukarno once said that there are three ways to promote nationalism, "first we point out to the people that they have a glorious past, secondly we intensify the notion among our people that the present time is dark, and the third way is to show them the promising, pure and luminous future and how to get there" (quoted in Oetomo, 1966: 633). But what from the past should be selected? Some countries, such as India, for example, have a vast and rich history from which to choose. What particular events support current hopes for cultural development and, perhaps a more difficult question, what events, if selected, will not promote disunity? For as Marriott (1963: 34) remarks, critical ". . . moments of history remembered as triumphant by one sector of society are all too often remembered as humiliating by other sectors." Because of this problem, India, for example, has not selected its new national past without difficulty. India's long, painful search for inspiring glories in the past has

"had to reach back beyond both documentary history and legend to seize upon an archaic figure once hardly known to exist outside the work of British epigraphers— the Buddhist emperor Asoka. Asoka, who reigned in about 269-232 B.C., has as much conscious continuity with modern India as the pyramids have with Abdel Nasser's Egypt. Asoka does, however, enjoy the advantage of having been a major indigenous ruler of spiritual pretensions who belonged to no known caste, no embattled region, and no threatened or threatening religion—at least as of 1947. Thus, the lion-ornamented capital of one Asoka's edict pillars, although it is a work of strongly Persian style and although it had been totally unknown to most Indians, nevertheless became the national emblem of India. Gandhian pacifists could reconcile themselves to the installation of these violent beasts by observing that the lions have drawn in their claws and are smiling" [Marriott, 1963: 35].

Although new states without the rich past of cultural traditions such as India's at first may appear at a disadvantage, they at least have less of a problem to face in the selection—or creation—of symbols that can serve to unite all their diverse peoples. In the West Indies, for example, where the whole population, except for a few Amerindians in Guyana, are immigrants from other lands and cultures, Dr. Eric Williams, Prime Minister of Trinidad and Tobago and renowned historian, issued, on the very first day of independence, his work (1962) which was explicitly committed to providing a unifying theory for a society marked by major racial and cultural divisions. Although cognizant of these divisive tendencies, Williams—as some other West Indian nationalists— stressed the idea that tendencies toward social and cultural pluralism need not weaken the new nation, that there is strength not only in unity but in diversity and that these factors are not irreconcilable. Most of the major ethnic and racial groups in Trinidad, he asserted, are bound together by a common history of exploitation and subordination under colonialism and all should therefore unite to build the new nation. Thus, he perceived the existence of cultural differences as requiring a "closing of ranks" rather than separate national allegiances. This argument is supported by the Enlightenment values of which he was a leading West Indian exponent: the presence of ascriptive ethnic and racial barriers need not and should not be a bar to equality of opportunity; the maintenance of a multiplicity of subcultural units can be reconciled with the goals of nationhood as long as all groups share a basic loyalty to the nation and to the democratic and egalitarian, if not the inclusivist, values that guided the nationalist movement (Bell and Oxaal, 1964).

In both the old and new states one of the functions of history is to define the character of a people and to provide self-esteem. During the colonial period, however, histories were usually provided for the colonial peoples by foreign historians, writing with the often unconscious, although sometimes deliberate, bias and ethnocentrism of the ruling power. Colonials "lucky" enough to get an education frequently had their identity and self-confidence thereby damaged by the image of themselves and their own people created for them by the distortions of foreign historians. For example, with respect to teaching about Africa, Ajayi (1966: 611) says:

"the education of the black man had to be controlled, not only through the prejudices of the white teacher and the white textbook author, but also sometimes by actual directives of the administrations in laws said to be designed for the best interests of the black man. Within this philosophy of education, the white man had a glorious and heroic history, the black man had none at all. The white man was always brave and courageous, the black man, if not lying and sneaking and lazing around, was only fierce and savage. White men fought wars and levied indemnities, black men only raided their neighbours and extorted tributes. Whatever cultural traits the white man had and the black man did not have, like writing, the wheel, the plough, and even eating forks, were essentials of civilization, but what the black man prided himself on, like rhythm, courtesy, respect of elders, and a stable philosophy of an ordered world, did not really count. Europe was the centre of the world, and all worthwhile achievements have been by white men. One witty geography book still in use in the 1930s proclaimed that Africa was the land of man-like apes and ape-like men. Others confirmed that the climate of Europe was the best in the world, temperate, equable; Africa was too hot and too humid for constructive work."

India fared no better in the history books written by Englishmen: "The most prominent vice of the Hindus is want of veracity, in which they outdo most nations even of the East. . . . [T]he inherent weakness of the greatest Asiatic armies when confronted with European skill and discipline. . ." India will relapse into political chaos "if the hands of the benevolent despotism which now holds her in its iron grasp should be withdrawn. . . . [T]he people of Europe, even during the feudal ages, were greatly superior to the Hindus. . . . In truth, the Hindu, like the Eunuch, excels in the qualities of a slave. . . . . [I]n the still more important qualities, which constitute what we call the moral character, the Hindu ranks very low." Majumdar (1966: 619-620), who reports these quotes, says that they were contained, along with similar statements, in books which were prescribed as textbooks for Indian history when he was a college student.

To take a final example, when last reported by Keur (1960: 801), on Saba in the Netherlands Antilles, where the population speaks an English Creole and is descended from African slaves, the history book in use in the public schools began with the sentence, "One hundred years before Christ, the Germans came to our land."

The writing of national histories by local scholars may redress the grievances and, along with cultural policies such as those having to do with official languages and proportional representation, is a major way of shaping both what is remembered of the past and the hoped for direction of future developments. Pride and consciousness will undoubtedly be falsely served by over eager historians of the new states, but no worse surely than the calumnies of the past. A Senegalese, Cheikh Anta Diop, has asserted, for example, that Negroes "were the first to invent mathematics, astronomy, the calendar, sciences in general, the arts, religion agriculture, social organization, medicine, writing, technical skills, and architecture" (Monteil, 1966: 594). Further, he alleges that the Wolofs of Senegal discovered America.

But this is an extreme case. The historical record is being set straight, both by the research of scholars and by the history-making actions of nationalist leaders.

In the West Indies, new histories have been—and are being—written. The important linkages between equality, a major goal of independence, and social and cultural development that may inform them can be seen from Table 2. The data are from West Indian leaders, as interviewed by Moskos. Eighty-nine percent of the egalitarians compared to 13 percent of the inegalitarians thought that the greatest need was for reducing social barriers at home rather than for

TABLE 2
PERCENTAGES OF WEST INDIAN LEADERS HAVING CERTAIN
ATTITUDES TOWARD SOCIAL AND CULTURAL DEVELOPMENT BY
EGALITARIANISM (in percentages)

Attitudes Toward Social and Cultural Development	Egalitarian	Inegalitarian
The Present: Priority of concern with social inclusiveness		
Greatest need is for reducing social barriers at home (inclusivist)	89	13
Greatest need is for increasing social contact abroad (exclusivist)	11	87
Total	100	100
Number of cases	(44)[a]	(68)
The Past: Teaching of West Indian history (Africa and slavery or India and indentured labor)		
Favors more emphasis	95	16
Opposes more emphasis	5	84
Total	100	100
Number of cases	(44)	(68)
The Future: Desired direction of future cultural development		
Uniquely West Indian	82	31
Basically Anglo-European	18	69
Total	100	100
Number of cases	(44)	(68)

SOURCE: Moskos and Bell, 1967: 111.

a. The number of cases on which the percentages are based is given in parentheses.

increasing social contact abroad. Ninety-five percent of the egalitarians wanted more of the history taught in the schools to be West Indian history with an emphasis on Africa and slavery (or in the case of East Indian respondents, India and indentured labor). And 82 percent of the egalitarians compared to 31 percent of the inegalitarians desired the future cultural development of their emergent nations to take a uniquely West Indian rather than a basically Anglo-European direction. Remembering that 100 percent of the egalitarians were also true nationalists (from Table 1), these findings show a rather tight connection between nationalist attitudes, favorable attitudes toward equality of opportunity, and a desire for social and cultural development leading toward incorporation of the lower socio-racial sections now, in the past (as it could be taught), and in the future (as it could be lived). A hopeful picture, perhaps, for the nation-builders who wish to make the state and nation coterminous, until one notes that of the 112 leaders interviewed by Moskos only 44 were egalitarians and true nationalists while 68 were inegalitarians, who largely rejected these same social and cultural developments.

The national motto of Jamaica is "Out of Many, One People." It is not a statement of present fact, but a hope, an aspiration for the future. How it can be achieved is partly a historical problem of factually showing the experiential basis of unity and partly a problem of design whereby enough significant present reality can be given to national organizations and national identity to make the state work. As in Switzerland and other multi-cultural states, however, the "Many" do not have to become "One" in all their cultural traditions for this to happen. Philip Mason (1972: x) reminds us of Shylock's words, "I will buy with you, sell with you, talk with you, walk with you . . . but I will not eat with you, drink with you nor pray with you." Mason continues to say, "I heard an even longer and more explicit catalogue of the same kind the first day I spent in Barbados. And surely it is on the lines of cultural diversity within an economic unity that a solution lies for minorities such as the East Indians or the Basques. The art of politics is to reconcile these dimensions." Yes, one can agree. Yet some level of national identity must exist if the state is to withstand its divisive and separatist forces and the creation of at least some elements of a national culture is a method that has tempted—and will continue to tempt—many a leader in both some of the old and new states. While the acceptance, even celebration, of diversity in a context of mutual respect, itself perhaps constituting an aspect of the new national culture, is a potentially viable policy, one of the prime dangers is that separate may not be equal. If it is not, then such a policy may rest on wobbly foundations since an existential basis for discontent, revolution, and, if the geography is right, partition remains.

CONCLUSION

It has not been possible in this essay to discuss fully the various decisions of nationhood. Only a few have been singled out for brief comment in relation to the factors of ethnicity and race. Nor has it been possible to give anything close to full treatment to the elements of the cybernetic-decisional theory that we (Bell and Mau, 1971) have formulated on the abstract level in an effort to account in a general way for our understanding of many of the important choices that exist in the transition to nationhood, the conditions that give rise to them and under which they are made, the beliefs and values that enter into the decision-making process, and the images of the future that guide historical action. Such concepts, I trust, are evident in the foregoing pages.

We have tried, throughout this volume, to move back and forth between the theoretical and the empirical, the general and the particular. The following four case studies leave us at the end with our feet firmly on the ground.

Moreover, these studies return from the abstract to the concrete not by focusing on new states as have the authors up to this point, but rather by concentrating upon a few of the old states. As I have tried to show in this chapter, a decisions-of-nationhood framework can be equally well applied to both.

In the chapters that follow, Paul F. Power discusses tradition and innovation as they affect ethnic and religious group relations in Northern Ireland, which is, of course, part of one of the oldest nations, Great Britain. Wracked by conflict and violence as we go to press, the divided people of Northern Ireland have, as Power points out, some integrative commonalities, but these are offset by conflicting loyalties to ethnic, religious, and political references that define a variety of discriminations and inequalities. Note in Power's analysis the cleavages of belief, lineage, structure, process, and governmental power. Furthermore, a shortfall between minority expectations for the future and demonstrable achievements preceded political violence.

A planner and a consultant to the group about which he writes, Harry Coblentz poignantly describes a microcosm of forgotten people. He tells of the present condition of an Indian community in the United States as it exists between past oppression and possible future inundation as a result of a new water project, plans for which may become a reality. Coblentz's contribution reminds us to look for the locus of power where relevant decisions are being—or can be—made. From the perspective of the Indian community the outside society poses seemingly insurmountable problems and the major decisions that affect it are made elsewhere.

Janet Merrill Alger moves back in history to revolutionary America and "interviews" nearly 200 colonial leaders by analysis of archival materials. Using basically the same typology of nationalist attitudes used by Moskos for the West Indies, she shows that, among other things, "Ethnicity and religion affected the position of elites on independence where those variables were important sources of internal cleavage apart from the issue of independence." That is, the attitude toward political independence of certain ethnic and religious groups differed in different American colonies depending on their position in the power structure.

After some preliminary observations on the formation of the modern state in Spain, Great Britain, France, Germany, and Italy, Pedro Gonzàlez Blasco gives a detailed analysis of the case of the Basques in Spain at several different historical periods. Basque land, as he points out, is more developed than most of the rest of Spain. Thus, Castilian-speaking workers migrate there and constitute "a minority within a minority." The results of his case study are in part contrary to the general relationship we have posited between equality and modern nationalism. At certain periods and among some sub-groups, Basque nationalism was not an outgrowth of an egalitarian movement. This does not, of course, violate the propositions as stated earlier, since they were stated in the form of "if a, then b" rather than "if, and only if, a, then b." But one would like to make the latter statement when possible. In this case, the "deviant case" is an important restraint. Political independence may be "merely" a means. "The ends that it can serve depend upon particular configurations of ethnicity, class, and power and upon where established and insurgent groups fit into those configurations." When the ends will include equality depends on the conditions of the situation, though conditions, more often than not, have linked equality and nationalism historically.

Finally, Helen I. Safa makes some concluding remarks in a commentary in which she stresses, once again, one of the major themes of this volume: the importance of the "demand for equality."

REFERENCES

AJAYI, J.F.A. (1966) "The place of African history and culture in the process of nation-building in Africa south of the Sahara," pp. 606-616 in I. Wallerstein (ed.) Social Change: The Colonial Situation. New York: John Wiley.

BELL, W. (1973) "New states in the Caribbean: a grounded theoretical account," in S.N. Eisenstadt and S. Rokkan (eds.) Building States and Nations. Beverly Hills, Calif.: Sage.

——— [ed.] (1967) The Democratic Revolution in the West Indies: Studies in Nationalism, Leadership, and the Belief in Progress. Cambridge: Schenkman.

——— (1964) Jamaican Leaders: Political Attitudes in a New Nation. Berkeley and Los Angeles: University of California Press.

——— (1962) "Equality and attitudes of elites in Jamaica." Social and Economic Studies 11 (December); 409-432.

——— and J. A. MAU [eds.] (1971) The Sociology of the Future. New York: Russell Sage Foundation.

BELL, W. and I. OXAAL (1964) Decisions of Nationhood: Political and Social Development in the British Caribbean. Denver, Colo.: The Social Science Foundation, University of Denver.

DESPRES, L. A. (1967) Cultural Pluralism and Nationalist Politics in British Guiana. Chicago: Rand McNally.

EULAU, H. (1958) "H. D. Lasswell's developmental analysis." Western Political Q. 11 (June): 229-242.

GEERTZ, C. (1963) "The integrative revolution," pp. 105-157 in C. Geertz (ed.) Old Societies and New States. New York: Free Press.

KEUR, D. L. (1960) "Metropolitan influences in the Caribbean." Annals of the New York Academy of Sciences 83 (January 20): 796-801.

MAJUMDAR, R. C. (1966) "Nationalist historians," pp. 617-630 in I. Wallerstein (ed.) Social Change: The Colonial Situation. New York: John Wiley.

MARRIOTT, M. (1963) "Cultural policy in the new states," pp. 27-56 in C. Geertz (ed.) Old Societies and New States. New York: Free Press.

MASON, P. (1972) "Preface," pp. v-ix in D. Lowenthal, West Indian Societies. London: Oxford University Press.

MAU, J. A. (1968) Social Change and Images of the Future: A Study of the Pursuit of Progress in Jamaica. Cambridge: Schenkman.

MONTEIL, V. (1966) "The decolonization of the writing of history," pp. 592-605 in I. Wallerstein (ed.) Social Change: The Colonial Situation. New York: John Wiley.

MOSKOS, C. C. Jr. (1967) The Sociology of Political Independence: A Study of Nationalist Attitudes Among West Indian Leaders. Cambridge: Schenkman.

——— and W. BELL (1967) "Attitudes toward equality," pp. 100-114 in W. Bell (ed.) The Democratic Revolution in the West Indies. Cambridge: Schenkman.

——— (1965) "Cultural unity and diversity in new states." Teachers College Record 66 (May): 679-694.

MURCH, A. (1971) Black Frenchmen: The Political Integration of the French Antilles. Cambridge: Schenkman.

OETOMO, B. (1966) "Some remarks on modern Indonesian historiography," pp. 631-642 in I. Wallerstein (ed.) Social Change: The Colonial Situation. New York: John Wiley.

OXAAL, I. (1971) Race and Revolutionary Consciousness. Cambridge: Schenkman.

——— (1968) Black Intellectuals Come to Power: The Rise of Creole Nationalism in Trinidad & Tobago. Cambridge: Schenkman.

PALMER, R. R. (1959, 1964) The Age of Democratic Revolution: A Political History of Europe and America, 1760-1800, 2 vols. Princeton, N.J.: Princeton University Press.

SHEVKY, E. and W. BELL (1955) Social Area Analysis. Stanford, Calif.: Stanford University Press.

SMITH, M. G. (1965) The Plural Society in the British West Indies. Berkeley and Los Angeles: University of California Press.

SYMMONS-SYMONOLEWICZ, K. (1970) Nationalist Movements: A Comparative View. Meadville, Pa.: Maplewood Press.

——— (1968) Modern Nationalism: Towards a Consensus in Theory. New York: The Polish Institute of Arts and Sciences in America, Inc.

WILLIAMS, E. (1962) History of the People of Trinidad and Tobago. Port of Spain, Trinidad: PNM Publishing.

WILSON, G. and M. WILSON (1945) Analysis of Social Change. London: Cambridge University Press.

Chapter 21

CONFLICT AND INNOVATION IN ULSTER

PAUL F. POWER

*A*lthough Northern Ireland is legally a part of a mature nation-state, recent and continuing disorder in the United Kingdom's only sub-system testifies to the persistence of disputes about the legitimacy, defense, and performance of its regime after a half-century of existence. Sources and analogies for these controversies may be found in the long history of Anglo-Irish interaction. The Ulster conflict involves ethnic, political, religious, and economic factors that predate the creation of the polity. Insights into these factors are necessary first steps towards understanding the unrest.

Our main concern is with the origins, course and results of the civil rights phase (1967-1969) of the disorder. During this time new attitudes, policies and structures emerged that tended to democratize the regime's performance and to promise a reduction in ascriptive and exclusivist features of community relations. But almost simultaneously the new forces came into conflict with a revival of ideological and physical disputes about regime defense or legitimacy, disputes interwoven with confessional and ethnic identities.

The uneven conflict and the British system's military intervention caused the civil rights movement to give way. The next period (1970-1971) was characterized by increasing tensions, desperate insurgency, and regime repression. Britain's suspension of the local regime in March 1972 produced Irish Nationalist hopes, and loyalist disarray and backlash. A year later London announced constitutional reforms, with divided responses. Whatever the current phase may bring, the civil rights phase was an important antecedent which at a higher level of generality demonstrated how in a context of unresolved social and political questions of basic sorts there appeared change that deserves to be called innovation.

I

Despite ecological, economic, legal, linguistic, and military forces that work for socio-political unity, Northern Ireland has two political communities, one of which controls the sub-system through a regime that endures despite dissensus. Richard Rose (1970, 1971) describes the condition as a "divided regime," a regime that is neither fully legitimate nor fully repudiated. He is impressed with survey evidence collected in early 1968 that there were potential repudiators of the regime within the majority, i.e., the Ultras who would use any means to defend the constitutional order as they define it, as well as revolutionary

AUTHOR'S NOTE: The author gratefully acknowledges support for field research from the Taft Memorial Committee of the University of Cincinnati and helpful comments on an earlier version of this paper by Anthony Coughlan and J. Bowyer Bell.

nationalists within the minority group usually identified with the nine-lived Irish Republican Army (IRA). Vital to the relationships of the communities are inequalities in access to and possession of power, differences which have created an ascendent community and a subordinate community. The inequalities have stemmed partly from the size of the Protestant majority (about 63 percent) in the total population of 1.5 million, but also from other sources that coincide and reinforce one another along the lines of belief, lineage, structure, and process. The outcome has not been two discontinuous, and autonomous nations. In particular, the Ulster land, the English language, and the economic order have provided some integrative commonalities. Yet they have been offset by conflicting loyalties to ethnic, political, and sectarian references that created the inequalities and a semi-polarized and low-consensus sub-system.

Historically, Northern Ireland is the product of (a) the Ulster Protestants' determination to remain part of the United Kingdom and avoid inclusion in a united, independent and predominantly Roman Catholic Ireland; (b) the provisions of the British Government of Ireland Act of 1920, which divided Ireland and Ulster, established a parliament for six of its nine counties, as well as a stillborn parliament in Dublin, and reserved crucial policy matters for Westminster; and (c) the 1921 treaty between Sinn Fein and London that created the Irish Free State within the Commonwealth and provided the North with the right to opt out of the new Irish regime. Prepared since 1912 to enter armed conflict with Westminster unless this right existed, the northern Unionists began their formal rule in 1921 with a clear commitment to preserve the Unionist ideology which had matured during the constitutional integration of Britain and Ireland (1801-1921) and to continue a Protestant-Parliamentary tradition, dating at least to William II's victory in the 1690 Battle of the Boyne, in at least part of the semi-colonized island.[1] Grounded on these impulses and organized through the Orange Order and the Unionist Party, the regime found no rationale to share power with the Catholic minority nor to treat it as allegiant. Confirmed by perceptions of minority beliefs or behavior, the declared religio-political bias of the regime lasted from its founding under Sir Edward Carson until Terence O'Neill became Prime Minister in 1963.

The emergence of O'Neill, an experienced Unionist minister, opened a creative, if discordant chapter of Northern Ireland. A descendent of Sir Arthur Chichester, London's head of the Irish government in 1607, O'Neill derives his surname from his great-grandfather who in 1855 by Crown authority assumed title to the ancestral O'Neill estates. Causing consternation or surprise, his government began to encourage the Unionist regime to approach Catholics as allegiant citizens, even as potential Unionist voters and party members.[2] Explanations for the shift include a benign reaction to the collapse of IRA warfare from 1956-1962 that had failed to attract important minority support; the impact of post-Johannus ecumenism in both religious communities, and the launching of economic development programs which would be aided by social harmony. A significant change, in 1965 Northern Ireland and the Republic entered a new relationship, dramatized by two meetings of O'Neill and Prime Minister Sean Lemass. A former revolutionist who in 1959 had succeeded de Valera as leader of the Fianna Fail Party, Lemass led the Republic away from economic isolation and political orthodoxy into an Anglo-Irish free trade pact and subsidized industrial growth. He held a federationist view of Anglo-Irish relations not found in the 1937 Irish Constitution which claims authority for the Dublin regime to legislate for the entire island.[3]

The appearance of a conciliationist government caused Ultras to protest, setting the scene for the civil rights phase. Partly identifiable with the Rev. Ian K. Paisley, the Ultras are largely petit bourgeoise and proletariat defenders of fundamentalist versions of the Reformation and Unionism who have worked through one or more structures—the Protestant Unionist Party, the Ulster Defense Committee, the Ulster Volunteer Force, Orange lodges, and to a degree, Unionist Party branches. The legal and illegal Ultra street protests in 1964-1967 against Republican symbols, Christain ecumenism, and the detente between the Dublin and Ulster governments preceded or overlapped the civil rights movement. Not only did the Ultras initiate unrest but by doing so they contributed to O'Neill's reluctance from fear of backlash to grant reforms implied by his conciliatory ideas and to hold to minimum concessions.

What O'Neill's original conciliationist policy had to deal with in the minority's political outlook and conduct may be briefly noted. The minority's ethnic self-view is one component. In the community there is a consciousness of ethnic solidarity with the all-Ireland majority which a half century of partition had not erased and may have intensified on the Captivity model. In early 1968, the Strathcylde survey found that 76 percent of the Catholics in the North viewed themselves as Irish, 15 percent as British, 5 percent as Ulstermen, 3 percent as British or Irish, and 1 percent as Anglo-Irish (Rose, 1971). (The majority's self-view reflected an "overseas" influence: 39 percent British, 32 percent Ulster, 20 percent Irish, 6 percent British or Irish, and 2 percent Anglo-Irish. Yet "Protestant" is widely used by the majority as an ethnic term to unite these self-identities). Accordingly, the northern "minority" may interpret social and political relations in the North as a meeting of the island's Irish majority and the British minority that controls the regime of six Ulster counties.

As to the minority's political action from partition to the civil rights phase, three forms can be identified: (1) a conspiratorial and periodically violent strategy, usually but not always attributable to the IRA;[4] (2) a non-partici-patory, agitational approach conducted by the Sinn Fein Republicans who boycotted elections or entry into the Northern Ireland and Westminster Parliaments; and (3) an opportunistic, parliamentary strategy represented by the Nationalist Party which traced to the Home Rule movement. Varying more in means than in ideology, all three sought a united Ireland. From the first (1921) through the 1965 general election the Nationalists and other anti-partitionists won from 9 to 12 members in the 52 seat House of Commons of Northern Ireland in the Parliament at Stormont near Belfast. The Unionists returned 33 to 40 members to form all of the governments that could depend on a few non-Unionist members to support the territorial settlement. Beginning with PR, the regime abandoned it in 1929 to safeguard Unionists from independents, but especially to ensure that electoral contests followed the community cleavage. In the eight general elections thereafter through 1965, electoral stagnation of no competition typified between 20-27 constituencies of the 52 total. Tacit electoral truces between Unionists and Nationalists accounted for much of this stagnation.

From the first through the 1965 elections the Nationalists provided the bulk of the anti-partitionist members in the Stormont House. They won nine seats in

1965. Because of their own convictions and those of Unionists, for many years the Nationalists functioned as sub-systemic, as well as governmental critics, and were so treated by the regime which claimed with some merit to have a legitimate monopoly over the defense of polity values. Yet, inconsistent with these realities, in 1965 the Nationalist leader, Eddie McAteer, became the Leader of Her Majesty's Opposition following the Dublin-Stormont detente.

In addition to the Nationalists, the opposition had these elements: the Liberal Party, revived in the 1950s, had minimal strength (one Stormont Commons seat in 1965), but some critical influence. The Northern Ireland Labor Party (NIL), bisectarian and from 1949 committed to partition, was an exception with the Liberals to the opposition's anti-partition character. But NIL never secured more than four seats and won only two in 1965. Another workers party, Republican Labor (RLP), attracted voters of Sinn Fein sympathies, especially in industrial Belfast, but it never won more than two seats. An RLP leader, Gerry Fitt, won a Westminster seat in 1966 and called there unsuccessfully for investigations into minority grievances.

The 1963 emergence of an attentive Unionist government facilitated the expression of the minority's charges. Because they were presented in new ideological and methodological contexts politics in Northern Ireland entered an innovative phase. The grievances themselves were rooted in basic systemic problems. But since the complaints focused on subsystemic structures and performance in the perspective of democratic theory and human rights and were not obviously linked to anti-systemic ideology and methods, they could not be denigrated as subversive by a "sensitive" government.

The grievances centered on partial disenfranchisement, plural voting, gerrymandering, discrimination in employment and housing, and regime emergency powers. All of these objections tended to support the image of a discredited Stormont. Yet the civil rights movement did not demand an end to the sub-system's autonomy through Westminster absorption. Influencing this view was pragmatic Irish nationalism, as opposed to some Republican traditions, which has considered Stormont as potentially a regional Irish government in a united Ireland. This possibility is recognized in Britain's 1920 Government of Ireland Act.[5] From the pragmatic view the abolition of Stormont might even enhance British power in Ireland through direct rule.

Franchise disability came from a property qualification for local elections (as in Britain before 1946) which excluded from the local registers about one-fourth of those entitled to vote for the Stormont House of Commons which had a universal adult franchise. Plural voting rested on a university bonus (abolished in Britain in 1948) that gave Queen's University in Belfast four seats in the Stormont House, and on a six-maximum-vote premium for certain corporations at local and Stormont levels.[6] Economic realities meant that these three distortions adversely affected the political power of the minority and aided the majority's electoral strength. That Northern Ireland retained property qualifications and plural voting after the balance of the United Kingdom had abandoned them was an especially active source of minority criticism of the regime's use of devolved authority.

Gerrymandering and related inequitable practices in 67 local units of varying population and territorial size supplied tangible grounds for minority protest. Unionist manipulation of ward or district lines and elector content to insure the maximum results for Unionist votes and the reverse for Labor, Nationalist and Sinn Fein oppositions were especially pronounced in the Fermanagh and Tyrone counties and Londonderry (Derry) City. These areas are the Punjab of Ireland. Derry is a dually holy city of St. Colomba, a sixth-century missionary to Iona, and the Rev. George Walker, who rallied Protestant defenders in 1689. Although Catholics have been in a slight majority since before partition in Fermanagh and Tyrone, the Unionist county councillors consistently outnumbered opposition representatives. Segregated Derry City (67 percent Catholic) had ward boundaries redrawn under Unionist control as recently as 1966, with the result that 10,274 Unionist votes elected 16 councilmen and 20,102 anti-Unionist votes elected eight. Reviewable by the Stormont Parliament but seldom upset, Unionist redistricting combined with the limited franchise and plural voting to ensure regime ascendency in most local governments even in areas where the sub-system minority was a majority.

Housing grievances included claims that too few public houses were being built and more credible charges that they were located to preserve voting imbalances and that allocations were biased. Minority interest in council housing had been accentuated by its modest per capita share of total income. This condition was linked to majority self-recruitment in government and industry, a custom reinforced by the loyalist syndrome and minority educational and psychological impediments. In the mid-1960s Catholics made up 12 percent of local government employees and 6 percent of the central bureaucracy. The regime had allocated one-third of the Royal Ulster Constabulary for Catholics, but had secured a representation of only one-seventh.

Economic development had a paradoxical effect. Through British subsidies, foreign investments and new industry, the O'Neill government reduced unemployment from the 15-20 percent rates of the 1950s to 5-8 percent levels in the mid-1960s. Northern Ireland acquired a percapita income 75 percent of England's and 150 percent of the Republic's. But the minority's participation in the economic progress lagged behind, e.g., its unemployment rate was still between 12-25 percent. Moreover, O'Neill's economic programs stressed industralized Belfast and other eastern areas with 67 percent of the total population and a minority community of 22-24 percent. Rational or not, charges developed of regime discrimination against Armagh, Londonderry, Fermanagh and Tyrone counties which were 40-55 percent Catholic.

Although the O'Neill government adopted a conciliatory idiom, it did not allay minority fear of the regime's emergency powers under the Civil Authorities (Special Powers) Act of 1922, intended as a temporary measure but made permanent in 1933.[7] Employed against the IRA in the 1950s, the statute permits orders that sanction a variety of measures, e.g., indefinite internment of alleged subversives without trial, as does a comparable law in the Republic.

Many Special Powers orders covering internment and other security measures were withdrawn in 1949-1951. The Act's continuation served to deter revolutionists and to unsettle the opposition and libertarians. Part of the network of Special Powers was the Ulster Special Constabulary (B Specials), a fully Protestant and armed police reserve with sectarian and militant qualities that distributed the minority. As Irish Catholics responded favorably, if cautiously, to O'Neillism, they escalated past charges that they were the potential objects of repression under a law which the United Kingdom had acknowledged to be in derrogation of the European Human Rights Convention. Although the statute was not significantly used until August 1971 because of its controversial nature and the availability of other public order laws, the Special Powers issue became more controversial after the O'Neill government had drawn back from the implications of its reformist notions in an effort to restore the equilibrium disturbed by Ultras.

That the O'Neill government wished to cool the sub-system became evident in early 1966 when the Prime Minister approved only the abolition of the business vote in local elections when pressed by the bisectarian Belfast Trades Council to fully democratize the franchise. That the Council demands were tied to British electoral practices and civil liberties organizations and did not raise any systemic controversies should not be overlooked as favorable elements which might have influenced but did not cause O'Neill's government to make more substantial concessions. Following murders in mid-1966 attributed to the revolutionist Ulster Volunteer Force, the regime did return individual convictions and proscribed the Ultras' counterpart to the IRA, which has roots in the Orange-Unionist determination to forcefully resist Irish Home Rule at the start of this century. Mention of these even-handed steps should not obscure the episode's warning signals to the government from revolutionary loyalists. Corroborating O'Neill's shift away from conciliation, he agreed in late 1966 with Home Minister William Craig, whom he later dismissed for Ultra tendencies, to refuse a demand for full democratic rights for all citizens.

The government's new posture helped to unify and provoke minority critics. Voluntary groups which had earlier helped to create a democratizing and reformist trend, notably the Campaign for Social Justice in Northern Ireland, coalesced after O'Neill's retrenchment to form the Civil Rights Association of Northern Ireland (CRA) in early 1967. Largely Catholic and Nationalist or Republican and including some Protestants, Laborites, Communists and a rare Unionist, the CRA began the main struggle for reforms. The CRA aggregated and prosecuted demands grounded on broad, humanistic and democratic values and avoided traditional appeals to Catholic loyalties and the anti-partition movement of the Pan-Irish. Consequently, for a time (1967-1969) the CRA attracted sympathetic attention and political support beyond the minority community, especially among British labor leaders. The CRA's invocation of principles with which the British constitution as distinct from the Northern Ireland regime presumably conforms was crucial for producing the eventual intervention in Stormont affairs by the Westminster Parliament under Section 75 of the 1920 Ireland Act which reserves final authority over Northern Ireland to London. In sum, the CRA tapped universalist ideals and secured a positive, systemic concern for Northern Ireland's relative correspondence to the values. For the North's regime, its opposition, and Westminster these were innovative, perhaps unique, developments.

The newly formed opposition departed not only from historic ideologies but also from conventional means. Rather than using parliamentary tactics, boycott of elections or office, manipulation of sectarian tensions, IRA-type violence or some combination thereof, the civil rights movement of 1967-1969 relied on nonviolent, secular demonstrations which were occasionally illegal but ostensibly civil, i.e., undertaken in the public order for its benefit by ethical means.[8] This development may be attributed to recent Continental, American or Indian influences. Possibly these demonstrations were adaptations of one of the following: underpublicized, nonviolent protest in Irish history (e.g., Daniel O'Connell's Catholic Emancipation marches in the last century), the well-established custom of religio-political parades conducted by both Ulster communities, and even the previous examples of Ultra unrest. Yet civil rights protests were more creatively adventuresome than any of these Irish precursors. For a sub-system where the dominant group has tended to equate illegality in politics with repudiation of the regime, they probed and extended the government's capacity to tolerate dissent and to democratize the regime.

From O'Neill to Paisley the regime became especially alarmed about civil rights rhetoric and tactics used by the People's Democracy (PD). More radical in idiom and purpose than other components of the civil rights movement, PD stemmed from the dissatisfaction of some Queen's University students and faculty with the CRA's ideology and methods and more concretely as a response to a police riot against a civil disobedience march in Derry on October 5, 1968. Seeking the peaceful or violent replacement of northern and southern Irish regimes with a vague socialist order in a united nation, PD provide temporary energy and leadership to the civil rights movement that altered the opposition and the regime in significant ways. Intellectualized by Kevin Boyle, Michael Farrell, and Cyril Toman, PD had and may still have in Bernadette Devlin a charter member who became an international personality.[9] PD did not monopolize public protest that led in some cases to illegal conduct. Whether linked to PD or not, civil rights protest became especially innovative when it refused to accept government restrictions limiting peaceful demonstrations to "safe," in this instance, minority territory, but tried, sometimes effectively as in Derry, to carry them into Unionist areas. These actions meant that the universalist ideology of the civil rights movement had succeeded over narrower rationales on both sides through the means of physically appealing on all streets to the rights of speech, assembly and petition and to the redress of specific injustices.

The civil rights phase of 1967-1969 included preparations for or the use of violence by members of the movement. A widely publicized instance was the lobbing of bricks toward police by Ms. Devlin, M. P. for Mid-Ulster since April 1969, during the police siege of Free Bogside that August. She justified her conduct as community-defense but was convicted and served four months imprisonment. At about the same time in West Belfast Catholics tried to defend themselves against shooting that was initiated, according to the Cameron Report, by the RUC and B Specials only to find that IRA cadres and guns were in low supply. The IRA's revival and split stems from this episode. Additionally, there were many instances of juvenile conduct that the actors considered as principled resistance, but the regime saw as criminal behavior.

Yet, overall, the civil rights protest of 1967-1969 was a period of considerable self-restraint on the part of the aggrieved minority who suffered far more violence than they inflicted.[10] A notable, successful test of self-discipline was the Bartollet Bridge episode, January 4, 1969, in which peaceful marchers were attacked by Ultras without retaliating as in Martin Luther King's activities which the leaders had studied. Contributing to the self-restraint of the civil rights protagonists was the divided condition of minority attitudes toward the regime and means of changing it. In early 1968 after the rights campaign had begun, according to Rose's study, minority opinion divided about equally among responses of acceptance, rejection, and agnosticism as to the legitimacy of the constitutional order. Thirteen percent approved, but 83 percent disapproved of IRA methods. Forty percent endorsed illegal, nonviolent protest against regime rules (Rose, 1970: 189-193). This divided opinion also helps to explain the impact of the civil rights conflict on the sub-system's institutions and processes.

II

After nearly a half-century of operating as if it were a whole rather than a partial system, Northern Ireland experienced a civil rights conflict that effected significant changes within the political sub-system and between it and environments. The more important of these may be noted under six headings:

(1) Due to elite conciliation and systemic (Westminster) and opposition pressures, the regime began to increase the exposure of governmental decision-making to minority influence, to distribute public services more equitably and to increase their quantity, and to discontinue or democratically alter structures and practices that had adversely affected the low-power minority or which it had believed had a repressive impact. Specifically, the O'Neill government announced on November 22, 1968, that the regime would

(a) abolish the business vote;

(b) replace the gerrymandering Londonderry government with a Development Commission having municipal authority;

(c) consider eventual withdrawal of parts of the Special Powers Act if civil order permitted;

(d) institute an ombudsman for central administration; and

(e) introduce a new objective formula for housing allocations.

Later, after additional conflict and systemic eldering, Stormont pledged a local franchise based on universal adult suffrage, a central Housing Executive for local housing, an ombudsman for local administration, a reduction in the number and powers of local governments, the disarming of police and the termination of the B Specials. That the regime conducted self-appraisals leading to many of these reforms (Government of Northern Ireland, Cameron, 1969a, 1969b; Hunt, 1969c; Macrory, 1970) lent it credibility for some supporters and critics. Compensation included the deployment and increase in the British Army to replace police, the creation of a bisectarian, provincial guard (Ulster Defense Regiment) to eventually keep order, and the enactment of public security laws. The outcome of the "reforms" was to democratize and centralize the regime's institutional performance but also to enlarge its capacity to enforce compliance. But a democratic "gain" was achieved.

(2) Conflict pluralized regime defenders into Unionist reformers, Unionist Ultras, and Ultras who formed a new organization—the Protestant Unionist Party. The divisions caused the original, conciliationist Prime Minister, O'Neill, to be replaced by a pragmatist, James Chichester-Clark, following a formal victory for reform Unionists in early 1969.

The process may be noted: Expecting to strengthen his position, O'Neill called the February 1969 General Election. With 48.2 percent of the total vote the Official Unionists won 36 seats in the 52-place Stormont House, the same number as in 1965. Unaccustomed to personal electoral challenge, O'Neill narrowly won his own seat against Paisley and Farrell of PD. Twelve of the Unionist victors were anti-O'Neill. Independent Unionists favoring O'Neill won three. Only one anti-O'Neill Unionist was defeated. Although the non-Unionist winners decreased from 16 in 1965 to 13 in 1969, there was no significant change in the percentage of the non-Unionist vote, 32.7 percent. Anticipating a Catholic shift to his Unionism that did not develop, O'Neill was left to face Unionist critics who unsettled his position sufficiently to produce his retirement. Chichester-Clark succeeded him in a narrow party contest.

(a) O'Neill's exit did not shift the Unionist government from a "reform" course during and even after the civil rights phase. For the structural reformers kept control of the dominant party, which still followed the community cleavage, and therefore of the divided regime despite Ultra opposition that eventually helped to displace Clark in favor of Brian Faulkner in March 1971. Centralization of party decision-making in the parliamentary elite at the expense of local party units and systemic guidance from Labor and Conservative governments in London aided the reformers to control the regime. Also helpful were the concessions granted to the minority, its principled nonviolence or weakness which did not represent a threat to regime authority, and the evolutionary stress of the regime policy in the contiguous system, the Republic of Ireland.

Notice should be taken of how the northern conflict caused strain and some movement away from traditionalism in the Republic. The Fianna Fail government of Lynch offered genuinely Republican reactions to the northern conflict, e.g., shifting of troops and nationalist U.N. speeches. But Dublin gave the most weight to its evolutionary approach to reunification and the Anglo-Irish objective of EEC entry (External Affairs, 1969, 1970). The formula owed something to a regime crisis over alleged arms smuggling to the North by government ministers, leading to inconclusive trials and a party struggle between evolutionists and ideologists, which the former won (O'Brien, 1971).

(b) Another result of conflict within "loyalist" circles was the creation of the liberal Alliance Party, an outgrowth of an ecumenical and integrationist group, the New Ulster Movement. Drawing from the Unionist, Labor and Liberal parties, the chiefly Protestant Alliance indicted Ultras for obscurantism, Nationalists for rejecting partition, Liberals and Laborites for stressing economics, and all extremists for direct action or violence. Untested at the polls, the Alliance Party is a reminder that Northern Ireland politics includes progressive, British nationalists who judged the sub-system with systemic values ("British standards"), finding that nearly all political actors were imperfect except the government when it reformed. The Alliance Party represents regime supporters who anticipated the governing party's dissolution and prepared a life-raft for reformist Unionists and Catholic moderates dissatisfied with other choices. Its purpose was not fully utilized in the civil rights phase.

(3) In the minority community the results of the civil rights conflict included the energizing of preexisting politicized elements, their adoption of new idioms and means and entry into a comprehensive structure (CRA). There followed the mobilization and participation of former parochials, the emergence of a mood of achievement and self-confidence, and the decline of optimism and solidarity.

(a) The civil rights conflict resulted in serious impairment to the Nationalist Party, Republican Labor Party, and the Northern Ireland Labor Party. The civil rights movment had roots in all three parties and received support from them. But the movement adopted an idiom and tactics that they had not often employed in their nationalist or working-class appeals and parliamentary or trade union methods. Facing rigid governments, these appeals and methods had not been productive of significant reforms whereas the civil rights movement—coupled with a meliorist government—produced some democratic changes despite Ultra resistence. The inadequacy of the minority's traditional opposition became evident in the 1969 decline of Nationalist Party seats in the Stormont House from nine to six due to the election of three civil rights independents, John Hume, Ivan Cooper and Patrick O'Hanlon. Although the NIL and RL maintained two MP's each, they, too, encountered adversity after the formal end of the civil rights phase when prominent leaders headed by RL Gerry Fitt, the Westminister MP with British Labor ties, joined the independents and some Nationalists to form the Social Democratic Labor Party (SDL) in August 1970. By this time civil rights protest had declined and violence had risen in minority areas to the embarrassment of most SDL founders.

(b) A beneficiary of but not an originator or prime component in the rights movement, the low-ebb IRA was revitalized and divided because of the conflict. An insurgency wing (Provisionals) began to grow in numbers and power as the rights phase ended without resolving its own dispute with the political and socialist wing (Officials) or offering a vital challenge to the regime.[11] The IRA was indebted to the rights movement for influencing the regime to nearly refrain from using live ammunition and the Special Powers Act until mid-1971.

(c) A prime factor in the civil rights conflict, People's Democracy experienced counter-influences from the regime and fellow oppositionists so that by the end of 1970 it was no longer at the center of the struggle as it had been in 1968-1969. Early in 1969 PD succeeded in penetrating the CRA to try to reduce communist and IRA influence and to make the organization a broadly-based, socialist agency. PD lost its CRA position a year later.

Mobilizing and prosecuting radical discontent which abandoned partition mentality to seek a socialist Ireland, PD had an impact on the North and the South which is beyond measurement at this stage of analysis. One may suggest that PD's influence on others exceeded contrary influence. Suspected within and outside the regime of being Trotskyite or anarchist, PD contributed to the new mode of politics and the advancement of civil rights only to be outflanked by civil rights politicians of the center. PD's relative decline is explainable by the gap between its philosophy and nationalist ideology, the granting of some reforms, and the escalation of violence and sectarianism which it rejected.

(d) The conflict generated citizens defense committees, prominently in Belfast and Derry, which mobilized and organized minority efforts to resist or negotiate with police and army authorities who sought with uneven success to enforce the law in Catholic locales. Attracting middle-class and clerical support, they tended to become nonrevolutionary power bases for future

SDL leaders. The emergency groups helped to preserve minority ethnocentricity and communal morale during stress.

(e) Disorder concerned the Roman Catholic Church. Entering the unrest with eclectic loyalties and objectives, the Church supported peaceful means and a redress of minority grievances. Assessments brought controversies. The Hierarchy responded to the serious disturbances in August 1969 with charges that Ultra militants were responsible, a judgment that drew criticism of Cardinal Conway, the Primate of Ireland, from Protestant spokesmen. Yet the Hierarchy's policy moved toward support of the regime when structural reforms were promised. This trend was confirmed subsequently. At the end of 1970 the Church accepted an invitation of two years' standing to name a chaplain to the Stormont Parliament. By this act the Catholic Church gave recognition to the northern regime which surpassed any earlier Petrine acknowledgement of Caesar and partition.

(4) Contrasting with earlier ideas and methods, the civil rights struggle troduced new ideas and methods into the minority's opposition to the regime. ithout replacing the older notions and techniques, the civil rights movement)ened Northern Ireland to the *possibility* of a new politics, grounded on ideals ore inclusive than the traditional norms of self-determination and confession 1 which both communities had depended.

(a) The civil rights movement declined under the influence of such factors as majority doubts about sincerity, attainment of several reforms, leadership diffusion, inexperience in non-sectarian politics, and the persistence of conventional idioms and means of opposition.

(b) Especially noteworthy as an adverse factor for the civil rights movement was the military response to the Ultras. The extraordinary introduction in August 1969 of the British Army guarded the rights movement against Ultras and later permitted the reformers to continue beyond their high period to exercise the right of dissent and to press for additional changes. Yet the intervention of a crisis military force, welcomed at the time by the non-Republican, minority members who had experienced Ultra civilian and police violence, deflated the atmosphere in which civil protest for minority rights had first appeared and begun to thrive.

The military buildup was a setback to any vision in which the Northern Ireland regime possessed stability without significant latent or manifest coercion. Beyond that disappointment the escalation was a reversal for one of the few creative developments in the recent political history of Ireland. Systemic governments in Westminster had let devolution and therefore Ultra Unionism to remain unsupervised except in broad outline for nearly a half-century. When the sub-system's first conciliationist government began to liberalize the regime and Ultras threatened it as well as the civil rights movement, the higher authorities responded with excessive military forces to replace inadequate or partisan police to keep the peace. That the minority had welcomed the British Army as "defenders" should not be given significant attention. For the police displacement and army buildup militarized the sub-system's political and social orders to the benefit of Ultras and the Provisional IRA and to the detriment of a humanistic and democratizing movement that had begun to link the two communities.

(5) The interaction of the political sub-system and its social environments 1s revealed to observers who may not have been fully aware of how the regime

and the minority relate to their divergent ethnic and confessional heritages and social institutions. Some detachment of governing segments (Unionist moderates) from political dependency on traditional socio-political structures, e.g., the Orange Order, can be identified, along with a slight shift in the ascendent ideology toward a secular idiom. Ecumenism first rose and then declined. The government's creation of a cabinet-level Community Relations Commission began to foster sociable attitudes and mutual respect through public and Catholic educational structures and voluntary associations without uniting or displacing them.

An experiment in direct anti-atavism, a law against incitement to hatred was passed. But pertinent systemic legislation on employment discrimination was not adopted, despite minority urgings. The new ombudsmen found few complaints about sectarian preference to have merit. Supportive of civil rights demands but critical of socialist and violent currents among communicants, the church of the minority began to detach itself from an ambivalent outlook on the regime and to move toward without reaching de jure acceptance in response to the granting of concessions and clerical inability to eliminate the IRA's appeal to Catholic workers.

(6) As a consequence of civil conflict and the central system's response to it indicated above, the sub-system's autonomy within the system decreased under political, administrative and military "intervention." Ideologically, British nationalism or liberal imperialism gained and Ulster nationalism receded. The London regime ended the parliamentary custom of not discussing sub-systemic problems in detail and implied the possibility of cancelling Stormont to govern directly unless it adopted reforms. Yet to bolster Unionism and dismay Irish nationalism the two governments reaffirmed that the sub-system would not cease to be a part of the system without the consent of the people of Northern Ireland.[12] "People" means the majority community unless and until the minority becomes the majority through population increase, an unlikely development in this century.[13]

III

During the civil rights phase slight progress was made in movement toward a secularized and universalistic political culture, enhanced capacity for attitudinal and structural innovation, and a detachment of the political subsystem from primordial and ascriptive sentiments and loyalties in the social environment. But by the end of 1969 these traditional forces had recovered to compete again.

As to a standard of autonomy for the political sub-system with respect to other political systems, conflict produced a reduction in Northern Ireland's devolved authority and power within its comprehensive system (U.K.). This may be listed as a gain in terms of conventional devolution's retardation of the sub-system according to democratic norms. Yet no prospect appeared of ending the dominant party's monopoly of the government or of parliamentary sharing of power. Northern Ireland experienced a strengthening of its legal and political posture in relation to a competitive system, the Republic of Ireland. Here one may note a possible achievement at the expense of another polity.

Developmental criteria of increased governmental power and greater consensus about the sub-system's legitimacy have unclear results. Governmental power may seem to have risen in repressive capacity. But what of support for a controversial regime? The relative absence of insurrection by minority and related dissidents during the civil rights phase suggests the possibility of an upswing in their consensual attitude in response to regime reforms. But even if this were true, and there is no survey evidence to help decide, the 1970-1972 conflict suggests that any upswing may have declined significantly in the next phase.

Huntington (1965) has argued that rapid mobilization and participation of citizens in systems without previous institutional adjustment to this kind of experience may lead to systemic decay. On this question sufficient data may not be available to judge Ulster's civil rights phase with any certainty. Yet one should not ignore that in the present case the sub-system survived a considerable mobilization, and to some degree, participation, of many previously alienated or passive minority members without decaying either in the meaning of regime collapse or shrinkage of participatory opportunities.

In the civil rights phase the sub-system of Northern Ireland was progressively altered in ways not previously accomplished by traditional means of opposition to the regime—parliamentary politics, constitutional boycott, and political violence. Not only was the regime partially reformed but so was the opposition owing to a diversification of its means of struggle through street politics and civil disobedience. There were two sides to "innovation" in the civil rights phase of Ulster's conflict.

NOTES

1. The forces at work in Northern Ireland are interpreted from an Irish nationalist and socialist perspective in De Paor (1970). Unionist assumptions and themes are found in Wilson (1955).
2. Terrence O'Neill's (1969: 112 ff.) strategy for improving community relations was paternalistic in style and integrationist in objective.
3. For the Lemass transition which had economic determinants, see MacDonagh (1968: 130-135), and Coogan (1966: 105-110, 164-165).
4. For the convoluted but ongoing history of the IRA, see Bell (1970).
5. For a positive estimate of devolution, see Wilson (1955: 183-211). An earlier study found that devolution had been a low-yield success: Mansergh (1936). A favorable judgment of public finance and public services is Lawrence (1965). Brett (1970) finds democratic shortfalls, and Coughlan (1969) asks for a special Bill of Rights to correct them.
6. The extent of the plural franchise can be measured by 1967 register data showing 28,883 additional eligibles for the Stormont Parliament than for the Westminster Parliament (909, 841) which had slightly different residence criteria. Franchise problems are discussed critically in Mertens (1969).
7. For elaboration and analysis of the Special Powers Act, see Calvert (1968: 380-389).
8. The functions of civil disobedience in an aspirant democratic system are suggested in Power (1972a). A functional evaluation of all actors using civil protest in Ulster is reported in Power (1972b).
9. Ms. Devlin's autobiography (1969) is a guide to recent unrest and her political socialization. PD leaders discuss their goals and strategy in Farrell (1969: 3-19).
10. Accounts are found in Edwards (1970), Orange and Green (1969), Hastings (1970), Riddell (1970), and Wallace (1970). The conflicts were reported in the Belfast Telegraph and the Irish Times and interpreted in the Observer and Hibernia.
11. The IRA divided soon after August 1969 when it was unable to defend Catholic areas in Belfast against Ultra invaders. The Provisionals adopted a military tactic and censured the Officials for unpreparedness and Marxist-Leninist notions.
12. See the Joint Declaration of the Wilson and Chichester-Clark governments on August 19, 1969, included in Stormont's effort to defend its pre-conflict record, explain reforms and call for mutuality and peaceful development: A Commentary ... Cmd. 534 (Government of Northern Ireland, 1969).

13. The minority's birth rate is 28.3 per thousand, 40 percent higher than the majority's. However, the minority's emigration rate is twice that of the majority's. Improved economic opportunity would reduce this gap. The projection of a Catholic majority for 2021 based on the most favorable set of assumptions for minority growth is made by the Economic and Social Research Institute: The Irish Times, June 11, 1970.

REFERENCES

BRETT, C.E.B. (1970) "The lessons of devolution in northern Ireland." Political Q. 41 (July-September): 261-280.

CALVERT, H. (1968) Constitutional Law in Northern Ireland. London and Belfast: Oxford University Press.

COOGAN, T. P. (1966) Ireland Since the Rising. New York: Praeger.

COUGHLAN, A. (1969) The Northern Crisis. Dublin: Solidarity Publications.

De PAOR, L. (1970) Divided Ulster. Baltimore: Penguin Books.

DEVLIN, B. (1969) The Price of My Soul. New York: Alfred A. Knopf.

EDWARDS, O. D. (1970) The Sins of Our Fathers: London: Gill and Macmillan.

FARRELL, M. (1969) "People's democracy: a discussion on strategy." New Left Rev. 55 (May-June): 3-19.

Government of Northern Ireland (1970) Report, Review Body on Local Government in Northern Ireland (P. A. Macrory, chairman; Cmd. 546). Belfast: Her Majesty's Stationery Office.

——— (1969a) Disturbances in Northern Ireland (Cameron Report, Cmd. 532). Belfast: Her Majesty's Stationery Office.

——— (1969b) A Commentary by the Government of Northern Ireland to Accompany the Cameron Report (Cmd. 534). Belfast: Her Majesty's Stationery Office.

——— (1969c) Report of the Advisory Committee on Police in Northern Ireland (Lord Hunt, chairman; Cmd. 535). Belfast: Her Majesty's Stationery Office.

HASTINGS, M. (1970) Ulster: 1969. London: Gollancz.

HUNTINGTON, S. P. (1965) "Political development and political decay." World Politics 18 (April): 386-430.

LAWRENCE, R. J. (1965) The Government of Northern Ireland. Oxford: Oxford University Press.

MacDONAGH, O. (1968) Ireland. Englewood Cliffs, N.J.: Prentice-Hall.

MANSERGH, N. (1936) The Government of Northern Ireland. London: Allen & Unwin.

MERTENS, C. (1969) "Report on civil and social rights in Northern Ireland." J. of International and Comparatiave Law 2, 3.

O'BRIEN, C. C. (1971) "Irish troubles: the boys in the back room." New York Rev. (April 8): 35-39.

O'NEILL, T. (1969) Ulster at the Crossroads. London: Faber & Faber.

ORANGE and GREEN (1969) A Quaker Study of Community Relations in Northern Ireland. N.P.

POWER, P. F. (1972a) "Civil disobedience as functional opposition." Journal of Politics 34 (February): 37-55.

——— (1972b) "Civil protest in Northern Ireland." J. of Peace Research 3: 223-236.

Republic of Ireland (1969, 1970) Bulletin of the Department of External Affairs (August 28, 1969 and July 13, 1970).

RIDDELL, P. (1970) Fire Over Ulster. London: Hamish Hamilton.

ROSE, R. (1971) Governing Without Consensus: An Irish Perspective. Boston: Beacon Press.

——— (1970) "The dynamics of a divided regime." Government and Opposition 5 (Spring): 166-192.

WALLACE, M. (1970) Drums and Guns: Revolution in Ulster. London: Geoffrey Chapman.

WILSON, T. [ed.] (1955) Ulster Under Home Rule. London: Oxford University Press.

Chapter 22

INTERNAL AND EXTERNAL CONFLICTS OF
AN AMERICAN INDIAN COMMUNITY

HARRY S. COBLENTZ

My involvement with the Fort McDowell Mojave-Apache Community, twenty miles northeast of Phoenix, Arizona, began about six years ago when I was asked to present a programmatic proposal for a community comprehensive plan to be funded under Section 701 of the U.S. Housing Act of 1965. The program although approved in 1968 was not funded until September 1970 but in the meantime working contacts were started with tribal officials and local Bureau of Indian Affairs representatives as well as other members of the community (Coblentz, 1971).

My professional concern for Fort McDowell dwells on several issues including social problems, housing, land development legislation, economic prognosis, a preliminary development plan and its relationship to the Central Arizona Project. The Report of the United States Senate Subcommittee on Indian Education—A National Tragedy—A National Challenge (1969: ix) begins by stating that:

"The American vision of itself is of a nation of citizens determining their own destiny; of cultural difference flourishing in an atmosphere of mutual respect; of diverse people shaping their lives and the lives of their children."

The future role of American Indians is based on a new piece of legislation rather than the colonial regulations of a benevolent nation. Treaties are now being re-examined with the benefit of principles which recognize the wrongs done to Indians and also their place in our total society.

At the local level, Fort McDowell Indian Community was more than aware of the need to project its concerns beyond that of a physical plan so from the outset the Tribal Council agreed that the preparation of a social plan was complementary to the traditional physical plan prepared by planners.

A public facilities plan showing the proposed location of a new school for tribal children seemed less than real or even necessary when the tribes' children were being subjected to rude pressures within the local school district because they were minority or Indian children. A value system for understanding and evaluating these problems and challenges is one of the significant purposes of the plan (Klein, 1968).

The question will doubtless arise what of these plans? Will they amount to anything simply because they are more humanistically oriented than simply physical in nature? A plan of action has been started by the tribal council using several types of funding provided by the Bureau of Indian Affairs (BIA) and involving tribal members. In addition, an entirely new and continuing resource has been made available to the Community by the consultant in his capacity as a faculty member in the College of Human Development at The Pennsylvania State

University. Every two terms four students of the Community Development Division will carry out their practicums for two terms under the direction and supervision of the BIA program coordinator at the Fort McDowell Community. This ongoing involvement is described later and it does constitute a new form of program implementation which is so vital for the success of this or any plan and its stated objectives. For the consultant, the practicum is invaluable because it provides an excellent method for obtaining information on current social events within the tribe and which can only be provided through the students' peers in the tribe.

CULTURAL BACKGROUND FOR DETERMINATION OF SOCIAL ISSUES

The Fort McDowell Indian Community is located twenty-eight miles northeast of downtown Phoenix and thirteen miles north of Mesa. The reservation is four miles wide, ten miles long, and is bisected lengthwise by the Verde River, one of Arizona's few flowing streams. Its south boundaries begin one and one-half miles above the junction with the Salt River. The Reservation contains 24,680 acres, none of which is allocated.

The Reservation is occupied almost entirely by the Mojave-Apache Tribe which numbers about 250 persons,[1] 230 of whom live at Fort McDowell. Most of the children attend public schools in Mesa but a few older students are in BIA schools in Phoenix and California.

Originally established as the Camp McDowell Reserve on January 1, 1873, the land was set aside as the Fort McDowell Indian Reservation pursuant to Executive Order of September 15, 1903. Lands of settlers who had moved into the area were purchased by an Act of April 2, 1904. There is little of what non-Indians call Indian culture in the tribe's outward actions but in its internal organization it has all the stresses and conflicts of many Indian groups. This is also its strength because it becomes its cohesive force.

Water rights for some 1,300 acres of irrigable land were granted to the Reservation by the Kent Decree in 1910. Little pastoral farming is carried out on the reservation although cattle raising by tribal families is becoming quite significant and these excellent water rights are a great asset to the tribe.

The riparian lands of the Verde River are already much in use as a recreational facility and as part of the comprehensive plan a section is devoted to the extended use of this natural feature. There is a considerable use of the river area by persons who pay a small fee to the tribal community and preliminary discussions have taken place with federal, state, and county officials as well as private investors to develop further this natural resource; the Verde is one of three flowing streams in Arizona. Such discussions may seem somewhat premature in view of the recently announced proposal to undertake construction of the Central Arizona Project (CAP) which will divert water from the Colorado River to urban communities and farming lands in central and southern Arizona. However it is by no means assured that the CAP will be built and during the early days of this plan's formulation two planning stages were proposed: pre-flooding and post-flooding.

The current plans of the U.S. Bureau of Reclamation indicate a central water storage facility to be located several miles south of the Reservation on the Verde River. This facility, called the Orme Dam, will create a lake which will submerge, at maximum level, about twelve to fifteen thousand acres of the Reservation's twenty-five-thousand acres as well as creating serious dysfunctions because of the various discrete parcels created. The economic impact[2] of this proposal to the Fort McDowell Indian Community has been undertaken in 1968 with a grant from the Bureau of Reclamation but it did not assume to interpret the feeling of the community with respect to the desirability of the project vis-a-vis Fort McDowell lands. In fact, recent indications suggest that the community seriously questions its approval of the project. Either way the Fort McDowell Indian Community clearly recognizes it has a most valuable piece of real estate. Although what the realizable value will be is another matter, particularly in view of the creation of numerous small land parcels.

Some of the problems arising from this uncertainty as to the future of the community's land and the CAP which has been projected for a completion date of 1985 did occur when the U.S. Public Health Service and the U.S. Department of Housing and Urban Development declined to install a water system for new housing because the facilities would become obsolete when the community would be submerged. However in mid-1970 these two federal agencies agreed to go ahead with their participation in a much-needed housing project because it could be expected to have at least a ten-year life (compare U.S. Department of Housing and Urban Development, 1969: 8). This illustrates a conflict point which in part has been satisfactorily resolved, and arose because the under thirty group wished to believe that their elders get priority treatment for new housing but found no evidence to support their belief (Jones, 1968: 21).

Concerns such as this may not seem uncommon but to a sub-cultural group such as the Fort McDowell Community it seems to be just another insurmountable problem posed in both instances by the outside society (but see Barnett, 1953: 40).

THE FORT McDOWELL CONCEPT OF PLANNING

The Fort McDowell Tribal Council in the preparation of this plan decided very early on that it did not want to see a grandiose document which did nothing more than paint a picture of things which could not be, or which failed to respond to the total needs of the community it represented (McLoughlin, 1969).

It was on this basis that the agreement between the Fort McDowell Community and the planning consultant was struck. The State Department of Economic Planning and Development, its predecessor organization the University of Arizona, and U.S. Department of Housing and Urban Development (HUD) have acknowledged this special relationship in their approvals of the planning contract for Fort McDowell. One of the points made is that with its relative economic emancipation, Fort McDowell has become a microcosm of its larger metropolitan society—Phoenix which was formerly an isolated southwestern small city but is now undergoing vast upheavals due to its general economic development and tremendous population growth.

THE NEW BIA POSTURE FOR PLANNING

The Commissioner of Indian Affairs, Louis R. Bruce, in a memorandum[3] dated August 14, 1970 amplified the President's message of July 8, 1970 to Congress on Indian policy; Commissioner Bruce said:

"I place absolute top priority on achieving Indian participation in program development. Until Indian people participate in planning and developing Bureau budgets at the Agency level, they will not be completely aware of the scope, commitment or, in some instances, the limitations of BIA programs or other BIA activities. Without this basic knowledge, local Indian leadership will be unable to make *our* system *their* system.

"The long-term goal that I seek through joint budget development is to give Indian leadership the opportunity to initiate a process of negotiating with local BIA administrators for the tribes to take over and administer a range of programs which we have traditionally administered for them. In certain instances it is likely that programs will be taken over intact; in other cases Indian people will find our existing programs unresponsive to their needs and undertake to restructure them radically. They must know the BIA system to do either.

"Tribal Participation

"One question the Indian people will want answered is: How do we translate their ideas into operational terms? Superintendents hold the key to success, and I have this general advice to offer before turning to specific program suggestions."

He continued:

"Tribal leaders cannot reasonably be expected to learn about budget development isolated from an understanding of the fundamentals of Agency operation. Many Indian people with whom I have talked seem convinced that we try to keep them in the dark in this area. Here is an opportunity to prove that we keep no secrets (other than personnel records, welfare case sheets, or similar documents involving individual privacy) from the tribes we serve.

"Planning, Objectives, and Goals

"One cannot intelligently talk about development without relating it to meeting the long-term goals which communities must set for themselves and to the development of practical strategies for achieving these objectives. This is the embodiment of sound planning, an element which has been generally absent in the development of reservation programs to date.

"What too often has passed for 'reservation planning' has been the fleeting efforts of outside experts. We could fill an archive with planning documents developed in this manner. Most not only do not reflect the goals of community members, but the few which do usually have failed to forge the vital links between the planning participants—the Indian people—and the ultimate solutions to the planning problems they face. Do not encourage any more planning of this sort.

"Clearly, there is a great deal of preliminary work of a generalist nature—that is, not requiring the retaining of experts—which first must be undertaken to assist a community to assemble the ideas which must precede developing a 'comprehensive' plan. I expect superintendents to plan key roles in this critical area by helping local leadership to rough in the parameters of a community plan and to sort out the logical alternatives for solving some of the problems uncovered in this effort.

"I also expect superintendents to take the initiative in compiling lists of resources that Indian leadership can draw upon in developing and implementing comprehensive development plans. Seven of the eleven Executive Departments provide clearly earmarked services to Indians, to say nothing of scores of other programs which can be shaped to meet Indian needs.

"While the general objective is to enhance the level of living for Indian people, this may be described in many ways by tribal people. One group might specify a particular change in per capita income as its goal; while another may state its desire to maintain the land base. There will be extremes in manner in which these objectives may be articulated. It is the BIA's job to make certain that local tribal objectives and priorities are defined in such a manner as to allow an assessment to be made to determine if BIA is responsive to these objectives. If our programs are not responsive, then it is BIA's task to work with local tribal people to define programs that will be responsive to tribal objectives."

To what degree this will occur remains very much a local matter involving both the American Indian group and the attitude of the BIA officials. For Fort McDowell the proposed mixture is perfect and fits in well with its present circumstances.

THE FORT McDOWELL
INDIAN COMMUNITY ORGANIZATION

The Fort McDowell group was organized most recently in 1936 and 1938 when the corporate charter and constitution and by-laws were approved by the appropriate groups at Fort McDowell and the U.S. Department of Interior.

The governing body of the Fort McDowell Community is the Tribal Council and consists of five members elected by qualified voters of the community serving as follows: three members elected at the end of one year and two members for the following year. There has been a great deal of factiousness at nomination times and several years ago when a dissident minority felt unhappy with the election results anonymous letters were mailed to certain tribal members, but the Tribal Council called in the Federal Bureau of Investigation and no more such activity has been reported. The threat was met with force.

The Tribe has been most concerned with revision of the by laws and the consultant has included it as part of his advisory role to assist in such an activity.[4]

Recognizing that with the impending development of its land and contiguous lands a new advisory group is required, the Tribal Council has agreed to the formation of a planning board, which will consist of persons from within and outside the council membership. This is important and significant since the community is small and planning and development should not be separated.

THE FORT McDOWELL
TRIBAL OFFICE ORGANIZATION

Reflection of the new role to be given Tribal organization is the upgrading of the status of the Fort McDowell tribal office with the appointment of Mr. Samuel L. Hilliard as full-time program coordinator from a prior joint appointment with the neighboring Salt River Reservation.

This primary role will be to "bring about a diminishment of the Bureau's conventional function in favor of strengthening the role of the Indian community."[5]

A statement of his duties clearly spells out the new BIA posture and provides a sense of direction for the administrative framework which is supportive to the community plan.

COMMUNITY INVOLVEMENT AND EDUCATION

Recently the community expressed concern and distress over degrading treatment meted its younger school population. Intensive discussions[6] took place between the group, the planning consultant, the community's psychiatric social worker, and the BIA program coordinator. It was felt that the insensitive treatment should be handled on a group basis so that one parent would not have to be concerned with future after-effects to his or her child or children while in school. This unfortunate incident and a subsequent school vehicle problem have become a catalytic process making it possible to organize a parents' group on a continuing basis which will be able to discuss the many problems confronting parents dealing with a school system in which they have no political representation[7] and from which they are geographically detached. In the summer of 1970 the writer taught twenty American Indian teachers at Pennsylvania State University who had been brought there under the aegis of the BIA as part of a special executive training program. These men and women wanted to have all schools for Indians operated by BIA since they felt they could manipulate the BIA system as opposed to the public school system.

The parents' group has held two meetings and judging by reports from a number of different sources its interests and concerns have been well defined and the group is actively pursuing various elements and their solutions. The new corporate strength of the group is demonstrated by the account of an incident at the second meeting when the Mesa Public School representative, who wished to enter the meeting hall, was denied admission until he was formally invited and then at the end of his presentation it was made clear that he could leave. This organization should be regarded as a new mechanism for taking community action on a wider range of points and issues such as the Central Arizona Project and land leases.

A tribal council newsletter is now published monthly and through it the parents group will inform other tribal members of their program and activities; the tribal young people also contribute items including poetry and stories.

All parents are concerned about the type of education their children receive but Fort McDowell parents are probably more sensitive than most because there are sufficient touch-points of discrimination to warrant immediate attention. Some of these touch-points can be classified as purely educational in terms of expectancy, although others are classically Indian versus white. With respect to the former the Tribal Council has renewed formerly unfruitful discussions with the Mesa Public Schools and notes that a newly founded project known as "Incentives Only" may be helpful to Fort McDowell school-age children. In a recent letter to the planning consultant the project director of the Center for Educational Advancement in Mesa wrote:

"Mesa has approximately 730 Indian students enrolled in Grades 1-12. The 'Incentives Only' Project has 69 students in the experimental classes and 59 students in the control schools.

"The Mesa Public Schools signed a contract with the Office of Economic Opportunity (OEO) and a subcontract with the Mesa Education Association. The purpose of our participation is to assist in the research regarding the use of incentives to accelerate achievement in reading and mathematics. The amount of the OEO grant is $38,376.

"Approximately 1200 students are involved in the Project. About 100 students per grade level at the 1, 2, 3, 7, 8, and 9 grades are included in the experimental sample. A similar number of students from a parallel sample will comprise the control group. Three elementary schools and one junior high constitute each experimental and control group.

"The educational materials utilized are the same as would normally be employed. This is not a machine oriented program, and there are no plans to initiate a machine program. The only added ingredient not normally available is the use of incentives to students and teachers.

"The Project administrators, teachers and the Mesa Education Association are developing models for the distribution of incentives. The exact types of incentives to students and teachers have not been finalized at this time. All types of incentives will probably be used to some degree; however, material incentives to students will probably be minimal [but see Suttles, 1968: 58—Author].

"The earnings possible in this Project are based upon a minimal performance level of the children involved. If students meet or exceed the minimal gain, the MEA will earn additional monies on a per month gain basis. All payments out of the escrow account will be based on gains on a per student per subject base. Some teachers involved are not concerned about incentives for themselves but rather to determine if incentives to students do, in fact, accelerate achievement in reading and mathematics.

"As with other OEO performance contacts, Battelle Memorial Institute of Columbus Ohio is conducting the testing and evaluation of this Project. Turnkey Systems of Washington, D.C. is serving as the management support agency."[8]

The adults of the Fort McDowell Community do not intend to set up a school monitoring process but they are themselves products of a system which they only too well know to be self-fulfilling. Thus, they are extremely concerned with the benefits to be gained from improvements in the system and in the sub-system which they contend exists for their children.

Recently Edward J. Meade Jr. in a foreword to the Ford Foundation publication *Toward Humanistic Education* (Weinstein and Fantini, 1970: ix) stated:

"Education takes the world as its subject; it is the process by which we learn of the past and the present in order to shape the future. At the same time, of course, education acts on the world of which it is a part; educational processes and programs are instruments for changing the world."

Although the parents of Fort McDowell school children may not quite phrase their concerns in this macro-fashion they are very much aware that their children may be denied what they need for fulfillment of their human potential. The parents are very willing to work with educators for they do not regard themselves as alien to the society in which they and their children are transported both metaphorically and physically.

Some of the high school students attend BIA boarding schools at Riverside, California, Stewart, Nevada, and Phoenix and one of the reasons given is that the students receive more attention and the costs[9] to parents are less in a number of different ways. For the students, there is the hardship of being away from home but in return there is an active school life including after hours recreation the lack of which at Fort McDowell is discussed later.

PRE-SCHOOL CHILDREN

There is an active headstart program conducted at the Salt River Reservation Centre on East McDowell Road and the Tribal Council has a station wagon which carries ten pupils the twenty mile one-way journey. As part of the continued expansion of Fort McDowell's communal activities it is most likely that a Headstart program will start there. This has distinct economic advantages since the community will benefit from additional tribal members being employed at the new centre.

ADULT EDUCATION AND WORK OPPORTUNITIES

As a concerted activity little has been done in this area and it includes job training, re-training, mid-career changes and the usual but often misconceived continuing education component. Some of the younger men wish to raise their educational levels and for a number it would mean an immediate income improvement since a large number work for local and federal government departments and educational attainment is continuously recognized. As part of the general social work and counselling area more opportunities need to be given adult tribal members. If during the next decade the Central Arizona Project is constructed, a large number of extant City of Phoenix Water Department employees may become redundant and should this happen job re-training and selection will have to be carried out promptly and efficiently. With new programs being made available to Indian Reservations and the simultaneous BIA process of "Buy Indian" there will be new job opportunities for Fort McDowell men and women as social work aides, para-professionals in health, child day-care centers, juvenile programs, recreational activities, and aides for care of the elderly.

Additionally new tribal enterprises are being planned at the entrance to the reservation which will require business and trades training. Adult education courses may be offered at the Salt River Indian Centre, Scottsdale or Mesa Community Colleges or later, even at a public school to be built at the northeast corner of neighboring Fountain Hills which Fort McDowell grade school children may attend.

It is clear from many discussions ranging over a period of several years that there are ample job opportunities in the greater Phoenix area, but with the change in the valley's agricultural economy more persons will be thrown into the non-skilled workers' cauldron of despair and the Fort McDowell worker must be trained to meet the more exacting demands of employers. This question must be posed: is the limitation of opportunities always resulting from discrimination or from a legitimate rejection of workers who lack skills? At this point of time there is absolutely no reason to believe the first condition is true and employers wanting to employ Fort McDowell Indians appear to be extremely flexible in their personnel practices.

HEALTH

This is a very complex problem with concerns ranging from infant health to comprehensive and continuous medical care for the aged. A U.S. Public Health Service Clinic is now held weekly[10] at Fort McDowell and a major hospital facility is available at the new Indian Hospital in Phoenix. Many go to private doctors in Mesa or Scottsdale because they have the income to do so although the above mentioned facilities are available to all tribal members. Additionally a large number of families is covered by the male worker's medical insurance plan (Kahn, 1969: 23).

An inspected and approved water supply is available to all but one or two houses so that a problem confronting many Indian and non-Indian rural persons is not found here.

Transportation to medical care facilities outside the reservation is not considered by tribal members to be a problem. Under a recent agreement elderly members of the Fort McDowell Community can be placed in a nursing home with all costs borne by the BIA, although now the consultant and the tribal council are considering a small care centre on the reservation serving Fort McDowell as well as a number of other small reservations.

Care of the elderly within the Fort McDowell Community will become an increasingly significant problem and a variety of solutions is being considered.

RECREATION

One of the main complaints aired by school-age children and the younger adults is lack of recreation.[11] A program is being re-activated and a building formerly used as the recreation center has been completely renovated with the assistance of the Penn State students. BIA will fund a program including the hiring of a part-time recreation director and for the last several months a number of young Fort McDowell adults have established an ongoing program with the assistance of the PSU Practicum students who came as resource persons and are in attendance each night.

The plans for the basketball court are now being implemented and the community center design will be developed by local architects with funds supplied by the federal government.

The basketball teams are transported to local matches by their trainer and volunteers but intra-community transportation is a problem particularly for the younger children since the residential section of the reservation extends over five miles and a preliminary investigation of need is being carried out under the direction of the consulting planner.

The isolation of the community has many advantages from a traditional standpoint but boredom is a disruptive and destructive force and immediate and continuing activities are being developed and sponsored by the community. Again the numbers of children and young adults, whose involvement is crucial, is small but the opportunities for future employment and education are relatively good so that to neglect this component of an individual's life is short-sighted and could prove to be disastrous in this changing society in which Fort McDowell is also undergoing such great change.

EVALUATION OF PROGRAMS
TO BE IMPLEMENTED BY TRIBE

The Tribal Council is very concerned with evaluation of programs being undertaken in the community and it can be said that it has considered a cybernetic approach to program fulfillment. In as much that the socio-cultural system acts as a buffer between the members of a community and their environment, the basic argument will be that any planned change in the environmental system must be actively sensitive to the laws of the system. The planning process and final plan must be contingent upon the sociocultural pheonomena to which it will be exposed and to the negative effects which its execution might create.

CONCLUSION

Poverty as a normative condition is not found at Fort McDowell although there are occasional problems. Its major problems focus around a desire to achieve greater individual economic emancipation and the work force profile shows this. The Tribal Council is not capable of recommending policies for modifying basic biological and psychological conditions for the community but it can, and does, intend to prepare plans for consideration by the community which will improve the quality of life in areas including education, economic opportunities, personal health, environmental health and community mental health, recreation, housing and community organization.

The future of Fort McDowell cannot be defined by a single goal, but by a combination of goals. Fort McDowell, as any other Indian community, has dependencies and relationships with the larger society but considering its proximity to Metropolitan Phoenix the relationship requires new levels of cooperation. The Comprehensive community plan will suggest the methods by which this integration can be imaginatively and realistically handled.

Today, people everywhere are living through a change in the human scene that challenges many ideas and institutions inherited from other days. Their awareness of their natural environment; their relationship with other people; and their sense of the possibilities in human life; all these have been transformed. Fort McDowell has as one of its problems to plan on the basis of a Central Arizona Project *or* no Central Arizona Project. Long-run successes cannot be assured by short-term changes. There is a tendency in humankind to see the immediate effects of a policy or the effects on a special group or situation, and not to inquire into the long-run effects.[12]

Fort McDowell is part of a system which must establish criteria for its validity. Recently Donald N. Michael (1968: 3) wrote that:

> "The general argument of this book is that the convergence of certain social and technological trends will lead to much more extensive use of long-range planning even though we are ill prepared institutionally, methodologically, and personally to do it well."

Trends must be identified within the Metropolitan Phoenix community and established as a policy on a cooperative basis. Metropolitan leadership in both the private and public sectors has been lacking and sub-sets of the system such as Fort McDowell will suffer if it is not forthcoming.

A belief commonly held by non-Indians is that the American Indian truly understands his relationship to his environment. It is not that this is not any longer so, he is simply living in another stage of environment (Brophy and Aberle, 1966: 11). The Fort McDowell community intends to re-establish this relationship and will do this because of its cohesiveness which is Indian based.

NOTES

1. Because of Tribal Census time differentials this figure differs from the Socio-Economic Profile prepared by the BIA, Phoenix office, June, 1969.

2. Confidential Report to the Tribal Council, "The Economic Development Potential of the Fort McDowell Indian Reservation Under Flowing-Stream and Under Orme Dam Conditions, January, 1968," 120 pp. and maps.

3. U.S. Department of Interior BIA, Fiscal Year 1973, Bureau of Indian Affairs Program Development, August 14, 1970.
4. Concern with the Constitution and By-Laws anent nominating procedures and opening hours of the election polls has been expressed formally in an action taken by a Tribal member to the U.S. District Court for the District of Arizona, Civil Action No. 71.47 Phoenix, January 28, 1971. The Plaintiff's complaint was rejected but the Tribal Council does intend to pursue an updating of its regulations.
5. Statement included in U.S. Civil Service Commission Classification Action December, 1970.
6. Tribal Council Meeting, September, 1970, Fort McDowell.
7. The Commissioner for Indian Affairs quoted earlier said in his August, 1970 Memorandum, section on Education, which suggests new procedures for BIA schools but which unfortunately cannot help Fort McDowell. "There are, however, important segments that can be planned and implemented immediately at the local level, specifically the control of local schools by Indian school boards and the use of volunteer services. In order to get the educational contracting program under way at last, I proposed a program of negotiation between superintendents and Indian leadership at the community level. The Washington staff will cooperate fully in the development of individual education contracts and provide advice and technical assistance to Agencies and tribal councils, school boards or other Indian interest groups undertaking negotiations in this area *I want to emphasize the necessity of moving from advisory Indian school boards to control of local schools*" (Commissioner's emphasis).
8. The parent's group will continue to follow this activity with the utmost interest using it as an evaluative tool by which to measure the quality of the educational product rendered their children.
9. All public high school students in Arizona pay for their text books which for many low-income parents is a real hardship. Presently means for obtaining textbooks through public funds is being investigated by the program coordinator at Fort McDowell.
10. The Health Center was a 1965 Tribal Council Goal.
11. Several years ago a tribal member ran a successful program but when he assumed outside duties he had to give it up and the program died.
12. See articles on CAP questioning validity of a quarter-century-old concept in Arizona Republic, Phoenix, June 28, 29, 30, July 1, 1970 by Walter Meek and July 2, 3, 4, and 5, 1970 by Ben Avery.

REFERENCES

BARNETT, H. G. (1953) Innovation: The Basis of Cultural Change. New York: McGraw-Hill.
BROPHY, W. A. and S. A. ABERLE (1966) The Indian America's Unfinished Business. Norman: University of Oklahoma Press.
COBLENTZ, H. S. (1971) Fort McDowell Indian Community Comprehensive Planning Program, Vol. II Social Issues Concept for Social Action, Vol. III Housing and Vol. IV an Economy in Transition. University Park, Pa.: U.S. Department of Housing and Urban Development.
JONES, J. A. (1968) Variables Influencing Behavior in Indigenous Non-Western Cultures. Tempe, Ariz.: Arizona State University
KAHN, A. J. (1969) Studies in Social Policy and Planning. New York: Russell Sage.
KLEIN, D. C. (1968) Community Dynamics and Mental Health. New York: John Wiley.
McLOUGHLIN, B. J. (1969) Urban and Regional Planning: A Systems Approach. London: Faber & Faber.
MICHAEL, D. N. (1968) The Unprepared Society: Planning for a Precarious Future. New York: Harper Colophon.
MICHELSON, W. (1970) Man and His Urban Environment: A Sociological Approach. Menlo Park, Calif.: Addison-Wesley.
SUTTLES, G. D. (1968) The Social Order of the Slum: Ethnicity and Territory in the Inner City. Chicago: University of Chicago Press.
U.S. Department of Housing and Urban Development (1969) Rosebud Indian Reservation: Report on the Transitional Housing Experiment. Washington, D.C.
U.S. Senate, 91st Congress, 1st Session (1969) Report of the Committee on Labor and Public Welfare, Indian Education: A National Tragedy—A National Challenge. Washington, D.C.: GPO.
WEINSTEIN, G. and M. D. FANTINI [eds.] (1970) Toward Humanistic Education. New York: Praeger.

Chapter 23

THE IMPACT OF ETHNICITY AND RELIGION
ON SOCIAL DEVELOPMENT IN
REVOLUTIONARY AMERICA

JANET MERRILL ALGER

*R*evolutionary America may be roughly designated as the period beginning with the Stamp Act controversy in 1765 and ending with the ratification of the U.S. Constitution by the last state in 1790. Though there are no accurate statistics on the ethnic and religious distribution of the population for this era, all existing records indicate that the colonies and early states were overwhelmingly English and Protestant.

At the time of the first U.S. census in 1790, 61 percent of the population were English, 10 percent Irish, 9 percent German, 8 percent Scotch, and the remaining 12 percent were distributed among several very minor groups or the unassigned (U.S. Department of Commerce, 1960). There is little reason to think that this distribution differed substantially at the time of the American Revolution.

In the case of religion, a rough census conducted in 1775 indicates that non-Protestants made up slightly over 1 percent of the population while Protestants were divided as follows: Congregationalists, 31 percent; Anglicans (Episcopalians),[1] 27 percent; Presbyterians, 22 percent; Quakers, 2 percent; and the remaining 16 percent were distributed among several minor groups which will not be distinguished in this paper (Morris, 1953: 550).

From a twentieth-century standpoint this evidence indicates a very homogeneous population because the distinctions made here among Protestants and among northern Europeans have little social significance in the contemporary United States. But before going on to conclude that ethnicity and religion were unimportant variables in revolutionary America, it must be realized that (1) these distinctions were of social significance at that time, and (2) these groups were not evenly distributed among the colonies or early states. The first point will be most easily demonstrated empirically in the following pages by correlating these variables with others. The second point may be demonstrated by a look at the available statistics for the period. The 1790 census indicates that the New England or northern states were the most ethnically homogeneous followed by the southern states. The middle states were the least ethnically homogeneous, and in New Jersey and Pennsylvania the English were less than 50 percent of the population, making these the only states without an English majority (U.S. Department of Commerce, 1960). Again, it is unlikely that this distribution differed at the time of independence. The situation was similar in the case of religion. At the time of the Revolution, Congregationalists were almost entirely from the north where they formed the majority of the population. Episcopalians were the major group in the south while the middle colonies were very mixed religiously. Almost all Quakers lived in Pennsylvania where they constituted about one-third (at most) of the population. Presbyterians had a majority in that colony by the time of the Revolution, were a significant minority in some southern colonies, and had churches in the north as well.[2]

In this paper I will deal with some aspects of the relationship between ethnicity and religion and the political realm in the years immediately preceding and following the Declaration of Independence in 1776 insofar as this relationship applies to the top leaders of the colonies and states of that time. The material to be presented is part of a larger study of 192 top leaders of the period beginning with the American Revolution and ending in 1790. This group was chosen randomly from a near-universe of top leaders who met at least one of six criteria. These men either held the highest positions available in the society of their time, were very wealthy during the specified period, were among the best known professionals, were the first to do something of significance in the New World (such as write the first history of their region), had great and unusual influence over contemporaries as a consequence of personal qualities, or were from the oldest, best-known families in their colony. Information on these leaders was acquired through an "interview schedule" applied to their own writings and the writings of others about them. That is, they were studied as if they were live subjects using a sociological survey design adapted to this historical situation.[3]

ETHNICITY, RELIGION AND INDEPENDENCE

The major relationships I wish to present are those between ethnicity and religion and support for independence during the year immediately preceding that event in 1776. Following the work of Charles C. Moskos (1967) on the West Indies, a typology was constructed to distinguish degrees of support for independence taking account of both the "respondents' " expressed attitude and behavior. True nationalists were those who expressed no reservations about immediate independence and lent their active support to the cause through such means as speeches, pamphlets, and service in the war which began in 1775. Acquiescing nationalists were those who expressed skepticism toward independence, at least in the immediate future, but who went along with the movement for a variety of reasons. Some of these men lent their active support to the cause while others engaged in no activity regarding it. Colonialists were against independence at any time and either actively opposed it or did nothing because the social climate was too hostile toward their views. Thus, three nationalist types were distinguished, ranging from those who fully supported immediate independence from Great Britain to those who strongly opposed it. Of the 154 respondents in the sample who answered the questions from which the typology was constructed, 64 percent were true nationalists, 16 percent were acquiescing nationalists, and 20 percent were colonialists.

When the nationalist types are correlated with ethnicity in Table 1, we see that leaders from the dominant ethnic group, the English, were less likely to support independence than those from the minority groups. Among the minorities, Irish leaders were the most likely to be true nationalists. Looking at

TABLE 1
NATIONALIST TYPES BY ETHNICITY (in percentages)

| | Nationalist Types | | | |
Ethnicity	True Nationalists	Acquiescing Nationalists	Colonialists	Total
English	58	24	18	100 (72)
Scotch[a]	66	7	27	100 (15)
Irish[a]	81	13	6	100 (16)
Other	78	4	18	100 (23)

X^2 = 8.87, 6df, (NS); C.C. = 0.26; .05 or better will be considered significant in this and all other tables to be presented.

a. Respondents were coded on the basis of their father's ethnicity to avoid the possibility of a large "mixed blood" category which would not lend itself to analysis. As a consequence, the "Scotch" and "Irish" categories may confuse the reader. Those in the "Scotch" category were primarily full-blooded highland Scotsmen. Those in the "Irish" category were largely Scotch-Irish. Both groups were Protestant, most often Presbyterian.

the other side of the table, we can see that the Scotch leaders were the most likely to support the colonial regime followed by the English and those in the "Other" category. Acquiescing nationalists were most likely to be drawn from the ranks of the English. Thus, although leaders from all minority groups were more likely to support independence than the dominant English, those of Scotch descent were also more likely to oppose it. In addition to the opposition of the Scots, when the "Other" category is broken down, it turns out that three of the four respondents who opposed independence were German. Since seven German leaders answered the questions on independence, in percentage terms this means that 43 percent of this group opposed independence. Thus, German leaders opposed independence even more strongly than the Scotch. Although the small number of cases renders this finding tenuous, it is consistent with other available information on this group, as will become clear later on.

Before attempting an interpretation of these findings, it will be instructive to look at the relationship between ethnicity and support for independence in each of the three major regions of the colonial period. These are the northern colonies (which encompassed Massachusetts, Rhode Island, Connecticut, and the New Hampshire territories), the middle colonies (which included New York, New Jersey, Pennsylvania, and Delaware), and the southern colonies (which were composed of Maryland, Virginia, North Carolina, South Carolina, and Georgia). Table 2 indicates that the north was ethnically too homogeneous to allow for comment. In the south the support of all groups was high, though English leaders were less likely than those of any minority group to be true nationalists. In the middle colonies, ethnicity had its greatest effect. Over 65 percent of all minority group leaders supported independence while only 33 percent of the English did so.

Thus, within each region non-English leaders remain more likely to support independence from Great Britain than England's own sons, but certain factors emerge from the comparison by region that were not visible in the original table. First, we may note that within the three major regions, Scotsmen were less likely to be colonialists than the dominant English. One of the four Scotsmen who were Loyalists lived in foreign parts during the critical years, another moved

TABLE 2
NATIONALIST TYPES BY ETHNICITY AND PLACE OF RESIDENCE
BETWEEN 1765-1776 (in percentages)

Ethnicity	Nationalist Types			
	True Nationalists	Acquiescing Nationalists	Colonialists	Total
(Northern Colony)				
English	68	23	9	100 (34)
Scotch	—	—	—	—
Irish	(2)	—	—	— (2)
Other	—	—	—	—

X^2 = 0.93, 6df, (NS); C.C. = 0.16

(Middle Colony)				
English	33	28	39	100 (18)
Scotch	67	0	33	100 (6)
Irish	71	29	0	100 (7)
Other	82	9	9	100 (11)

X^2 = 10.68, 6df, p $<$.01; C.C. = 0.45

(Southern Colony)				
English	80	10	10	100 (10)
Scotch	100	0	0	100 (6)
Irish	100	0	0	100 (5)
Other	(4)	—	—	— (4)

X^2 = 3.26, 6df, (NS); C.C. = 0.34

(Other) [a]				
English	50	30	20	100 (10)
Scotch	—	(1)	(2)	— (3)
Irish	—	—	(1)	— (1)
Other	62	0	38	100 (8)

X^2 = 7.77, 6df, (NS); C.C. = 0.51

a. The cateogry "Other" includes those who moved between regions during the specified period and those who spent all or part of the time in a foreign country.

between regions, and the other two lived in the middle colonies. Second, in the south, English leaders were considerably more likely to be true nationalists than they were overall. Third, it was only in the middle colonies that the English were a major source of opposition to independence. The situation, then, is clear. The English viewed themselves as the legitimate rulers of the American colonies and their support for independence varied with the ethnic heterogeneity of their local region. Where their position in the power structure was secure, as in the ethnically homogeneous north and south, the majority of them supported independence. Where their power was threatened by other groups of growing or almost equal strength, they felt safer under colonial protection from "home."

There is still a difference in support for independence among northern and southern leaders of English stock which requires explanation. We might suppose that since the north was ethnically slightly more homogeneous than the south, northern Englishmen would be slightly more pro-independence than their southern counterparts, and this was not the case. But the English were not in danger of losing their hegemony in either region. Once this degree of security was reached, ethnic factors would no longer affect position on independence, and other factors would become more important. One of these other factors operating in the north to lower the support of the English for independence was religion. For in the north, the English were split into two religious camps (Congregational and Episcopal), while in the south they were largely of one religion (Episcopal). In fact, the findings on ethnicity and independence cannot be fully understood until we look at the relationship between religion and independence.

A man's religion was a stronger determinant of his position on independence than his ethnicity. Ninety-two percent of Presbyterian leaders were true nationalists. They were followed rather closely by Congregationalists with 81 percent. Only 46 percent of Quakers and 45 percent of Episcopalians, on the other hand, supported the Revolution. Quakers and Episcopalians provided the largest proportion of Tory leadership, and Episcopalians were more likely to be acquiescing nationalists than any other group.

Once again it will be profitable to look at this same relationship within the three major regions before an interpretation of these findings is attempted. In the north, the only comparison possible is between Congregationalists and Episcopalians, and the difference between these two groups is striking. Eighty-four percent of the Congregationalist top leaders were true nationalists, and there were no colonialists among them. In contrast, only 25 percent of Episcopalian top leaders wholeheartedly supported independence, and they were the major source of support for the colonial regime in that region. In the middle colonies, independence received its only major support from the Presbyterians and, though the number of cases is very small, this is consistent with all other information on this region. Quakers and Episcopalian leaders strongly opposed independence as did those placed in the "Other" category though the small number of "responses" prevents comment on a mixed category of that sort. In the south, the top leaders of all religious groups strongly supported independence including the Episcopalians, eighty-four percent of whom were true nationalists. In order to make these findings on ethnicity and religion intelligible, we must now describe the position of each group within the three major regions.

As has already been indicated, the overwhelming majority of northerners were of English stock, and this is reflected in their top leadership. But this

TABLE 3

NATIONALIST TYPES BY RELIGION IN 1776 (in percentages)

Religion in 1776	Nationalist Types			
	True Nationalists	Acquiescing Nationalists	Colonialists	Total
Presbyterian	92	8	0	100 (12)
Congregationalist	81	19	0	100 (21)
Quaker	46	15	39	100 (13)
Episcopalian	45	23	32	100 (44)
Other	69	15	15	99[a](13)

$X^2 = 18.59, 8df, p < .02;$ C.C. = 0.39

a. Percentages do not add up to 100 due to rounding.

TABLE 4

NATIONALIST TYPES BY RELIGION IN 1776 AND PLACE OF RESIDENCE BETWEEN 1765-1776 (in percentages)

	Nationalist Types			
Religion in 1776	True Nationalists	Acquiescing Nationalists	Colonialists	Total
(Northern Colony)				
Presbyterian	(1)	—	—	— (1)
Congregationalist	84	16	0	100 (19)
Quaker	—	—	(1)	— (1)
Episcopalian	25	37	37	99[a] (8)
Other	(1)	(1)	—	— (2)

$X^2 = 18.71$, 8df, p $<$ .02; C.C. = 0.61

(Middle Colony)				
Presbyterian	100	0	0	100 (5)
Congregationalist	—	—	—	—
Quaker	40	20	40	100 (10)
Episcopalian	29	29	42	100 (14)
Other	40	20	40	100 (5)

$X^2 = 7.90$, 8df, (NS); C.C. = 0.43

(Southern Colony)				
Presbyterian	100	0	0	100 (5)
Congregationalist	(1)	—	—	— (1)
Quaker	—	—	—	—
Episcopalian	84	8	8	100 (13)
Other	(2)	—	—	— (2)

$X^2 = 1.38$, 8df, (NS); C.C. = 0

(Other)				
Presbyterian	—	(1)	—	— (1)
Congregationalist	—	(1)	—	— (1)
Quaker	(2)	—	—	— (2)
Episcopalian	33	22	45	100 (9)
Other	(3)	—	—	— (3)

$X^2 = 12.89$, 8df, (NS); C.C. = 0.67

a. Percentages do not add up to 100 due to rounding.

leadership was split along religious lines with a Congregationalist majority and an Episcopalian minority. This minority tended to be wealthy, to hold many of the administrative or Crown offices that were available and, as elsewhere, to see itself as the legitimate temporal and spiritual authority. These tacit claims of the descendants of the Church of England stood little chance of producing anything but hostility and alarm among the northern descendants of Calvin around them.

Until the early eighteenth century, the Church of England had no hold whatsoever in the north. At about that time, the zeal of the early Puritans began to subside making the social climate less hostile to splits within the dissenting framework and to the growth of Anglicanism. The Society for the Propagation of the Gospel in Foreign Parts was established in England in 1701 and began sending its missionaries to the northern colonies soon after. With the financial support of this group, churches were established in spite of the privileged position of the dissenters, and by the middle of the century the Church of England had made substantial progress among the upper classes. These prosperous, worldly and well-educated descendants of Calvin had begun to find the old orthodoxy too severe and were attracted to the more easygoing ways of the Episcopal church. Thus, the northern Episcopal church was entirely dependent on English financial support and through its native membership eventually became the main upholder of British authority in the region.

In the 1760s, the Anglicans made an all-out effort to establish an American episcopacy in the colonies. From their own point of view it was an unnecessary inconvenience to have their ministers ordained in London. From the standpoint of the dissenting clergy, the founding of an American episcopacy would mean the eventual development of an Anglican establishment. The Congregationalist and Presbyterian clergies strongly and successfully resisted this move, but this issue had by then merged into the general political quarrel with Great Britain which was to result in independence. John Adams noted that "[i]f any gentleman supposes this controversy to be nothing to the present purpose, he is grossly mistaken. It spread an universal alarm against the authority of Parliament. It [the scheme for a colonial episcopate] excited a general and just apprehension, that bishops, and dioceses, and churches, and priests, and tithes, were to be imposed on us by Parliament. . . . If Parliament could tax us, they could establish the Church of England" (quoted in Nelson, 1961: 14).

None of this means that members of the Anglican church were initially less disturbed than the dissenters about Parliamentary measures directed at the colonies, and there is a good deal of evidence which indicates their early opposition to Parliamentary Acts. But their ability to oppose Parliament was hindered by their desire for an American episcopate and by their generally high class position in a region in which downward mobility among other top elites was very high as a consequence of British policies. Hence, as the opposition movement grew, they began to drop out, and it is clear from the data presented above that by the time events had progressed to the point of independence, they had become the main upholders of British authority in the north.

In the middle colonies ethnicity and religion both operated as major determinants of position on independence. The case of Pennsylvania, the most populous colony of this region, provides the most interesting example of the impact of these variables.

Pennsylvania was settled by Quakers who sought a refuge for their persecuted fellows and a new land in which to try a Holy Experiment. The government they set up was, in many respects and for its time, highly enlightened and liberal. For instance, religious freedom, curtailed in other colonies, was fully practiced here, and war was banished as an instrument of foreign policy. Treaties were made with the Indians and were largely upheld, which was unusual in the colonies. As a consequence of the policy of religious freedom as well as of the location and natural richness of the soil, immigrants of many different ethnic and religious backgrounds flocked to Pennsylvania. At first they were heartily welcomed and even invited to come though their world views were quite different from that of the Quakers. As time went on, these groups grew large, outnumbering the Quakers, and sought their share of political power. For the first time, the

Quakers began to view the situation with alarm. They feared that such groups would pass legislation inconsistent with Quaker scruples about taking oaths and fighting wars. They feared that religious toleration would be curtailed, and that they would face the persecution in their own colony they had faced elsewhere. As the threat became greater, the Quakers became more withdrawn and intolerant of deviance within their own ranks. They also disenfranchized the newcomers by establishing a property qualification for voting and a rotten borough system. The former disenfranchized urban dwellers (including some Quakers) while the latter denied representation in the government to those in the newer western counties that did not have a Quaker majority. We will look at these more closely in a moment.

After the death of William Penn, his own family deserted Quakerism and turned Episcopalian. In other words, the same phenomenon of the successful abandoning the discipline of sect membership that was noted in the north occurred in the middle colonies. This caused a shift in political alignments, and eventually the Episcopalians gained control of most administrative offices while the Quakers retained control of the Assembly and, therefore, the purse-strings of the colony. They used this power of the purse to withhold funds earmarked for military purposes.

Concurrent with these events, the flow of immigrants began pushing west and settling the frontiers of Pennsylvania. As their numbers grew, they applied for representation and services for their area from the eastern government. Their most pressing problem, of course, was the Indians. It was the usual story. The settlers violated lands given the Indians by treaty, and the Indians retaliated by murdering the settlers. Grossly unrepresented in the Assembly in Philadelphia, they had few legal means to change their situation. Their petitions were to no avail. The Quakers would not appropriate funds to fight the Indians. The latter had a right to the lands, and war was not a means of solving problems.

To further complicate matters, while the unresponsive government was largely Quaker, the western settlers were largely Scotch-Irish Presbyterians. Thus, each antagonist belonged to an easily defined ethnic or religious group. The Quakers were particularly leery of the Presbyterians. They strongly resembled the Congregationalists who, a century ago, had so enjoyed hanging Quakers. Enfranchizing this group raised the spectre of religious persecution in one's own homeland as well as the violation of Quaker scruples against war.

The result of this quarrel was the formation of a group called the Paxton boys who massacred a group of harmless Indians under Quaker protection and then marched on the Quaker stronghold of Philadelphia itself. They were stopped and persuaded to return home by the Germans who were the only one of the newer groups to remain loyal to the Quakers. The Quakers, thoroughly alarmed, did at this point offer some protection to the hard-pressed western settlers. Their bitterness, however, did not abate. One of these settlers put his thought into verse. Speaking to the Quakers, he said:

"Encourage ev'ry friendly savage,
To murder, burn, destroy and ravage;
Of Scotch and Irish let them kill
As many thousands as they will
That you may lord it o'er the land,
And have the whole and sole command"
[quoted in Wertenbaker, 1938: 224].

Given these circumstances, it is not surprising that the Scotch-Irish Presbyterians as well as the other newer and smaller sects turned wholeheartedly to independence as a means of overthrowing the Quaker government and gaining some share of power and protection for themselves. The Quakers, knowing that independence would mean their final demise both politically and religiously and being unwilling to take arms, opposed independence. The Episcopalians, now the proprietors of the colony and as insecure in their power as the Quakers in theirs, also opposed independence. The Germans, loyal to the Quakers who invited them to live in Pennsylvania in peace and religious freedom, also opposed independence. Hence, the movement in Pennsylvania was carried by the Scotch-Irish Presbyterians and the smaller disenfranchised sects. The situation just described pitted whole ethnic and religious groups against each other, obscuring the class differences that existed within them to a greater degree than in the north where class and religion were more closely intertwined in the case of the Episcopalians.

In the other middle colonies there were few Quakers, but there were many Episcopalians who also fought against the rise of the smaller sects. Their pretensions to "the throne" in America, so to speak, and their relative insecurity in the middle colonies, made them strong supporters of colonialism. Hence, in all the middle colonies, independence was carried by the smaller ethnic and religious groups.

Unlike their northern and middle-colony counterparts, southern Episcopalians formed a clear majority of the population and of the top leadership in the region. Further, in contrast to the position of the northern Congregationalists who were also a clear majority in their region, there was no high-status minority religious group seeking to supplant them. Hence, in the south the overwhelming majority of Episcopalians were true nationalists, and neither ethnicity nor religion had an important impact on position on independence. The small variations which did exist were consistent with the original findings, and the English and Episcopalians were slightly less likely than other groups to support independence.

The findings on ethnicity and religion may be generally summarized as follows:

(1) Ethnicity and religion affected the position of elites on independence where those variables were important sources of internal cleavage apart from the issue of independence.

(2) The stance of leaders from high status ethnic and religious groups on independence was dependent upon the ethnic and religious heterogeneity of their local region. Where the high status of such groups was not threatened by competing groups, elite members largely supported and fostered independence. Northern Congregationalists, southern Episcopalians, and Englishmen from both regions would be examples of this pattern of behavior. Where that high status was threatened by competing groups of near equal or superior strength and size, elite members largely opposed independence. Northern and middle-colony Episcopalians and middle-colony Quakers would be examples of this pattern of behavior. For in the first case, independence could only increase the share of political and social rewards accruing to elites from these high-status groups, whereas in the second case it might well oust them from their already precarious position of favor.

(3) The stance of leaders from low-status ethnic and religious groups was less variable, and they seemed to generally support independence as a means of improving their position in their own region. But great care must be exercized in generalizing about these elites because data on them is largely from the middle colonies where they stood a strong chance of success. It is possible that in a more homogeneous region in

which they were much weaker in size or organization than a single dominant group, they might feel safer under colonial protection. For instance, as in the case of Pennsylvania, Scotch-Irish Presbyterians had settled the back country of North and South Carolina. When their peaceful efforts to win concessions for their counties from the eastern seabord planters failed, they formed a Regulation Movement and rebelled. This rebellion was successfully defeated by the easterners in 1771 just before the final series of events leading to independence got under way. Some historians have argued (for instance Nelson, 1961: 112-113) that as a consequence of their experience with the native elite, this group supported the colonial regime in the War for Independence. The evidence is far from conclusive (Alden, 1957: 162), and no further light can be shed on the issue here. That is, the size of the sample in this study was too small to have drawn heavily from these less populous southern colonies, and this group was so successfully kept out of the top elite that a much larger sample would have been required to draw enough of them to make a statement on the issue.

ETHNICITY, RELIGION, AND THE HOLDING OF PUBLIC OFFICE

Given the variation found in support for independence by ethnicity and religion, it would be of interest to know how these same groups fared politically after independence was declared. The following tables show the relationship between ethnicity and religion and the holding of public office before and after the Revolution.

Looking first at ethnicity, we see that from 1765-1776, the Irish and those classified as "Other" were less likely than the English or Scotch to hold public office. Further, when they did hold public office they were less likely than the English or Scotch to hold only a Crown position for the entire period.

When we look at these same relationships from 1777 to the formation of the national government in 1789, several changes are apparent. First, leaders from all groups gained somewhat because of the increased number of offices available under conditions of independence. Second, more than four times as many Irish leaders held office in the second period as in the first, and this represents the most spectacular gain in the table. Third, among office holders, all of the minority groups were more likely than the English to hold a national office or combined national and local offices, while the English were more likely than all

TABLE 5

TYPE OF PUBLIC OFFICE HELD BETWEEN 1765-1776 BY ETHNICITY
(in percentages)

Ethnicity	Type of Public Office Held Between 1765-1776				
	Crown[a]	Both	Non-Crown[a]	No Office	Total
English	10	7	26	57	100 (76)
Scotch	23	23	0	54	100 (13)
Irish	0	15	23	62	100 (13)
Other	4	0	22	74	100 (27)

X^2 = 16.53, 6df, (NS); C.C. = 0.34

a. Crown offices were those in which the incumbent was selected by, responsible to, and dependent on the king or his ministers. Non-crown offices were those in which the incumbent was selected by, responsible to, and dependent upon the colonial electorate or its representatives for his position.

TABLE 6
TYPE OF PUBLIC OFFICE HELD BETWEEN 1777-1789 BY ETHNICITY
(in percentages)

Ethnicity	Type of Public Office Held Between 1777-1789			
	National or Both	Local Only	No Office	Total
English	26	34	40	100 (61)[b]
Scotch	42	25	33	100 (12)[b]
Irish	46	38	15	99[a] (13)
Other	32	14	54	100 (22)[b]

X^2 = 7.96, 6df, (NS); C.C. = 0.26

a. Percentages do not add up to 100 due to rounding.
b. The main cause of the smaller population in the second period is that many of those who opposed independence left the country during the war.

but the Irish to hold a local office. These national offices were those that existed under the Articles of Confederation and prior to the formation of our present government in 1789.

Since the age distribution of the different ethnic groups was very similar, age cannot account for these findings. Rather, it appears that the Irish, who were the strongest supporters of independence among ethnic groups, also reaped the greatest political benefits from the Revolution in so far as these are reflected in the gaining of political office.

The second important finding in the table is that, apart from the Irish, the political gains made by leaders of minority groups as a consequence of independence, do not appear to have greatly altered local power structures. Instead, it appears that the achievements of these leaders were more the consequence of the creation of a new set of offices which had not previously existed on the national level. The English, on the other hand, appear to have retained local offices but did not succeed in making large gains among the newly created offices.

Among the minority groups, only the Irish seem to have done almost as well on the local as the national level. This is probably largely accounted for by the case of Pennsylvania where the local government was actually overthrown.

The findings on religion and public office holding in the two periods are equally interesting, but more complex, and, once again, they are not attributable to age.

As in the case of ethnicity, all groups gain in office holding to some extent because of the increased number of offices available. The key to an explanation of the distribution of offices found among office holders must be sought in the case of the Episcopalians. At first glance it appears that they made large gains and these were primarily on the national level. In the light of their record on the issue of independence, this seems to be a contradictory finding though it is not. The reader will first note that the difference in the marginals for the two periods is far greater for Episcopalians than for any other group. The bulk of those missing in the second period are those who left the country after independence because of their opposition to that issue. The remainder are those who retired so far into private life after the Revolution that no information on this question could be obtained. Hence, the greatly decreased pool of 31 Episcopalians who

TABLE 7
TYPE OF PUBLIC OFFICE HELD BETWEEN 1765-1776 BY RELIGION
IN 1776 (in percentages)

Religion in 1776	Type of Public Office Held Between 1765-1776				
	Crown	Both	Non-Crown	No Office	Total
Presbyterian	14	21	7	57	99[a] (14)
Congregationalist	4	4	27	65	100 (26)
Quaker	0	0	46	54	100 (13)
Episcopalian	13	13	31	42	99[a] (45)
Other	6	0	6	88	100 (16)

X^2 = 22.04, 12df, p $<$.05; C.C. = 0.40

a. Percentages do not add up to 100 due to rounding.

"answered the question" are those whose lives remained sufficiently public to have left a record. Among these, none of the non-office holders was from the south and two-thirds of them were from the north. Eighty-six percent of those who held local office were from the south as were 60 percent of those who held national or combined national and local offices. Hence, those Episcopalians who held public office after independence were largely from the south where they strongly supported the Revolution.

Congregationalists made the largest gains in office holding, and these were primarily on the local level. Always an insular group, suspicious of others and arousing suspicion in others, they made little national impact in spite of their strong support for independence. Instead, they successfully ousted their Episcopalian competitors at home and took these local offices for themselves.

The position of the Quakers as reflected in office-holding was remarkably unaltered by independence in spite of the Revolution which took place in Pennsylvania at the time of the Declaration. The data on Episcopalian leaders from the middle colonies indicate that none of them continued to hold only

TABLE 8
TYPE OF PUBLIC OFFICE HELD BETWEEN 1777-1789 BY RELIGION AT
THE TIME OF FEDERATION (in percentages)

Religion at Federation	Type of Public Office Held Between 1777-1789			
	National or Both	Local Only	No Office	Total
Presbyterian	37	13	50	100 (16)
Congregationalist	19	48	33	100 (21)
Quaker	16	50	34	100 (12)
Episcopalian	45	26	29	100 (31)
Other	29	6	65	100 (17)

X^2 = 17.51, 8df, p $<$.03; C.C. = 0.39

a. When collecting the data for this study, it appeared that the colonists changed religions rather frequently. Hence, as a precaution, religion was coded separately for the period preceding and the period following the Revolution. As it turned out, very few of these shifts took place in the second period, and the separate coding was unnecessary. For instance, the two additional Presbyterians were additions by immigration rather than conversion, and the losses among Episcopalians and Quakers were a consequence of flight from the country at the time of independence. Thus, only the one addition under the "Other" category came about through conversion, and this one case could not alter the findings.

local offices. It is possible, then, that they took the brunt of the consequences of opposition to independence in that region and colony. Since it was in the middle colonies that the Tory forces were most highly organized and active, and these forces were clearly led by Episcopalians rather than Quakers, this is probably what occurred.

Presbyterians and those classified as "Other" made their greatest gains on the national level. Presbyterians, however, made the lowest overall gain in office-holding which is surprising in the light of their overwhelming support for independence. This result in the table was caused by the fact that 3 of the 8 non-office-holding Presbyterians were either geographically mobile across regions during the second period, or had only recently emigrated to America. Both of these conditions would have made it difficult or impossible for these men to hold public office at that time. If these are withdrawn, only 38 percent of this group were non-office holders.

In general, these findings on ethnicity and religion and office-holding may be summarized by saying that there was a strong though imperfect relationship between support for independence and the gaining of political office in the period following that event up to the formation of the national government. Since support for independence in the northern and particularly the middle colonies was closely related to ethnic and religious cleavage, we may fairly say that the Revolution did open up political offices to many of those who did not previously have adequate representation. Much of this change, however, was a consequence of the creation of new offices on the national level and the extent of change on the local level was very variable.

NOTES

1. The terms "Anglican" and "Episcopalian" both refer to followers of the Church of England in America. The colonists used the former word until the very end of the eighteenth century when the word "Episcopalian" came into use. In this paper these terms will be used interchangeably to refer to the American followers of the Church of England.
2. This information can be found in any basic history text covering the period under discussion.
3. See Chapter II of my dissertation (Alger, 1971) for a detailed discussion of the method used in this study.

REFERENCES

ALDEN, J. R. (1957) The South in the Revolution, 1763-1789. Louisiana: Louisiana State University Press.
ALGER, J. M. (1971) The Sociology of the American Revolution. Yale University, Ph.D. dissertation.
MORRIS, R. B. [ed.] (1953) Encyclopedia of American History. New York: Harper & Bros.
MOSKOS, C. C., Jr., (1967) The Sociology of Political Independence. Cambridge: Schenkman.
NELSON, W. H. (1961) The American Tory. Oxford: Clarendon Press.
U.S. Department of Commerce (1960) Historical Statistics of the United States: Colonial Times to 1957, A Statistical Abstract Supplement. The Bureau of the Census.
WERTENBAKER, T. J. (1938) The Founding of American Civilization: The Middle Colonies. New York: Charles Scribner's Sons.

Chapter 24

MODERN NATIONALISM IN OLD NATIONS AS A CONSEQUENCE OF EARLIER STATE-BUILDING: THE CASE OF BASQUE-SPAIN

PEDRO GONZALEZ BLASCO

"If this society becomes rational, very probably, there is no solution for the Catalan problem, without a solution for the Spanish problem, nor is there a solution of the Spanish problem without a solution of the Catalan problem. . . . A rational society cannot maintain such stupid and absurd tensions as exist today about these problems."

Josep Mª Castellet

Where Castellet said "Catalan," one now must say "Basque."

This paper presents an overview of Basque nationalism as a case of later peripheral nationalism resulting from early state-building (Linz, 1970a). In addition some references are made to Basque nationalism in France for the purpose of comparison with the Spanish Basques.

This is a case of continuing peripheral nationalism in an old European country; but it may be relevant for new states, founded in our century and now in the process of nation-building. Basque nationalism probably was and might again be a contributing factor in the difficulties of institutionalizing competitive democracy in Spain (Dahl, 1971). Certainly, a democratic majority rule offers no obvious solution to the integration into a polyarchy of localized, relatively small, linguistic and cultural minorities. Yet, in the Spanish case, it can be seen that many of the conditions for "consociational democracy," as defined by Lijphart, were not present. In this chapter, I aim to contribute to the analysis of the conditions needed for and the obstacles operating against a stable democracy (see Lijphart, 1968, 1969,; Lorwin, 1971).

Presented first is a review of the historical context in which several Western European countries reached their unification, a context clearly different from that of the new states of the twentieth century. The different road to unification created different situations and problems for the later process of nation-building. In fact, in some cases, the creation of a nation-state was not fully achieved. Spain is, in some degree, an example of the failure to build a fully shared sense of nationhood.

Second is a description of the Basque country, its emergence from the centralist state in the nineteenth century in the form of a religious and particularist popular movement—Carlism—its transformation in the first decades of this century to a regionalist movement, the Basque Nationalist Party (PNV), and in recent years the split of the Basque movement into a left and a right.

AUTHORS' NOTE: I am indebted to Professor Juan J. Linz of Yale University for his assistance and suggestions in the preparation of this paper, and to Mrs. Alice Murphy for her assistance in typing the successive versions.

Third is an explanation of Basque nationalism in relation to Spain's political situation and development. And, finally, Basque nationalism is discussed in a comparative context, with an explanation of Basque nationalist attitudes.

HISTORICAL FRAMEWORK

The state-building process in Europe in the last four centuries has been a very complex one. Spain began its unification with the joining of the crowns of Castile and Aragón in 1476 and the conquest of Granada in 1492 and completed it with the annexation of Navarre in 1512. The dynastic union of the crowns of Castile-Aragón and Navarre, like that of Aragón and Catalonia before it, did not destroy the distinctive political and legal institutions of each of these kingdoms, as the Hapsburgs discovered in 1640 when their attempts to reduce the autonomy and distinctiveness of these areas resulted in the rebellion of Catalonia. Although the Basque-speaking area, except for Navarre, had been part of Castile since the middle ages, it tended to maintain its distinctive institutions more than other parts of Spain.

France as a nation emerged slowly through the incorporation of territories into the core of the Ile de France (Philip Augustus, 1214; Louis IX, 1270; Philip IV, 1308); it was almost as we know it now when Charles VIII inherited the crown of France from his parents and married Anne, Duchess of Brittany (1488). Finally, in 1589 part of the former kingdom of Navarre was incorporated into France.

The United Kingdom is another example of state-building through monarchies. England and Wales were united in 1485 under the crown of Henry VII, both nations establishing their union by an agreement (Act of Parliament) in 1535. England and Scotland were joined when King James VI of Scotland inherited the crown of England in 1603. Although ruled by one king, they remained two separate and distinct monarchies (England and Wales, England-Scotland). In 1707 with the Union Act between England and Scotland these kingdoms became Great Britain, and in 1801 the United Kingdom was established with the inclusion of Ireland (Rose, 1970: 7). In this case, different kingdoms participated in the formation of a new state. The role played by the monarchies was to achieve a union under the crown and in later periods the rise of the British Empire became an important element in the creation of unity.

A different example of state-building in Europe is the case of Italy. There, popular movements led by men like Garibaldi or Mazzini aroused important minorities against absolute rulers and foreign domination, while the diplomatic capabilities of the government of the kingdom of Savoy, its monarchy, military, and bureaucratic capacity, took over the unification process that culminated in the occupation of the Papal states in 1871. This dual character of unification and renaissance, however, left a heritage of tension not finally resolved until the proclamation of the republic.

In many respects Italy followed the model of the Napoleonic states, but it may never be as centralized as France or Portugal. The social and economic heterogeneity of the peninsula and the role of large and wealthy cities created a country with a multi-centered economy that resisted the centralizing tendencies of the new state and led to the present regional autonomies.

In addition, the incorporation of German-speaking areas after World War I and the persistence of French as a language in the Val D'Aosta were restraints on total homogeneity. The smallness and relative insignificance of these territories and their link to foreign powers contributed to special regulations of their status after World War II. However, despite the phrase of Massimo D'Azeglio in 1860, "Italy is made; now we must make Italians" (Seton-Watson, 1967: 13), the *Rissorgimento* had created a powerful Italian national consciousness, which had its agressive component furthered by the *Irredenta,* the Austrian rule in World War I, and fascism. The character of the new monarchy was defined by the phrase, king "by the grace of God and by the will of the nation" (Seton-Watson, 1967: 13), in contrast to the title of the King of Great Britain: King of England, King of Wales, and King of Scotland, or in the Spanish case, King of Castile, King of Aragón, Duke of Milan, and so on.

The German unification that took place almost at the same time had many similarities with the Italian but also had important differences. The German-speaking lands had been divided throughout centuries into many sovereign states which persisted, despite attempts at integration into the nineteenth century when a new nationalism emerged as a reaction to the French invasion and as a reflection of ideas of the French Revolution.

The Austro-Hungarian Empire in the south and the kingdom of Prussia in the north and east were strong poles of attraction, but the Austrian government's lack of close ties with the German government and the authoritarian character of the military bureaucratic monarchy of Prussia created serious difficulties for the nationalist democrats who wanted unification. The Frankfurt National Assembly of 1848 floundered when faced with these dilemmas. In addition, the powerful dynastic states had control of extensive territories, particularly Bavaria, and there were proud city-states such as Hamburg and Bremen. Economic development created among the northwestern German bourgeoisie strong pressure for integration that crystallized in the *Zollverein,* a custom union of northwestern and northern German states. It took the skill of the Prussian prime minister Bismarck to engineer the unification of northern German states under the hegemony of Prussia by first defeating Austria (1866) and then combining the various political efforts for the struggle against Napoleon III. The solution was the German Reich proclaimed in Versailles in 1871 with a confederal constitution which did not recognize the rights of the various sovereigns who would be represented in the Bundesrat. The hybrid formula of a democratic early Reichstag, a confederation of princes, kings, and city-states represented in the Bundesrat in which the non-democratically elected government of Prussia had assured its majority, was very different from the more constitutional monarchy of Italy.

The 1918 revolution did away with the non-democratic elements of Bismarck's constitution and retained an important degree of federalism, but it did not destroy the hegemonic position of Prussia. Thus, Bismarck's unification by "blood and iron" and manipulation sacrificed much of the liberal democratic ideology of early German nationalism; because of Protestant dominance important segments of the Catholic population were alienated and an authoritarian paternalistic spirit forced the labor movement into negative integration. Germany also was unable to integrate Alsace-Lorraine and the Poles in the eastern territories. These legacies contributed to the tensions of the Weimar Republic and the rise of Nazism. Today Germany could be an integrated

	TYPE I		TYPE II	TYPE III	
	Centralizing Patterns: Strong		Light	Noncentralizing Patterns	
	Spain	France	Great Britain	Italy	Germany
Date of Unification	1492-1512	1223 Philip August 1720 Louis IX 1308 Philip IV 1488 Charles VIII	1525 { England Henry VIII Wales 1602 { England James I Scotland 1707 "Act Unions"	1861-(1871)	1871 (June 18)
Head of State	Ferdinand and Isabella	Philip August Charles VIII		Cavour (Garibaldi and Mazzini) V. Emmanuele I	Bismarck William I
Core	Castilia	Ile de France	England	Piedmont	Prussia
Act of Unification of State	Marriage Ferdinand and Isabella Conquest Granada Incorporation Navarre	Conquest, marriage of Duchess of Brittany (Charles VIII) (Navarre 1589)	Dynastic succession and inheritance Act Unions	Civil struggles	Treaties
Place of Crown	Kings of Castile, Kings of Aragon, Lord of Vizcaya, Duke of Milano	King of France	King of England King of Wales King of Scotland	King of Italy	German Emperor supported by the army
National Unity	Successful state but failure of full nation-building.	Successful state-building and successful nation-building later. Existing "old" minorities, (Basque, Britanny, Alsace).	Successful state building and successful pluri-national building, failure to assimilate minorities as Ireland, Scotland.	Successful state and nation, more centralized government than Germany.	Successful state and nation under federal state.

Figure 1

nation-state, reduced to its ethnic-linguistic borders, with Prussia democratized in its institutions, the working class integrated throughout the Socialist Party, and the Protestants and Catholics more willing to ignore their differences after the experiences of anti-religious Nazism. But World War II created two states and two societies out of what might have been a single nation.

While this process of state-building of the powerful monarchies was going on in France, Great Britain, and even Spain, Italy and Germany remained divided into many kingdoms, dukedoms, republics, and city-states with large parts dominated by foreign powers, mainly Spain.

Germany retained some formal unity in the form of empire, while a large part of the German-speaking area was dominated by the Austrian Hapsburgs who were also rulers of a multi-national eastern European empire. The unification of these areas would take place in the nineteenth century, in the age of romantic nationalism, when the King of Piedmont and the Prussian monarch became the head of new nation-states. However the process of aggregation was not the same as in previous centuries through dynastic alliances and inheritances. In their case a revolutionary democratic nationalist movement was used or controlled by the diplomatic statesmanship of Cavour and Bismarck, the prime ministers of the two most modern states.

In addition to these large states created in the period of patrimonial state-building, we find in Europe those countries in which states grew out of the complex political, social, and economic structure with elements of city or peasant republics, state-societies with continuous representative institutions like Switzerland, the Netherlands, Belgium and, after World War II, Austria.

Thus, one can think of state-building in this area of Europe as constituting three main types:

Type I: Countries unifying by centralizing patterns, where the parts of the new state are very different in land size and population, the core being dominant, as in Spain and France.

Type II: Countries unifying by light centralizing patterns, where there is a relative balance in some important aspect between the parts forming the new state and unifying after a period of maturation of the national idea, as in Great Britain.

Type III: Countries basing their new state on former states or on the cultural heritage of their city-states, as Italy or Germany, where actual unification in a centralizing or federal form came later through a slow process and where the role played by the popular rulers was very important [see Figure 1].

To these three main types, one could add the new states created on self-determination of national principle after World War I in eastern and Balkan Europe. The lack of conjuncture between linguistic cultural borders and geographic, economic, and historical borders there make the nation-state-building process difficult.

In summary, there were: the partimonial monarchies, some retaining traces of the political pluralism of the pre-absolutist states (like the United Kingdom, Austro-Hungary), others centralized by absolute monarchs and liberal demo-cratic centralist revolutions (France, Portugal, Spain to a degree), nation-states built in the nineteenth century with more or less popular support by traditional oligarchies of the modern bureaucratic monarchies (Italy with strong democratic national components, Germany with authoritarian and populist components); the peripheral consociational democracies and the eastern European nation-states emerging from the disintegration and defeat of the Hapsburg, Turkish, and Tzarist empires.

Spain in the eighteenth and even more in the nineteenth century abandoned the pattern of a united kingdom of formally separate monarchies, following the French centralizing model, but for reasons difficult to specify it did not succeed in the linguistic, cultural, social, and economic homogenization to the extent that France did. The fact that a Spanish state was created before the era of romantic nationalism differentiated it from Italy and Germany, even when the fight against Napoleon (1808-1815) had created a national consciousness. However the mixture of democratic liberal ideals and religious traditional values in that struggle only a few years later divided the country in a dynastic civil war. The support for the clerical traditionalist monarchy reinforced the sentiment of distinctiveness and legitimized the defense of traditional rights and privileges *(fueros)*. The differences in language between Castilian (inexactly called "Spanish"), and Catalan, Galician, and even more Basque are greater than the dialectical differences within other European states. The crisis of the Spanish state, due to loss of empire, delayed economic development, and social conflict, in addition to the linguistic, economic, and social structure differences in an age of cultural nationalism, led to the emergence of regional peripheral nationalism first in Catalonia, then in the Basque country, and finally by diffusion in other regions.

These divisive tendencies make Spain *servata distancia* similar to Belgium and Yugoslavia as multi-lingual as any developed countries. However, the early state-building and the long historical tradition of Spain distinguish it from some of the multi-lingual new states.

The degree of integration achieved was and is great compared to the multi-national empires that disintegrated in 1918. A common history and imperial past, a deep-seated culture in Castile, and a common struggle against Napoleonic invasion created Spanish Castilian nationalism, although it could not in the crisis of the political, economic, and social revolution at the end of the last century incorporate all Spaniards. Neither a state without nationalism nor fully a nation-state without the institutional heritage allowing the transition to consociational forms, Spain fell somewhere between the three main types delineated above. Many Catalans and Basques feel a regional national identity, some feel Spanish national identity, and still others have a dual allegiance. The Basque country, whatever the nationalists may say, is not Spain's Ireland, and therefore the prospects for secession are quite different. The principality of Catalonia is not a united link to the Spanish crown as Norway and Hungary were to Sweden and Austria.

There are basic differences, but also surprising similarities, between Spain and new nations born in the struggles against colonial domination. Four-and-one-half centuries of independence, an imperial role, and the absence of political or cultural dependency save Spain from the emotional, sometimes neurotic, nationalism of the Third World. However, some countries carved out by the European powers, crossing ethnic and linguistic boundaries as created states, find it infinitely more difficult than Spain to create nations out of those states. In many of them, for example the Congo, Nigeria, Pakistan, Indonesia, we find a similarity to Spain in unbalanced economic and social development coinciding more or less with ethnic-linguistic boundaries and complicated by internal immigration.

Before turning to the case of the Basques in modern Spain, I summarize below some general facts of state-building in Spain that are relevant to ethnic differentiation. In this summary, I follow the formulations of Juan J. Linz (1970a):

(1) Spain is a case of early state-building, in which the political, linguistic, cultural, and social integration of its territorial components was not fully accomplished before the age of nationalism.

(2) For the minorities, Spain is a state, but it is not their nation. Therefore, Spain is not fully a nation-state. [see Aguirre, 1944: 346; Madariaga, 1967: 10:141].

(3) Although the Spanish elites succeeded in building a state, these minorities constitute a failure in the process of nation-building. Some of the reasons for that failure may be:
    (a) Spanish state-building went on before the age of nationalism, therefore the Spanish nation-building process was carried out without the emotional components of nation-state building, without the symbolic elements. (The Spanish national anthem has no text but is a march predating the French Revolution and the series of singable anthems of nationalist movements.)
    (b) Defeat overseas, civil war between liberal and traditionalists delaying economic development, inefficient administration, and corrupt democratic Parliamentary forms are all characteristics which make many Spaniards reject the unitary state.
    (c) While it was asking for taxes, recruits for unsuccessful ventures, and support for an apparently inefficient overgrown administration, the Madrid center and its government had, at least from a superficial point of view, little to offer to the peripheral, wealthy, linguistically distinct regions. Conveniently forgotten was the protectionist economic policy that assured a relatively large internal market to the capitalist of the periphery who probably could not have competed at the international level.

(4) In modern times, the efforts to achieve cultural unity failed because:
    (a) The different economic, social, and, in the Catalan case, cultural development of some of the peripheral regions and financial weakness of the central government often raised the quality of the cultural representatives in the periphery.
    (b) The arbitrary and inexpediant attempts to impose the Castilian language and to weaken or destroy the vernacular culture sometimes bordered on the ridiculous.

(5) The overlap between regional-linguistic problems and other deeply felt issues complicated matters. In Catalonia the bitter struggles between Catalan manufacturing bourgeoisie and the anarchosyndicalist proletarians, in large part immigrants from other parts of the country, led to a complex three-cornered relationship between the bourgeoisie, the workers, and a large part of the population who were deeply religious. The relationship reinforced the periphery-center conflict when it collided with the classical anti-clerical forces.

(6) Given the limited national integration and the persistence of regional distinctiveness particularly in language, why did Spain not try early federal or other consociational solutions? Linz notes that the more or less authoritarian periods were not favorable to such experiments. However this is not the only or most important explanation, since there are other basic differences between Spain and the countries that have tried such solutions specifically for the question of nationality.
    First, in contrast to other countries, the linguistically distinct regions are more highly developed economically and socially than the rest of Spain; at some points Barcelona was a more modern city than the national capital. The central government could not offer economic or development assistance without giving up a moderate position. Neither the Basque country nor Catalonia was in this respect comparable to Brittany, Wales, Slovakia, Sicily, Macedonia, or even Flanders.

Second, the proportions of each minority and even all of them together are only a small part of the national population. This is different,for example, than the Belgian case, where the Walloons and the Flemish are each close to half of the population, or to the proportion of German and French Swiss, or even to the proportions of Serbs and Croats.

Third, the rapid economic development of Catalonia and the Basque country has attracted Castilian-speaking labor, who in the Basque case are particularly difficult to assimilate, and who constitute minorities within a minority which often identify, or are linked with the Castilian majority in Spain. This is not the case with most peripheral nationalist areas in Europe which (with exception to Alsace-Lorraine and Slovenia) tend to be more underdeveloped and therefore do not attract immigration from the dominant nationality group.

BASQUE COUNTRY

It is not easy for the Basque nationalist to define the boundaries of his homeland, since all the Basque-language territories have never been combined into a single political unit and the Basque-speaking area has constantly grown smaller in the last centuries.

Maximal nationalist aspirations define almost imaginary borders, based on a remote and mythical history, outlining the territory between Bordeaux-Toulouse-Zaragosa and west of Bilbao, leaving out the French and Aragonese metropolises. A more realistic definition is that territory west of the historical boundaries of the kingdom of Navarre across the Pyrenees, covering part of France and Spain, and the Lordom of Vizcaya, and those parts of Spain which in the middle ages and modern times enjoyed a certain degree of communal self-government or special feudal relationship to the crown of Castilia (see Saenz de Buruaga, 1969: 281-296).

The Spanish-French border established in the sixteenth century cuts across the Basque lands which are designated by the nationalists as *Euskalerria*. Today, the linguistic area where Euskera in its various dialects is spoken is even narrower, with Castilianization of a large part of Alava, Navarre, and even of the large cities, and the penetration of French as a language in the departments that are considered Basque. The nationalist formula, 3 + 4 = 7 = 1[1] is based on modern administrative divisions, rather than on language borders or historical frontiers.

Some of the difficulties encountered by the Basque nationalist movement are the result of the undetermined boundaries. Spanish Navarre has Basque-speaking areas and the Navarrese at some points were willing to collaborate on an autonomist solution, but at other times they were too strongly attracted to Spain. While the Carlist movement has been defending the traditional *fueros*, distinctive political, administrative, and financial laws, of the Basque-Navarrese region, its leaders also joined with the centralist army in 1936, keeping some of the privileges of Alava and especially of Navarre. In contrast, the boundaries of Catalonia coincided with linguistic borders even where the Castilian language extended into the Aragonese, and Castilian-Aragonese penetrated long ago into some parts of Catalonia.

The core of the Basque country is made up of the three Spanish provinces of Vizcaya, Guipúzcoa, and Alava, to which Navarre may be added and the French department of Basses Pyrénées. The tabulation below demonstrates the similarities between the Euskera names and the Spanish and French administra-

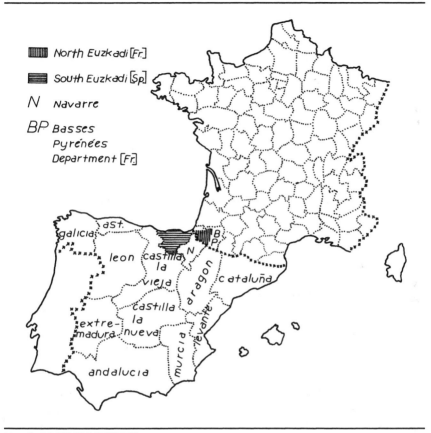

Map 1: BASQUE COUNTRY

tive divisions of the traditional Basque regions (see also Estornés, 1965: 103; Caro Baroja, 1958a: 23).

The Spanish Basque country is largely mountainous, and the population is settled along river valleys and the coast. The green valleys perpendicular to the sea make communications between the Basques difficult and foster a certain isolation. The region is highly industrial with factories spreading out into small

	Euskera	Spanish	French
South Euskadi	1. Bizkaia	Vizcaya	
	2. Gipuzkoa	Guipuzcoa	
	3. Araba	Alava	
	4. Nafarroa[a]	Navarra	
North Euskadi	5. Basa Nafarra		Basse Navarre
	6. Xuberoa		Soule
	7. Lapurdi		Labourd

a. Sometimes Nafarroa and Basa Nafarra are considered as one, thus leaving six provinces instead of seven.

Map 2: BASQUE-SPEAKING AREAS FROM THE 16th TO 20th CENTURIES (from Caro
Baroja, 1946: 265).

communities where some of the laborers combine industrial work with
cultivating land around their ancestral farmhouses called *caseríos* (Caro Baroja,
1958: 163). On the coast there are fishing villages and two important harbors,
Bilbao and Pasajes. The French Basque country is more like a plateau, a factor
that makes for easier integration. The French side is relatively underdeveloped,
while the Spanish side of Vizcaya and Guipúzcoa enjoys two of the highest per
capita incomes in the country.

The largest population claimed by the Basques is 4,844,852[2] (Sarrailh,
1962: 177), but this figure includes provinces like Logrono and Huesca and areas
of Castile where hardly anyone identifies with the Basques. The same
exaggeration is true for the French part.

Today, the so-called Basque country in Spain is very far from such a Basque
maximalist approach. The three Basque provinces of Alava, Guipúzcoa, and
Vizcaya represented 4.5 percent of the whole Spanish population in 1960, 4.8
percent in 1964, and 5.2 percent in 1965 (FOESSA, 1970: 155; Linz, 1970b).

TABLE 1
POPULATION OF THE BASQUE COUNTRY

Provinces	Population			Number of Square Kilometers	Persons per Square Kilometer
	1945	1960	1967		
Alava	117,500	138,934	182,916	3,047	46
Guipúzcoa	370,114	478,337	598,224	1,997	240
Vizcaya	579,978	754,383	971,029	2,217	340
Navarre	347,369	402,042	432,439	10,421	39

SOURCES: Barbancho, 1967: 129; Anuario Estadistico, 1965: 472).

Even from this average one should subtract 1.2 percent born outside of those provinces. The population for the three provinces was 1,371,654 inhabitants in 1960.

The new nationalists, as the old PNV, operate with this reality, but they do not forget their maximalist ideas.

Navarre with its population of 402,042 was 1.3 percent of the Spanish population in 1960 but it is a region with a tradition of administrative and fiscal autonomy, and is not necessarily favorable to linguistic autonomy or local nationalism.

The Basque country had almost half the population of Madrid Province (8.6 percent) or West Andalusia (10.8) percent in 1960 (FOESSA, 1970: 155).

The distribution of the active population of the Basque country, considering agriculture, industry, and services, is 14 percent, 55 percent, 31 percent, corresponding with a relatively post-industrial situation. With Madrid and Barcelona, the Basque country is far ahead of other Spanish areas, not only the underdeveloped Extremadura or Galicia Interior but western Andalusia or even Levante (FOESSA, 1970: 172). Such differences as these are a relevant factor in the regional problem. In general, we can say that the Basque country is an area with a high density of population (282 inhabitants per square kilometer for 1965) compared to the whole of Spain (60 inhabitants per square kilometer in 1960), but within the Basque country there is also a difference between Vizcaya and Guipúzcoa (above the mean) and Alava and Navarre.

The natural increase, despite the relatively high birth rates for industrial-urban regions, particularly because of religious beliefs, is insufficient to keep up with the labor needs. This leads to a large-scale migration into the Basque country which threatens denationalization.

There is a great polarization of the Spanish population toward three main centers: Madrid (center), Barcelona (coast), Basque country (coast). For the Basque country, in the period of 1901 to 1930 there were 39,687 net migrants, between 1931 and 1950 there were 189,248, and between 1951 to 1960 there were 152,226. Thus, migration into the area has been large and has risen rapidly. In the future the process can be expected to continue.

The migrants came generally from Castilia or areas outside of the Basque country, the net migration among Basque procinces themselves being low.

The recently growing mobility of the population within the same province is not high, even though it is, in some cases such as within Vizcaya and within Guipúzcoa, among the highest in Spain (FOESSA, 1970: 581).

By sex, there is a relative balance between the number of men and women who enter the Basque country. For example, between 1941 and 1960, there were 97,973 men and 90,011 women (Barbancho, 1967: App 16).

The direction of this migration is toward urban areas and toward industrial-ized centers but not toward rural areas of the Basque country, with the historical immigration having been toward Vizcaya and Guipúzcoa. Only recently is it directed also to Alava.

The Basque country, with Madrid and Barcelona, has a low average of persons living in the same region where they were born. The immigration usually consists of young people coming from rural areas because in the Basque country there are new jobs and because the level of living in the small villages is not high. Thus, the Basque country is growing largely owing to the immigration of Castilian-

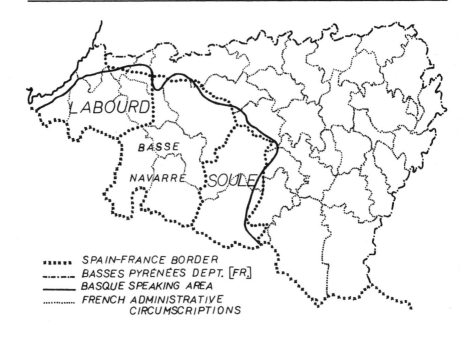

••••• SPAIN-FRANCE BORDER
—••—••— BASSES PYRÉNÉES DEPT. [FR.]
————— BASQUE SPEAKING AREA
············· FRENCH ADMINISTRATIVE
              CIRCUMSCRIPTIONS

MAP 3: BASSES PYRENEES DEPARTMENT, FRANCE (from Micheu-Puyou, 1965: 36).

speaking people. This flow of immigration toward the Basque country is increasing.

The situation of the Basque country population is very different on the French side, where in part the Basque population emigrates to other parts of France.

At the time of Spanish state-building, the Basque people were part of the Kingdom of Aragón, the Kingdom of Castile, and the Kingdom of Navarre.

It is important to remember that there was no King of Spain, but rather a King of Castile, a King of León, a Lord of Vizcaya (Basque), a Duke of Milan (Italy today), a Count of Flanders (Belgium today), and so on. All these people, through their kingdoms, became part of the new state of Spain, by conquest, by heritage, or by marriage. (Alava was incorporated into Castilia in 1322 and Vizcaya in 1370.)

From the time of the incorporation of Navarre into Spain in 1512 to our day, the Basque people were part of Spain. During the Spanish Independence War against Napoleon, the Spanish people fought together, and a strong national feeling rose uniting all groups in the defense of Spain. The attempts of the French army to bring the entire Basque country into France were rejected by the Basque people. But the French Administration of Bonaparte imposed their centralizing patterns that "ordained the suppression of *Diputaciones* or *Juntas* for all the Lordom of Vizcaya, and for all the Provinces of Guipúzcoa and Alava" (Garcia Venero, 1968: 134).

The Basque deputies, with the Castilian, Aragonese, Andalusian, and other deputies from all of Spain signed the constitution for a united Spain in 1812 (Cortes de Cádiz). This constitution was heavily influenced by ideas of the Enlightenment—"that liberty, equality, and property are natural, God-given rights which men protect when they enter society. . . . In the name of these principles the Cortes produced on paper (for neither the constitution nor its legislative consequences were ever effective) a Spain that would have delighted the monarchial bureaucrats: A clumsy tax system, with endless provincial divergencies, was to be replaced by a uniform income tax. The machinery of the *ancien regime* with its characteristic confusion of administrative and judicial functions was dismantled. The bizarre quasi-federal structure of local government vanished, to be replaced by a system of uniform municipalities and provinces under a *jefe politics,* ancestor of the all-powerful Civil Governor" (Carr, 1966: 98). Article 2 of the Constitution states: "The Spanish Nation is free and independent, is not and cannot be the property of any family or person" (Sainz de Varanda, 1957: 75).

The Provincial Organization of 1827 gave a new form to the land of Spain, at which time the Basque territory took its present shape. Since that time the Basque country has generally been known as the Provinces of Guipúzcoa, Vizcaya, and Alava. The former Kingdom of Navarre in Spain became the present Province of Navarre.

Before the Cádiz Constitution in 1812, the local government in the Basque country was the Junta Forales (representative meetings for the defense of the Basque country). These Juntas took place under "the tree" of Guernika representing the traditional freedom of the Basque people, where each municipality sent its deputies. In fact the Juntas were separate for each Province, and there were for several centuries two different Juntas in Vizcaya, one for "villas" and one for "merindades." The Basque people asked for recognition of their former laws and customs (fueros) within the Spanish state. Later on, a political party named Fuerista or Foralista was born, with the goal of defending their fueros, but this party only existed for a few years after 1876. The Carlist Party (also called Comunión) fought mainly against the liberal monarchy (Isabelle II, Alfonso XII, Alfonso XIII) defending the legitimate monarchy of Carlos, brother of Ferdinand VII and his descendents. This political party, even though different than the Fuerista party, supported in later times the idea of the fueros. The Carlist Party was supported by the clergy and a large part of the Basques, except in the coastal mercantile-industrial cities.

The effects of the Fuerista and the Carlist were noted by Linz: "The 19th century religious dynastic conflict left a legacy of questioning the authority of the state, of hostility to the parties of the liberal monarchy, of Catholic questioning of the new political order" (Linz, 1970a: 38).

The Basque Nationalist Party (PNV) founded in 1894 by Sabino Arana Goiri, a former Carlist, was aimed at creating a new Basque nation from the six Basque provinces (three in Spain and three in France). It was based on two major unifying features: the Basque race and a deep Catholic feeling. Sabino Arana claimed the Basque nation would be "Constituted, if not exclusively, mainly of the families of Euskerian face" (Linz, 1970a: 78). Sabino Arana's Catholic feeling is reflected in another statement made at a time when religious problems were creating a breakdown among his followers: "I proclaim Catholicism for my country because its traditions and its religious and political character are essentially Catholic. . . . If my people resist it, I would reject my race. Without God, we want nothing" (Basaldúa, 1953: 69).

Arana's personality strongly influenced the PNV on this point,[3] and the party was supported by a large part of the Basque clergy, mainly in rural areas. Outside the Basque country, the PNV represented a defense of traditional Basque Catholicism against the anti-clericalism of the liberals.

In 1898, Arana Giori was elected to the provincial Council of Vizcaya. With few followers, they fought in the Basque country against the two strong parties (Conservative and Liberal) and against the minority Carlist Party (Payne, 1970: 113). In fact, the PNV moved pragmatically from the creation of a separate Basque Nation toward a desire for more autonomy within the Spanish state.

Between 1889 and 1923, the PNV grew slowly (Mtnez. Cuadrado, 1969: 906, Ybarra, 1948). Little by little PNV was replacing the Carlist Party, as Payne (1967) stated especially after the Carlist Party split into two branches: Carlist and Integrist.

During this period the number of PNV seats in the Spanish Cortes was insignificant, but gains were made in municipal and provincial councils (for Biscay, see Ybarra, 1948). In 1931, the fall of the dictatorship of Primo de Rivera was followed by the proclamation of the Spanish Second Republic that followed an anti-clerical and laicist course. At a time when there was no Catholic party in all of Spain, the PNV guided the Catholic feelings of the Basques. In addition, the Jesuits also supported the PNV hoping, perhaps, a concordat could be signed between the Basque country and the Vatican.

Then in the general elections of 1931 (Cortes Constituyentes) the PNV running with the Carlists won 15 seats. The arrangement between the PNV and the Carlist Party is not clear. The PNV were looking for autonomy for Basques, the Carlists possibly thought that, with four strongly Catholic Basque provinces, the rest of Spain might be "reconquered" for the Catholic faith and for the legitimate king; at the same time they hoped to gain support for the fueros.

During the period 1931 to 1933 when the Socialist Party controlled the power in the Spanish Cortes, the PNV worked in support of the Church. By 1933 when the PNV won 12 seats in the Spanish Cortes, the coalition between PNV and the Carlist Party had been broken. In that election the CEDA, (Confederación Española de Derechas Autónomas) came to power, and the PNV in the next three years switched from collaboration with the right to support for the leftist parties. The reasons for this change could have been that although CEDA claimed the defense of Catholic interests, they were at the same time opposed to regional-nationalist movements. The PNV also believed that the wine tax, imposed during the CEDA government, affected the tax autonomy of the Basque provinces. In addition, a new generation of leaders had grown up in the PNV with a more open political approach: J. Antonio Aguirre, Irujo, and Leizaola.

As a consequence of the change from right to left collaboration, the PNV lost votes. In the general elections of 1936 the PNV went from 12 seats in the Spanish Cortes to 7 seats and from 46 percent of the total vote to 35 percent. But also during this period, non-nationalistic parties taken together were stronger than the Basque Nationalist Party. In Vizcaya and Guipúzcoa the PNV was the strongest single party but had only a plurality.

According to the Constitution of the Spanish Republic (December 9, 1931) the minorities of Spain could ask for a special statute within the Spanish state; this the Basque leaders began to do. The Basque Studies Society (Sociedad de Estudios Vascos) wrote a proposal of a Basque statute in May 1931. In a meeting that took place in Lizarra (Estella) on June 14, 1937, the mayors of the Basque country accepted the model as a first draft of the future Basque statutes.

The proposed Basque statute was submitted by a Basque delegation to the government of the Republic in Madrid, but it was cooly received. The government assigned the writing of the Basque statute to the Provincial Councils of Alava, Guipúzcoa, Vizcaya, and Navarre, and practically ignored the proposal written by the Basque Studies Society. Thus a committee of delegates wrote a new proposal that was voted on in a meeting of the Basque mayors in 1932 at Pamplona (June 19). Navarre rejected the statute removing their province from a Basque proposal of autonomy. The results are shown in Table 2.

The other three Basque provinces then tried to get a new statute passed excluding Navarre. The new proposal for Alava, Guipúzcoa, and Vizcaya provinces was approved by the Basque mayors in Vitoria (August 6, 1933) by a vote of 249 in favor and only 28 against. With a general plebiscite the Basque people of those provinces supported the Basque statute. The results were: in favor: 411,756; against: 14,576; abstentions: 64,784; electorate population: 491,116 (Garcia Venero, 1968: 534 and La Cierva, 1969: 204).

It is interesting to note that in Alava only 46 percent of the population voted in favor of the Basque statute, in contrast with Vizcaya, 88.4 percent, and Guipúzcoa, 89.5 percent. However, the Spanish Republican government, dealing with important problems such as the Asturias Revolution, the Catalan Revolution, and agrarian reform did not accept the Basque statute. Only in October 1936 under very special circumstances was it accepted by the government. With the outbreak of the Spanish Civil War in July of that year, the government recognized tha autonomy of the Basques, thus assuring the cooperation of Vizcaya, Guipúzcoa, and part of Alava in the fight against Franco's army. José Antonio Aguirre became president of the autonomous Basque country in Spain (October 7, 1936).

In addition to the reasons already mentioned, the relative success of Basque nationalism between 1931 and 1936 can also be credited to the Republican government's desire to find a rational solution for the problem of Spanish peripheral nationalism in several regions and to the flexibility of the PNV in accepting autonomy of the Basque country within the Spanish Republic rather than in seeking full separation. Perhaps most significant was the religious

TABLE 2
PROVINCIAL VOTE FOR DRAFT OF "STATUTE" BY PROVINCES, JUNE 19, 1932

	Municipalities				
	Yes	No	Blank	Total	Inhabitants
Alava	52	11	15	78	106,099
Guipúzcoa	84	2	3	89	296,269
Navarra	109	123	35	267	351,107
Vizcaya	109	1	6	116	482,211

SOURCES: Sarrailh, 1962: 449; Lacierva, 1969: 203.

problem and the threat of anticlericalism, especially with the anti-clerical feeling of several Spanish Republican leaders, such as Prime Minister Azaña: "The history of some part of the peripheral opposition might well have started as a religious cleavage, reinforced perhaps by some socio-economic crisis situations, and slowly turned into a regionalist, autonomist sentiment, and finally toward nationalist parties" (Linz, 1970a: 31). In short, when PNV linked its own purposes with the different desires of different groups, it became strong enough to achieve one of its goals: the autonomy of the Basque country.

In 1939, the statute was canceled by Franco's government because Basque nationalists fought against Franco's army (Lizarra, 1944: 25). Two of the provinces siding with Franco during the Civil War, Navarre completely and Alava partially, retained the privileges granted to them in 1839 (Rodriguez-Garraza, 1968: 313-371). This situation, more or less, remains today. These two provinces have a special agreement with the Spanish Administration on Economic Affairs.

In general, the PNV based its legitimacy on history, in the past more than in the future. It is a movement of the traditional communal society versus bourgeois society, dealing with an ethnocentric dimension and a strong folk feeling. It seems a reaction to the denationalization of the Basque country, not only because the Basque language was disappearing but also because the industrialization process was changing the traditional rural moralistic values. Immigration accelerated this process.

The PNV was rejected, in general, by the bourgeoisie of the Basque country and was supported by the Basque clergy, as Linz claimes (1970a: 66): "In the Basque country, the PNV identified deeply with the Church hoping to build a separate social and perhaps political community that would help to defend religious values from the secularizing tendencies perceived as coming from the center and to isolate the Basques from the unbelief of many immigrant workers."

The Basque Nationalist Party rejected the Socialist Party as a foe of the Basque country. PNV had its own worker's union, Solidaridad de Trabajadores Vascos (STV),[4] a relatively successful organization linked with the Catholic Workers International Union and with the Internacional de Sindicatos Libres. Partially, the formation of STV was a reaction against immigrant workers from other parts of Spain and the secular labor movement. The STV participated in the Alianza Sindical Obrera (ASO), a labor union of anarchists, socialists, and Catholics created in 1962.

Today, PNV, within Basque nationalist movement, seems to be a moderate party, with Christian Democratic tendencies. Its followers are mainly bourgeois middle class. One of its most critical problems is dealing with the Basque youth.

Another nationalist party was Basque National Action (ANV), a small group, more radical than PNV. Its influence was overpowered by the stronger PNV.

After the decline of the fueristas, Carlistas, and the old nationalists parties such as PNV and ANV, new nationalist organizations arose during the 1960s especially in Guipúzcoa, perhaps the most active nationalist area, today. In many cases these new parties are very different from the old ones. A brief discussion of each follows.

BASQUE NATIONALIST CHRISTIAN SOCIALIST MOVEMENT

An ideological stream, rather than a concrete organization, it has no proper name, but "Christian Socialist" may be a fair descriptive label. It is rather difficult to learn about its ideological context because it is illegal. It is not very different from other new Basque nationalist movements, although it presents some differences in organizations from ETA or EMBATA. My understanding of the movement was gained from private conversations, booklets, and so on. (An understanding of something about it can be gained by reading the New York *Times* article, December 15, 1970; see also, Vilar, 1968: 712).

The main characteristics are:

  (a) has an interest in Catholicism, in the direction of a "new left Catholicism," a willingness to consider pluralism, a belief in separation of the state and church, a concern with the lower class, anti-war feelings;

  (b) favors "socialism in freedom," participation of the workers in industry, freedom of expression, association, a certain degree of nationalization, and unity of labor unions;

  (c) supports Basque nationalism, independent of the French and Spanish nations, in the sense of a Basque unity on the basis of a Basque common will, in order to integrate into a new Europe of the regions.

Euzkadi Ta Azkatasuna (ETA)
Basque Nation and Its Freedom

Basque Nation is a revolutionary movement of national liberation that proclaims: independence of all other political organizations, the use of whatever means that each historical situation requires in order to gain the liberty of the Basques, perhaps to join the other supranational structures, and, most important, that the Basque country should be formed by the six Basque provinces now divided between Spain and France.

In the political field, the ETA demands:

  (a) a democratic regime neither fascist nor communist, without a dictatorship and without any class domination;

  (b) decentralization on the basis of municipalities and regions;

  (c) a European federation of nationalities but not of states;

  (d) no borders between nation and nation;

  (e) rejection of race;

  (f) suppression of the army; and

  (g) a non-confessional religion.

If we look at the social content of this platform we find a rejection of economic liberalism, a new system of property stressing the social dimension, planning the whole economy, and the rule of work above the capital. Also, we find the need for the labor union as an instrument of the democratic economy. On the cultural level, ETA stands for an officially required Basque language.

ETA claims they are for peaceful opposition to French or Spanish oppression, but if such means are not enough they claim the right to a war of liberation, revolutionary war, urban or rural guerrillas, and so on. Although the psychological component is more important than military action, it is possible that some of its groups are being trained outside of Spain for such action, but one must be careful about discussions of a political organization like this since much of it is underground.

In the beginning it was an intellectual, bourgeois movement, but little by little it has changed to a revolutionary activist organization, with more of a proletarian conception on the basis of class struggles in or out of the Basque country.

In 1966 ETA was split into two groups mainly as a consequences of its inner conflict between action and thought. Thus, there is a mostly activist group, named ETA-ZARRA or ETA-BAI, and a mostly intellectual minority group, named ETA-BERRI.

In 1967, another important group left ETA because of the strong Marxist-Leninist orientation that ETA was taking. But this is the normal process of such groups, working outside the law, mainly with young followers, far from, but at the same time, close to the old Basque political organizations, and supporting the pressures of historical political parties (PSOE, PCE, and so on) in and outside of Spain. It is difficult to know the degree of penetration of the Communist Party into the ETA, but it is wrong to think that ETA is only a branch of the Spanish Communist Party. The problem is more complex, but in this paper we can mention it only in passing (see Hermet, 1971: 152).

Even though it is difficult to know definitely the relationship between the new Basque nationalist groups and the Spanish Communist Party (PCE), it is possible to observe some general trends. The Spanish communists desire "a plurinational state, rather than Federal, accepting without doubt the rights of Catalonia, Basque Country, and Galicia. Within the Spanish state those three nations would have a statute of autonomy as would other Spanish provinces. The Spanish provinces themselves would have regional and decentralized institutions. The future Spanish Parliament, in which the regions with a statute of autonomy would be represented, would be formed by one assembly, elected by proportional representation" (Hermet, 1971: 170).

One other significant point in this problem is the Spanish communist suggestion of separation between church and state, but collaboration between them, stressing the principle of religious freedom, maintaining the possibility of Catholic educational institutions, and also supporting financial aid for the churches (see Hermet, 1971: 168-170).

The problem is even more complex because the Basque Communist Party (Partido Communista de Euzkadi), today following the Spanish Communist Party (PCE), could become in the future a centralizing element in the Basque country. On the other hand, when an anti-Franco regime is not the main issue, then probably the strong Basque Catholic feeling will be a difficult obstacle for the Basque Communist Party, especially the situation of the Basque clergy. Third, the Communist Party, as a political organization, hardly admits that the revolutionary groups are out of its control, especially when those groups could become critical against its rigid or reformist organization. All of these points, however, do not mean that the Spanish Communist Party and the Basque Communist Party are not now collaborating with Basque nationalist groups for their common interest.

Embata

The new Basque nationalist party in France is called Embata. It is concerned with three problems: the separation of the Basque country, the disappearance of the Basque language, and the shrinking of the Basque-French economy. Embata is also concerned that neither France nor the formation of a new Europe has considered the interests of the Basque people. Embata demands: (1) for the present, within the framework of the French Constitution and respecting French law, the formation of a Basque Department, with the Basque provinces of Labourd, Soule, and Basse Navarre, with a statute for the Basque language; (2) in the future, within the new Europe, the creation of a region, politically, culturally, and administratively autonomous, joined with the Spanish-Basque provinces, in federation with other European institutions. The demands of Embata are similar in part to those of the old PNV of the Spanish provinces.

Besides these parties, there are the Socialist Party of the Basque Workers and Peasants (ELNAS) and Euzkadi Gaztedi (EGI) mainly an activist group. In general, we could summarize the movements as social-democratic or revolutionary-socialist. Ambiguous in their formulation, they want to create a public opinion in favor of Basque freedom, but they have no concrete definition of goals.

The program of ETA is unclear enough so that any future orientation is possible. The relationship among these groups is not well organized; in many cases the only two links are the pull of Basque nationalism and their opposition toward the Spanish and French regimes. The popular support is limited, coming from young people, students, and urban middle classes. Some workers participate in these movements, but in general, most of the workers are interested in more general problems of justice, economic development, relative order, and peace. The Castilian-speaking worker population within the Basque country, the historical rejection of the Socialist Party by the ONV, and the inability of the Basques to integrate non-Basque workers are important elements in this problem.

The fact that the demands of ETA and Embata, to Spain and France, are different may be a result of the different economic situations of the Basque population, wealthy in the Spanish case and relatively poor in the French case.

The Roman Catholic Church was especially strong in the Basque country. Thus, the first breakout of Basque nationalism was tied in with the desire to defend the Catholic faith against the liberal centralist government of Madrid during liberal and republican periods.

As mentioned earlier, the Basque Nationalist Party, proposed "politics under the Catholic religion." The support of rural priests for the Basque Nationalist Party was one of the keystones of their success. The role of the Catholic hierarchy, however, was ambiguous, as it was in Belgium toward Flemish nationalism, despite its appeal among the low clergy and the faithful.

After the Spanish Civil War, even though the whole country was secularized, the Basques remained very Catholic in feeling. By several indicators of religiosity, the Catholic feeling is still strong especially in Navarre (Linz, 1970a: 134-145). Additionally, the degree of participation in lay Catholic organizations is high. The change of attitude of the Roman Catholic Church, after the Second Vatican Council was important, in the Basque country, permitting the use of the Basque language in liturgical ceremonies, the support of the new clergy (many young Jesuits) for social movements, and the feeling against the pharisaic official Catholicism of the Spanish state.

Yet the gap between younger and older clergy, the lack of understanding between priests and bishops, and the stress on political or social issues create confusion in the thoughts of Basque Catholics. The working class (with the migrant worker population), the students, and the young intellectuals in the Basque country, as in the whole of Spain, are more and more critical of the Catholic Church (as against the Spanish Catholic Church) and little by little are turning away from it.

The situation is reflected in the new Basque nationalistic organizations. The ETA is a non-confessional organization, with strong Marxist approach on the socioeconomic level, while other organizations have a tendency we might call Catholic-socialist, maintaining their Catholic feeling but desiring separation of state and church while being influenced by Marxist thought in their orientation toward socialism. The old Catholic issue of the PNV seems now to have passed away. The new clergy in many cases supports the new nationalism in the urban areas, and in rural areas not only the priest but also the old monasteries (as Arantzazu) support it.

BASQUE NATIONALISM IN THE CONTEXT OF SPAIN'S POLITICAL SITUATION

The larger context of the general political situation in Spain, of course, influences the forms that Basque nationalism takes. The present government, as an authoritarian regime, centralized and controlled power, but it is different from totalitarian systems in that it permits political movement within the regime at certain levels (see Linz, 1970b). Furthermore, compared with the other European states, the Spanish administration is centralized but not very much bureaucratized.

In general, the desire for a relatively strong government is not only a characteristic of the Franco regime but also of a large part of the Spanish people. It is possible that the unrest of the years before the Civil War gave the Spanish people the need for an authority strong enough to maintain social order. In any case, today the desire for order and peace has a popular base in Spain.

For example, in a recent FOESSA Survey (FOESSA, 1970: Ch. 5 App. 78-79), 49 percent of the executives, 74 percent of the clerical workers, 81 percent of skilled workers, and 84 percent of the non-skilled workers have first placed to the importance of "order and peace." Corresponding figures for other groups are: high school students, 67 percent; doctors, 65 percent; employees, 68 percent; and workers, 82 percent. Only two groups fall below 50 percent: lawyers, 48 percent, and graduate students, 21 percent. The mean equaled 58 percent.

But this conservative attitude does not change the strong desire of many segments of the Spanish population for progress, social and political change, and participation in government. In the same survey, for example, a significant proportion chose liberal over conservative items as more important: conservative, 180 items, liberal, 486 items.

The Spanish people today seem to be more and more interested in success and money and less interested in remembering the Civil War. And they are not greatly concerned with political affairs (FOESSA, 1970: Ch. 5). However, the situation will change in the next few years when Franco will no longer be in control and the political situation may become more problematic. Also, young people are conscientious about the need to participate in politics. The university has been an important factor for politicization and for rejecting the Franco regime.

Accepting the necessity of political parties and choosing not one, but two or more parties, a large segment (49.4 percent) of the Spanish people generally prefer a republic rather than the present situation or a monarchy (FOESSA, 1970 Ch. 5). This possibility, of course, is rejected in the present law and in the future monarchy of Franco's heir Juan Carlos de Borbon.

It is important to note that 55 percent of the workers but only one percent of the university students chose the present regime (see Table 3). The Carlist Party received a very low percentage; neither its dynastic issue nor fueros issue seems to have the power to attract today.

In any event, the future political situation is not clear. Data on choice of political party give an idea of the strength of the nationalist parties throughout present-day Spain. Table 4 shows the answers to the question: what party would you elect if it were possible to do so? The possibility of listing the Communist Party perhaps would change these data a little, but probably not the future for the nationalist parties. It should be noted that within the two percent shown for the latter are included the Catalonian, Galician, and Basque nationalist parties.

However, in a freer situation, after a political period of unrest with a more important role for the young people, it is possible that the nationalist parties could polarize economic interests, regionalist feelings, and religious misgivings, gaining additional support. This would not be exactly true nationalism, but rather acquiescing nationalism, as will be discussed later.

Connected with the problem of nationalism is another important issue—regionalism.

The idea of regionalism includes four main elements:

(a) Deconcentration—a central authority remains at the center of the nation (capital), but powers are delegated to various local representatives of the ministries.

(b) Decentralization—the power is scattered among the local representatives of the people, and the central power is a kind of coordination.

TABLE 3
POLITICAL SYSTEM PREFERRED AFTER FRANCO (in percentages)

Political System Preferred	Students	Lawyers	Employees	Doctors	Workers
Present regime	1	8	37	20	55
Regency	4	5	6	9	4
Bourbon monarchy	11	23	5	8	5
Carlist monarchy	3	—	1	1	—
Monarchy	5	10	7	19	6
Republic	76	53	45	43	30
Total	100	99	101	100	100
Number of cases	(227)	(77)	(179)	(122)	(185)

SOURCE: FOESSA, 1970: ch. 5.

TABLE 4
CHOICE OF PARTY

Parties	Percentage
Movimento-Falange	21
Christian dmeocracy } Social democracy }	52.4
Socialist	16.3
Carlist	2
Nationalist	2
Others	7.3
Total	101.0
Number of cases	(605)

SOURCE: FOESSA, 1970: ch. 5.

(c) the region, not the province, as a geographic base for economic development and therefore as the administrative unit.

(d) Recognition of the specific peculiarities of the region such as language, folk customs, costumes, and so on, permitting practical channels for its development.

Region, as most suitable for present-day Spain, is defined here as:

"a space, smaller than the nation, directly or indirectly articulated around an urban center, which is thought of as such by the people interrelated with it, and therefore such space is capable of a communal specific organization . . . even though in most cases this organization doesn't exist yet" [FOESSA, 1970: 126].

Regionalism is not only an old traditional desire, but also a new revolutionary idea, expressing nationalism in a special way and also the feelings of many non-separatists. For example, in many cases opposition toward the authoritarian Franco regime and the regionalist feeling of many Spanish people are joined in the Basque nationalist movement in a mixture difficult to clarify.

There are four areas of linguistic differences. Castilian is spoken in both Castilias (old and new) and Andalusia; Catalan is spoken in Catalonia, Baleares, and Valencia. Basque is spoken in the Basque country, and Galician is spoken in Galicia. In multi-lingual speaking areas the degree of familiarity with the different regional languages is shown in Table 5.

TABLE 5
PERCENTAGE OF HOUSEWIVES HAVING SPECIFIED DEGREE OF FAMILIARITY WITH THE REGIONAL LANGUAGE BY REGION
(in percentages)

Region	Familiarity with Regional Language:			
	Understand	Speak	Read	Write
Galicia	96	92	42	24
Balearic Islands	94	91	51	10
Catalonia	90	77	62	38
Valénćian country	88	69	46	16
Basque country	50	46	25	12

SOURCE: FOESSA, 1970: 1264-1304.

The Basque language is spoken or understood by only half the Basque population. Even this average is very difficult in terms of the degree of urbanization. In general, Basque is spoken in rural areas, but not in big cities. Thus 82 percent of the rural area Basque population are Basque speaking, 51 percent in urban areas and 19 percent in big cities (FOESSA, 1970: 1304).

The proportion of people writing the Basque language is low (12 percent), but in this case it is not very relevant for the rural area. When education is high the use of the Basque language decreases (FOESSA, 1970: 1264). Basque housewives reported their attitudes about their children speaking Basque as follows: 40 percent would like it very much; 29 percent would like it; and 31 percent believe it is necessary (FOESSA, 1970: 1265, 1306, 1307). Attitudes did not vary with social class. This attitude is a cultural characteristic, not a social one in that, in the same way as in other Spanish areas, the desire to maintain the regional language is because of cultural-symbolic-folk reasons rather than utility. Of course, everyone also speaks Castilian, the official language.

The importance of this language can be measured in a certain sense by the percentage of persons that learn it first. Thus, we note 40 percent of the housewives interviewed learned to speak Basque before Castilian and even 9 percent to write it as a first language. These and other data on language indicate that in the Basque country there is a linguistic minority that is significant.

Spain's wealthiest region, the northeastern part of the peninsula, is almost three times wealthier than the poorest. Yet differences in regional income in Spain are slowly lessening. In 1955 the wealthiest province had a per capita income 3.7 times that of the poorest; in 1967 the comparable figure was 2.7 (see Table 6).

Thus, in 1967, Madrid and Vizcaya were the two wealthiest provinces, but the differences between them and the poorest were decreasing, within a total increase of the national per capita income of 6.1 percent in 1970. Important aspects of the differentials in wealth are government revenues and the expenditures in the Basque country. There is a general belief that the Basque country gives to the rest of Spain, and in two of the three Basque provinces this is true. But it is interesting to note that the third, Alava, in fact through 1967 received more than it gave. This suggests that the government is not systematically discriminating against the Basque country, but is simply trying to help poor provinces, wherever they happen to be located. Finally, on this economic point it should be noted that Alava and Navarre are the only two provinces in all of Spain that have a special economic agreement of régimen foral with the Spanish state, the remainder of the old fueros.

TABLE 6 HERE

TABLE 6
EVOLUTION OF THE REGIONAL INDEX OF INCOME PER CAPITA
(in U.S. dollars)

Regions	1955	1960	1967	Difference 1967-1960	1967-1955
Madrid	160	151	153	+2	−7
Basque country	205	165	148	−17	−57
Barcelona	154	154	142	−8	−12
National mean	100	100	100		

SOURCE: Foessa, 1970: Table 4.59.

BASQUE NATIONALIST ATTITUDES

Attitudes Toward Nationalism

In this paper, nationalism is defined as the active solidarity (including beliefs, attitudes, emotions, and actions) of a human collectivity which is bounded in geographical space and which shares a common culture or a common fund of significant experiences or interests, conceives of itself as a unit or a potential unit, and strives to create or maintain political unity and self-government. Put in terms of a movement in a politically dependent territory, "A nationalist movement is a collection of politico-social beliefs, attitudes, emotions, and actions aimed at the creation of a nation-state, politically independent and autonomous, self-governing, and geographically distinct" (Bell, this volume). Yet, this is an "all-or-none" definition and we should make allowances for various degrees of independence or autonomy aimed for. A desire for more political autonomy even within the old state framework may be considered at least a "quasi-nationalist" attitude, differing not in kind but in amount.

The following is a discussion of the attitudes of five Basque political groups as they relate to the question of more political autonomy and separate nationhood for the Basque region:

(a) The Foralistas, Carlistas groups accept Spain not only as a state but also as a nation. They do not question the national unity of Spain, but they seek recognition for the privileges of the former Kingdoms of which Spain is composed. They are against Basque nationalism because of its desire for a new nation separate from the Spanish state. They demand more independence in local government versus the central government, but they recognize the central power as the only national Spanish government.

(b) The Old Basque Nationalist group (PNV) stressed the differences between the Basque Country and Spain or France, but they wanted to be one nation with either Spain or France. They demanded a legal statute as a guarantee of local autonomy for the Basque people on certain matters in the Basque country, but since the Republican period this group has been integrated into the Spanish nation. They look for an autonomy of the Basque *pais* in a kind of Spanish "Federal" Nation.

(c) The Regionalists stress the necessity and the practical recognition for channels of expression of Basque culture. They are against full Basque nationalism, but they believe it is necessary to develop units to improve the development of the whole Spanish (or French) nation. In their plans, not the province but the region would be the unit of national Spanish (or French) affairs.

(d) Modern Basque Nationalists in France want more stress on Basque characteristics and to obtain more power in France. In fact, they recognize France as their nation. They do not look for full political independence or for a Basque self-government completely separate from French power. They want now to become a *Basque* department in the French administration.

(e) Modern Basque Nationalists in Spain represent a true nationalist movement, as defined above. They are looking for a Basque nation separated politically and geographically from Spain and France and for full self-government in a new nation-state in the world.

If one can generalize these findings as a comparison with the nationalisms of the new states since World War II, two hypotheses can be ventured:

(1) Because the nationalists in the old nations are not fighting against a completely foreign power, the attitudes favoring political independence are not as strong as in the new nations with a colonial background.

(2) The integrationalists of one kind or another, such as Groups A, B, C, and D above, are stronger in numbers of population than in new nations with a colonial background.

With respect to the future, if economic, political, or social conditions become difficult for France or Spain, then it is possible that the political groups of the Basque country will move toward greater desire for more independence. The Carlista-Foralista groups might remain integrationists, but the old Basque nationalists and regionalists might become at least acquiescing nationalists and the modern Basque Nationalists, both Spanish and French, might become militantly active in pursuing complete nationhood status. The following Table is a summary of the attitudes of the different groups.

Attitudes Toward Inequalities

To say that the Basques, in general, feel superior to the Spanish is an empty truth, as will be seen by the following analysis of the concept of inequality related to the variables of race, culture and economy.

Race. Basically, it is the old Basque Nationalist Party (PNV) that stressed the issue of race. This group believes the Basque race is different not only from the Spanish people but from all the other races in the world. They recognized common origins perhaps only with the Celtic race. There is no trustworthy work on this matter. All of the available work deals with the problem of race on romantic or non-scientific grounds by modern standards. It is not easy to discover the origins of the Basque people. Through history they have been mixed with many of the European peoples, especially with those living on the Iberian Peninsula. It is difficult to distinguish race, when the concept of race is not easily clarifiable in the way that the Basque nationalists claim (see Caro Baroja, 1943: 39; Harris, 1968: 263-269).

The snobbish regionalist has a feeling of superiority, but in a superficial way,

TABLE 7
ATTITUDES TOWARD NATIONALISM AMONG DIFFERENT GROUPS

Basque Groups	Full Political Independence	Self-Government	Geographical Separation	Supported By
Foralistas Carlistas	No	At local level	No	Mass of people (decreasing)
Old Basque Nationalists	Ambiguous	Legal recognition local and regional level	No	Selected groups only
Regionalists	No	At local and regional level	No	Mass of people
Modern Basque Nationalists in France	No	Basque dept. in France	No	Small minorities
Modern Basque Nationalists in Spain	Yes	Full	Yes	Minorities

stressing the masculinity of the Basque man. This has become the subject of jokes in Spain.

Today the modern Basque nationalists reject the feeling of race superiority because they are aware of the unpopularity of such an issue in the political arena.

Culture. Culturally there is a feeling of inferiority on the part of the Basques. Basque nationalism is fighting with a stagnant Basque culture and it is not easy for the nationalists to recognize this fact. As an escape they blame Basque stagnation on France or Spain. There is certain anguish in pushing their fight for a dying Basque culture. This is clear in the case of the French Basques because of the force of French culture. Thus, the attitudes are very different: old Basque nationalists demand a bilingual culture, but the modern Basque Nationalists in Spain want the Basque language as the only one. The regionalists and the modern Basque nationalists in France are oriented toward maintaining the Basque language and culture within the family and local business. They are willing to use Spanish or French in external relations.

Economically, we find differences between Basques living in Spain and Basques living in France. The Spanish Basques have a higher level of living than the rest of the Spaniards. Thus, from an economic point of view the other Spaniards regard Basque nationalism as an egoistic separatist movement and reaction against it is strong. But the French Basques generally have a lower level of living than the rest of the French. The situation influences the attitude of the Basques toward Spain and France.

In Spain, it is necessary to distinguish two types among the Basques: (a) business elites and (b) young modern intellectuals. The business elites of the wealthy bourgeoisie, the upper class, feel that their economic superiority rests on the national Spanish state's protectionism; thus, the Basque upper class has a pro-Spain attitude. In Bilbao, for instance, Basques control not only Basque business but also many Spanish businesses including banks.

However, young professionals, graduate students, artists, writers, and, in general, a middle range intellectual group think in terms of a future socialist state for the Basque country and are against the inegalitarian Basque upper bourgeoisie. This latter type is mainly equalitarian and anticapitalist, fighting not only Spanish capitalism, but also Basque capitalism. Now, this second type is supporting a new generation of Basque clergy, thinking that socialism will be the outcome for Spanish political systems. Yet today economic relations, perhaps, are the most important link joining the Basque and Spanish people.

The regionalists are in an ambiguous position: they are inegalitarian in the sense that they want to maintain their superior economic status, but at the same time they accept their higher economic level as a fact that does not make them superior to other Spaniards. They look for a common national economic development, in which each will play its own role.

ENLIGHTENMENT VALUES AND BASQUE NATIONALISM

Wendell Bell (1967) in his work on the West Indies, jointly with Ivar Oxaal, Charles C. Moskos, James A. Mau, and other collaborators, has given us a set of related ideas on Engllightenment, egalitarianism, and attitudes toward political independence. The explanation of nationalist attitudes and actions given by this group of writers has relevance to the case of Basque nationalism and invites comparison. Moskos and Bell say that "of all the Enlightenment values, equality is the key element in the images of the future that are shaping the new nations" (Bell, 1967: 101). Such equality is important, not only before independence takes place when it fuels the nationalist movements, but also after that event when it functions as a guide while leaders are involved in the decisions of nationhood.

Another important fact of this study is the importance that certain elites play in the nationalist movements. In order to measure the leaders as "egalitarian," Moskos, in one study, used two indicators: equality of opportunity and the classless society, in the sense that "if features such as equality of opportunity, the classless society, or related notions were mentioned, the leaders were called 'egalitarians'" (Bell, 1967: 102). In this research several relationships became clear:

(1) Attitudes toward equality were more frequent among non-wealthy leaders, and among political or labor leaders.

(2) Egalitarians tend to be democrats. But it is important to note that "there is some disagreement—especially among egalitarians—concerning the most desirable political system" (Bell, 1967: 107).

(3) There is a strong correlation (a) between attitudes toward equality and nationalist types, and (b) between (darker) skin color and egalitarianism.

These authors also suggest ways of thinking about and investigating equality and inequality when they say that one should:

(1) consider existing inequalities in fact,

(2) distinguish between perceived and actual inequalities,

(3) study the ideology (attitudes and values) concerning civil, political, cultural and social inequalities and inequalities, all of which are, in their view, linked to Enlightenment values,

(4) examine, when dealing with nationalist movements, how it is possible for the elites to get power in order to construct an egalitarian society, and

(5) determine the feasibility of political nationalist movements under the conditions of particular situations.

Thinking of the Basque Nationalist movement, let us quote another statement from Moskos and Bell's work (Bell, 1967: 105): "In general . . . egalitarians like democrats were characteristically leaders of secular, mass-based organizations who held legitimate change most directly in their hands. Contrariwise, inegalitarians tended to be leaders who represented the established vested interests of West Indian Society." Dealing with nationalist movements in old European nations, such as the present application to the Basque case to be given below, one finds some interesting differences.

Finally, Enlightenment beliefs and values were considered to include "a belief in the possibility of progress, the use of reason, skepticism of the old order, the equality of man, the removal of inherited privilege, and a faith in men collectively to govern themselves under democratic procedures" (Moskos, 1967b: 59). Moskos goes on to say that "attitudes toward political democracy, egalitarianism, and social inclusiveness can be paired with their equivalents embodied in the rights of man. That is 'liberty' corresponds to political democracy, 'equality' is egalitarianism, and 'fraternity' comes close to our meaning of social inclusiveness" (Moskos, 1967b: 59).[5] Let us turn, now, to the Basque-Spain case.

Certainly, the colonial situation of the West Indies in some sense predetermined who would uphold Enlightenment values and how they would be linked to the political independence movements. The case of Spain is different in a number of respects and, therefore, the linkage between Enlightenment values and the nationalist movement in the Basque country also is different. Only grossly distorting the facts can the situation of the Basque be compared with that of a colonial population, where there is a racially and ethnically stratified society and an economy controlled largely from the outside. In a colonial context the realization of many of those values can be closely, almost necessarily, linked with the national independence movement. In the Basque case, for complex reasons to which we have in foregoing sections already referred, we find two historically different situations or patterns.

Pattern one. By the eighteenth century, and particularly in the nineteenth, Enlightenment values penetrated Spain and crystallized in the Constitution of 1812. A large part of the elite identified with them, but soon counter-revolutionary forces with considerable support in popular strata rose against them, particularly in the countryside of the periphery, Navarre, the Basque country, and part of Catalonia. In the war between the traditionalist supporters of Don Carlos and the liberals fighting for his niece Isabelle II, most of the army, the urban bourgeoisie, even the aristocracy, sided with the liberals. The strong Catholic tradition of parts of the periphery and the defense of traditional institutions like the "fueros"—that is, all of the corporative freedoms rather than individual freedoms or privileges in matters of taxation and military service— were against the equality of all citizens in such matters. The struggle against the centralized egalitarianism aligned most of the Basque country, with the exception of a few cities, *against* the Enlightenment values represented by the government in Madrid with the support of the majority of Castilian-speaking Spain. Basque Nationalism, as it emerged at the turn of the century, stands, therefore, against individualistic democracy, against equality of all citizens of the state, and against tendencies toward secularization even when the latter no longer contained the commitment to a traditional monarchy. However imperfectly realized in the political culture, the link to Enlightenment values in this period is represented by the opponents of Basque nationalism.

The PNV in the course of the Republic emphasized less its clerical-traditionalist position and stressed more the ideas of Christian-democracy and, thereby, articulated some democratic values as well. But by emphasizing an ethnic nationalism in a multi-ethnic region the PNV tended to an ambivalence toward the equality of citizens of Castilian background, who constituted a large proportion of the population, mostly industrial workers.

In a recent phase of Basque Nationalism things have changed somewhat.

Pattern two. Many writers have pointed out that the central government is an authoritarian regime. Two of the Basque provinces had been on the Republican side, and the PNV was among the defeated in the Civil War against Franco. Thus, at the time they stood for many of the values we identify with the Enlightenment tradition. Not so the Navarrese, who in the past were also Basques, who fought on Franco's side, and even the Carlist minority in the Basque country.

In recent years a new type of Basque Nationalism has emerged which links its demands of social and economic equality with nationalism, including a revolutionary tendency. The linkage between class conflict and nationalism was in part established through the fact that a large part of the business bourgeoisie, particularly financial sections and large enterprises, does not identify with the regional nationalism but with the Spanish state. In the emergent nationalist movements the emphasis has been less on political democracy than on social change. For example, the Communist Party has a separate Basque organization whose commitment to liberal democracy is at least dubious. Other Basque Nationalists are also less concerned about political democracy than about creating a socialist Basque society. This ideal includes socialist, populist, and revolutionary elements which would be compatible with political democracy if they were to have the support of the majority of the population, but if imposed by a minority might very well be in conflict with it. They are, however, strongly egalitarian in ideology.

Yet, the radical nationalism of the linguistic-cultural minority combined with the radical economic and social program, in a region like the Basque country, is not necessarily identified with democratic political institutions and equality for *all* citizens. Since some of the nationalist demands might be unacceptable to many citizens of Castilian language and origin, and even to some Basques who do not identify with the nationalist interpretation of their destiny but are more or less loyal to the Spanish state, such a minority might turn dictatorial. Those opposed to the nationalist demands might very well be supporters of democracy, equality of opportunity, and even socialism in a *Spanish* state and society. Many, but not all of them, would also be willing to support a certain degree of regional autonomy in cultural matters and administration. The same would be true for Spaniards outside of the Basque country and any of the regional-cultural nationalist movements. Therefore, we cannot, like in some colonial situations, distinctively identify the commitments to values of political freedom, social egalitarianism, or even socialism with support for the nationalist movements, particularly in its more extreme forms.

In fact, the imposition of the Basque national culture which today represents only a minority, would require, almost inevitably, restrictions on freedoms of those not committed to it.

Let us not forget, that while the upper-bourgeoisie is largely identified with Spain and to a considerable degree is influential under the Franco regime, controlling large parts of the Spanish economy, it is Basque. On the other side, a large proportion of the working class in the Basque country is first or second generation immigrant Castilian-speaking. Thus, the way class and ethnic identity differ in their relationship from the new states since World War II and the way each in turn relates to the central administration ("imperial powers" in the case of the new states) clearly affects the extent to which nationalist movements are egalitarian and democratic. This is not to say Bell, Moskos, and their associates are wrong, but it is to point to the conditions under which their findings for the new states of the Caribbean will hold and other conditions under which they won't. As Bell and Moskos say, political independence is a means. The ends that it can serve depend upon particular configurations of ethnicity, class, and power and upon where established and insurgent groups fit into those configurations.

CONCLUSION

Our analysis has stressed the complexity of Basque Nationalism as the result of the long historical process and the accumulation of multiple social cleavages in Basque society. The first division, back in history, is that of the Basque-speaking area between France and Spain, and the different assimilative capacities of the French nation and state in contrast to the Spanish. The response of Basque Nationalism to both situations is different and the problems posed by the small, largely rural French Basques to the state is very different from the large minority of Spanish Basques in one of the most developed industrial regions.

Another basic consideration is the importance of the linkage established in the 19th century between regional autonomy, and later nationalism, and the defense of traditional Catholicism against a central state tending to a greater secularization. A third source of conflict within the Spanish Basque society has been the persistence of rural-urban tension, reflected, at first, in the support for the liberals by the cities and for the Carlism of the countryside and small towns and later in the greater support for the PNV in the countryside than the capitals.

A fourth line of cleavage that in the 1930s was still bridged by the Christian-Democratic Nationalist Party, but that with the impact of social revolutionary ideas fast became more open in recent years is to be found in the class conflicts within advanced industrial society. The existence of the Basque Communist Party and the social revolutionary nationalist movements, competing with the old PNV has complicated further the struggle for the nationalist cultural demands. Fifth, the fact that the Spanish Basque country is a highly industrialized region attracting immigrant laborers from the rest of Spain to work in Basque-owned enterprises is an additional source of conflict. These multiple cross-cutting lines of cleavage in a regional society forming part of an old and well established state makes interesting contrasts between its nationalism and that of many of the colonial peoples of the twentieth century.

The additional fact that Spain today is ruled by an authoritarian regime further confuses the issues and lines of cleavage. Many Spaniards strongly opposed to the regime due to their commitment to democratic, liberal values and in some cases even to the dictatorship of the proletariat, are not necessarily in sympathy with Basque Nationalism in some or all of its manifestations, either because of its social radicalism or its clericalism, and certainly because of its secessionist talk. Unfortunately, this sometimes indirectly benefits some branches of the Franco Regime.

The solution of the Basque problem has to be found in political arrangements like those described by Lijphart (1968) in his model of consociational democracies. However, in contrast to other multi-linguistic societies those solutions in the Spanish case are far from easy to institutionalize. Some of the nationalists in peripheral Spain have hoped-for images of the future that stress the disintegration of the European historical states, including even those of such long tradition as France, and their substitution by a united Europe based on ethnic-linguistic-historical fatherlands or regions rather than states, reversing the process of national unification that took place through the last few centuries. Such a possibility, though it could, perhaps, contribute to solving the problems of Spain, seems very remote, given the weakening in many European states of regional identities and the strength of the economic and social networks created by modern states. The solution in the immediate future may have to be found in federal arrangements or consociational democracy as attempted in Belgium, Switzerland, and other multi-linguistic countries. Another alternative, obviously, would be a multi-linguistic federal state tied together by a Communist Party, like in Yugoslavia. But such a solution would certainly not insure many of the liberal values cherished by many Basque and Spaniards.

As Linz (1970a: 18) has written, "No final optimal solution to the problem is in sight. A fact that doesn't exclude partial solutions on an evolutive basis, somewhat like Belgium or Canada, far from satisfactory to all concerned."

NOTES

1. Three Basque provinces in France + four Basque provinces in Spain = seven Basque provinces = 1 Basque nation.
2. About 2,465,049 inhabitants in the Spanish part and 2,379,803 inhabitants in the French part.
3. In connection with Arana's personality, we should mention his tendency to hurl invective at the Spanish in general.
4. The Basque name is EUZKO LANGILIEN ALKARTASUNA, which has been sometimes translated as Solidaridad de Obreros Vascos (SOV).
5. It seems to me that such a conception of Enlightenment thought in relation to the rights of man is too gross. Enlightenment values today are expressed in a plurality of forms. For example, roughly speaking, they could be expressed in non-socialist or socialist terms. But even within socialism, the problem is complex, as we see in the Basque case.

REFERENCES

AGUIRRE, J. A. (1944) Escape Via Berlin. New York: Macmillan.
ARRARAS, J. (1956) Historia de la Segunda República Española. Vol. I. Madrid: Editora Nacional.
BALDINGUER, K. (1963) La Formacion de Los Dominios Lingüísticos en la Península Iberica. Madrid: Gredos.
BARBANCHO, A. G. (1967) Las Migraciones Interiores Españolas. Madrid: Instituto de Desarrollo Económico.
BASALDUA, P. de (1953) El Libertador Vasco Sabino Arana. Buenos Aires: Edit. Vasca Ekin.
BELL, W. (1967) The Democratic Revolution in the West Indies. Cambridge, Mass.: Schenkman.
BLADE, M.J.F. (1869) Etudes sur L'origine des Basques. Paris: A. Franck.
CARO BAROJA, J. (1958) Los Vascos. Madrid: Minotauro.
––– (1946) Los Pueblos de España. Barcelona: Barna.
––– (1943) Los Pueblos del Norte de la Peninsula Iberica. Madrid: C.S.I.C.
CARR, R. (1966) Spain 1808-1939. Oxford University Press.
CASTELLET, J. M. (1968) pp. 295-305 in S. Vilar. Protagonistas de la España Democratica, La Oposicion a la Dictadura 1939-1969. Paris: Ediciones Sociales.
DAHL, R. A. (1971) Polyarchy: Participation and Opposition. New Haven: Yale Univ. Press.
DEUTSCH, K. W. (1953) Nationalism and Social Communication–An Inquiry into the Foundations of Nationalism. New York: John Wiley.
EGUREN y BENGOA, E. (1914) Estudio Antropológico del Pueblo Vasco. Bilbao: Elexpura Hnos.
ESTORNES, B. (1965) Origenes de los Vascos. Tomo III. San Sebastian: Auñamendi.
FOESSA (1970) Informe Sociologico sobre la Situacion Social de España. Madrid: Euramerica. (Chapter 5 is an unpublished part of this Report.)

GARCIA VENERO, M. (1968) Historia del Nacionalismo Vasco. Madrid: Edit. Nacional.
GIRADET, R. (1962) "Raport Introductif," in Etude Comparative des Nationalisms Contemporains. Unpublished Paper. Association Francaise de Science Politique. Serie I. No. 1. (Mai).
——— and SEMIDEI, M. (1962) "Itinerrires et definitions terminologiques." in Etude Comparative des Nationalisms Contemporains. Unpublished Paper. Association Francaise de Science Politique. Serie I, No. 2 (Mai).
HARRIS, M. (1968) "Race," pp. 263-269 in D. L. Sills (ed.) International Encyclopedia of Social Sciences. New York: Free Press.
HERMET, G. (1971) Les Comunistes en Espagne, Etude d'un Movement Politique Clandestin. Paris: Armand Colin.
HOLBORN, H. (1959) A History of Modern Germany 1840-1945. New York: Alfred A. Knopf.
HUMBERTZ-DORZ, J. (1970) Origines et Débuts des Partis Comunistes des Pays Latins (1919-1923). Holland: D. Reidel.
LA CIERVA, R. de (1969) Historia de la Guerra Civil Española, Perspectivas y Antecedentes 1898-1963. Madrid: San Martin.
LAYABURU, E. (1959) Historia General del Señorio de Vizcaya. Bilbao: Biblioteca de la Gran Enciclopedia Vasca.
LEFEVRE, TH. (1933) Les Modes de Vie dan les Pyrénées Atlantiques Orientales. Paris: Armand Colin.
LIJPHART, A. (1969) "Consociational democracy." World Politics XXI (January): pp. 207-225.
——— (1968) "Typologies of democratic systems." Comparative Political Studies I (April): pp. 3-44.
LINZ, J. J. (1970a) "Early state-building and late peripheral nationalisms against the state: the case of Spain." Unpublished paper for the UNESCO Conference of Nation-Building. New Haven: Yale University.
——— (1970b) "An authoritarian regime: Spain." pp. 281-293 in E. Allard and S. Rokkan (ed.) Mass Politics. New York: Free Press.
——— (1967) "The party system of Spain: past and future." pp. 197-282 in S. M. Lipset and S. Rokkan (ed.) Party System and Voter Alignments.
LIZARRA, A. de (1944) Los Vascos y la Republica Española. Buenos Aires: Editorial Vasca Ekin.
LOWRIN, V. R. (1971) "Segmented pluralism" Comparative Politics 2 (January): 141-175.
MTNEZ. CUADRADO, M. (1969) Los Vascos y la Republica Española. Buenos Aires: Editorial Vasca Ekin.
MADARIAGA, S. de (1967) Memorias de un Federalista. Buenos Aires: Editorial Sudamericana.
MARQUET, J. (1962) "Le nationalisme espagnol," in Etude Comparative des Nationalisms Contemporains. Unpublished Paper. Association Francaise de Science Politique. Serie II. No. 2 (Mai).
MAUROIS, A. (1968) A History of France. New York: Minerva Press.
MICHEU-PUYOU, J. (1965) Histoire Electorale de Département des Basses-Pyrénées sous la III et la IV Republic. Paris: Librairie Generale de Droit et de Jurisprudence.
MOSKOS, C. C. (1967a) The Sociology of Political Independence. Cambridge, Mass.: Schenkman,
——— (1967b) "Attitudes toward political independence," pp. 49-67 in W. Bell (ed.) The Democratic Revolution in the West Indies. Cambridge, Mass.: Schenkman.
PALMER, R. R. (1961) Historical Atlas of the World. New York: Rand McNally.
PALMER, R. R. and J. COLTON (1965) A History of the Modern World. New York: Alfred A. Knopf.
PAYNE, S. (1970) The Spanish Revolution. New York: W. W. Norton.
——— (1967) Politics and the Military in Modern Spain. Stanford: Stanford University Press.
PFLANZE, O. (1963) Bismarck and the Development of Germany. The Period of Unification 1815-1871. Princeton, N.J.: Princeton University Press.
RAMA, C. M. (1960) La Crisis Española del Siglo XX. Mexico: Fondo de Cultura Economica.
RODRIGUEZ-GARRAZA, R. (1968) Navarra de Reino a Provincia 1828-1841. Pamplona: Ediciones Universidad de Navarra.

ROMIER, L. (1953) A History of France. New York: St. Martin's Press.
ROSE, R. (1970) "The United-Kingdom as a multinational state." Occasional Paper. u° 6. Glasgow: University of Strathclyde.
SAENZ DE BURUAGA, G. (1969) Ordenacion del Territorio el Caso del Pais Vasco y su Zona de Influencia. Madrid: Guadiana.
SAINZ DE VARANDA, R. (1957) Coleccion de Leyes Fundamentales. Zaragoza: Acribia.
SARRAILH, F. (1962) Vasconia. Buenos Aires: Norbait.
SETON-WATSON, C. (1967) Italy from Liberalism to Fascism 1870-1925. London: Methuen.
VICENS VIVES, J. (1940) España Geopolitica del Estado y del Imperio. Barcelona: Yunque.
VILAR, S. (1968) Protagonistas de la España Democratica la Oposicion a la Dictadura 1939-1969. Paris: Ediciones Sociales.
YBARRA, J. de (1948) Politica Nacional en Vizcaya. Madrid: Instituto de Estudios Politicos.

Chapter 25

ETHNICITY AND NATION-BUILDING:
A COMMENTARY

HELEN ICKEN SAFA

At first glance, the papers in this section appear to deal with problems of nation-building quite different than the problems of new nations dealt with in other sections. Great Britain, Spain, and even the United States are not "new" nations, recently emerged from the throes of colonial conflict. Indeed, they have themselves been colonizers, and still retain strong colonial or neo-colonial ties in many Third World countries. It is difficult for social scientists to explain why Great Britain and the United States, who have served as "models" of democratic government to the rest of the world, should have unrest within their own boundaries.

This unrest is not recent. The Basque separatist movement, the Catholic-Protestant split in northern Ireland, and the movement for greater self-determination among American Indians are long, festering sores which have only recently again been inflamed. One may ask, why now? At least part of the explanation must lie in the example provided by the new nations in their determination to throw off the colonial yoke. If these new nations have succeeded in achieving political sovereignty, then long suppressed minorities like the Basques in Spain (or the Catalans), the Catholics in northern Ireland (or the Welsh), and the American Indians (or the blacks, Chicanos, and Puerto Ricans) in the United States should also have a chance at greater self-determination.

Though the authors of these papers may not agree, I feel that the causes of conflict between these minorities and the dominant ruling elite are not really that different from those formerly prevalent between new nations and their colonial powers. In both cases, the demand is for equality, in the full political, economic and social sense of that term. The disenfranchisement of minorities like the Catholics in northern Ireland, described by Power, and the American Indians in the United States (who cannot vote while they reside on reservation land) is not that different from the disenfranchisement of native peoples under colonial rule. Political disenfranchisement of the subordinate group serves to reinforce the power of a ruling elite, whose primary interest is in the economic exploitation of native people or minority groups as a cheap labor reservoir and market for manufactured goods. As Frank (1969: 388) has pointed out for Latin America, the classical colonial relationship has changed from the monopolistic exchange of manufactured goods for raw materials to a new form of exploitation through foreign investment in manufacturing subsidiary facilities abroad. Thus, a rapidly growing part of industry in northern Ireland consists of subsidiaries of British firms (Boserup, 1970: 22) which now produce locally the formerly imported consumer and some producer goods—with equipment and skilled manpower imported from the home office, but relying on cheap, local labor.

The multi-national corporation, as this phenomenon is called, is now of increasing importance in most Third World countries.

The growth of foreign industry and investment does not necessarily lead to a rise in the standard of living of the masses in these countries, since most of the increase in wealth accrues to the local managerial and professional classes, who serve as junior partners to these foreign-owned firms. Thus, the standard of living of American Indians is the lowest of any ethnic group in the United States, while that of Catholics in northern Ireland is below that of Protestants, which in turn is well below that of England. The Basque case discussed by Blasco at first would appear to be an anomaly, since the Basques have a higher level of living than the rest of the Spaniards. However, the riches of this region flow largely to the central government in Madrid and to a handful of Basque business elite who, according to Blasco, are strongly opposed to Basque nationalism.

Blasco explains further that the opposition of the business elite to Basque separatism is on the grounds that their economic superiority rests on the national Spanish State's protectionism. Here again we find another parallel with the political independence movement in new nations, though Blasco is reluctant to make such a comparison. The elites who have benefited from foreign domination, through access to political power or economic privileges, naturally oppose political independence. This is brought out most vividly in the paper by Janet Merrill Alger on revolutionary America. Those who stood to gain from political independence from England, like the smaller disenfranchised Irish Catholics or Scotch-Irish Presbyterians, supported it, while those who stood to lose, like the English Episcopalians, especially in New England, opposed independence. In fact, support for independence by the English, who "viewed themselves as the legitimate rulers of the American colonies" varied directly with the security of their position in the power structure.

The legitimacy of the local bourgeoisie, however, is often weakened as a result of their dependence on a foreign power. As in the new nations, the ruling elite may attempt to use reform or repression in a struggle to maintain control. Concessions are made to widen the franchise, as in northern Ireland. Attempts are made at economic development, as on the Fort McDowell Mojave-Apache Indian community, which becomes all the more attractive as it is discovered that these Indians are occupying "a most valuable piece of real estate." Repression is easier than reform in an autocratic regime like Franco Spain, as the recent arrests and life sentences of the Basque clergy reveal. However, the threat of violence and repression is there even in democratic regimes as exemplified by the emergency power granted and utilized by the Ulster government permitting indefinite internment of alleged subversives without trial.

However, reform and repression may not work. In northern Ireland, for example, it would appear that reforms no longer satisfy the demands of the Catholic minority who now seek nothing short of unification with the Irish Republic. Reforms also lack the backing of the Protestant majority, who fear any loss of their power and any reduction of status differences between them and Catholics (Boserup, 1970: 29). Repression may produce a backlash, as it did in revolutionary America and has again most recently in Bangladesh. The alternative is revolution.

Revolutions based on ethnic nationalism can take many forms, depending on the nature of the conflict with the ruling power, and the basis of support among the mass populace. These forms can also be seen as stages in the process of revolutionary consciousness through which many new nations and ethnic groups demanding equality have passed. Originally, the conflict is seen largely in cultural terms. As in the Basque country or among the Irish of Ulster, the minority often possesses a distinct language and/or religion[1] which sets them apart as a separate ethnic group. The struggle for independence often focuses first on the maintenance or revival of these separate cultural traditions. The early appeal to black nationalism in the United States similarly stressed the African heritage and differences in diet, language and other customs distinguishing blacks from the dominant white culture.

As revolutionary consciousness develops, however, cultural nationalism may take on added political dimensions. Revolutionary leaders, who are themselves usually members of the local elite come to recognize that political sovereignity is no guarantee of political and economic equality for their people. A change of rulers is no longer enough, especially since so many new nations have suffered as much oppression at the hands of the local bourgeoisie as at the hands of the foreign colonial power.

Increasingly, political movements for independence or separatism such as the ETA among the Basque and the IRA in northern Ireland have adopted a socialist or Marxist platform, which promises a more equal distribution of wealth in the society as well as political sovereignty. Similarly, the black nationalist movement in the United States developed more political forms of expression, such as the Black Panther Party, which is overtly Marxist in its orientation. These Marxist movements feel that it is only under socialism that their demands for equality can be truly satisfied. They are not content with seeking recognition of their distinct cultural traditions, and, in fact, have tried to minimize cultural differences in establishing class alliances, as among Catholic and Protestant workers in northern Ireland. Thus far, most attempts at establishing class alliances between sharply antagonistic ethnic groups have failed. Catholics in northern Ireland still tend to see all Protestants as their natural enemy (and vice versa), much as the Basque Nationalists think that all their problems would be solved by independence and an end of exploitation from Madrid. The battle has been fought so long in ethnic terms that it is difficult to convince workers to abandon cultural allegiances in favor of new class alliances. Most workers have not passed beyond the cultural nationalist stage of revolutionary consciousness and fail to recognize capitalism as the real source of their exploitation. As in the Third World countries, the battle against colonialism must be fought first. Then the struggle for socialism may begin.

NOTES

1. Though strong Catholics, the Basque people and clergy view their Catholicism as different from that of the rest of Spain.

REFERENCES

BOSERUP, A. (1970) "The politics of protracted conflict." Trans-action 7 (March): 22-31.
FRANK, A. G. (1969) Latin America: Underdevelopment of Revolution. New York: Monthly Review Press.

CONTRIBUTORS

JANET MERRILL ALGER was born in Brooklyn, New York in 1938 and was educated at Columbia University and Yale University from which she received her Ph.D. in 1972. She has taught at Michigan State University, the University of Akron, and is Assistant Professor of Sociology at the University of Illinois at Chicago Circle. Her academic interests include political sociology, social change, and the development of techniques for the incorporation of historical data into sociological research. She is presently engaged in a comparative study of leaders of the American and West Indian independence movements. A small portion of the American data is reported in this volume.

FREDERICK C. BARGHOORN is Professor of Political Science, Yale University. He was born in New York City in 1911, receiving his A.B. from Amherst College in 1934 and his Ph.D. from Harvard University in 1941. He has taught at the University of Chicago and Columbia University and was employed by the Department of State from 1941 through 1947, during which time he served for four years on the staff of the U.S. Embassy in Moscow. In addition to his many other writings he is the author of *The Soviet Image of the United States* (1950), *Soviet Russian Nationalism* (1956), *The Soviet Cultural Offensive* (1961), *Soviet Foreign Propaganda* (1964), and *Politics in the USSR* (1966).

WENDELL BELL was born in Chicago, Illionis in 1924 and was educated at Fresno State College (B.A.) and the University of California, Los Angeles (M.A. and Ph.D.). He was a member of the faculty of Stanford Univeristy, Northwestern University, and UCLA before joining the faculty of Yale University in 1963 as Professor of Sociology. He was Chairman of the Department from 1965 to 1969 and presently is Director of a training program in comparative sociology. His research has been in the fields of urban sociology, social change, and political sociology. In addition to his contributions to professional journals, he has authored, coauthored, or edited *Social Area Analysis* (1955), *Public Leadership* (1961), *Decisions of Nationhood* (1964), *Jamaican Leaders* (1964), *The Democratic Revolution in the West Indies* (1967), and *The Sociology of the Future* (1971). He has been both a pre- and post-doctoral Social Science Research Council Fellow and spent a year at the Center for Advanced Study in the Behavioral Sciences.

PEDRO GONZALEZ BLASCO was born in Valdeavellano de Tera, Soria, Spain in 1937. He lived in Madrid from 1939 and was educated at Our Lady of Pillar College, the Central University of Madrid (M.D. Sciences. Physics) and at the Counciliar Seminary of Madrid, Divinity School (Philosophy Diploma). He was a

Fellow of the Education and Science Ministry of Spain, then he traveled in France and England. He was Professor at High School from 1961 to 1965 and Sub-Director of Chaminade Hall of Graduate Students at the University of Madrid from 1966 to 1969. His former research has been in the field of Physics, on radioactive elements ("Radiations of the Radon"). In addition to his contributions to several social or educational associations, he has written for the Spanish political magazine, "Cuadernos para el Diálogo." Since 1970, he has been a Fellow in Sociology at Yale University where he is a candidate for the Ph.D. degree.

JEFFREY BUTLER was born in Cradock, Cape Province, South Africa in 1922, and was educated at Rhodes University and Oxford. He taught in South Africa, Oxford and in the African Studies Program at Boston University, before joining the History Department at Wesleyan University in 1964. His research has been into African politics and into the history of British policymaking in South Africa. He has written articles on trade unions and politics in Africa, edited a series of papers on African history, and made a study of a South African question in British politics, *The Liberal Party and the Jameson Raid* (1968).

HARRY S. COBLENTZ was born in England and educated at Cambridge University, the University of Durham (B.A. with First Class Honours in Town and Country Planning) and the University of North Carolina (Master of Regional Planning). He has worked as a planner with large cities and joint agencies in England, United States, Canada, and Mexico and has held teaching appointments in universities in communities where he has also been engaged in planning practice. He was on the faculty of Arizona State University prior to his present appointment in the College of Human Development at the Pennsylvania State University as Associate Professor of Urban Planning in 1969. He is also Chairperson of Penn State's Committee of the Inter-Disciplinary Graduate Program in Regional Planning. His professional work and research have been in the fields of social planning, planning with ethnic groups, regional planning and housing. In addition to contributions to professional journals, he is the author of the Canadian Government's three-year pilot multi-governmental research study of the Halifax Region, *The Halifax Housing Survey 1960-63.* He has been a Fulbright Scholar and was the 1971 Gastprofessor at the Institut Für Verkewesen, Universität Fridericiana (TH) Karlsruhe, Germany.

JOEL C. EDELSTEIN was born in Long Branch, New Jersey in 1941 and was educated at the New School for Social Research and the University of California, Riverside. He was a visiting assistant professor at California State College, Los Angeles, before joining the faculty of The Concentration in Modernization Processes at The University of Wisconsin-Green Bay in 1971. His research has been in the fields of political economy of underdevelopment in Latin America with special emphasis on Cuba, and contemporary North American political economy. In addition to his contributions to professional journals, he is co-editor, with Ronald Chilcote, of *Latin America: The Struggle with Dependency and Beyond* (1973).

LOCKSLEY EDMONDSON was born in Jamaica (West Indies) in 1934, where he received his early education and then worked for five years in the Jamaican civil service. He subsequently pursued undergraduate studies in Economics, Politics, and Sociology at the University of Birmingham, England, and graduate studies in political science at Queen's University at Kingston, Ontario, Canada. He taught at the University of Waterloo, Ontario, and Makerere University, Kampala, Uganda, before joining the faculty of Cornell University in 1970. He is now Senior Lecturer in the Department of Government, University of the West Indies, Kingston, Jamaica. His research has been in the fields of international and comparative race relations, African and Caribbean politics and international relations, and Afro-American politics. He has contributed to various edited volumes and professional journals and is presently working on a number of monographs and books. His *The Internationalization of Race* is scheduled for publication shortly.

CYNTHIA ENLOE was born in New York City in 1938 and was educated at Connceticut College and the University of California, Berkeley (Ph.D.) She has been a member of the Political Science Faculty at Berkeley and Northeastern University and is currently an Associate Professor at Miami University (Ohio). Her research has been in the fields of political development and ethnic politics, with a special interest in Southeast Asia. In addition to articles in professional journals, she has authored *Multi-ethnic Politics: The Case of Malaysia* (1970) and *Ethnic Conflict and Political Development* (1972). She has conducted research under a Fulbright grant and under a grant from the National Endowment for the Humanities. For the year 1971-1972 she was Fulbright Lecturer at the University of Guyana.

WILLIAM J. FOLTZ was born in Mount Vernon, New York, in 1936. He did his undergraduate work at Princeton University and at the Institut d'Etudes Politiques in Paris, and received his Ph.D. from Yale University, where he is now Associate Professor of Political Science. African politics have been his special interest, and from 1967-1970 he was Chairman of Yale University's Council on African Studies. He has held visiting appointments at Wesleyan and Makerere Universities, and Ford Foundation and Guggenheim fellowships for research in Africa. He spent 1971-1972 as a visiting researcher at the Christian Michelsen Institute, Bergen, Norway. His principal publications include *Nation Building* (with Karl W. Deutsch et al., 1963), *From French West Africa to the Mali Federation* (1965), and *Resolving Conflict in Africa: The Fermeda Workshop* (with L. W. Doob, R. B. Stevens et al., 1970).

DAVID P. FORSYTHE was born in North Carolina in 1941 and was educated at Wake Forest University and Princeton University (Ph.D.). He has been on the research staff of the Princeton Center of International Studies and the Carnegie Endowment for International Peace and has taught at Agnes Scott College and Georgia State University. He is currently an Associate Professor in the Department of Political Science at the University of Nebraska–Lincoln. His research interests are international law and organization and the Middle East. He is the author of many journal articles and of *United Nations Peacemaking* (1971).

WALTER E. FREEMAN was born in Oak Park, Illinois in 1925 and was educated at Northern Illinois State University and Michigan State University (Ph.D.). He was a member of the Michigan State University faculty as a Professor of Sociology and Chief of Research for the Institute of Community Development before coming to The Pennsylvania State University in July, 1968 as a Professor of Human Development where he is currently Professor and Director of the Division of Community Development. He has been advisor to the Academy for Rural Development in Peshawar, Pakistan and has served as specialist in social organization for the United Nations Technical Assistance Team for Community Development in Jamaica, Barbados, and Trinidad-Tobago. He has also directed area studies for the Peace Corps and served with a team from the International World Bank for Reconstruction and Finance, in evaluating the proposed community development program (5-year plan) in Kenya. In addition to his contributions to professional journals he has co-authored *Community Development* (1957) and is a contributor to *Perspectives on the American Community: A Book of Readings* (1969) and *Patients, Physicians, and Illness* (1972).

MARGARET E. GALEY was born in Pittsburgh, Pennsylvania and was educated at Vassar College and the University of Pennsylvania where she received her Ph.D. in International Relations in 1970. Her research interests have focused on international organization, social anthropology and science and public policy. From 1970-1971 she held a Post-Doctoral Maurice Falk Fellowship in Race, Ethnicity and Mental Health, at the University of Pittsburgh. Following a Research Associateship with the United Nations Institute for Training and Research in New York, she became Assistant Professor of Political Science at Purdue University, Lafayette, Indiana.

HARMANNUS HOETINK was born in Groningen, The Netherlands in 1931 and studied sociology and history at Amsterdam and Leiden Universities (Ph.D.). From 1953 to the present he has lived in the Caribbean (Curacao, Dominican Republic, Puerto Rico), except for the years 1964-1968 when he set up and directed the Center for Latin American Research and Documentation in Amsterdam and was a Professor Extraordinary at Rotterdam. At present he is Director of the Institute of Caribbean Studies and Professor of Sociology at the University of Puerto Rico, Rio Piedras. He has contributed to a dozen books, wrote *Het Patroon van de Oude Curacaose Samenleving* (1958, 3rd ed. 1971). *The Two Variants in Caribbean Race Relations* (1967), *El Pueblo Dominicano: 1850-1900* (1970), and *Slavery and Race Relations in the Americas* (in press), and edited the *Encyclopedie van de Nederlandse Antillen* (1969). He was co-winner of the 1970 Prize of the Conference on Latin American History.

LEO KUPER was born in Johannesburg, South Africa, and received his education at the University of Witwatersrand and the University of Birmingham (Ph.D.). Prior to joining the faculty of the University of California, Los Angeles in 1961 as Professor of Sociology, he lectured at the University of Birmingham and was Chairman of the Department of Sociology and Social Work at the University of Natal. He is currently Director of the African Studies Center at UCLA. Besides his contributions to scholarly journals, he has authored or coedited *Living in Towns* (1953), *Passive Resistance in South Africa* (1957), *Durban: A Study in Racial Ecology* (1958), *An African Bourgeoisie* (1965), and *Pluralism in Africa* (1969). Working under a grant from the National Science Foundation, he has focused his present research on theories of pluralism, revolution, and revolutionary violence in race relations.

JOSEPH B. LANDIS was born in Carlisle, Pennsylvania, in 1942 and received his undergraduate education at Fisk University and the College of Wooster. He did his graduate work at Yale University and has been an acting instructor of sociology at Yale. He is now an Assistant Professor of Sociology at Western Michigan University teaching courses in race relations, political sociology, and comparative ethnic relations. He has contributed to professional journals and is now working on a book on race relations and politics in Guyana.

RENE LEMARCHAND was born in Nantes (France) in 1932 and was educated at the University of California, Los Angeles (Ph.D.). He is currently Professor of Political Science at the University of Florida and was at one time Director of the African Studies Center there. His research has been primarily focused on problems of social change and political development. Besides having contributed numerous articles to professional journals, he is the author of *Political Awakening in the Congo: The Politics of Fragmentation* (1964) and *Rwanda and Burundi* (1970). The latter work earned him the Herskovits Award for 1971.

ALBERT E. LEVAK was born in Etna, Pennsylvania in 1922 and was educated at Shippensburg State College, Pa., the University of Pittsburgh, and Michigan State University, earning a Ph.D. in Sociology and Anthropology in 1954. He served in the U.S. Army in Italy and North Africa. He was a member of the faculty of Michigan Technological University, the Ohio State University, and Mississippi State University before joining the faculty of the Department of Social Science at Michigan State University where he is now a Professor. During 1958-1959 he devised and implemented a training program in Pakistan and on the MSU campus for the faculties of the two Academies for Rural Development located at Peshawar and Comilla. During 1960-1961 he served as an Advisor to the Academy at Peshawar. He was former Director of the Office of Human Relations in the Institute of Community Development, Michigan State University. His research interests include minority peoples, social problems, and community development. Publications related to Pakistan include: *Social Research for Basic Democracies* (1961), *Community Development in Pakistan: Some Selected Problems* (1962), *Underdeveloped Areas and Community Development* (1963), and *Social Research in the Formulation and Implementation of Development Plans* (1963). He has been a post-doctoral Senior Fellow (1963-1964) at the Urban Studies Center, Rutgers—The State University, New Jersey.

GORDON K. LEWIS received his B.A. in Modern History from the University of Wales, his M.A. from Oxford, and his Ph.D. in Government from Harvard University. He has been Visiting Professor of Political Science variously at the University of Chicago, Michigan State University, Brandeis University, and the University of California, Los Angeles. Since 1955, he has been a faculty member at the University of Puerto Rico where he is currently Professor of Political

Science. His many publications include *Puerto Rico: Freedom and Power in the Caribbean* (1963), *The Growth of the Modern West Indies* (1968) and *The Virgin Islands, A Caribbean Lilliput* (1972).

ANTHONY P. MAINGOT was born in Trinidad in 1937. He received his B.A. from the University of Florida and after some graduate work in Sociology at UCLA returned to the University of Florida where he received his Ph.D. in History and Sociology in 1967. He was an Assistant Professor of Sociology and History at Yale University before moving in 1973 to a position as Professor of International Relations at the University of the West Indies in St. Augustine, Trinidad. In addition to his interest in the Caribbean, he has done field research in Colombia. His substantive interests include research on historical consciousness and the rewriting of history. In addition to his many contributions to professional journals and to edited volumes, he has written *Gentlemen and Officers: Civil-Military Relations in Colombia to 1965* which will soon be published. At present, he is serving as a member of the Constitutional Reform Commission of Trinidad and Tobago.

ROBERT MAST is a native of Pittsburgh, Pennsylvania. Prior to receiving his Ph.D. in Sociology at the University of Pittsburgh he worked in various community organization settings specializing in race relations. He taught for a number of years at Chatham College and the University of Pittsburgh and directed research into urban problems, race relations, and police-community relations at the latter institution. He was Associate Director of the International Race Studies Program at the Institute of Race Relations in London, England, for three years, where he concentrated on comparative studies of Europe and North America, the Third World and the West, and analysis of change in the United States. At present, he is Research Associate at the Center for Black Studies, Wayne State University.

ROBERTA MAPP McKOWN did her undergraduate and some graduate work in Economics at the University of Oregon. After several years of nonacademic activity she returned to graduate study in Political Science at Oregon and received the Ph.D. in 1968. She is presently an Assistant Professor of Political Science at the University of Alberta and Associate Chairman of the Department. Her research has been on integration in Ghana and Kenya and she is also a participant in the Multi-National Student Survey Project (La Jolla and Copenhagen). She currently holds a grant from the Canada Council to begin work on a long-range study of African political integration processes and political stability. Her published work includes a theoretical model of student politicization and analyses of student activism in Ghana and Kenya.

PAUL F. POWER is Professor of Political Science at the University of Cincinnati where he has taught since 1961. Born in Wilmington, Delaware in 1925 he is a graduate of Yale University and New York University (Ph.D.). His research has been in political ethics and the political thought and foreign relations of former colonial nations. He is co-author or editor of *The Meanings Of Gandhi* (1971), *Indian Nonalignment* (1967), *Neutralism and Disengagement* (1964), and author of articles in Asian Survey, Journal of Modern African Studies, and The American Political Science Review.

HELEN ICKEN SAFA is an anthropologist who has worked primarily in Latin America, especially Puerto Rico, and with ethnic minorities in the U.S. She received a Ph.D. in anthropology from Columbia University in 1962 and taught for four years at Syracuse University before joining the faculty at Livingston College, Rutgers University, where she is now Professor of Urban Planning and Policy Development and Director of the Latin American Institute. Her research has been largely in the areas of urban anthropology, poverty, and the processes of modernization. She is presently completing a book, *The Urban Poor of Puerto Rico,* soon to be published. She is also the author of numerous articles and guest editor of a special issue of the American Behavioral Scientist (March 1972) on "The City as a Social System."

JAMES LARRY TAULBEE was born in Dayton, Kentucky in 1942 and was educated at Purdue University and The Johns Hopkins University (Ph.D.) He is currently Assistant Professor of Political Science at Emory University in Atlanta, Georgia. His research has focused on the control of force in international politics, the radical left and American foreign policy, and the use of gaming as a teaching tool. He is a member of a special panel to assess the status of the law of reprisal and retaliation sponsored by the American Society of International Law. His essays have appeared in The Journal of Public Law as well as in a number of edited collections.

AUTHOR INDEX

revolution(s): Rwanda and Algerian, similarity of, 27; contribution of black under-class of Americans to theory and practice of, 91; potential for, in modernization, 139; social, result of ethnic conflict in situations of vertical differentiations, 141-142;–ary America, impact of ethnicity and religion on, 327-339 passim; based on ethnic nationalism, various forms of, 376-377

ruling class: inherant conflicts of, with working class, 49; of American empire, 50, 52

scapegoating: and stereotyping, 106-107; definition of, 107; function of, 178

self-determination: (see also autonomy); national, Palestinian claim to and difficulties concerning, 190; sought by minorities in "old" nations, 375

slave: master relations and race relations, spurious causality between, 31

slavery: institutionalization of, trans-Atlantic, 75; in Caribbean, 76, 78; and capitalism, institutionalized relationship between, 91

social: changes, large, as indicators of future conflict, 182; changes, major forces of, 182; scale, increases in, 283-289; organizations, trend toward increasing complexity and number of, 284; scale, race and ethnicity, 285-287; increased by nationalist movements, 287-289; plan, preparation of, by Indian community, 315, 317-319; changes in Indian community and larger society, relationship between, 324

social science: relative to one's orientation, 59, 61; history of and criticisms of, 59-62; relevancy as main responsibility of, 60; theories limited by prevailing philosophies, 60; and middle-range theory, 61; need for general theory (and description thereof), 61; needs aid from the oppressed, 66-67; needs redirection, 88; past deficiencies and new trends of, 90; must seek reconciliation between concepts of race and class, 91; criticism of argument for a "peoples", 97; suggested roles of, 99

social structure: total, elements of and

importance of, in determining social consciousness, 34; heterogeneous society, defined, 45; homogeneous society, definition and characteristics of, 45, 48; transformation of homogeneous society to structural pluralism, 48; taxonomies of, 180-181; homogenity and heterogenity of, 180-181; horizontal patterns of, 181-182; vertical dimensions of, 181-182

socialism: and ethnic harmony, 14; and nationalism, relationship between, 97; and supposed elimination of oppression, 118-119; aim of Marxist movements to achieve equality, 377

solidarity: as result of competing interaction, 178; ethnic, transcending formal boundaries, 303; as related to nationalism, 364

somatic norm image: criticism of theory of, 21; definition of, on existence of socio-racial continuum in a society, 43; alternative theories to, 95

state: as creator of ethnic cleavages, 147, 148, 171-174; importance of its formal institutions in study of ethnic relations, 171 174; Soviet, questionable viability of, 129ff; and need for third-party legal inquiry, 196; soft, definition of, 233; and nation, distinction between, 293-294, 297; building pattern, European typology of, 344-346

status: inconsistencies, in every society, 35; and ethnicity, interaction of and effect on group conflict, 103-116 passim; discrepancy or disequilibrium, limitation of, as explanations of group conflict, 111-112; discrepancies, roles of, in ethnic conflict, 114; predominance of ethnicity over–in conflict, 108-109, 115; discrepancies, concerning criteria for evaluating, 136; discrepancies (objective and perceived) as related to ethnic conflict, 136-137ff; solidarities, affected by perceptions, 136-137; discrepancies, indicators of, 137-140; discrepancies, importance of intra-caste or intra-class cleavage in understanding of, 137; discrepancies, mutability of indicators of, 138; incongruencies, result of Rwanda revolution, 142; socio-economic, of ethnic groups in Guyana, 260